The Paralegal Professional

ESSENTIALS

Henry R. Cheeseman, JD, LLM

CLINICAL PROFESSOR OF LAW
DIRECTOR, LEGAL STUDIES PROGRAM
MARSHALL SCHOOL OF BUSINESS
UNIVERSITY OF SOUTHERN CALIFORNIA

Thomas F. Goldman, JD

PROFESSOR OF LAW AND MANAGEMENT
DIRECTOR, PARALEGAL STUDIES
DIRECTOR, CENTER FOR LEGAL STUDIES
BUCKS COUNTY COMMUNITY COLLEGE

PEARSON
Prentice
Hall

Upper Saddle River, New Jersey 07458

Photo Credits, by page

Page 2 PhotoDisc; **Page 16** Gary Conner/ PhotoEdit; **Page 21** Margot Granitsas/The Image Works; **Page 32** PhotoDisc; **Page 34** Tony Freeman/PhotoEdit; **Page 43** Jeff Cadge/Getty Images Inc. Image Bank; **Page 54** PhotoDisc; **Page 75** Jeff Greenberg/ PhotoEdit; **Page 78** Michael Newman/ PhotoEdit; **Page 90** PhotoDisc; **Page 106** Nancy P. Alexander/PhotoEdit; **Page 108** Jeff Greenberg/PhotoEdit; **Page 118** Photo-Disc; **Page 131** Jeff Greenberg/ PhotoEdit; **Page 135** Courtesy of the Library of Congress; **Page 148** PhotoDisc; **Page 155** U.S. Department of Agriculture; **Page 157** Jeff Greenberg/PhotoEdit; **Page 174** Photo-Disc; **Page 187** Jeff Greenberg/PhotoEdit; **Page 204** Rudi Von Briel/PhotoEdit; **Page 214** PhotoDisc; **Page 220** Richard Lord/ The Image Works; **Page 234** Jeff Greenberg PhotoEdit; **Page 252** PhotoDisc; **Page 254** Paul Conklin/PhotoEdit; **Page 267** Charles C. Place/Getty Images Inc-Image Bank; **Page 284** PhotoDisc; **Page 287** A. Ramey/Photo-Edit; **Page 292** Michael Newman/Photo-Edit; **Page 314** PhotoDisc; **Page 318** Barry Winiker/Index Stock Imagery, Inc.; **Page 322** Bob Rowan, Progressive Image/CORBIS.

Editor-in-Chief: Stephen Helba
Director of Production and Manufacturing: Bruce Johnson
Manufacturing Manager: Ilene Sanford
Manufacturing Buyer: Cathleen Petersen
Executive Editor: Elizabeth Sugg
Editorial Assistant: Cyrenne Bolt de Freitas
Managing Editor: Mary Carnis
Production Liaison: Denise Brown
Director, Image Resource Center: Melinda Reo
Manager, Rights and Permissions: Zina Arabia
Interior Image Specialist: Beth Brenzel
Cover Image Specialist: Karen Sanator
Image Permission Coordinator: Nancy Seise
Full Service Production: Gay Pauley/Holcomb Hathaway
Photo Research: Teri Stratford
Design Director: Cheryl Asherman
Design Coordinator: Christopher Weigand
Cover Design: Kevin Kall
Compositor: Aerocraft Charter Art Service
Cover Printer: Phoenix Color Corp.
Printer/Binder: Von Hoffman Press, Inc.

Pearson Prentice Hall™ is a trademark of Pearson Education, Inc.
Pearson® is a registered trademark of Pearson plc
Prentice Hall® is a registered trademark of Pearson Education, Inc.

Pearson Education Ltd.
Pearson Education Singapore Pte. Ltd.
Pearson Education Canada, Ltd.
Pearson Education–Japan

Pearson Education Australia Pty. Limited
Pearson Education North Asia Ltd.
Pearson Educación de Mexico, S.A. de C.V.
Pearson Education Malaysia Pte. Ltd.

10 9 8 7 6 5 4 3 2 1
ISBN 0-13-110461-6

Dedicated to the memory of my parents,
Morris and Ethel Goldman,
who guided me through life,
encouraged me to pursue an education,
and delighted in my becoming a teacher.

—THOMAS GOLDMAN

In memory of
Henry B. and Florence Cheeseman

A grain of sand
has been
ten thousand mountains.

Who are we
to hold it?

—HENRY CHEESEMAN

CONTENTS *in Brief*

CONTENTS

PART III
PARALEGAL SKILLS   251

CHAPTER 9

Interviewing and Investigation Skills   252

CHAPTER 10

Traditional and Computer Legal Research   284

FROM THE AUTHORS

W hen we were asked to write this text for Pearson Prentice Hall, we welcomed the opportunity to create a text that would present essential information for paralegal students in a memorable way, using a format that is easy to read and enjoyable to use. We worked with an award-winning design and production group who thought outside the box and understood the need to present information for traditional and returning students in a unique format. What we have produced is, we hope, the best combination of paralegal career and skill information and substantive law concepts.

For the student, we have tried to present the material in a visual format that has been referred to as a *textbook magazine*. Topics are broken down and presented in a variety of formats, including traditional text, brief sidebar items, and contemporary perspective and ethical issues boxes.

Because many legal assistant students today work in law offices, we have tried to provide a number of practical checklists, sample documents, tips, and resources for use in the working environment. Beginning students of paralegal studies are provided with a series of checklists to stimulate their thinking and help guide their educational pursuits. With these materials they can start the process of employment planning by preparing resumes and refining the art of interviewing.

We have incorporated exercises and material focused on skill development and knowledge acquisition as recommended in a report approved and adopted by the Board of Directors of the American Association for Paralegal Education that states

> . . . a person must not only possess a common core of legal knowledge, but also must have acquired vital critical thinking, organizational, communication, and interpersonal skills.

We have tried to address in one text the varying needs of instructors teaching Introduction to Law classes and Introduction to Legal Assistant Studies classes. In this book, planned variety in presentation gives students the best opportunity to excel. Each chapter contains an assortment of real-world cases.

The importance of ethics in business and in the American legal system has become clear in the post–Enron era. Our text emphasizes business and legal ethics, and numerous questions and review problems challenge readers to consider various forms of ethical responsibility borne by paralegals, lawyers, and businesspersons. In solving the exercises, using citations to actual cases and references to related websites, readers develop critical thinking skills while enhancing their research and communication skills.

No one today can be properly prepared to work in the modern legal environment without knowledge of technology. In this text we provide students with a foundation in the use of computers in the law office and in conducting legal research, and students get ample opportunity for technology practice by completing the *Working the Web* exercises.

In-class discussions are encouraged by the feature *Cases for Discussion*. These cases, variable in length, present students with opportunities to develop verbal communications skills and public speaking opportunities and to think critically about issues.

It is our wish that our commitment to these goals shines through in this labor of love. We hope you have as much pleasure using this text as we have had in creating it for you.

Henry Cheeseman
Thomas Goldman

PREFACE

Written by an award-winning author team, ***The Paralegal Professional: Essentials*** provides a solid introduction to the paralegal profession. The fully up-to-date and extensive coverage of technology in the law office, legal and business ethics, international perspectives, and diversity prepares students for today's work environment.

CAREER GUIDANCE + THE LAW

The Paralegal Professiona: Essentials provides a critical combination of topics designed to enhance the course teaching structure in any environment. Paralegal programs differ widely in the nature of the student body, the academic environment in which they are grounded, the business environment in which the school resides, and the talent available for driving the program. Each program emphasizes the skills students need to succeed in the world around them.

Paralegal students come from various backgrounds and have a variety of learning skills and styles and differing professional interests. ***The Paralegal Professional*** was created for every kind of learner, whether they already possess a 4-year degree or are working on their first 2-year degree; whether they are employed in law offices or returning to the workforce; whether they are enhancing their careers or exploring a career change.

Chapter Outlines, Chapter Objectives, and *Chapter Summaries* guide students through the logic of the course. *Boldface terms* in text, chapter-end *Legal Terminology* lists, and the text *Glossary* work hand-in-hand to introduce a new vocabulary and reinforce its proper use. Colorful *exhibits* guide visual learners through the material. These basic features are enhanced with:

- Numerous examples of *cases*
- Integrated coverage of *diversity*
- *Ethics* guidelines for action
- Legal applications for *technology tools* in the law office
- Sample *documents*

PROFESSIONALISM

The paralegal profession is one of the fastest growing occupations in the United States today. By understanding the role paralegals play, students gain a respect and perspective appropriate for their chosen field.

- In each chapter, *Ethics Questions for Analysis and Discussion* provide readers the opportunity to strengthen ethical reasoning. In addition, on-going discussion of both *legal* and *business ethics* demonstrates the connection between the two worlds.

- *Contemporary Perspective* boxes include *articles, interviews,* and *essays* about the critical issues that impact careers.

- Numerous *Meet the Courthouse Team* boxes describe the roles of personnel paralegals are likely to encounter.

- Each chapter's *Case for Briefing* walks students through one of the most important tasks they will perform as professionals; the briefing task is reinforced with *legal reasoning, legal writing, legal research,* and *ethics research* questions.

- *Critical Legal Thinking and Writing* questions provide practice for practitioners in all areas of the law.

INTERNATIONAL PERSPECTIVE

- *International Perspective* features explore global legal and economic issues.

INFORMATION TECHNOLOGY

- *Information Technology* boxes highlight digital advancements and legislation relevant to legal personnel.

SIDEBAR

- *Sidebars* emphasize facts and issues relevant to the surrounding discussions.

PRACTICE

In addition to the *Cases for Briefing*, chapter-end features encourage review through such features as *Working the Web*, *Cases for Discussion*, and others.

QUICK REFERENCE

Every feature of the book is designed to be a quick reference for professionals and a study review for new learners. Features include:

- Marginal references to *related websites*.

- *Checklists* for career guidance and for paralegal procedures.
- *Appendices* on the U.S. Constitution, English/Spanish Legal Terminology, Internet Resources, Case Briefing, and Professional Rules of Conduct
- Guide on *pronunciation of Latin terms*

SUPPLEMENTS

The Paralegal Professional: Essentials is backed by digital and print *course supplements* that support distance learning and lifelong skills. These include a complete *Online Course* and a time-limited version of *LexBrief* legal briefing software and the *Lexiverse Legal Dictionary*.

The book can be packaged with *state-specific materials* at a reduced price:

California Courts
Texas Courts
Florida Courts
New York Courts
New York Civil Practice
Civil Litigation

- **Instructor's Manual** is free to instructors and available on CD-ROM complete with lecture notes and test questions available in files ready for word processing and printing. The CD also includes PowerPoint files for overheads and handouts.

- **Prentice Hall Test Manager** is available with more than 350 test questions to be selected at random or individually. Quizzes, tests, and exams can be created and printed when needed. All output can be scrambled into several different versions of the same test to discourage students from imitating one another's answers.

- *WebCT Course* for the book is fully classroom-tested and is available for Distance Learning students or as an online study enhancement to the classroom. It is a complete package with reference links, sample documents, and handouts as well as all the course management features offered as a part of any WebCT course.

- *Premium Companion Website* is available for use as a classroom study enhancement or in cartridges that easily translate into Blackboard or Course-Compass learning environments. The Prentice Hall Companion Website technology course support program includes course management, bulletin boards, and class organization features such as online syllabi.

- *FREE Companion Website* is a limited version of the Premium Companion Website. It gives students an online study guide and review with immediate hints and feedback for completing review questions.

- **LexBrief**™ software is a tool designed to help students develop the analytical, organizational, and summation skills needed to have a successful career in the legal industry. Once these skills are mastered, LexBrief™ continues its utility as an unparalleled management tool.
  LexBrief™ allows users to easily and efficiently create and manage their case briefs. LexBrief™ comes with a customizable dictionary and the ability to cross-reference between briefs, as well as to organize briefs according to class.

- **The Lexiverse Dictionary** is a stand-alone, customizable legal dictionary for today's legal and paralegal students. This program allows students to augment the program's existing terminology and definitions database through the easy-to-use customization feature.
  Students can now tailor their studies through the continual use of this program by building up a customized database of terms and definitions unique to the individual user. The program is ideal for use in class via a laptop, at home, or even in the office.

NOTE: Every effort has been made to provide accurate and current Internet information in this book. However, the Internet and information posted on it are constantly changing, so it is inevitable that some of the Internet addresses listed in this textbook will change.

ACKNOWLEDGMENTS

A special acknowledgement goes to Jodi McMaster and Erin McAuliffe at San Antonio College for hours of dedicated work and attention.

A round of applause to those whose insights contributed to the learning aspects of the book. Special thanks to:

Michael Fitch, for his guidance and encouragement early in the development of the project.

Kathryn Myers, for her generosity and kindness in allowing the use of her material on portfolios and for the guidance she unknowingly gave by her example of enthusiasm, dedication, and hard work in support of paralegal education.

The inspiring panelists and speakers at the AAfPE annual and regional meetings over the past five years, who provided insights, guidance, suggestions, and encouragement.

To the officers and members of the local and national professional associations, including NALA, NFPA, NALS, and ALA, for allowing the use of materials but mostly for their suggestions regarding topics and real life issues to be covered.

Paralegals Edie Hannah and Elma Quinn for tireless reviews, detail checking, encouragement and support, countless hours on the phone getting materials and networking with other professionals to obtain comments and input to make this textbook relevant to working paralegals as well as to students preparing for the profession.

The students in Tom Goldman's classes, for testing the text and WebCT materials in a class setting and graciously providing suggestions and feedback.

Finally, much gratitude to the reviewers, whose thorough responses helped to complete this project:

Chelsea Campbell, Lehman College CUNY

Anderson Castro, Florida International University

Stephanie Delaney, Highline Community College

Linda Hornsby, Florida International University

Nance Kriscenski, Manchester Community College

Linda Cabral Marrero, Mercy College

Leslie Miron, Mercy College

R. Eileen Mitchell, University of New Orleans

Anthony Piazza, Dan N. Myers University

Alex A. Yarborough, Virginia College at Birmingham

Henry R. Cheeseman is an award-winning author of several business law textbooks published by Prentice Hall publishing, including the definitive, highly-regarded *Business Law*. He has earned six degrees, including a Juris Doctor degree from the UCLA School of Law, an LLM degree from Boston University, and an MBA degree from the University of Chicago. Professor Cheeseman is a clinical professor of law and the Director of Legal Studies at the Marshall School of Business, University of Southern California. Students there voted him best teacher of the year, earning him the "Golden Apple" Teacher Award. Professor Cheeseman recognizes the importance of the paralegal to the practice of law, and has joined with Thomas Goldman to write this new and exciting introduction to paralegal studies.

Thomas F. Goldman is a Professor of Law and Management, Director of the Center for Legal Studies, and Director of the Paralegal Studies Program at Bucks County Community College in Pennsylvania. An accounting and economics graduate of Boston University and of Temple University School of Law, Professor Goldman now has an active international law, technology law, and litigation practice. He has worked extensively with paralegals and received the award of the Legal Support Staff Guild. He was elected the Legal Secretaries Association Boss of the Year for his contribution to cooperative education by encouraging the use of paralegals and legal assistants in law offices. He also received the Bucks County Community College Alumni Association Professional Achievement Award. He has been an educational consultant on technology to major corporations and a frequent speaker and lecturer on educational, legal, and technology issues.

The

Paralegal

Profession

CHAPTER 1
The Professional Paralegal

CHAPTER 2
Ethics, Regulation, and
Professional Responsibility

CHAPTER 3
Careers in the Paralegal Profession

CHAPTER 4
Paralegal Workplace Skills

PART I

THE PARALEGAL PROFESSION

The paralegal, or legal assistant, profession has seen explosive growth since the late 1960s. As we will discuss in Part I, opportunities and career choices for the paralegal have never been better. Possible employers are just as diverse as the duties paralegals are asked to perform. Federal, state, and local governments, including regulatory bodies, employ many paralegals.

Today's paralegals need specialized skills, and formal programs of study and continuing education programs have developed to help individuals obtain needed skills. As with other professions, ethical rules and regulations have evolved to help paralegals avoid conflicts and possible malpractice. These topics will be discussed in Part I.

CHAPTER 1

CHAPTER OBJECTIVES

After studying this chapter, you should be able to

1. Define the terms *paralegal* and *legal assistant.*

2. Explain what paralegals do and their role in the legal profession.

3. Explore job opportunities for the paralegal.

4. Explain the need for education and training, to be recognized as a member of the paralegal profession.

5. Describe the different educational paths available to become a paralegal.

6. Outline the history of the paralegal profession.

7. Understand the American Bar Association standards for approval of legal assistant education programs.

8. Understand the American Association for Paralegal Education core competencies for paralegals/legal assistants.

9. Articulate your current level of skills and knowledge.

10. Define your personal goals.

The Professional Paralegal

The great can protect themselves, but the poor and humble require the arm and shield of the law.

ANDREW JACKSON

Introduction

The paralegal or legal assistant profession has seen an explosive growth since the late-1960s. Like other professions, this one has evolved over time to meet a need. Prior to the late 1960s, many of the functions of paralegals today were performed by those with titles such as legal secretary, lay assistant, and legal clerk or law clerk (the latter of which was usually reserved for the recent graduate of law school who had not yet passed the bar exam).

WHAT IS A PARALEGAL?

A great deal of confusion has arisen as to what the professional in this field should be called or what the professionals should call themselves. The most popular terms, *paralegal* and *legal assistant*, are used interchangeably in most of the United States. In particular, these are the terms used interchangeably by the American Bar Association (ABA), the National Federation of Paralegal Associations (NFPA), and the National Association of Legal Assistants (NALA). The confusion stems in part from the shift from the title of *secretary* to the title *administrative assistant* and, in some offices and educational institutions, *law office assistant*.

The exact definition of legal assistant has been the subject of discussions by national organizations including the ABA, NFPA, and NALA, as well as many state legislatures, supreme courts, and bar associations.

ABA definition of *paralegal* online: www.abanet.org/legal services/legalassistants/def 98.html

NFPA definition of *paralegal* online: www.paralegals.org/ development/NFPA_def.htm

The American Bar Association's 1997 version of the definition, which also has been adopted by the National Association of Legal Assistants, is:

A legal assistant or paralegal is a person, qualified by education, training, or work experience who is employed or retained by a lawyer, law office, corporation, governmental agency or other entity and who performs specifically delegated substantive legal work for which a lawyer is responsible.

The National Federation of Paralegal Associations defines a paralegal as follows:

A paralegal/legal assistant is a person qualified through education, training or work experience to perform substantive legal work that requires knowledge of legal concepts as customarily, but not exclusively performed by a lawyer. This person may be retained or employed by a lawyer, law office, governmental agency or other entity or may be authorized by administrative, statutory or court authority to perform this work.

WHAT DO PARALEGALS DO?

The primary function of paralegals is to assist attorneys in preparing for hearings, trials, meetings, and closings. In many cases paralegals do the preparatory work, helping to draft documents, assisting in the preparation of other documents and forms, coordinating the activities and functions required in some cases, and in many offices maintaining the financial records of the firm.

People tend to think of paralegals as working in a private law office directly under the supervision of attorneys. Actually, employers of the paralegal are just as diverse as the duties they are asked to perform. Many paralegals are employed by the federal government, as well as state and local governments including regulatory bodies. The paralegal's activities might include analyzing legal material for internal use and collecting and analyzing data, as well as preparing information and explanatory material, for use by the general public.

More and more paralegals are coming to the profession from other professions, such as nursing, bringing with them a specialized body of knowledge that they combine with the legal skills they learned in a paralegal program. With this expertise they frequently are hired to analyze case materials for trial attorneys, both plaintiff and defense, and also are employed as case analysts and as claims representatives for health insurance companies. Their knowledge of medicine, combined with their legal knowledge, gives them a unique ability to analyze specialized material.

Other specialties are expected to take the same career path. Those with engineering and other bachelor of science degrees also bring a special point of view to the law. A paralegal with a forensic science background, for example, may well be the ideal paralegal to work with criminal defense attorneys and prosecutors.

Prior to the recognition of a separate paralegal profession, individuals had typically acquired specialized knowledge of a narrow legal field through on-the-job training. Someone working with a lawyer, usually a secretary, would learn the daily routine tasks and become knowledgeable about that specific area of law. Many of these individuals became the resource person for information, such as the documentation requirements for real estate settlements, the preparation and filing of estate and trust accountings, and the procedures for preparing and filing cases and appeals. These were the first paralegals. Today, many of the skills and procedures formerly acquired over an extended time on the job are taught at institutions specializing in the education of paralegals or legal assistants, offering a certificate program, a two-year associate degree program, or a four-year bachelor's degree program.

In 1968 the American Bar Association formed a committee to investigate the use of lay assistants in the legal office. The result was the American Bar Association's forming the Standing Committee on Legal Assistants. The ABA gave this committee jurisdiction over training and standards for the education of legal assistants. Within this jurisdiction the Standing Committee on Legal Assistants monitors trends in the field and recommends to the House of Delegates—the policymaking body of the American Bar Association—training programs that meet its standards for quality education.

ABA Standing Committee on Legal Assistants: www.abanet.org/legalservices/ legalassistants/home.html

NALA Model Standards & Guidelines: www.nala.org/ stand.htm

National Association of Legal Assistants Model Standards and Guidelines

Proper utilization of the services of legal assistants affects the efficient delivery of legal services. Legal assistants and the legal profession should be assured that some measures exist for identifying legal assistants and their role in assisting attorneys in the delivery of legal services. Therefore, the National Association of Legal Assistants, Inc., hereby adopts these Model Standards and Guidelines as an educational document for the benefit of legal assistants and the legal profession.

Standards. A legal assistant should meet certain minimum qualifications. The following standards may be used to determine an individual's qualifications as a legal assistant:

1. Successful completion of the Certified Legal Assistant (CLA) certifying examination of the National Association of Legal Assistants;

2. Graduation from an ABA approved program of study for legal assistants;

3. Graduation from a course of study for legal assistants which is institutionally accredited but not ABA approved, and which requires not less than the equivalent of 60 semester hours of classroom study;

4. Graduation from a course of study for legal assistants, other than those set forth in (2) and (3) above, plus not less than six months of in-house training as a legal assistant;

5. A baccalaureate degree in any field, plus not less than six months in-house training as a legal assistant;

6. A minimum of three years of law-related experience under the supervision of an attorney, including at least six months of in-house training as a legal assistant; or

7. Two years of in-house training as a legal assistant.

For purposes of these Standards, "in-house training as a legal assistant" means attorney education of the employee concerning legal assistant duties and these Guidelines. In addition to review and analysis of assignments, the legal assistant should receive a reasonable amount of instruction directly related to the duties and obligations of the legal assistant.

"Give Us Respect" Say Paralegals

Fulton County Daily Report　　　　April 16, 2001

WANTED: Bright, articulate individual with college degree and computer skills willing to work hard in a dead-end job. About half your peers feel underpaid, but in general they find the work interesting and appreciate the flexibility this career offers.

Interested?

Then, become a paralegal, legal secretary, or legal assistant. Because that's essentially how they describe their jobs in the *Daily Report*'s survey of the salary and working conditions of legal support staff. The *Daily Report* collected data from 255 respondents at law firms, businesses, and corporations of all types and sizes around the state, including Dye, Tucker, Everitt, Long & Brewton in Augusta; Goodman McGuffey Aust & Lindsey; King & Spalding; Mead Corporation; Scientific–Atlanta; Sutherland Asbill & Brennan; Tisinger Tisinger Vance & Greer in Carrollton; Troutman Sanders; and United Parcel Service.

Those surveyed are almost evenly divided about whether they are fairly compensated: 50 percent say yes, 47 percent say no; 3 percent didn't answer. Among the paralegals surveyed, the highest percentage in one salary category earns $45,001 to $55,000; for legal assistants and legal secretaries, it's $35,001 to $45,000.

In addition to answering objective, multiple-choice questions about compensation, the respondents were invited to write detailed comments about their careers, and many did. Though some wrote glowingly about their jobs and excellent relationships with co-workers and lawyers, others worried about dwindling benefits, poor chances for advancement, as well as salaries that seem less and less adequate in light of increased workloads and escalating associate pay.

One paralegal who requested anonymity sums it up this way: "I didn't realize I would hit the proverbial ceiling so quickly," she says. "I'm in my early 30s, have been with my current employer for several years, and have already exhausted, via promotions, all advancement opportunities for paralegals with my employer."

The other thing she's exhausted is her employer's pay scale. Paralegals are a part of cash flow, she says. At firms, many do lawyer-level work, freeing up attorneys for more complex and better-paying tasks. In-house, paralegal work can reduce bills the company pays to outside counsel.

"You can't have paralegals doing attorney-level work but treat them like staff when it comes to compensation," she says. "If your clients are being billed for your services, but you're not seeing any of that at bonus time and the attorneys are, it's an annual slap in the face."

Disparities in Pay

A major factor fueling dissatisfaction with pay, according to survey responses, comes when legal support staff compares raises—usually 4 percent to 6 percent—with the double-digit increases given to greenhorn associates already earning $100,000 or more.

Of course, management and support staff see pay issues differently. That's illustrated by comments from Troutman Sanders' managing partner and some of the firm's staffers. Of the 20 Troutman Sanders support staff members who responded to the survey, 16 complained about compensation.

One Troutman legal secretary writes about lawyer–staff pay disparity through the lens of Troutman's merger with Mays & Valentine. When the merger was announced, management told staffers that it meant "partners will now experience double-digit increases in their compensation," the secretary wrote. "This was particularly galling since the staff raises have been held at 4 percent for four years, and 4 percent of $35,000 to $45,000 doesn't come close to 10 percent of $300,000."

Robert W. Webb Jr., the firm's managing partner, says he finds those survey responses upsetting. "That's just not true," he says, explaining that average merit increases have run [approximately 4] percent, and that raises have never been held at 4 percent.

In addition to merit increases, the firm spent about $350,000 on market-based pay raises for staff just this year, he says. Over the past three years, the total is $750,000. Partner pay increases were in the double digits before the Mays & Valentine merger, he says. According to the *Daily Report Dozen*, a ranking of the city's wealthiest firms, pay increases have been at 10 percent or above since 1997.

Janet L. Conley, jconley@amlaw.com

Advancement Opportunities

High associate salaries ironically may be helping paralegals get the advancement opportunities they want, says Chris Cole, director of professional staffing at Bellon & Associates, a legal recruiting firm. "As a result of the salary increases for associates, a lot of the firms have stopped hiring first-year associates," he says. "Paralegals have taken over some of those tasks."

Firms also offer supervisory positions, but there's a rub. According to Cole, supervisory paralegals usually have the same billable requirements as those without the extra responsibilities. In addition, paralegals and legal assistants are doing more of their own secretarial work—a situation shared by lawyers.

Shortage of Secretaries

Part of the shift in who handles secretarial work can be attributed to a shortage of legal secretaries. Anne Rubin, owner of the placement firm Atlanta Secretaries, says that although there's a big demand for intelligent, competent legal secretaries, there are fewer and fewer of them. Women—who hold most legal secretary jobs—now go to law school or pursue other goals, she says.

According to Rubin, the dwindling supply has pushed up pay, and top legal secretaries can make as much as $53,000. To attract good legal secretaries, she says, firms must offer more flexible working hours, especially to women with long suburban commutes and children in daycare centers that charge by the minute after 6 p.m.

Daycare Bonus at A&B

Cathy A. Benton, Alston & Bird's director of human resources, says "Alston and Bird is doing something incredible." The firm plans to open a daycare center this fall. It will be housed a few blocks from A&B's offices, and its services will be affordable and available to lawyers and support staff on an equal basis, she says.

Alston & Bird was motivated in part by Georgia's new, higher tax credits for employer-sponsored childcare, but, says Benton, "We think it is important in balancing work and family and think it is the right thing to do in today's market, to be able to recruit people and keep people."

The Benefits Factor

Benefits of all types were an important factor in job satisfaction—or dissatisfaction—according to the *Daily Report*'s survey results. Among those surveyed, 93 percent receive some form of employer-subsidized health coverage; 87 percent get life insurance; and 78 percent are covered by disability insurance. Retirement benefits also were offered widely: 89 percent had a 401(k) or other retirement plan, and 31 percent were offered a pension plan. One Georgia-Pacific Co. legal assistant praised the company's benefits: reimbursement for MARTA [rapid transportation] and membership in professional organizations, flex time, on-site daycare and access to a chiropractor.

Other support staff at other employers weren't as happy. "We have been losing benefits in the last few years," wrote one legal secretary at a firm in the 201- to 400-lawyer range. When her firm changed insurance companies recently, she says, coverage costs went up and prescription co-pays rose from $5 to $15. The firm also abolished a pension plan to which it had contributed at 4 percent of employees' salaries.

Four out of five Sutherland Asbill respondents complained about insurance benefits. One wrote next to the survey question about life insurance, "Just enough for a cheap funeral! Maybe a pine box!"

Melissa R. Todd, Sutherland Asbill's director of human resources, says secretaries get a $25,000 life insurance policy from the firm, plus a $25,000 policy for accidental death and dismemberment. Paralegals get $50,000 for each. Support staff also can purchase supplemental insurance. "Certainly that would be enough for a funeral," she says. But she adds that the firm may consider offering equal benefits to all staffers. In addition, the firm pays 90 percent of employee health insurance costs and buys monthly MARTA cards, she says.

Taking on More Work

As firms cut costs—to pay higher associate salaries, some respondents speculated—support staff are required to take on more work. Wrote one Troutman Sanders legal secretary, "The day is coming in the near future when I am going to have to take on three attorneys (some already have four people!). At that time, I will no longer have the time to do anything other than churn out a work product that I normally would never consider approving."

Webb, the firm's managing partner, says that any situations where work quality is affected by overload will be corrected. He also points out that it's not unusual among Atlanta firms for secretaries to serve three timekeepers. Troutman's firmwide ratio of secretaries to timekeepers is 2.2 to 1; the secretaries-to-lawyers ratio is 1.9 to 1, and fewer than 10 secretaries serve four lawyers, he says.

Two paralegals, each from a firm of 15 or fewer lawyers, also lament increasing workloads. "My firm doesn't replace employees when they leave—I am doing the job of three people at $14 an hour," wrote one, who also said she worked more than 40 hours a week at a firm that refused to pay overtime or bonuses.

The other paralegal wrote of being extremely disillusioned by the lack of support her firm gives its staff. "We have lost fantastic paralegals over the years due to pay and professionalism issues," she wrote. "At times, they have been replaced by individuals with no four-year degree and no formal paralegal education, causing a decline in morale of the remaining professional paralegals, who feel diminished as a class." (The jobs were necessarily "dumbed down" to accommodate the low skill level of new recruits.) "Rather than retain their experienced, professional paralegals, the firm simply finds new candidates they can pay cheaply regardless of the difference in skill-value to the practice."

Keys to Contentment

Sheri H. Kornblum, director of paralegal recruitment at The Partners Group, says firms must change to keep paralegals happy. They'll have to treat paralegals more like professionals and not micromanage them or tie them to time-clocks. But she says salaries already are pretty good, especially with overtime that's often in the $10,000 to $15,000 range. The highest base salary at which she's placed a paralegal is $62,000, she says, adding, "There are attorneys in this city who are making only $45,000." The most highly compensated paralegal in the *Daily Report*'s survey reported earning $75,000 to $85,000 and had 11 years to 15 years of experience.

Salary caps, however, may compress pay as legal support staff gain experience, Kornblum says. According to the *Daily Report* survey, about 20 percent of respondents said their employers had salary caps. But there's more to it than money, according to Kornblum. She says paralegals leave big firms for small ones because they're bored. Though smaller firms might pay less, she says, paralegals like the work because they may get to attend depositions, or sit second-chair to manage papers during a trial.

Kornblum's observation runs parallel to the survey finding that one of support staffers' biggest complaints is about poor chances for advancement. Some of the survey respondents who exhibited the most job satisfaction attributed their happiness to high levels of autonomy and responsibility.

"In my department, my job as a bankruptcy paralegal offers an opportunity for court appearances handled exclusively by paralegals," wrote one paralegal at an Atlanta firm. "Most other specialties are not as accommodating. . . . Although we deal with high-volume cases, we are treated very professionally and are given lots of freedom, and with that comes greater responsibility."

OPPORTUNITIES

Paralegals held about 188,000 jobs in 2000, according to the U. S. Department of Labor, Bureau of Labor Statistics, *Occupational Outlook Handbook*. In 2000 full-time paralegals had median annual earnings of $35,360. Salaries in the industries employing the largest numbers of paralegals in 2000 were:

Department of Labor,
Occupational Outlook Handbook:
www.bls.gov/oco/ocos114.htm

- Federal government, $48,560
- Local government, $34,120
- Legal services, $34,230
- State government, $32,680

In a 1998 survey by the American Bar Association,

Almost two-thirds of the lawyers who responded, 65.5 percent, employ legal assistants at their firms; 60.2 percent of respondents actively work with paralegals.

> The general responsibilities most often assigned to paralegals are maintaining client files, drafting correspondence, and performing factual research.
>
> Legal assistants are more likely to be employed by large firms than small firms.
>
> Lawyers in smaller firms delegate a wider array of responsibilities to legal assistants than lawyers in bigger firms do.
>
> Lawyers with business/corporate, probate/estate planning, and litigation practices make more extensive use of paralegals than do lawyers in other practice areas.

The ABA survey demonstrates that clients who choose to work with larger firms are much more likely to have a portion of their work completed by paralegals than those who choose a lawyer from a small firm. Almost all (99 percent) of the lawyers practicing in firms with more than 100 lawyers reported that their firms use legal assistants. By contrast, only 34.8 percent of those working at firms of three or fewer lawyers employ paralegals. Of the lawyers who indicated that their firms do not employ paralegals, 56.8 percent reported that their firm's size would not support legal assistants and 44.1 percent said that their secretaries assume tasks that would be assigned to legal assistants.

Exhibit 1.1 compares 2001 and 2002 salaries for paralegals, from a survey by The Affiliates, broken down by experience and size of law firm.

THE FUTURE

Clients who are unwilling or unable to pay what they see as inflated fees for lawyers may determine the future of the paralegal profession. The future also could be dictated by the courts, which, looking at the fairness of charging higher rates for attorneys' tasks that could properly be delegated to a paralegal, would result in a lower charge to the client. Two of the future concerns involving paralegals and billings are:

1. The cases in which secretarial or clerical tasks are charged to the client as paralegal fees. These tasks are considered overhead (part of the cost of running the office) and should be performed at no additional cost to the client. This is one of the areas in which the definition of paralegal has come into play in the courts. Courts are allowing charges for paralegal fees but not for secretarial fees.

2. The fairness of charging higher rates for attorneys' performing tasks that could properly be delegated to a paralegal, thereby resulting in a lower charge to the client.

ABA 1998 Survey: www.abanet.org/media/sept98/leg-asst.html

Meet THE COURTHOUSE TEAM

Introduction to the Team

As a paralegal, you will work with a number of different individuals outside of the law office. Many of these people are part of the local, state, and federal court system. Others, though located within the courthouse, are not directly part of the court system but, because of the nature of governmental administration and record keeping, might be related to your job as a paralegal. This text will introduce some of these people to you.

Most courthouses contain offices and personnel involved in administration of the legal process. Generally, the three main areas of law with separate administrative offices are: civil matters; criminal cases; and wills, probate and orphans court.

In addition, many courthouses house government offices such as the local tax authorities, recorder of deeds, central records office, district attorney/prosecutor, and public defender.

exhibit 1.1   *Survey of paralegal salaries.*

	2001	2002	% Change
SENIOR/SUPERVISING PARALEGAL (7+ years' exp.)			
Large law firm	$49,000 − $66,250	$49,000 − $65,250	−0.9%
Midsized law firm	$46,250 − $59,000	$45,750 − $57,250	−2.1%
Small/midsized law firm	$42,500 − $53,500	$40,750 − $52,500	−2.9%
Small law firm	$37,250 − $46,250	$36,500 − $46,750	−0.3%
MIDLEVEL PARALEGAL (4–6 years' exp.)			
Large law firm	$42,250 − $54,250	$42,000 − $54,250	−0.3%
Midsized law firm	$39,000 − $51,750	$39,000 − $49,750	−2.2%
Small/midsized law firm	$37,750 − $47,750	$37,000 − $46,750	−2.0%
Small law firm	$32,500 − $40,250	$33,250 − $41,750	3.1%
JUNIOR PARALEGAL (2–3 years' exp.)			
Large law firm	$33,000 − $41,000	$33,250 − $41,000	0.3%
Midsized law firm	$32,500 − $39,750	$31,750 − $39,000	−2.1%
Small/midsized law firm	$31,250 − $38,500	$30,500 − $37,750	−2.2%
Small law firm	$28,000 − $35,250	$27,250 − $35,000	−1.6%
CASE CLERK (0–2 years' exp.)			
Large law firm	$24,250 − $29,750	$25,750 − $30,500	4.2%
Midsized law firm	$24,250 − $29,250	$25,000 − $29,500	1.9%
Small/midsized law firm	$24,000 − $28,000	$24,250 − $28,250	1.0%
Small law firm	$22,000 − $26,250	$22,500 − $26,250	1.0%
LAW FIRM DEFINITIONS			
Large law firm	75+ attorneys		
Midsized law firm	35–75 attorneys		
Small/midsized law firm	10–35 attorneys		
Small law firm	up to 10 attorneys		

For instance, summarizing depositions traditionally has been a task delegated to paralegals. Assume that the paralegal takes two hours to complete the task and the paralegal's time is billed to the client at $75 per hour (don't get excited—that doesn't necessarily have any bearing on what you may be paid); the client would be charged $150. For a lawyer to do the same work, if billed out at $175 per hour, the client would be charged $350. Unless there is good reason for the lawyer to do the work, the decision not to delegate the work to a paralegal seems unfair to the client. A number of court decisions are beginning to draw upon these fundamental questions of the fairness and propriety of attorney billings for their services. As other federal and state courts weigh in on this line of decisions, law firms may have to hire more paralegals.

The U. S. Department of Labor has included the paralegal profession among the fastest growing occupations in the economy through the year 2010. This encompasses additional growth of the occupation as well as the need for individuals to replace existing employees. The Labor Department estimates might be increased further by the de facto requirement found in the court opinions that more paralegals be used to perform services instead of attorneys' performing the services. Exhibits 1.2 and 1.3 give projected job openings and replacement needs for various occupational groups.

Job openings by major occupational group. **exhibit 1.2**

Job openings due to growth and replacement needs by major occupational group, projected 1998–2008.

Source: Chart 11, *Occupational Outlook Handbook,* U. S. Department of Labor, Bureau of Labor Statistics.

exhibit 1.3   *Occupations with the largest numerical growth.*

Occupations with fast growth and high pay that have the largest numerical growth, projected 1998–2008.

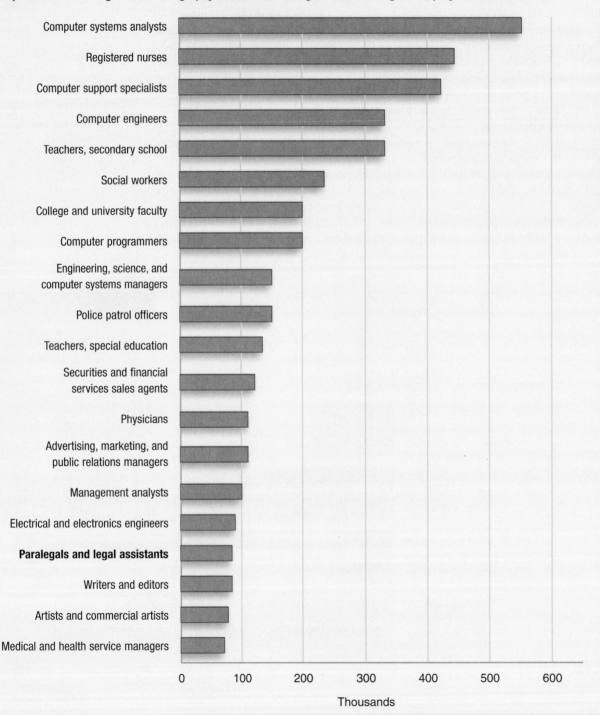

Source: Chart 8, *Occupational Outlook Handbook,* U. S. Department of Labor, Bureau of Labor Statistics.

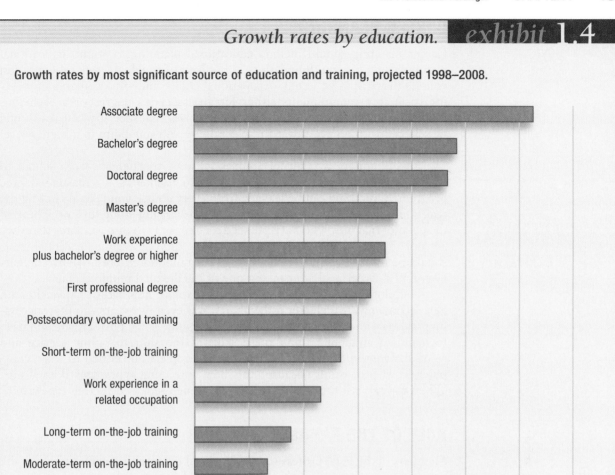

Growth rates by education.   *exhibit* 1.4

Growth rates by most significant source of education and training, projected 1998–2008.

Source: Chart 4, *Occupational Outlook Handbook,* U. S. Department of Labor, Bureau of Labor Statistics.

According to the Department of Labor, "The changing pattern of occupational employment also means changes in educational requirements. Occupations requiring an associate degree or higher education, which account for 25 percent of all jobs in 1998, will account for 40 percent of job growth from 1998 to 2008." Exhibit 1.4 shows projected growth rates by amount of education and training.

The best trained, most skilled individual clearly will be the one to get the job. The challenge in obtaining your first job is demonstrating that you are the best person for the job. Consider the prospective employer comparing the resumes of a number of paralegal job applicants. One paralegal has a high school diploma and a paralegal certificate. Another applicant has an associate degree or even a bachelor's degree in paralegal studies. Which would you hire?

Monthly Labor Review,
Nov. 1999, Charles Bowman:
www.bls.gov/opub/mlr/1999/
11/art1exc.htm

CAREER PLANNING

Career planning should include educational planning. A sound educational plan builds on a sound foundation, at the base of which are general education courses that will assist in any occupational choice and are acceptable in meeting basic core requirements either for an associate's degree or a bachelor's degree. Occupation-related courses such as paralegal specialty courses should be selected with an eye toward transferability and suitability in a higher-level educational pursuit.

This is not to say that all courses must be transferable from school to school or from associate-degree program to bachelor's- or master's-degree program. Something can be learned from every course you take, including the realization that you do not wish to pursue this area of study further. Think of the people you know who have pursued a career only to discover later that they are not interested in this line of work. One of your early educational goals should be to explore areas of your actual or potential interest. Many students even find a career goal after taking one of the dreaded required courses.

Therefore, you should be prepared to explore new areas of specialty and new technology. It is clearer today than it was even five years ago that successful paralegals have a good foundation in computer skills. Further, you will have to maintain and build upon these skills as the shift to online service and resources continues to grow. Think of the people who refused to learn computer word processing because "this new correcting typewriter does it all." When was the last time you even saw, let alone used, a correcting typewriter?

ROLE OF THE PARALEGAL

Members of the legal profession and the legal community increasingly see the paralegal as a member of the legal services delivery team. As the paralegals' educational level increases, so will the responsibility given to them. Tasks that were once handled solely by an attorney are now being handled by the paralegal under the supervision of an attorney.

In many areas of law, the cost of legal services has increased. The use of paralegals in many cases permits the delivery of quality legal services at a reduced cost to the client. As concern for access to legal services increases, and discussions about mandatory pro bono service by lawyers expand, so does the possibility of involving paralegals in serving low- and moderate-income populations of the United States.

NATIONAL ASSOCIATIONS OF PARALEGALS

In addition to numerous local and state paralegal and legal assistant organizations, a number of national paralegal/legal assistant organizations support the profession. Four of these are described briefly below.

National Association of Legal Assistants

National Association of Legal Assistants: www.nala.org

National Association of Legal Assistants (NALA) is a leading professional association for legal assistants, providing continuing education and professional certification programs for paralegals. Incorporated in 1975, NALA has a membership of more than 18,000 paralegals, through individual members and through its 90 state- and local-affiliated associations.

National Federation of Paralegal Associations

National Federation of Paralegal Associations (NFPA) is a professional organization of state and local paralegal associations founded in 1974 by eight paralegal associations in response to the growing interest in development of the paralegal profession. NFPA has member associations representing more than 17,000 North American paralegals.

National Federation of Paralegal Associations: www.paralegals.org

Association of Legal Administrators

The Association of Legal Administrators (ALA) was founded in 1971 to provide support to professionals involved in the management of law firms, corporate legal departments, and government legal agencies.

Association of Legal Administrators: www.alanet.org

Legal Assistant Management Association

Legal Assistant Management Association (LAMA) is a North American management association founded in 1984. It has more than 400 members in 16 metropolitan chapters in the United States and Canada. Its members are managers of legal assistants in law firms, corporate law departments, and governmental, judicial, and legal agencies. LAMA members manage more than 5,000 legal assistants.

Legal Assistant Management Association: www.lamanet.org

QUALIFICATIONS OF A PARALEGAL

What are the qualifications that permit one to call oneself a paralegal or a legal assistant, and to be billed as a paralegal? The answer is not easy to come by. Just as the practice of law falls to the individual states for regulation, so does regulation of the paralegal profession. At present there is a lack of uniformity in regulation either by statute or by court rules. Without a state law or a court rule, perhaps the most consistent and universal recognition of minimum qualifications are those established by the educational guidelines of the American Bar Association's Standing Committee on Legal Assistants and the American Association for Paralegal Education (AAfPE), a national educational association of legal educators. The minimum educational requirements for certification of the educational institutions' program of study have become the de facto standard of the minimum qualifications to call oneself a paralegal or legal assistant.

While other state legislatures and courts wrestle with the minimum standards, California has addressed the requirements in a 2000 amendment to the Business and Professional Code that requires a paralegal to possess at least one of the following:

ABA Educational Guidelines:
www.abanet.org/legalservices/
legalassistants/resource.html

1. A certificate of completion of a paralegal program approved by the American Bar Association.

2. A certificate of completion of a paralegal program at an institution that requires a minimum of 24 semester, or equivalent, units in law-related courses, accredited by a national or regional accreditation organization or approved by the Bureau for Private Postsecondary and Vocational Education.

3. A baccalaureate or advanced degree and minimum of one year of law-related experience under an attorney who is an active member of the State Bar of California.

4. A high school diploma or general equivalency diploma and a minimum of three years' law-related experience under the supervision of a California attorney, with this training being completed before December 31, 2003.

Other states might look to the California statute in deciding the question of who is qualified by education, training, or work experience.

PARALEGAL EDUCATION IN THE UNITED STATES

AAfPE: www.aafpe.org

An estimated 800+ paralegal education programs are available in the United States. Some of these programs have obtained ABA approval of their paralegal education program. More than half of the institutions offering paralegal education programs are members of the American Association for Paralegal Education, which, as a condition of institutional membership, requires substantial compliance with the ABA guidelines for approval of a paralegal program.

The American Bar Association and the American Association for Paralegal Education are voluntary programs. Lack of approval of a program does not necessarily mean that the school or the program does not provide a good quality education but, rather, that it has chosen not to undergo the cost or process for approval by the ABA or for membership in the AAfPE.

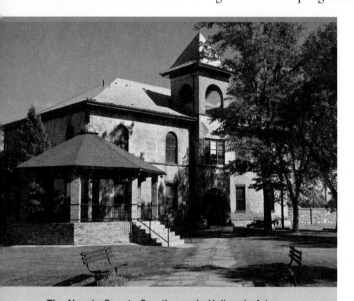

The Navajo County Courthouse in Holbrook, Arizona.

American Bar Association Paralegal Education Standards

The American Bar Association is the largest professional legal organization in the United States. The ABA has indicated that one of its highest priorities is to increase access to legal services.

The American Bar Association Standing Committee on Legal Assistants was formed more than 25 years ago to "work within the ABA and with other groups to help make quality legal services more accessible and affordable, primarily by fostering the increasingly effective integration of legal assistants—or paralegals—into the legal services delivery team." The Committee has jurisdiction within the ABA over matters relating to the education, train-

Formal Mission Statement of the American Bar Association

Goal I   To promote improvements in the American system of justice.

Goal II   To promote meaningful access to legal representation and the American system of justice for all persons regardless of their economic or social condition.

Goal III   To provide ongoing leadership in improving the law to serve the changing needs of society.

Goal IV   To increase public understanding of and respect for the law, the legal process, and the role of the legal profession.

Goal V   To achieve the highest standards of professionalism, competence, and ethical conduct.

Goal VI   To serve as the national representative of the legal profession.

Goal VII   To provide benefits, programs, and services that promote professional growth and enhance the quality of life of the members.

Goal VIII   To advance the rule of law in the world.

Goal IX   To promote full and equal participation in the legal profession by minorities, women, and persons with disabilities.

Goal X   To preserve and enhance the ideals of the legal profession as a common calling and its dedication to public service.

Goal XI   To preserve the independence of the legal profession and the judiciary as fundamental to a free society.

ing, and use of legal assistants or legal paraprofessionals. Through its Approval Commission, the committee sets the standards for ABA-approved educational programs for legal assistant education and training.

In 1974 the committee adopted the first guidelines for the approval of legal assistant education programs by the House of Delegates of the ABA. These guidelines require that

> the institution shall maintain a program for the education of legal assistants that is designed to qualify its graduates to be employed in law-related occupations, including public and private law practice and/or corporate or government law-related activities. (Guidelines G-301)

The process for ABA approval starts with the submission of a self-study report intended "to provide a comprehensive description of all program components with emphasis on the following areas: organization and administration; financial and other resources; advisory committee; educational program, faculty, and program leadership; admissions and student services; placement; library; and physical plant."

After submission and review of the self-study report, an onsite visit is conducted by a three-member team composed of a representative of the ABA Standing Committee on Legal Assistants, an experienced legal assistant, and an educator from another paralegal program, to verify information provided in the self-study and to acquire supplementary information essential to making an evaluation and recommendation to the House of Delegates at its semi-annual meetings in February and August. On each site visit the faculty, staff, administration, and students of the institution meet to review various documents such as course outlines, faculty evaluations, placement records, and student files.

As stated by the ABA, "Seeking approval from the American Bar Association is a voluntary process initiated by the institution offering the program. Therefore, the lack of approval does not necessarily mean a paralegal program is not of good quality and reputable."

The ABA Standing Committee Guidelines require that instruction be at the post-secondary level and contain at least 60 semester hours including general educational and legal specialty courses. Of these 60 hours, at least 18 must be general education courses and at least 18 must be legal specialty courses.

For purposes of the Guidelines, a "legal specialty course" is interpreted in Guideline G-303(c)d as a course (1) in a specific area of law, procedure, or legal process, (2) which has been developed for legal assistants and emphasizes legal assistant skills, forms, documents, procedures, and legal principles and theories, and (3) which is pertinent to the legal assistants' performance of a job.

To meet the American Bar Association requirements for approval, the program must (1) have been in operation for at least two academic years, (2) have graduated students, and (3) have satisfied the requirements of the ABA Guidelines for Paralegal Education Programs.

AAfPE Role in Paralegal Education

The American Association for Paralegal Education is a national organization of paralegal educators and institutions offering paralegal education programs. It has more than 380 members, of which more than 324 are educational institutions. Of these, 33 educational institutions are associate members (programs less than 2 years old or not meeting the criteria for institutional membership). According to the AAfPE Directory for 2001, the member schools have more than 41,000 students and more than 191,000 graduates.

Since its founding, the AAfPE has become the leading professional organization for paralegal education. Paralegal faculty and program directors

Goals of the American Association for Paralegal Education

- Promote high standards for paralegal education.
- Provide a forum for professional improvement for paralegal educators.
- Plan, promote, and hold annual conferences and seminars.
- Provide technical assistance and consultation services to institutions, educators, and employers.
- Promote research and disseminate information on the paralegal profession.
- Cooperate with the ABA and other institutions and professional associations in developing an approval process for paralegal education programs.
- Promote the goals of the AAfPE through cooperation with other national, regional, and local groups and organizations interested in paralegal education.

represent the institutional members in all aspects of the organization's decision-making. As an organization of paralegal educators, it has strived to set minimum educational standards to ensure that graduates of member institutions are well qualified to enter the workforce.

As the profession has advanced, employers and educators have recognized that successful paralegals need to possess certain basic skills. AAfPE looked at the issue and published a report that was approved and adopted by its Board of Directors, the Preamble to which states "A person must not only possess a common core of legal knowledge, but also must have acquired vital critical thinking, organizational, communication, and interpersonal skills."

Those entering the profession or seeking to develop the necessary skills and knowledge for professional growth and advancement must have an understanding of the basic skills and knowledge. They might possess some of the skills at one level of competency or another. They might have acquired some of the knowledge. They might need to further develop some skills to higher levels of competency and to gain or update additional knowledge as part of their professional education. In any case, they should look at these core competencies as skills and knowledge that should be continually upgraded and updated. Many of the core competencies can be acquired by completing a paralegal education program, whether a certificate program, associate's degree, bachelor's degree, or other continuing professional education programs and courses.

Individuals must take responsibility for their own professional education and growth. A good starting point is an honest and careful review of one's individual skill levels and knowledge in certain categories. The accompanying box, listing skills and knowledge competencies, is a useful guide.

> ## *Relevant Skills and Topics*
>
> ### SKILL DEVELOPMENT
>
> - Critical thinking skills
> - Organizational skills
> - General communication skills
> - Interpersonal skills
> - Legal research skills
> - Legal writing skills
> - Computer skills
> - Interviewing and investigation skills
>
> ### ACQUISITION OF KNOWLEDGE
>
> - Organization and operation of the legal system
> - Organization and operation of law offices
> - The paralegal profession and ethical obligations
> - Contracts
> - Torts
> - Business organizations
> - Litigation procedures

AAfPE Statement of Academic Quality

Selecting an appropriate educational institution for a basic education or an advanced education can be a difficult task. The AAfPE Statement of Academic Quality is a good starting point for measuring the appropriateness of an institution for an individual's education even if the institution is not a member of the association.

The AAfPE Statement of Academic Quality provides, in part:

> Paralegal education is a unique academic curriculum, composed of both substantive legal knowledge and professional skills, that incorporates legal theory with an understanding of practical applications. This intellectually demanding course of study is derived from the responsibilities of paralegals as legal professionals. It is the philosophy of this organization that a person is qualified as a paralegal with (1) an associate or baccalaureate degree or equivalent course work; and (2) a credential in paralegal education completed in any of the following types of educational programs: associate degree, baccalaureate degree

(major, minor or concentration), certificate, or master's degree. AAfPE recognizes these essential components of quality paralegal education programs:

Curriculum Development

Quality paralegal education programs monitor the responsibilities and competencies expected by employers on an ongoing basis. . . .

Facilities

Quality paralegal education programs have a physical learning environment that provides: (1) access to legal research library facilities that include computer-based resources; (2) classrooms that provide opportunities for interaction among students and between students and the instructor and include the necessary equipment and technology to facilitate learning; (3) a convenient physical location for administration/support staff and the provision of student services; and (4) accessibility pursuant to the Americans with Disabilities Act (ADA) requirements.

Faculty

The faculty of quality paralegal education programs consists of legal professionals and, where appropriate, other similarly qualified persons in good standing in their profession who (1) possess expertise and experience in their subject area; (2) have background working as or with paralegals; (3) can demonstrate teaching ability; (4) hold a graduate degree or possess exceptional expertise in the legal subject to be taught; and (5) are committed to the role of paralegals in the delivery of legal services. . . .

Paralegal Instruction

Quality paralegal education programs maintain standards of excellence and include, either as separate classes or with the overall course of study, the following topics: ethics, substantive and procedural law, the American legal system, delivery of legal services, law offices and related environments, the paralegal profession, legal research and writing, law-related computer skills, legal interviewing and investigation, and areas of legal practice such as those described in AAfPE's Core Competencies for Paralegal Programs; and offer an experiential learning component, such as internship, practicum, or clinical experience.

Related Competencies

Quality paralegal education programs assist their students in acquiring these essential related competencies, primarily in general education: (1) critical thinking skills (analysis, judgment, research, and problem-solving); (2) communication skills (oral, written, nonverbal, and interpersonal); (3) computer skills; (4) computational skills; (5) understanding of ethics; and (6) organizational skills. Graduates also possess a basic understanding of American history, business, and political systems.

Reprinted with the permission of the AAfPE.

Types of Programs

The goal of the educational experience is to get a job and be able to perform at a professional level. The demands on paralegals today require them to have greater skills and ability than in the past. Whereas basic typing, office, and business communications skills might have been acceptable for a starting position in a law firm twenty years ago, these are not the skills demanded for those looking for a paralegal position today. The core competencies as set by the AAfPE are essential for getting a job and succeeding in the profession today. More and more employers today also are asking for transcripts showing the courses taken and the minimum number of hours of study as spelled out in the ABA guidelines, even for graduates of educational institutions that have not obtained ABA certification of their programs. The reality is that many attorneys do not know the educational requirements to obtain a paralegal degree or certificate. And in many cases they do not know the elements of the ABA, NFPA, or NALA definitions of paralegal or legal assistant.

Paralegal/legal assistant educational programs generally fall into two categories—those offering a certificate and those offering a degree, either an associate's degree or a bachelor's degree. These programs of study may be offered by a two-year community or junior college or a four-year college or university. A number of business and private (proprietary) schools also offer paralegal/legal assistant programs of study.

Students' educational and professional backgrounds will determine, in many cases, which of the programs to select. Those with bachelor's and higher academic degrees may need only the legal specialty courses. Those who come from a specialty background, such as nursing or one heavy in science courses, may want to broaden their education by taking courses of a general nature in addition to the legal specialty courses.

Certificate Programs

Most educational institutions with paralegal/legal assistant programs, both public and private, offer a certificate. The certificate recognizes completion of a program of study that requires less than is required to receive a degree. Some certificates award college credits; some do not. For students already possessing a baccalaureate degree, obtaining additional college credits probably isn't an issue. For students without an undergraduate degree, programs that do not offer college credit can still be valuable but should be carefully considered. At the very least, the actual time spent in the classroom should be equivalent to the minimums of college credit courses.

Students' concerns should be for what is acceptable in the community in which they intend to work. Those planning to transfer should consider the acceptability of the course for transfer credit to another credit-granting institution. Even if they have no immediate intention of continuing in school, it is wise to plan ahead and not lose the hours and credits they have earned, in the event they later decide to transfer or go on to obtain a degree. Many professional paralegal organizations are reporting that a bachelor's degree is becoming more necessary to enter the paralegal field and some programs. The U. S. Attorney's Office, for example, is requiring at least a four-year degree to consider individuals for a paralegal position.

Statue of Justice, Wiblingen, Germany.

Associate Degree Programs

Many community colleges and junior colleges offer an associate degree in science (AS degree) or in arts (AA degree) or applied arts (AAS degree) in paralegal or legal assistant studies. For many students the two-year community college or junior college programs offer a community-based transition into higher education. For others it is a way of getting back into higher education while working at a full-time job or after being in another occupation. Support services for returning students or students needing additional help are often available. Many of these schools offer English courses for those for whom English is a second language and those returning to school who need a refresher course or help with study skills after years away from school. This also tends to be a cost-effective educational environment for trying different areas of study before finding an area of concentration.

Baccalaureate Programs

Some of the earliest paralegal programs were built on a model in which a bachelor's degree was the prerequisite to entering the paralegal program of study. A number of programs now offer a bachelor's degree in paralegal studies. One national organization has recommended the bachelor's degree as the minimum qualification to enter the profession. The increase in professional recognition of paralegals has resulted in their gaining more responsibility, as well as a growing demand for the skills required to perform the assigned tasks. As the standing of the paralegal on the legal team rises, so will the demand for people with a broad-based educational background to serve in those positions. Four-year programs of study are attempting to meet that demand by merging traditional four-year study core requirements and legal specialty courses.

Consider the family law attorney or paralegal. In the frequently highly charged emotional environment of custody and divorce, knowledge of family and child psychology is essential. For those in an intellectual property practice, an understanding of science and engineering is a basic requirement. The four-year timeframe allows more flexibility to explore and build skills and knowledge, as well as to meet the increasing demand for more education for paralegals.

Graduate Programs

A few colleges and universities now offer graduate degrees in legal studies. Others offer advanced degrees in related areas such as legal administration.

Specialty Certificates

Specialty certificates, such as the paralegal certificate or the legal nurse consultant certificate, offer an excellent entry point into a paralegal career. Such certificates combined with degrees in other fields of study, such as nursing, journalism, and computer science, are like a capstone program preparing one for entry into a new career. One of the greatest demands has been for those with a background in nursing combined with a paralegal education. A growing number of colleges are offering a certificate in Legal Nurse Consulting.

Paralegal Certification

The National Federation of Paralegal Associations (NFPA) administers a certification program. Its exam, known as PACE (Paralegal Advanced Competency Exam), requires that the paralegal have two years' experience and a bachelor's degree and have completed a paralegal course at an accred-

American Association of
Legal Nurse Consultants:
www.aalnc.org

NFPA PACE:
www.paralegals.org/PACE/
home.html

ited school. The two-day exam covers federal procedure and law and tests paralegal skills such as communication and interviewing, as well as areas such as family and contract law. Those who successfully pass the exam may use the designation "RP" after their names. Continued use of the designation requires 12 additional hours of continuing legal or specialty education every two years.

Since 1976, the National Association of Legal Assistants has conferred the CLA (Certified Legal Assistant) designation on those who pass its national certification program's two-day comprehensive examination. The first day contains a 1.5-hour exam on communications and a 2.5-hour exam on judgment and analytical ability. The second day consists of a 1-hour test on ethics, a 1.5-hour test on legal research, and a 2-hour test on substantive law, which includes tests on general law and four practice areas selected by the examinees. All of the sections of this exam are on the federal level, with no testing on state laws or procedures.

To maintain use of the CLA designation, the legal assistant must submit evidence of completion of 5 units of continuing legal assistant education every five years. Ten hours of education equals one unit of CLE (continuing legal education), including a college course in the field. For those who have achieved the initial designation, NALA also offers specialist credentials for those practicing in specific areas of law, including bankruptcy, intellectual property, civil litigation, probate and estate planning, corporate and business, criminal, or real estate. Successful completion of these 4-hour examinations permits the additional designation CLAS, Certified Legal Assistant–Specialty.

NALA CLA: www.nala.org/cert.htm

LAMA Position Paper: www.lamanet.org/resources/pp-edu.cfm

PERSONAL GOALS

If you are reading this book, you probably have made at least a tentative career goal to enter the paralegal profession, with the ultimate goal of obtaining a job. It should not be "just a job" but, rather, a job that will give you satisfaction and one that you will get up and go to with anticipation, not dread. The paralegal field offers many paths and many and varied specialties. One of your goals should be to take courses that will introduce you to the specialty you would enjoy most. Maybe you already are well versed in something that will lead to a specialty, such as nursing, one of the sciences, or law enforcement.

One of the first steps is to assess your own skills. What are your other educational skills? What are your personality traits? Do you like working under deadlines or working with certain groups of people, such as elderly people or those with disabilities?

As you will see, the paralegal profession offers opportunities in many areas of legal specialty and in many types of working environments. Understanding your interests, skills, and desired working conditions and job locations will help you select the best educational path toward achieving your professional goals.

Minimum Education

The position of the Legal Assistant Management Association (LAMA) is that a baccalaureate degree should be the minimum requirement for employment as a legal assistant. Legal assistants have assumed many responsibilities formerly handled by lawyers. Working with complex legal issues requires that a legal assistant possess clear writing, researching, and critical thinking abilities. Because a strong academic background is essential, LAMA believes that a baccalaureate degree should be the minimum requirement for employment as a legal assistant. LAMA believes this accepted professional standard of academic achievement lends greater credibility and respect to the legal profession.

Source: LAMA's *Position Paper on Legal Assistant Education.*

SIDEBAR

Collecting Lunch Stories: The Hidden Perk

Facts & Findings   August 1998

Collecting good stories is one of the top benefits of working in the legal profession. In a field that operates at an intense level most of the time and demands diligence, commitment, and excellence, it's no wonder that on occasion we crack. When this happens, we can either get upset or take a good story to Happy Hour now and then. I prefer the latter alternative. This way, when I crack, I don't think of it so much as having a breakdown as that I am contributing to the story exchange.

While working on my master's thesis, I learned four tips from legal assistants through their stories. Here are their tips and a few of their stories. Enjoy.

Tip #1: Take charge.

Refusing to take control of a situation left a legal assistant sitting in the dark—literally. Mary needed to leave on time one evening, so she asked a colleague to stay late and help an attorney who had a deadline the next day. Mary warned the paralegal before she left, "You must go in and see [the attorney] every half hour or he'll forget you're here. He'll eventually tell you to go home, but you have to go in every half hour." Mary explained that when this attorney focused on a project, he forgot everything else, including other lawyers and paralegals working with him.

The paralegal filling in for Mary didn't want to disturb the attorney, so she stayed in her office, letting the attorney come to her with work to do throughout the evening. At some point, the lawyer stopped coming, and at 4:00 a.m., after he had taken his midnight nap and gained a second wind, the attorney found the paralegal sitting in her office. He had forgotten she was there. The paralegal's fear of disturbing the attorney had kept her up all night. Worse, he was ready to work, and the paralegal was tired.

Tip #2: Learn to roll your eyes.

Sometimes it just doesn't pay to get angry. On some days it's better to do what Sabrina does: rolls her eyes and keeps on going. Sabrina, a paralegal helping a team of attorneys keep up with a hectic deposition schedule, stayed at work late one night preparing a set of documents for an attorney to use at a deposition the next day. The attorney had gone back to his hotel to work and asked Sabrina to drop off the documents on her way home.

The paralegal arrived at the hotel around 10:00 p.m. and asked the desk clerk to call up to the attorney's room to let him know she had arrived.

"He's in the bar," announced the clerk, who had gotten to know the attorney during his stay at the hotel.

Sabrina, thinking the clerk had to be mistaken, asked again. This attorney had a deposition the next day.

"In the bar," the man said, smiling, pointing toward the door.

Sabrina stepped into the bar area, and found the attorney laughing with a member of the co-counsel's trial team.

When the attorney saw Sabrina, he waved her over to the table.

"Here are your documents for tomorrow," she said.

"Oh, the deposition has been canceled. Didn't anyone call you?" the attorney grinned.

"He was the only person I was working late for that night. Who else was going to call me?" the paralegal said to me, rolling her eyes. In Sabrina's case, she respected this attorney, and the deposition cancellation was a nice break in the tough schedule.

Tip #3: Learn to laugh at yourself.

When I first moved to Massachusetts, I was working with a team of legal assistants who made fun of the way I talked and looked at me like I was a nut case when I asked the location of the closest Whataburger (only those who know Whataburger can appreciate my need . . .). It turned out no one in Massachusetts or in the several surrounding states had ever heard of Whataburger. So . . . I stood looking down at a woman on the floor surrounded by notebooks, asking her, "How much more do you lack?" (I didn't understand why she looked up at me as if I had asked why grocery stores up here keep chili on the ethnic food aisles.) "How much more do you lack?" I asked again, speaking English, I'm sure. We were tired; maybe I slurred all the words.

"How much more do I like what?" she cried. I could see frustration in her eyes. She had been working so hard. "How much more do I like sitting on the floor than I like sitting at my desk? What are you talking about?"

"I mean," I said, finally realizing I was displaying some slang (and very poor slang at that) that I had picked up in the South, "how much more do you have to do?"

She laughed. She told everyone else in the office. They laughed. We met our deadlines. We had lunch. We laughed some more.

No matter how overwhelming the situation seems, laugh. Even in the worst situations, think of yourself as if you are standing in the middle of a cartoon strip. Are the circumstances as ridiculous as the Dilbert cartoon's spoofs on corporate life?

Tip #4: Recognize the story, remember the story, repeat the story.

"Don't be too sensitive," is the advice from Karen, a legal assistant coordinator in Texas. "The way [attorneys] talk to you may be intimidating," so you can't get caught up in that.

A Boston legal assistant used all of [the above] advice (taking charge, eye rolling, . . . and laughing) to keep in perspective a heated exchange that occurred during an intense session of deposition preparation.

The paralegal went to New York to help an attorney with a deposition. She traveled with the warning that this particular attorney, though well-respected and one of the firm's top rainmakers, could be "extremely intense." During their preparation for the deposition, the attorney asked her to call another paralegal to have him send some documents for the next day. While she was in the middle of speaking into the paralegal's voice mail, the attorney barked, "Look, you have to get off the phone. We have work to do."

"Intense," was not the word that came to mind.

"Look," she said to the attorney, "you told me to call him. So just give me a break." Both stressed that the exchange allowed both paralegal and attorney to release some tension.

After the frustration wore off, she was able to recognize the situation for what it was: a great story about the well-respected attorney known for his "intensity," one that would earn respect among her colleagues.

Even if we're confident, comfortable, and able to laugh, we still experience occasional frustration; it's part of the profession. But if our polished skills don't make the situation any better, at least we'll be able to recognize a good lunch story when it happens.

CONTEMPORARY PERSPECTIVE CONTEMPORARY PERSPECTIVE CONTEMPORARY PERSPECTIVE

Checklist

SKILLS & GOALS

○ My personal goals are:

○ My professional goals are:

○ I have these skills:

○ Languages	○ Communication	○ Organizational
○ Computer	○ Written	○ Resourcefulness
○ Academic background	○ Oral	○ Cultural awareness
○ Occupational background	○ Public speaking	○ Analytical

○ Skills I need to develop:

○ Skills I need to improve:

CASES FOR BRIEFING

Throughout this text, actual court cases will be presented to familiarize you with the language of law and the courts and to expose you to topics of interest, including issues of practice and ethics. Questions at the beginning of each case will guide your reading. Your instructor also might ask you to brief the case—that is, to prepare a brief abstract of the case. If briefing is assigned, read Appendix A: How to Brief a Case.

le′gəl tur′mə näl′ə je

LEGAL TERMINOLOGY

American Association for Paralegal Education (AAfPE)
American Bar Association (ABA)
Associate's degree
Bachelor's degree
Certified Legal Assistant (CLA)
Legal assistant
National Association of Legal Assistants (NALA)
National Federation of Paralegal Associations (NFPA)
Paralegal (legal assistant)
Paralegal Advanced Competency Exam (PACE)
Proprietary school

Summary

CHAPTER 1 THE PROFESSIONAL PARALEGAL	

What Is a Paralegal?

Definition	A paralegal, or legal assistant, is "a person qualified by education, training, or work experience who is employed or retained by a lawyer, law office, corporation, governmental agency, or other entity who performs specifically delegated substantive legal work for which a lawyer is responsible."

What Do Paralegals Do?

Functions of Paralegals	The primary function of paralegals is to assist attorneys in preparing for hearings, trials, meetings, and closings.

Opportunities

Numbers and Salaries	In 2000, paralegals held about 188,000 jobs in the United States, with median annual earnings of $35,360. The U. S. Department of Labor projects that this profession will continue to be among the fastest growing through the year 2010.

Career Planning

Education	1. General education courses. 2. Associate's degree or bachelor's degree.

Role of the Paralegal

Level of Responsibility	The paralegal is a member of the legal services delivery team with responsibilities commensurate with his or her education and experience.

National Associations of Paralegals

Major Associations	1. National Association of Legal Assistants 2. National Federation of Paralegal Associations 3. Association of Legal Administrators 4. Legal Assistant Management Association

Qualifications of a Paralegal

Minimum Qualifications	Established by the educational guidelines of the American Bar Association's Standing Committee on Legal Assistants and American Association for Paralegal Education.

(continued)

Paralegal Education in the United States	
Standards	1. American Bar Association Paralegal Education Standards 2. AAfPE in Paralegal Education 3. AAfPE Statement on Academic Quality
Types of Programs	1. Certificate programs 2. Associate degree programs 3. Baccalaureate programs 4. Graduate programs 5. Specialty certificates

Working the Web

1. Check the NFPA site at www.paralegals.org for:
   a. Various information pertaining to the paralegal profession.
   b. Current definition from your jurisdiction, in the Professional Development section.
   c. Information on career outlook, salary, and other pertinent facts, in the Career Center.

2. Visit the NALA site at www.nala.org for information on
   a. Certified Legal Assistant (CLA) program
   b. Links to recent surveys on paralegal utilization and compensation

3. Check the American Bar Association subcommittee on the utilization of legal assistants website at www.abanet.org.

4. Take a look at the American Association for Paralegal Education website at www.aafpe.org for:
   a. Core competencies
   b. A guide to quality paralegal education
   c. Links to other sites

5. Check the latest information on the paralegal occupation in the U. S. Department of Labor, Bureau of Labor Statistics' *Occupational Outlook Handbook* at www.bls.gov/oco/ocos114.htm.

Questions
CRITICAL LEGAL THINKING AND WRITING

1. Why should those planning to become paralegals or legal assistants get a well-founded education and develop the necessary skills?
2. What skills are required to be a paralegal and why are they important?
3. What is the difference between the job of a legal secretary, legal administrator, or legal assistant manager, and that of a paralegal?
4. How can a paralegal demonstrate the qualifications for employment as a paralegal?
5. How can one satisfy the court that he or she is qualified as a paralegal and not as a legal secretary?
6. Based on the AAfPE core competencies, what sorts of assignments and tasks should you expect in your paralegal education?
7. What educational plan makes the most sense for you? Why?
8. Complete the checklist "Skills & Goals." Based on your answers, how well prepared are you for a career as a paralegal? What skills need development?
9. Prepare a plan of action, based on the AAfPE core competencies, for improving your skills and knowledge.
10. Why would an employer, such as the U. S. Attorney's office, require a four-year degree for those seeking a paralegal position?

Questions
ETHICS: ANALYSIS AND DISCUSSION

1. Search your state statutes, code, or court rules for the definition of "Paralegal" or "Legal Assistant."
2. Does your state have a statute or court rule on the regulation of the paralegal or legal assistant practice?
3. Does your state have minimum educational requirements for paralegals?

Use of the Title "Paralegal"

There are few certainties in the area of ethics, for paralegals or in any profession. What qualifies as ethical conduct is in most cases based on state law and court interpretation applied to a set of facts. For the following:

- *Prepare a written statement based on your state law.*
- *Use your state bar association website as a starting point.*

You hold a bachelor's degree in paralegal studies from a prestigious college. You want to work as an independent paralegal. May you advertise in the local newspaper and put a sign on the door of your office that uses the term "paralegal," according to your state law?

Missouri v. Jenkins

491 U.S. 274 (1989)   Supreme Court of the United States

Read the following case excerpts. Information on preparing a briefing is provided in Appendix A: How to Brief a Case. In your brief, prepare a written answer to each of the following questions.

1. What is the difference between "market rates" for paralegals and cost to the attorney for paralegal service?

2. Does billing for paralegal services at market rates unfairly benefit the law firm?

3. According to this court, how is a reasonable attorney's fee calculated?

4. How does the public benefit from allowing paralegals to be billed at market rates?

5. Does this court believe that a reasonable attorney's fee should include paralegal fees?

Brennan, J., delivered the opinion of the Court.

This is the attorney's fee aftermath of major school desegregation litigation in Kansas City, Missouri. We [are hearing this case to decide] should the fee award compensate the work of paralegals and law clerks by applying the market rate for their work?

I

This litigation began in 1977 as a suit by the Kansas City Missouri School District (KCMSD), the school board, and the children of two school board members, against the State of Missouri and other defendants. The plaintiffs alleged that the State, surrounding school districts, and various federal agencies had caused and perpetuated a system of racial segregation in the schools of the Kansas City metropolitan area. . . . After lengthy proceedings, including a trial that lasted 7 1/2 months during 1983 and 1984, the District Court found the State of Missouri and KCMSD liable. . . . It ordered various intradistrict remedies, to be paid for by the State and KCMSD, including $260 million in capital improvements and a magnet-school plan costing over $200 million.

The plaintiff class has been represented, since 1979, by Kansas City lawyer Arthur Benson and, since 1982, by the NAACP Legal Defense and Educational Fund, Inc. (LDF). Benson and the LDF requested attorney's fees under the Civil Rights Attorney's Fees Awards Act of 1976, 42 U.S.C. § 1988. Benson and his associates had devoted 10,875 attorney hours to the litigation, as well as 8,108 hours of paralegal and law clerk time. For the LDF, the corresponding figures were 10,854 hours for attorneys and 15,517 hours for paralegals and law clerks. Their fee applications deleted from these totals

3,628 attorney hours and 7,046 paralegal hours allocable to unsuccessful claims against the suburban school districts. With additions for postjudgment monitoring and for preparation of the fee application, the District Court awarded Benson a total of approximately $1.7 million and the LDF $2.3 million. . . .

Both Benson and the LDF employed numerous paralegals, law clerks (generally law students working part-time), and recent law graduates in this litigation. The court awarded fees for their work based on Kansas City market rates for those categories. As in the case of the attorneys, it used current rather than historic market rates in order to compensate for the delay in payment. It therefore awarded fees based on hourly rates of $35 for law clerks, $40 for paralegals, and $50 for recent law graduates. [. . .]

III

Missouri's second contention is that the District Court erred in compensating the work of law clerks and paralegals (hereinafter collectively "paralegals") at the market rates for their services, rather than at their cost to the attorney. While Missouri agrees that compensation for the cost of these personnel should be included in the fee award, it suggests that an hourly rate of $15—which it argued below corresponded to their salaries, benefits, and overhead—would be appropriate, rather than the market rates of $35 to $50. According to Missouri, § 1988 does not authorize billing paralegals' hours at market rates, and doing so produces a "windfall" for the attorney.

We begin with the statutory language, which provides simply for "a reasonable attorney's fee as part of the costs." Clearly, a "reasonable attorney's fee" cannot have been meant to compensate only work performed personally by members of the bar. Rather, the term must refer to a reasonable fee for the work product of an attorney.

Thus, the fee must take into account the work not only of attorneys but also of secretaries, messengers, librarians, janitors, and others whose labor contributes to the work product for which an attorney bills her client; and it also must take account of other expenses and profit. The parties have suggested no reason why the work of paralegals should not be similarly compensated, nor can we think of any. We thus take as our starting point the self-evident proposition that the "reasonable attorney's fee" provided for by statute should compensate the work of paralegals, as well as that of attorneys.

The more difficult question is how the work of paralegals is to be valuated in calculating the overall attorney's fee.

The statute specifies a "reasonable" fee for the attorney's work product. In determining how other elements of the attorney's fee are to be calculated, we have consistently looked to the marketplace as our guide to what is "reasonable." In *Blum v. Stenson*, 465 U.S. 886 (1984), for example, we rejected an argument that attorney's fees for nonprofit legal service organizations should be based on cost. We said: "The statute and legislative history establish that 'reasonable fees' under § 1988 are to be calculated according to the prevailing market rates in the relevant community. . . ." A reasonable attorney's fee under § 1988 is one calculated on the basis of rates and practices prevailing in the relevant market, i.e., "in line with those [rates] prevailing in the community for similar services by lawyers of reasonably comparable skill, experience, and reputation," and one that grants the successful civil rights plaintiff a "fully compensatory fee," comparable to what "is traditional with attorneys compensated by a fee-paying client."

If an attorney's fee awarded under § 1988 is to yield the same level of compensation that would be available from the market, the "increasingly widespread custom of separately billing for the services of paralegals and law students who serve as clerks," all else being equal, the hourly fee charged by an attorney whose rates include paralegal work in her hourly fee, or who bills separately for the work of paralegals at cost, will be higher than the hourly fee charged by an attorney competing in the same market who bills separately for the work of paralegals at "market rates." In other words, the prevailing "market rate" for attorney time is not independent of the manner in which paralegal time is accounted for. Thus, if the prevailing practice in a given community were to bill paralegal time separately at market rates, fees awarded the attorney at market rates for attorney time would not be fully compensatory if the court refused to compensate hours billed by paralegals or did

so only at "cost." Similarly, the fee awarded would be too high if the court accepted separate billing for paralegal hours in a market where that was not the custom.

We reject the argument that compensation for paralegals at rates above "cost" would yield a "windfall" for the prevailing attorney. Neither petitioners nor anyone else, to our knowledge, has ever suggested that the hourly rate applied to the work of an associate attorney in a law firm creates a windfall for the firm's partners or is otherwise improper under § 1988, merely because it exceeds the cost of the attorney's services. If the fees are consistent with market rates and practices, the "windfall" argument has no more force with regard to paralegals than it does for associates. And it would hardly accord with Congress' intent to provide a "fully compensatory fee" if the prevailing plaintiff's attorney in a civil rights lawsuit were not permitted to bill separately for paralegals, while the defense attorney in the same litigation was able to take advantage of the prevailing practice and obtain market rates for such work. Yet that is precisely the result sought in this case by the State of Missouri, which appears to have paid its own outside counsel for the work of paralegals at the hourly rate of $35.

Nothing in § 1988 requires that the work of paralegals invariably be billed separately. If it is the practice in the relevant market not to do so, or to bill the work of paralegals only at cost, that is all that § 1988 requires. Where, however, the prevailing practice is to bill paralegal work at market rates, treating civil rights lawyers' fee requests in the same way is not only permitted by § 1988, but also makes economic sense. By encouraging the use of lower cost paralegals rather than attorneys wherever possible, permitting market-rate billing of paralegal hours "encourages cost-effective delivery of legal services and, by reducing the spiraling cost of civil rights litigation, furthers the policies underlying civil rights statutes."

Such separate billing appears to be the practice in most communities today. In the present case, Missouri concedes that "the local market typically bills separately for paralegal services," and the District Court found that the requested hourly rates of $35 for law clerks, $40 for paralegals, and $50 for recent law graduates were the prevailing rates for such services in the Kansas City area. Under these circumstances, the court's decision to award separate compensation at these rates was fully in accord with § 1988.

IV

The courts below correctly granted a fee enhancement to compensate for delay in payment and approved compensation of paralegals and law clerks at market rates. The judgment of the Court of Appeals is therefore Affirmed.

CHAPTER 2

CHAPTER OBJECTIVES

After studying this chapter, you should be able to:

1. Explain the reasons for the Unauthorized Practice of Law (UPL) regulation.

2. Understand the basic areas of concern for the paralegal in the area of UPL.

3. Discuss issues involving the conflicting views on regulation of the paralegal profession.

4. Understand the difference between the attorneys' and the paralegals' rules of ethics and the obligations of each profession.

5. Explain the ethical responsibilities established by statutes, court decisions, and court rules.

6. Understand the concept of conflict of interest for the legal profession.

7. Explain how the ethical wall protects client confidentiality.

8. Understand how a paralegal can have a conflict of interest in working a second job.

9. Explain the concept of the work product doctrine.

10. Understand the lawyer supervision requirements and obligations in utilizing legal assistants.

Ethics, Regulation, and Professional Responsibility

Morality cannot be legislated, but behavior can be regulated. Judicial decrees may not change hearts, but they can restrain the heartless.

MARTIN LUTHER KING, JR.

Introduction

Every profession develops a set of guidelines for those in the profession to follow. These may be the rules of practice, such as court rules of procedure; ethical guidelines, such as the ABA Model Rules of Professional Conduct; or statutorily mandated rules, such as professional licensing statutes. By their own efforts, lawyers have developed a combination of organizational guidelines such as the rules of ethics, and have lobbied for licensing regulation of the profession through the courts and the legislature.

The paralegal profession is going through a growth phase in developing these guides. Even though these rules and regulations are in the development stage, the legal assistant must have some sense of the rules to be followed. The legal assistant in many workplaces today is a substitute for the recent law school graduate, frequently referred to as a junior associate, who may not have taken the bar examination and been admitted to practice. In any case, ethics rules must be followed to avoid conflict, potential violation of client rights and statutory regulation, and possible malpractice.

ABA Model Rules of Professional Conduct, 2002 Edition: www.abanet.org/cpr/mrpc/mrpc_toc.html

UNAUTHORIZED PRACTICE OF LAW (UPL)

Regulations are put into place in an attempt to prevent abuses in the practice of law. Two relevant issues involve giving advice and filling out forms.

Regulation of the Practice of Law

All of the states regulate the practice of law, in an attempt to protect the public from incompetent and unscrupulous practitioners, just as they regulate the practice of medicine and many other professions. States such as Pennsylvania have specifically addressed the issue of unauthorized practice of law by paralegals and legal assistants. The Pennsylvania statute on the unauthorized practice of law makes it a misdemeanor for "any person, including, but not limited to, *a paralegal or legal assistant* . . . within this commonwealth [to] practice law."

The Pennsylvania statute seems to address concerns that the general public will misinterpret the title of paralegal or legal assistant as denoting a person admitted to practice law in the commonwealth. An unresolved issue in Pennsylvania, and in other states, is to define what specific conduct the courts will hold to be the practice of law. Because the interpretation will vary from state to state, the paralegal must be aware of the local requirements and limitations that define the unauthorized practice of law within that jurisdiction. What constitutes the practice of law under these statutes usually is decided on a case-by-case basis.

Certain conduct required or requested by an attorney or client should at the very least cause the paralegal to pause. A client who asks you to prepare a power of attorney without "bothering the lawyer," or to "go with me to the support conference" should raise a caution flag in the paralegal's mind. The difficulty is in knowing what the individual courts allow or will permit in individual circumstances. Some jurisdictions and administrative agencies do permit those who are not admitted to practice to appear in court or before administrative law judges or referees on behalf of clients. Typically, these are law students acting under the guidance and supervision of an attorney under limited circumstances, but they may include paralegals. Depending upon the jurisdiction, nature of the action, and level of the court, the paralegal might be permitted to appear with or on behalf of a client—for example, before a Social Security Administration Administrative Law Judge.

County courthouse in Bridgeport, California.

Giving Advice

Is the giving of advice an unauthorized practice of law? Yes, if legal rights may be affected. The question of what advice is legal advice is not easy to answer. Consider the seemingly innocent question, "How should I sign my name?" In most circumstances the answer might be, "Just sign it the way you normally write your name." But when a person is signing a document in a representative capacity, for example as the officer of a corporation or on behalf of another person under a power of attorney, telling the client to just "sign your name" might be giving legal advice because the client's legal rights could be affected if he or she does not indicate representative capacity.

Filling Out Forms

Filling out forms for clients also can be a source of trouble. In some jurisdictions paralegals are permitted to assist clients in the preparation of certain documents. Other courts, however, view this assistance as rendering legal advice. One of the more interesting decisions in this context was by a federal judge who ruled the Quicken Family Lawyer computer program, which provides legal forms, as the unauthorized practice of law [*Unauthorized Practice of Law v. Parsons Tech.*, 179 F.3d 956 (5th Cir. 1999)].

REGULATION OF THE PARALEGAL PROFESSION

Regulation and licensing of the paralegal profession has been one of the hottest topics in the legal and paralegal communities. Each state, through its respective legislature and court, regulates and licenses the practice of law. The original UPL issues were simply those of the licensing of attorneys and laws preventing the unauthorized practice of law. With the development of the paralegal profession has come a new set of concerns and controversy surrounding what is the unauthorized practice of law, who should be permitted to render legal services, and under what conditions.

The conflict is between the paralegal profession and the bar organizations, such as the American Bar Association, which does not see the need for the additional time, effort, and cost for certification of paralegals and legal assistants. The ABA position is broadly based on the argument that the public is protected by the attorney's obligation to supervise the paralegal and responsibility to the public.

For the most part, the paralegal profession has sought some level of regulation, certification, or licensure. Somewhere in the middle are increasing numbers of employers of paralegals who want some level of assurance that those they hire who claim to be paralegals are qualified for those positions. As the responsibilities undertaken by paralegals have increased, so have the educational requirements. Within the profession has come a concern that those who hold themselves out as paralegals are truly qualified to perform the work they have undertaken. This is no different from the organized bar monitoring the activities of those holding themselves out as being lawyers.

State Licensing Attempts

Individual states have attempted to set up licensing systems. A case in point is the proposal rejected in 1999 by the New Jersey Supreme Court to license traditional paralegals, which had been developed after five years of study by that court's committee on paralegal education and regulation. If it had been approved, this proposal would have made New Jersey the first state to license traditional paralegals.

Ethical PERSPECTIVE

Unauthorized Practice of Law

Check those items you believe to be the unauthorized practice of law.

- ☐ I have been asked to appear in court for a client.
- ☐ The client has asked for my advice on a legal matter.
- ☐ The client has asked me to fill out forms that affect legal rights.

It is not always clear what conduct will be considered UPL. If you are not sure, ASK.

Ethical PERSPECTIVE

Filling Out Forms

It is the unauthorized practice of law "to fill out bankruptcy forms even when simply plugging in information and letting the computer program pick the exemptions."

In re Kaitangian, *218 B.R.102 (Bankr. S.D. Cal. 1998).*

California leads the nation in setting stringent educational requirements that may become a model for other states (refer to the California statute mentioned in Chapter 1, p. 15).

The Washington State Bar adopted a rule to establish a "Practice of Law Board" that authorizes nonlawyers to practice law in limited areas as needed to assure access to affordable legal services.

After a number of efforts, a Hawaii State Bar Association task force on paralegal certification developed a compromise "voluntary" certification proposal for consideration by the Hawaii Supreme Court, which recognized the opposition from some segments of the bar.

It is obvious to some observers that the organized bar is fearful in many cases of the incursion of the paralegal profession into the practice of law. For some, the issue is loss of income. Others are concerned for the delivery of quality legal services by all those who hold themselves out as being members of the legal profession. For the paralegal, it is a question of status as well as job opportunities. With the establishment of minimum standards for holding oneself out as a paralegal comes a status that members of a profession are entitled to enjoy. For those who have worked hard to develop the necessary paralegal skills by way of education and experience it eliminates the unqualified from taking those jobs that should be performed by qualified individuals. The stated goals of the different groups are not that far apart: delivery of quality legal services at affordable prices with a reasonable standard of living for the legal profession and the paralegal profession.

The traditional role of the attorney in advising and representing clients is limited to those who are admitted to practice as lawyers under the applicable state law. Some exemptions do exist that allow nonlawyers to perform certain services under state law, such as document preparation under California law. Under federal law, the Social Security system provides an example.

PERSPECTIVE

Backup Attorney

To avoid possible claims for the unauthorized practice of law, have your supervising attorney select a backup attorney with whom you are authorized to consult when your primary supervising attorney is not available. Ensure you have contact information, including home phone number, cell phone number, and pager number.

Social Security Administration

Under federal law, certain specific exemptions permit nonlawyers to act on behalf of clients and to appear before administrative agencies. Most notable is that of the Social Security Administration. Under federal regulation, a paralegal can, without supervision, represent individuals before the Social Security Administration, including appearing before Administrative Law Judges on behalf of clients. Paralegals may appear as representatives of claimants for disability claims; Medicare parts A, B, and C; and cases of overpayment and underpayment.

As representative of a claimant, the paralegal in practice before the Social Security Administration may obtain information, submit evidence, and make statements and arguments. The difference between the paralegal and the attorney is only in the matter of direct versus indirect payment for services. The Social Security Administration pays the attorney directly, whereas the paralegal must bill the client for services rendered. Within the Social Security Administration, paralegals are employed as decision writers and case technicians.

SIDEBAR

Social Security

An estimated 500,000 cases are presented annually before Administrative Law Judges of the Social Security Administration. As the population ages, that number is expected to increase.

Paralegal Regulations Encouraged

The Indiana Lawyer, February 28, 2001   Rachel E. Faulkner, Director of Public Relations, Indianapolis Bar Association

A community of legal professionals exist who are distinguished by the work they perform, yet no specific standards of regulations currently exist to mandate specific educational requirements or duties. These professionals are paralegals/legal assistants, and they provide a very necessary service to the legal community.

The American Bar Association defines a paralegal/legal assistant as an individual qualified by education, training, or work experience, who is employed or retained by a lawyer, law office, corporation, governmental agency or other entity, and who performs specifically delegated substantive legal work for which a lawyer is responsible. Similar variations of this popular definition exist from organizations such as the National Federation of Paralegal Associations, Indiana State and Indianapolis Bar Associations, the Indiana Paralegal Association, etc.

According to Edna Wallace, RP, a practicing paralegal with the law firm of Kroger, Gardis & Regas, LLP and immediate past chair of the Indianapolis Bar Association Paralegal Committee, this issue goes beyond titles and descriptions, as its significance impacts the standards of performance for the profession. Without regulation, any person employed by a lawyer, law office, corporation, government agency, or other entity can use the title of "legal assistant" without qualification by education, work experience, or training and without the knowledge to perform substantive legal work that would require knowledge of legal concepts and normally would be performed by a lawyer, and can sign [his or her] name with a designation of legal assistant, Wallace said.

Some law firms utilize the title "legal assistant" to describe their support staff who more accurately should be referred to as administrative assistants. This practice, along with the lack of regulation, perpetuates the devalued image of the profession. Many paralegals advocate formalizing standards for the profession to combat the problem and to ensure that paralegals/legal assistants truly obtain and maintain the knowledge and expertise in substantive and procedure law that their profession requires.

While mandated licensing and other regulations, such as required continuing legal education (CLE), will add value to the paralegal/legal assistant profession, like everything else it comes at a price. Will law firms agree to pay for obtaining and maintaining the license and the necessary CLE hours, as well as association dues?

Many paralegals, like Wallace, believe they should. She said that ultimately lawyers are responsible for the professional services of the paralegal/legal assistant pursuant to the Indiana Rules of Professional Responsibility (Rule 9.1). This requirement alone should inspire attorneys to take reasonable measures to ensure that their paralegal/legal assistant is experienced, qualified, and educated to maintain the integrity of the profession.

According to Wallace, encouraging regulations will work to move the profession forward. In a challenge to other paralegals/legal assistants, she asked: Are you willing to sit back and watch everything you worked hard for, went to school for, and believe in slip back to the same status as several years ago? It's an uphill battle. Are you ready for the challenge?

ETHICAL RULES AND OBLIGATIONS

Lawyers generally need to follow only one set of ethics guidelines. Although it may be a set enacted by the state legislature, it usually is one adopted by the supreme court of the state in which they practice.

The most widely adopted is the *Model Rules of Professional Conduct* (see Appendix B for excerpts of the Model Rules, 2002 edition) prepared by the American Bar Association, originally released in 1983. The prior release, the Model Code of Professional Conduct (Model Code) is still in use in some jurisdictions. Procedurally, each state reviews the Model Rules or Model Code and

Taking the Stand: Ethics

Ellen Lockwood, C.L.A.   State Bar of Texas, Chair, Ethics Committee, Legal Assisting Division

Q: How did you become the chair of the Ethics Committee?

A: The position became vacant at the time my first stint on the board of directors ended. Ethics interested me, so I asked to be appointed. The president was just thrilled to have someone volunteer!

Q: What is the most common ethics question you are asked?

A: Questions regarding giving legal advice. Usually the questions are in the gray area between giving basic information and giving legal advice.

Q: What has been the oddest ethics question you've encountered?

A: I don't recall any ethics questions that I would consider odd. I do receive many questions that surprise me because the answers appear so obvious to me.

This makes me believe that we cannot stress ethics enough in paralegal programs as well as in CLE. We particularly need examples of ethical dilemmas in everyday situations so that ethics is not just an abstract list of rules.

Q: What was the most costly ethics mistake by a paralegal that you've become aware of?

A: Other than embezzling (I'm aware of two cases in Texas), I think the most costly ethics mistake any paralegal can make is become too comfortable with your knowledge. Not only is it important to keep up your CLE; it is important to remember that you are not the attorney and cannot give legal advice. Even when you are sure of the answer, ask your attorney so you can honestly tell the client, "Attorney X asked me to tell you _____."

NFPA Ethics Code: www.
paralegals.org/Development/
model code.html

NALA Ethics: www.nala.org/
stand.htm

adopts the entire recommended set of Model Rules or the Model Code, or portions as it thinks appropriate for its jurisdiction.

Unlike the ABA for lawyers, no single source of ethical rules is set out for the legal assistant. Absent a single unified body of ethical rules, legal assistants must follow state statutes and conduct themselves in conformity with the rules of professional conduct applicable to attorneys and with the ethics opinions of their professional associations. The two major legal assistant organizations providing an ethical code for its members are the National Federation of Paralegal Associations (NFPA) and the National Association of Legal Assistants (NALA).

Although legal assistants are not governed directly by the American Bar Association ethical rules, there is an intertwined relationship between the lawyer, the client, and the paralegal. What the paralegal does or does not do can have a real impact on the lawyer's duty and obligation to the client. The lawyer is ultimately responsible for the actions of the legal assistant under the Model Rules.

ABA Model Guidelines for the Utilization of Legal Assistant Services

In 1991 the American Bar Association's policy-making body, the House of Delegates, adopted a set of guidelines intended to govern the conduct of lawyers when utilizing paralegals or legal assistants. These guidelines are given as Exhibit 2.1.

Attorneys are bound by the ethical code adopted by the state in which they practice. The ethical guidelines for the paralegal are a combination of the ethical rules imposed on the supervising attorney and the paralegal professional association rules imposed on paralegals. As a general rule, whatever the ethical rules forbid the attorney from doing, they also forbid the paralegal from doing. Paralegals therefore can look to their state's adopted set of rules, or code, of

Guidelines for the utilization of legal assistant services.   *exhibit 2.1*

GUIDELINE 1: A lawyer is responsible for all of the professional actions of a legal assistant performing legal assistant services at the lawyer's direction and should take reasonable measures to ensure that the legal assistant's conduct is consistent with the lawyer's obligations under the ABA Model Rules of Professional Conduct.

GUIDELINE 2: Provided the lawyer maintains responsibility for the work product, a lawyer may delegate to a legal assistant any task normally performed by the lawyer except those tasks proscribed to one not licensed as a lawyer by statute, court rule, administrative rule or regulation, controlling authority, the ABA Model Rules of Professional Conduct, or these Guidelines.

GUIDELINE 3: A lawyer may not delegate to a legal assistant:

(a) Responsibility for establishing an attorney–client relationship.

(b) Responsibility for establishing the amount of a fee to be charged for a legal service.

(c) Responsibility for a legal opinion rendered to a client.

GUIDELINE 4: It is the lawyer's responsibility to take reasonable measures to ensure that clients, courts, and other lawyers are aware that a legal assistant, whose services are utilized by the lawyer in performing legal services, is not licensed to practice law.

GUIDELINE 5: A lawyer may identify legal assistants by name and title on the lawyer's letterhead and on business cards identifying the lawyer's firm.

GUIDELINE 6: It is the responsibility of a lawyer to take reasonable measures to ensure that all client confidences are preserved by a legal assistant.

GUIDELINE 7: A lawyer should take reasonable measures to prevent conflicts of interest resulting from a legal assistant's other employment or interests insofar as such other employment or interests would present a conflict of interest if it were that of the lawyer.

GUIDELINE 8: A lawyer may include a charge for the work performed by a legal assistant in setting a charge for legal services.

GUIDELINE 9: A lawyer may not split legal fees with a legal assistant or pay a legal assistant for the referral of legal business. A lawyer may compensate a legal assistant based on the quantity and quality of the legal assistant's work and the value of that work to a law practice, but the legal assistant's compensation may not be contingent, by advance agreement, upon the profitability of the lawyer's practice.

GUIDELINE 10: A lawyer who employs a legal assistant should facilitate the legal assistant's participation in appropriate continuing education and pro bono publico activities.

Source: ABA Model Guidelines for Utilization of Legal Assistant Services. Copyright © 2001 by the American Bar Association. Reprinted with permission. All rights reserved.

ABA Model Guidelines for
Utilization of Legal Assistant
Services: www.abanet.org/
legalassts/modguide.html

professional responsibility for guidance in deciding what is appropriate or inappropriate from an ethical perspective.

By definition, the paralegal works under the supervision of an attorney. As such, the paralegal is the agent of the attorney and therefore owes a duty to the supervising attorney similar to that of the traditional agent–servant relationship found in agency law—that of a fiduciary obligation. Among the fiduciary obligations of an agent are the duty to exercise reasonable care, skill, and diligence. The agent also owes a duty of loyalty to the principal. This includes the obligation to act for the employer's benefit rather than for his or her own benefit or the benefit of another whose interest may be adverse to that of the employer.

By extension of the rule of agency, the paralegal, as a subagent of the supervising attorney, becomes an agent of the client. The attorney is an agent of the client, and the paralegal is a subagent. As an agent of the client, the same duties that are owed to the law firm as the employer are also owed to the client.

One of the questions that arise in firms engaged in corporate practice and in securities practice is whether the paralegal can purchase stock (securities) in a client corporation. Some firms have written policies prohibiting members of the firm, including paralegals, from purchasing the securities (stock) of client corporations. At the forefront is the propriety of using the information leading to the purchase or the transaction in client securities. Among the issues is whether the purchase was made based upon material inside information, information not generally available to the public, the knowledge of which would cause a person to buy or sell a corporate security. Use of material inside information of publicly traded stocks is generally a violation of federal securities laws prohibiting insider transactions.

For the attorney, guidance is available from Model Rule 1.7 and the comments to the Model Rule and under the previous Model Code DR 5–101A, which provides that an attorney must refuse employment when personal interests, including financial interests, might sway professional judgment. To the extent that this rule applies to the attorney, good judgment would dictate that it applies to the paralegal as well.

Paralegal Associations Ethics Codes

The two leading national paralegal membership organizations are the National Federation of Paralegal Associations and the National Association of Legal Assistants. Each of these groups has formulated a set of ethical guidelines for its respective membership, as well as for others looking for ethical guidance in the regulation of the paralegal profession.

National Federation of Paralegal Associations

NFPA Guidelines for Enforcement of the Model Code:
www.paralegals.org/develop
ment/modelcode.html

The National Federation of Paralegal Associations, Inc. is a professional organization composed of paralegal associations and individual paralegals throughout the United States and Canada. Members of NFPA have varying backgrounds, experiences, education, and job responsibilities that reflect the diversity of the paralegal profession. NFPA promotes the growth, development, and recognition of the paralegal profession as an integral partner in the delivery of legal services. Exhibit 2.2 presents a brief version of the NFPA Model Code. The full version is reproduced in Appendix B.

THE HINDU LAW SYSTEM

More than 20 percent of the world's population is Hindu. Most Hindus live in India, where they make up about 80 percent of the population. Others live in Burma, Kenya, Malaysia, Pakistan, Singapore, Tanzania, and Uganda. Hindu law is a religious law. As such, individual Hindus apply this law to themselves regardless of their nationality or place of domicile.

Classical Hindu law rests neither on civil codes nor on court decisions but, rather, on the works of private scholars that were passed along for centuries by oral tradition and eventually were recorded in the smitris (law books). Hindu law—called dharmasastra in Sanskrit, that is, the doctrine of proper behavior—is linked to the divine revelation of Veda (the holy collection of Indian religious songs, prayers, hymns, and sayings written between 2000 and 1000 B.C.). Most Hindu law is concerned with family matters and the law of succession.

After India became a British colony, British judges applied a combination of Hindu law and common law in solving cases. Once India gained its independence, this Anglo–Hindu law, as it was called, was ousted. In the mid-1950s, India codified Hindu law by enacting the Hindu Marriage Act, the Hindu Minority and Guardianship Act, the Hindu Succession Act, and the Hindu Adoptions and Maintenance Act. Outside of India, Anglo–Hindu law applies in most other countries populated by Hindus.

In April 1997, NFPA adopted the Model Disciplinary Rules (Model Rules) to make possible the enforcement of the Canons and Ethical Considerations contained in the NFPA Model Code. At present, unlike a violation by an attorney of the state-adopted rules that can result in loss of the right to practice (disbarment), no such sanction exists for the paralegal breach of association rules except loss of membership.

NFPA Code of Ethics and Professional Responsibility.	*exhibit 2.2*

§1. NFPA model disciplinary rules and ethical considerations

1.1 A paralegal shall achieve and maintain a high level of competence.

1.2 A paralegal shall maintain a high level of personal and professional integrity.

1.3 A paralegal shall maintain a high standard of professional conduct.

1.4 A paralegal shall serve the public interest by contributing to the improvement of the legal system and delivery of quality legal services, including pro bono publico services.

1.5 A paralegal shall preserve all confidential information provided by the client or acquired from other sources before, during, and after the course of the professional relationship.

1.6 A paralegal shall avoid conflicts of interest and shall disclose any possible conflict to the employer or client, as well as to the prospective employers or clients.

1.7 A paralegal's title shall be fully disclosed.

1.8 A paralegal shall not engage in the unauthorized practice of law.

Source: Copyright © 2002 by National Federation of Paralegal Associations. Excerpts reprinted with permission.

National Association of Legal Assistants

The National Association of Legal Assistants, formed in 1975, is a leading professional association for legal assistants. NALA provides continuing professional education, development, and certification. It may best be known in the profession for its Certified Legal Assistant (CLA) examination. The ABA Standing Committee on Legal Assistants has recognized the CLA designation as a designation marking a high level of professional achievement. Exhibit 2.3 gives the NALA Code.

exhibit 2.3   *NALA Code of Ethics and Professional Responsibility.*

A legal assistant must adhere strictly to the accepted standards of legal ethics and to the general principles of proper conduct. The performance of the duties of the legal assistant shall be governed by specific canons as defined herein so that justice will be served and goals of the profession attained.

CANON 1. A legal assistant must not perform any of the duties that attorneys only may perform nor take any actions that attorneys may not take.

CANON 2. A legal assistant may perform any task which is properly delegated and supervised by an attorney, as long as the attorney is ultimately responsible to the client, maintains a direct relationship with the client, and assumes professional responsibility for the work product.

CANON 3. A legal assistant must not: (a) engage in, encourage, or contribute to any act which could constitute the unauthorized practice of law; and (b) establish attorney–client relationships, set fees, give legal opinions or advice, or represent a client before a court or agency unless so authorized by that court or agency; and (c) engage in conduct or take any action which would assist or involve the attorney in a violation of professional ethics or give the appearance of professional impropriety.

CANON 4. A legal assistant must use discretion and professional judgment commensurate with knowledge and experience but must not render independent legal judgment in place of an attorney. The services of an attorney are essential in the public interest whenever such legal judgment is required.

CANON 5. A legal assistant must disclose his or her status as a legal assistant at the outset of any professional relationship with a client, attorney, a court or administrative agency or personnel thereof, or a member of the general public. A legal assistant must act prudently in determining the extent to which a client may be assisted without the presence of an attorney.

CANON 6. A legal assistant must strive to maintain integrity and a high degree of competency through education and training with respect to professional responsibility, local rules and practice, and through continuing education in substantive areas of law to better assist the legal profession in fulfilling its duty to provide legal service.

CANON 7. A legal assistant must protect the confidences of a client and must not violate any rule or statute now in effect or hereafter enacted controlling the doctrine of privileged communications between a client and an attorney.

CANON 8. A legal assistant must do all other things incidental, necessary, or expedient for the attainment of the ethics and responsibilities as defined by statute or rule of court.

CANON 9. A legal assistant's conduct is guided by bar associations' codes of professional responsibility and rules of professional conduct.

Conflict of Interest

A conflict of interest exists if the representation of one client will be directly adverse to the interest of another client. Conflict of interest may best be explained by the biblical adage that "no one can serve two masters." If the master is entitled to complete loyalty, any conflict in loyalties presents a conflict of interest in which neither master can be certain of the loyalty of his or her servant. It's easy to see the conflict that would arise in a lawyer's going to court representing both the plaintiff and the defendant. Less obvious are situations in which the attorney represents two parties with a common interest, such as a husband and wife purchasing a new home. In most cases, the interests would be the same and no conflict would exist. When these clients are seeking counseling for marital problems, however, the conflict becomes more obvious as one of them seeks a greater share of the common property or other rights and the lawyer is called upon to give legal advice as to the right to the parties. Finally, lawyers clearly cannot represent both husband and wife in court in the marital dissolution trial.

The American Bar Association Model Rules of Professional Conduct provide a guideline in Rule 1.7, Conflict of Interest: General Rule, which provides in part that a lawyer shall not represent a client if the representation of that client will be directly adverse to another client, unless the lawyer reasonably believes the representation "will not adversely affect the relationship with the other client; and each client consents after consultation."

The essence of the rule is that of loyalty to the client. The 1981 version of the American Bar Association Model Code of Professional Responsibility provides in Canon 5:

> A lawyer should exercise independent professional judgment on behalf of a client.

A lawyer and her client consult in court.

The ethical considerations comment to Canon 5 states:

> EC5–1 The professional judgment of a lawyer should be exercised, within the bounds of the law, solely for the benefit of his client and free of compromising influences and loyalties. Neither his personal interests, the interests of other clients, nor the desires of third persons should be permitted to dilute his loyalty to his client.

Clearly, a lawyer should not accept the employment if the lawyer's personal interests or desires will, or if there is a reasonable probability that they will, adversely affect the advice to be given or services to be rendered to the prospective client. The information that may be considered to create a conflict of interest is not limited solely to that of the attorney representing a client. It also includes the information held by another member of the legal team, including the legal assistant.

The National Federation of Paralegal Associations Model Code of Ethics provides in Canon 8:

> A paralegal shall avoid conflicts of interest and shall disclose any possible conflict to the employer or client, as well as to their prospective employers or clients.

The ultimate obligation to determine the conflict of interest of the paralegal or legal assistant rests with the supervising attorney. Standard procedure in law firms is to check for conflicts of interest within the law firm before accepting a new client or undertaking a new matter for an existing client. Just as other attorneys are asked to review lists of new clients and new matters, so must paralegals check to be certain they do not have a conflict of interest.

Conflicts of interest may arise for paralegals when they change from one employer to another. If the previous employer represented a client or handled certain matters for a client during the period in which the paralegal was employed, a conflict of interest may exist. A more difficult concern for the paralegal is the conflict of interest that can arise from a law firm's representation of family members and personal friends. Paralegals frequently refer family and friends to the attorney or the law firm where they work. The mere relationship or friendship itself might not create conflict but in some cases could give rise to a claim of undue influence wherein the paralegal may stand to benefit from the action of the law firm. Examples are the drafting of wills and trusts in which the paralegal may be named as a beneficiary or instances in which the paralegal may be named as the executor of the estate or as a trustee receiving compensation.

Ethical Wall

Law firms use the term *ethical wall*—also called a Chinese wall—to describe an environment in which an attorney or a paralegal is isolated from a particular case or client to avoid a conflict of interest or to protect a client's confidences and secrets. By creating this boundary or wall, any potential communications, whether written or oral, are prevented between the members of the legal team handling a particular matter or client and the person with whom there may be a conflict of interest.

In an age of consolidation of law firms in many areas, the number of individual employers has diminished while the number of clients has increased. As a result, professionals today may find themselves in firms that were on the opposite side of cases in the past. Creating an ethical wall permits the professional to accept employment with the other firm. It also permits greater mobility by professionals, as they can go to a new firm in which there may have been a conflict.

Moonlighting

Freelance or independent paralegals who work for more than one firm or attorney face the potential problem of conflict of interest. Special caution has to be taken to avoid accepting employment in cases where conflicts may exist. Freelance and independent paralegals are keenly aware of this and generally take precautions to prevent conflicts. The law firms and attorneys for whom they work usually are aware of the potential and also take special precautions to isolate potential conflict situations. Full-time paralegals who seek outside income should pay special attention to potential conflicts that may arise.

PERSPECTIVE

Uniformity of Paralegal Ethics

The paralegal profession has no unified code of ethics. State regulations and ethics opinions are not uniform. National organizations such as the National Association of Legal Assistants and the National Federation of Paralegal Associations each provide a uniform code of ethical conduct for members.

Not all of these conflicts are obvious. Consider the case of a paralegal working for a plaintiffs negligence firm handling cases against a major retail store. That paralegal's acceptance of employment at the retail store the firm is suing presents a conflict of interest. Knowledge of the strategy of the case would be of interest to the retail store employer. But divulging the information would breach the confidence of the law firm and the confidence of the law firm's client. Failure to disclose information to the retail store that directly affects its business breaches the duty of loyalty to that employer.

Attorney–Client Privilege

Attorney–client privilege is founded on the belief that clients should be able to tell their attorneys everything about their case so the attorney can give proper legal advice to the client. For the attorney, the ABA Model Rules provide in Rule 1.6, Confidentiality of Information, that "a lawyer shall not reveal information relating to representation of a client unless the client consents after consultation, except for disclosures that are impliedly authorized."

Work Product Doctrine

Work product is broadly defined to include the certain written statements and memoranda prepared by counsel in representation of a client, generally in preparation for trial. In *Hickman v. Taylor* [329 U.S. 495 (1947)] the court recognized a qualified immunity from discovery for the "work product of the lawyer"; such material could be discovered only upon a substantial showing of "necessity or justification." An exemption from discovery was necessary because, as the Hickman court stated:

> Were such materials open to opposing counsel on mere demand, much of what is now put down in writing would remain unwritten. An attorney's thoughts, heretofore inviolate, would not be his own. Inefficiency, unfairness and sharp practices would inevitably develop in the giving of legal advice and in the preparation of cases for trial. The effect on the legal profession would be demoralizing. And the interests of the clients and the cause of justice would be poorly served.

The work product doctrine is an extension of the attorney–client privilege wherein the nonlawyer is assisting the lawyer in trial preparation. Litigation practice today requires that attorneys use nonlawyers including paralegals, secretaries, law clerks, and others. The client will communicate through these members of the legal team, and the same privileges must exist [*U. S. v. Koval*, 196 F.2d 918, quoting 8 Wigmore, Evidence 2290, 2201]. The attorney's work prod-

Ethical PERSPECTIVE

The Paralegal and the Claim of Attorney–Client Privilege

As stated by the federal court in the case of Claus Von Bulow:

"The law is clear in this circuit the person claiming the attorney–client privilege has the burden of establishing all the essential elements thereof. The question is a simple one. Was Reynolds [a friend of Claus Von Bulow claiming that information given to her by the defendant was privileged] an agent of an attorney and has she presented sufficient evidence of this relationship? In other words, were communications made to her, in confidence, in her capacity as an agent of an attorney for the purpose of obtaining legal advice from that attorney? We think not.

"The attorney–client privilege is founded on the assumption that encouraging clients to make the fullest disclosure to their attorneys enables the latter to act more effectively. We have recognized that an attorney's effectiveness depends upon his ability to rely on the assistance of various aides, be they secretaries, file clerks, telephone operators, messengers, clerks not yet admitted to the bar, and aids of other sorts. The privilege must include all the persons who act as the attorney's agents."

Source: Von Bulow v. Von Bulow, 811 F. 2d 136 (2d Cir. 1987).

SIDEBAR

Federal Rules of Civil Procedure Rule 26

General Provisions Governing Discovery; Duty of Disclosure

(b)(3) Trial Preparation: Materials. . . . A party may obtain discovery of documents and tangible things otherwise discoverable . . . and prepared in anticipation of litigation or for trial by or for another party or by or for that other party's representative (including the other party's attorney, consultant, surety, indemnitor, insurer, or agent) only upon a showing that the party seeking discovery has substantial need of the materials in the preparation of the party's case and that the party is unable without undue hardship to obtain the substantial equivalent of the materials by other means. . . . The court shall protect against disclosure of the mental impressions, conclusions, opinions, or legal theories of an attorney or other representative of a party concerning a litigation.

uct has been the subject of extensive litigation. The distinction between what is discoverable and what is trial preparation is not always clear. The courts must balance the needs of the opposing sides.

THE FUTURE

What can you expect in the future? Certainly the demands of employers and courts will dictate that educational requirements be increased as the paralegal becomes a more and more important member of the legal services team. As an organization, the American Association of Legal Administrators, representing the law office administrators who do much of the hiring of paralegals, advocates a four-year degree as a minimum standard.

As courts mandate that certain activities be performed by paralegals and not by lawyers, the demand for better qualified paralegals will follow. The courts will look to credentials and training in making determinations of who may act and bill for services as a paralegal. If lawyers are responsible for the activities delegated to their paralegals, they will insist that paralegals be better trained and qualified. Hiring decisions in the future may be based on educational minimums. Years of experience as a legal secretary may not count as much as being a graduate of an educational institution with a minimum set of standards such as those of the American Association for Paralegal Education.

American Association of Legal Administrators: www.alanet.org/home.html

AAfPE Regulations Statement: www.aafpe.org/acadqual.html

LEGAL TERMINOLOGY

Attorney–client privilege

Conflict of interest

Ethical wall

Model Guidelines for the Utilization of Legal Assistant Services

Model Rules of Professional Conduct

Unauthorized practice of law (UPL)

Work product doctrine

AAfPE Position on Educational Standards for Paralegal Regulation

The American Association for Paralegal Education (AAfPE), in existence since 1981, is the only national organization serving paralegal educators and institutions that offer paralegal programs. AAfPE presently has more than 450 members. AAfPE-member schools currently enroll more than 41,000 students and have graduated nearly 191,000 students.

As the national resource for paralegal education, AAfPE has set minimum recommended educational standards for paralegal education programs to become institutional members. AAfPE believes that the paralegal profession requires training of sufficient length, sophistication, intensity, and quality to produce a functional entry-level paralegal.

Certain educational components should be required in any paralegal regulatory plan. AAfPE recommends that state legislatures, courts, and/or bar associations considering paralegal regulation should adopt or include the AAfPE educational minimum standards described below.

FORMAL PARALEGAL EDUCATION

It is the position of AAfPE that some form of formal paralegal education should be present as a meaningful requirement in any paralegal regulation plan. This formal paralegal education should be offered through a program specifically designed to provide paralegal education.

MINIMUM LENGTH OF STUDY

A person is qualified as a paralegal with (1) an associate or baccalaureate degree or equivalent coursework, and (2) a credential in paralegal education from a paralegal program associated with an educational institution accredited by a nationally recognized agency completed in any of the following types of educational programs: associate degree, baccalaureate degree (major or minor), certificate, or master's degree.

A paralegal's education shall include, either as separate courses or within the overall course of study, coursework in substantive and procedural law, the American legal system, law offices and related environments, the paralegal profession, legal research and writing, ethics, and areas of legal practice such as those described in AAfPE's Core Competencies for Paralegal Programs.

The paralegal's credential shall include no fewer than 18 semester-credit hours of substantive paralegal classes and shall be from a paralegal education program that, at the time the paralegal credential is granted, is:

1. An institutional member of the American Association for Paralegal Education or
2. A paralegal educational program approved by the American Bar Association or
3. A paralegal education program at the post-secondary (college) level that requires the student to have completed a minimum of sixty (60) semester hours (or the equivalent) of total study prior to graduation. A semester hour is equivalent to 15 classroom hours of at least 50 minutes in duration. The course offerings may be for credit or not for credit, but they should meet these minimum time periods.

OTHER EDUCATIONAL INSTITUTION REQUIREMENTS

The educational institution should be accredited by a nationally recognized accrediting agency. Additionally, the institution should meet the educational standards described in the AAfPE Statement of Academic Quality.

Minimum educational requirements are essential in any paralegal regulation plan. Paralegal education is a unique academic curriculum, composed of both substantive legal knowledge and professional skills, which incorporates legal theory with practical application. Any proposal for regulation of paralegals should contain provisions incorporating the level of paralegal education necessary to enable graduates to meet the responsibilities of paralegals as legal professionals.

In recent years there has been a proliferation of short-term entry-level paralegal training programs of very limited duration, some with as few as 125 clock hours (which is less than 9 semester credit hours). These programs do a fundamental disservice to the legal profession by creating unrealistic expectations in both employers and students that a quality paralegal education has been delivered when such is not the case. State regulatory bodies are urged to adopt the educational minimums defined in this document as a requisite element of any paralegal regulation plan.

The AAfPE Board of Directors adopted this Position Statement on February 24, 2001, at San Antonio, Texas. Reprinted with permission of AAfPE.

Summary

CHAPTER 2 ETHICS, REGULATION, AND PROFESSIONAL RESPONSIBILITY

Unauthorized Practice of Law (UPL)

Relevant Issues	1. Regulation of the practice 2. Giving advice 3. Filling out forms

Regulation of the Paralegal Profession

State Function	Done by legislatures and courts of each state

Ethical Rules and Obligations

ABA Rules	1. ABA Model Rules of Professional Conduct 2. ABA Guidelines for the Utilization of Legal Assistant Services
Paralegal Associations Ethics Codes	1. National Federation of Paralegal Associations Model Code 2. National Association of Legal Assistants (CLA exam) Code of Ethics and Professional Responsibilities
Conflict of Interest	Association Guidelines 1. ABA Model Rules of Professional Conduct 2. ABA Model Code of Professional Responsibility 3. NFPA Model Code of Ethics
Ethical Wall	Definition: An environment in which an attorney or a paralegal is isolated from a case or client to avoid a conflict of interest or to protect a client's confidences and secrets
Moonlighting	Definition: Working for more than one firm or attorney
Attorney–Client Privilege	1. Definition: A rule that says a client can tell his or her lawyer anything about the case without fear that the attorney will be called as a witness against the client 2. Governed by ABA Model Rules, Confidentiality of Information
Work Product Doctrine	1. Work products are certain written statements and memoranda prepared by counsel in representation of a client 2. Doctrine extends attorney–client privilege to paralegals

The Future

Education	1. NALA (recommends four-year degree) 2. AAfPE standards

Working the Web

1. Check the NALA website at www.NALA.org for the latest ethics rules and opinions.
2. Check the NFPA at www.paralegal.org for ethics updates.
3. Check the ABA website at www.abanet.org for ethics updates.
4. Find your state bar association website, providing guidance or opinions on legal ethics, by using an Internet search engine such as www.Yahoo .com or www.google.com.
5. Check the NFPA website for agencies that allow nonlawyer practice at www.paralegals.org/Development/Roles/allow.html.

Questions

CRITICAL LEGAL THINKING AND WRITING

1. What is the general theory for regulating the practice of law? How is this applied?
2. Why is "just giving advice" potentially the unauthorized practice of law?
3. How would regulation of the paralegal profession assure the public of quality legal services?
4. What is the advantage to the paralegal in obtaining the PACE or CLA designation?
5. Why should the paralegal be familiar with the ABA Model Rules of Professional Conduct?
6. How do the ABA Model Guidelines for the Utilization of Legal Assistant Services define the role of the paralegal in the law office?
7. Do violations by a paralegal of the ethics rules of the national paralegal associations have the same impact as violation of the ethical rules of attorneys on the right to practice?
8. Would a paralegal dating a client have a conflict of interest caused by compromising influences and loyalties?
9. Under what circumstances might a paralegal have a conflict of interest in taking a new job in a law firm?
10. How does an ethical wall protect the client?
11. Does a client have an attorney–client privilege regarding information given to a paralegal during the preparation of a case?
12. Should a paralegal be considered an "other representative" under the Federal Rules of Civil Procedure, Rule 26? Why or why not?

Questions

ETHICS: ANALYSIS AND DISCUSSION

1. Are paralegals held to the same standard as attorneys when there is no supervising attorney?
2. What is the paralegal's duty to the client when the paralegal's employer breaches its duty to the client?
3. Who is responsible for the quality of the legal work performed for a client, the attorney or the paralegal?

Unauthorized Practice of Law—Form Completion

There are few certainties in the area of ethics, for paralegals or in any profession. What qualifies as ethical conduct is in most cases based on state law and court interpretation applied to a set of facts. The citation listed below represents one legal opinion and is provided as a research starting point. Do not assume that the same rule applies in your jurisdiction. For the following:

- *Prepare a written statement based on your state law.*
- *Use your state bar association website as a starting point.*

You have graduated from a paralegal program at a local college. While you are looking for a job where your talents can be properly utilized, a friend asks you to help him fill out a set of bankruptcy forms using a computer program he has purchased at the local office supply mega warehouse. The program is designed to pick out the exemptions after the requested information is plugged in. [*In Re Kaitangian*, Calif. 218 BR 102 (1998).] Is this the unauthorized practice of law?

Case

FOR DISCUSSION

In Re *Estate of Devine*   263 Ill. App.3d 799 (1994)

A paralegal working in a small office became friendly with a client of the attorney and assisted the client in personal matters outside of the office, including helping him to shop and handle personal finances. In that role the paralegal was given power to sign checks for the client. After the client died, the paralegal withdrew $165,958 from the joint account with the deceased client.

Is a lawyer responsible for the actions of a paralegal?

The court held both the paralegal and the attorney liable for breach of fiduciary duty, holding that if the attorney, who performed work including writing a will leaving a bequest to the attorney and the paralegal, was a fiduciary, so then was the paralegal as a matter of law. Further, the court noted that the law in a number of states holds the attorney liable for a paralegal's acts including the responsibility for unethical conduct by nonlawyer employees of the lawyer. The Illinois court quoted New York and New Jersey cases holding the employing attorney in violation of the Code of Professional Conduct for failing to properly supervise employed paralegals.

Questions

1. Does this case effectively extend the lawyer's ethical rules to the conduct of paralegals?
2. May a paralegal maintain a personal relationship with a client of the firm?
3. Should a paralegal be as familiar as the supervising (employing) attorney with the ABA Model Rules of Professional Conduct?

Tegman v. Accident and Medical Investigations

30 P.3d 8 (Wash. Ct. App. 2001)   Court of Appeals of Washington, Division One

Read the following case excerpted from the Court of Appeals opinion. Review and brief the case. In your brief, answer the following questions.

1. How does this court define "the practice of law"?

2. What is the standard or duty of care that this court imposes on a paralegal who does not have a supervising attorney?

3. What action does this court suggest that a paralegal take when it becomes clear that there is no supervising attorney?

4. Why should a paralegal contact the supervising attorney immediately upon being given a case to handle?

5. Based on this case, should a paralegal advise the client that he or she is a paralegal? If so, when? Why?

Becker, Mary K., A.C.J.

Between 1989 and 1991, plaintiffs Maria Tegman, Linda Leszynski, and Daina Calixto were each injured in separate and unrelated automobile accidents. After their accidents, each plaintiff retained G. Richard McClellan and Accident & Medical Investigations, Inc. (AMI) for legal counsel and assistance in handling their personal injury claims. . . . Each plaintiff signed a contingency fee agreement with AMI, believing that McClellan was an attorney and AMI a law firm. McClellan has never been an attorney in any jurisdiction. McClellan and AMI employed Camille Jescavage, . . . [a] licensed attorney. . . .

Jescavage . . . learned that McClellan entered into contingency fee agreements with AMI's clients and that McClellan was not an attorney. [Attorneys for AMI] settled a number of cases for AMI, and learned that McClellan processed settlements of AMI cases through his own bank account. . . .

In July 1991, McClellan hired Deloris Mullen as a paralegal. Mullen considered Jescavage to be her supervising attorney, though Jescavage provided little supervision. Jescavage resigned from AMI in the first week of September 1991. McClellan told Mullen that her new supervising attorney would be James Bailey. Mullen did not immediately contact Bailey to confirm that he was her supervising attorney. [He] later told Mullen he was not.

While at AMI, Mullen worked on approximately 50–60 cases, including those of [the] plaintiffs. . . .

Mullen was aware of some of McClellan's questionable practices and knew that there were substantial improprieties involved with his operation. Mullen stopped working at AMI on December 6, 1991, when the situation became personally intolerable to her and she obtained direct knowledge that she was without a supervising attorney. When she left, she did not advise any of the plaintiffs about the problems at AMI. After Mullen left, McClellan settled each plaintiff's case for various amounts without their knowledge or consent, and deposited the funds in his general account by forging their names on the settlement checks.

The "practice of law" clearly does not just mean appearing in court. In a larger sense, it includes "legal advice and counsel, and the preparation of legal instruments and contracts by which legal rights are secured." Mullen contends that her status as a paralegal precludes a finding that she was engaged in the practice of law. She argues that a paralegal is, by definition, someone who works under the supervision of an attorney, and that it is necessarily the attorney, not the paralegal, who is practicing law and owes a duty to the clients. Her argument assumes that she had a supervising attorney. The trial court's determination that Mullen was negligent was dependent on the court's finding that Mullen knew, or should have known, that she did not have a supervising attorney over a period of several months while she was at AMI. . . .

The label "paralegal" is not in itself a shield from liability. A factual evaluation is necessary to distinguish a paralegal who is working under an attorney's supervision from one who is actually practicing law. A finding that a paralegal is practicing law will not be supported merely by evidence of infrequent contact with the supervising attorney. As long as the paralegal does in fact have a supervising attorney who is responsible for the case, any deficiency in the quality of the supervision or in the quality of the paralegal's work goes to the attorney's negligence, not the paralegal's.

In this case, Mullen testified that she believed James Bailey was her supervising attorney after Jescavage left. The court found Mullen was not justified in that belief. . . . Mullen testified that she had started to distrust McClellan before he informed her that Bailey would be her supervising attorney. Mullen also testified that she did not contact Bailey to confirm that he was supervising her. Bailey testified at a deposition that he did not share Mullen's clients and she did not consult him regarding any of her ongoing cases. He also said that one of the only conversations he remembers having with Mullen with respect to AMI is one where he told her that he was not her supervising attorney after she raised the issue with him. This testimony amply supports the trial court's finding that Mullen was unjustified in her belief that Bailey was her supervising attorney.

[Mullen] continued to send out demand and representation letters after Jescavage left AMI. Letters written by Mullen before Jescavage's departure identify Mullen as a paralegal after her signature, whereas letters she wrote after Jescavage's departure lacked such identification. Even after Mullen discovered, in late November 1991, that Bailey was not her supervising attorney, she wrote letters identifying "this office" as representing the plaintiffs, neglecting to mention that she was a paralegal and that no attorney was responsible for the case. This evidence substantially supports the finding that Mullen engaged in the practice of law.

Accordingly, we conclude the trial court did not err in following *Bowers* and holding Mullen to the duty of an attorney. The duty of care owed by an attorney is that degree of care, skill, diligence, and knowledge commonly possessed and exercised by a reasonable, careful, and prudent lawyer in the practice of law in Washington. . . .

The court found that the standard of care owed by an attorney, and therefore also by Mullen, required her to notify the plaintiffs of: (1) the serious problems concerning the accessibility of their files to persons who had no right to see them, (2) the fact that client settlements were not processed through an attorney's trust account but, rather, McClellan's own account, (3) the fact that McClellan and AMI, as nonlawyers, had no right to enter into contingent fee agreements with clients and receive contingent fees, (4) the fact that McClellan was, in fact, engaged in the unlawful practice of law, and that, generally, (5) the clients of McClellan and AMI were at substantial risk of financial harm as a result of their association with AMI. Mullen breached her duty to her clients in all of these particulars.

We conclude the finding is supported by substantial evidence. Accordingly, the trial court did not err in concluding that Mullen was negligent. . . .

Although Mullen was a paralegal, she is held to an attorney's standard of care because she worked on the plaintiffs' cases during a period of several months when she had no supervising attorney. The fact that she did not render legal advice directly does not excuse her; in fact, her failure to advise the plaintiffs of the improper arrangements at AMI is the very omission that breached her duty. Under these circumstances it is not unjust to hold her accountable as a legal cause of the plaintiffs' injuries. As all the elements of negligence have been established, we affirm the judgment against Mullen. Affirmed.

WE CONCUR: AGID, J., COLEMAN, J.

This case will also be published in the Washington Appellate Reports, and if cited in the courts of Washington, will require that citation as well. This case has a Lexis number of 2001 Wash. App. LEXIS 1890.

CHAPTER 3

Careers in the Paralegal Profession

The law relating to public policy cannot remain immutable; it must change with the passage of time. The wind of change blows on it.

L. J. DANCKWERTS, *NAGLE V. FEILDEN* (1966)

Introduction

Opportunities and career choices for the paralegal have never been better. Twenty years ago the role of the paralegal was a limited, behind-the-scenes role with little client contact except, possibly, as a receptionist or a legal secretary. Today, paralegals are employed in every area of the law. They interview clients, conduct factual investigations, do legal research, prepare legal documents, assist at the counsel table in trials, and even represent clients in some administrative hearings. They are employed in law firms of all sizes, federal, state, and local government, insurance companies, and corporations.

COMPENSATION ISSUES FOR THE PARALEGAL

Paralegal compensation is as varied as the variety of working environments and regional locations. As with most jobs and professions, salaries tend to be higher in large metropolitan areas and lower in small and rural areas. Large firms tend to pay more and small firms tend to pay less. At times these variations in compensation can be justified by the costs of working in certain locations, such as higher taxation and the cost of commuting. Exhibit 3.1 gives a breakdown of hourly rates for paralegals by level and geographic region.

exhibit 3.1 *Hourly compensation for legal assistants/paralegals.*

SURVEY COVERS THREE LEVELS OF LEGAL ASSISTANT PAY

To assist in setting competitive pay levels, the *ECS Geographic Report on Professional and Technical Personnel Compensation* from Watson Wyatt Data Services breaks down the hourly wages for three levels of legal assistants/paralegals by geographic region. Highlights of the report are as follows:

FOR-PROFIT COMPANIES

Overall median rate for a legal assistant/paralegal:	$18.83/hour
Level 1, entry level, three or fewer years of experience, standardized tasks:	$15.20/hour
Highest rate: Middle Southeast states:	$17.43/hour
Level 2, intermediate, three to five years of experience, advanced skills:	$18.47/hour
Highest rate: Pacific Southwest states:	$21.16/hour
Next highest rate: Lower Mountain states:	$21.06/hour
Level 3, senior, five or more years of experience; tasks with substantial variety and complexity:	$20.90/hour
Highest rate: Pacific Southwest states:	$24.00/hour
Next highest rate: Central Plains states:	$23.04/hour

NOT-FOR-PROFIT COMPANIES

Entry-level paralegal:	$13.80/hour
Intermediate paralegal:	$15.84/hour
Senior paralegal:	$18.86/hour

Copyright © 2000 IOMA.

SELECTING A SPECIALTY

It is never too early to set career goals. The decision to pursue a paralegal profession offers many and varied opportunities and specialties. The final career path you take will no doubt have many bends and turns as you start your first job and learn about the different areas of practice that are available to you. Your ultimate specialty or employer might result from your educational background, such as journalism or medicine, or an area of special interest such as environmental issues, or possibly just a preference to work with certain types of clients such as the elderly or infirm.

And it is never too late to make a career adjustment. Many successful individuals begin a career later in life. Colonel Sanders started Kentucky Fried Chicken late in life. Schools are full of nontraditional students seeking a career change. In the paralegal field we are seeing more and more nurses who, having worked in the medical field for years, are making a career change to the legal field.

What is important is to find a career that will give you satisfaction and in which you look forward to going to work. The decision should start with a self-evaluation of your likes and dislikes, interests, passions, and any physical or geographic limitations. If you hate to fly, you probably do not want a job that requires travel. If you are not comfortable with strangers, you probably do not want a job as a paralegal investigator for a litigation firm. If you like books and research, you might want to work as the firm librarian or researcher. Consider the characteristics in the career-planning checklist on page 61.

Paralegals as Exempt Employees Under Federal Law

Employees classified as exempt employees under the Fair Labor Standards Act are exempt from the rules requiring payment of overtime for working more than 40 hours per week. Under the Fair Labor Standards Act (FLSA), certain classes of employees—loosely defined as executive, administrative, or professional—are exempt from the Act's provisions of minimum wage and overtime pay. In many professional occupations compensation is based not on hourly labor rates but, rather, on an annual salary. As consideration for the salary, employees are not bound to the traditional 40-hour work week but may work hours in excess without being paid extra.

In certain types of practices, working in excess of the 40 hours, sometimes substantially, is common. This is particularly true in litigation practices during the course of a trial in which much preparation work is done at night and on weekends when the litigation team is not in actual court. Similarly, those in taxation practices work many extra hours during "tax season," generally mid-January to April 15. In recognition of the additional demands for time during these periods, many firms pay a flat salary and attempt to avoid hourly timekeeping altogether.

The Department of Labor, in the case of *DOL v. Page & Anderson P.C.,* attempted to have paralegals treated as nonexempt, which would have required the firm to pay overtime under the FLSA. Even though the DOL lost and abandoned its appeal with prejudice, preventing relitigating that case, the case is fact-specific to the paralegals in that firm and cannot be relied upon by other law firms.

The problem with classifying the paralegal as an exempt employee comes from the definition of "exempt employee" under the FLSA. To come under the *executive* exemption, the employee must customarily and regularly exercise discretionary powers; to come under the *administrative* exemption, one must customarily and regularly exercise discretion and independent judgment; and to come under the *professional* exemption, the work requires the consistent exercise of discretion and judgment. In describing the duties of a paralegal, most lawyers and paralegals use these phrases to describe the duties and obligations of the profession. But one of the definitions of a paralegal includes the phrase "under the direction and control of the supervising attorney." If the actions are "under the direction and control" of someone else, the person is not exercising "independent judgment and discretion," and therefore does not qualify under most interpretations of the FLSA.

Because of the rigid position of the United States Department of Labor in interpreting the FLSA, many employers classify the paralegal as an hourly employee, not out of disrespect but, rather, out of fear of a DOL audit. Failure to comply can result in claims by the DOL for willful violation of the act, which can result in penalties, including liquidated damages, and civil penalties of up to $10,000 and potential imprisonment for up to six months.

The Paralegal's Portfolio

Kathryn Myers, Coordinator, Paralegal Studies   Saint Mary-of-the-Woods College, Paralegal Studies Program

INTERVIEW

Q: How did the practice of assembling a portfolio come about?

A: This portfolio is actually based on the old concept of the "artist's portfolio." Anyone who is involved in a "hands-on" profession has utilized this concept for years.

Q: Instead of pictures, what do you mean when you speak of a portfolio for paralegal students?

A: A portfolio for paralegal students consists of two parts. One part is for my use in the program. The students have growth papers for each class, plus a series of other papers. I look at the collection of work to determine whether the paralegal program is doing what it says it will and whether it needs to be changed. I have modified a number of classes based on the material in this portfolio.

    The other part is a professional portfolio. The students pull material from the above portfolio and create their own professional portfolio to take on interviews. This contains a copy or copies of their resume, transcripts, selected writing samples, projects, or any other document they believe would be useful at the interview. Employers have been very impressed with this presentation.

Q: Do potential employers ever balk at seeing something that bulky? If so, how would you suggest handling it?

A: This has not been a problem for my students. As indicated earlier, we "create" two portfolios—one program-related and the other for professional purposes. I think this eliminates any problems at the interview.

Q: What is the most important thing about a portfolio?

A: The most important thing in the professional portfolio appears to be that the employer has another tool to assess the quality of the potential employee. Grades do not mean that much anymore. An "A" at [our college] may well come from a more demanding curriculum than an "A" at another institution. There is no basis for comparison unless the employer knows the grading scales/demands of the different programs. However, having a portfolio of material allows the employer to see what an interviewee can do.

Q: With that in mind, what should a paralegal student keep in mind when putting together the portfolio?

A: How a student puts a portfolio together says a lot about the student. I encourage students to incorporate both good and "not so good" work. That shows the employer that the interviewee can learn and can improve. Students collect material as they go through the program rather than waiting until the end.

    Students should highlight their growth, their abilities, and their determination. They need to provide documentation that can show abilities that counter any poor grades that might appear on the transcript. This shows potential employers that test-taking is not necessarily the be-all, end-all to grades.

    Most of all, the students need to let themselves shine through within the portfolio materials. Each students is unique and each has different talents to highlight. That is the value of the portfolio.

THE STUDENT PORTFOLIO

The following is an excerpt from Kathryn Myers' article on portfolios on the American Association for Paralegal Education website at www.aafpe.org/smwc.html.

A portfolio is a purposeful collection of student work that is accumulated over time. The material reveals the extent of student learning, achievement, and development. The "portfolio system" is intended to specify knowledge and competence in areas considered necessary to successfully work as a paralegal/ legal assistant while leaving the selection of means of documentation of competency to the individual student. Documentation of knowledge and skill acquisition can take a variety of forms including, but not limited to, letters of support

diaries

videotapes and audiotapes of work

pleadings

memoranda

course projects

registration receipts from continuing education and other conferences attended

proof of membership in professional organizations

subscriptions to legal publications

Typically, much of the material can be compiled from projects and activities required within courses.

Procedure

The portfolio shall contain documentation of knowledge and skill acquisition based on the Core Competencies established by the American Association for Paralegal Education. Those core competencies are divided into two areas—skill development and acquisition of knowledge. Within those areas are competencies based on:

Skill Development

critical thinking skills

organizational skills

general communication skills

interpersonal skills

legal research skills

legal writing skills

computer skills

interviewing and investigation skills

Acquisition of Knowledge

organization and operation of the legal system

organization and operation of law offices

the paralegal profession and ethical obligations

contracts

torts

business organizations

litigation procedures

It is understood that the areas may overlap somewhat and that these areas do not cover all competencies associated with the program, student growth, or professional success. However, students who perfect these competencies and who perform from this educational base have a foundation for success.

It is suggested that the student purchase a secure container to collect and organize the material [such as] a hanging file folder or file box. This portfolio may be maintained on computer disk; however, you will not have any graded materials if this is the only method of collection you use.

Students should keep a log of all materials completed. When completing each assignment, [they should] enter the document in the log, with a column to check for inclusion in the campus portfolio and another to check for inclusion in the professional portfolio. Some documents may, of course, overlap in their application.

Students are responsible for the contents of their portfolios. The student should periodically review the contents of the portfolio and add or remove materials based on decisions as to the extent to which the contents adequately represent knowledge and skill acquisition in each of the areas outlined below. This portfolio is not intended to be a compilation of senior level work; rather, it is useful to provide work of varying levels of efficiency to show, among other things, growth and improvement.

Content

To be a successful paralegal/legal assistant, the student must possess a common core of legal knowledge as well as acquire vital critical thinking, organizational, communication, and interpersonal skills. Courses in a student's program should provide the student with the means to develop the competencies, which have been divided into the following sections:

Area 1   Understanding the Profession and Its Ethical Obligations

Area 2   Research

Area 3   Legal Writing

Area 4   Basic Skills

Area 5   Acquisition of Legal Knowledge

Area 6   Professional Commitment Beyond Course-work

Area 7   Evaluation of Professional Growth/ Evaluation of Program

Appendix

Guidelines for Selecting Entries

When selecting entries, students should bear in mind that each piece is part of a much larger whole and that, together, the artifacts and rationale make a powerful statement about individual professional development. Asking the following questions may help with decision making.

1. What do I want my portfolio to show about me as a paralegal? What are my attributes as a paralegal?

2. What do I want my portfolio to demonstrate about me as a learner? How and what have I learned?

3. What directions for my future growth and development does my self-evaluation suggest? How can I show them in my portfolio?

4. What points have been made by others about me as a paralegal and learner? How can I show them in my portfolio?

5. What effect does my professionalism have upon my peers? How can I show this in my portfolio?

6. What overall impression do I want my portfolio to give a reviewer about me as a learner and as a paralegal?

When decision making about what to include becomes a challenge, it may be helpful to look at each artifact and ask yourself, "What would including this item add that has not already been said or shown?" Remember that portfolios create representative records of your professional development; they are not intended to be comprehensive.

Values and Attitudes

Values and attitudes determine the choices we make in our lives. They cross the boundaries of subject-matter areas. Thus, in this final section of your portfolio, you are asked to look at your own values and attitudes and then write a one- to three-page paper in which you reflect upon your own values. Identify one or more values that are important to you. Explain how they influence your choices as a person, parent, future paralegal, voter, and/or citizen of the global community. Include specific examples.

The following questions may help you choose a topic for your essay: What does it mean to be honest? fair? tolerant? open to new ideas and experiences? respect evidence? Which is more important—decreasing the production of greenhouse gases or preserving jobs? The right to choose how many children we want or controlling world population growth? Freedom to produce pornographic art or the right of children to be sheltered from such experiences? Spending more time with your children or getting a second job so you can buy things you want?

There are no easy answers to these questions. Have fun thinking about your own values. Remember to include specific examples from your own life!

Transcripts

Include copies of unofficial transcripts from all colleges and universities that you have attended.

Degree evaluation	Include a copy of your degree evaluation, if you received one.
Graduation evaluation	Include a copy of your graduation evaluation.
Awards or recognitions	Include copies of awards or recognitions you have received.

PROFESSIONAL PORTFOLIO

Modify this inclusive portfolio into a professional portfolio. This professional portfolio will be representative, not comprehensive. Each artifact chosen for inclusion should represent at least one significant aspect of you and/or your accomplishments that can be translated into employability. Use these guidelines to prepare your professional portfolio:

1. Prepare your portfolio as a showcase of your best work—your highest achievements. This will involve selecting from artifacts in your portfolio and adding new ones.

2. Do not send your portfolio when you apply for a job. Rather, include in your cover letter a statement concerning your portfolio. For example: "Throughout my paralegal studies program at _____ College, I developed a professional

portfolio that clearly and concisely exhibits my attributes as a paralegal. I would be pleased to share this portfolio with you during an interview."

3. If granted an interview, take your portfolio with you. Be prepared to present the highlights. Practice presenting it effectively. In some instances, you might be asked to present it at the beginning of the interview, and in other instances you might use it as a source of evidence or enhancement of a point you make in the interview. Interviewing practices vary widely from employer to employer. Portfolios are most likely to be reviewed in situations where the employer is familiar with the abilities of a paralegal.

4. If the interviewer(s) is particularly interested and would like to examine your portfolio more closely, offer to leave it if at all possible. You should make explicit arrangements for collecting it and, of course, follow through as planned. It could be that your portfolio will create the impression that tips the scales in your favor.

5. Remember—it is likely that some people in a position to hire are not familiar with professional portfolios as you know them. Take time to con-cisely explain that developing your portfolio has been a process of reflection and evaluation that has helped you to know yourself as a paralegal and to establish a foundation for career-long professional development. To some extent, presenting your portfolio will inform the interviewer about both you and the portfolio concept and process.

6. Keep your portfolio up to date. As you continue to gain experience and to grow professionally, alter it to reflect your development. It is not only your first job application that may be enhanced by a well prepared and presented portfolio but developing your portfolio is an excellent foundation for meeting any expectation of continuing legal education.

Conclusion

It is my hope and intention that by your creating this portfolio, you have an opportunity to reflect upon your education and to emphasize to yourself and others that you are capable and qualified to perform as a paralegal. It is time to believe in you. Good luck!

Reproduced with permission of the author.

Checklist

CAREER PLANNING

- ○ My current paralegal job-related skills are:
- ○ My special interests are:
- ○ My passions are:
- ○ My personality traits are:
- ○ My geographical work and living desires are:
- ○ My willingness to accept responsibility is:
- ○ My level of self-motivation is:

ASSESSING YOUR BACKGROUND

As the law has become more specialized, so has the demand for paralegals with more than just paralegal skills. Law firms specializing in an area such as medical malpractice frequently look for paralegals who also have a medical background such as nursing. Firms with large, complex litigation cases often look for someone with computer database skills who can manage the files. Paralegals with journalism experience and training frequently are sought out for their interviewing and writing skills.

Your personal background can be an asset when added to your paralegal certificate or degree. As you begin your professional training, take stock of your entire educational background, special skills, and talents, as well as personal areas of interest.

ASSESSING YOUR SKILLS

You may well have a number of personal skills that will benefit you in the future as a paralegal. You might have great interpersonal skills, communicate well orally and in writing, and be a highly motivated person—all qualities of a good paralegal. Individuals with language skills are particularly in demand in international law, as well as in working with clients who lack English-language skills. The paralegal who understands a second language and the cultural nuances of the client's background can be invaluable.

ASSESSING YOUR INTERESTS

What are your personal interests? Are you an active outdoors person in your free time, for whom working on environmental issues would be of great interest and satisfaction? Do you find yourself drawn to volunteering or working in your free time with shut-ins and elderly people?

Doing a self-assessment early in your studies offers you an opportunity to recognize your strengths and develop them and to acknowledge weaknesses that you need to work on to permit your personal and professional growth. Becoming aware of your interests and background knowledge enables you to select the elective course that can qualify you for work in a specialty field of law.

SELECTING YOUR ELECTIVES

If you have a career goal for a specific legal specialty, taking electives is a good way to gain additional knowledge in the specialty area of interest. Taking electives also is a good way to explore an area in which you think you might be interested, without committing to more than one semester or a few credits of study. Many students find new interests and a potential career direction after taking courses in areas they had not considered previously. For example, you may have been reading in newspapers and magazines, and following on television, stories about the high technology industries and wondered how your

SIDEBAR

When Spanish Is Not Spanish

A witness might testify in Spanish and the translation may not be correct. For example, there are enough differences between Castilian Spanish (the official language of Spain) and Puerto Rican Spanish to require a translator who is knowledgeable about the dialect or native origin of the witness to give a proper translation.

career goal as a paralegal would fit into this growth area. One of the fastest growing fields is that of intellectual property law.

In an age of dot coms, computers, and a growing global marketplace, protection of intellectual property has become a critical concern for individuals and companies alike. Taking a three-credit course in intellectual property may well introduce the paralegal student to a new area of interest in a potential growth area of the paralegal profession. This is also true for other emerging areas in the paralegal profession, such as environmental law and legal nurse consulting.

PREPARING YOUR RESUME

A resume is a short description of a person's education, a summary of work experience, and other related and supporting information that potential employers use in evaluating a person's qualifications for a position in a firm or an organization. Exhibit 3.2 provides an example. You should prepare a resume as you see yourself today. Look at your resume from the perspective of a future employer. What areas do you need to strengthen to demonstrate your ability to perform the type of job you would like to have? You should look at your resume as being a continuing work in progress. Constantly update your resume to include any new job responsibilities, part-time employment skills and qualifications, and special achievements. Add meaningful items to your resume in the form of courses, skills, and outside interests that will land you that first paralegal job after you complete your training.

After you have gathered all of the necessary information, put it into a proper resume form, then review it. Does the resume reflect the information you want to communicate to a prospective employer? Try to look at it with an open, objective mind. Employers are looking for individuals who demonstrate a good work ethic, willingness to accept responsibility and take direction, and the skills necessary for the job for which they are applying.

Set your roadmap for the job you wish to obtain. What additional educational skills are required? This will determine your future course of study. Work-study programs in your field or cooperative education are good ways of demonstrating on-the-job training. Depending upon your goals, resources, and timeframe, a specialized certificate such as a paralegal certificate, an associate's degree in paralegal studies, or a bachelor's degree in paralegal studies will certainly demonstrate your level of interest and ability to achieve the minimum level of education for the job.

Creating an Electronic Resume

A growing number of employers are using computers to search the Internet for job applicants and to sort electronically through the resumes they receive. Human resources managers search through resumes received online or through Internet sites by entering a few words or phrases that describe the required skills and qualifications for the position they are trying to fill. Only the resumes in the computer system that match these electronic sorting terms and phrases are considered for the job offered. To have your resume considered, you need to have an electronic resume in addition to the traditional printed resume.

exhibit **3.2** *Sample resume.*

JANE DOE

1234 N. Maple Street, Anytown, USA 90000 • Home: (213) 555-1111 • Work: (213) 555-3333 • jane.doe@att.net

LITIGATION PARALEGAL

EDUCATION

University of Paralegal Studies, Fremont, CA
  Paralegal Specialist Certificate, 2002, Honors graduate
  Approved by ABA
  Course of study: Legal Research and Writing, Contracts, Torts, Ethics, Litigation
    Specialization

University of California at Berkeley
  Bachelor of Arts Degree in History, 2001
  Graduated Cum Laude

SKILLS AND ABILITIES

- Ability to analyze documents, digest depositions, draft discovery, and prepare cases for trial
- Knowledge of torts and contract law, legal research techniques, and basic civil procedure
- Fluent in French, both written and spoken
- Proficient in Word for Windows, WordPerfect and Excel

LEGAL INTERNSHIP

Jones, Smith, Smythe and Smooth, Los Angeles, 2001–2002
- Digested depositions for complex litigation case
- Organized multiple documents using several software programs

WORK EXPERIENCE

Los Angeles Unified School District, 1998–1999
  Secondary School Teacher
- Arranged classroom materials
- Supervised student teachers
- Chaired English Department
- Created curricula for advanced students

PROFESSIONAL ASSOCIATIONS

Los Angeles Paralegal Association
University of Paralegal Studies Alumni Association

References and writing samples available upon request.

Checklist

Personal information
- ○ Name
- ○ Address

Education
- ○ High school
  - ○ Year of graduation
- ○ College
  - ○ Year of graduation
  - ○ Degree
  - ○ Grade point average or class rank

Work experience
- ○ Current or last employer
  - ○ Position(s) held
- ○ Prior employer
  - ○ Position held and dates

Specific skills
- ○ Office skills   ○ Computer skills   ○ Language skills   ○ Other job-related skills

Other
- ○ Organizational memberships   ○ Licenses/certifications

Converting a Traditional Resume into an Electronic Resume

If you already have created a resume using a word-processing program, open the file containing your resume and save it as a plain ASCII text file. You will want to change the name of the new text file to distinguish it from the file name used for the traditional printed version.

Text-only files cannot accommodate type formatting and special characters, so be sure that your electronic resume appears in one simple font and one font size. You also must remove justification, tables, rules (lines), and columns. If you have tabs in your document, remove them and use the space bar to align your text (better yet, align all text at the left so that indentation problems do not occur). Change every bullet to an asterisk or a lowercase letter o, as shown in the sample electronic resume in Exhibit 3.3.

exhibit **3.3**   *Sample electronic resume.*

JANE DOE
1234 N. Maple Street
Anytown, USA 90000
Home: (213) 555-1111 * Work: (213) 555-3333
jane.doe@att.net

LITIGATION PARALEGAL

Education
University of Paralegal Studies, Fremont, CA
Paralegal Specialist Certificate, 2002, Honors graduate
Approved by ABA
Course of study: Legal Research and Writing, Contracts, Torts, Ethics, Litigation Specialization

University of California at Berkeley
Bachelor of Arts Degree in History, 2001
Graduated Cum Laude

Skills and Abilities
* Ability to analyze documents, digest depositions, draft discovery, and prepare cases for trial
* Knowledge of torts and contract law, legal research techniques, and basic civil procedure
* Fluent in French, both written and spoken
* Proficient in Word for Windows, WordPerfect 6.0, and Excel

Legal Internship
Jones, Smith, Smythe and Smooth, Los Angeles, 2001–2002
* Digested depositions for complex litigation case
* Organized multiple documents using several software programs

Work Experience
Los Angeles Unified School District, 1998–1999
Secondary School Teacher
* Arranged classroom materials
* Supervised student teachers
* Chaired English Department
* Created curricula for advanced students

Professional Associations
Los Angeles Paralegal Association
University of Paralegal Studies Alumni Association

References and writing samples available upon request.

The first line of your resume should contain only your full name. Type your street address, phone and fax numbers, and email address on separate lines below your name. Next count the number of characters in each line and create a new line whenever the number of characters (including spaces) exceeds 65. This will ensure that the text will fit on a line with appropriate margins.

Because many human resource managers search by key words, you'll want to include a key word section near the top of your resume. List nouns that describe your job-related skills and abilities. If you have work experience with specific job titles such as "paralegal," list these key words as well. Also include language proficiency or other specialty qualifications such as "nurse–paralegal" or "fluent in Spanish."

After you have created your resume, save it again as an ASCII plain text file. Email the resume to yourself or to a friend to see how it looks when sent over the Internet.

Checklist

MY CAREER ROADMAP

- ○ Skills I need to acquire:

- ○ Skills I need to strengthen:

- ○ Courses I should take:

- ○ Extracurricular activities for the resume:

- ○ Interim work experience I should seek:

- ○ Volunteer activities:

- ○ Short-term career goals:

- ○ Long-term career goals:

INTERVIEWING FOR A JOB

Most students today work at part-time or full-time jobs while pursuing their education. These might be summer jobs, holiday fill-in positions, or full-time jobs. Look at the interview for the part-time, summer, or holiday positions, or the interview for a new full-time position as an opportunity to perfect your interviewing skills. Interviewing for a job can be highly stressful. Careful interview preparation can help to eliminate some of the stress and help you put your best foot forward so you can get that dream job you want.

Checklist

Getting Ready

- ○ Write resume.
- ○ Make contacts.
- ○ Network.
- ○ Make appointments from mass mailings, telephone solicitations, and network contacts.

Before the Interview

- ○ Know your resume.
- ○ Be familiar with a typical application form.
- ○ Know something about the company or firm. Check the Martindale Hubbell or Standard and Poor's directories.
- ○ Have a list of good questions to ask the interviewer, and know when to ask them.
- ○ Rehearse your answers to possible interview questions, then rehearse again.
- ○ Plan a "thumbnail" sketch of yourself.
- ○ Know the location of the interview site and where to park, or become familiar with the public transportation schedule.
- ○ Be at least 10 minutes early.
- ○ Go alone.
- ○ Bring copies of your resume, list of references, and writing samples in a briefcase or portfolio.
- ○ Check local salary ranges for the position.
- ○ Be prepared to answer questions regarding your salary expectations.
- ○ Try to anticipate problem areas, such as inexperience or gaps in your work history.
- ○ Be prepared to handle difficult questions, and know how to overcome objections.

The Introduction

- ○ Dress the part.
- ○ Do not smoke, eat, chew gum, or drink coffee prior to or during the interview.
- ○ Maintain good eye contact and good posture.
- ○ Shake hands firmly.
- ○ Establish rapport and be cordial without being overly familiar.
- ○ Be positive—convert negatives to positives.
- ○ Keep in mind that the first impressions are lasting impressions.

(continued)

INTERVIEW STRATEGIES, continued

The Interview

- ○ Provide all important information about yourself.
- ○ Sell yourself—no one else will.
- ○ Use correct grammar.
- ○ Do not be afraid to say, "I don't know."
- ○ Ask questions of the interviewer.
- ○ Do not answer questions about age, religion, marital status, or children unless you wish to. Try to address the perceived concern.
- ○ Find out about the next interview or contact.
- ○ Find out when a decision will be made.
- ○ Shake hands at the end of the interview.

After the Interview

- ○ Immediately document the interview in your placement file.
- ○ Send personalized thank-you letters to each person who interviewed you.
- ○ Call to follow up.

Source: Adapted from *How to Land Your First Paralegal Job,* 3/e, by Andrea Wagner (Upper Saddle River, NJ: Prentice Hall, 2001), pp. 163–164.

Checklist

QUESTIONS TO ASK AT THE INTERVIEW

- ○ How does the firm evaluate paralegals?
- ○ What is the growth potential for a paralegal in the firm?
- ○ Why did the prior paralegal leave?
- ○ How is work assigned?
- ○ What support services are available to paralegals?
- ○ What consideration is given for membership in paralegal associations?
- ○ Does the firm provide any assistance for continuing education for paralegals?

After the interview, you should review what happened and the results of the interview as a way of learning how to improve your interviewing skills. Even if you obtain the job, you'll want to learn what you did correctly that helped you to get the job as well as what you could have done better for the next time.

Checklist

ANALYZING HOW I HANDLED THE INTERVIEW

- ○ I arrived early for the interview.

- ○ I greeted the interviewer warmly, with a smile and a firm handshake.

- ○ I maintained good posture.

- ○ I did not smoke or chew gum during the interview.

- ○ I spoke clearly, using good grammar.

- ○ I demonstrated enthusiasm and interest.

- ○ I was able to answer questions asked of me.

- ○ I sent a thank-you note within 24 hours after the interview.

ARRANGEMENTS AND ORGANIZATION OF LAW OFFICES AND LAW FIRMS

The classic image of the law firm was of the solo practitioner working alone in a small office in a small town. The more modern view portrayed in movies and on TV is that of a large national or global law firm. In between are small partnerships and other environments—corporations, insurance companies, government agencies, and consulting firms composed of accountants, lawyers, and management consultants. Exhibit 3.4 shows organization charts for four typical types of arrangements in which the paralegal may find work.

Solo Practice

Solo practice refers to one lawyer practicing alone without the assistance of other attorneys. The solo practitioner still exists, not only in small towns but in large metropolitan areas as well. The solo practitioner may well be the employer who is most dependent upon the skills of the paralegal in running the office, working with clients, and assisting at trial. A solo practice offers perhaps the greatest challenge for the paralegal who wishes to be involved in every aspect of a law practice. Tasks that otherwise might be assigned to an associate will fall to the legal assistant to perform.

In a litigation practice or a practice in which the attorney is frequently out of the office attending meetings, the paralegal becomes the main point of contact and coordination between clients and the supervising attorney. Jobs that might be done in larger firms by an accounting staff, such as preparation of payroll and maintenance of client escrow accounts, frequently are done by the paralegal in solo practices. Many solo practitioners consider their paralegal to be a key resource in the practice of law.

Small Offices

Small-office arrangements range from individual practitioners sharing space to partnerships. For the small practitioner, the cost of maintaining an adequate law library, conference room, office space, and office support services such as photocopy and fax machines is daunting. Therefore, practices frequently share these common services while separating client practices. The lawyers might have a similar type of practice, such as criminal law or family law, or dissimilar practices, such as family law and insurance defense work. Depending upon the arrangement, the practitioners might refer clients back and forth. The responsibility for the client and the client relationship is a personal one for the attorney.

Depending upon the arrangement, personnel, such as the receptionist, secretary, or paralegal, might be shared. In these situations the paralegal must be certain which of the attorneys is the supervising attorney with regard to each client. The paralegal who is working for more than one attorney in a sharing arrangement might be privy to confidential information that may not be shared with the other attorneys in the office. In some respects this can be thought of as an ethical wall environment. At the very least, the paralegal and the attorneys must clearly understand the ethical issues involved.

Partnerships

A partnership arrangement is two or more natural or artificial (corporation) persons who have joined together to share ownership and profit or loss. Partnerships in small-office arrangements may take the form of true partnerships, sharing all aspects of the practice, or may be partnerships in name only. In this latter case, the same ethical issues that the paralegal faces in the pure office-sharing arrangement must be considered.

If all of the attorneys are partners with complete responsibility for each other and the practice, paralegals may find themselves working for more than one of the partners. In effect, the partners share the paralegal's services. This can give rise to

---

Meet THE COURTHOUSE TEAM

The Courtroom

The first time you enter a courtroom, you may be surprised to find a number of people working as part of the courtroom team. Obviously there is a judge presiding. Less obvious are the support personnel—the people who keep the courtroom organized and handle trial details such as scheduling and processing documents. Also, they sometimes act as the interface between jury and judge. Depending on the state and the court, they are called minutes clerk, bailiff, or court deputy. In addition, there usually is a court reporter whose job is to make a contemporaneous record of the proceeding. Frequently the judge's law clerk will sit in on hearings as well.

Ethical PERSPECTIVE

Lawyers Who Share Offices

It is "impermissible for unaffiliated attorneys to have unrestricted access to each other's electronic files (including email and word-processing documents) and other client records. If separate computer systems are not utilized, each attorney's confidential client information should be protected in a way that guards against unauthorized access and preserves client confidences and secrets."

District of Columbia Ethics Opinion 303

certain issues for the paralegal when more than one of the partners demand something at the same time with the same sense of urgency. The fact that each of the partners will consider himself or herself to be "boss" can create a delicate situation for the paralegal.

A common solution in many offices is for one of the partners to be the primary supervising attorney for the paralegal, through whom the other partner (or partners) funnels work and requests. From an ethical point of view this solves the problem of who the supervising attorney is for the clients and files on which the paralegal is working and at the same time clarifies the lawyers' responsibilities under the lawyers' Rules of Professional Conduct.

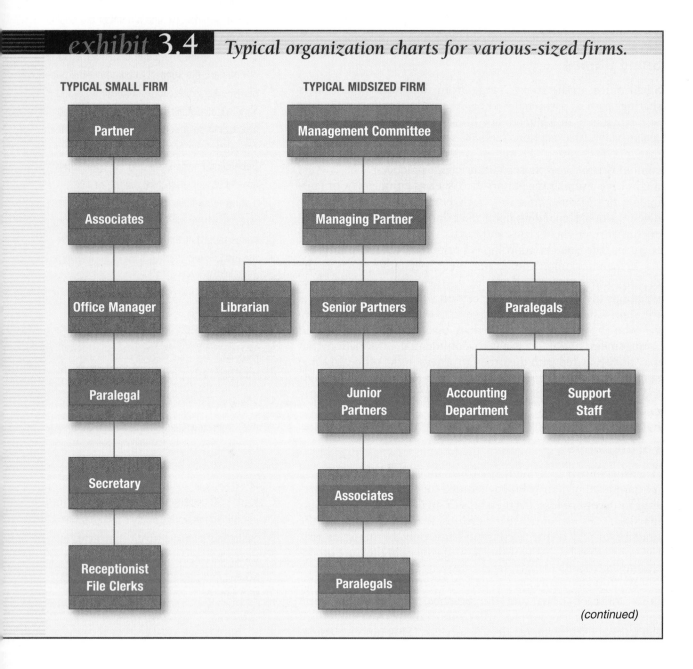

exhibit 3.4 *Typical organization charts for various-sized firms.*

TYPICAL SMALL FIRM

- Partner
- Associates
- Office Manager
- Paralegal
- Secretary
- Receptionist File Clerks

TYPICAL MIDSIZED FIRM

- Management Committee
- Managing Partner
  - Librarian
  - Senior Partners
    - Junior Partners
      - Associates
        - Paralegals
  - Paralegals
    - Accounting Department
    - Support Staff

(continued)

Continued.   *exhibit* 3.4

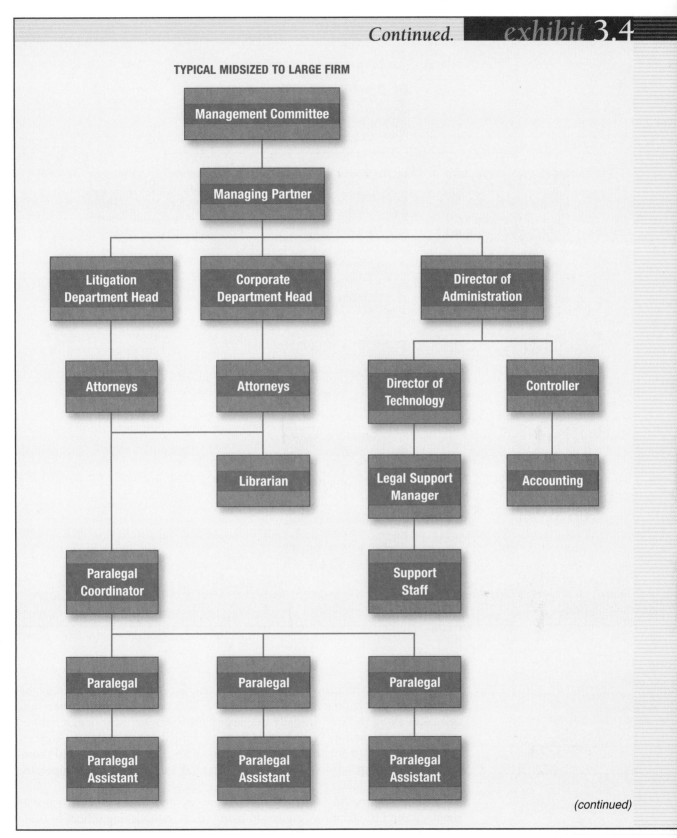

TYPICAL MIDSIZED TO LARGE FIRM

(continued)

exhibit **3.4** *Continued.*

TYPICAL LEGAL DEPARTMENT OF CORPORATION

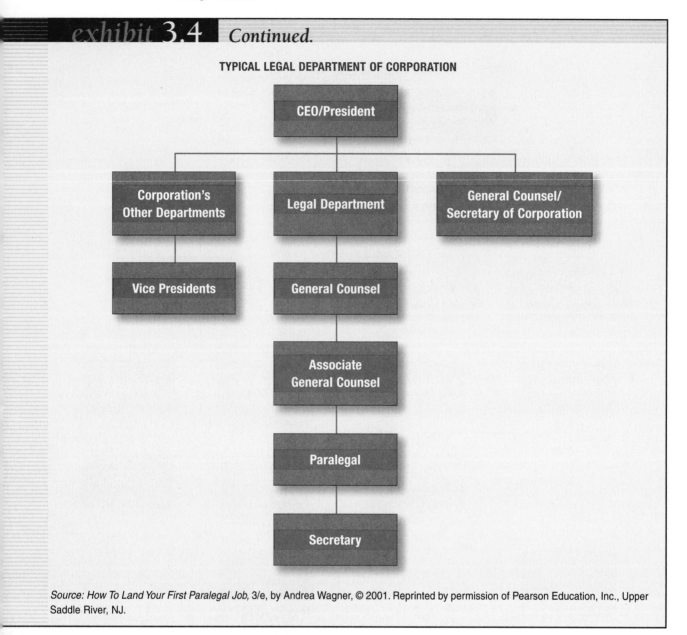

Large Offices

Historically, what are now viewed as large law offices are an outgrowth of traditional law offices that have expanded over the years, adding partners and associates along the way. Initially the larger law firms were regional, confined to major cities such as New York, Chicago, Philadelphia, and Los Angeles. With the growth of government at the national level, many firms found themselves establishing offices in the nation's capital to service clients appearing before federal agencies.

Continued growth of the national economy and business and corporate clients around the country resulted in many firms' establishing offices in other large cities, giving them a presence on each of the coasts as well as central locations such as Chicago, with offices in Washington, D.C., and elsewhere. Growth of the global economy has taken us one step farther, with law firms establishing offices in foreign countries. As a result, the large law firm has taken on the characteristics of many corporations, with firms merging to bring specialty areas of law within one firm while expanding the global availability of legal services.

For the paralegal the large office can be an exciting and dynamic area of practice. Paralegals may be called upon to travel with other members of the legal team or on their own as part of the practice. Even when no travel is required, the paralegal might be called upon to work with clients with diverse backgrounds, both domestically and internationally. One of the values of the large law firm for clients is the availability of a number of legal specialties within one legal services provider. For the paralegal this offers the opportunity to work in different areas of legal specialty.

Working in a large law firm also has some disadvantages. The larger the firm, the greater is the potential for less personal relationships and contacts with clients and other members of the legal team. In some firms, just as in any large organization, "playing politics" becomes very real. A paralegal's status, as well as some of the perks and benefits of the job, may depend on the status of the individual's supervising attorney. At the same time, the opportunities for advancement in a large firm might outweigh the disadvantages.

Large Firms

Unlike the small office, in which the paralegal also might be the bookkeeper, office manager, receptionist, and second chair in litigation, a department within a large firm generally hires support staff for each of these functions. The first contact for a paralegal with a large firm may be with the human resources department as part of the job application process. Bookkeeping or accounting departments usually handle payroll, check requests, and other financial issues. In the larger firms even the function of making copies takes place in a duplicating department, and the firm might have a mailroom for handling incoming and outgoing mail.

The large law firm has specialized components. In some ways this is similar to the structure of the English legal system, in which the solicitor deals directly with clients and the barrister litigates the cases. U. S. law firms frequently have litigation spe-

Courthouse built circa 1823 in Ohio.

cialists who spend their time in the actual litigation of cases while other attorneys within the same firm rarely, if ever, go to court. The role of the latter is to work with clients and, when the need arises, prepare the materials for the litigation department.

Just as the law has become more complex, lawyers also have come to specialize in narrow areas of practice such as environmental law, intellectual property law, health-care law, insurance law, tort law, and family law. This means that paralegals in large law firms also become specialists within their supervising attorney's primary field of law. Large-practice firms encourage clients to use the firm for all of their legal needs, so a lawyer within the firm frequently refers clients to other specialists in the firm while maintaining primary contact with the clients. Some firms have lawyers whose expertise is in getting new clients. These lawyers, often former politicians and government officials, are frequently referred to as the "rainmakers." They use their contacts to obtain clients and then refer the clients to the specialists within the firm.

Compensation for attorneys within large firms is generally based on how much new business the attorney has brought in, as well as how many billable hours the supervising attorneys have been able to bill for themselves and their paralegals. In this kind of environment, the paralegal who is able to maintain relationships with clients is an invaluable asset to the firm.

General Practice

A general law practice is one that handles all types of cases. This is what people usually think of as the small-town lawyer, the generalist to whom everyone in town comes for advice. The reality is that the same generalists practice in cities as well as small towns throughout the country. Their practices are as diverse as the law itself, handling everything from adoptions to zoning appeals. As general practitioners, they serve the same function in law as the general family practice doctor does in medicine.

Lawyers in this type of practice often work in several areas of law within the same day—attending a hearing in small claims court in the morning, preparing a will before lunch, having a luncheon meeting with an opposing attorney to discuss settlement of an accident case, then helping someone who is forming a corporation, and finally appearing at a municipal government meeting in the evening to seek a zoning approval. For many, the general practice is the most exciting type of practice, with a continually changing clientele offering all sorts of legal challenges. The paralegal in this environment has the opportunity to work with different types of clients on different types of legal matters on a constant basis. The challenge in this type of practice is to stay current in each of the areas of law of the practice.

Specialty Practice

A specialty practice is involved in practice in one area of law. Lawyers with specialty backgrounds, such as engineering, might choose to work in patent law or intellectual-property law. Those coming into the legal profession with accounting backgrounds might specialize in tax matters. Others have special interests and passions such as working with senior citizens in an elder law practice, or protecting the interests of children as child advocates, or practicing criminal law.

With the increasing complexity of the law, legal specialists are frequently receiving referrals from attorneys in other specialties or in general practice. The paralegal working for a specialist often acquires such a high level of knowledge in a specific area of law that it rivals that of many general practitioners. One of the dangers for the paralegal with this extent of specialty knowledge is that other attorneys could ask the paralegal questions to which the answers border on, or actually result in, the unauthorized practice of law. Because the paralegal in a specialty law practice is dependent—as are the supervising attorney and the practice—on referrals from other attorneys, the natural tendency is to accommodate referral attorneys by trying to answer questions of a legal nature. The paralegal must diplomatically avoid giving legal advice even to an attorney from another firm, to avoid a potential claim of UPL.

Maintaining relationships with other law firms and their paralegals and secretaries becomes a primary job function for the paralegal in a specialty practice. The paralegal commonly obtains referrals for the supervising attorney and the firm as a result of relationships developed in professional associations with other paralegals who recommend their friend who works for a lawyer specializing in the area sought.

In many areas of specialty, the paralegal has become a vital team member. Legal assistants with specialty skills in specific substantive areas perform services that allow the attorney to concentrate on other substantive issues of law. In addition, the legal assistant handles office management tasks and functions. These encompass intraoffice support including coordination between members of the professional team and the client. Some areas of specialty are discussed next.

Legal Nurse Consultant and Nurse Paralegal

Nurse paralegals or legal nurse consultants are nurses who have gained medical work experience and combine it with paralegal skills. Becoming a legal nurse consultant or a nurse paralegal is an ideal career opportunity for nurses with clinical nursing experience who want to work in the legal environment. Entry to most education programs requires a current license as a Registered Nurse and a minimum of 2,000 to 6,000 hours of clinical nursing experience, usually one to three years. Some programs are open to those with an associate degree in nursing, but usually a bachelor's degree in nursing is requested or desired.

Nurse paralegals draw upon their knowledge of medical terminology, medical procedures, and nursing practice to decipher medical records for the legal community. The most obvious advantage is their ability to analyze medical records from both medical and legal standpoints. Their experience also enables them to conduct more effective interviews with clients, fact witnesses, and expert witnesses in cases of medical malpractice and cases involving injury and damage investigation. Graduates of these programs often work as independent nurse consultants for law firms and insurance companies. Others find positions with insurance companies and law firms specializing in medical malpractice and personal injury.

Although the ABA considers the nurse paralegal and legal nurse consultant to be part of the paralegal profession, the American Association of Legal Nurse Consultants (AALNC) views this role as a subspecialty of nursing. In March 1998, the Standing Committee on Legal Assistants of the American Bar Association decided that "legal nurses and legal nurse consultants fall squarely within the ABA definition of 'paralegal/legal assistant.'" In contrast, AALNC has defined the legal nurse consultant as a specialty practitioner of nursing

Networking

SIDEBAR

Networking is the establishment of contact with others with whom questions and information are shared. For the paralegal, networking may be the key to obtaining a job, finding a new job, and performing at the highest level in a job. As is frequently said, it is not *what* you know but *whom* you know. Knowing the right person or a person who can refer you to the right person is a valuable asset. Many paralegals develop a referral list of other paralegals they can call to get a quick answer in their own jurisdiction and others. Most paralegals facing a deadline are not too proud to call their contacts, whether across the street, across the state, or across the nation, to meet a deadline or get the necessary form. During interviews, hiring attorneys have been known to ask about the paralegal's networking activities.

American Association of
Legal Nurse Consultants:
www.aalnc.org

whose education should be developed and presented as specialty nursing curricula by nurse educators in partnership with legal educators.

Real Estate

Paralegals or legal assistants with real estate experience in sales or from title insurance agencies can perform many of the tasks associated with a real estate practice, such as communicating between buyers and sellers, coordinating the documentation for settlement, and preparing documents for recording purposes. In most jurisdictions becoming a licensed salesperson or a real estate broker requires the completion of a course of study that provides a foundation in the practices and procedures of real estate practice and equips the paralegal with a terminology base that facilitates effective communication with the supervising attorney.

In large cases, paralegals might be responsible for summarizing discovery documents.

Complex Litigation

Complex litigation takes many forms, from class-action lawsuits to complex product liability cases. Paralegals working in complex litigation generally oversee the requests for document production and maintain indexes, usually on computer databases, of the paperwork generated from litigation. In large cases the paralegal might supervise a staff of other paralegals or law students in summarizing discovery documents. At trial, these paralegals frequently coordinate the production of exhibits.

Environmental Law

Environmental law covers everything from toxic waste dumps to protection of wildlife and the environment. A challenge for the environmental paralegal is in locating and obtaining public records and other documents necessary to establish the areas of concern and claims, some of which predate computer records, such as toxic waste dumps created during World War II and the early 1950s.

Intellectual Property

In a survey by The Affiliates, a company providing temporary and full-time legal personnel, 48 percent of the surveyed attorneys indicated intellectual property as the fastest growing field in law. The intellectual-property paralegal is concerned with the formalities of protecting intellectual-property interests including patent rights, trade secrets, and copyrights and trademarks. The two main areas are *prosecution*, which involves establishing the priority of the claims that will result in granting of the patent or copyright, and *litigation*, which protects those rights against claims by others, such as in patent infringement cases.

The Affiliates: www.futurelaw office.com/practice.html

Elder Law

With the aging of the population has come an increased need to protect the rights of the elderly and obtain all the benefits to which they are entitled. This includes such simple tasks as assisting individuals to apply for Social Security benefits, Medicare benefits, or Medicaid benefits. It also entails working with the elderly to create estate plan documents, powers of attorney, and health-care directives. More and more, the paralegal or legal assistant is becoming an advocate for the elderly, in many cases working in a pro bono capacity or through social service agencies. Elder law has come to include the additional issues of helping the elderly work through the maze of health care and government benefits.

Legal Assistant Manager

As legal assistant staffs have grown, even at some of the smaller firms, the position of legal assistant manager has emerged. With higher turnover rates and increased specialization comes the associate's need for someone to hire, supervise, train, and evaluate legal assistants. In many firms this person is the interface between the legal assistants and the attorneys.

As paralegals gain specialized knowledge in specific fields, they find themselves working for different attorneys as their expertise demands. Attorneys, for the most part, do not have the time to handle the nonlegal aspects of managers, such as acting as leader, mentor, employee advocate, supervisor, trainer, evaluator, problem solver, and resource manager. The largest firms appoint a managing partner to handle the management tasks and human resources issues. In many smaller firms, these duties fall to the individual with the title of legal assistant manager. The new specialty is well recognized and supported by its own organization, the Legal Assistant Management Association.

Legal Assistant Management Association: www.LAMANET.org

Pro Bono Paralegals

Pro bono means working without compensation on behalf of individuals and organizations that otherwise could not afford legal assistance. Increasingly, the legal profession has taken on the role of working without compensation in legal aid offices and community legal service programs. Paralegals, as members of professional associations, participate in pro bono activities at varying levels and time commitments.

Government Employment

Federal, state, and local governments are large employers of paralegals, and paralegals are expected to be utilized even further at every level in the future. Many of the federally employed paralegals are found in administrative agencies. A good example is the work of paralegals in the Social Security Administration as decision writers, case schedulers, and case specialists. Just as the private law firm has discovered the value of the paralegal on the legal team, so have government law offices such as the U. S. Attorney's Office and the Office of the Solicitor General. These offices are involved with both criminal prosecutions and civil litigation where the government is a party. Many other agencies that conduct administrative hearings utilize paralegals at all levels.

SIDEBAR

Document Specialist or Paralegal?

Under the definition enacted by the Maine legislature, anyone calling himself or herself a paralegal or legal assistant must work under the supervision of an attorney. Independent paralegals no longer can use the title *paralegal* or *legal assistant*. This has resulted in some changing the name of their freelance business to *document specialist* (*Bangor Daily News,* August 16, 1999).

The California legislature passed a law prohibiting self-help legal document service providers from receiving compensation unless the legal document assistant is registered in the county where the service is provided and provides a bond of $25,000.

SIDEBAR

The DuPont Experience

In an effort to reduce costs, DuPont, one of the largest companies in America, changed the way it uses legal assistants—elevating the work, positions, and numbers of legal assistants. Legal assistants have been given more responsibility in handling documents, technology, and investigations. In doing so, DuPont reportedly reduced by almost 90 percent the number of outside law firms and services it formerly used. As of 2000, the DuPont legal department had 51 paralegals working with 140 lawyers. In the DuPont model the legal department acts as counsel to the other DuPont-owned companies and deals with them as clients much in the way that the outside law firms had in the past.

Source: Paralegals Are Part of DuPont's Legal Team, by D. L. Hawley, *Legal Assistant Today,* March 4, 2000.

Legal Departments of Corporations

Many people think of a corporate legal department as a laid-back, conservative environment with little activity other than drafting minutes of meetings and filing corporate records with the federal and state governments. The reality today is that, in the new global economy, more and more corporations with in-house staffs are engaged in international trade. A whole body of law relates to compliance for imports and exports. For example, the transfer and sale of certain high-tech equipment and technology must have prior government approval. Sales involving shipments to other countries require letters of credit and currency conversion. International trade creates a whole host of unique issues related to the laws of the countries with which the domestic corporation may be doing business.

The paralegal is in the middle of these transactions, juggling the requirements from both the legal perspective and the sales and marketing perspective. Paralegals with foreign language skills find themselves in even greater demand in handling communication issues. Those with cultural ties to or background in the countries with which the corporation is doing business will find their knowledge frequently tapped to avoid cultural mistakes resulting from miscommunication.

Self-Employment

The paralegal has some opportunities to be self-employed, although state regulation may limit the opportunities or restrict paralegal self-employment. Where authorized by federal law, the paralegal may actively represent clients without the supervision of an attorney, such as before the Social Security Administration. Many paralegals work as freelancers for different attorneys, usually on a case-by-case basis. In addition to the normal ethical obligations regarding confidentiality and conflict of interest, the freelance paralegal must observe the ethical guidelines on advertising in the local jurisdiction and avoid creating the appearance of being available to render legal advice except where authorized.

ADMINISTRATIVE PROCEDURES IN THE LAW OFFICE

Certain administrative procedures are common to most, if not all, law offices. Two of the main administrative functions are timekeeping and conflict checking.

Timekeeping

As Abraham Lincoln has been quoted as saying, "A lawyer's time and advice are his stock-in-trade." Keeping track of billable time becomes a critical function to ensure that the law firm

Timeslips input screen.   *exhibit 3.5*

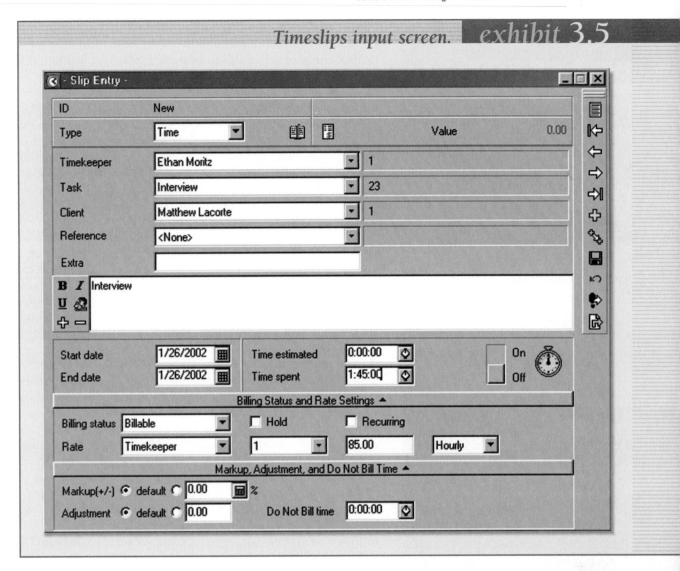

will be compensated properly for its advice and efforts on behalf of clients. Timekeeping extends beyond attorneys to paralegals and, in some cases, secretaries and file clerks. The task has been automated by the use of software, such as Timeslips, that accurately captures, stores, and processes this information. Exhibit 3.5 illustrates a Timeslips input screen.

Conflict Checking

Conflict checking is necessary to verify that current and prior representations of parties and matters handled will not present a conflict of interest for the firm in accepting a new client or legal matter. Checking for conflicts of interest is an essential function designed to avoid the ethical violations of representing competing interests. Many offices use computer database software for conflict checking.

Ethical PERSPECTIVE

Proof of Supervision

Accurate contemporaneously recorded time records for the paralegal and for the attorney may be used to show the level of supervision of the paralegal by the supervising attorney.

Ethical
PERSPECTIVE

Adequate Screening

"The court does not subscribe to the argument that, as a matter of law, screening would be ineffective when a nonlawyer switches employment to 'the other side.' The ABA opinions indicate that a law firm can set up appropriate screening and administrative procedures to prevent nonlawyers from working on the other side of those common cases and disclosing confidential information."

Connecticut Trial Court, unpublished decision, Devine v. Beinfield, *1997 Ct. Sup. 7674, 1997 Conn Super Lexis 1966, No. CV93 0121721 S (Jul.1,1997).*

SIDEBAR

Billing for Paralegal Time

The 11th Circuit Court of Appeals has said, "We have held that paralegal time is recoverable as part of a prevailing party's award for attorney's fees and expenses, [but] only to the extent that the paralegal performs work traditionally done by an attorney." Quoting from *Allen v. United States Steel Corp.,* 665 F.2d 689, 697 (5th Cir. 1982): "To hold otherwise would be counterproductive because excluding reimbursement for such work might encourage attorneys to handle entire cases themselves, thereby achieving the same results at a higher overall cost."

Jean v. Nelson, 863 F. 2d 759 (11th Cir. 1988).

Names of clients, opposing parties, counsel, and law firms can be quickly searched electronically. Some firms still rely on a manual check of paper lists and file-card indexes containing the names of clients, opposing parties, and opposing attorneys in cases. To determine conflicts where there has been only indirect representation is difficult.

Attorneys and paralegals who change firms may have to do a preliminary conflict check before they accept or start employment. The conflict comes when the former firm and the new firm are, or were, on opposite sides of a case. It may be a conflict for someone who has had access to information about a case to switch to the firm representing the opposing party. Confidential disclosure for the limited purpose of checking for a conflict before starting employment could prevent a serious or perceived ethical breach in the form of a breach of confidentiality or conflict of interest. In some cases the conflict of interest may result from a financial interest such as stock ownership or investments. Making full disclosure of these potential conflict situations to the supervising attorney or to the appropriate conflict checker with the firm is important.

In many cases the conflict can be resolved by isolating the individual from information about the case—sometimes called building an ethical wall. An ethical wall, also known as a Chinese wall, is an attempt to shield a paralegal or lawyer from access to information about a case when there is the possibility of a conflict of interest. Most courts permit the establishment of an ethical wall to protect the parties from the conflict of interest or breach of confidentiality. But a Nevada court, based on a 1994 ethics opinion, prohibits paralegals from working for a firm that represents any client that has an adversarial relationship to any client of the former employer law firm [*Ciaffone v. District Court*, 113 Nev. 1165 (1997), 945 P.2d 950].

LEGAL TERMINOLOGY

Barrister
Conflict checking
Elective course
Ethical wall
General practice
Networking
Nurse paralegal (legal nurse consultants)
Partnership
Pro bono
Resume
Solicitor
Solo practice
Specialty practice
Timekeeping

Summary

CHAPTER 3 CAREERS IN THE PARALEGAL PROFESSION

Compensation Issues for the Paralegal

1. Salaries tend to be higher in large metropolitan areas and lower in small towns and rural areas.
2. Large firms tend to pay more and small firms, less.
3. There are regional variations.

Selecting a Specialty

1. Career satisfaction is vital.
2. Start with a self-evaluation.

Assessing Your Background

1. Personal background.
2. Paralegal certificate or degree.

Assessing Your Skills

1. Interpersonal.
2. Communication.
3. Motivation.

(continued)

Assessing Your Interests

1. Recognize your strengths.
2. Work on weaknesses.

Selecting Your Electives

1. Gain additional knowledge.
2. Explore areas of possible interest.

Preparing Your Resume

1. Traditional paper resume
2. Electronic resume
3. Constant updating

Interviewing for a Job

1. Prepare carefully to reduce stress.   2. Put your best foot forward.

Arrangements and Organization of Law Offices and Law Firms

1. Solo Practice
2. Small Offices
3. Partnerships
4. Large Offices
5. Large Firms
6. General Practice
7. Specialty Practice
    a. Legal Nurse Consultant and Nurse Paralegal
    b. Real Estate
    c. Complex Litigation
    d. Environmental Law
    e. Intellectual Property
    f. Elder Law
    g. Legal Assistant Manager
    h. Pro Bono Paralegals
8. Government Employment
9. Legal Departments of Corporations
10. Self-Employment

Administrative Procedures

1. Timekeeping
2. Conflict Checking

Working the Web

1. Check the websites of the various paralegal professional associations for information on paralegal occupational opportunities:
   a. National Association of Legal Assistants at www.nala.org
   b. National Federation of Paralegal Associations at www.paralegals.org
   c. Legal Assistant Management Association at www.lamanet.org
   d. American Association of Legal Nurse Consultants at www.aalnc.org
   e. The American Association of Nurse Attorneys at www.taana.org

2. Check online employment information source at www.monster.com

3. Check online sources for help creating resumes:
   a. Purdue University at www.owl.English.purdue.edu/files/35.html
   b. College of William and Mary at www.wm.edu/csrv/career/stualum/resmdir/contentrs.html

4. Check online career sources at:
   a. Career Resource Library at www.labor.state.ny.us/html/library.htm
   b. America's Job Bank at www.ajb.dni.us/index.html
   c. Wall Street Journal at www.careers.wsj.com
   d. CareerWEB at www.cweb.com

5. Check the Martindell-Hubbell Legal Directory for law firms in your area that have a website.

Questions

CRITICAL LEGAL THINKING AND WRITING

1. What additional costs might a paralegal incur in working in a large-city practice in contrast to a small-town office?
2. What advantages might a person have in entering the paralegal profession later in life?
3. How does assessing your interests and skills help in choosing a career path?
4. How does assessing your interests and skills help in preparing your personal resume?
5. Prepare the resume you would like to have five years from now. How would this resume help you in selecting courses, extracurricular activities, and interim employment?
6. Complete the "My Career Roadmap" checklist in this chapter.

7. Start to network by setting up a meeting with a working paralegal and preparing a list of questions to ask at that meeting.
8. Why would a paralegal who specializes in one legal field be at greater risk for unauthorized practice of law?
9. Other than revealing potential employment opportunities, what advantages does networking have for a paralegal?
10. Why is accurate timekeeping important to the paralegal and the law firm?

ETHICS: ANALYSIS AND DISCUSSION

1. In changing jobs from one firm to another, how does the paralegal avoid a conflict of interest?
2. What ethical and UPL problems do freelance paralegals face that those working in a single firm do not?
3. What ethical issues might arise in determining the paralegal's supervising attorney when the paralegal is working in a small firm of three attorneys?

Confidentiality—Conflict of Interest

There are few certainties in the area of ethics, for paralegals or in any profession. What qualifies as ethical conduct is in most cases based on state law and court interpretation applied to a set of facts. The citation listed below represents one legal opinion and is provided as a research starting point. Do not assume that the same rule applies in your jurisdiction. For the following:

- *Prepare a written statement based on your state law.*
- *Use your state bar association website as a starting point.*

You are working as a paralegal in a small law office. The office is shared by three attorneys, each of whom is a solo practitioner. To save money they share a law library and a fax machine, and they use a common computer network with separate workstations but with a common file server to save files because it has an automatic backup system. You work for each of the lawyers as the need arises, answering phones, and generally performing paralegal services. [*District of Columbia Ethics Opinion 303.*] What issues of confidentiality should be considered? As the office paralegal, are there any conflicts of interest problems for you?

FOR DISCUSSION

Jean v. Nelson   863 F.2d 759 (11th Cir. 1988)

Reimbursement for Paralegal Time under Federal Statute

The district court awarded, and the 11th Circuit Court of Appeals upheld, reimbursement for time spent by paralegals and law clerks where the work was normally done by an attorney. The hourly rate awarded was $40. This is the rate at which the law firm whose paralegals and clerks were involved bills its clients.

The government challenges the rate awarded, and contends that paralegal time is compensational only at the actual cost to the plaintiffs' counsel. In the context of a Title VII case, [the court] held that paralegal time is recoverable as "part of a prevailing party's award for attorney's fees and expenses, [but] only to the extent that the paralegal performs work traditionally done by an attorney. To hold otherwise would be counterproductive because excluding reimbursement for such work might encourage attorneys to handle entire cases themselves, thereby achieving the same results at a higher overall cost."

Questions

1. Does this rationale encourage lawyers to use paralegals?
2. Does this decision facilitate the availability of lower-cost quality legal services?
3. Should an attorney be allowed to charge more than out-of-pocket costs for paralegal services?

CASE FOR BRIEFING

Doe v. Condon

532 S.E.2d 879 (S.C. 2000)

Supreme Court of South Carolina

Read the following case, then review and brief the case. In your brief, answer the following questions.

1. According to this court, why is the practice of law limited to licensed attorneys?

2. What tasks does this court indicate that a paralegal may perform?

3. What tasks does this court indicate that a paralegal may not perform?

4. Why is answering legal questions about the need for a will or a trust the unauthorized practice of law (UPL)?

5. In this court's interpretation, what is the reason for prohibiting a fee-splitting arrangement between a lawyer and a paralegal?

Per curiam

This is a declaratory judgment action. Petitioner, a paralegal, has submitted a generalized list of tasks he wishes to perform and has inquired whether performing them constitutes the unauthorized practice of law. Petition also seeks a determination of the propriety of the proposed fee-splitting arrangement with his attorney–employer.

To protect the public from unsound legal advice and incompetent representation, South Carolina, like other jurisdictions, limits the practice of law to licensed attorneys.

Our Supreme Court has set forth a succinct standard for the proper role of paralegals:

> The activities of a paralegal do not constitute the practice of law as long as they are limited to work of a preparatory nature, such as legal research, investigation, or the composition of legal documents, which enables licensed attorney–employer to carry a given matter to a conclusion through his own examination, approval, or additional effort.

While the important support function of paralegals has increased through the years, the guidelines stand the test of time. The paralegal plays a supporting role to the supervising attorney. Here the roles are reversed. The attorney would support the paralegal. Petitioner would play the lead role, with no meaningful attorney supervision and the attorney's presence and involvement only surfaces on the back end. Meaningful attorney supervision must be present throughout the process. The line between what is and what is not permissible conduct by a non-attorney is sometimes unclear as a potential trap for the unsuspecting client.

The conduct of the paralegal contemplated here clearly crosses the line into the unauthorized practice of law. It is well settled the paralegal may not give legal advice, consult, offer legal explanations, or make legal recommendations.

Petitioner intends to conduct unsupervised "wills and trusts" seminars for the public, "emphasizing" living trusts during the course of his presentation. Petitioner also plans to answer estate-planning questions from the audience.

I find, as other courts have, that the very structure of such "educational" legal seminars suggests that the presenter will actually be giving legal advice on legal matters. At the very least, petitioner will implicitly advise participants that they require estate planning services. Whether a will or trust is appropriate in any given situation is a function of legal judgment. To be sure, advising a potential client when his or her need for a living trust (or other particular estate-planning instrument or device) fits squarely within the practice of law. These matters cry out for the exercise of professional judgment by a licensed attorney. Thus, in conducting these informational seminars, petitioner would engage in the unauthorized practice of law as a non-attorney offering legal advice.

I fully recognize the prevailing popularity of "financial planners" and others jump[ing] on the estate planning bandwagon. This trend in no way affects the decision before the court. This paralegal would not be presenting the estate-planning seminar as a financial planner. The seminar would be conspicuously sponsored by the paralegal's attorney–employer.

Petitioner intends to get client information and answer general estate planning questions during his proposed "initial client interviews." While petitioner may properly compile client information, petitioner may not answer estate-planning questions. Petitioner's answering legal questions would constitute the unauthorized practice of law for the reasons stated above. Wall law firm in which the petitioner is employed plans to direct clients to an attorney for follow up consultations. A paralegal may not give legal advice in any event. Moreover, permissible preparatory tasks must be performed while under the attorney supervision. The proposed after-the-fact review comes too late.

Petitioner's law firm intends to compensate him based upon the volume and type of cases he "handles." A paralegal, of course, may not handle any case. This fee arrangement directly violates Rule 5.4 of the Rules of Professional Conduct. This limitation serves to "discourage the unauthorized practice of law by lay persons and to prevent a non-lawyer from acquiring a vested pecuniary interest in an attorney's disposition of a case that could possibly take preeminence over a client's best interest. This compensation proposal arrangement, coupled with petitioner's desire to market the law firm's services via the educational seminars and meet individually with clients, creates a situation ripe for abuse. Indeed, the proposal by petitioner presents the very evil Rule 5.4 was designed to avoid. Accordingly, I find petitioner's proposed compensation plan violates both the letter and spirit of Rule 5.4 prohibiting fee-splitting with non-attorneys.

Note: If in South Carolina, include the parallel citation: 341 S.C. 22. The Lexis citation for this case is 2000 S.C. LEXIS 125.

CHAPTER 4

CHAPTER OBJECTIVES

After studying this chapter, you should be able to:

1. Explain what a paralegal does.

2. Describe the skills necessary to work as a paralegal.

3. Articulate personal goals and skills.

4. Understand the concept of commitment.

5. Understand the concept of resourcefulness.

6. Understand the concept of interpersonal skills.

7. Understand the concept of professional communications.

8. Understand the concept of analysis.

9. Understand the need for cultural sensitivity.

Paralegal Workplace Skills

It is when merchants dispute about their own rules that they invoke the law.

J. BRETT, ROBINSON V. MOLLETT, 1875

Introduction

As the paralegal profession has evolved, so, too, have the duties and roles of the paralegal within the legal system and elsewhere. The earliest legal assistant was probably a legal secretary who developed specialized skills while working for an attorney in one of the legal specialties. As the need for specialized skills became more obvious, legal assistant programs and paralegal programs were created to teach the requisite skills. In the classic sense, a paralegal performs those tasks and activities that assist the supervising attorney in representing clients. The broader view is that the paralegal performs many of the same functions that attorneys perform, under the supervision of an attorney but limited by laws and regulations on the unauthorized practice of law (UPL).

PARALEGAL TASKS AND FUNCTIONS

The actual tasks and functions the paralegal performs vary according to the type of practice, size of the firm or organization, and skill of the individual paralegal. Some of the more generic tasks include:

Clerk or Minutes Clerk

The clerk is the judge's administrative assistant in the courtroom. It has been said that the clerk controls access to the judge in the courtroom. Clerks control the flow of documents to and from the bench and generally act as the judge's right hand. Frequently they arrange the schedules and coordinate requests to the judge and facilitate communication between counsel and judge. And as the judge's left and right ears, clerks convey to the judge your courtesy or lack of it. Because clerks usually are in the courtroom before anyone else, it is good practice to introduce yourself and offer a smile. When the court asks who you are, the clerk will let the court know, which is less embarrassing than having the judge ask, "Who is that?"

- Conducting interviews
- Maintaining written and verbal contacts with clients and counsel
- Setting up, organizing, and maintaining client files
- Preparing pleadings and documents
- Reviewing, analyzing, summarizing, and indexing documents and transcripts
- Assisting in preparing witnesses and clients for trial
- Maintaining calendar and tickler systems
- Performing research, both factual and legal
- Performing office administrative functions including maintaining time and billing records

Client Interviews

Many paralegals act as the first line of contact with clients. Paralegals may not ethically or legally give legal advice or set legal fees, but they frequently conduct the initial interview with the client. This might involve taking the initial client information and preparing the client data sheet (see Exhibit 4.1) or conducting a more in-depth interview to determine the facts of the matter for the attorney's review. Frequently, the paralegal continues to function as the contact point with the client and the supervising attorney or the law firm. Paralegals frequently establish rapport with clients and earn their confidence.

The paralegal always must be keenly aware of the ethical limitations in dealing with clients. This is especially true when the client develops a high level of confidence in dealing with the paralegal. Clients come to the attorney for advice. When they have confidence in a paralegal, they might tend to ask the paralegal for advice and recommendations instead of "bothering" the attorney. Providing such advice or recommendations may constitute the rendering of legal advice in violation of UPL restrictions. For example, to the client, the question "Should I make my son my power of attorney?" seems simple. But the answer is not so simple and involves many legal consequences so it must be referred to the supervising attorney. Another UPL might be to help the client complete blank legal forms, such as bankruptcy forms or will forms purchased at the stationery store.

Investigations

The paralegal may be asked to act as the direct representative of the supervising attorney in conducting an investigation into a pending case. A paralegal trained in the specific area of law understands the factual needs of a case and the sources of information available. A paralegal who has had the opportunity to observe or work with an attorney and has watched the presentation of evidence in a trial obtains a good sense of what will make good demonstrative evidence, such as models and photographs. In the case of photos, an understanding of the kind of questions that might be asked in direct examination and

Client data sheet.   *exhibit* 4.1

CLIENT DATA SHEET

ACTION TAKEN/REQUIRED

1. Client Name:

2. Client/Matter Number:

3. Client Address:

4. Phone: Work:

        Home:

        Fax:

5. Email address:

6. Social Security No.:

7. Date of Birth:

8. Marital Status:

9. Client Contact:

10. Matter:

    (a) Adverse Party:

    (b) Date of Incident:

    (c) Statute of Limitations Period:

    (d) Statute of Limitations Date:

11. Opposing Counsel:

12. Opposing Counsel Address:

13. Opposing Counsel Phone:

Approximately 20 percent of the world's population is Muslim. Islam is the principal religion of Afghanistan, Algeria, Bangladesh, Egypt, Indonesia, Iran, Iraq, Jordan, Kuwait, Libya, Malaysia, Mali, Mauritania, Morocco, Niger, North Yemen, Oman, Pakistan, Qatar, Saudi Arabia, Somalia, South Yemen, Sudan, Syria, Tunisia, Turkey, and the United Arab Emirates. Islamic law (or Sharía) is the only law in Saudi Arabia. In other Islamic countries, the Sharía forms the basis of family law but coexists with other laws.

The Islamic law system is derived from the *Koran,* the Sunnah (decisions and sayings of the Prophet Muhammad), and reasoning by Islamic scholars. By 10 A.D., Islamic scholars decided that divine law could not be further improved, so they closed the door of ijtihad (independent reasoning) and froze the evolution of Islamic law at that point.

Islamic law prohibits riba, or the making of unearned or unjustified profit. Making a profit from the sale of goods or the provision of services is permitted. The most notable consequence of riba is that it forbids the payment of interest on loans. To circumvent this result, the party with the money is permitted to purchase an item and resell it to the other party at a profit or to advance the money and become a trading partner who shares in the profits of the enterprise.

Today, Islamic law is used primarily in the areas of marriage, divorce, and inheritance and, to a limited extent, in criminal law. To resolve the tension between Sharía and the practice of modern commercial law, the Sharía is often ignored in commercial transactions.

cross-examination about the photographs offered as evidence enables the paralegal to be certain that the photographs are taken from the correct angles with the correct landmarks or measurements included. Interviews conducted by the paralegal in preparation for trial could qualify as privileged for the attorney–client privilege just as they do when conducted by attorneys. The paralegal must be aware of how interview material may be used and potentially obtained by opposing parties and act to protect clients' privileged communication with the paralegal as a representative of the supervising attorney.

Legal Writing

Paralegals frequently are called upon to maintain the written communications with clients, opposing attorneys, and the court. These may be in the form of correspondence, memos of law, or briefs for the court. Many paralegals become extremely adept at drafting complaints and supporting memoranda of law and briefs. Although the content is the ultimate responsibility of the supervising attorney, the paralegal with good writing skills is an invaluable asset. Well-written and well-reasoned documentation is easy to review for signature and transmittal and is a major timesaver for the attorney.

Legal Research

In the modern law office legal research is conducted with hard copy books and also with electronic media, including extensive use of the Internet. The ability to conduct research into case law, statutory enactments, and regulatory rules and procedures gives the paralegal a major advantage in getting the job in the first place and advancing in most firms. Legal research today requires the ability to use online legal services such as Lexis, Westlaw, VersusLaw, and Loislaw, as well as the ability to find information on government websites and private websites.

Lexis: www.lexisnexis.com/

Westlaw: www.westlaw.com/about/

VersusLaw: www.versuslaw.com

Loislaw: www.loislaw.com

WHAT PARALEGALS IN LEGAL SPECIALTIES DO

In addition to the various generic tasks that most paralegals or legal assistants perform, paralegals working in specialty areas find themselves performing additional and more specialized tasks that frequently require special knowledge, education, or skill beyond the basic skills and knowledge required of all paralegals. Some of the tasks performed by paralegals in specialty practice are as follows.

GENERAL BUSINESS PRACTICE:

- Draft lease agreements
- Draft partnership agreements
- Draft noncompetition agreements
- Prepare agreements of sale and attend real estate settlements
- Draft contracts for business arrangements and new ventures
- Draft employee agreements

DEBTOR RIGHTS AND CREDITOR REMEDIES:

- Draft correspondence complying with state and federal regulations concerning debt collection
- Prepare documentation to support garnishment proceedings
- Arrange for execution and support judgments, including publication of notice of sales and levies on personal property
- Transfer judgments to other jurisdictions
- Prepare, file, and terminate Uniform Commercial Code financing statements (see Exhibit 4.2)
- Assist clients in filing bankruptcy petitions, including the preparation of schedules and proofs of claim
- Prepare Chapter 11 debtor's financial statements
- Attend Chapter 13 confirmation hearings

CORPORATE PRACTICE:

- Determine availability and reserve fictitious or corporate name
- Prepare and file fictitious name registrations
- Prepare articles of incorporation, minutes, and bylaws for corporation
- Prepare, issue, and transfer stock certificates
- Prepare shareholder agreements
- Prepare applications and file for employer identification numbers and tax registration numbers

exhibit **4.2** *Uniform Commercial Code Form UCC-1.*

PARTIES
Debtor name (last name first if individual) and mailing address:

1

Debtor name (last name first if individual) and mailing address:

1a

Debtor name (last name first if individual) and mailing address:

1b

Secured Party(ies) name(s) (last name first if individual) and address for security interest information:

2

Assignee(s) of Secured Party name(s) (last name first if individual) and address for security interest information:

2a

Special Types of Parties (check if applicable):

☐ The terms "Debtor" and "Secured Party" mean "Lessee" and "Lessor," respectively.

☐ The terms "Debtor" and "Secured Party" mean "Consignee" and "Consignor," respectively.

☐ Debtor is a Transmitting Utility.

3

SECURED PARTY SIGNATURE(S)

This statement is filed with only the Secured Party's signature to perfect a security interest in collateral (check applicable box(es)) —

a. ☐ acquired after a **change of name, identity or corporate structure** of the Debtor.

b. ☐ as to which the **filing has lapsed.**

c. already subject to a security interest in **another county in Pennsylvania** —
  ☐ when the **collateral was moved** to this county.
  ☐ when the **Debtor's residence or place of business was moved** to this county.

d. already subject to a security interest in **another jurisdiction** —
  ☐ when the **collateral was moved** to Pennsylvania.
  ☐ when the **Debtor's location was moved** to Pennsylvania.

e. ☐ which is **proceeds** of the collateral described in block 9, in which a security interest was previously perfected (also describe proceeds in block 9, if purchased with cash proceeds and not adequately described on the original financing statement).

Secured Party Signature(s)
(required only if box(es) is checked above):

_____

_____

_____

4

FINANCING STATEMENT
Uniform Commercial Code Form UCC-1
IMPORTANT — Please read instructions on
reverse side of page 4 before completing

Filing No. (stamped by filing officer):   Date, Time, Filing Office (stamped by filing officer):

5

This **Financing Statement** is presented for filing pursuant to the Uniform Commercial Code, and is to be filed with the (check applicable box):

☐ Secretary of the Commonwealth.
☐ Prothonotary of _____ County.
☐ real estate records of _____ County.

6

Number of Additional Sheets (if any): _____ 7

Optional Special Identification (Max. 10 characters): _____ 8

COLLATERAL

Identify collateral by item and/or type:

☐ (check only if desired) Products of the collateral are also covered.   9

Identify related real estate, if applicable: The collateral is, or includes (check appropriate box(es)) —

a. ☐ **crops** growing or to be grown on —
b. ☐ goods which are or are to become **fixtures** on —
c. ☐ **minerals** or the like (including oil and gas) as extracted on —
d. ☐ **accounts resulting from the sale of minerals** or the like (including oil and gas) at the wellhead or minehead on —

the following real estate:
  Street Address:
  Described at: Book _____ of (check one) ☐ Deeds ☐ Mortgages , at Page(s) _____ ,
  for _____ County. Uniform Parcel Identifier _____ .
  ☐ Described on Additional Sheet.

Name of record owner (required only if no Debtor has an interest of record):

10

DEBTOR SIGNATURE(S)

Debtor Signature(s):

1 _____

1a _____

1b _____ 11

RETURN RECEIPT TO:

STANDARD FORM — FORM UCC-1
Approved by Secretary of Commonwealth of Pennsylvania

- Prepare and file annual reports
- Prepare and file articles of dissolution
- Prepare and file securities registrations and required filings with state regulatory agencies and with the United States Securities & Exchange Commission

ENVIRONMENTAL LAW:

- Track information with regard to Superfund sites
- Determine applicability of brown fields to client property
- Research history of properties to determine environmental activity
- Obtain the appropriate information about sites from state and federal environmental agencies
- Obtain documentation and assist in the preparation of environmental audits
- Organize and index documentation

FAMILY LAW:

- Collect information from clients with regard to marital status and prior marital status
- Interview client and collect information with regard to child support (see Exhibit 4.3)
- Draft prenuptial agreements
- Draft divorce complaints and responsive pleadings
- Prepare motions for support
- Prepare motions for custody and visitation
- Prepare property settlement agreements
- Prepare protection from abuse petitions
- Prepare petitions for termination of parental rights
- Prepare adoption petitions

IMMIGRATION LAW:

- Prepare applications and petitions for filing with the Immigration and Naturalization Service (INS) (see Exhibit 4.4 for a sample)
- Coordinate translation of foreign documents
- Prepare immigration and nonimmigration visa applications
- Coordinate activities with clients in foreign jurisdictions seeking visa and entry into the United States
- Assist clients in obtaining work visa to work in foreign countries
- Assist clients in the preparation of documentation to prove claim of marital status for submission to INS

INTELLECTUAL PROPERTY:

- Prepare patent search
- Prepare trademark search
- Prepare applications for patent, trademark, or copyright (Exhibit 4.5 is a sample)

exhibit 4.3   *Child support data form.*

_____ v. _____ No. _____

THIS FORM MUST BE FILLED OUT

(If you are self-employed or if you are salaried by a business of which you are owner in whole or in part, you must also fill out the Supplemental Income Statement which appears on the last page of this Income and Expense Statement.)

INCOME AND EXPENSE STATEMENT OF

_____

I verify that the statements made in this Income and Expense Statement are true and correct. I understand that false statements herein are made subject to the penalties of 18 Pa.C.S. §4904 relating to unsworn falsification to authorities.

Date: _____   Plaintiff or Defendant _____

INCOME

Employer: _____

Address: _____

Type of Work: _____

Payroll Number: _____

Pay Period (weekly, biweekly, etc.): _____

Gross Pay per Pay Period: $ _____

Itemized Payroll Deductions: Federal Withholding $ _____
                                Social Security   _____
                                Local Wage Tax   _____
                                State Income Tax   _____
                                Retirement   _____
                                Savings Bonds   _____
                                Credit Union   _____
                                Life Insurance   _____
                                Health Insurance   _____
                                Other (specify)   _____
                                _____
                                Net Pay per Pay Period $ _____

OTHER INCOME: (Fill in Appropriate Column)

	Weekly	*Monthly*	*Yearly*
Interest	$ _____	$ _____	$ _____
Dividends	_____	_____	_____
Pension	_____	_____	_____
Annuity	_____	_____	_____
Social Security	_____	_____	_____
Rents	_____	_____	_____
Royalties	_____	_____	_____
Expense Account	_____	_____	_____
Gifts	_____	_____	_____
Unemployment Comp.	_____	_____	_____
Workmen's Comp.	_____	_____	_____
Total	_____	_____	_____

TOTAL INCOME $ _____

Sample Immigration and Naturalization Service form.   *exhibit* 4.4

U.S. Department of Justice
Immigration and Naturalization Service

Notice of Entry of Appearance as Attorney or Representative

Appearances - An appearance shall be filed on this form by the attorney or representative appearing in each case. Thereafter, substitution may be permitted upon the written withdrawal of the attorney or representative of record or upon notification of the new attorney or representative. When an appearance is made by a person acting in a representative capacity, his personal appearance or signature shall constitute a representation that under the provisions of this chapter he is authorized and qualified to represent. Further proof of authority to act in a representative capacity may be required. **Availability of Records** - During the time a case is pending, and except as otherwise provided in 8 CFR 103.2(b), a party to a proceeding or his attorney or representative shall be permitted to examine the record of proceeding in a Service office. He may, in conformity with 8 CFR 103.10, obtain copies of Service records or information therefrom and copies of documents or transcripts of evidence furnished by him. Upon request, he/she may, in addition, be loaned a copy of the testimony and exhibits contained in the record of proceeding upon giving his/her receipt for such copies and pledging that it will be surrendered upon final disposition of the case or upon demand. If extra copies of exhibits do not exist, they shall not be furnished free on loan; however, they shall be made available for copying or purchase of copies as provided in 8 CFR 103.10.

In re: Lim Chi

Date: 09-15-2002
File No. A1357

I hereby enter my appearance as attorney for (or representative of), and at the request of the following named person(s):

Name: Lim chi
☑ Petitioner   ☐ Applicant
☐ Beneficiary

Address: (Apt. No.)   (Number & Street)   (City)   (State)   (Zip Code)
275 Swamp Road   Newtown   Pa 18940

Name:
☐ Petitioner   ☐ Applicant
☐ Beneficiary

Address: (Apt. No.)   (Number & Street)   (City)   (State)   (Zip Code)

Check Applicable Item(s) below:

☑ 1. I am an attorney and a member in good standing of the bar of the Supreme Court of the United States or of the highest court of the following State, territory, insular possession, or District of Columbia
Pennsylvania   Supreme Court   and am not under a court or administrative agency
Name of Court
order suspending, enjoining, restraining, disbarring, or otherwise restricting me in practicing law.

☐ 2. I am an accredited representative of the following named religious, charitable, social service, or similar organization established in the United States and which is so recognized by the Board:

☐ 3. I am associated with
the attorney of record previously filed a notice of appearance in this case and my appearance is at his request. (*If you check this item, also check item 1 or 2 whichever is appropriate.*)

☐ 4. Others (Explain Fully.)

SIGNATURE

COMPLETE ADDRESS
138 North State Street
Newtown, pa 18940

NAME (Type or Print)
Thomas F. Goldman

TELEPHONE NUMBER
215 555 4321

PURSUANT TO THE PRIVACY ACT OF 1974, I HEREBY CONSENT TO THE DISCLOSURE TO THE FOLLOWING NAMED ATTORNEY OR REPRESENTATIVE OF ANY RECORD PERTAINING TO ME WHICH APPEARS IN ANY IMMIGRATION AND NATURALIZATION SERVICE SYSTEM OF RECORDS:
Thomas F. Goldman

(Name of Attorney or Representative)
THE ABOVE CONSENT TO DISCLOSURE IS IN CONNECTION WITH THE FOLLOWING MATTER:

Name of Person Consenting   Signature of Person Consenting   Date

(NOTE: Execution of this box is required under the Privacy Act of 1974 where the person being represented is a citizen of the United States or an alien lawfully admitted for permanent residence.)

This form may not be used to request records under the Freedom of Information Act or the Privacy Act. The manner of requesting such records is contained in 8CFR 103.10 and 103.20 Et.SEQ.

Form G-28 (09/26/00)Y

exhibit 4.5 Copyright form.

FEE CHANGES
Fees are effective through June 30, 2002. After that date, check the Copyright Office Website at www.loc.gov/copyright or call (202) 707-3000 for current fee information.

FORM TX
For a Nondramatic Literary Work
UNITED STATES COPYRIGHT OFFICE

REGISTRATION NUMBER

TX TXU

EFFECTIVE DATE OF REGISTRATION

Month Day Year

DO NOT WRITE ABOVE THIS LINE. IF YOU NEED MORE SPACE, USE A SEPARATE CONTINUATION SHEET.

1 TITLE OF THIS WORK ▼

PREVIOUS OR ALTERNATIVE TITLES ▼

PUBLICATION AS A CONTRIBUTION If this work was published as a contribution to a periodical, serial, or collection, give information about the collective work in which the contribution appeared. Title of Collective Work ▼

If published in a periodical or serial give: Volume ▼ Number ▼ Issue Date ▼ On Pages ▼

2 a NAME OF AUTHOR ▼ DATES OF BIRTH AND DEATH Year Born ▼ Year Died ▼

Was this contribution to the work a "work made for hire"? ☐ Yes ☐ No
AUTHOR'S NATIONALITY OR DOMICILE Name of Country OR { Citizen of ▶ USA / Domiciled in ▶
WAS THIS AUTHOR'S CONTRIBUTION TO THE WORK Anonymous? ☐ Yes ☐ No Pseudonymous? ☐ Yes ☐ No If the answer to either of these questions is "Yes," see detailed instructions.

NATURE OF AUTHORSHIP Briefly describe nature of material created by this author in which copyright is claimed. ▼
Sole Author

b NAME OF AUTHOR ▼ DATES OF BIRTH AND DEATH Year Born ▼ Year Died ▼

Was this contribution to the work a "work made for hire"? ☐ Yes ☐ No
AUTHOR'S NATIONALITY OR DOMICILE Name of Country OR { Citizen of ▶ / Domiciled in ▶
WAS THIS AUTHOR'S CONTRIBUTION TO THE WORK Anonymous? ☐ Yes ☐ No Pseudonymous? ☐ Yes ☐ No If the answer to either of these questions is "Yes," see detailed instructions.

NATURE OF AUTHORSHIP Briefly describe nature of material created by this author in which copyright is claimed. ▼

c NAME OF AUTHOR ▼ DATES OF BIRTH AND DEATH Year Born ▼ Year Died ▼

Was this contribution to the work a "work made for hire"? ☐ Yes ☐ No
AUTHOR'S NATIONALITY OR DOMICILE Name of Country OR { Citizen of ▶ / Domiciled in ▶
WAS THIS AUTHOR'S CONTRIBUTION TO THE WORK Anonymous? ☐ Yes ☐ No Pseudonymous? ☐ Yes ☐ No If the answer to either of these questions is "Yes," see detailed instructions.

NATURE OF AUTHORSHIP Briefly describe nature of material created by this author in which copyright is claimed. ▼

NOTE
Under the law, the "author" of a "work made for hire" is generally the employer, not the employee (see instructions). For any part of this work that was "made for hire" check "Yes" in the space provided, give the employer (or other person for whom the work was prepared) as "Author" of that part, and leave the space for dates of birth and death blank.

3 a YEAR IN WHICH CREATION OF THIS WORK WAS COMPLETED This information must be given in all cases. ◀ Year
b DATE AND NATION OF FIRST PUBLICATION OF THIS PARTICULAR WORK Complete this information ONLY if this work has been published. Month ▶ Day ▶ Year ▶ USA ◀ Nation

4 COPYRIGHT CLAIMANT(S) Name and address must be given even if the claimant is the same as the author given in space 2. ▼

See instructions before completing this space.

TRANSFER If the claimant(s) named here in space 4 is (are) different from the author(s) named in space 2, give a brief statement of how the claimant(s) obtained ownership of the copyright. ▼
By written agreement.

DO NOT WRITE HERE OFFICE USE ONLY: APPLICATION RECEIVED / ONE DEPOSIT RECEIVED / TWO DEPOSITS RECEIVED / FUNDS RECEIVED

MORE ON BACK ▶ • Complete all applicable spaces (numbers 5-9) on the reverse side of this page. • See detailed instructions. • Sign the form at line 8.

DO NOT WRITE HERE
Page 1 of ____ pages

EXAMINED BY FORM TX
CHECKED BY
☐ CORRESPONDENCE Yes
FOR COPYRIGHT OFFICE USE ONLY

DO NOT WRITE ABOVE THIS LINE. IF YOU NEED MORE SPACE, USE A SEPARATE CONTINUATION SHEET.

5 PREVIOUS REGISTRATION Has registration for this work, or for an earlier version of this work, already been made in the Copyright Office?
☐ Yes ☐ No If your answer is "Yes," why is another registration being sought? (Check appropriate box.) ▼
a. ☐ This is the first published edition of a work previously registered in unpublished form.
b. ☐ This is the first application submitted by this author as copyright claimant.
c. ☐ This is a changed version of the work, as shown by space 6 on this application.
If your answer is "Yes," give: Previous Registration Number ▶ Year of Registration ▶

6 DERIVATIVE WORK OR COMPILATION
a Preexisting Material Identify any preexisting work or works that this work is based on or incorporates. ▼

b Material Added to This Work Give a brief, general statement of the material that has been added to this work and in which copyright is claimed. ▼

See instructions before completing this space.

7 a DEPOSIT ACCOUNT If the registration fee is to be charged to a Deposit Account established in the Copyright Office, give name and number of Account.
Name ▼ Account Number ▼

b CORRESPONDENCE Give name and address to which correspondence about this application should be sent. Name/Address/Apt/City/State/ZIP ▼

Area code and daytime telephone number ▶ 480-991-7881 Fax number ▶
Email ▶

8 CERTIFICATION* I, the undersigned, hereby certify that I am the
Check only one ▶ { ☐ author / ☐ other copyright claimant / ☐ owner of exclusive right(s) / ☑ authorized agent of ____ }
Name of author or other copyright claimant, or owner of exclusive right(s) ▲
of the work identified in this application and that the statements made by me in this application are correct to the best of my knowledge.

Typed or printed name and date ▼ If this application gives a date of publication in space 3, do not sign and submit it before that date.

Date ▶

Handwritten signature (X) ▼
X ________________________________

9 Certificate will be mailed in window envelope to this address:
Name ▼
Number/Street/Apt ▼
City/State/ZIP ▼

YOU MUST:
• Complete all necessary spaces
• Sign your application in space 8
SEND ALL 3 ELEMENTS IN THE SAME PACKAGE:
1. Application form
2. Nonrefundable filing fee in check or money order payable to *Register of Copyrights*
3. Deposit material
MAIL TO:
Library of Congress
Copyright Office
101 Independence Avenue, S.E.
Washington, D.C. 20559-6000

As of July 1, 1999, the filing fee for Form TX is $30.

*17 U.S.C. § 506(e): Any person who knowingly makes a false representation of a material fact in the application for copyright registration provided for by section 409, or in any written statement filed in connection with the application, shall be fined not more than $2,500.
June 1999—200,000
WEB REV: June 1999

☆U.S. GOVERNMENT PRINTING OFFICE: 1999-454-879/49

- Assist in preparation of documentation in opposition, interference, infringement, and similar proceedings
- Coordinate activities and filings with foreign patent, trademark, and copyright attorneys and agents
- Work with engineers in preparation of applications and defense of patents and trade secrets
- Draft licensing agreements for intellectual property items

HUMAN RESOURCES LAW:

- Draft plan documents for tax-sheltered employee benefit plans
- Draft deferred compensation plans
- Prepare and file for an Internal Revenue Service determination letters of plans
- Prepare and file annual reports including 5500 series Internal Revenue Service forms
- Calculate employer and employee contribution levels and limitations
- Draft, review, and distribute summary plan descriptions

LITIGATION:

- Investigate factual allegations of case
- Help to locate witnesses and physical evidence
- Draft summons, complaint, answers, and other defenses and responsive pleadings
- Organize and maintain litigation files
- Assist in the preparation of trial notebooks
- Gather, review, summarize, and index documents for use at trial
- Locate and arrange for interviews with expert witnesses
- Prepare written interrogatories
- Assist in preparing and conducting oral depositions, including videotape depositions
- Prepare or obtain subpoenas (see sample in Exhibit 4.6) and arrange for service upon witnesses
- Coordinate, assist, and arrange for trial exhibits
- Obtain jury-pool information, and assist in the selection of appropriate jury members
- Attend trial and assist in the handling of witnesses, exhibits, and evidence
- Prepare contemporaneous summaries of witness statements during trial

PARALEGAL SKILLS

The skills needed by a paralegal are varied and depend, in some cases, on the nature of the legal specialty in which one works. Common to all paralegals are certain basic skills and attributes including communication skills, initiative, resourcefulness, commitment or "stick-to-itiveness," and self-motivation, among others.

exhibit 4.6   *Subpoena.*

Commonwealth of Pennsylvania
County of Philadelphia

In the matter of:

Henry Thomas
(Plaintiff)   *(Demandante)*

vs.

Thomas Cheese
(Defendant)   *(Demandado)*

COURT OF COMMON PLEAS

October _____ Term, Yr. 2002

No. 68-96874

Subpoena

To: Elizabeth Rhodes

        (Name of Witness)   *(Nombre del Testigo)*

    1.   YOU ARE ORDERED BY THE COURT TO COME TO *(El tribunal le ordena que venga a)*
Court room 654 _____, AT PHILADELPHIA, PENNSYLVANIA ON *(en Filadelfia,*
Pennsylvania el) November 4, 2002 _____, AT *(a las)* ____10____ O'CLOCK ___A___.M., TO
TESTIFY ON BEHALF OF *(para atestiguar a favor de)* Henry Thomas _____ IN THE ABOVE
CASE, AND TO REMAIN UNTIL EXCUSED *(en el caso arriba mencionado y permanecer hasta que le autoricen irse)*.

    2.   AND BRING WITH YOU THE FOLLOWING *(Y traer con usted lo siguiente)*:

_____

_____

NOTICE	AVISO
If you fail to attend or to produce the documents or things required by this subpoena, you may be subject to the sanctions authorized by Rule 234.5 of the Pennsylvania Rules of Civil Procedure, including but not limited to costs, attorney fees and imprisonment.	**Si usted falla en comparecer o producir los documentos o cosas requeridas por esta cita, usted estara sujeto a las sanciones autorizadas por la regla 234.5 de las reglas de procedimiento civil de Pensilvania, incluyendo pero no limitado a los costos, remuneracion de abogados y encarcelamiento.**

INQUIRIES CONCERNING THIS SUBPOENA SHOULD BE ADDRESSED TO *(Las preguntas que tenga acerca de esta Citacion deben ser dirigidas a)*:
ISSUED BY:

Edith Hannah

    (Attorney)   *(Abogado/Abogada)*

ADDRESS *(Direccion)* 8 North Broad Street, Philadelphia, PA

TELEPHONE NO. *(No. de Telefono)* 215 555 9999

ATTORNEY *(Abogado ID #)* A5B6

BY THE COURT *(Por El Tribunal)*
JOSEPH H. EVERS
PROTHONOTARY *(Protonotario)*

PRO _____
    (Clerk)   *(Escribano)*

10-200 (Rev. 7/99)   Completed Subpoena must be signed and sealed by the Prothonotary (Room 266 City Hall) before service.

Everyone has goals in life. You might be a great jogger who longs to win the Boston Marathon, or a skilled writer who wants to write the great American novel. Achieving most goals requires some set of skills. If your goal is to be a successful paralegal, you will need certain basic skills. You may already possess some of these, and may need to acquire others. Some of the basic skills you already have are:

- the ability to read English—unless someone is reading this book to you

- the ability to communicate at some level in writing or speaking

- initiative—because you have signed up for this course or have picked up this book to read and learn about the paralegal profession.

In addition, you may have skills such as:

- facility with computers and the Internet

- the ability to speak a second or third language

- a background in medicine, engineering, business, or other academic or occupational area.

Some other skills are less obvious—resourcefulness, commitment or stick-to-itiveness, analytical skills and interpersonal skills including cultural sensitivity—so we will explore them in more depth. We cannot all run a marathon, or type 160 words a minute, but we all can acquire most of the basic skills by making an effort to improve ourselves and attain the knowledge base to achieve most, if not all, of our goals. Many people achieve much more than they, themselves, and others believed they were capable of achieving, by just plain hard work. If you want something bad enough and are willing to work hard enough, you can achieve your personal and professional goals. A good starting point in achieving your goals is to understand your strengths and weaknesses, capitalize on the strengths, and work on improving the weaknesses.

Checklist

STRENGTHS & WEAKNESSES

○ My strengths:

○ How I can capitalize on my strengths:

○ My weaknesses:

○ How I can overcome my weaknesses:

Resourcefulness

Resourcefulness is the ability to meet and handle a situation and find solutions to problems. It is one of the most valuable skills anyone can have—and one that is not easily taught. A resourceful person in the office is sometimes referred to as the "can do" person on the team. This is the person who usually finds some creative way to accomplish what everyone else has given up on. Certainly, creativity is involved—solving the problem by thinking outside the box and not limiting the solution to tried-and-true methods.

When everyone else says, "I can't find this witness," the resourceful person tries a new approach and finds the witness. When others use only the standard telephone directories, the resourceful person uses the cross-reference directory. When local telephone directories do not yield results, resourceful people use the national telephone directories on CD and the online Internet telephone directories.

In the legal workplace the person who gets noticed is the one who finds a way to get the job done in time for the hearing, meeting, or arbitration. This is the person who is willing to use unconventional ways to get the job finished, such as when the power goes out or the computer system crashes just before a deadline. Lawyers want resourceful people on their team and reward them to keep them on the team.

Commitment

Commitment means finishing that which one starts out to do or complete. From our childhood we remember the story of the tortoise and the hare (rabbit), in which the tortoise wins the race by being "slow and steady." The tortoise wins in part because of commitment—putting everything into the race and not stopping until the job is done.

Many people start jobs and don't finish them. Others start what seems to be an insurmountable task and—to their amazement and maybe ours—finish, and finish well. Taking on an assignment in a law office requires commitment. Team members are expected to finish the task, whether it is researching a case, writing a brief, filing a pleading, or organizing a file.

As a professional, you are expected to finish the tasks within the assigned timeframe. There is no excuse for not doing some tasks, such as filing the complaint with the court before the statute of limitations expires, or getting the brief to the court by the court-imposed deadline. Even a simple thing like getting to court on time requires commitment.

Not everyone has the necessary commitment or wants to take on the responsibility of meeting commitments. You have to decide whether you are willing to make the commitment. Others will be depending on you, and if you do not want to commit, admit it to yourself and to the others who are depending on you, and then choose some other activity or profession. Choosing a profession, whether it is the legal profession, the paralegal profession, the medical profession, or the accounting profession, requires a commitment to serve others. As a professional, you are making a commitment to your clients that you will provide the best professional advice, skill, and effort. They depend on this professionalism and the necessary commitment.

SIDEBAR

Organizing

The skill of organizing includes the ability to

1. Categorize
2. Prioritize
3. Organize
4. Utilize time efficiently

Analytical Skills

Analytical skills allow one to follow a step-by-step process to solve a problem. It could be finding a missing witness by looking in telephone books, or determining that the person is part of a group, such as a professional society or organization that publishes a membership directory. Solving these types of problems requires analytical skills to figure out, for instance, what made a bottle explode, injuring a client. Determining the actual cause requires a step-by-step analysis of the potential reasons and the narrowing down of possible causes.

One of the basic skills that law students and paralegal students are taught is *legal analysis*, the ability to identify the facts and legal issues and contrast and compare them to the law and to other cases. This is a skill that develops with time. As you learn the elements of crimes, torts, and other areas of law, you will learn the individual parts of each. In contracts law, you will learn what conduct is a valid acceptance of a contract offer, and in tort law, what constitutes reasonable conduct under the circumstances.

Interpersonal Skills

Critical to paralegal success, as well as to success in other endeavors, is the ability to work with other people. To categorize people, co-workers, colleagues, and employers might be unfair, but we all do it. We think, and sometimes say, things like, "He's a pleasure to work with" or, "She has clients eating out of her hand." Conversely, we might also say things like, "She's the most negative person I know" or "He's only out for himself." These comments are a reflection of the other person's interpersonal skills, the ability to work with and effectively communicate with others.

How we relate to others can make the job easier or harder. These people include not just co-workers as members of the legal team but also clients, witnesses, and opposing parties. Obviously, everyone in the firm or on the team must have a level of trust and confidence in the others on the team. People who have a good working relationship accomplish more and enjoy doing it. In contrast, conflict and tension make the job harder and can lead to people taking shortcuts and avoiding contact, which can result in poor performance and potential malpractice.

Not everyone has the personality to deal with every type of situation and every type of personality—for example, dealing with clients. But everyone on the legal team has to develop the skills to work with people and recognize when they may have to have someone else handle certain aspects of a case or client. The skill is in recognizing when and how they can affect relationships and desired results. Some might call this "sensitivity"—to other people's needs, desires, wants, likes, and dislikes. Cultural differences are discussed later, but in the American culture, for example, people tend to be sensitive to odors—breath, body, environmental. We do not want to offend. Our use of language is another area of sensitivity. We try to avoid using words that we believe will offend the other person in a particular circumstance, such as telling off-color jokes in a religious setting in front of a person of the cloth.

SIDEBAR

Thinking Outside the Box

This exercise is widely used to demonstrate thinking outside the box. Without lifting your pencil from the paper, connect all the dots with only four lines.

```
•     •     •


•     •     •


•     •     •
```

(Answer on p. 116)

The starting point in working with attorneys, paralegals, and support staff, clients and opposing counsel, court personnel and others, is to be sensitive to issues such as these. What offends you probably offends others. Being sensitive to how others react to your words, conduct, and actions can provide good clues as to what is acceptable and what is not.

In the past, how we related to others and how others perceived us was measured by direct face-to-face contact, telephone contact, and written communications. Today we have to add to those forms of communication the way we write emails and use electronic communications. These technological advances make our communications more immediate. Too many happy faces and frowning faces, such as :) or :(in an email, could be interpreted as overfamiliarity. THE USE OF ALL CAPITAL LETTERS might be interpreted as shouting at the reader. Poor spelling and bad grammar in emails are likely to be seen as less than professional or pure sloppiness or carelessness. In the past, letters were dictated, typed, proofread, and then signed. Today we dash off an email without much thought—and sometimes it reflects just that. How our clients view our capabilities and skill now might be measured by that quick email response.

The Tarrant County Courthouse in Fort Worth, Texas.

Communication Skills

Communication means expressing ideas effectively. The practice of law requires good communication, both oral and written. The lawyer and the paralegal who work together must be able to communicate assignments and information with clarity and, frequently, brevity. Over time, communication will improve, with each person coming to understand what the other is really asking or saying.

Communication is made complex by subtleties, nuances, and expressions that may require interpretation or explanation. For example, older attorneys who are used to using traditional methods of research may ask the new paralegal (who has a deep understanding of computer research methods and little traditional book experience) to "check the pocket parts." This means checking for the latest update or change to a statute or case law. Or asking a paralegal to "Shepardize" a case may have no meaning to one who has learned only the West system, in which the method for checking other cases is called KeyCiting, or the Loislaw system, which refers to this as GlobalCiting.

Although communication may not be a major issue in the typical office environment, it can be a major problem in the fast-paced office when the litigation attorney sends a message from court in the middle of a case to the support paralegal at the office, by a two-way pager, after the other side has brought up an unexpected case in argument to the court.

Nowadays there is rarely the luxury of time to develop a common written and oral language base for communication among the paralegal, clients, opposing attorneys, and court personnel. Letters, pleadings, contracts, and other written documents must be clear and accurate. In many situations only one document must carefully communicate the idea, request, or demand. Oral communication also must be clear and precise.

The old adage still holds true: First impressions matter. If the first impression is a poorly written communication with misspelled words and unconventional grammar, or a discussion in person or by telephone that is filled with slang and poor grammar, the impression may affect the client's or court's view of the firm's professionalism, ability, and legal skills. It can influence the client's decision to stay with the firm or not, the judge's granting the request, or the court clerk's giving you the help you need.

Analyzing the Audience

There are many ways to address those with whom you communicate. Here we will point out some general differences in the way men and women communicate. The following section describes some cultural background considerations.*

IF YOUR RECEIVER IS A MAN, IT IS POSSIBLE THAT:

- He has been socialized to perform aggressively and boast of his successes.
- His childhood games taught him that competition is fun and winning is good.
- He is motivated by competition.
- He views conflict as impersonal, a necessary part of working relationships.
- He is impressed by power, ability, and achievement.
- He may hear only your literal words and miss your underlying emotion.
- He will not express his true feelings through facial expression.
- His communication style tends to be direct.

IF YOUR RECEIVER IS A WOMAN, IT IS POSSIBLE THAT:

- She has been socialized to work cooperatively and to be modest about her success.
- Her childhood games taught her to compromise and collaborate, and she continues to be motivated by affiliation.
- She competes primarily with herself—with her own expectations of what she should be able to accomplish.
- She takes conflict personally.
- She is impressed by personal disclosure and professional courage.
- She has the ability to focus on several projects at the same time.

*These discussions are adapted from *Crosstalk: Communicating in a Multicultural Workplace,* by Kenton and Valentine. Copyright © 1997 by Prentice Hall, Upper Saddle River, NJ.

SIDEBAR

Communication Skills

How well do you . . .

- Read with comprehension?
- Listen effectively and accurately and interpret nonverbal communication?
- Write in clear, concise, and grammatically correct English?
- Speak in clear, concise, and grammatically correct English?
- Use language to persuade?
- Tailor the nature of the communication to maximize understanding in the intended audience, including people with different levels of education and different cultural backgrounds?

Source: American Association for Paralegal Education.

- She is proficient at decoding your nonverbal meanings and likely to display her feelings through facial expression or body language.
- Her style will be indirect, except with other women of equal rank.

CONSIDER YOUR RECEIVER'S ATTITUDES ABOUT YOU:

- Man-to-man: He may afford you instant credibility based on similarity.
- Woman-to-woman: She may expect you to be friendly, nurturing, and concerned. She may afford you instant credibility based on similarity.
- Man-to-woman: She may expect that you will not really listen to her.
- Woman-to-man: He may expect you to be friendly and nurturing, even passive-dependent. Any aggressive behavior or deviation from his expectation can cause him discomfort and confusion, or produce negative responses. He may simply disregard you.

CULTURAL SENSITIVITY

The culturally sensitive person is aware of the reasons for differences in the way people behave, based on religious and ethnic background and belief system. As the cultural makeup of the United States has become more diverse, the need for cultural awareness and sensitivity in the legal and paralegal professions has grown. Just as men and women are said to think differently, so do Europeans, Asians, Latinos, and Africans.

To communicate effectively, you must be aware of the possible interpretations of what you are communicating and what the other person is saying. Interviewing a Latino male, for example, may require a different approach than interviewing an Asian female. Even subtleties of eye contact can affect an interview. Whereas Americans view eye contact as a sign of sincerity, some Asian cultures view it as aggressive. As you develop your communication skills, you must become sensitive to how you are perceived and learn to fashion your approach to maximize accuracy of communication.

The effectiveness of paralegals also is influenced by how well they "read" the cultural backgrounds of those with whom they interact. This involves manner of speaking, dressing, and acting, and whether one is a man or a woman in that culture. What is heard may not be what was intended. What you perceive may not be what the other person perceives, because of cultural differences that affect the interpretation of the words and body language. We will briefly highlight some general characteristics of four cultural groups.*

Effective communication is essential in dealings between paralegal and client.

European Background

Generally the countries of Western Europe, including Scandinavia, comprise the group of European background. This group is extraordinarily large and

---

*These discussions are adapted from *Crosstalk: Communicating in a Multicultural Workplace,* by Kenton and Valentine. Copyright © 1997 by Prentice Hall, Upper Saddle River, NJ.

JAG Competition Showcases Soldier Skills

Soldiers, September 2001, Volume 56, Issue 9

Deana Willis

Forget all the lawyer jokes you've heard. The 21st Theater Support Command's Office of the Staff Judge Advocate's "Iron JAG" competition demonstrated that Army attorneys and paralegals have the right stuff to bring to the battlefield—soldier-style. Iron JAG is a grueling set of events, including a 400-meter relay swim, a field march with full combat load, a modified PT test, an operational law exam, a cross-country run, and tests on common-task training and JAG mission-essential tasks.

The organizer of this year's Iron JAG, SGM Mike Broady, used his experience from a previous assignment with a ranger regiment to create a competition to reinforce the standard CTT, JAG METL, and physical training that is conducted at unit level. The 11-hour competition tested attorneys and enlisted paralegals on all facets of their missions, promoting the JAG team concept and validating and evaluating JAG training.

"The competitors happen to be lawyers, legal NCOs and legal specialists, but they're always soldiers first and they have to maintain those soldier skills," said MG John D. Altenburg, the assistant judge advocate general. "That's why we want to push this so hard."

NCOs at individual law centers throughout U. S. Army, Europe, independently trained their soldiers in annual CTT tasks and specific JAG METL tasks, then team members trained each other. Enlisted soldiers trained their officer partners in CTT, and the attorneys trained their paralegals in battlefield law to prepare for the difficult operational law test.

"The operational law test is unique," said Broady. "It's based on rules of engagement, the laws of land warfare, the Hague and Geneva conventions, collateral claims damage, and other issues that JAG teams could encounter on the battlefield."

The competition was so fierce that a winning team did not emerge until the last event. The first-place trophy was captured by the 1st Infantry Division's team number 4, CPT Joseph Ratermann and PFC Michael Rea. Second place went to CPT John Hyatt and SGT Stephen Newsome, also of the 1st Infantry Division. The 21st TSC team of CPT Robert Borcherding and SSG Geriberto Dragon placed third.

From *Soldiers*, Vol. 56, No. 9, September 2001, U. S. Government Printing Office.

---

complex, which limits attempts to make cultural generalities. In terms of gender differences, men and women with roots in the European culture may have different initial reactions to you and attitudes about your topic. Male and female listeners alike tend to perceive men as having more credibility than women of equal rank, experience, and training. Men tend to be more credible to other men, and women may be more credible to other women.

Now consider the cultural implications of graphic pictures of physical injuries from car crashes. These would be acceptable in the United States, but Germans tend to dislike the sight of blood, and the British are likely to be offended by violence.

According to Kenton and Valentine, if you are of European–American appearance, receivers of communication may be concerned that you will:

- Reject their opinions
- Take advantage of them or hold them back
- Consider them different in a negative way
- Deny them equal opportunities (p. 56)

Latino Background

Collectively, Latin America encompasses 51 countries. Latin American countries are generally considered to be those south of the U. S. border, including

Mexico and the countries of Central America, South America, and the Caribbean islands. With so vast an area, there are many differences from country to country and even from city to city. The languages, too, are not the same. Portuguese is spoken in Brazil, and the Spanish spoken in South America differs from the Spanish spoken in Puerto Rico. The Latino–American population has moved closer to becoming the largest minority group in the United States.

According to Kenton and Valentine, individuals with roots in the Latino culture tend to:

- Value family and loyalty to family
- Honor nationalism
- Exhibit a strong sense of honor
- Have a fatalistic view of the world
- Express passion in speech, manner, and deed (pp. 98–99)

Asian Background

More than 30 countries can be considered Asian, among them China, Malaysia, Japan, the Philippines, India, and Korea. They, too, demonstrate vast differences in the individual cultures. Some generalizations may be made, however. Being direct and to the point is generally considered rude in Asian cultures, in which relationships are considered top priority. For example, the Japanese tend to prefer an indirect style of communication. In communicating with people who have an Asian background, it might be best to begin with pleasantries about the weather, sports, or general well-being of the individual and his or her family.

Roots in the African Culture

African Americans represent the largest ethnic group in the United States. A distinction should be made between African Americans of recent immigration with stronger cultural ties to the African culture and African Americans with long family ties within the United States whose cultural roots are American. According to Kenton and Valentine, some of the African core beliefs and cultural values that may influence attitudes and behavior are:

- A holistic worldview
- Emotion and expressiveness
- A keen sense of justice or fairness
- A belief in the uniqueness of the individual as defined by the ethnic group (p. 54)

LEGAL TERMINOLOGY

Analytical skill	Cultural sensitivity
Commitment	Interpersonal skills
Communication	Resourcefulness

Summary

Paralegal Tasks and Functions

1. Conducting interviews
2. Conducting investigations
3. Legal writing
4. Legal research
5. Review, analysis, summarizing, and indexing
6. Assisting in preparation of witnesses and clients for trial
7. Maintaining calendar and tickler systems
8. Performing research
9. Performing office administration functions

Paralegal Skills

1. Resourcefulness
2. Commitment
3. Analytical skills
4. Interpersonal skills
5. Communication skills
6. Cultural sensitivity

Analyzing the Audience

1. Men versus women
2. Cultural background

Working the Web

1. Check the online features of
   a. Westlaw at www.westlaw.com
   b. Lexis-Nexis at www.lexisnexis.com
   c. Lexisone at www.lexisone.com
2. Check the cultural awareness programs of the Office of Civil Rights of the U. S. Department of Commerce at www.doc.gov/ocr/cultural.html
3. Review Executive Order 13166: Improving Access to Services for Persons with Limited English Proficiency at www.doc.gov/ocr/eo13166.html
4. Visit the Library of Congress Country Studies website at http://lcweb2.loc.gov/frd/cs/cshome.html
5. Check the list of national holidays at the Department of State website at www.state.gov/s/cpr/rls/dpl/index.cfm?docid=3003

Questions
CRITICAL LEGAL THINKING AND WRITING

1. Why should a paralegal tell clients in the initial interview that he or she is a paralegal?
2. Why are good English writing and speaking skills important for the paralegal?
3. Complete the "Strengths & Weaknesses" checklist in this chapter.
4. How can you use the "Strengths & Weaknesses" checklist in preparing your personal career roadmap?
5. What actions have you observed in other people that demonstrated their resourcefulness? Have others ever told you that you are resourceful?
6. As a paralegal job applicant, how can you demonstrate the characteristic of commitment?
7. What cultural differences have you observed that have limited open communications?
8. Why and how might you modify your manner of dress or choice of words in interviewing a client? A witness?
9. Can you think of a situation in which an interview would be better conducted by a woman? By a man? Explain.
10. How does the "Thinking Outside the Box" activity demonstrate this type of thinking?

Questions
ETHICS: ANALYSIS AND DISCUSSION

1. Why do paralegals have to tell clients and witnesses that they are paralegals?
2. In a meeting with a client, can the paralegal use the phrase "in my opinion"?
3. Why might an ethical issue of competence be raised if the paralegal is not aware of the language and cultural differences of a client?

Unauthorized Practice of Law—Fee Splitting

There are few certainties in the area of ethics, for paralegals or in any profession. What qualifies as ethical conduct is in most cases based on state law and court interpretation applied to a set of facts. The citation listed below represents one legal opinion and is provided as a research starting point. Do not assume that the same rule applies in your jurisdiction. For the following:

- *Prepare a written statement based on your state law.*
- *Use your state bar association website as a starting point.*

You are offered the opportunity to work with a local law firm providing living trust services to the public. Your responsibility would be to make a presentation on the advantages of living trusts to community groups and in other public meetings. Any interested person would meet with you after the general session and you would fill out the forms, collect the fee, and send the completed form and half the fee collected to the law firm for review and transmittal to the client. You would retain half the amount collected as your fee. [*Cincinnati Bar Assn. v. Kathman*, 92 Ohio St.3d 92 (2001).] What ethical issues are involved? Explain.

FOR DISCUSSION

In Re *Busy Beaver Bldg. Centers, Inc.*   19 F.3d 833 (3rd Cir. 1994)

Paralegal Fees Based on Skill Level

In deciding the propriety of awarding paralegal fees in bankruptcy cases, the court held:

As is true with recently graduated attorneys, entry-level paralegals perform the more mundane tasks in the paralegal work spectrum, some of which may resemble those tasks generally deemed "clerical" in nature. Yet, even with these tasks, paralegals may have to bring their training or experience to bear, thereby relieving attorneys of the burden of extensive supervision and ensuring the proper completion of tasks involving the exercise, or potential exercise, of some paraprofessional judgment. Of course, the appropriate rate the attorney will command for paralegal services will ordinarily parallel the paralegal's credentials and the degree of experience, knowledge, and skill the task at hand calls for. . . . [P]urely clerical or secretarial tasks should not be billed at a paralegal rate, regardless of who performs them.

The short of it is that the market-driven approach of the [bankruptcy act] § 330 permits compensation for relatively low-level paralegal services if and only if analogous non-bankruptcy clients agree to pay for the same, and then only at that rate. [T]hose services not requiring the exercise of professional legal judgment . . . must be included in "overhead."

We cannot agree that in all cases the general ability of a legal secretary to perform some particular task determines whether a paralegal or a legal secretary is the appropriate, read most efficient, employee to perform it at any given instant. At times temporal constraints may foreclose the delegation option. At other times a paralegal—or, for that matter, an attorney—can more productively complete a clerical task, such as photocopying documents, than can a legal secretary.

Questions

1. How can the attorney prove the skill level of paralegals when seeking compensation for paralegal services?
2. Will this kind of reasoning by the court force attorneys to hire more skilled paralegals?
3. Would the existence of a certificate or degree in paralegal studies be useful in proving that the person who worked on a case was a paralegal?

Ramirez v. Plough, Inc.

12 Cal. Rptr. 2d 423 (Cal., Ct. App. 1992)*   **Court of Appeal of California**

* If citing in a California court, add "15 Cal. App. 4th 1110" after the case name and before the citation from the California Reporter, set off by commas. Ramirez v. Plough, Inc., 15 Cal. App. 4th 1110, 12 Cal. Rptr. 2d 423 (1992)

Read, and if assigned, brief this case. Prepare a written answer to each of the following questions.

1. How does this case illustrate the cultural differences of clients?

2. Are the views and conduct of the parent in this case the same as you have and would have taken?

3. What ethical obligation does the paralegal have to be sure the client who does not speak the same language understands the advice given? Does it matter if it is medical directions as in this case, or legal advice?

4. Does a law firm have a higher duty to a non–English-speaking client than a drug company, such as the defendant in this case, does in selling a product?

5. Does the law firm have a duty to explain cultural differences in the American legal system and its procedures to non-English speaking, non-native born clients?

Thaxter, Judge.

Jorge Ramirez, a minor, by his guardian ad litem Rosa Rivera, appeals from a summary judgment in favor of Plough, Inc. Appellant sued Plough alleging negligence, product liability, and fraud. The action sought damages for injuries sustained in March of 1986 when Jorge, who was then four months old, contracted Reye's Syndrome after ingesting St. Joseph Aspirin for Children (SJAC). Plough marketed and distributed SJAC.

Reye's Syndrome is a serious disease of unknown cause characterized by severe vomiting, lethargy, or irritability which may progress to delirium or coma.

....

In December 1985, the Food and Drug Administration (FDA) requested that aspirin manufacturers voluntarily place a label on aspirin products warning consumers of the possible association between aspirin and Reye's Syndrome. Plough voluntarily complied and began including a warning and insert in SJAC packaging. On June 5, 1986, the Reye's Syndrome warning became mandatory.

In March 1986, SJAC labeling bore the following warning: "Warning: Reye's Syndrome is a rare but serious disease which can follow flu or chicken pox in children and teenagers. While the cause of Reye's Syndrome is unknown, some reports claim aspirin may

increase the risk of developing this disease. Consult a doctor before use in children or teenagers with flu or chicken pox." In addition, the SJAC package insert included the following statement: "The symptoms of Reye's Syndrome can include persistent vomiting, sleepiness and lethargy, violent headaches, unusual behavior, including disorientation, combativeness, and delirium. If any of these symptoms occur, especially following chicken pox or flu, call your doctor immediately, even if your child has not taken any medication. Reye's Syndrome is serious, so early detection and treatment are vital."

Rosa Rivera purchased SJAC on March 12, 1986, and administered it to appellant, who was suffering from what appeared to be a cold or upper respiratory infection. She gave appellant the aspirin without reading the directions or warnings appearing on the SJAC packaging. The packaging was in English and Ms. Rivera can speak and understand only Spanish. She did not seek to have the directions or warnings translated from English to Spanish, even though members of her household spoke English.

The trial court granted Plough's motion for summary judgment on the grounds that "there is no duty to warn in a foreign language and there is no causal relationship between plaintiff's injury and defendant's activities."

It is undisputed SJAC was marketed and intended for the treatment of minor aches and pains associated with colds, flu, and minor viral illnesses. The SJAC box promised "fast, effective relief of fever and minor aches and pains of colds." . . . In March 1986, federal regulations requiring a Reye's Syndrome warning had been promulgated and were final, although not yet effective. . . . The scientific community had already confirmed and documented the relationship between Reye's Syndrome and the use of aspirin after a viral illness. There is no doubt Plough had a duty to warn of the Reye's Syndrome risk.

The question thus is whether the warning given only in English was adequate under the circumstances. Respondent argues that, as a matter of law, it has no duty to place foreign-language warnings on products manufactured to be sold in the United States and that holding manufacturers liable for failing to do so would violate public policy.

While the constitutional, statutory, regulatory, and judicial authorities relied on by respondent may reflect a public policy recognizing the status of English as an official language, nothing compels the conclusion that a manufacturer of a dangerous or defective product is immunized from liability when an English-only warning does not adequately inform non-English literate persons likely to use the product.

Plough's evidence showed that over 148 foreign languages are spoken in the United States and over 23 million Americans speak a language other than English in their homes. That evidence plainly does not prove that Plough used reasonable care in giving an English-only warning. Plough, then, resorts to arguing that the burden on manufacturers and society of requiring additional warnings is so "staggering" that the courts should preclude liability as a matter of law. We are not persuaded.

Certainly the burden and costs of giving foreign-language warnings is one factor for consideration in determining whether a manufacturer acted reasonably in using only English. The importance of that factor may vary from case to case depending upon other circumstances, such as the nature of the product, marketing efforts directed to segments of the population unlikely to be English-literate, and the actual and relative size of the consumer market which could reasonably be expected to speak or read only a certain foreign language. Plough presented no evidence from which we can gauge the extent of the burden under the facts of this case.

Ramirez submitted evidence that Plough knew Hispanics were an important part of the market for SJAC and that Hispanics often maintain their first language rather than learn English. SJAC was advertised in the Spanish media, both radio and television. That evidence raises material questions of fact concerning the foreseeability of purchase by a Hispanic not literate in English and the reasonableness of not giving a Spanish-language warning. If Plough has evidence conclusively showing that it would have been unreasonable to give its label warning in Spanish because of the burden, it did not present that evidence below.

. . . [I]f we accepted Plough's arguments in this case, in effect we would be holding that failure to warn in a foreign language is not negligence, regardless of the circumstances. Such a sweeping grant of immunity should come from the legislative branch of government, not the judicial. In deciding that Plough did not establish its right to judgment as a matter of law, we do not hold that manufacturers are required to warn in languages other than English simply because it may be foreseeable that non-English literate persons are likely to use their products. Our decision merely recognizes that under some circumstances the standard of due care may require such warning.

Because the evidence shows triable issues of material fact and because Plough did not establish its immunity from liability as a matter of law, its motion for summary judgment should have been denied.

Answer: Thinking Outside the Box

The instructions did not say you needed to stay within the dots!

The

American

Legal

System

CHAPTER 5
The Constitution and
Sources of American Law

CHAPTER 6
Judicial and Alternative
Dispute Resolution

CHAPTER 7
Civil Litigation

CHAPTER 8
Criminal Law and Process

PART II

THE AMERICAN
LEGAL SYSTEM

This unit introduces you to the American legal system and process. As a paralegal student, you must understand the main provisions of the U.S. Constitution and the sources of the law in the United States. These issues are addressed in Chapter 5. Chapter 6 discusses the state and federal court systems and the litigation process in the courts, as well as non-judicial alternative dispute resolution procedures such as arbitration. The next two chapters of this unit describe in sufficient detail for paralegal studies the following necessary information: the pretrial and trial civil litigation process (Chapter 7), and criminal law and procedure (Chapter 8). In summary, this unit will provide you with the comprehensive knowledge of the American legal system and process that is needed for paralegal studies.

CHAPTER 5

CHAPTER OBJECTIVES

After studying this chapter, you should be able to:

1. Define *law* and describe the functions of law.

2. Describe the fairness and flexibility of the law.

3. List and describe the schools of jurisprudential thought.

4. Explain how English common law was adopted in the United States.

5. List and describe the sources of law in the United States and the doctrine of *stare decisis*.

6. Describe the concept of federalism and the doctrine of separation of powers.

7. Define and apply the Supremacy Clause of the U. S. Constitution.

8. Explain the federal government's authority to regulate commerce.

9. Explain the Bill of Rights and its freedoms.

10. Describe due process and its forms.

The Constitution and
Sources of American Law

The nation's armour of defence against the passions of men is the Constitution. Take that away, and the nation goes down into the field of its conflicts like a warrior without armour.

HENRY WARD BEECHER
PROVERBS FROM PLYMOUTH PULPIT, 1887

Introduction

Every society makes and enforces laws that govern the conduct of the individuals, businesses, and other organizations that function within it. In the words of Judge Learned Hand, "Without law we cannot live; only with it can we insure the future which by right is ours. The best of men's hopes are enmeshed in its success" (*The Spirit of Liberty,* 1960).

Although U.S. law is based primarily on English common law, other legal systems, such as Spanish and French civil law, also influenced it. The sources of law in this country are the U.S. Constitution, state constitutions, federal and state statutes, ordinances, administrative agency rules and regulations, executive orders, and judicial decisions by federal and state courts.

Businesses that are organized in the United States are subject to its laws. They also are subject to the laws of other countries in which they operate. Businesses organized in other countries must obey the laws of the United States when doing business here. In addition, businesspeople owe a duty to act ethically in the conduct of their affairs, and businesses owe a responsibility not to harm society.

Paralegals need to know the history of the law in the United States and how the law developed to be what it is today. Every person in the United States, and in particular paralegals, should have knowledge of this country's constitutional framework and many of the most important provisions of the U.S. Constitution. This chapter addresses the nature and definition of law, the history and sources of law, and the U.S. Constitution.

THE COURTHOUSE TEAM

Judge's Law Clerk

Each judge has one or more law clerks to assist in researching and writing opinions. Technically not part of the courtroom team, they typically sit in the courtroom near the judge or at a table in front of the judge. Motions, briefs, and proposed orders are frequently routed through law clerks, who usually are lawyers. Some administrative law judges, however, have a paralegal serve as a "clerk." For example, Social Security Administration administrative law judges use paralegals as decision writers. They play a major role in researching and writing orders, opinions, and briefs.

Law clerks are the ones who usually communicate with the lawyers when questions arise about pleadings and other documents filed with the court. They also may set up settlement conferences and pretrial meetings. They also are a good source of information on how the judge does things. It is a good idea to take their calls almost as quickly as the judge's calls!

WHAT IS LAW?

The law consists of rules that regulate the conduct of individuals, businesses, and other organizations within society. Laws are intended to protect persons and their property from unwanted interference from others and forbid persons from engaging in certain undesirable activities.

The concept of **law** is broad. Although it is difficult to state a precise definition, *Black's Law Dictionary*, 5th edition, gives one that is sufficient for this text:

Law, in its generic sense, is a body of rules of action or conduct prescribed by controlling authority, and having binding legal force. That which must be obeyed and followed by citizens subject to sanctions or legal consequences is a law.

Functions of the Law

The law is often described by the functions it serves within a society. The primary *functions* served by U.S. law are:

1. Keeping the peace, which includes making certain activities crimes.
2. Shaping moral standards (e.g., enacting laws that discourage drug and alcohol abuse).
3. Promoting social justice (e.g., enacting statutes that prohibit discrimination in employment).
4. Maintaining the status quo (e.g., passing laws that prevent the forceful overthrow of the government).
5. Facilitating orderly change (e.g., passing statutes only after considerable study, debate, and public input).

Every year millions of students arrive on college campuses and unpack an array of items—clothes, books, furniture, decorations, and their computers. College students used to be judged by the size of their stereo speakers. Today they are judged by their computer and Internet savvy. More than 90 percent of college students now own personal computers.

The Internet has revolutionized campus life. Computer kiosks abound around college campuses, occupying space in libraries, dorm rooms, and hallways of athletic departments. Traditional libraries have become obsolete for many students as they conduct their research online. More than 60 percent of college students check out the Web daily, communicate through email, pick up course assignments, download course notes, and socialize online. Wired to modern technology, current university and college students will lead their parents and employers (and sometimes even their professors!) into the new world of high technology. Today's college students are the leaders of the e-generation.

Universities and colleges now are rated not only on how well they are connected with alumni but also on how well they are connected to computer technology. Some universities have installed software that allows their students to sit anywhere on campus with their laptops and plug into the school's computers. The computer is no longer just a study tool. It has become totally integrated into the lives of college students. The new generation of students studies online, shops online, and even dates online.

With this new technology comes one other thing that a student should know about: e-commerce and Internet law. The use of new computer technology has developed so rapidly that aspects of the law have not kept up. For example, purchase of goods and items over the Internet is exploding, but state and federal governments are struggling to develop laws to handle these transactions. How is the contract formed? What about signatures? Is a purchaser's credit card information protected? What laws protect privacy over the Internet? Can an Internet user crack a wrapper and use certain software? What criminal laws apply to fraud over the Internet? The number of legal questions pertaining to this new technology is endless.

6. Facilitating planning (e.g., designing commercial laws to allow businesses to plan their activities, allocate their productive resources, and assess the risks they take).

7. Providing a basis for compromise (approximately 90 percent of all lawsuits are settled prior to trial).

8. Maximizing individual freedom (e.g., the rights of freedom of speech, religion, and association granted by the First Amendment to the U.S. Constitution).

Fairness of the Law

On the whole, the American legal system is one of the most comprehensive, fair, and democratic systems of law ever developed and enforced. Nevertheless, some misuses and oversights of our legal system—including abuses of discretion and mistakes by judges and juries, unequal applications of the law, and procedural mishaps—allow some guilty parties to go unpunished.

In *Standefer v. United States* [447 U.S. 10, 100 S.Ct. 1999 (1980)] the Supreme Court *affirmed* (let stand) the criminal conviction of a Gulf Oil Corporation executive for aiding and abetting the bribery of an Internal Revenue Service agent. The agent had been acquitted in a separate trial. In writing the opinion of the Court, Chief Justice Warren Burger stated, "This case does no more than manifest the simple, if discomforting, reality that different juries may reach different results under any criminal statute. That is one of the consequences we accept under our jury system."

SIDEBAR

The Nature of Law

"Hardly anyone living in a civilized society has not at some time been told to do something or to refrain from doing something, because there is a law requiring it, or because it is against the law. What do we mean when we say such things? Most generally, how are we to understand statements of the form 'X is law'?"

"Introduction," *The Nature of Law: Readings in Legal Philosophy*, edited by M. P. Golding (New York: Random House, 1966).

Flexibility of the Law

One of the main attributes of American law is its *flexibility*. The law is generally responsive to cultural, technological, economic, and social changes. For example, laws that are no longer viable—such as those that restricted the property rights of women—are often repealed.

Sometimes it takes years before the law reflects the norms of society. Other times, society is led by the law. The Supreme Court's landmark 1954 decision in *Brown v. Board of Education* [347 U.S. 483, 74 S.Ct. 686 (1954)] is an example of the law leading the people. The Court's decision overturned the old "separate but equal" doctrine that condoned separate schools for Black children and White children. U.S. law evolves and changes along with the norms of society, technology, and the growth and expansion of commerce in the United States and the world.

Laws cannot be written in advance to anticipate every dispute that could arise in the future. Therefore, *general principles* are developed to be applied by courts and juries to individual disputes. This flexibility in the law leads to some uncertainty in predicting results of lawsuits. The following quote by Judge Jerome Frank addresses the value of the adaptability of law (*Law and the Modern Mind*, 1930):

> The law always has been, is now, and will ever continue to be, largely vague 7and variable. And how could this be otherwise? The law deals with human relations in their most complicated aspects. The whole confused, shifting helter-skelter of life parades before it—more confused than ever, in our kaleidoscopic age.
>
> Men have never been able to construct a comprehensive, eternalized set of rules anticipating all possible legal disputes and formulating in advance the rules which would apply to them. Situations are bound to occur which were never contemplated when the original rules were made. How much less is such a frozen legal system possible in modern times?
>
> The constant development of unprecedented problems requires a legal system capable of fluidity and pliancy. Our society would be straightjacketed were not the courts, with the able assistance of the lawyers, constantly overhauling the law and adapting it to the realities of ever-changing social, industrial, and political conditions; although changes cannot be made lightly, yet rules of law must be more or less impermanent, experimental and therefore not nicely calculable.
>
> Much of the uncertainty of law is not an unfortunate accident; it is of immense social value.

Feminist Legal Theory

In the past, the law treated men and women unequally. For example, women were denied the right to vote, could not own property if they were married, were unable to have legal abortions, and could not hold the same jobs as men. The enactment of statutes, the interpretation of constitutional provisions, and the courts have changed all of these things. The Nineteenth Amendment gave women the right to vote. States have repealed constraints on the ability of women to own property. The famous U.S. Supreme Court decision in *Roe v. Wade* gave women the constitutional right to have an abortion [410 U.S. 959 (1973)].

Title VII of the Civil Rights Act of 1964 prohibits employment discrimination based on sex. In addition, the equal protection clause of the U.S. and state constitutions provides that the government cannot treat women differently from men (and vice versa) unless some imperative reason warrants different treatment.

But is it enough for women to be treated like men? Should the female perspective be taken into account when legislators and judges develop, interpret, and apply the law? A growing body of scholarship known as *feminist legal theory*, or *feminist jurisprudence*, is being created around just such a theory.

The so-called battered woman's syndrome illustrates how this type of theory works. It has been introduced into evidence to prove self-defense in homicide cases where a woman is accused of killing her husband or another male. This defense asserts that sustained domestic violence against a woman may justify such a murder. Although rejected by many courts, some courts have recognized battered woman's syndrome as a justifiable defense.

Other areas of the law in which a woman's perspective might differ from a man's include male-only combat rules in the military, rights to privacy, family law, child custody, surrogate motherhood, job security for pregnant women, rape, sexual assault, abortion, and sexual harassment.

Even the traditional "reasonable man standard," so prevalent in American law, is being attacked as gender-biased. Those who seek change argue that merely renaming it the "reasonable person theory" is not enough. They assert that women will be judged by the reasonable actions expected of men until this standard is redefined to take into account females' unique values.

This view seems to be gaining ground. For instance, in one sexual harassment case, the court recognized that a "reasonable woman standard" should be used to determine whether a male's conduct toward a female co-employee violated Title VII. The court stated, "We prefer to analyze harassment from the victim's perspective. A complete understanding of the victim's view requires, among other things, an analysis of the different perspectives of men and women. Conduct that many men consider unobjectionable may offend many women" [*Ellison v. Brady*, 924 F.2d 872 (9th Cir. 1991)].

Critics of feminist legal theory argue that existing laws adequately protect the equal rights of females in society. Feminist legal theorists counter that justice for women will remain elusive until the law recognizes the female perspective.

Schools of Jurisprudential Thought

The philosophy or science of the law is referred to as **jurisprudence.** Several different philosophies have been advanced about how the law developed. These range from the classical natural theory to modern theories of law and economics and critical legal studies. Legal philosophers can be grouped into the following major categories, which are summarized in Table 5.1.

- The *natural law school* of jurisprudence postulates that the law is based on what is "correct." Natural law philosophers emphasize a *moral theory of law*—that is, law should be based on morality and ethics. People "discover" natural law through reasoning and choosing between good and evil.

Documents such as the U.S. Constitution, the Magna Carta, and the United Nations Charter reflect this theory.

- The *historical school* of jurisprudence believes that the law is an aggregate of social traditions and customs that have developed over the centuries. Changes in the norms of society will be reflected gradually in the law. The law is an evolutionary process. Thus, historical legal scholars look to past legal decisions (precedent) to solve contemporary problems.

- The *analytical school* of jurisprudence maintains that the law is shaped by logic. Analytical philosophers believe that results are reached by applying principles of logic to the specific facts of the case. The emphasis is on the logic of the result rather than how the result is reached.

- The *sociological school* of jurisprudence asserts that the law is a means of achieving and advancing certain sociological goals. Followers of this philosophy, known as *realists*, believe that the purpose of law is to shape social behavior. Sociological philosophers are unlikely to adhere to past law as precedent.

- The philosophers of the *command school* of jurisprudence believe that the law is a set of rules developed, communicated, and enforced by the ruling party rather than reflecting the society's morality, history, logic, or sociology. This school maintains that the law changes when the ruling class changes.

- The *critical legal studies school* proposes that legal rules are unnecessary and are used as an obstacle by the powerful to maintain the status quo. Critical legal theorists (the *"crits"*) argue that legal disputes should be solved by applying arbitrary rules based on broad notions of what is "fair" in each circumstance. Under this theory, subjective decision-making by judges would be permitted.

The Law and Economics School of Jurisprudential Thought

Should free-market principles, like the supply-and-demand and cost-benefit theories, determine the outcome of lawsuits and legislation? U.S. Court of Appeals Judge Richard Posner thinks so, and so do a growing number of other judges and legal theorists. These people are members of the *law and economics school* (or the "Chicago school") of jurisprudence, which had its roots at the University of Chicago.

According to the law and economics school, which is unofficially headed by Judge Posner, promoting market efficiency should be the central goal of legal decision making. In the area of antitrust law, for example, law and economics theorists would not find corporate mergers and takeovers to be illegal simply because they resulted in market domination. Instead, they would find this practice to be illegal only if it rendered the overall market less efficient.

Focusing on cold economic categories such as market efficiency may seem appropriate when making decisions in cases that involve businesses. But proponents of law and economics theory use this type of analysis in cases involving everything from freedom of religion to civil rights. For example, in a 1983 dissenting opinion, Judge Posner suggested that the practice of appointing counsel, free of charge, to prisoners who bring civil rights cases should be abolished. If a prisoner cannot find a lawyer who will take the case on a contingency-fee basis, it probably means that the case is not worth bringing.

Despite the naysayers who warn that the morality of certain rights and liberties must be safeguarded even if it is unpopular or costly from an economic point of view, proponents of law and economics are gaining increased acceptance in law schools and increased appointments to the judiciary.

	Comparison of schools of jurisprudential thought.	*table* 5.1
SCHOOL	**PHILOSOPHY**	
Natural law	Postulates that law is based on what is "correct." Emphasizes a moral theory of law—that is, law should be based on morality and ethics.	
Historical	Believes that law is an aggregate of social traditions and customs.	
Analytical	Maintains that law is shaped by logic.	
Sociological	Asserts that the law is a means of achieving and advancing certain sociological goals.	
Command	Believes that the law is a set of rules developed, communicated, and enforced by the ruling party.	
Critical legal studies	Maintains that legal rules are unnecessary and that legal disputes should be solved by applying arbitrary rules based on fairness.	
Law and economics	Holds that the central concern of legal decision making should be to promote market efficiency.	

HISTORY OF AMERICAN LAW

When the American colonies were first settled, the English system of law was generally adopted as the system of jurisprudence. This was the foundation from which American judges developed a common law in the United States.

English *common law* was law developed by judges who issued their opinions when deciding a case. The principles announced in these cases became **precedent** for later judges deciding similar cases. The English common law can be divided into cases decided by the law courts, chancery or equity courts, and merchant courts.

Law Courts

Prior to the Norman Conquest of England in 1066, each locality in England was subject to local laws as established by the lord or chieftain in control of the local area. There was no countrywide system of law. After 1066, William the Conqueror and his successors to the throne of England began to replace the various local laws with one uniform system of law.

To accomplish this, the king or queen appointed loyal followers as judges in all local areas. These judges were charged with administering the law in a uniform manner in what were called **law courts.** Law at this time tended to emphasize form (legal procedure) over the substance (merit) of the case. The only relief available in law courts was a monetary award for damages.

Chancery (Equity) Courts

Because of the at times unfair results and the limited remedy available in the law courts, a second set of courts—the *Court of Chancery* (or *equity court*)—was established, under the authority of the Lord Chancellor. Those who believed that the decision of the law court was unfair or that the law court could not grant an appropriate remedy could seek relief in the Court of Chancery.

The legal systems of all the states except Louisiana are based primarily on the English common law. Because of its French heritage, Louisiana bases its law on the *civil law*. Elements of California and Texas law, as well as law in other southwestern states, are rooted in civil law. In the United States, the law, equity, and merchant courts have been merged. Thus, most U.S. courts permit the aggrieved party to seek both law and equitable orders and remedies.

The importance of common law to the American legal system is described in the following excerpt from Justice William Douglas's opinion in the 1841 case of *Penny v. Little* [4 Ill. 301 (Ill. 1841)]:

The common law is a beautiful system, containing the wisdom and experiences of ages. Like the people it ruled and protected, it was simple and crude in its infancy, and became enlarged, improved, and polished as the nation advanced in civilization, virtue, and intelligence. Adapting itself to the conditions and circumstances of the people and relying upon them for its administration, it necessarily improved as the condition of the people was elevated. The inhabitants of this country always claimed the common law as their birthright, and at an early period established it as the basis of their jurisprudence.

The Chancery Court inquired into the merits of the case rather than emphasize legal procedure. The Chancellor's remedies were called *equitable remedies* because they were shaped to fit each situation. Equitable orders and remedies of the Court of Chancery took precedence over the legal decisions and remedies of the law courts.

Merchant Courts

As trade developed in the Middle Ages, the merchants who traveled about England and Europe developed certain rules to solve their commercial disputes. These rules, known as the "law of merchants" or the *law merchant*, were based upon common trade practices and usage. Eventually, a separate set of courts, called the **Merchant Court,** was established to administer these rules. In the early 1900s, the Merchant Court was absorbed into the regular law court system of England.

SOURCES OF LAW IN THE UNITED STATES

In more than 200 years since the founding of this country and the adoption of the English common law, U.S. lawmakers have developed a substantial body of law. The sources of modern law in the United States are the U.S. and state constitutions, treaties, statutes and ordinances (codified law), administrative agency rules and regulations, executive orders, and judicial decision.

Constitutions

The **Constitution of the United States of America** is the *supreme law of the land*. This means that any law—federal, state, or local—that conflicts with the U.S. Constitution is unconstitutional and, therefore, unenforceable.

The principles enumerated in the Constitution are extremely broad, as the founding fathers intended them to be applied to evolving social, technological, and economic conditions. The U.S. Constitution often is referred to as a "living document" because it is so adaptable.

The U.S. Constitution established the structure of the federal government by creating three branches of government and giving them the following powers:

1. **Legislative branch** (Congress: Senate and House of Representatives): power to make (enact) the law
2. **Executive branch** (President): power to enforce the law
3. **Judicial branch** (courts): power to interpret and determine the validity of the law

Powers not given to the federal government by the U.S. Constitution are reserved to the states. States also have their own constitutions, often patterned after the U.S. Constitution, though many are more detailed. State constitutions establish the legislative, executive, and judicial branches of state government and establish the powers of each branch. Provisions of state constitutions are valid unless they conflict with the U.S. Constitution or any valid federal law.

Treaties

The U.S. Constitution provides that the President, with the advice and consent of the U.S. Senate, may enter into **treaties** with foreign governments. Treaties become part of the supreme law of the land. With increasing international economic relations among nations, treaties will become an even more important source of law affecting business in the future.

Codified Law

Statutes are written laws that establish certain courses of conduct to which the covered parties must adhere. The U.S. Congress is empowered by the Commerce Clause and other provisions of the U.S. Constitution to enact *federal statutes* to regulate foreign and interstate commerce. Federal statutes include antitrust laws, securities laws, bankruptcy laws, labor laws, equal employment opportunity laws, environmental protection laws, consumer protection laws, and such. State legislatures enact *state statutes*, which include corporation laws, partnership laws, workers' compensation laws, the Uniform Commercial Code, and the like. The statutes enacted by the legislative branches of the federal and state governments are organized by topic into code books, often called **codified law.**

State legislatures often delegate lawmaking authority to local government bodies, including cities and municipalities, counties, school districts, water districts, and so on. These governmental units are empowered to adopt **ordinances.** Examples of ordinances are traffic laws, local building codes, and zoning laws. Ordinances are also codified.

Administrative Agencies

The legislative and executive branches of federal and state governments are empowered to establish **administrative agencies** to enforce and interpret statutes enacted by Congress and state legislatures. Many of these agencies regulate business. For example, Congress has created the Securities and Exchange Commission (SEC) and the Federal Trade Commission (FTC), among others.

The U.S. Congress or the state legislatures usually empower these agencies to adopt administrative rules and regulations to interpret the statutes that the agency is authorized to enforce. These rules and regulations have the force of law. Administrative agencies usually have the power to hear and decide disputes. Their decisions are called *orders*. Because of their power, administrative agencies are often informally referred to as the "fourth branch" of government.

Executive Orders

The executive branch of government, which consists of the President of the United States and state governors, is empowered to issue **executive orders.** This power is derived from express delegation from the legislative branch and is implied from the U.S. Constitution and state constitutions. For example, on October 8, 2001, President George W. Bush by Executive Order established within the Executive Office of the President an Office of Homeland Security to be headed by the Assistant to the President for Homeland Security.

Judicial Decisions

When deciding individual lawsuits, federal and state courts issue **judicial decisions.** In these written opinions the judge or justice usually explains the legal reasoning used to decide the case. These opinions often include interpretations of statutes, ordinances, administrative regulations, and the announcement of legal principles used to decide the case. Many court decisions are printed (reported) in books available in law libraries.

Table 5.2 summarizes the sources of law in the United States.

PRIORITY OF LAW IN THE UNITED STATES

Again, the U.S. Constitution and treaties take precedence over all other laws. Federal statutes take precedence over federal regulations, and valid federal law takes precedence over any conflicting state or local law. State constitutions rank as the highest state law, and state statutes take precedence over state regulations. Valid state law takes precedence over local laws.

The Doctrine of *Stare Decisis*

Based on the common law tradition, past court decisions become precedent for deciding future cases. Lower courts must follow the precedent established by higher courts. That is why all federal and state courts in the United States must follow the precedents established by U.S. Supreme Court decisions.

The courts of one jurisdiction are not bound by the precedent established by the courts of another jurisdiction, although they may look to each other for guidance. Thus state courts of one state are not required to follow the legal precedent established by the courts of another state.

Summary of sources of law in the United States.   *table 5.2*

SOURCE OF LAW	DESCRIPTION
Constitutions	The U.S. Constitution establishes the federal government and enumerates its powers. Powers not given to the federal government are reserved to the states. State constitutions establish state governments and enumerate their powers.
Treaties	The U.S. President, with the advice and consent of the U.S. Senate, may enter into treaties with foreign countries.
Codified law (statutes and ordinances)	Statutes are enacted by the U.S. Congress and state legislatures. Ordinances, enacted by municipalities and local government agencies, establish courses of conduct that the covered parties must follow.
Administrative agency rules and regulations	Administrative agencies are created by the legislative and executive branches of government. They may adopt rules and regulations that regulate the conduct of covered parties.
Executive orders	Executive orders, issued by the U.S. President and governors of states, regulate the conduct of covered parties.
Judicial decisions	Courts decide controversies. A court issues decisions that state the holding of the case and the rationale the court used in reaching that decision.

Adherence to precedent is called ***stare decisis*** ("to stand by the decision"). The doctrine of *stare decisis* promotes uniformity of law within a jurisdiction, makes the court system more efficient, and makes the law more predictable for individuals and businesses. A court may change or reverse its legal reasoning later if a new case is presented to it and change is warranted.

THE CONSTITUTION OF THE UNITED STATES OF AMERICA

Prior to the American Revolution, each of the thirteen original colonies operated as a separate sovereignty under the rule of England. In September 1774, representatives of the colonies met as a Continental Congress. In 1776, the colonies declared independence from England, and the American Revolution ensued.

The Constitutional Convention was convened in Philadelphia in May 1787, with the primary purpose of strengthening the federal government. After substantial debate, the delegates agreed to a new U.S. Constitution, reported to Congress in September 1787. State ratification of the Constitution was completed in 1788. Since that time, many amendments, including the **Bill of Rights,** have been added to the Constitution.

Stare Decisis

The doctrine of *stare decisis* is discussed in the following excerpt from Justice Musmanno's decision in *Flagiello v. Pennsylvania* [208 A.2d 193 (PA 1965)].

Without *stare decisis,* there would be no stability in our system of jurisprudence. *Stare decisis* channels the law. It erects lighthouses and flies the signals of safety. The ships of jurisprudence must follow that well-defined channel which, over the years, has been proved to be secure and worthy.

SIDEBAR

Ethical PERSPECTIVE

Firestone Tires Shred

On October 16, 1998, 14-year-old Jessica LeAnn Taylor, a junior high school cheerleader, was a passenger in a Ford Explorer SUV being driven to a homecoming football game. She never made it to the game. On the way, the left-rear Firestone ATX tire shredded, causing the SUV to roll over, killing Jessica. Randy Roberts, a small-town lawyer from East Texas, was hired by Jessica's parents to take on corporate giants Firestone Tire Company, which made the tire, and Ford Motor Company, which manufactured the Explorer SUV. At the time, Ford Explorer had become the number-one SUV in sales worldwide, and Firestone, the exclusive manufacturer of ATX and Wilderness tires for the Explorer, could hardly keep up with demand.

When attorney Roberts sought to discover any consumer complaints or other lawsuits that had been brought against Firestone concerning shredding tires, Firestone refused to disclose any documents but told Roberts that it knew of only one other similar accident. Undeterred, Roberts brought the issue to court, and the judge ordered Firestone to hand over the documents. The information, released in February 2000, showed 1,100 complaints had been reported to Firestone about its ATX and Wilderness tires shredding, and 57 lawsuits had been filed already.

Attorney Roberts notified the National Highway Traffic Safety Administration (NHTSA), the federal government administrative agency responsible for automobile safety, about the findings. The NHTSA instituted an investigation, which further found that more than 80 people had died and more than 250 people had been injured in accidents involving shredding Firestone ATX and Wilderness tires, the majority on Ford Explorer SUVs.

Further investigation showed that there had been deaths and injuries in other countries, including Saudi Arabia, Venezuela, Colombia, and Ecuador. The Firestone tires tended to shred under hot temperatures, so countries and areas of the United States with hotter temperatures witnessed more tire-shredding accidents. Evidence also showed that Ford had replaced the

Firestone tires in Saudi Arabia in the summer of 1998 but did not notify the NHTSA (no law required Ford to do so).

With mounting pressure, in August 2000 Firestone recalled more than 6 million ATX and Wilderness tires, the largest tire recall in U.S. history (the second largest involved the Firestone 500 tire scandal of the 1970s). Consumers all over America flocked to have their Firestone ATX and Wilderness tires replaced, but because of the demand Firestone began allocating recalls first to the states having the hottest climates, with others to follow. The public was incensed, so tires other than those made by Firestone were used for replacements as well, at Firestone's expense.

Ford blamed Firestone for all the problems, stating "This is a tire issue, not a vehicle issue." Firestone countered, alleging that Ford instructed its dealers to sell Ford Explorers with tires underinflated to 26 pounds per square inch (psi), instead of Firestone's suggested 30 psi. Firestone said Ford did this to lower the chance of the somewhat unstable Explorer rolling over. Ford denies responsibility.

Hundreds of civil lawsuits now have been filed against Firestone and Ford, alleging design defect, defect in manufacturing, and failure to warn. The lawsuits seek not only compensatory damages for the loss of loved ones and to pay for injuries, but also large punitive damage awards to punish Firestone and Ford for acting recklessly. It will take years for all the trials and appeals to be sorted out to determine who is financially culpable. In the meantime, substantial ethical issues have been raised questioning the conduct of Firestone and Ford.

1. Do you think Firestone acted quickly enough in instituting the recall of its ATX and Wilderness tires?

2. Did Ford act ethically in this case? Should it have done anything earlier? Explain.

3. If you were a juror in Jessica's parents' lawsuit against Firestone and Ford, would you award punitive damages? Why or why not?

The U.S. Constitution serves two major functions:

1. It creates the three branches of the federal government (the executive, legislative, and judicial branches) and allocates powers to these branches.
2. It protects individual rights by limiting the government's ability to restrict those rights.

The Constitution itself provides that it may be amended to address social and economic changes.

Federalism and Delegated Powers

The U.S. form of government is referred to as **federalism,** which means that the federal government and the 50 state governments share powers. When the states ratified the Constitution, they *delegated* certain powers to the federal government. These **enumerated powers** authorize the federal government to deal with national and international affairs. State governments have powers that are not specifically delegated to the federal government by the Constitution and are empowered to deal with local affairs.

Doctrine of Separation of Powers

The first three Articles of the Constitution divide the federal government into three branches:

1. Article I of the Constitution establishes the *legislative branch* of government, which is bicameral—consisting of the Senate and the House of Representatives—collectively referred to as *Congress.* Each state is allocated two senators. The number of representatives to the House of Representatives is determined by the population of each state. The current number of representatives is determined from the 2000 census.
2. Article II of the Constitution establishes the *executive branch* of government by providing for the election of the President and Vice President. The President is not elected by popular vote but, instead, by the *Electoral College*, whose representatives are appointed by state delegations.
3. Article III establishes the *judicial branch* of the government in the Supreme Court and provides for the creation of other federal courts by Congress.

The Polk County Courthouse in Bartow, Florida.

Checks and Balances

Certain checks and balances are built into the Constitution to ensure that no one branch of the federal government becomes too powerful. Some of the checks and balances in our system of government are as follows:

1. The judicial branch has authority to examine the acts of the other two branches of government and determine whether these acts are constitutional.
2. The executive branch can enter into treaties with foreign governments only with the advice and consent of the Senate.

Geier v. American Honda Motor Co., Inc.

120 S.Ct. 1913 (2000)   Supreme Court of the United States

FACTS

The United States Department of Transportation is the federal administrative agency responsible for administering and enforcing federal traffic safety laws, including the National Traffic and Motor Vehicle Safety Act of 1966. Pursuant to this Act, in 1987 the Department of Transportation adopted a Federal Motor Vehicle Safety Standard requiring automobile manufacturers to equip 10 percent of their 1987 vehicles with passive restraints, including automatic seat belts or airbags.

In 1992, Alexis Geier, driving a 1987 Honda Accord automobile in the District of Columbia, collided with a tree and was seriously injured. The car was equipped with manual shoulder and lap belts, which Geier had buckled up at the time of the accident; the car was not equipped with airbags, however.

Geier sued the car's manufacturer, the American Honda Motor Company, Inc., alleging that American Honda had negligently and defectively designed the car because it lacked a driver's side airbag, thus violating the District of Columbia's tort law.

The trial court dismissed Geier's lawsuit, finding that the District of Columbia's tort law conflicted with the federal passive restraint safety standard and was therefore preempted under the Supremacy Clause of the U.S. Constitution. The court of appeals affirmed. Geier appealed to the U.S. Supreme Court, which granted review.

ISSUE

Does the federal passive restraint safety standard preempt the District of Columbia's common law tort action in which the plaintiff claims that the defendant American Honda, which was in compliance with the federal standard, should nonetheless have equipped the 1987 automobile with airbags?

IN THE LANGUAGE OF THE COURT

Breyer, Justice.

In effect, petitioner Geier's tort action depends upon his claim that the manufacturer had a duty to install an airbag when it manufactured the 1987 Honda Accord. Such a state law—i.e., a rule of state tort law imposing such a duty—by its terms would have required manufacturers of all similar cars to install airbags rather than other passive restraint systems, such as automatic belts or passive interiors. It would have required all manufacturers to have installed airbags in respect to the entire District of Columbia-related portion of their 1987 new car fleet, even though the federal safety standard at that time required only that 10% of a manufacturer's nationwide fleet be equipped with any passive restraint device at all.

Regardless, the language of the federal passive restraint standard is clear enough: The federal standard sought a gradually developing mix of alternative passive restraint devices for safety-related reasons. The rule of state tort law for which petitioner Geier argues would stand as an "obstacle" to the accomplishment of that objective. And the federal statute foresees the application of ordinary principles of preemption in cases of actual conflict. Hence the tort action is preempted.

DECISION AND REMEDY

The U.S. Supreme Court held that the federal passive restraint safety standard preempted petitioner Geier's tort lawsuit under the District of Columbia's law against American Honda.

Questions

1. What is the purpose of the Supremacy Clause of the U.S. Constitution? What would be the consequences if there were no Supremacy Clause? Explain.

2. Do you think American Honda owed a duty to equip all of its 1987 vehicles with airbags even though federal law did not require this?

3. Do laws ever protect—rather than harm—businesses? Do you think defendant American Honda would say "There are too many laws" in this case?

3. The legislative branch is authorized to create federal courts and determine their jurisdiction and to enact statutes that change judicially made law.

Supremacy Clause

The **Supremacy Clause** establishes that the federal Constitution, treaties, federal laws, and federal regulations are the supreme law of the land [Article VI, Section 2]. State and local laws that conflict with valid federal law are unconstitutional. The concept of federal law taking precedence over state or local law is called the **preemption doctrine.**

Congress may expressly provide that a particular federal statute *exclusively* regulates a specific area or activity. No state or local law regulating the area or activity is valid if there is such a statute. More often, though, federal statutes do not expressly provide for exclusive jurisdiction. In these instances, state and local governments have *concurrent jurisdiction* to regulate the area or activity. But any state or local law that "directly and substantially" conflicts with valid federal law is preempted under the Supremacy Clause.

Commerce Clause

The **Commerce Clause** of the U.S. Constitution grants Congress the power "to regulate commerce with foreign nations, and among the several states, and with Indian tribes" [Article I, Section 8, clause 3]. Because this clause authorizes the federal government to regulate commerce, it has a greater impact on business than any other provision in the Constitution. Among other things, this clause is intended to foster the development of a national market and free trade among the states.

The Commerce Clause also gives the federal government the authority to regulate **interstate commerce.** Originally, the courts interpreted this clause to mean that the federal government could regulate only commerce that moved *in* interstate commerce. The modern rule, however, allows the federal government to regulate activities that *affect* interstate commerce.

Under the *effects on interstate commerce test*, the regulated activity does not itself have to be in interstate commerce. Thus, any local (**intrastate**) activity that has an effect on interstate commerce is subject to federal regulation. Theoretically, this test subjects a substantial amount of business activity in the United States to federal regulation.

For example, in the famous case of *Wickard, Secretary of Agriculture v. Filburn* [317 U.S. Ill, 63 S.Ct. 82 (1942)], a federal statute limited the amount of wheat a farmer could plant and harvest for home consumption. Filburn, a farmer, violated the law. The U.S. Supreme Court upheld the statute on the grounds that it prevented nationwide surpluses and shortages of wheat. The Court reasoned that wheat grown for home consumption would affect the supply of wheat available in interstate commerce.

Commerce Regulation

The federal government may regulate:

1. *Interstate* commerce that crosses state borders.

2. *Intrastate* commerce that affects interstate commerce.

SIDEBAR

State Police Power

The states did not delegate all power to regulate business to the federal government. They retained the power to regulate *intrastate* and much interstate business activity that occurs within their borders. This is commonly referred to as states' **police power.**

The Commerce Clause of the U.S. Constitution gives the federal government the exclusive power to regulate commerce with foreign nations. Direct and indirect regulation of foreign commerce by state or local governments that discriminates against foreign commerce violates the Foreign Commerce Clause and is therefore unconstitutional.

Consider the following examples. The state of Michigan is the home of General Motors Corporation, Ford Motor Company, and Chrysler Corporation, the three largest automobile manufacturers in the United States. Suppose the Michigan state legislature enacts a law imposing a 100 percent tax on any automobile imported from a foreign country that is sold in Michigan but does not impose the same tax on domestic automobiles sold in Michigan. The Michigan tax violates the Foreign Commerce Clause and therefore is unconstitutional and void.

If, on the other hand, Michigan enacts a law that imposes a 100 percent tax on all automobiles sold in Michigan, domestic and foreign, the law does not discriminate against foreign commerce and therefore does not violate the Foreign Commerce Clause. But the federal government could enact a 100 percent tax on all foreign automobiles but not domestic automobiles sold in the United States, and that law would be valid.

Police Power

SIDEBAR

States may enact laws that protect or promote the public health, safety, morals, and general welfare as long as the law does not unduly burden interstate commerce.

Police power permits states (and, by delegation, local governments) to enact laws to protect or promote the *public health, safety, morals, and general welfare.* This includes the authority to enact laws that regulate the conduct of business. Zoning ordinances, state environmental laws, corporation and partnership laws, and property laws are enacted under this power.

Bill of Rights

In 1791, the states approved the 10 amendments commonly referred to as the Bill of Rights, and they became part of the U.S. Constitution. The Bill of Rights guarantees certain fundamental rights to natural persons and protects these rights from intrusive government action. Most of these rights, or "freedoms," also have been found applicable to so-called artificial persons (i.e., corporations).

The First Amendment to the Constitution guarantees the rights of free speech, assembly, religion, and the press. Because these rights are continually litigated and are frequent subjects of U.S. Supreme Court opinions, they are singled out for special attention, along with the due process clause.

Freedom of Speech

One of the most honored freedoms guaranteed by the Bill of Rights is the *freedom of speech* of the First Amendment. Many other constitutional freedoms would be meaningless without it. The First Amendment's Freedom of Speech Clause protects speech only, not conduct. The U.S. Supreme Court places speech into three categories: (1) fully protected, (2) limited protected, and (3) unprotected speech.

1. **Fully protected speech.** *Fully protected speech* is speech that the government cannot prohibit or regulate. Political speech is an example of such speech. For example, the government could not enact a law that forbids citizens from criticizing the current administration. The First Amendment protects oral, written, and symbolic speech.

2. **Limited protected speech.** The Supreme Court has held that certain types of speech have only *limited protection* under the First Amendment. The government cannot forbid this type of speech, but it can subject this speech to time, place, and manner restrictions. The following types of speech are accorded limited protection:

- *Offensive speech* is speech that offends many members of society. (It is not the same as obscene speech, however.) The Supreme Court has held that offensive speech may be restricted by the government under time, place, and manner restrictions. For example, the Federal Communications Commission (FCC) can regulate the use of offensive language on television by limiting such language to time periods when children would be unlikely to be watching (e.g., late at night).

- *Commercial speech*, such as advertising, was once considered unprotected by the First Amendment. The Supreme Court's landmark decision in *Virginia State Board of Pharmacy v. Virginia Citizens Consumer Council, Inc.* [425 U.S. 748, 96 S.Ct. 1817 (1976)] changed this rule. In that case, the Supreme Court held that a state statute prohibiting a pharmacist from advertising the price of prescription drugs was unconstitutional because it violated the Freedom of Speech Clause. However, the Supreme Court held that commercial speech is subject to proper time, place, and manner restrictions. For example, a city could prohibit billboards along its highways for safety and aesthetic reasons as long as other forms of advertising (e.g., print media) were available.

3. **Unprotected speech.** The Supreme Court has held that the following types of speech are not protected by the First Amendment and may be totally forbidden by the government:

- Dangerous speech (including such things as yelling "fire" in a crowded theater when there is no fire)

- Fighting words that are likely to provoke a hostile or violent response from an average person

- Speech that incites the violent or revolutionary overthrow of the government; the mere abstract teaching of the morality and consequences of such action is protected

- Defamatory language

- Child pornography

- Obscene speech

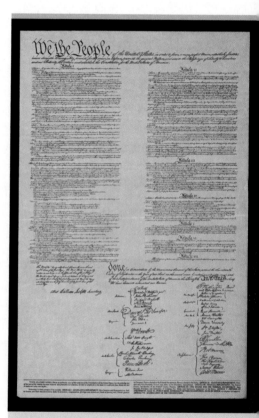

The Constitution of the United States.

The definition of *obscene speech* is quite subjective. One Supreme Court justice stated, "I know it when I see it" [Justice Stewart in *Jacobellis v. Ohio*, 378

Once or twice a century a new medium seems to come along that presents new problems in applying freedom-of-speech rights. This time it is the Internet. Congress enacted the *Telecommunications Act of 1996* to regulate telecommunications, including the Internet. Two provisions of this federal statute restricted the ability of cyberspace operators to transmit certain images.

1. *Computer Decency Act.* This part of the statute made it a felony to knowingly make "indecent" or "patently offensive" materials available on computer systems, including the Internet, to persons under 18 years of age.

2. *Signal Bleed Provision.* This provision of the statute required cable operators either to limit sexually explicit programming on cable channels to the hours between 10:00 P.M. and 6:00 A.M. or to scramble sexually explicit channels in full.

The Act provided for fines, prison terms, and loss of licenses for anyone convicted of violating the terms of these provisions. Immediately, cyberspace providers and users filed lawsuits challenging these provisions of the Act as violating their free speech rights granted under the First Amendment to the Constitution. Proponents of the Act countered that these provisions were necessary to protect children from indecent materials. The plaintiffs won both cases at trial, and the U.S. Supreme Court granted review to decide the free speech issues.

The Supreme Court also came down on the plaintiff's side in each case. The Court overturned the Computer Decency Act, finding that the terms "indecent" and "patently offensive" were too vague to define and criminally enforce. The Court decided that the signal-bleed provision imposed an overly broad illegal content-based restriction on speech. In both cases, the Supreme Court reasoned that limiting the content on the Internet to what is suitable for a child resulted in unconstitutional limiting of adult speech. The Court noted that children are far less likely to trip over indecent material on the Internet than on TV or radio because the information must be actively sought out on the Internet. The Court also stated that parents can regulate their children's access to the Internet and can install blocking and filtering software programs to protect their children from seeing adult materials.

The Supreme Court declared emphatically that the Internet must be given the highest possible level of First Amendment free-speech protection, greater than that afforded to TV and radio. The Court concluded that the Internet allows an individual to reach an audience of millions at almost no cost, setting it apart from TV, radio, and print media, which are prohibitively expensive to use. The Supreme Court stated, "As the most participatory form of mass speech yet developed, the Internet deserves the highest protection from government intrusion." The Court also reasoned that, because the Internet is a global medium, even if the challenged provisions of the Act were upheld, there would be no way to prevent indecent material from flowing over the Internet from abroad.

Reno v. American Civil Liberties Union, 117 S.Ct. 2329 (1997); *United States v. Playboy Entertainment Group, Inc.*, 120 S.Ct. 1878 (2000)

U.S. 184, 84 S.Ct. 1676 (1963)]. In *Miller v. California*, the Supreme Court determined that speech is obscene when

1. The average person, applying contemporary community standards, would find that the work, taken as a whole, appeals to the prurient interest.
2. The work depicts or describes, in a patently offensive way, sexual conduct specifically defined by the applicable state law.
3. The work, taken as a whole, lacks serious literary, artistic, political, or scientific value. [413 U.S. 15, 93 S.Ct. 2607 (1973)]

States are free to define what constitutes obscene speech. Movie theaters, magazine publishers, and so on are often subject to challenges that the materials they display or sell are obscene and therefore not protected by the First Amendment.

Freedom of Religion

The U.S. Constitution requires federal, state, and local governments to be neutral toward religion. The First Amendment actually contains two separate religion clauses:

1. The *Establishment Clause* prohibits the government from either establishing a state religion or promoting one religion over another. Thus, it guarantees that there will be no state-sponsored religion. The Supreme Court used this clause as its reason for ruling that an Alabama statute that authorized a one-minute period of silence in schools for "meditation or voluntary prayer" was invalid [*Wallace v. Jaffree*, 472 U.S. 38, 105 S.Ct. 2479 (1985)]. The Court held that the statute endorsed religion.

2. The *Free Exercise Clause* prohibits the government from interfering with the free exercise of religion in the United States. Generally, this clause prevents the government from enacting laws that either prohibit or inhibit individuals from participating in or practicing their chosen religion. For example, in *Church of Lukumi Babalu Aye, Inc. v. City of Hialeah, Florida* [113 S.Ct. 2217 (1993)], the U.S. Supreme Court held that a city ordinance that prohibited ritual sacrifices of animals (chickens) during church services violated the Free Exercise Clause. Of course, this right to be free from government intervention in the practice of religion is not absolute. For example, human sacrifices are unlawful and are not protected by the First Amendment.

Due Process Clause

The **Due Process Clause** provides that no person shall be deprived of "life, liberty, or property" without due process of the law. It is contained in both the Fifth and Fourteenth Amendments. The Due Process Clause of the Fifth Amendment applies to federal government action; that of the Fourteenth Amendment applies to state and local government action. The government is not prohibited from taking a person's life, liberty, or property, but the government must follow due process to do so. There are two categories of due process: *substantive* and *procedural*.

Substantive due process. **Substantive due process** requires that government statutes, ordinances, regulations, or other laws be clear on their face and not overly broad in scope. The test of whether substantive due process is met is whether a "reasonable person" could understand the law to be able to comply with it. Laws that do not meet this test are declared *void for vagueness*.

Suppose, for example, that a city ordinance made it illegal for persons to wear "clothes of the opposite sex." Such an ordinance would be held unconstitutional as void for vagueness because a reasonable person could not clearly determine whether his or her conduct violates the law.

THE CIVIL LAW SYSTEM

One of the major legal systems that has developed in the world, in addition to the Anglo–American common law system, is the **Romano–Germanic civil law system.** This legal system, commonly called the **civil law,** dates to 450 B.C., when Rome adopted the Twelve Tables, a code of laws applicable to the Romans. A compilation of Roman law, called the *Corpus Juris Civilis* (the Body of Civil Law), was completed in A.D. 534. Later, two national codes—the French Civil Code of 1804 (the Napoleonic Code) and the German Civil Code of 1896—became models for countries that adopted civil codes.

In contrast to the Anglo–American common law, in which laws are created by the judicial system as well as by congressional legislation, the Civil Code and parliamentary statutes that expand and interpret it are the sole sources of the law in most civil law countries. Thus, the adjudication of a case is simply the application of the Code or the statutes to a specific set of facts. In some civil law countries, court decisions do not have the force of law.

Today, Austria, Belgium, Greece, Indochina, Indonesia, Japan, Latin America, the Netherlands, Poland, Portugal, South Korea, Spain, Sub-Saharan Africa, Switzerland, and Turkey follow the civil law.

Procedural due process. Procedural due process requires that the government give a person proper *notice* and *hearing* of the legal action before that person is deprived of his or her life, liberty, or property. The government action must be fair.

For example, if the government wants to take a person's home by eminent domain to build a highway, the government must (1) give the homeowner sufficient notice of its intention, and (2) provide a hearing. Under the **Just Compensation Clause** of the Fifth Amendment, the government must pay the owner just compensation for taking the property.

LEGAL TERMINOLOGY

Administrative agencies	Interstate commerce
Bill of Rights	Intrastate commerce
Civil law system	Judicial branch of government
Codified law	Judicial decision
Commerce clause	Jurisprudence
Commercial speech	Just Compensation Clause
Due Process Clause	Law
Enumerated powers	Law court
Executive branch of government	Legislative branch of government
Executive order	Merchant court
Federalism	Ordinances

Police powers	Substantive due process
Precedent	Supremacy Clause
Preemption doctrine	Treaty
Procedural due process	U.S. Constitution
Stare decisis	

Summary

CHAPTER 5 THE CONSTITUTION AND SOURCES OF AMERICAN LAW

What Is Law?

Definition	A body of rules of action or conduct prescribed by controlling authority and having binding legal force.
Functions	1. Keep the peace 2. Shape moral standards 3. Promote social justice 4. Maintain the status quo 5. Facilitate orderly change 6. Facilitate planning 7. Provide a basis for compromise 8. Maximize individual freedom
Fairness	Although the American legal system is one of the fairest and most democratic systems of law, abuses and mistakes in the application of the law still occur.
Flexibility	The law must be flexible to meet social, technological, and economic changes.

Schools of Jurisprudential Thought

Natural Law	Postulates that law is based on what is "correct"; it emphasizes a moral theory of law—that is, law should be based on morality and ethics.
Historical	Believes that law is an aggregate of social traditions and customs.
Analytical	Maintains that law is shaped by logic.
Sociological	Asserts that the law is a means of achieving and advancing certain sociological goals.
Command	Believes that the law is a set of rules developed, communicated, and enforced by the ruling party.

(continued)

Critical Legal Studies	Maintains that legal rules are unnecessary and that legal disputes should be solved by applying arbitrary rules based on fairness.
Law and Economics	Believes that promoting market efficiency should be the central concern of legal decision making.

History of American Law

Foundation of American Law	English common law (judge-made law) forms the basis of the legal systems of most states in this country. Louisiana bases its law on the French civil code.

Sources of Law in the United States

Constitutions	U.S. Constitution establishes the federal government and enumerates its powers. Powers not given to the federal government are reserved to the states. State constitutions establish state governments and enumerate their powers.
Treaties	The President, with the advice and consent of the Senate, may enter into treaties with foreign countries.
Codified Law	1. *Statutes* are enacted by Congress and state legislatures. 2. *Ordinances* and statutes are passed by municipalities and local government bodies to establish courses of conduct that must be followed by covered parties.
Administrative Agency Rules and Regulations	Administrative agencies are created by the legislative and executive branches of government; they may adopt rules and regulations that govern the conduct of covered parties.
Executive Orders	Issued by the President and governors of states, executive orders regulate the conduct of covered parties.
Judicial Decisions	Courts decide controversies by issuing decisions that state the holding of each case and the rationale the court used to reach that decision.

Doctrine of *Stare Decisis*

Definition	Means "to stand by the decision"; doctrine that provides for adherence to precedent.

Constitution of the United States of America

Scope	Consists of seven articles and 26 amendments; establishes the three branches of the federal government, enumerates their powers, and provides important guarantees of individual freedom. The Constitution was ratified by the states in 1788. *(continued)*

Basic Constitutional Concepts	1. *Federalism:* The Constitution created the federal government, which shares power with the state governments.
	2. *Delegated powers:* When the states ratified the Constitution, they delegated certain powers, called *enumerated powers,* to the federal government.
	3. *Reserved powers:* Those powers not granted to the federal government by the Constitution are reserved to the states.
	4. *Separation of powers:* Each branch of the federal government has separate powers.
	a. Legislative branch—power to make the law.
	b. Executive branch—power to enforce the law.
	c. Judicial branch—power to interpret the law.
	5. *Checks and balances:* Certain checks and balances are built into the Constitution to ensure that no one branch of the federal government becomes too powerful.

Supremacy Clause

| Purpose | Stipulates that the U.S. Constitution, treaties, and federal law (statutes and regulations) are the *supreme law of the land.* State or local laws that conflict with valid federal law are unconstitutional. This is called the *preemption doctrine.* |

Commerce Clause

| Purpose | 1. *Commerce Clause:* Authorizes the federal government to regulate commerce with foreign nations, among the states, and with Indian tribes. |
| | 2. *Interstate commerce:* Under the broad *effects test*, the federal government may regulate any activity (even intrastate commerce) that *affects* interstate commerce. |

Bill of Rights

| Scope | Consists of the first 10 amendments to the Constitution. They establish basic individual rights. The Bill of Rights was ratified in 1791. |

Due Process Clause

Purpose	Provides that no person shall be deprived of "life, liberty, or property" without due process. Two categories of due process:
	1. *Substantive due process:* Requires that laws be clear on their face and not overly broad in scope. Laws that do not meet this test are *void for vagueness.*
	2. *Procedural due process:* Requires that the government give a person proper *notice* and *hearing* before that person is deprived of his or her life, liberty, or property. An owner must be paid *just compensation* if the government takes his or her property.

Working the Web

1. The U.S. government is the largest source of information anywhere in the world, and for the most part this information is free and available online. Two good starting points are www.uncle-sam.com, a private website, and www.firstgov.gov, an official government website.

2. The White House has made a serious commitment to provide access to government information via the Internet. Information ranging from facts about the President and Vice President and their families and events at the White House, to current executive orders and press releases is available on the White House website. One may even listen to speeches and view photos at www.whitehouse.gov.

3. Imagine you are interested in a bill that was introduced into the U.S. House of Representatives last month. You want to read the full text of the bill and find out what happened to it (its legislative history). Using the U.S. House of Representatives website at www.house.gov, retrieve a current House bill and its legislative history.

4. Get information on recent legislative actions, scheduled activities, committee information, senators and Senate leadership, Senate history, procedures, terminology, and links to other information at www.senate.gov.

5. Imagine you want to find out who your representative is in the House of Representatives. Using the U.S. House of Representatives website, determine who your representative is. Print out the biographical material about him or her. Find out what his or her email address is.

6. Suppose you want to find out what is online from the Internal Revenue Service. Using the www.firstgov.gov website, navigate your way to the Internal Revenue Service's home page.

Questions

CRITICAL LEGAL THINKING AND WRITING

1. If you briefed the case of *Lee v. Weisman* (at the end of the chapter), did your personal feelings affect the way you presented the information in your brief? Review your brief of the case; after reflection, did you write the brief from the majority or minority viewpoint?

2. What is the role of the paralegal in briefing cases for the supervising attorney?

3. Does the Establishment Clause protect the rights of the individual, or does it take them away?

4. How do the priorities of the U.S. Constitution protect the average citizen of a state?

5. How does the doctrine of *stare decisis* promote uniformity of laws?

6. How has the inherent flexibility of the American legal system enabled the United States to grow and survive challenges such as wars, domestic unrest, and terrorist threats?

7. Are money damages always a satisfactory solution to a legal dispute?

8. Should federal courts be permitted to make decisions that affect only local matters, such as the limitation on prayer in school or viewing of material on cable television?

9. What is the value in allowing the President to issue executive orders instead of Congress enacting a law?

10. Do the biblical Ten Commandments offer a sufficient set of rules of conduct for a modern society? Why or why not?

ETHICS: ANALYSIS AND DISCUSSION

1. What ethical obligations does the paralegal have in briefing cases for the supervising attorney?

2. Are there any ethical issues in allowing one's personal feelings to be expressed in working on a case? What if you have strong feelings against the position of the client, such as in the prayer in school case, or the pornography on cable case?

3. Does the American system of law depend on the legal team to put aside its personal beliefs and work diligently on unpopular cases or issues? How does this ensure equal justice and allow for change in the system?

Competent Representation

There are few certainties in the area of ethics, for paralegals or in any profession. What qualifies as ethical conduct is in most cases based on state law and court interpretation applied to a set of facts. The citation listed below represents one legal opinion and is provided as a research starting point. Do not assume that the same rule applies in your jurisdiction. For the following:

- *Prepare a written statement based on your state law.*
- *Use your state bar association website as a starting point.*

You are working in a law firm for an attorney who has had a series of strokes that have caused a permanent reading disability and memory impairment [Philadelphia Ethics Opinion 2002-12 (2000); also, see Texas Ethics Opinion 522 (1997)]. Do you have any ethical obligtation to the attorney's clients? Do you have any ethical obligation to the firm and to the attorney?

Youngstown Co. v. Sawyer, Secretary of Commerce

343 U.S. 579, 72 S.Ct. 863, 96 L.Ed.2d 1153 (1952)

5.1 FACTS

In 1951, a dispute arose between steel companies and their employees about the terms and conditions that should be included in a new labor contract. At the time, the United States was engaged in a military conflict in Korea that required substantial steel resources from which to make weapons and other military goods.

On April 4, 1952, the steelworkers' union gave notice of a nationwide strike called to begin at 12:01 A.M. on April 9. The indispensability of steel as a component in weapons and other war materials led President Dwight D. Eisenhower to believe that the proposed strike would jeopardize the national defense and that governmental seizure of the steel mills was necessary to ensure the continued availability of steel. Therefore, a few hours before the strike was to begin, the President issued Executive Order 10340, which directed the Secretary of Commerce to take possession of most of the steel mills and keep them running. The steel companies obeyed the order under protest, and brought proceedings against the President.

ISSUE

Was the seizure of the steel mills constitutional?

Bonito Boats, Inc. v. Thunder Craft Boats, Inc.

489 U.S. 141, 109 S.Ct. 971, 103 L.Ed.2d 118 (1989)

5.2 FACTS

Article 1, Section 8, clause 8 of the U.S. Constitution grants Congress the power to enact laws to give inventors the exclusive right to their discoveries. Pursuant to this power, Congress enacted federal patent laws that establish the requirements to obtain a patent. Once a patent is granted, the patent holder has exclusive rights to use the patent.

Bonito Boats, Inc. developed a hull design for a fiberglass recreational boat that it marketed under the trade name Bonito Boats Model 5VBR. The manufacturing process involved creating a hardwood model that was sprayed with fiberglass to create a mold. The mold then served to produce the finished fiberglass boats for sale. Bonito did not file a patent application to protect the utilitarian or design aspects of the hull or the manufacturing process.

After the Bonito 5VBR was on the market for six years, the Florida legislature enacted a statute prohibiting the use of a direct molding process to duplicate unpatented boat hulls and forbade the knowing sale of hulls so duplicated. The protection afforded under the state statute was broader than that provided for under the federal patent statute.

Subsequently, Thunder Craft Boats, Inc. produced and sold boats made by the direct molding process. Bonito sued Thunder Craft under Florida law.

ISSUE

Is the Florida statute valid?

Heart of Atlanta Motel v. United States

379 U.S. 241, 85 S.Ct. 348, 13 L.Ed.2d 258 (1964)

5.3 FACTS

The Heart of Atlanta Motel, in the state of Georgia, has 216 rooms available to guests. The motel is readily accessible to interstate highways 75 and 85 and to state highways 23 and 41. The motel solicits patronage from outside the state of Georgia through various national advertising media, including magazines of national circulation, and it maintains more than 50 billboards and highway signs within the state. Approximately 75 percent of the motel's registered guests are from out of state.

Congress enacted the Civil Rights Act of 1964, which made it illegal for public accommodations to discriminate against guests based on their race. Prior to that, the Heart of Atlanta Motel had refused to rent rooms to Blacks. After the act was passed, it alleged that it intended to continue not to rent rooms to Blacks. The owner of the motel brought an action to have the Civil Rights Act of 1964 declared unconstitutional, alleging that Congress, in passing the Act, had exceeded its powers to regulate commerce under the Commerce Clause of the U.S. Constitution.

ISSUE
Who wins?

Rostker, Director of the Selective Service v. Goldberg

453 U.S. 57, 101 S.Ct. 2646, 69 L.Ed.2d 478 (1981)

5.4 FACTS
In 1975, after the war in Vietnam, the U.S. government discontinued draft registration for men in this country. In 1980, after the Soviet Union invaded Afghanistan, President Jimmy Carter asked Congress for funds to reactivate draft registration. President Carter suggested that both males and females be required to register. Congress allocated funds only for the registration of males. Several men who were subject to draft registration brought a lawsuit that challenged the law as being unconstitutional in violation of the Equal Protection Clause of the U.S. Constitution. The U.S. Supreme Court upheld the constitutionality of the draft registration law, reasoning as follows.

The question of registering women for the draft not only received considerable national attention and was the subject of wide-ranging public debate, but also was extensively considered by Congress in hearings, floor debate, and in committee. The foregoing clearly establishes that the decision to exempt women from registration was not the "accidental by-product of a traditional way of thinking about women."

This is not a case of Congress arbitrarily choosing to burden one of two similarly situated groups, such as would be the case with an all-black or all-white, or an all-Catholic or all-Lutheran, or an all-Republican or all-Democratic registration. Men and women are simply not similarly situated for purposes of a draft or registration for a draft.

Justice Marshall dissented, stating that "The Court today places its imprimatur on one of the most potent remaining public expressions of 'ancient canards about the proper role of women.' It upholds a statute that requires males but not females to register for the draft, and which thereby categorically excludes women from a fundamental civic obligation. I dissent."

ISSUE
Was the decision fair? Has the law been a "progressive science" in this case? Is it ethical for males, but not females, to have to register for the draft?

Lee V. Weisman

120 L.Ed.2d 467, 112 S.Ct. 2649 (1992)

Read the following case, excerpted from the U.S. Supreme Court's opinion. Review and brief the case. In your brief, answer the following questions.

1. Who are the plaintiff and defendant?
2. What does the Establishment Clause provide?
3. Was the fact that the prayer was nonsectarian important to the Supreme Court's decision?
4. What argument did the dissenting opinion make in support of allowing prayer at high school graduation ceremonies?
5. How close was the vote by the justices in this case?
6. What test did the court use to determine if the practice violates the Establishment Clause?
7. Can a school persuade a student to participate in religious exercises?
8. Is nonsectarian prayer permitted under the Establishment Clause?

Kennedy, Justice (joined by Blackmun, Stevens, O'Conner, and Souter).

Deborah Weisman graduated from Nathan Bishop Middle School, a public school in Providence, Rhode Island, at a formal ceremony in June 1989. She was about 14 years old. For many years it has been the policy of the Providence school committee and the Superintendent of Schools to permit principals to invite members of the clergy to give invocations and benedictions at middle school and high school graduations. Many, but not all, of the principals elected to include prayers as part of the graduation ceremonies. Acting for himself and his daughter, Deborah's father, Daniel Weisman, objected to any prayers at Deborah's middle school graduation, but to no avail. The school principal, petitioner Robert E. Lee, invited a rabbi to deliver prayers at the graduation exercises for Deborah's class. Rabbi Leslie Gutterman, of the Temple Beth El in Providence, accepted.

It also has been the custom of Providence school officials to provide invited clergy with a pamphlet entitled "Guidelines for Civic Occasions," prepared by the National Conference of Christians and Jews. The Guidelines recommended that public prayers at nonsectarian civic ceremonies be composed with "inclusiveness and sensitivity," though they acknowledge that "prayer of any kind may be inappropriate on some civic occasions." The principal gave Rabbi Gutterman the pamphlet before the graduation and advised him that the invocation and benediction should be nonsectarian.

Deborah's graduation was held on the premises of Nathan Bishop Middle School on June 29, 1989. Four days before the ceremony, Daniel Weisman, in his individual capacity as a Providence taxpayer and as next friend of Deborah, sought a temporary restraining order in the United States District Court for the District of Rhode Island to prohibit school officials from including an invocation or a benediction in the graduation ceremony. The court denied the motion for lack of adequate time to consider it. Deborah and her family attended the graduation, where the prayers were recited.

In July 1989, Daniel Weisman filed an amended complaint seeking a permanent injunction barring petitioners, various officials of the Providence public schools, from inviting the clergy to deliver invocations and benedictions at future graduations.

The case was submitted on stipulated facts. The District Court held that petitioners' practice of including invocations and benedictions in public school graduations violated the Establishment Clause of the First Amendment, and it enjoined petitioners from continuing the practice. The court applied the three-part Establishment Clause test. Under that test, to satisfy the Establishment Clause a governmental practice must (1) reflect a clearly secular purpose, (2) have a primary effect that neither advances nor inhibits religion, and (3) avoid excessive government entanglement with religion. On appeal, the United States Court of Appeals for the First Circuit affirmed.

These dominant facts mark and control the confines of our decision: State officials direct the performance of a formal religious exercise at promotional and graduation ceremonies for secondary schools. Even for those students who object to the religious exercise, their attendance and participation in the state-sponsored religious activity are in a fair and real sense obligatory, though the school district does not require attendance as a condition for receipt of the diploma.

The controlling precedents as they relate to prayer and religious exercise in primary and secondary public schools compel the holding here that the policy of the city of Providence is an unconstitutional one. It is beyond dispute that, at a minimum, the Constitution guarantees that government may not coerce anyone to support or participate in religion or its exercise, or otherwise act in a way which "establishes a state religion or religious faith, or tends to do so."

We are asked to recognize the existence of a practice of nonsectarian prayer within the embrace of what is known as the Judeo-Christian tradition, prayer which is more acceptable than one which, for example, makes explicit references to the God of Israel, or to Jesus Christ, or to a patron saint. If common ground can be defined which permits once conflicting faiths to express the shared conviction that there is an ethic and a morality which transcend human invention, the sense of community and purpose sought by all decent societies might be advanced. But though the First Amendment does not allow the government to stifle prayers which aspire to these ends, neither does it permit the government to undertake that task for itself.

The sole question presented is whether a religious exercise may be conducted at a graduation ceremony in circumstances where, as we have found, young graduates who object are induced to conform. No holding by this Court suggests that a school can persuade or compel a student to participate in a religious exercise. That is being done here, and it is forbidden by the Establishment Clause of the First Amendment.

For the reasons we have stated, the judgment of the Court of Appeals is affirmed.

Scalia, Justice (joined by Rehnquist, White, and Thomas) dissenting, expressed the view that (1) the establishment of religion clause should not have been interpreted so as to invalidate a long-standing American tradition of nonsectarian prayer at public school graduations, (2) graduation invocations and benedictions involve no psychological coercion of students to participate in religious exercises, (3) the only coercion that is forbidden by the establishment of religion clause is that which is backed by a threat of penalty, and (4) the middle school principal did not direct or control the content of the prayers in question, and thus there was no pervasive government involvement with religious activity.

CHAPTER 6

CHAPTER OBJECTIVES

After studying this chapter, you should be able to:

1. Describe the state court systems.

2. Describe the federal court system.

3. Apply a cost-benefit analysis for bringing and defending a lawsuit.

4. Explain how a justice is chosen for the U.S. Supreme Court.

5. Explain subject-matter jurisdiction and venue of federal and state courts.

6. Describe in personam jurisdiction of courts.

7. Explain how personal jurisdiction applies to website operators.

8. Compare the Japanese and American legal systems.

9. Explain the use of arbitration.

10. Explain the use of other nonjudicial methods of alternative dispute resolution.

Judicial and Alternative Dispute Resolution

I was never ruined but twice; once when I lost a lawsuit, and once when I won one.

VOLTAIRE

Introduction

The two major court systems in the United States are: (1) the federal court system, and (2) the court systems of the 50 states and the District of Columbia. Each of these systems has jurisdiction to hear different types of lawsuits. The process of bringing, maintaining, and defending a lawsuit is called **litigation.** Litigation is a difficult, time-consuming, and costly process that must comply with complex procedural rules. Although it is not required, most parties employ a lawyer to represent them when they are involved in a lawsuit.

Several forms of *nonjudicial* dispute resolution have developed in response to the expense and difficulty of bringing a lawsuit. These methods, collectively called **alternative dispute resolution (ADR),** are being used more and more often to resolve commercial disputes.

Paralegals are especially valuable in providing support to lawyers who are engaged in litigation—that is, representing clients in lawsuits. In this area, paralegals interview clients, prepare documents submitted to courts, conduct legal research, and assist lawyers during trial.

This chapter discusses the various court systems, the jurisdiction of courts to hear and decide cases, the litigation process, and alternative dispute resolution.

U.S. Courts: www.uscourts.gov

STATE COURT SYSTEMS

Each state and the District of Columbia have separate court systems. Most state court systems include the following:

- Limited-jurisdiction trial courts
- General-jurisdiction trial courts
- Intermediate appellate courts
- A supreme court (or highest state court)

Limited-Jurisdiction Trial Court

State **limited-jurisdiction trial courts,** which sometimes are referred to as *inferior trial courts,* hear matters of a specialized or limited nature. Examples of these courts in many states are traffic courts, juvenile courts, justice-of-the-peace courts, probate courts, family law courts, and courts that hear misdemeanor criminal law cases and civil cases involving lawsuits less than a certain dollar amount. Because these courts are trial courts, evidence can be introduced and testimony given. Most limited-jurisdiction courts keep a record of their proceedings. Their decisions usually can be appealed to a general-jurisdiction court or an appellate court.

Many states also have created **small-claims courts** to hear civil cases involving small dollar amounts (e.g., $5,000 or less). Generally, the parties must appear individually and cannot have a lawyer represent them. The decisions of small claims courts are often appealable to general-jurisdiction trial courts or appellate courts.

General-Jurisdiction Trial Court

Every state has a **general-jurisdiction trial court.** These courts often are called **courts of record** because the testimony and evidence at trial are recorded and stored for future reference. These courts hear cases that are not within the jurisdiction of limited-jurisdiction trial courts, such as felonies, civil cases above a certain dollar amount, and so on. Some states divide their general-jurisdiction courts into two divisions, one for criminal cases and another for civil cases. General-jurisdiction trial courts hear evidence and testimony. The decisions handed down by these courts are appealable to an intermediate appellate court or the state supreme court, depending on the circumstances.

Intermediate Appellate Court

In many states, **intermediate appellate courts** (also called appellate courts or *courts of appeal*) hear appeals from trial courts. These courts review the trial court record to determine any errors at trial that would require reversal or modification of the trial court's decision. Thus, the appellate court reviews either pertinent parts or the whole trial court record from the lower court. No

Meet THE COURTHOUSE TEAM

Judge's Secretary

The judge's secretary is the guardian of the gate to the judge, whether this is the physical entrance to the judge's chambers, the telephone, email or mail. Judges' secretaries rarely spend time in the courtroom. Their province is the judge's office or, as it is called, the judge's chambers. Many judges refer to their secretary as the "Boss." Judges' secretaries keep the calendar and monitor phone calls and requests for the judge's time. A good relationship with the judge's secretary can be the secret to "just a moment with the judge." Although not every act of kindness or act of politeness is relayed to the judge, *every* act of rudeness, belligerence, or hostility *will* be reported, and judges have long memories—almost as long as judges' secretaries!

new evidence or testimony is permitted. The parties usually file legal briefs with the appellate court stating the law and facts that support their positions. Appellate courts usually grant a short oral hearing to the parties. Appellate court decisions are appealable to the state's highest court. In less populated states that do not have an intermediate appellate court, trial court decisions can be appealed directly to the state's highest court.

Highest State Court

Each state has a highest court in its court system. Most states call this highest court the *supreme court*. The function of a state supreme court is to hear appeals from intermediate state courts and certain trial courts. The highest court hears no new evidence or testimony. The parties usually submit pertinent parts of or the entire lower court record for review. The parties also submit legal briefs to the court and usually are granted a brief oral hearing. Decisions of state supreme courts are final, unless a question of law is involved that is appealable to the U.S. Supreme Court. Exhibit 6.1 depicts a typical state court system.

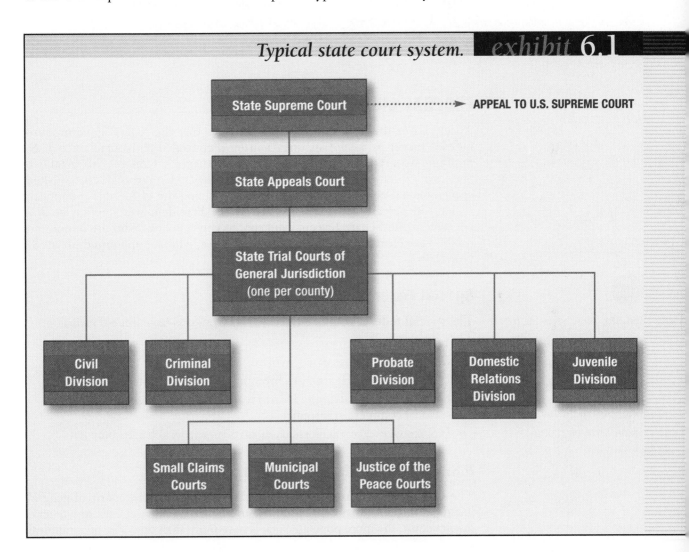

Typical state court system.   exhibit 6.1

Specialized Courts Hear Commercial Disputes

In most states, the same judges who hear and decide criminal, landlord–tenant, matrimonial, medical malpractice, and other nonbusiness-related cases also hear most business and commercial disputes. The one major exception to this standard has been the state of Delaware, where a special Chancery Court hears and decides business litigation. This special court, which deals mainly with cases involving corporate government disputes, has earned a reputation for its expertise in handling and deciding corporate matters. Perhaps the existence of this special court and a corporation code that tends to favor corporate management are the primary reasons that more than 60 percent of the corporations listed on the New York Stock Exchange are incorporated in Delaware.

New York is one state that is following Delaware's lead in this area. New York has designated four courts within its general court system to hear commercial disputes. These courts, which began operating in 1993, hear contract, sales, insurance, unfair competition, libel and slander, shareholder, business-related tort, and other commercial cases. Other states are expected to establish courts that specialize in commercial matters in the near future.

Businesses tend to favor special commercial courts because the judges presiding over them are expected to have the expertise to handle complex commercial lawsuits. Also, the courts are expected to be more efficient in deciding business-related cases, thereby saving time and money for the parties.

FEDERAL COURT SYSTEM

Article III of the U.S. Constitution provides that the federal government's judicial power is vested in one "supreme court." This court is the U.S. Supreme Court. The Constitution also authorizes Congress to establish "inferior" federal courts. Pursuant to this power, Congress has established special federal courts, the U.S. district courts, and the U.S. courts of appeal. Federal judges are appointed for life by the President with the advice and consent of the Senate (except bankruptcy court judges, who are appointed for 14-year terms, and U.S. Magistrate Judges, who are appointed for an 8-year term).

U.S. Tax Court: www.ustax
court.gov/ustcweb.htm

U.S. Court of Federal Claims:
www.uscfc.uscourts.gov/

U.S. Court of International
Trade: www.uscit.gov/

Special Federal Courts

The **special federal courts** established by Congress have limited jurisdiction. They include:

- *U.S. tax court:* Hears cases involving federal tax laws
- *U.S. claims court:* Hears cases brought against the United States
- *U.S. Court of International Trade:* Hears cases involving tariffs and international commercial disputes
- *U.S. bankruptcy court:* Hears cases involving federal bankruptcy laws

U.S. District Courts

The **U.S. district courts** are the federal court system's trial courts of general jurisdiction. The District of Columbia and each state have at least one federal district court; the more populated states have more than one. The geographical area that each court serves is referred to as a *district*. There are presently 96 federal district courts. The federal district courts are empowered to impanel juries, receive evidence, hear testimony, and decide cases. Most federal cases originate in federal district courts.

U.S. Courts Of Appeals

The **U.S. courts of appeals** are the federal court system's intermediate appellate courts. The federal court system has 13 circuits. **Circuit** refers to the geographical area served by a court. Eleven are designated by a number, such as the "First Circuit," "Second Circuit," and so on. The Twelfth Circuit court is located in Washington, D.C., and is called the District of Columbia Circuit.

As appellate courts, these circuit courts hear appeals from the district courts located in their circuit, as well as from certain special courts and federal administrative agencies. The courts review the record of the lower court or administrative agency proceedings to determine if any error would warrant reversal or modification of the lower court decision. No new evidence or testimony is heard. The parties file legal briefs with the court and are given a short oral hearing. Appeals usually are heard by a three-judge panel. After the panel renders a decision, a petitioner can request a review *en banc* by the full court.

The Thirteenth Circuit court of appeals was created by Congress in 1982. Called the **Court of Appeals for the Federal Circuit** and located in Washington, D.C., this court has special appellate jurisdiction to review the decisions of the Court of Federal Claims, the Patent and Trademark Office, and the Court of International Trade. This court of appeals was created to provide uniformity in the application of federal law in certain areas, particularly patent law.

The map in Exhibit 6.2 shows the 13 federal circuit courts of appeals.

U.S. Supreme Court

The highest court in the land is the Supreme Court of the United States, located in Washington, D.C. This court is composed of nine justices who are nominated by the President and confirmed by the Senate. The President appoints one justice as **chief justice,** responsible for the administration of the Supreme Court. The other eight justices are *associate justices*.

The Supreme Court, which is an appellate court, hears appeals from federal circuit courts of appeals and, under certain circumstances, from federal district courts, special federal courts, and the highest state courts. The Supreme Court hears no evidence or testimony. As with other appellate courts, the lower court record is reviewed to determine whether an error has been committed that warrants a reversal or modification of the decision. Legal briefs are

THE COURTHOUSE TEAM

U.S. Magistrate Judge

Magistrate judges are appointed by the district court to serve for an 8-year term. Their duties fall into four general categories: (1) conducting most of the initial proceedings in criminal cases; (2) trying certain criminal misdemeanor cases; (3) trying civil cases with the consent of a party; and (4) conducting a wide variety of other proceedings referred to them by district judges.

U.S. Court for the Federal Circuit: www.fedcir.gov/

THE COURTHOUSE TEAM

Courtroom Deputy Clerk

In some courts, such as the U.S. District Court for the Eastern District of Pennsylvania, each judge is assigned a courtroom deputy clerk to act as liaison between judge and counsel. The courtroom deputy clerk schedules dates and times for hearings on motions, pretrial hearings, and trials, and confers with attorneys on any special trial procedures.

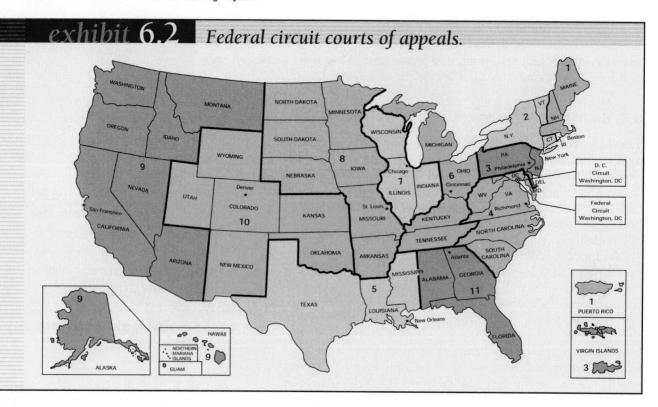

exhibit **6.2** *Federal circuit courts of appeals.*

Meet

THE COURTHOUSE TEAM

U.S. Supreme Court Clerks

Each of the nine Supreme Court justices has three law clerks—recent law school graduates usually chosen from the elite law schools across the country—who assist them. The justices rarely read the appellate petitions but instead delegate this task to their law clerks. The clerks then write a short memorandum discussing the key issues raised by the appeal and recommend to the justices whether they should grant or deny a review.

U.S. Supreme Court:
www.supremecourtus.gov

filed, and the parties are granted a brief oral hearing. The Supreme Court's decision is final.

Exhibit 6.3 illustrates the federal court system.

The U.S. Constitution gives Congress the authority to establish rules for the appellate review of cases by the Supreme Court, except in the rare case where mandatory review is required. Congress has given the Supreme Court discretion to decide what cases it will hear.

A petitioner must file a **petition for certiorari** asking the Supreme Court to hear the case. If the Court decides to review a case, it will issue a **writ of certiorari.** Because the Court issues only about 150 to 200 opinions each year, writs usually are granted only in cases involving constitutional and other important issues.

Each justice of the Supreme Court, including the chief justice, has an equal vote. The Supreme Court can issue the following types of decisions:

- *Unanimous decision.* If all of the justices voting agree as to the outcome and reasoning used to decide the case, it is a unanimous opinion. Unanimous decisions are precedent for later cases.

- *Majority decision.* If a majority of the justices agree to the outcome and reasoning used to decide the case, it is a majority opinion. Majority decisions are precedent for later cases.

- *Plurality decision.* If a majority of the justices agree to the outcome of the case, but not to the reasoning for reaching the outcome, it is a plurality opinion. A plurality decision settles the case but is not precedent for later cases.

- *Tie decision.* Sometimes the Supreme Court sits without all nine justices being present, because of illness or conflict of interest, or because a justice has not been confirmed to fill a vacant seat on the court. In the case of a tie vote, the lower court decision is affirmed. These votes are not precedent for later cases.

A justice who agrees with the outcome of a case but not the reason proffered by other justices can issue a **concurring opinion** setting forth his or her reasons for deciding the case. A justice who does not agree with a decision can file a **dissenting opinion** that sets forth the reasons for his or her dissent.

U.S. Supreme Court building, Washington D.C.

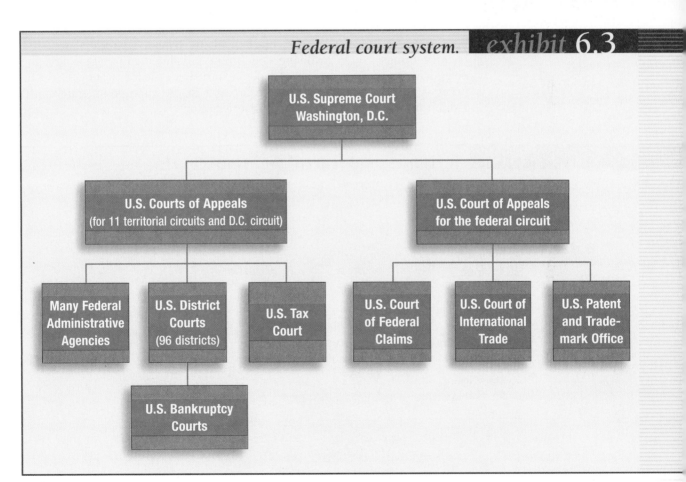

Federal court system.   exhibit 6.3

JURISDICTION OF FEDERAL AND STATE COURTS

Article III, Section 2, of the U.S. Constitution sets forth the jurisdiction of federal courts. Federal courts have *limited jurisdiction* to hear cases involving:

- **Federal questions:** Cases arising under the U.S. Constitution, treaties, and federal statutes and regulations. There is no dollar-amount limit on federal question cases that can be brought in federal court.
- **Diversity of citizenship:** Cases between (a) citizens of different states, (b) a citizen of a state and a citizen or subject of a foreign country, and (c) a citizen of a state and a foreign country where the foreign country is the plaintiff. A corporation is considered to be a citizen of the state in which it is incorporated and in which it has its principal place of business. The reason for providing diversity of citizenship jurisdiction was to prevent state court bias against nonresidents. The federal court must apply the appropriate state's law in deciding the case. The dollar amount of the controversy must exceed $75,000. If this requirement is not met, the action must be brought in the appropriate state court.

Federal courts have *exclusive jurisdiction* to hear cases involving federal crimes, antitrust, bankruptcy, patent and copyright cases, suits against the United States, and most admiralty cases. State courts cannot hear these cases.

State and federal courts have *concurrent jurisdiction* to hear cases involving diversity of citizenship and federal questions over which federal courts do not have exclusive jurisdiction (e.g., cases involving federal securities laws). If a plaintiff brings a case involving concurrent jurisdiction in state court, the defendant can remove the case to federal court. If a case does not qualify to be brought in federal court, it must be brought in the appropriate state court. Exhibit 6.4 illustrates the overlapping jurisdiction.

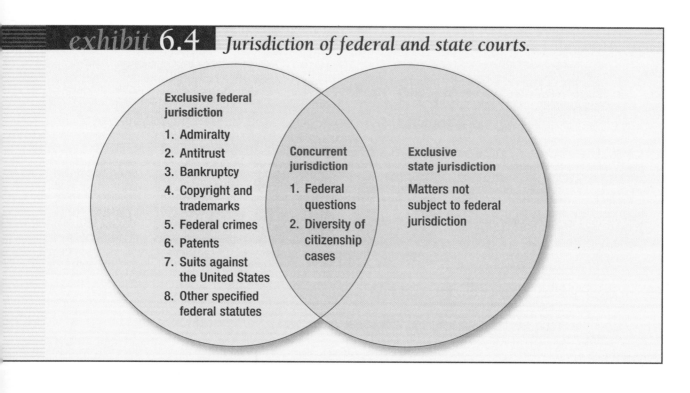

exhibit 6.4   *Jurisdiction of federal and state courts.*

Exclusive federal jurisdiction

1. Admiralty
2. Antitrust
3. Bankruptcy
4. Copyright and trademarks
5. Federal crimes
6. Patents
7. Suits against the United States
8. Other specified federal statutes

Concurrent jurisdiction

1. Federal questions
2. Diversity of citizenship cases

Exclusive state jurisdiction

Matters not subject to federal jurisdiction

Not every court has the authority to hear all types of cases. First, to bring a lawsuit in a court the plaintiff must have *standing to sue.* In addition, the court must have *jurisdiction* to hear the case, and the case must be brought in the proper *venue.*

Standing to Sue

To bring a lawsuit, a plaintiff must have **standing to sue.** The plaintiff must have some stake in the outcome of the lawsuit.

Consider this example: Linda's friend Jon is injured in an accident caused by Emily. Jon refuses to sue. Linda cannot sue Emily on Jon's behalf because she does not have an interest in the result of the case.

Courts hear and decide actual disputes involving specific controversies. Hypothetical questions will not be heard and trivial lawsuits will be dismissed.

The Franklin County Courthouse in Framington, Maine.

Types of Jurisdiction

A court must have **jurisdiction** to hear and decide a case. There are two types of jurisdiction: (1) subject-matter jurisdiction and (2) in personam, in rem, or quasi in rem jurisdiction.

1. *Subject-matter jurisdiction.* Some courts have only limited jurisdiction. To hear and decide a case, a court must have **subject-matter jurisdiction** over the type of case. For example, federal courts have jurisdiction to hear only certain types of cases (discussed later in this chapter) and certain state courts, such as probate courts and small-claims courts, can hear only designated types of cases. If a court does not have subject-matter jurisdiction, it cannot hear the case.

2. *In personam, in rem, and quasi in rem jurisdictions.* Jurisdiction over the person is called **in personam jurisdiction,** or **personal jurisdiction.** By filing a lawsuit with a court, a plaintiff gives the court in personam jurisdiction over himself or herself. The court must also have in personam jurisdiction over the **defendant,** which usually is obtained by having that person served a summons within the territorial boundaries of the state (i.e., **service of process**).

    Service of process usually is accomplished by personally serving the summons and complaint on the defendant. If this is not possible, alternative forms of notice, such as mailing the summons or publishing a notice in a newspaper, may be permitted. A corporation is subject to personal jurisdiction in the state in which it is incorporated, has its principal office, and is doing business. A party who disputes the jurisdiction of a court can make a *special appearance* in that court to argue against the imposition of jurisdiction. Service of process is not permitted during such an appearance.

    A court may have jurisdiction to hear and decide a case because it has jurisdiction over the property of the lawsuit. This is called **in rem jurisdiction** ("jurisdiction over the thing"). For example, a state court would have jurisdiction to hear a dispute over the ownership of a piece of real estate located within the state. This is so even if one or more of the disputing parties lives in another state or states.

Sometimes a plaintiff who obtains a judgment against a defendant in one state will try to collect the judgment by attaching property of the defendant that is located in another state. This is permitted under **quasi in rem jurisdiction,** or **attachment jurisdiction.**

Long-Arm Statutes

In most states, a state court can obtain jurisdiction over persons and businesses located in another state or country through the state's **long-arm statute.** These statutes extend a state's jurisdiction to nonresidents who were not served a summons within the state. The nonresident must have had some *minimum contact* with the state [*International Shoe Co. v. Washington,* 326 U.S. 310, 66 S.Ct. 154, 90 L.Ed. 95 (1945)]. In addition, maintenance of the suit must uphold the traditional notions of fair play and substantial justice.

The exercise of long-arm jurisdiction is generally permitted over nonresidents who have (1) committed torts within the state (e.g., caused an automobile accident in the state), (2) entered into a contract either in the state or that affects the state (and allegedly breached the contract), or (3) transacted other business in the state that allegedly caused injury to another person.

Parties to a contract may include a **forum-selection clause** that designates a certain court to hear any dispute concerning nonperformance of the contract. In the case discussed next, under "Venue," the U.S. Supreme Court upheld a forum-selection clause in a contract.

Venue

Venue requires lawsuits to be heard by the court with jurisdiction nearest the location in which the incident occurred or where the parties reside. For example, Harry, a Georgia resident, commits a felony crime in Los Angeles County, California. The California Superior Court, located in Los Angeles, is the proper venue because the crime was committed there, the witnesses are probably from the area, and so on.

Occasionally, pretrial publicity may prejudice jurors located in the proper venue. In these cases, a *change of venue* may be requested so that a more impartial jury can be found. The courts generally frown upon *forum shopping* (i.e., looking for a favorable court without a valid reason).

SIDEBAR

ADR

Litigation is expensive and time-consuming. Businesses should consider alternative dispute resolution (ADR) to solve their disputes.

ALTERNATIVE DISPUTE RESOLUTION

Use of the court system to resolve business and other disputes can take years and cost thousands, if not millions, of dollars in legal fees and expenses. In commercial litigation, the normal business operations of the parties are often disrupted. To avoid or lessen these problems, businesses are increasingly turning to methods of alternative dispute resolution (ADR) and other aids to resolving disputes. The most common form of ADR is *arbitration*. Other forms of ADR are *mediation, conciliation, minitrial, fact-finding*, and a *judicial referee*.

Carnival Cruise Lines, Inc. v. Shute

499 U.S. 585, 111 S.Ct. 1522, 113 L.Ed.2d 622 (1991)   United States Supreme Court

FACTS

Mr. and Mrs. Shute, residents of the state of Washington, purchased passage for a seven-day cruise on the *Tropicale*, a cruise ship operated by the Carnival Cruise Lines, Inc. (Carnival). They paid the fare to the travel agent, who forwarded the payment to Carnival's headquarters in Miami, Florida. Carnival prepared the tickets and sent them to the Shutes. Each ticket consisted of five pages, including contract terms. The ticket contained a forum-selection clause that designated the state of Florida as the forum for any lawsuits arising under or in connection with the ticket and cruise. The Shutes boarded the *Tropicale* in Los Angeles, which set sail for Puerto Vallarta, Mexico. While the ship was on its return voyage and in international waters off the Mexican coast, Mrs. Shute was injured when she slipped on a deck mat during a guided tour of the ship's galley. Upon return to Washington, she filed a negligence lawsuit against Carnival in U.S. district court in Washington seeking damages. Carnival filed a motion for summary judgment contending that the suit could be brought only in a court located in the state of Florida. The district court granted Carnival's motion. The court of appeals reversed, holding that Mrs. Shute could sue Carnival in Washington. Carnival appealed to the U.S. Supreme Court.

ISSUE

Is the forum-selection clause in Carnival Cruise Line's ticket enforceable?

IN THE LANGUAGE OF THE COURT

Blackmun, Justice.

As an initial matter, we do not adopt the court of appeals' determination that a nonnegotiated forum-selection clause in a form ticket contract is never enforceable simply because it is not the subject of bargaining. Including a reasonable forum clause in form contract of this kind may well be permissible for several reasons: First, a cruise line has a special interest in limiting the fora in which it potentially could be subject to suit. Because a cruise ship typically carries passengers from many locales, it is not unlikely that a mishap on a cruise could subject the cruise line to litigation in several different fora.

Additionally, a clause establishing the forum for dispute resolution has the salutary effect of dispelling any confusion where suits arising from the contract must be brought and defended, sparing litigants the time and expense of pretrial motions to determine the correct forum, and conserving judicial resources that otherwise would be devoted to deciding these motions. Finally, it stands to reason that passengers who purchase tickets containing a forum clause like that at issue in this case benefit in the form of reduced fares reflecting the savings that the cruise line enjoys by limiting the fora in which it may be sued.

DECISION AND REMEDY

The forum-selection clause in Carnival's ticket is fair and reasonable and therefore enforceable against Mrs. Shute. If she wishes to sue Carnival, she must do so in a court in the state of Florida, not in a court in the state of Washington. The U.S. Supreme Court reversed the decision of the court of appeals.

Questions

1. Should forum-selection clauses be enforced? Why or why not?

2. Did Carnival Cruise Lines act ethically by placing the forum-selection clause in their tickets?

3. Do forum-selection clauses serve any legitimate business purpose? Explain.

Obtaining personal jurisdiction over a defendant located in another state has always been a difficult issue for the courts. States have enacted long-arm statutes that permit the courts located in one state to reach out and make people in another state come to court and defend themselves. To make sure this is not overly burdensome, the U.S. Supreme Court has held that out-of-state defendants must have had certain "minimum contacts" with the state before they are made to answer to a lawsuit there [*International Shoe Co. v. Washington*, 326 U.S. 310, 66 S.Ct. 154 (1945)].

Today, with the advent of the Internet and the ability of persons and businesses to reach millions of people in other states electronically, the application of the *International Shoe* minimum-contacts standard is even more difficult.

Several courts have decided cases involving the reach of a state's long-arm statute to obtain jurisdiction over someone in another state because of his or her Internet activities. In one case, Zippo Manufacturing Company (Zippo) sued Zippo Dot Com, Inc. (Dot Com) in federal district court in Pennsylvania. Zippo manufactures its well-known line of Zippo tobacco lighters in Bradford, Pennsylvania, and sells them worldwide. Dot Com, a California corporation with its principal place of business and its servers located in Sunnyvale, California, operates an Internet website that transmits information and sexually explicit material to its subscribers. Of Dot Com's 140,000 paying subscribers worldwide, 3,000 are located in Pennsylvania.

Zippo sued Dot Com in federal district court in Pennsylvania for trademark infringement. Dot Com alleged that it was not subject to personal jurisdiction in Pennsylvania. The district court applied the *International Shoe* "minimum-contacts" standard and held that Dot Com was subject to personal jurisdiction under the Pennsylvania long-arm statute and ordered Dot Com to defend itself there [*Zippo Manufacturing Company v. Zippo Dot Com, Inc.,* 952 F.Supp. 1119 (W.D.Pa. 1997)].

In another case, the court held that maintaining a passive website that merely provides advertising and other information is not sufficient to draw the website operator into another state's courts. The case involved Circus Circus Hotel (Circus Circus), a hotel and casino located in Las Vegas, Nevada, which maintains an Internet website advertising its services.

Janice and Robert Decker, two New Jersey residents, brought a lawsuit against Circus Circus in federal district court in New Jersey for alleged personal injuries suffered at the Las Vegas hotel. On Circus Circus's motion, the district court dismissed the action, finding that Circus Circus's passive website did not subject it to personal jurisdiction in New Jersey even though its advertisements were seen by the Deckers in New Jersey. The court held that mere Internet advertising, without selling products or services over the Internet, does not meet *International Shoe's* minimum-contacts standard necessary to haul a defendant into court [*Decker v. Circus Circus Hotel,* 49 F.Supp.2d 743 (D.N.J. 1999)].

Arbitration

National Mediation Board:
www.nmb.gov

American Arbitration
Association: www.adr.org

In **arbitration,** the parties choose an impartial third party to hear and decide the dispute. This neutral party is called the *arbitrator.* Arbitrators usually are selected from members of the American Arbitration Association (AAA) or another arbitration association. Labor union agreements, franchise agreements, leases, and other commercial contracts often contain arbitration clauses that require disputes arising out of the contract to be submitted to arbitration. If there is no arbitration clause, the parties can enter into a *submission agreement,* whereby they agree to submit a dispute to arbitration after the dispute arises.

Federal Arbitration Act

The Federal Arbitration Act (FAA) was originally enacted in 1925 to reverse the longstanding judicial hostility to arbitration agreements that had existed as English common law and had been adopted by American courts. The Act provides that arbitration agreements involving commerce are valid, irrevocable, and enforceable contracts, unless some grounds exist at law or equity (e.g., fraud, duress) to revoke them. The FAA permits one party to obtain a court order to compel arbitration if the other party has failed, neglected, or refused to comply with an arbitration agreement.

In *Gilmer v. Interstate/Johnson Lane Corporation,* [S.Ct. 1647 (1991)], the Supreme Court upheld an arbitration clause in an employment contract. In that case, a 62-year-old employee who was dismissed from his job sued his employer for alleged age discrimination in violation of the federal Age Discrimination in Employment Act (ADEA).

The employer countered with a motion to compel arbitration. The Supreme Court upheld the motion and stated, "By agreeing to arbitrate a statutory claim, a party does not forgo the substantive rights afforded by the statute, it only submits to their resolution in an arbitral, rather than judicial, forum."

Critics contend that this gives the advantage to employers. Employers argue that arbitration is the only way to combat skyrocketing jury verdicts.

Evidence and testimony are presented to the arbitrator at a hearing held for this purpose. Less formal evidentiary rules usually are applied in arbitration hearings than at court. After the hearing, the arbitrator reaches a decision and enters an *award.* The parties often agree in advance to be bound by the arbitrator's decision and award. If the parties have not so agreed, the arbitrator's award can be appealed to court. The court gives great deference to the arbitrator's decision.

Congress enacted the Federal Arbitration Act to promote the arbitration of disputes [9 U.S.C. §§ 1 et. seq.]. About half of the states have adopted the Uniform Arbitration Act, which promotes the arbitration of disputes at the state level. Many federal and state courts have instituted programs to refer legal disputes to arbitration or another form of alternative dispute resolution.

Mediation and Conciliation

In **mediation,** the parties choose a neutral third party to act as the *mediator* of the dispute. Unlike an arbitrator, a mediator does not make a decision or award. Instead, the mediator acts as a conveyor of information between the parties and assists them in trying to reach a settlement of the dispute. A mediator often meets separately with each of the parties. If the mediator is successful, a settlement agreement is reached. If not, the case proceeds to trial. In a **conciliation,** the parties choose an interested third party, the *conciliator,* to act as the mediator.

Arbitrators and Mediators

SIDEBAR

Arbitrators usually are selected by the court, from a pool of attorneys admitted to the appointing court who have been in practice a minimum period of time and/ or have taken a qualifying course for arbitrators. They usually receive a minimum payment per case, such as $100 in some jurisdictions, or a daily rate of, say, $150–$300 per day regardless of the number of cases heard. Mediators are chosen in the same manner as arbitrators but usually serve without pay as a pro bono service and must be certified as a mediator.

Businesses often complain that there are too many lawyers and too much litigation in the United States. Currently there are more than 800,000 lawyers and more than 20 million lawsuits per year in this country. In contrast, Japan, a country with about half the population of the United States, has only 15,000 lawyers and little litigation. Why the difference?

Much of the difference is cultural: Japan nurtures the attitude of avoiding confrontation. Litigious persons in Japan are looked down upon. Thus, companies rarely do battle in court. Instead, they opt for private arbitration of most of their disputes.

Other differences are built into the legal system itself. For example, there is only one place to go to become a *bengoshi,* or lawyer, in Japan—the government-operated National Institute for Legal Training. Only 2 percent of 35,000 applicants are accepted annually, and only 400 new *bengoshi* are admitted to Japan's exclusive legal club per year.

The Japanese legal system has other obstacles, too. For example, no class actions or contingency-fee arrangements are allowed. Plaintiffs must pay their lawyers a front fee of up to 8 percent of the damages sought, plus a nonrefundable filing fee to the court of one-half of 1 percent of the damages. To make matters even more difficult, no discovery is permitted. Thus, plaintiffs are denied access to an opponent's potential evidence before trial. And, even if the plaintiff wins the lawsuit, damage awards are low.

Some experts argue that Japan has more legal practitioners than the statistics reveal. For example, approximately 5,000 non-*bengoshi* patent specialists perform services similar to U.S. patent attorneys. Another 50,000 licensed tax practitioners offer services similar to U.S. tax attorneys. Many non-*bengoshi* legal experts handle tasks such as contract negotiation and drafting. In addition, sales personnel and front-line managers often act as problem-solvers.

The Japanese bias against courtroom solutions remains strong. The current system is designed to save time and money and to preserve long-term relationships. The belief that disputes can be solved amicably without litigation is a concept that U.S. businesses are starting to embrace.

Minitrial

A *minitrial* is a session, usually lasting a day or less, in which the lawyers for each side present their cases to representatives of each party who have authority to settle the dispute. In many cases, the parties hire a neutral person (e.g., a retired judge) to preside over the minitrial. Following the presentations, the parties meet to try to negotiate a settlement.

Fact-Finding

Fact-finding is a process whereby the parties hire a neutral person to investigate the dispute. The *fact-finder* reports his or her findings to the adversaries and may recommend a basis for settlement.

Judicial Referee

If the parties agree, the court may appoint a *judicial referee* to conduct a private trial and render a judgment. Referees, who often are retired judges, have most of the powers of a trial judge, and their decisions stand as a judgment of the court. The parties usually reserve their right to appeal.

LEGAL TERMINOLOGY

Alternative dispute resolution (ADR)

Arbitration

Briefs

Chief justice

Circuits

Conciliation

Concurring opinion

Court of Appeals for the Federal Circuit

Court of record

Defendant

Dissenting opinion

Diversity of citizenship

Federal question

Forum-selection clause

General-jurisdiction trial court

In personam jurisdiction (personal jurisdiction)

In rem jurisdiction

Intermediate appellate courts (courts of appeal)

Jurisdiction

Limited-jurisdiction trial courts

Litigation

Long-arm statute

Mediation

Petition for certiorari

Quasi in rem jurisdiction (attachment jurisdiction)

Service of process

Small-claims courts

Special federal courts

Standing to sue

Subject-matter jurisdiction

U.S. courts of appeal

U.S. district courts

Venue

Writ of certiorari

Summary

State Court Systems

Limited-Jurisdiction Trial Court	State court that hears matters of a specialized or limited nature (e.g., misdemeanor criminal matters, traffic tickets, civil matters under a certain dollar amount). Many states have created small claims courts that hear small-dollar-amount civil cases (e.g., under $3,000) where the parties cannot be represented by lawyers.
General-Jurisdiction Trial Court	State court that hears cases of a general nature that are not within the jurisdiction of limited-jurisdiction trial courts.
Intermediate Appellate Court	State court that hears appeals from state trial courts. The appellate court reviews the trial court record in making its decision; no new evidence is introduced at this level.
Highest State Court	Each state has a highest court in its court system. This court hears appeals from appellate courts, and where appropriate, trial courts. This court reviews the record in making its decision; no new evidence is introduced at this level. Most states call this court the supreme court.

Federal Court System

Federal Court System	1. *Special federal courts:* Federal courts that have specialized or limited jurisdiction. They include:
	
	  a. *U.S. tax court:* Hears cases involving federal tax laws.
	  b. *U.S. claims court:* Hears cases brought against the United States.
	  c. *U.S. Court of International Trade:* Hears cases involving tariffs and international commercial disputes.
	  d. *U.S. bankruptcy courts:* Hear cases involving federal bankruptcy law.
	
	2. *U.S. district courts:* Federal trial courts of general jurisdiction that hear cases not within the jurisdiction of specialized courts. There is at least one U.S. district court per state; more populated states have several district courts. The area served by one of these courts is called a *district*.
	
	3. *U.S. courts of appeals:* Intermediate federal appellate courts that hear appeals from district courts located in their circuit, and in certain instances from special federal courts and federal administrative agencies. There are 12 geographical *circuits* in this country. Eleven serve areas that are comprised of several states, while another is located in Washington, D.C. A thirteenth circuit court—the *Court of Appeals for the Federal Circuit,* is located in Washington, D.C., and reviews patent, trademark, and international trade cases.
	
	(continued)

Federal Court System, *continued*	4. *U.S. Supreme Court:* Highest court of the federal court system. It hears appeals from the circuit courts and, in some instances, from special courts and U.S. district courts. The Court, located in Washington, D.C., comprises nine justices, one of whom is named chief justice.
Decisions by U.S. Supreme Court	*Petition of certiorari and writ of certiorari:* To have a case heard by the U.S. Supreme Court, a petitioner must file a *petition for certiorari* with the Court. If the Court decides to hear the case, it will issue a *writ of certiorari.*
Voting by the U.S. Supreme Court	1. *Unanimous decision:* All of the justices agree as to the outcome and reasoning used to decide the case; the decision becomes precedent. 2. *Majority decision:* A majority of justices agrees as to the outcome and reasoning used to decide the case; the decision becomes precedent. 3. *Plurality decision:* A majority of the justices agrees to the outcome but not to the reasoning; the decision is not precedent. 4. *Tie decision:* If there is a tie vote, the lower court's decision stands; the decision is not precedent. 5. *Concurring opinion:* A justice who agrees as to the outcome of the case but not the reasoning used by other justices may write a concurring opinion setting forth his or her reasoning. 6. *Dissenting opinion:* A justice who disagrees with the outcome of a case may write a dissenting opinion setting forth his or her reasoning.
Jurisdiction of Federal and State Courts	Federal courts may hear the following cases: 1. *Federal question:* Cases arising under the U.S. Constitution, treaties, and federal statutes and regulations; there is no dollar-amount limit. 2. *Diversity of citizenship:* Cases between (a) citizens of different states and (b) citizens of a state and a citizen or subject of a foreign country; federal courts must apply the appropriate state law in such cases. The controversy must exceed $75,000 for the federal court to hear the case.
Jurisdiction of State Courts	State courts hear some cases that may be heard by federal courts. 1. *Exclusive jurisdiction:* Federal courts have exclusive jurisdiction to hear cases involving federal crimes, antitrust, and bankruptcy; patent and copyright cases; suits against the United States; and most admiralty cases. State courts may not hear these matters. 2. *Concurrent jurisdiction:* State courts have concurrent jurisdiction to hear cases involving diversity of citizenship cases and federal question cases over which the federal courts do not have exclusive jurisdiction. The defendant may have the case removed to federal court. *(continued)*

Standing to Sue	To bring a lawsuit, the plaintiff must have some stake in the outcome of the lawsuit.
Subject-Matter Jurisdiction	The court must have jurisdiction over the subject matter of the lawsuit; each court has limited jurisdiction to hear only certain types of cases.
In Personam Jurisdiction (or Personal Jurisdiction)	The court must have jurisdiction over the parties to a lawsuit. The plaintiff submits to the jurisdiction of the court by filing the lawsuit there. Personal jurisdiction is obtained over the defendant by serving that person *service of process*.
In Rem Jurisdiction	A court may have jurisdiction to hear and decide a case because it has jurisdiction over the property at issue in the lawsuit (e.g., real property located in the state).
Quasi In Rem Jurisdiction (or Attachment Jurisdiction)	A plaintiff who obtains a judgment against a defendant in one state may utilize the court system of another state to attach property of the defendant's located in the second state.
Long-Arm Statutes	Permit a state to obtain personal jurisdiction over an out-of-state defendant as long as the defendant had the requisite minimum contact with the state. The out-of-state defendant may be served process outside the state in which the lawsuit has been brought.
Venue	A case must be heard by the court that has jurisdiction nearest to where the incident at issue occurred or where the parties reside. A *change of venue* will be granted if prejudice would occur because of pretrial publicity or another reason.
Forum-Selection Clause	A clause in a contract that designates the court that will hear any dispute that arises out of the contract.

Alternative Dispute Resolution (ADR)

Description	*Nonjudicial* means of solving legal disputes. ADR usually saves time and money required by litigation.

Types of ADR	1. *Arbitration:* An impartial third party, called the arbitrator, hears and decides the dispute. The arbitrator makes an award. The award is appealable to a court if the parties have not given up this right. Arbitration is designated by the parties pursuant to:
	
	  a. *Arbitration clause:* Agreement contained in a contract stipulating that any dispute arising out of the contract will be arbitrated.
	
	  b. *Submission agreement:* Agreement to submit a dispute to arbitration after the dispute arises.
	
	<div align="right">*(continued)*</div>

Types of ADR, *continued*	2. *Mediation:* A neutral third party, called a *mediator,* assists the parties in trying to reach a settlement of their dispute. The mediator does not make an award.
	3. *Conciliation:* An interested third party, called a *conciliator,* assists the parties in trying to reach a settlement of their dispute. The conciliator does not make an award.
	4. *Minitrial:* A short session in which the lawyers for each side present their case to representatives of each party who have the authority to settle the dispute.
	5. *Fact-finding:* The parties hire a neutral third person, called a *fact-finder,* to investigate the dispute and report his or her findings to the adversaries.
	6. *Judicial referee:* With the consent of the parties, the court appoints a judicial referee (usually a retired judge or lawyer) to conduct a private trial and render a judgment. The judgment stands as the judgment of the court and may be appealed to the appropriate appellate court.

Working the Web

1. The official website for the U.S. Supreme Court is www.supreme courtus.gov/; however, information on the U.S. Supreme Court can also be found at the Cornell University site at www.supct.law.cornell.edu/ supct.

2. Obtain information on the U.S. Courts of Appeals at the Emory University website at www.law.emory.edu.

3. Find information on the U.S. District Courts at www.vls.law.vill.edu/ locator/fedcourt.html.

4. A number of sites offer links to state court information, and many state courts have their own Web pages. Information and links can be found at the Villanova University website at www.vls.law.vill.edu/locator/state court.htm.

5. The American Arbitration Association website, www.adr.org, offers information on alternative dispute resolution, labor relations, employment, commerce, and international disputes. It includes rules, forms, and articles about alternative dispute resolution.

6. Using the Cornell website (see above), click on the gallery of current justices. Read the biography of justice Ginsburg.

7. Using the Emory gateway (see above), find the U.S. Court of Appeals for the circuit in which your state is located. Find a recent decision.

8. Using the Emory gateway, find out if any U.S. District Courts for your state publish opinions on the Internet. List the courts and dates of coverage for each court.

9. Find the home page for courts in your state. Which courts in your state are reporting cases on the Internet? What are the dates of coverage for each court in your state?

10. Using the American Arbitration Association website (see above), click on Customer Service. Find a form for submission of a dispute resolution.

CRITICAL LEGAL THINKING AND WRITING

1. Is the action of a court in not hearing a case because of a lack of case or controversy really a decision by the court or a way of it saving time?

2. How does the Case for Briefing, *Adler v. Duval*, demonstrate the court's recognition of the case or controversy issue?

3. How does the *Adler v. Duval* case contrast with the Chapter 5 case of *Lee v. Weisman?*

4. What if an executive's calendar contains both business and personal information? Is it protected by the Fifth Amendment's privilege against self-incrimination?

5. May email be introduced as evidence to prove a case of sexual harassment?

6. How can a forum-selection clause be used to limit a client's exposure to suit?

7. What factors should be considered in advising a client in which court to bring action when there is concurrent jurisdiction?

8. What are the practical considerations in selecting a forum for trial of a case?

9. What are the advantages and the disadvantages in using the different methods of alternative dispute resolution?

10. Why might someone agree not to appeal a case decided by an arbitrator?

ETHICS: ANALYSIS AND DISCUSSION

1. May a paralegal represent a client before an arbitration panel?

2. Are a paralegal's time records or calendar subject to the attorney–client privilege?

3. May a paralegal sign a pleading?

Unauthorized Practice of Law—Court Appearance

There are few certainties in the area of ethics, for paralegals or in any profession. What qualifies as ethical conduct is in most cases based on state law and court interpretation applied to a set of facts. The citation listed below represents one legal opinion and is provided as a research starting point. Do not assume that the same rule applies in your jurisdiction. For the following:

- *Prepare a written statement based on your state law.*
- *Use your state bar association website as a starting point.*

You have been appointed as a trustee of a client's children's educational trust. You need to petition the court for a release of the funds for non-educational purposes—paying the taxes on the trust income. [*Ziegler v. Harrison Nickel*, 64 Cal. App. 4th 545; 1998 Lexis 500.] May you appear alone as the trustee and represent the trust in the court proceedings? Would a nonlawyer, nonparalegal be permitted to appear?

CASES *for Discussion*

Allison v. ITE Imperial Corp.

729 F.Supp. 45 (S.D. Miss. 1990)

6.1 FACTS

James Clayton Allison, a resident of Mississippi, was employed by the Tru-Amp Corporation as a circuit breaker tester. As part of his employment, Allison was sent to inspect, clean, and test a switch gear located at the South Central Bell Telephone Facility in Brentwood, Tennessee. On August 26, 1988, he attempted to remove a circuit breaker manufactured by ITE Corporation (ITE) from a bank of breakers, when a portion of the breaker fell off. The broken piece fell behind a switching bank and, according to Allison, caused an electrical fire and explosion. Allison was severely burned in the accident. Allison brought suite against ITE in Mississippi state court, claiming more than $50,000 in damages.

ISSUE

Can this suit be removed to federal court?

AMF Inc. v. Brunswick Corp.

621 F.Supp. 456 (E.D.N.Y. 1985)

6.2 FACTS

AMF Incorporated and Brunswick Corporation both manufacture electric and automatic bowling center equipment. In 1983 the two companies became involved in a dispute over whether Brunswick had advertised certain automatic scoring devices in a false and deceptive manner. The two parties settled the dispute by signing an agreement that any future problems between them involving advertising claims would be submitted to the National Advertising Council for arbitration. In March 1985, Brunswick advertised a new product, Armor Plate 3000, a synthetic laminated material used to make bowling lanes. Armor Plate 3000 competed with wooden lanes produced by AMF. Brunswick's advertisements claimed that bowling centers could save up to $500 per lane per year in maintenance and repair costs if they switched to Armor Plate 3000 from wooden lanes. AMF disputed this claim and requested arbitration.

ISSUE

Is the arbitration agreement enforceable?

Calder v. Jones

465 U.S. 783, 104 S.Ct. 1482, 79 L.Ed.2d 804 (1984)

6.3 FACTS

The National Enquirer, Inc., is a Florida corporation with its principal place of business in Florida. It publishes the *National Enquirer*, a national weekly newspaper with a circulation of more than 5 million copies. About 600,000 copies, almost twice the level of the next highest state, are sold in California. On October 9, 1979, the *Enquirer* published an article about Shirley Jones, an entertainer. Jones, a California resident, filed a lawsuit in California state court against the *Enquirer* and its president, a resident of Florida. The suit sought damages for alleged defamation, invasion of privacy, and intentional infliction of emotional distress.

ISSUE

Are the defendants subject to suit in California?

Burnham v. Superior Court of California

495 U.S. 604, 110 S.Ct. 2105, 109 L.Ed.2d 631 (1990)

6.4 FACTS

Dennis and Francis Burnham were married in 1976 in West Virginia. In 1977, the couple moved to New Jersey, where their two children were born. In July

1987, the Burnhams decided to separate. Mrs. Burnham, who intended to move to California, was to have custody of the children. Mr. Burnham agreed to file for divorce on grounds of "irreconcilable differences." In October 1987, Mr. Burnham threatened to file for divorce in New Jersey on grounds of "desertion." After unsuccessfully demanding that Mr. Burnham adhere to the prior agreement, Mrs. Burnham brought suit for divorce in California state court in early January 1988. In late January, Mr. Burnham visited California on a business trip. He then visited his children in the San Francisco Bay area, where his wife resided. He took the older child to San Francisco for the weekend. Upon returning the child to Mrs. Burnham's home, he was served with a California court summons and a copy of Mrs. Burnham's divorce petition. He then returned to New Jersey. Mr. Burnham made a special appearance in the California court and moved to quash the service of process.

ISSUE

Did Mr. Burnham act ethically in trying to quash the service of process? Did Mrs. Burnham act ethically in having Mr. Burnham served on his visit to California? Is the service of process good?

Adler v. Duval County School Board

112 F.3d 1475 (11th Cir. 1997)   United States Court of Appeals, Eleventh Circuit

Read the following case, excerpted from the court of appeals opinion. Review and brief the case. In your brief, answer the following questions.

1. What is the doctrine of mootness?
2. What was the action the plaintiffs complained of?
3. When would the plaintiffs have had to file and have their case heard for the court to rule on their claim?
4. How would bringing the cases as a class action have allowed the court to hear the case under the Case or Controversy requirement?
5. How does this case differ from the case of *Lee v. Weisman* in Chapter 5?

Tjoflat, Circuit Judge.

Appellants are four former high school students in the Duval County, Florida, school system who brought this action under 42 U.S.C. § 1983 (1994), alleging that a Duval County school policy permitting student-initiated prayer at high school graduation ceremonies (the "policy") violated their rights under the First and Fourteenth Amendments.

On June 7, 1993, three of the appellants graduated from Mandarin, one of the schools in the Duval County system. A fourth appellant graduated in June 1994. Because all four appellants have graduated, we find that to the extent they seek declaratory and injunctive relief, their case is moot. The only justiciable controversy in this case is the appellants' claim for money damages. We affirm the district court's grant of summary judgment for the appellees on this claim, but we do so without reviewing the merits of the district court's constitutional analysis. We begin by noting that appellants' claims for declaratory and injunctive relief are moot. All appellants have graduated, and none is threatened with harm from possible prayers in future Duval County graduation ceremonies. . . .

Article III of the Constitution limits the jurisdiction of the federal courts to the consideration of certain "Cases" and "Controversies." . . . The doctrine of mootness is derived from this limitation because an action that is moot cannot be characterized as an active case or controversy. "[A] case is moot when the issues presented are no longer 'live' or the parties lack a legally cognizable interest in the outcome." Any decision on the merits of a moot case would be an impermissible advisory opinion.

To apply the doctrine of mootness to this case, we must distinguish the appellants' claims for equitable relief from their claim for money damages. . . .

Equitable relief is a prospective remedy, intended to prevent future injuries. In contrast, a claim for money damages looks back in time and is intended to redress a past injury. The plaintiff requests money damages to redress injuries caused by the defendant's past conduct and seeks equitable relief to prevent the defendant's future conduct from causing future injury. When the threat of future harm dissipates, the plaintiff's claims for equitable relief become moot because the plaintiff no longer needs protection from future injury. This is precisely what happened in this case.

Appellants argue that, despite their graduation from high school, their claims for declaratory and injunctive relief are not moot because the original injury is "capable of repetition, yet evading review." This exception to the mootness doctrine is narrow. In the absence of a class action, the "capable of repetition, yet evading review" doctrine is limited to the situation where two elements combine: (1) the challenged action [is] in its duration too short to be fully litigated prior to its cessation or expiration, and (2) there is a reasonable expectation that the same complaining party will be subjected to the same action again. This case does not satisfy the second element. Because the complaining students have graduated from high school, there is no reasonable expectation that they will be subjected to the same injury again.

Having disposed of the appellants' claims for equitable relief, we are left with their claim for money damages, which we now address. Because the appellants' claim for money damages does not depend on any threat of future harm, this claim remains a live controversy. We accordingly turn our focus to the basis for the appellants' claim for damages. The complaint alleges that a "senior class chaplain" delivered a prayer at the June 7,

1993, Mandarin graduation ceremony at which appellants Adler, Jaffa, and Zion graduated. The only past injury for which the appellants could seek redress is being subjected to this prayer at their graduation ceremony. To prove that the appellees caused this injury, the appellants alleged in their complaint that the prayer was "a direct consequence" of the school's policy. In their answer, the appellees admitted that a student said the prayer, but denied that the prayer was a consequence of the policy.

The only issue the appellants raise on appeal is whether the district court erred in holding the policy constitutional. While the constitutionality of the policy may have been central to the now moot issue of whether equitable relief is warranted to prevent the policy from being implemented at future graduations, it does not dispose of the issue of whether the appellants should be awarded money damages for being subjected to the prayer at their graduation. In other words, any claim for damages does not depend on the constitutionality of the policy in the abstract or as applied in other Duval County schools. Even if the policy is unconstitutional, the defendants might not be liable if, for example, they did not implement the policy at the ceremony in question or if the prayer would have been delivered without the policy. On the other hand, if the district court was correct in finding the policy constitutional, defendant Epting, Mandarin's principal, might nonetheless be liable if he implemented the policy in an unconstitutional manner.

The constitutionality of the policy, therefore, has little independent relevance to the appellants' damages claim. Whether they are entitled to damages depends entirely on the circumstances under which the prayer was delivered at their graduation ceremony. In order to prevail, the appellants must have some theory connecting the individual defendants to the prayer. For these reasons, even if we were to find fault with the district court's constitutional analysis of the policy, this conclusion by itself would not answer the question of whether the court erred in granting the appellees summary judgment on the damages claim. The appellants offer no other grounds in their briefs for finding trial court error.

After considering the appellants' briefs and oral argument, we are convinced that they either fail to understand the basis for their damages claim or do not seriously seek damages. They have offered us no connection between the prayer and their damages claim; their briefs offer no indication as to any of the circumstances surrounding the Mandarin graduation prayer. They failed to argue that the prayer was a "direct consequence" of the policy, or any other theory connecting the defendants' actions to the Mandarin prayer. Their briefs do not even include the allegation made in their complaint that a prayer was delivered at Mandarin.

For all these reasons, we hold that they have waived their damages claim on appeal. We therefore affirm the district court's order to the extent it denied the appellants' motion for summary judgment and granted the appellees' motions for summary judgment on the appellants' damages claim. For the foregoing reasons, we *vacate* the district court's order granting the appellees summary judgment on the appellants' claims for declaratory and injunctive relief and *remand* the case with instructions that the district court dismiss those claims. We *affirm* the district court's denial of the appellants' motion for summary judgment and its grant of summary judgment for the appellees on the appellants' damages claim. It is *so ordered.*

UPDATE TO CASE:

After a rehearing en banc the court, upon a majority vote of the judges of the court, issued a subsequent opinion on June 3, 1999, and on March 15, 2000 on further proceeding the Court ruled that the policy on prayer did not violate the Establishment Clause. On June 19, 2000, the Supreme Court rendered a decision in *Santa Fe Independent School District v. Doe*, 530 U.S. 290, which invalidated a Texas school board's policy permitting students to vote on a prayer subject to officials' approval at home football games. The Duval Court proceeded to rehear the case based on the *Santa Fe* decision and ruled again in favor of the Duval School Board because the prayer there was not subject to official approval or input [*Adler v. Duval County Sch. Bd.*, 250 F.3d 1330 (11th Cir. 2001)].

CHAPTER OBJECTIVES

After studying this chapter, you should be able to:

1. Outline the litigation process.

2. Define the term *pleading.*

3. Describe a complaint and summons.

4. Describe an answer and cross-complaint.

5. Explain how depositions are used in discovery.

6. Explain how interrogatories and production of documents are used in discovery.

7. Define a *statute of limitations.*

8. Describe pretrial settlement conferences.

9. List and describe the stages in a trial.

10. Explain how verdicts and judgments are rendered at trial.

Civil Litigation

*The law wherein, as in a magic mirror, we see reflected,
not only our own lives, but the lives of all men that have
been! When I think on this majestic theme, my eyes dazzle.*

OLIVER WENDELL HOLMES, THE LAW, SPEECHES 17 (1913)

Introduction

The bringing, maintaining, and defense of a lawsuit comprise the **litigation process,** or **litigation. Civil litigation** involves legal action to resolve disputes between parties as contrasted with criminal litigation, which is brought by the government against a party accused of violating the law. The parties to the civil litigation may be individuals, businesses, or in some cases, government agencies. The fundamental process is the same, but the court and the procedure may vary.

Many lawyers specialize in civil litigation, in which a plaintiff sues a defendant to recover money damages or other remedy for the alleged harm caused by the defendant to the plaintiff. This may be an automobile accident case, a suit alleging a breach of a contract, a claim of patent infringement, or any of a myriad of other civil wrongs. A paralegal often spends considerable time researching, preparing documents, interviewing clients, and consulting with the attorney on civil litigation matters. This chapter discusses the process of civil litigation in detail.

THE LITIGATION PROCESS

The American litigation process is sometimes called an *adversarial system*. From the point of view of the layperson and some foreigners, it is a derogatory term. But "adversarial system" merely means that both of the litigants present their side of the case before a fact finder in the form of a jury or a judge. Each side tests the other side through questions before a neutral finder of fact who must determine the truth of the allegations made by each side. Also, with limited exception, by statute or court rule, each side typically pays its own cost of litigation, including attorney's fees and court costs irrespective of who wins or loses. In contrast, some foreign jurisdictions provide for the winner to be reimbursed for some of the cost of litigating the claim. Exhibit 7.1 is an example of a litigation timeline.

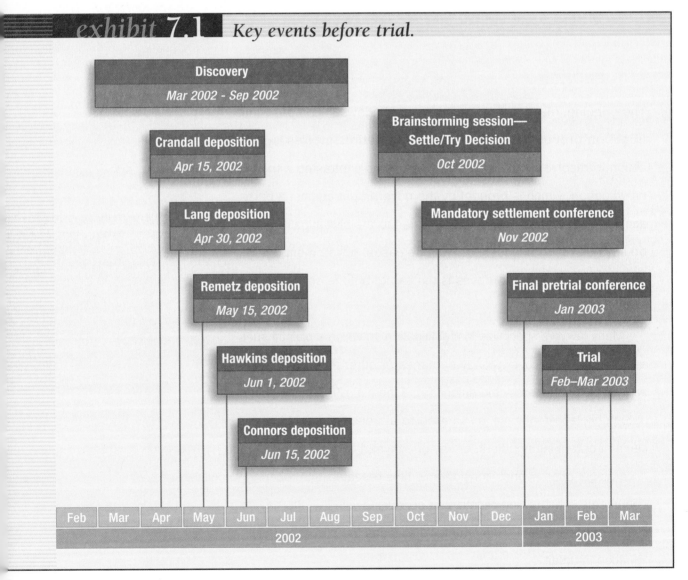

exhibit 7.1 *Key events before trial.*

Prepared with TimeMap, courtesy of CaseSoft, a division of DataQuest.

Cases or Controversies

The first issue is: Is there an actual legal dispute? This is also referred to as *cases or controversies*. Courts will not attempt to answer hypothetical questions. If there is an actual controversy, the party seeking a remedy must be the one who has been wronged or aggrieved by the defendant.

Before a court may hear a case, it must have the authority or the "power" to hear the case. The judicial power of the federal courts comes from the U.S. Constitution. Cases not within the power of the federal courts are within the authority of the state courts, which derive their authority from the individual state constitutions.

Differences Between Civil and Criminal Actions

The most significant difference between a civil action and a criminal action is the burden of proof required. In a criminal case, every accused is presumed innocent and the prosecution must prove the defendant guilty "beyond a reasonable doubt." In civil actions, cases are decided in favor of the party that has the *preponderance of the evidence*, when one party has presented slightly more evidence than the other party. In a civil action, both sides place in turn their evidence on the scales of justice, and one side wins.

The result of a conviction in a criminal action is usually a loss of freedom, which could be incarceration—in jail or under house arrest—or probation, and the possible loss of property in the form of fines, forfeiture, and costs. Civil suits, in contrast, generally result in the payment of damages in the form of money, or a court prohibition, under the penalty of being held in **contempt of court,** against certain forms of action, called an **injunction,** or an order to do something. In a civil action, the parties each pay for their own lawyers. In criminal cases, the government pays the lawyers who prosecute the cases. Persons accused of crimes pay for their own private counsel or, if the accused can't afford to pay for an attorney, the government provides and pays for a lawyer.

Meet THE COURTHOUSE TEAM

Civil Clerk/Prothonotary

The office of the Civil Clerk, Clerk of Courts, or Prothonotary, as it is called in some jurisdictions, is the office in which civil actions are generally filed and the records are maintained. This includes the official court-pleading file and, in many cases, the court docket records including judgments awarded and liens filed.

Civil Lawsuits

Civil lawsuits seek the recovery of dollar damages or the obtaining of other legal or equitable remedy.

SIDEBAR

PRELITIGATION

Many cases that are brought to a lawyer are resolved before institution of suit. This may involve as little effort as a letter from the lawyer advising the other party of a claim that results in settlement. For example, a collection letter from a lawyer may result in the debt being paid. It may involve correspondence between attorneys for the parties and telephone discussions that result in an agreement to settle negotiated between attorneys. A majority of cases in which litigation is commenced by the filing of pleadings are settled before actual trial of the case.

Key events before trial are shown in the timeline of Exhibit 7.1. The pretrial litigation process can be divided into the following major phases:

1. Pleadings
2. Discovery
3. Pretrial motions
4. Settlement conference.

Pleadings

The paperwork that is filed with the court to initiate and respond to a lawsuit is referred to as the **pleadings.** The major pleadings are the complaint, the answer, the cross-complaint, and the reply.

Complaint and Summons

The party who is suing (the **plaintiff**) must file a **complaint,** also called a plaintiff's original petition or summons in some jurisdictions, with the proper court. The content and form of the complaint will vary depending on local court procedural rules. Many courts follow the federal practice of "notice pleading." Other state courts follow the traditional form requiring detailed allegations of the basis for the action. The complaint must name the parties to the lawsuit, allege the ultimate facts and law violated, and state the remedy desired, and the "prayer for relief" to be awarded by the court. The complaint can be as long as necessary, depending on the case's complexity. Exhibit 7.2 is a sample state trial court complaint filed in Pennsylvania. Exhibit 7.3 is a federal pleading. Exhibit 7.4 is a bilingual notice to plead a complaint.

Once a complaint has been filed with the court, the court issues a **summons,** a court order directing the **defendant** to appear in court and answer the complaint. A fundamental requirement is that notice be given to the defendant. A sheriff, another government official, or a private process server may serve the complaint and, where required, the summons on the defendant. In some cases, the defendant may be served by other means, such as by publication when the defendant cannot otherwise be found to be served personally.

Answer

The defendant must file an **answer** to the plaintiff's complaint. The defendant's answer is filed with the court and served on the plaintiff. In the answer, the defendant admits or denies the allegations contained in the plaintiff's complaint. A judgment will be entered against a defendant who admits to all of the allegations in the complaint. The case will proceed if the defendant denies all or some of the allegations.

If the defendant does not answer the complaint, a **default judgment** is entered against him or her. A default judgment establishes the defendant's liability. The plaintiff then has only to prove damages.

In addition to answering the complaint, a defendant's answer can assert *affirmative defenses.* For example, if a complaint alleges that the plaintiff was personally injured by the defendant, the defendant's answer could state that he or she acted in self-defense. Another affirmative defense would be an assertion

IN THE COURT OF COMMON PLEAS OF BUCKS COUNTY, PA.
CIVIL ACTION-LAW

COUNTY LINE FENCE CO., INC. 2051 W. County Line Road Warrington, PA 18976	:	NO.
	:	
V.		ATTORNEY I.D. #12204
WAYNE YARNELL 5707 Dunbar Court Bensalem, PA 19020	:	
	:	

<u>COMPLAINT</u>

1. Plaintiff is County Line Fence Company, Inc., a Pennsylvania corporation duly authorized to do business in Pennsylvania, with a place of business at 2051 W. County Line Road, Warrington, Bucks County, Pennsylvania.

2. Defendant, WAYNE YARNELL, is an adult individual residing at 5707 Dunbar Court, Bensalem, Pennsylvania.

3. On or about April 30, 2002, Defendant entered into a contract with the Plaintiff for a 140 ft. Bufftech fence to be installed on Defendant's property at 5707 Dunbar Court, Bensalem, PA 19020. (See Exhibit "A")

4. Plaintiff properly and adequately installed the fencing per the contract.

5. Defendant agreed to pay a total of $5,300.00 for the fence.

6. Demand was made upon the Defendant by Plaintiff for payment of the amount due for fencing and installation.

7. In spite of the demand for payment, Defendant has failed and refused, and continues to fail and refuse to pay Plaintiff the balance due.

WHEREFORE, Plaintiff demands judgment in the amount of $5,300.00, together with attorneys fees, costs of suit and any additional amounts as the court deems proper.
THOMAS F. GOLDMAN & ASSOCIATES

Thomas F. Goldman

Thomas F. Goldman, Esquire
Attorney for Plaintiff

exhibit 7.3 *Complaint filed in federal court.*

UNITED STATES DISTRICT COURT
FOR THE DISTRICT OF COLUMBIA

UNITED STATES OF AMERICA)	CASE NUMBER 1:01CV01660
)	JUDGE: Ricardo M. Urbina
)	DECK TYPE: General Civil
Plaintiff,)	DATE STAMP: 08/01/2002
)	
v.)	
)	Civ. No.
)	COMPLAINT FOR CIVIL
ENHANCED SERVICES BILLING, INC.)	PENALTIES, PERMANENT
BILLING CONCEPTS, INC.,)	INJUNCTION, CONSUMER
Delaware Corporations,)	REDRESS AND OTHER
both with their principal place of business at)	EQUITABLE RELIEF
411 John Smith Drive, Suite 200)	
San Antonio, Texas 78229,)	
)	
NEW CENTURY EQUITY HOLDINGS CORP.)	
A Delaware Corporation,)	
10101 Reunion Place, Suite 450)	
San Antonio, Texas 78216)	
)	
)	
Defendants.)	

Plaintiff, the United States of America, acting upon notification and authorization to the Attorney General by the Federal Trade Commission ("FTC" or "Commission"), for its complaint alleges that:

1. Plaintiff brings this action under Sections 5(a)(1), 5(m)(1)(A), 9, 13(b), 16(a) and 19 of the Federal Trade Commission Act, 15 U.S.C. §§45(a)(1),

Complaint filed in federal court, continued.   exhibit 7.3

45(m)(1)(A), 49, 53(b), 56(a) and 57b, and the Telephone Disclosure and Dispute Resolution Act of 1992 ("TDDRA"), 15 U.S.C. §§ 5701 *et. seq.*, to obtain injunctive relief and consumer redress for violations of Section 5(a)(1) of the Federal Trade Commission Act, 15 U.S.C. § 45(a)(1), and to obtain monetary civil penalties, consumer redress and injunctive and other relief for Defendants' violations of the Commission's Trade Regulation Rule Pursuant to the Telephone Disclosure and Dispute Resolution Act of 1992 ("900-Number Rule"), 16 C.F.R. Part 308.

JURISDICTION AND VENUE

2. This court has jurisdiction over this matter under 28 U.S.C. §§ 1331, 1337(a), 1345 and 1355 and under 15 U.S.C. §§ 45(m)(1)(A), 49, 53(b), 56(a), 57b, 5721 and 5723. This action arises under 15 U.S.C. § 45(a)(1).

3. Venue in the District of Columbia is proper under 15 U.S.C. § 53(b) and 28 U.S.C. §§ 1391(b) and (c) and 1395(a).

DEFENDANTS

4. Defendant Enhanced Services Billing, Inc. is a Delaware corporation with its principal place of business at 7411 John Smith Drive, Suite 200, San Antonio, Texas 78229. Enhanced Services Billing, Inc. provides or provided billing and collection services for vendors who market Internet Web sites, psychic memberships, voice mail and hospital telephone and television rental, and other enhanced services. Enhanced Services Billing, Inc. was incorporated on March 17, 1994. Enhanced Services Billing, Inc. transacts or has transacted business in this district.

5. Defendant Billing Concepts, Inc. is a Delaware corporation with its principal place of business at 7411 John Smith Drive, Suite 200, San Antonio, Texas 78229. Billing Concepts, Inc. provides or provided billing and collection services for vendors who market . . .

exhibit **7.4**   *Bilingual notice to plead a complaint.*

IN THE COURT OF COMMON PLEAS
OF PHILADELPHIA COUNTY, PENNSYLVANIA
CIVIL ACTION LAW

KATHRYN KELSEY   : NO.

    vs.   : ATTORNEY I.D. NO.

KATHRYN CARROLL   : COMPLAINT IN EQUITY

COMPLAINT – CIVIL ACTION

NOTICE

You have been sued in court. If you wish to defend against the claims set forth in the following pages, you must take action within twenty (20) days after this complaint and notice are served, by entering a written appearance personally or by attorney and filing in writing with the court your defenses or objections to the claims set forth against you. You are warned that if you fail to do so the case may proceed without you and a judgment may be entered against you by the court without further notice for any money claimed in the complaint or for any other claims or relief requested by the plaintiff. You may lose money or property or other rights important to you.

You should take this paper to your lawyer at once. If you do not have a lawyer or cannot afford one, go to or telephone the office set forth below to find out where you can get legal help.

Philadelphia Bar Association
Lawyer Referral and
Information Service
One Reading Center
Philadelphia, Pennsylvania 19107
215-238-1701

AVISO

Le han demandado a usted en la corte. Si usted quiere defenderse de estas demandas expuestas en las paginas siguientes, usted tiene veinte (20) dias de plazo al partir de la fecha de la demanda y la notificacion. Hace falta asentar una compancia escrita o en persona o con un abogado y entregar a la corte en forma escrita sus defensas o sus objeciones a las demandas en contra de su persona. Sea avisado que si usted no se defiende, la corta tomara medidas y puede continuar la demanda en contra suya sin previo aviso o notificacion. Ademas, la corte puede decidir a favor del demandante y requiere que usted cumpla con todas las provisiones de esta demanda. Usted puede perer dinero o sus propiedades u oetros derechos importantes para usted.

Lieva esta demanda a un abogado immediatamente. Si no tiene abogado o si no tiene el dinero suficiente de pagartal servicio, vaya en persona o llame por telefono a la oficina cuya direccion se encuentra escrita abajo para averiguar donde se puede conseguir asistencia legal.

Asociacion de Licenciados de Filadelfia
Servicio de Referencia e
Informacion Legal
One Reading Center
Filadelfia, Pennsylvania 19107
215-238-1701

that the plaintiff's lawsuit is barred because the **statute of limitations** (time within which to bring the lawsuit) has expired. Exhibit 7.5 is a sample answer in state court, and Exhibit 7.6 recaps the pleadings process.

Cross-Complaint and Reply

A defendant who believes that he or she has been injured by the plaintiff can file a **cross-complaint,** or counterpetition as it is called in some jurisdictions, against the plaintiff in addition to an answer. In the cross-complaint, the defendant (now the *cross-complainant*) sues the plaintiff (now the *cross-defendant*) for damages or some other remedy. The original plaintiff must file a **reply** (answer) to the cross-complaint. The reply—which can include affirmative defenses—must be filed with the court and served on the original defendant.

Intervention and Consolidation

If other persons have an interest in a lawsuit, they may step in and become parties to the lawsuit. This is called an **intervention.** For instance, a bank that has made a secured loan on a piece of real estate can intervene in a lawsuit between parties who are litigating ownership of the property.

If several plaintiffs have filed separate lawsuits stemming from the same fact situation against the same defendant, the court can initiate a **consolidation** of the cases into one case if it would not cause undue prejudice to the parties. Suppose, for example, that a commercial airplane crashes, killing and injuring many people. The court could consolidate all of the lawsuits against the defendant airplane company.

Statute of Limitations

For some crimes, such as murder, there is no limitation on the time in which a defendant can be charged. In civil actions, however, the plaintiff must bring suit within a certain period of time after the action that gives rise to the complaint or lose the right to use the courts to enforce the civil right and remedy.

A statute of limitations establishes the period during which a plaintiff must bring a lawsuit against a defendant. If a lawsuit is not filed within this period, the plaintiff loses his or her right to sue. A statute of limitations usually begins to "run" at the time the plaintiff first has the right to sue the defendant (e.g., when the accident happens, or when the breach of contract occurs). Depending on state law, it also may begin to run when the plaintiff knows or should have known of the defendant's wrongful action that gives rise to a cause of action. In the case of minors, the statute may not begin to run—regardless of the time of discovery of the accrual of the cause of action—until the minor reaches the age of majority.

Federal and state governments have established statutes of limitations for each type of lawsuit. Most are from one to four years, depending on the type of lawsuit. For example, a one-year statute of limitations is common for ordinary negligence actions. Thus, if on July 1, 2000, Otis negligently causes an automobile accident in which Cha-Yen is injured, Cha-Yen has until July 1, 2001, to bring a negligence lawsuit against Otis. If she waits longer than that, she loses her right to sue him.

THE COURTHOUSE TEAM

Meet

Sheriff

In most jurisdictions, the sheriff's office performs several tasks related to the administration of court proceedings. In civil cases, the sheriff may be the designated official for serving all complaints and carrying out additional components of the litigation process. In criminal court cases, sheriffs may act as guards and escorts for prisoners and maintain the courthouse holding facility. Increasingly, sheriffs also provide courthouse security for the building and the individual courtrooms.

exhibit **7.5**   *Sample state answer.*

DATZ and GOLDBERG

BY: MARC C. BENDO, ESQUIRE

IDENTIFICATION NO.   80075   ATTORNEY FOR   DEFENDANT

1311 SPRUCE STREET

PHILADELPHIA, PENNSYLVANIA 19107

(215) 545-7960

COUNTY LINE FENCE CO., INC.   *COURT OF COMMON PLEAS*
2051 W. County Line Road
Warrington, PA 18976
                                     BUCKS COUNTY DIVISION
vs.
                                     TERM

WAYNE YARNALL
5707 Dunbar Court
Bensalem, PA 19020   *NO.* 99004879-23-1

ANSWER OF DEFENDANT, WAYNE YARNALL, TO PLAINTIFF'S CIVIL ACTION
WITH NEW MATTER

1. Denied. Plaintiff is without knowledge or information sufficient to form a belief as to the truth or falsity of this
   averment. Accordingly, same is denied with strict proof
   demanded at time of Trial.

2. Admitted. By way of further answer, however, Plaintiff's
   Civil Action has misspelled Defendant's proper name, which is
   Wayne Yarnall.

3. Denied. These allegations constitute conclusions of law to
   which no response is required pursuant to the applicable
   Pennsylvania Rules of Civil Procedure . . .

When litigation ensues, the clients, lawyers, and judges involved in the case usually are buried in paper—pleadings, interrogatories, documents, motions to the court, briefs, and memoranda; the list goes on and on. By the time a case is over, reams of paper are stored in dozens, if not hundreds, of boxes. Further, court appearances, no matter how small the matter, must be made in person. For example, lawyers often wait hours for a 10-minute scheduling or other conference with the judge. Additional time is required to drive to and from court, which in an urban area may amount to hours.

Some forward-thinking judges and lawyers envision a day when the paperwork and hassle are reduced or eliminated in a "virtual courthouse." The technology currently is available for implementing electronic filing—*e-filing*—of pleadings, briefs, and other documents related to a lawsuit. E-filing would include using CD-ROMs for briefs, scanning evidence and documents into a computer for storage and retrieval, and e-mailing correspondence and documents to the court and the opposing counsel. Scheduling and other conferences with the judge or opposing counsel could be held via telephone conferences and email.

Some courts have instituted e-filing already. For example, in the Manhattan bankruptcy court, e-filing is now mandatory. Other courts around the world are doing the same. Companies such as Microsoft and Lexis-Nexis have developed systems to manage e-filings of court documents.

Court personnel in some venues are resisting the "electronic courthouse" because they perceive it as a means of reducing personnel needs and court funding. Some lawyers are resisting e-filing because they have to learn how to deal with new technology and because it might reduce their billable hours when they no longer get paid for shuffling paper or sitting and waiting to appear before a judge. Eventually, though, courts and lawyers will be brought into this new technological age.

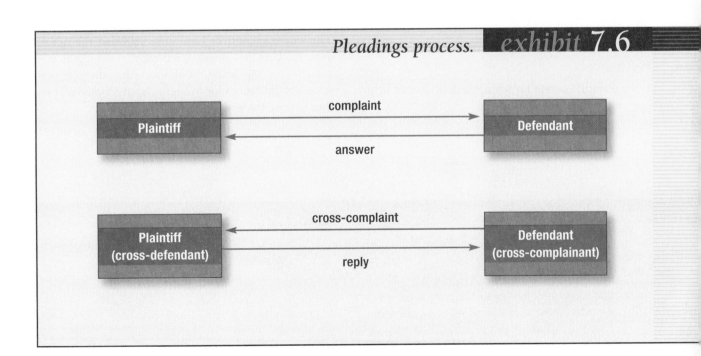

Pleadings process. exhibit 7.6

Norgart v. the Upjohn Company

21 Cal.4th 383, 87 Cal.Rptr.2nd 453 (1999)   Supreme Court of California

FACTS

Kristi Norgart McBride lived with her husband in Santa Rosa, California. Kristi suffered from manic-depressive mental illness (now called bipolar disorder). In this disease, the person cycles between manic (ultrahappy, expansive, extrovert) episodes to depressive episodes. The disease is often treated with prescription drugs. In April 1984, Kristi attempted suicide. A psychiatrist prescribed an antianxiety drug. In May 1985, Kristi attempted suicide again by overdosing on drugs. The doctor prescribed Halcion, a hypnotic drug, and added Darvocet-N, a mild narcotic analgesic. On October 16, 1985, after descending into a severe depression, Kristi committed suicide by overdosing on Halcion and Darvocet-N.

On October 16, 1991, exactly six years after Kristi's death, Leo and Phyllis Norgart, Kristi's parents, filed a lawsuit against the Upjohn Company, the maker of Halcion, for wrongful death based on Upjohn's alleged failure to warn of the unreasonable dangers of taking Halcion. The trial court granted Upjohn's motion for summary judgment based on the fact that the one-year statute of limitations for wrongful death actions had run. The court of appeals reversed, and Upjohn appealed to the Supreme Court of California.

ISSUE

Is the plaintiff's action for wrongful death barred by the one-year statute of limitations?

IN THE LANGUAGE OF THE COURT

Mosk, Justice.

Statute of limitations is the collective term commonly applied to a great number of acts that prescribe the periods beyond which a plaintiff may not bring a cause of action. It has a purpose to protect defendants from the stale claims of dilatory plaintiffs. It has a related purpose to stimulate plaintiffs to assert fresh claims against defendants in a diligent fashion. Inasmuch as it necessarily fixes a definite period of time, it operates conclusively across the board and not flexibly on a case-by-case basis.

Under the statute of limitations, a plaintiff must bring a cause of action from wrongful death within one year of accrual. The limitations period is thus defined by the Legislature. That means that the date of accrual of a cause of action for wrongful death is the date of death. Under the statute of limitations, the Norgarts had to bring the cause of action for wrongful death within one year of accrual. They did not do so. Pursuant to this rule, the Norgarts were too late, exactly five years too late.

DECISION AND REMEDY

The supreme court of California held that the defendant, the Upjohn Company, was entitled to judgment as a matter of law based on the fact that the one-year statute of limitations for wrongful death actions had run, thus barring the plaintiff's lawsuit. Reversed.

Questions

1. What is the public policy behind having statutes of limitations? What is the public policy against having such statutes? Which policy should dominate and why?

2. Was it ethical for the Upjohn Company to avoid facing the merits of the lawsuit by asserting the one-year statute of limitations?

3. What are the business implications for having statutes of limitations?

Discovery

The legal process provides for a detailed pretrial procedure called **discovery.** During discovery, both parties engage in various activities to learn facts of the case from the other party and witnesses prior to trial. Discovery serves several functions, including preventing surprise, allowing parties to prepare thoroughly for trial, preserving evidence, saving court time, and promoting the settlement of cases. The major forms of discovery are depositions, interrogatories, production of documents, and physical and mental examination.

Depositions

A **deposition** is the oral testimony given, under oath, by a party or witness prior to trial. The person giving the deposition is called the **deponent.** The *parties* to the lawsuit must give their depositions, if the other party calls them to do so. The deposition of a **witness** can be given voluntarily or pursuant to a **subpoena** (court order). The deponent can be required to bring documents to the deposition.

Depositions are used to preserve evidence (e.g., if the deponent is deceased, ill, or otherwise not available at trial) and to impeach testimony given by witnesses at trial. Most depositions are taken at the office of one of the attorneys. The deponent is placed under oath and then asked oral questions by one or both of the attorneys. The questions and answers are recorded in written form by a court reporter. Depositions also can be videotaped. The deponent is given an opportunity to correct his or her answers prior to signing the deposition, depending on local practice or rules.

Interrogatories

Interrogatories are written questions submitted by one party to a lawsuit to another party. The questions can be very detailed, as illustrated by the sample interrogatory in Exhibit 7.7. In addition, in some jurisdictions it might be necessary to attach certain documents to the answers. A party is required to answer the interrogatories in writing within a specified time period (e.g., 60 to 90 days). An attorney usually helps with the preparation of the answers. The answers are signed under oath.

Production of Documents

Often, particularly in complex business cases, a substantial portion of the lawsuit may be based on information contained in documents (e.g., memoranda, correspondence, company records). One party to a lawsuit may request that the other party produce all documents that are relevant to the case

The Appomatox Courthouse in Appomatox, Virginia, site of General Robert E. Lee's surrender on April 9, 1865.

PERSPECTIVE CONTEMPORARY PERSPECTIVE

Video Deposition Know-How

Ann T. Greeley, Ph.D., DecisionQuest

While transcribed and video depositions have many similarities, there are a number of important skills involved in effective video deposition testimony that are not involved in a transcribed deposition. The most important thing to remember is that the "camera doesn't forget"! This fact has three important implications:

You're on Stage

Witnesses must look credible at all times—not only during responses, but also between questions, between answers, and during any delays. When giving a video deposition, a witness must develop a level of self-awareness beyond that which is required for a transcribed deposition.

Nonverbal Behaviors Are Key

Nonverbal behaviors are extremely important in communicating credibility, and due to the nature of the camera, these behaviors are magnified. Therefore, distracting behaviors must be eliminated or minimized. Straightening a tie, twirling a piece of hair, adjusting glasses, or shifting around in a chair are signs of nervousness. Nervousness can be interpreted as defensiveness or as having something to hide. A calm and credible presence is crucial in a video deposition.

Possible Trial Testimony

In some states, video depositions can be used in lieu of live testimony even if the witness is present in the courtroom. As such, you need to prepare the witness as you would for testimony in front of a jury. Substantive preparation is extremely important for video depositions because unprepared deponents not only make errors, but they also appear nervous. As noted earlier, the camera exaggerates this appearance.

Given these aspects of video depositions, keep in mind the following points for effective testimony.

1. Be aware of nonverbal communication.
2. Conservative clothing is a must for a video deposition.
3. Keep the background simple.
4. Be aware that time has greater significance in a video deposition.
5. Beware of technical problems and plan ahead.

Overall, the video deposition presents distinct challenges for attorneys and witnesses. We find the best way to assure that a video deposition is successful is to conduct the witness preparation on videotape, before the actual deposition takes place. The attorney and a communications specialist can provide feedback to the witness long before the session is scheduled. In this way, you can be assured that the witness's performance will be one you and the camera won't want to forget.

prior to trial. This is called **production of documents.** If the documents sought are too voluminous to be moved or are in permanent storage, or if moving the documents would disrupt the ongoing business of the party who is to produce them, the requesting party may be required to examine the documents at the other party's premises. Exhibit 7.8 is an example of a request for production of documents.

Physical and Mental Examination

In cases that concern the physical or mental condition of a party, a court can order the party to submit to certain physical or mental examinations to determine the extent of the alleged injuries. This would occur, for example, where the plaintiff has been injured in an accident and is seeking damages for physical injury and mental distress.

exhibit **7.7**   *Sample interrogatory, continued.*

(d) The dates on which each such treatment or examination by a doctor or practitioner was rendered and the charges for each;

(e) All reports regarding any medical treatment or examinations, setting forth the author and date of such reports.

OTHER EXPENSES*

3. If you have incurred any bills or expenses in connection with the injuries or diseases which you suffered because of the accident referred to in the Complaint, identify each such bill or expense, the service for which the bill or expense was incurred, and the identity of the person who rendered the bill or who was involved in the expense.

PRIOR OR SUBSEQUENT INJURIES OR DISEASES

4. Either prior to or subsequent to the accident referred to in the Complaint, have you ever suffered any injuries or diseases in those portions of the body claimed by you to have been affected by the accident referred to in the Complaint?
   If so, identify:
   (a) The injuries or diseases you suffered;
   (b) The date and place of any accident, if such an injury or disease was caused by an accident;
   (c) All hospitals, doctors or practitioners who rendered treatment or examinations because of any such injuries or diseases;
   (d) Anyone against whom a claim was made, and the Court, term or number of any claim or lawsuit that was filed, in connection with any such injuries or diseases.

EARNINGS BEFORE THE ACCIDENT*

5. For the period of three years immediately preceding the date of the accident referred to in the complaint, state:
   (a) The name and address of each of your employers or, if you were self-employed during that period, each of your business addresses and the name of the business while self-employed;
   (b) The dates of commencement and termination of each of your periods of employment or self-employment;
   (c) A detailed description of the nature of your occupation in each employment or self-employment;
   (d) The amount of income from employment and self-employment for each year. (Attach your federal income tax return for each year.)

EARNINGS AFTER THE ACCIDENT*

6. If you have engaged in one or more gainful occupations subsequent to the date of the accident referred to in the Complaint, state:
   (a) The name and address of each of your employers or if you were self-employed, each of your business addresses and the name of the business while self-employed;
   (b) The dates of commencement and termination of each of your periods of employment or self-employment;
   (c) A detailed description of the nature of your occupation in each employment or self-employment;
   (d) The wage, salary or rate of earnings received by you in each employment or self-employment. (Attach your federal income tax return for each year subsequent to the accident);
   (e) The dates of all absences from your occupation resulting from the injuries and diseases suffered in this accident. Set forth the amount of any earnings or other benefits lost by you because of such absences.

Sample interrogatory.   exhibit 7.

THOMAS F. GOLDMAN & ASSOCIATES
138 N. State Street
Newtown, PA 18940
(123) 555-1234

KATHRYN KELSEY	: COURT OF COMMON PLEAS
	: PHILADELPHIA COUNTY
	:
vs.	: APRIL TERM, 2002
KATHRYN CARROLL	: NO. 1234

INTERROGATORIES ADDRESSED TO KATHRYN KELSEY

You are to answer the following interrogatories under oath or verification pursuant to the Pa. R.C.P. 4005 and 4006 within thirty days from the service hereof. The answering party is under a duty to supplement responses to any questions with information discovered after these answers were given.

Also, a party or expert witness must amend prior responses if he/she obtains information upon the basis of which:

(a) he/she knows the response was incorrect when made; or

(b) he/she knows that the response, though correct when made, is no longer true.

The words "your vehicle" as used in the following interrogatories are defined as the motor vehicle you were operating at the time of the accident.

When a Standard Interrogatory uses the word: "identify", the party served with the Interrogatory must identify all documents, things and persons known to that party or to that party's attorney, and the address of all persons identified MUST be set forth.

Where a Standard Interrogatory is marked with an asterisk (*), a Request for Production may accompany the Interrogatory.

STANDARD INTERROGATORIES PURSUANT TO
PHILADELPHIA RULE OF CIVIL PROCEDURE *4005

INJURIES AND DISEASES ALLEGED

1. State in detail the injuries or diseases that you allege that you suffered as a result of the accident referred to in the Complaint.

MEDICAL TREATMENT & REPORTS*

2. If you received medical treatment or examinations (including x-rays) because of injuries or diseases you suffered as a result of the accident, identify:

(a) Each hospital at which you were treated or examined;

(b) The dates on which each such treatment or examination at a hospital was rendered and the charges by the hospital for each;

(c) Each doctor or practitioner by whom you were treated or examined;

LIMITATIONS OF DUTIES AND ACTIVITIES AFTER THE ACCIDENT

7. State whether, as a result of this accident, you have been unable to perform any of your customary occupational duties or social or other activities in the same manner as prior to the accident, stating with particularity (a) the duties and/or activities you have been unable to perform, (b) the periods of time you have been unable to perform, and (c) the names and last known addresses of all persons who have knowledge thereof.

WITNESSES AND THOSE WITH KNOWLEDGE OF ACCIDENT

8. (a) Identify each person who (1) was a witness to the accident through sight or hearing and/or (2) has knowledge of facts concerning the happening of the accident or conditions or circumstances at the scene of the accident prior to, after, or at the time of the accident.

    (b) With respect to each person identified in the answer to the interrogatory above, state that person's exact location and activity at the time of the accident.

STATEMENTS

9. Have you or has anyone acting on your behalf obtained from any person any statement (as defined by the Rules of Civil Procedure) concerning this action or its subject matter?
        If so, identify:

    (a) Each such person;

    (b) When, where, by whom and to whom each statement was made, and whether it was reduced to writing or otherwise recorded;

    (c) Any person who has custody of any such statements that were reduced to writing or otherwise recorded.

STATEMENTS MADE BY PARTY TO WHOM INTERROGATORY IS ADDRESSED*

10. Have you given any statement (as defined by the Rules of Civil Procedure) concerning this action or its subject matter?
        If so, identify:

    (a) Each person to whom a statement was given;

    (b) When and where each statement was given;

    (c) Any person who has custody of any such statements that were reduced to writing or otherwise recorded.

DEMONSTRATIVE EVIDENCE*

11. Do you or does anyone acting on your behalf know of the existence of any photographs, motion pictures, video recordings, maps, diagrams or models of the site of the accident, the parties or any other subject matter involved in this action?
        If the answer is in the affirmative, identify:

    (a) The date(s) when they were made and what they are;

    (b) The name and address of the person making them;

    (c) The subject that each represents or portrays.

TRIAL PREPARATION MATERIAL

12. Have you or has anyone on your behalf conducted any investigations of the accident which is the subject matter of the complaint?
        If the answer is in the affirmative, identify:

exhibit **7.7**   *Sample interrogatory, continued.*

(a) Each person, and the employer of each person, who conducted any investigation;

(b) The dates of the investigations;

(c) All notes, reports or other documents prepared during or as a result of the investigations and the identity of the persons who have possession thereof.

EXPERTS*

13. (a) State the name and address of each person whom you expect to call as an expert witness at trial and state the subject matter on which the expert is expected to testify.

(b) For each such expert, have the expert state the substance of the facts and opinions to which the expert is expected to testify and summarize the grounds for each such opinion.

(c) Set forth the qualifications of each expert, listing the schools attended, years of attendance, degrees received, and experience in any particular field of specialization or expertise.

INSURANCE

14. (a) State whether you are covered by any type of insurance including any excess or umbrella insurance, in connection with this accident.

  If the answer is in the affirmative, state the following with respect to each policy:

(b) The name of the insurance carrier which issued each policy of insurance;

(c) The name insured under each policy and the policy number;

(d) The type of each policy and the effective dates;

(e) The amount of coverage provided for injury to each person, for each occurrence, and in the aggregate for each policy;

(f) Each exclusion, if any, in the policy which is applicable to any claim thereunder and the reasons why you or the company claims the exclusion is applicable.

(g) Whether you have made a claim under the policy and if so set forth the nature of the claim, the amount recovered and the date of recovery.

NONSTANDARD INTERROGATORIES

15. State your full name, address, date of birth and social security number.

16. Have you ever used any names other than the one listed above? If yes, state all names used and when each additional name was used.

17. To the extent known to you, your attorney or other representative, set forth the name and home and business address of the following:

(a) Those who actually saw the accident;

(b) Those who were present at or near the scene at the time of the accident;

(c) Those who have any knowledge of, or information concerning the circumstances and manner in which the accident occurred or the nature of the injuries sustained in the accident.

18. At the time of the accident or immediately thereafter, did you have any conversation with or make any statements to any of the parties or witnesses, or did any of them make any statements to you or in your presence? If so state the substance of any such conversation or statement and in whose presence it took place.

19. If you, your representative, attorney, consultant, surety, indemnitor, insurer or agent obtained a statement or statements as defined in Pennsylvania Rules of Civil Procedure 4003.4(1) and (2), concerning this action and/or its subject matter from any party to this action, any witness, or any person not a party to this action then state:

    (a) The name and address of the person who gave such statement, including the name and address of each person's employer;

    (b) The date each statement was given;

    (c) The name and address of the person who obtained each statement;

    (d) The date when each statement was obtained;

    (e) The place where each statement was obtained;

    (f) Whether each statement is written, signed by the person making it or if there is a stenographic, mechanical, electrical or other recording, or a transcription thereof;

    (g) The names and addresses of all persons and/or entities who presently have custody of each original statement identified in your answer above;

    (h) Please attach to your Answer to Interrogatories a copy or like reproduction of each statement identified in your answer above.

20. State the exact date, time and place the accident occurred and describe in detail how you claim the accident occurred.

21. State:

    (a) The exact portion of the highway where the accident occurred;

    (b) The positions of the respective vehicles prior to impact;

    (c) Distance from you when you first observed the other vehicle;

    (d) Positions of vehicles after impact;

    (e) What part of your vehicle came in contact with what part of the other vehicle;

    (f) The weather and road conditions at the time of the accident;

    (g) If weather was inclement, state whether windshield wipers were in use at the time of the collision;

    (h) What type of traffic signals controlled the place where the accident occurred;

    (i) Speed of all vehicles immediately prior to impact;

    (j) Lighting conditions at time of accident, including whether any artificial light illuminated place of accident. If there were artificial lights, state type and distance from accident.

22. State the name and address of the owner of the vehicle in which you were traveling.

23. State the registration number, year, make and model of above vehicle.

24. With regard to the vehicle listed above, state the name, address, age and driver's license number of operator of vehicle.

25. State whether the vehicle or any part thereof in which you were traveling at the time of the accident was defective, or not in safe working order. Identify defects, if any:

26. State whether repairs were made to the vehicle after accident. If yes, identify name and address of person/business making repairs, date and type of work performed. Attach copy of repair bill.

27. State where you were coming from and where you were going at time of the accident.

28. State how long you had been traveling and approximately how many miles traveled prior to the accident.

29. State whether you had been at the location of the accident previously; if yes, approximately how many times.

30. State whether you had consumed any alcohol, medication or drugs within 24 hours of the accident. If so, identify substance and when, where, and amount consumed.

31. State whether you have a prescription for any corrective lenses. If so, identify type of prescription and whether you were wearing same at time of accident.

32. Please identify your driver's license number and the State which issued the license. Identify any restriction on your license.

exhibit **7.7**   *Sample interrogatory, continued.*

33. If your driver's license has ever been revoked, suspended or withdrawn, state where, when and for what offense.

34. State when you first experienced pain following accident.

35. State nature of pain experienced.

36. State name and address of family physician.

37. State name and address of all physicians, clinics, hospitals, therapists, etc. where you sought consultation or treatment within five (5) years prior or subsequent to this accident and reason for consultation and/or treatment.

38. Did you know any of the witnesses or the individuals in any of the other vehicles involved in this accident or any of the witnesses to the occurrences?

    (a) If answer is yes, state name(s) of individual(s) you knew, how long you knew the individual(s) and the nature of your relationship with the individual(s) named.

    (b) As to the individual(s) named in 38(a) who were in another vehicle involved in this accident, did you know the individual(s) would be traveling near you on the highway?

39. As to each party traveling in the vehicle you were in, state your relationship (i.e., friend, relative, stranger, etc.).

40. As to each party named in #39, state how long you have known this person.

41. As to each witness, state your relationship (i.e., friend, relative, stranger, etc.) and where each witness was at the time of the accident.

42. State whether or not you knew or had ever before seen any of the occupants of the other vehicle(s) involved in this accident. If yes, state:

    (a) Who it is you knew or had seen prior to this accident;

    (b) How you know the person(s) identified;

    (c) For what length of time prior to the accident you knew this person(s);

    (d) Whether you knew the individual(s) named above would be traveling near you;

    (e) Whether you were traveling to the same location for the same purpose.

43. State whether or not you reside in a household where a relative owns a motor vehicle. Identify this individual and his/her relationship to you.

    (a) Identify the vehicle owned by year, make, model, license and vehicle identification number.

    (b) State whether this vehicle is insured. If yes, attach a copy of the declaration page indicating whether or not the limited tort option was selected.

44. State whether or not the police were called to the locale of the accident. If yes, state:

    (a) Who called police;

    (b) Whether or not the police responded to the call;

    (c) How long it took the police to respond;

    (d) The name(s) and badge(s) of the officer(s);

    (e) Whether you left the location prior to the police arrival;

    (f) Whether you provided your name to the police;

    (g) What, if anything, you told police;

    (h) Whether or not a police report was prepared. If answer is yes, please attach a copy of the police report and/or identify police department involved and police reference number for accident report.

45. If you were taken to the hospital for treatment, state how and by whom you were transported.

    THOMAS F. GOLDMAN & ASSOCIATES
    BY: _____

Sample request for production of documents.   **exhibit 7.8**

THOMAS F. GOLDMAN & ASSOCIATES
138 N. State Street
Newtown, PA 18940
(123) 555-1234

KATHRYN KELSEY	:	COURT OF COMMON PLEAS
	:	PHILADELPHIA COUNTY
vs.	:	APRIL TERM, 2002
KATHRYN CARROLL	:	NO. 1259

REQUEST TO PRODUCE UNDER PA R.C.P. 4033 and 4009
<u>DIRECTED TO PLAINTIFFS</u>

Within thirty (30) days of service, please produce for inspection and copying at the office of THOMAS F. GOLDMAN & ASSOCIATES, 138 North State Street, Newtown, Pennsylvania 18940, the following:

1. All photographs and/or diagrams of the area involved in this accident or occurrence, the locale or surrounding area of the site of this accident or occurrence, or any other matter or things involved in this accident or occurrence.

2. All property damage estimates rendered for any object belonging to the Plaintiffs which was involved in this accident or occurrence.

3. All property damage estimates rendered for any object belonging to the Defendant which was involved in this accident or occurrence.

4. All statements concerning this action or its subject matter previously made by any party or witness. The statements referred to here are defined by Pa. R.C.P. 4003.4.

5. All transcriptions and summaries of all interviews conducted by anyone acting on behalf of the Plaintiff or Plaintiff's insurance carrier of any potential witness and/or person(s) who has any knowledge of the accident or its surrounding circumstances.

6. All inter-office memorandum between representative of Plaintiffs' insurance carrier or memorandum to Plaintiffs' insurance carrier's file concerning the manner in which the accident occurred.

7. All inter-office memorandum between representative of Plaintiffs' insurance carrier or memorandum to Plaintiffs' insurance carrier's file concerning the injuries sustained by the Plaintiffs.

8. A copy of any written accident report concerning this accident or occurrence signed by or prepared by Plaintiff for Plaintiffs' insurance carrier or Plaintiff's employers.

9. A copy of the face sheet of any policy of insurance providing coverage to Plaintiffs for the claim being asserted by Plaintiff in this action.

10. All bills, reports, and records from any and all physicians, hospitals, or other health care providers concerning the injuries sustained by the Defendants from this accident or occurrence.

11. All photographs and/or motion pictures of any and all surveillance of Defendant performed by anyone acting on behalf of Plaintiff, Plaintiffs' insurer and/or Plaintiffs' attorney.

12. All photographs taken of Plaintiffs' motor vehicle which depict any damage to said vehicle which was sustained as a result of this accident.

13. All photographs taken of defendant's motor vehicle which depict any damage to said vehicle which was sustained as a result of this accident.

14. Any and all reports, writings, memorandum, Xeroxed cards and/or other writings, lists or compilations of the Defendant and others with similar names as indexed by the Metropolitan Index Bureau, Central Index Bureau or other Index Bureau in possession of the Plaintiffs or the Plaintiffs' insurance carrier.

Pretrial Motions

Parties to a lawsuit can make several pretrial motions to try to dispose of all or part of a lawsuit prior to trial. The two major pretrial motions are the motion for judgment on the pleadings, and the motion for summary judgment.

Motion for Judgment on the Pleadings

Either party can make a **motion for judgment on the pleadings** once the pleadings are complete. This motion alleges that if all of the facts presented in the pleadings are true, the party making the motion would win the lawsuit when the proper law is applied to these facts. In deciding this motion, the judge cannot consider any facts outside the pleadings.

Motion for Summary Judgment

The trier of the fact (i.e., the jury, or, if no jury, the judge) determines *factual issues.* A **motion for summary judgment** asserts that there are no factual disputes to be decided by the jury and that the judge should apply the relevant

PERSPECTIVE   *Calendars Ordered Into the Daylight*

Most executives keep some form of calendar that contains lists of things to do, appointments, and "what I've done" notes. If a calendar contains business-related information exclusively, it is discoverable by the prosecution in a criminal case. If the calendar is personal in nature, its owner can shield it from discovery under the Fifth Amendment's self-incrimination privilege. What if an executive's calendar contains both business and personal information? Is it discoverable or not? The court had to decide this issue in the following case.

John Doe I and John Doe II are two executives of a company that is the subject of an ongoing grand jury investigation into possible illegal price-fixing in a certain industry. Both executives kept calendars that contained both business and personal notes. The grand jury sought production of the calendars, but the executives refused to produce them, alleging Fifth Amendment protection. After examining the evidence, the district court determined that the calendars were corporate in nature and ordered them disclosed. The court also issued an order holding the executives in contempt for their failure to turn over their calendars. The executives appealed.

The court of appeals decided that where a calendar contains a mixture of business and personal notes, a mul-

tifactor approach should be applied to determine if they are discoverable. The court will look at ownership, preparation, access, content, purpose, and ratio of business to personal entries in determining whether a document is corporate or personal in nature. This balancing test asks, "What is the essential nature of the document?" No single factor is dispositive, and the final determination whether the calendar is business or personal in nature is a question of fact.

Applying this multifactor approach to the instant case, the court found that the executives' calendars contained a majority of business-related entries. There were notes concerning business travel, job-related "to do" lists, and entries about compensation at work. The court found that the executives' self-serving affidavits to the contrary were not credible. The court of appeals stated, "In the totality of these circumstances, the district court's conclusion that the daytimers were prepared, maintained, and used for business, not personal purposes, is not clearly erroneous."

The court held that the executives' calendars were discoverable and were not protected by the Fifth Amendment's privilege against self-incrimination. [In Re *Grand Jury Proceedings,* 55 F.3d 1012 (1995)]

Email has made it faster and easier to communicate with others, whether for business or personal reasons. Email messages also have become a source of evidence to be used at both criminal and civil trials. Consider the following case.

Karen Strauss worked for Microsoft Corporation as an assistant editor for the *Microsoft Systems Journal*. When she was passed over for a promotion and subsequently dismissed from her job, she brought a sex-discrimination case against Microsoft. She alleged that her supervisor, Jon Lazarus, sexually harassed her by making certain remarks and sending messages to her by email. She alleged that Lazarus referred to another woman in the office as "Spandex Queen," told another woman that he would pay her $500 if he could call her "Sweet Georgia Brown," and referred to himself as the "president of the Amateur Gynecology Club." Strauss also wanted to introduce email evidence that Lazarus followed these remarks with email messages to Strauss containing a satirical essay entitled "Alice in UNIX Land," an advertisement for the replacement of "Mouse Balls," and a parody on a play entitled *A Girl's Guide to Condoms*.

The email messages had been erased, but the plaintiff retrieved them from backup tapes automatically made by the company's computer network.

Microsoft made a motion to the court to preclude this evidence, including the email messages, from being introduced at trial. The district court denied Microsoft's motion. The court stated that the email messages, when viewed in light of Strauss's other evidence, could lead a reasonable jury to conclude that Microsoft engaged in the challenged conduct. The court noted that although the email messages may be embarrassing to Microsoft, such evidence is admissible. The court stated, "The Federal Rules of Evidence favor placing even the nastier side of human nature before the jury if to do so would aid its search for the truth." The court permitted Strauss to sue Microsoft for sexual harassment using the email messages as evidence.

As email continues to increase in use, it will become a greater—and very tangible—source of evidence at criminal and civil trials. [*Strauss v. Microsoft Corporation,* 68 Fair Empl. Prac. Cases (BNA) 1576 (S.D.N.Y. 1995)]

law to the undisputed facts to decide the case. Motions for summary judgment, which can be made by either party, are supported by evidence outside the pleadings. Affidavits from the parties and witnesses, documents (e.g., a written contract between the parties), depositions, and such are common forms of evidence. If, after examining the evidence, the court finds no factual dispute, it can decide the issue or issues raised in the summary judgment motion. This may dispense with the entire case or with part of the case. If the judge finds that a factual dispute exists, the motion will be denied and the case will go to trial.

Pretrial Settlement Conference

Federal court rules and most state court rules permit the court to direct the attorneys or parties to appear before the court for a **pretrial hearing,** or **settlement conference.** One of the major purposes of these hearings is to facilitate settlement of the case. Pretrial conferences often are held informally in the judge's chambers. If no settlement is reached, the pretrial hearing is used to identify the major trial issues and other relevant factors.

THE COURTHOUSE TEAM

U.S. Magistrate Judge

In the federal court system, a magistrate judge typically handles pretrial criminal matters. Under some local rules, by virtue of the authority in 28 U.S.C. 636(c), this judge may conduct, upon consent of all parties in a civil case, any or all proceedings, including a jury or non-jury trial, and order the entry of a final judgment. Appeals of a judgment may be made directly to the Court of Appeals, unless in the parties' consent they elected to have the case reviewed by the appropriate district judge (in which event any further appeal to the court of appeals would only be by petition for leave to appeal).

PERSPECTIVE

Oregon Rule on Visiting Adversaries' Websites

Visiting the website of a client's adversary in litigation does not violate the rule against lawyers' communicating with persons known to be represented by other counsel.

[Oregon State Bar Legal Ethics Commission Opinion 2001–164]

Utah Rule on Unencrypted Email

In ordinary circumstances a lawyer may use unencrypted Internet email to transmit client confidential information. *[Utah 00–01]*

More than 90 percent of all cases are settled before they go to trial. In cases that do proceed to trial, the trial judge may advise the attorneys of the rules or timetable of the individual judge. The judges also will advise the attorneys of any deadlines for discovery and the deadline for submitting any final motions with regard to what may be offered at the trial, called *motions in limine*.

In a number of jurisdictions, cases are referred to arbitration or other forms of alternative dispute resolution. Depending on the amount of money in controversy, some cases are required to be submitted before court-approved panels of attorneys sitting as arbitrators of the dispute. In other courts, the litigants may elect to have the case heard before an arbitration panel. Appeal rights from arbitration panel decisions vary, but cases typically may be appealed *de novo* to the trial court as if no arbitration had occurred, except possibly the payment of an appeal fee to cover part of the cost of the arbitration.

THE TRIAL

Pursuant to the Seventh Amendment to the U.S. Constitution, a party to an action at law is guaranteed the right to a *jury trial* in cases in federal court. Most state constitutions contain a similar guarantee for state court actions. If either party requests a jury, the trial will be by jury. If both parties waive their right to a jury, the trial will be without a jury. In non-jury trials, the judge sits as the **trier of fact.** These trials also are called *waiver trials* or **bench trials.** At the time of trial, the parties usually submit trial briefs to the judge that contain legal support for their side of the case.

Trials are usually divided into the following phases:

- Jury selection
- Opening statements
- Plaintiff's case
- Defendant's case
- Rebuttal and rejoinder
- Closing arguments
- Jury instructions
- Jury deliberation
- Entry of judgment

Jury Selection

The pool of the potential jurors usually is selected from voter or automobile registration lists. Potential jurors are asked to fill out a questionnaire such as that shown in Exhibit 7.9. Individuals are selected to hear specific cases through the process called **voir dire** ("to speak the truth"). Lawyers for each party and the judge can ask prospective jurors questions to determine if they would be biased in their decision. Jurors can be "stricken for cause" if the court believes that the potential juror is too biased to render a fair verdict. Lawyers may also use preemptory challenges to exclude a juror from sitting on a particular case without giving any reason for the dismissal. Once the appropriate number of jurors is selected (usually 6 to 12 jurors), they are impaneled to hear the case and are sworn in. The trial is ready to begin. In cases in which the Court is concerned for the safety of the jury, such as a high-profile murder case, it can **sequester,** or separate it from the outside world. Jurors are paid minimum fees for their service. Courts can hold people in contempt and fine or jail them for willful refusal to serve as a juror.

Opening Statements

Each party's attorney is allowed to make an **opening statement** to the jury. In opening statements, attorneys usually summarize the main factual and legal issues of the case and describe why they believe their client's position is valid. The information given in this statement is not considered as evidence. It is the attorney's opportunity to tell the trier of fact what he or she intends to tell them through witnesses and evidence.

Plaintiff's Case

Plaintiffs bear the **burden of proof** to persuade the trier of fact of the merits of their case. This is called the **plaintiff's case.** The plaintiff's attorney calls witnesses to give testimony. After a witness has been sworn in, the plaintiff's attorney examines (questions) the witness. This is called **direct examination.** Documents and other evidence can be introduced through each witness. After the plaintiff's attorney has completed his or her questions, the defendant's attorney can question the witness in **cross-examination.** The defendant's attorney can ask questions only about the subjects that were brought up during the direct examination. After the defendant's attorney completes his or her questions, the plaintiff's attorney can ask questions of the witness in **redirect examination.** The defendant's attorney can then again ask questions of the witness. This is called **recross examination.** Exhibit 7.10 illustrates this process.

Defendant's Case

After the plaintiff has concluded his or her case, the **defendant's case** proceeds. The defendant's case must

1. rebut the plaintiff's evidence.
2. prove any affirmative defenses asserted by the defendant.
3. prove any allegations contained in the defendant's cross-complaint.

The defendant's witnesses are examined in much the same way as the plaintiff's attorney cross-examines each witness. This is followed by redirect and recross examination.

SIDEBAR

Attorneys' Fees

In most civil lawsuits, each party is responsible for paying its own attorney's fees, whether the party wins or loses. This is called "the American rule." The court can award attorney's fees to the winning party if a statute so provides, if the parties have so agreed (e.g., in a contract), or if the losing party has acted maliciously or pursued a frivolous case. Accused parties in criminal cases are responsible for paying their own attorney's fees if they can afford to do so. If the accused is indigent, the government will provide an attorney (e.g., a public defender) free of charge.

An attorney in a civil lawsuit can represent the plaintiff on an hourly, project, or contingency fee basis. Hourly fees usually range from $75 to $500 per hour, depending on the type of case, the expertise of the lawyer, and the locality of the lawsuit. Under a *contingency fee arrangement,* the lawyer receives a percentage of the amount recovered for the plaintiff upon winning or settling the case. Contingency fees normally range from 20 to 50 percent of the award or settlement, with an average of about 35 percent. Lawyers for defendants in lawsuits normally are paid on an hourly basis.

exhibit 7.9 *Sample jury questionnaire.*

JURY QUESTIONNAIRE

(Please Print)

NAME _____ JUROR NO. _____
   (Last)   (First)   (Middle initial)

SECTION OF CITY _____
   (Currently)   (Other sections of city lived in within past ten years)

Marital Status ☐ Married ☐ Single ☐ Divorced ☐ Separated ☐ Widowed

Occupation _____
   (Currently)   (Other occupations within past ten years)

Occupation of ☐ Spouse *(or deceased spouse)* ☐ Other _____

_____
   (Currently)   (Other occupations within past ten years)

No. of Male Children _____ Ages _____

No. of Female Children _____ Ages _____

Your Level of Schooling Completed _____

Race ☐ White ☐ Hispanic ☐ Black ☐ Other

STOP HERE
Writing below this line is prohibited until the juror video is shown

QUESTIONS TO BE ANSWERED IN THE JURY ASSEMBLY ROOM

1. Do you have any physical or psychological disability or are you presently taking any medication? ☐ YES ☐ NO

2. (a) Have you ever been a juror before? ☐ YES ☐ NO

   (b) If so, were you ever on a hung jury? ☐ YES ☐ NO

Questions 3 through 15 apply to criminal cases only

3. Do you have any religious, moral or ethical beliefs that would prevent you from sitting in judgment in a criminal case and rendering a fair verdict? ☐ YES ☐ NO

4. Have you or anyone close to you ever been a victim of a crime? ☐ YES ☐ NO

5. Have you or anyone close to you ever been charged with or arrested for a crime, other than a traffic violation? ☐ YES ☐ NO

6. Have you or anyone close to you ever been an eyewitness to a crime, whether or not it ever came to Court? ☐ YES ☐ NO

7. Have you, or has anyone close to you, ever worked as a police officer or in other law enforcement jobs? This includes prosecutors, public defenders, private criminal defense lawyers, detectives, and security or prison guards. ☐ YES ☐ NO

8. Would you be more likely to believe the testimony of a police officer or any other law enforcement officer just because of his job? ☐ YES ☐ NO

9. Would you be less likely to believe the testimony of a police officer or any other law enforcement officer just because of his job? ☐ YES ☐ NO

10. Would you have any problem following the Court's instruction that the defendant in a criminal case is presumed to be innocent until proven guilty beyond a reasonable doubt? ☐ YES ☐ NO

11. Would you have any problem following the Court's instruction that the defendant in a criminal case does not have to take the stand or present evidence, and it cannot be held against the defendant if he or she elects to remain silent? ☐ YES ☐ NO

12. Would you have any problem following the Court's instruction in a criminal case that just because someone is arrested, it does not mean that the person is guilty of anything? ☐ YES ☐ NO

13. In general, would you have any problem following and applying the judge's instructions on the law? ☐ YES ☐ NO

14. Would you have any problem during jury deliberations in a criminal case discussing the case fully but still making up your own mind? ☐ YES ☐ NO

15. Is there any other reason you could not be a fair juror in a criminal case? ☐ YES ☐ NO

Questions 16 through 24 apply to civil cases only

16. Have you or anyone close to you ever sued someone, been sued, or been a witness? ☐ YES ☐ NO

17. Have you or anyone close to you been employed as a lawyer or in a law-related job? ☐ YES ☐ NO

18. Have you or anyone close to you been employed as a doctor or nurse or in a medical-related job? ☐ YES ☐ NO

19. In a civil case, would you have any problem following the Court's instruction that the plaintiff has the burden or proof, but unlike in a criminal case, the test is not beyond a reasonable doubt but "more likely than not"? ☐ YES ☐ NO

20. In a civil case, would you have any problem putting aside sympathy for the plaintiff and deciding the case solely on the evidence? ☐ YES ☐ NO

21. In a civil case, would you have any problem following the Court's instruction to award money for damages for things like pain and suffering, loss of life's pleasures, etc., although it is difficult to put a dollar figure on them? ☐ YES ☐ NO

22. Would you have any problem during jury deliberations in a civil case discussing the case fully but still making up your own mind? ☐ YES ☐ NO

23. Is there any reason in a civil case that you cannot follow the Court's instructions on the law? ☐ YES ☐ NO

24. Is there any reason in a civil case that you cannot otherwise be a fair juror? ☐ YES ☐ NO

exhibit 7.10 *Sequence for examining witnesses.*

Rebuttal and Rejoinder

After the defendant's attorney has completed calling witnesses, the plaintiff's attorney can call witnesses and put forth evidence to rebut the defendant's case. This is called a **rebuttal.** The defendant's attorney can call additional witnesses and introduce other evidence to counter the rebuttal. This is called the *rejoinder.*

Closing Arguments

At the conclusion of the evidence, each party's attorney is allowed to make a **closing argument** to the jury. Each attorney tries to convince the jury to render a verdict for his or her clients by pointing out the strengths in the clients' case and the weaknesses in the other side's case. Information given by the attorneys in their closing statements is not evidence. It is a chance for the attorneys to tell the jury what they said they would tell the jury through witness and evidence in the opening statements and how they had done that during the trial.

Jury Instructions

Once the closing arguments are completed, the judge reads **jury instructions** (or **charges**) to the jury. These instructions inform the jury about what law to apply in deciding the case (see Exhibit 7.11). For example, in a criminal trial the judge will read the jury the statutory definition of the crime charged. In an accident case, the judge will read the jury the legal definition of *negligence.*

Jury Deliberation

The jury then goes into the jury room to deliberate its findings. **Jury deliberation** can take from a few minutes to many weeks. After deliberation, the jury announces its **verdict.** In a civil case, the jury also assesses damages. The judge assesses penalties in criminal cases.

Allowable Costs

Under F.R.C.P. Rule 54, "costs shall be allowed as of course to the prevailing party unless the court otherwise directs."

Under 28 U.S.C. 1920, costs may include:

1. Fees of the clerk or marshal;

2. Fees of the court reporter for all or any part of its stenographic transcript necessarily obtained for use in the case;

3. Fees and disbursements for printing and witnesses;

4. Fees for exemplification and copies of papers necessarily obtained for use in the case;

5. Docket fees under section 1923 of this title [28 U.S.C.];

6. Compensation of court appointed experts, compensation of interpreters, and salaries, fees, expenses, and costs of special interpretation services under section 1828 of this title [28 U.S.C.].

Sample jury instructions.   exhibit 7.11

6.01J (Civ) PROPERTY DAMAGE

The plaintiff is entitled to be compensated for the harm done to his (her) property. If you find that the property was a total loss, damages are to be measured by either its market value or its special value to plaintiff, whichever is greater. If the property was not a total loss, damages are measured by (the difference in value before and after the harm) (the reasonable cost of repairs) and you may consider such evidence produced by defendant by way of defense to plaintiff's claim. In addition, plaintiff is entitled to be reimbursed for incidental costs or losses reasonably incurred because of the damage to the property, such as (rental of a replacement vehicle during repairs), (towing charges), (loss of use of the property), (etc.).

SUBCOMMITTEE NOTE

Damage to property is covered generally by Restatement of Torts, §§ 927 and 928. Section 927 provides for damages to be measured by the "market value" or "damages based upon its special value to [plaintiff] if that is greater than its market value." Restatement of Torts, § 927, Comment c (1934). Section 928 provides, in the case of damages not amounting to total destruction, damages measured by "the difference between the value of the chattel before the harm and the value after the harm or, at plaintiff's election, the reasonable cost of repair or restoration." This accounts for the parenthesized phrases (the difference in value before and after the harm) and (the reasonable cost of repairs).

Incidental costs will depend on the nature of the property damage. Rental of a substitute vehicle has long been recognized as one such compensable item. *Bauer v. Armour & Co.*, 84 Pa.Super. 174 (1924). Compensation for loss of use is specifically authorized by Restatement of Torts, § 928(b), in the case of less than total loss. The Subcommittee can see no logical reason why such damages should not be awarded under Section 927 in the case of total loss. *Nelson v. Johnson*, 55 D. & C. 2d 21 (Somerset C.P. 1970). Any further expense, proximately resulting from the loss or damage is recoverable under general provisions of tort law. *Nelson v. Johnson, supra*, at 33-34.

In the case of damage to automobiles, however, the appellate courts have adhered to the ancient rule requiring testimony of the one who supervised or made the repairs, prior to admission of damage estimates. *Mackiw v. Pennsylvania Threshermen & Farmers Mut. Cas. Ins. Co.*, 201 Pa.Super. 626, 193 A.2d 745 (1963). This rule has been criticized as time-consuming and "technical" by the very courts adhering to it. *Mackiw, supra*, 193 A.2d at 745. It further creates an intolerable burden on the courts, in a period when backlog has led to "compulsory" arbitration in many counties of cases valued below $10,000. E.g., *Loughery v. Barnes*, 181 Pa.Super. 352, 124 A.2d 120 (1956) (appeal after verdict of $341.30 for property damage); *Wilk v. Borough of Mt. Oliver*, 152 Pa.Super. 539, 33 A.2d 73 (1943) (new trial ordered after verdict of $175). The Subcommittee therefore adopts a rule requiring only the submission of a repair bill or estimate in proof of damages to automobiles (such bill being submitted prior to trial to defense counsel); should defendant wish to challenge such an estimate, he may do so through cross-examination and through the introduction of evidence in his own case. See *Watsontown Brick Co. v. Hercules Powder Co.*, 265 F.Supp. 268, 275 (M.D.Pa.), *aff'd*, 387 F.2d 99 (3rd Cir. 1967) (after introduction of damage evidence, burden shifts to defendant to show reduction).

Absent stipulation, the issue of reasonable compensation remains a jury issue.

6.01F (Civ) FUTURE PAIN AND SUFFERING

The plaintiff is entitled to be fairly and adequately compensated for such physical pain, mental anguish, discomfort, inconvenience and distress as you believe he (she) will endure in the future as a result of his (her) injuries. [. . .]

Entrepreneurs have been leaders in developing start-up companies that currently dominate the area of e-commerce and the Internet. Entrepreneur Bill Gates created Microsoft Corporation and is now the richest person in the world. The entrepreneurs who started Netscape, Yahoo, AOL, Amazon.com, and eBay are also multimillionaires. Many new entrepreneurs are hatching the successful Internet and e-commerce businesses of the future in their dorm rooms, juice bars, and chat rooms on the Net. These Internet and e-commerce entrepreneurs are members of a new breed who think big, move fast, and are willing to take risks.

These new cyberspace entrepreneurs need a new type of lawyer who understands their mindset. These lawyers practice "entrepreneur law" in that they must be able to give competent legal and business advice on a moment's notice. Although having to be careful to protect the interests of their clients, and to give correct legal advice, entrepreneurial lawyers must recognize that e-commerce and Internet businesses sometimes must act faster than traditional businesses. In such cases, the client may be willing to skip some of the minute details that lawyers would insist on for traditional clients. These "techie-owners" often find "Wall Street" lawyers too slow, too expensive, and too risk-adverse. The new entrepreneur lawyer is more to their liking.

There is a growing need for lawyers who know e-commerce and Internet law, have specialized skills in handling transactional law, and know small-client management. At the start, entrepreneur lawyers need strong skills in finance law, e-commerce contract law, selecting and drafting business entity formation documents, preparing transactional documents of shipping, drawing licensing agreements, drafting shareholder agreements, drafting employment agreements, and protecting trademarks, service marks, and trade secrets. Eventually, the lawyer would be looking at handling the Internet company's initial public offering (IPO) and debt financing. It is hoped that after the Internet company is successful, it will not trade in its entrepreneur lawyer for the "traditional" lawyer.

Civil cases include personal injury cases, such as those against airlines, in which a judgment may be awarded to the plaintiff if successful.

Entry of Judgment

After the jury has returned its verdict, in most cases the judge enters **judgment** to the successful party based on the verdict. This is the official decision of the court. But the court may overturn the verdict if it finds bias or jury misconduct. This is called a **judgment notwithstanding the verdict** or **judgment n.o.v.** or **j.n.o.v.,** for the Latin *judgment non obstante verdicto.* In a civil case, the judge may reduce the amount of monetary damages awarded by the jury if he or she finds the jury to have been biased, emotional, or inflamed. This is called *remittitur.* The trial court usually issues a *written memorandum* setting forth the reasons for the judgment. This memorandum, together with the trial transcript and evidence introduced at trial, constitutes the permanent *record* of the trial court proceeding.

LEGAL TERMINOLOGY

Answer

Bench trial

Burden of proof

Civil litigation

Closing arguments

Complaint

Consolidation

Contempt of court

Cross-complaint

Cross-examination

Default judgment

Defendant

Defendant's case

Deponent

Deposition

Direct examination

Discovery

Injunction

Interrogatories

Intervention

Judgment

Judgment notwithstanding the verdict (j.n.o.v.)

Jury deliberation

Jury instructions/charges

Litigation/litigation process

Motion for judgment on the pleadings

Motion for summary judgment

Opening statement

Plaintiff

Plaintiff's case

Pleadings

Pretrial hearing (or settlement conference)

Production of documents

Rebuttal

Recross examination

Redirect examination

Reply

Sequester

Settlement conference

Statute of limitations

Subpoena

Summons

Trier of fact

Verdict

Voir dire

Witness

Summary

The Pleadings

Description	Paperwork that initiates and responds to a lawsuit.
Complaint	Filed by the plaintiff with the court and served with a summons on the defendant. It sets forth the basis of the lawsuit.
Answer	Filed by the defendant with the court and served on the plaintiff. It usually denies most allegations of the complaint.
Cross-Complaint	Filed and served by the defendant if he or she countersues the plaintiff. The defendant is the cross-complainant and the plaintiff is the cross-defendant. The cross-defendant must file and serve a reply (answer).
Intervention	A person who has an interest in a lawsuit may intervene and become a party to the lawsuit.
Consolidation	Separate cases against the same defendant arising from the same incident may be consolidated by the court into one case if it would not cause prejudice to the parties.

Discovery

Description	The pretrial litigation process for discovering facts of the case from the other party and witnesses.
Depositions	Oral testimony given by a *deponent*, either a party or witness. Depositions are transcribed.
Interrogatories	Written questions submitted by one party to the other party. They must be answered within a specified period of time.
Production of Documents	A party to a lawsuit may obtain copies of all relevant documents from the other party.
Physical and Mental Examination	These examinations of a party are permitted upon order of the court where injuries are alleged that could be verified or disputed by such examination.

Dismissals and Pretrial Judgments

Motion for Judgment on the Pleadings	Alleges that if all facts as pleaded are true, the moving party would win the lawsuit. No facts outside the pleadings may be considered.

(continued)

Motion for Summary Judgment	Alleges that there are no factual disputes, so the judge may apply the law and decide the case without a jury. Evidence outside the pleadings may be considered (e.g., affidavits, documents, depositions).

Pretrial Settlement Conference

Description	Conference prior to trial between the parties in front of the judge to facilitate the settlement of the case. Also called *pretrial hearing*. If a settlement is not reached, the case proceeds to trial.

The Trial

Jury Selection	Jury selection. Done through a process called *voir dire*. Biased jurors are dismissed and replaced.
Opening Statements	Made by the parties' lawyers. Are not evidence.
The Plaintiff's Case	The plaintiff bears the burden of proof. The plaintiff calls witnesses and introduces evidence to try to prove his or her case.
The Defendant's Case	The defendant calls witnesses and introduces evidence to rebut the plaintiff's case and to prove affirmative defenses and cross-complaints.
Rebuttal and Rejoinder	The plaintiff and defendant may call additional witnesses and introduce additional evidence.
Closing Arguments	Made by the parties' lawyers. Are not evidence.
Jury Instructions	Judge reads instructions to the jury as to what law they are to apply to the case.
Jury Deliberation	Jury retires to the jury room and deliberates until it reaches a *verdict*.
Entry of Judgment	The judge may: a. Enter the verdict reached by the jury as the court's *judgment*. b. Grant a motion for *judgment* n.o.v. if the judge finds the jury was biased. This means that the jury's verdict does not stand. c. Order *remittitur* (reduction) of any damages awarded if the judge finds the jury to have been biased or emotional.

Working the Web

1. Use the court links in the federal courts website to locate the U.S. District Court for your jurisdiction and download, if available, the local rules at www.uscourts.gov/links.html.

2. Visit the national archives and review the grant of judicial power in Article III of the U.S. Constitution at www.nara.gov/exhall/charters/constitution/constitution.html.

3. Read the rights granted by the Fifth Amendment to the Constitution at www.nara.gov/exhall/charters/billrights/billrights.html.

4. Use the Lexisone website state resource locator to find the online resources of your state at www.lexisone.com/legalresearch/legalguide/states/states_resources_index.htm.

5. Use the Martindale–Hubbell website to locate available expert witnesses and process servers in your jurisdiction at www.martindale.com/xp/martindale/experts_and_services/search_experts_and_services/leg_search.xml.

Questions
CRITICAL LEGAL THINKING AND WRITING

1. What is the reason for having a statute of limitations in civil actions?

2. Why would a court in the administration of justice ever make a finding of judgment notwithstanding the verdict?

3. What is the possible reason for granting a summary judgment? When will it be granted?

4. Why is the burden of proof in civil cases different from that in criminal cases?

5. Do you believe that the general availability of liability insurance influences jury awards? Would knowing that a defendant was insured affect your judgment as a member of a jury?

6. Why would a named defendant not file an answer to a complaint?

7. If both sides of a case have taken complete and thorough discovery in a case, are they more or less likely to settle before trial? Why?

8. What are the advantages, disadvantages, and benefits of using video depositions?

9. What characteristics would you want in a juror in a case involving a charge of possession of drugs for personal use by a college student, an automobile accident involving a senior citizen, and an injury to a child caused by a defective toy resulting in visible scarring to the lower leg? Why?

10. How does the legal team determine that there are sufficient facts to go to a jury?

ETHICS: ANALYSIS AND DISCUSSION

1. Is there an ethical obligation not to file certain lawsuits?
2. What are the implications for a paralegal in failing to file a pleading before expiration of the statute of limitations? For the supervising attorney? For the client?
3. Should the email of lawyers and paralegals be treated as confidential and not subject to use as evidence in a case? Why or why not?

Unauthorized Communication

There are few certainties in the area of ethics, for paralegals or in any profession. What qualifies as ethical conduct is in most cases based on state law and court interpretation applied to a set of facts. The citation listed below represents one legal opinion and is provided as a research starting point. Do not assume that the same rule applies in your jurisdiction. For the following:

- *Prepare a written statement based on your state law.*
- *Use your state bar association website as a starting point.*

You have been advised in your orientation of the ethical rule prohibiting communication with an opponent who is represented by counsel. While surfing the web, you decide to see if the opposing party has a website, you locate it and check it carefully for any information that might help the investigation of the case assigned to you. You send a request to the site and get back information related to the lawsuit. [Oregon State Bar Op2001–164.] Have you violated the ethical prohibition barring communications with a represented party?

Conrad v. Delta Airlines, Inc.

494 F.2d 914 (7th Cir. 1974)

8.1 FACTS

Captain Conrad was a pilot for Delta Airlines. In 1970, Conrad was forced to resign by the airline. He sued, alleging that he was discharged because of his pro-union activities and not because of poor job performance, as claimed by Delta.

During discovery, a report written by a Delta flight operations manager was produced that stated: "More than a few crew members claimed that Conrad professed to being a leftist-activist. His overactivity with the local pilots' union, coupled with inquiries regarding company files to our secretary, led to the conclusion that potential trouble will be avoided by acceptance of his resignation."

Conrad claims that the report is evidence of the anti-union motivation for his discharge. Delta made a summary judgment motion to the trial court.

ISSUE

Should its summary judgment motion be granted?

Haviland & Co. v. Montgomery Ward & Co.

31 F.R.D. 578 (S.D.N.Y. 1962)

8.2 FACTS

Haviland & Company filed suit against Montgomery Ward & Company in U.S. district court, claiming that Ward used the trademark "Haviland" on millions of dollars worth of merchandise. As the owner of the mark, Haviland & Company sought compensation from Ward. Ward served notice to take the deposition of Haviland & Company's president, William D. Haviland. The attorneys for Haviland told the court that Haviland was 80 years old, lived in Limoges, France, and was too ill to travel to the United States for the deposition. Haviland's physician submitted an affidavit confirming these facts.

ISSUE

Must Haviland give his deposition?

Simblest v. Maynard

427 F.2d 1 (2d Cir. 1970)

8.3 FACTS

On November 9, 1965, Mr. Simblest was driving a car that collided with a fire engine at an intersection in Burlington, Vermont. The accident occurred on the night on which a power blackout left most of the state without lights. Mr. Simblest, who was injured in the accident, sued the driver of the fire truck for damages. During the trial, Simblest testified that when he entered the intersection, the traffic light was green in his favor. All of the other witnesses testified that the traffic light had gone dark at least 10 minutes before the accident. Simblest testified that the accident was caused by the fire truck's failure to use any warning lights or sirens. Simblest's testimony was contradicted by four witnesses who testified that the fire truck had used both its lights and sirens. The jury found that the driver of the fire truck had been negligent and rendered a verdict for Simblest. The defense made a motion for judgment n.o.v.

ISSUE

Who wins?

Harris v. Time, Inc.

191 C.A.3d 449, 237 Cal. Rptr. 584 (Cal.App. 1987)

8.4 FACTS

One day Joshua Gnaizda, a three-year-old, received in the mail what he (or his mother) thought was a tantalizing offer from Time, Inc. The front of the envelope contained a see-through window that revealed the following statement: "Joshua Gnaizda, I'll give you this versatile new calculator watch free just for opening this envelope before Feb. 15, 1985." Beneath the offer was a picture of the calculator watch itself. When Joshua's mother opened the envelope, she realized that the see-through window had not revealed the full text of Time's offer. Not viewable through the see-through window were the following words: "and mailing this certificate today." The certificate required Joshua to purchase a subscription to *Fortune* magazine in order to receive the free calculator watch.

Joshua (through his father, a lawyer) sued Time in a class action, seeking compensatory damages in an amount equal to the value of the calculator watch and $15 million in punitive damages. The trial court dismissed the lawsuit as being too trivial for the court to hear. Joshua appealed.

ISSUE

Should Joshua be permitted to maintain his lawsuit against Time, Inc.? Did Time act ethically? Should Joshua's father have sued for $15 million?

CASE FOR BRIEFING

Gnazzo v. G.D. Searle & Co.

973 F.2d 136 (1992)   **United States Court of Appeals, Second Circuit**

Read the following case, excerpted from the court of appeals opinion. Review and brief the case. In your brief, answer the following questions.

1. What is a statute of limitations? What purposes does such a statute serve?

2. What was the Connecticut statute of limitations for the injury alleged by the plaintiff?

3. What is summary judgment? When will it be granted?

4. What was the decision of the trial court? Of the court of appeals?

Pierce, Circuit Judge.

On November 11, 1974, Gnazzo had a CU-7 intrauterine device (IUD) inserted in her uterus for contraceptive purposes. The IUD was developed, marketed, and sold by G.D. Searle & Co. (Searle). When Gnazzo's deposition was taken, she stated that her doctor had informed her that "the insertion would hurt, but not for long," and that she "would have uncomfortable and probably painful periods for the first three to four months." On October 11, 1975, Gnazzo found it necessary to return to her physician due to excessive pain and cramping. During this visit she was informed by her doctor that he thought she had pelvic inflammatory disease (PID). She recalled that he stated that the infection was possibly caused by venereal disease or the use of the IUD. The PID was treated with antibiotics and cleared up shortly thereafter. Less than one year later, Gnazzo was again treated for an IUD-associated infection. This infection was also treated with antibiotics. Gnazzo continued using the IUD until it was finally removed in December of 1977.

Following a laparoscopy in March of 1989, Gnazzo was informed by a fertility specialist that she was infertile because of PID-induced adhesions resulting from her prior IUD use. Subsequent to this determination, and at the request of her then-attorneys, Gnazzo completed a questionnaire dated May 11, 1989. In response to the following question, "When and why did you first suspect that your IUD had caused you any harm?," Gnazzo responded "sometime in 1981" and explained: "I was married in April 1981, so I stopped using birth control so I could get pregnant—nothing ever happened (of course), then I started hearing and reading about how damaging IUDs could be. I figured that was the

problem; however, my marriage started to crumble, so I never pursued the issue."

On May 4, 1990, Gnazzo initiated the underlying action against Searle. In an amended complaint, she alleged that she had suffered injuries as a result of her use of the IUD developed by Searle. Searle moved for summary judgment on the ground that Gnazzo's claim was time-barred by Connecticut's three-year statute of limitations for product liability actions. Searle argued, inter alia, that Gnazzo knew in 1981 that she had suffered harm caused by her IUD. Gnazzo contended that her cause of action against Searle accrued only when she learned from the fertility specialist that the IUD had caused her PID and subsequent infertility.

In a ruling dated September 18, 1991, the district court granted Searle's motion for summary judgment on the ground that Gnazzo's claim was time-barred by the applicable statute of limitations. In reaching this result, the court determined that Connecticut law provided no support for Gnazzo's contention that she should not have been expected to file her action until she was told of her infertility and the IUD's causal connection. This appeal followed.

On appeal, Gnazzo contends that the district court improperly granted Searle's motion for summary judgment because a genuine issue of material fact exists as to when she discovered, or reasonably should have discovered, her injuries and their causal connection to the defendant's alleged wrongful conduct. Summary judgment is appropriate when there is no genuine issue as to any material fact and the moving party is entitled to judgment as a matter of law. We consider the record in the light most favorable to the non-movant. However, the non-movant "may not rest upon the mere allegations of denials of her pleading, but must set forth specific facts showing that there is a genuine issue for trial."

Under Connecticut law, a product liability claim must be brought within "three years from the date when the injury is first sustained or discovered or in the exercise of reasonable care should have been discovered." In Connecticut, a cause of action accrues when a plaintiff suffers actionable harm. Actionable harm occurs when the plaintiff discovers or should discover, through the exercise of reasonable care, that he or she has been injured and that the defendant's conduct caused such injury.

Gnazzo contends that "the mere occurrence of a pelvic infection or difficulty in becoming pregnant does not necessarily result in notice to the plaintiff of a cause of action." Thus, she maintains that her cause of action did not accrue until 1989 when the fertility specialist informed her both that she was infertile and that this condition resulted from her previous use of the IUD.

Under Connecticut law, however, "the statute of limitations begins to run when the plaintiff discovers some form of actionable harm, not the fullest manifestation thereof. Therefore, as Gnazzo's responses to the questionnaire indicate she suspected "sometime in 1981" that the IUD had caused her harm because she had been experiencing trouble becoming pregnant and had "started hearing and reading about how damaging IUDs could be and had figured that was the problem."

Thus, by her own admission, Gnazzo had recognized, or should have recognized, the critical link between her injury and the defendant's causal connection to it. In other words, she had "discovered, or should have discovered through the exercise of reasonable care, that she had been injured and that Searle's conduct caused such injury." However, as Gnazzo acknowledged in the questionnaire, she did not pursue the "issue" at the time because of her marital problems. Thus, even when viewed in the light most favorable to Gnazzo, the non-moving party, we are constrained to find that she knew by 1981 that she had "some form of actionable harm." Consequently, by the time she commenced her action in 1990, Gnazzo was time-barred by the Connecticut statute of limitations.

Since we have determined that Gnazzo's cause of action commenced in 1981, we need not address Searle's additional contention that Gnazzo's awareness in 1975 of her PID and her purported knowledge of its causal connection to the IUD commenced the running of the Connecticut statute of limitations at that time.

We are sympathetic to Gnazzo's situation and mindful that the unavoidable result we reach in this case is harsh. Nevertheless, we are equally aware that "it is within the Connecticut General Assembly's constitutional authority to decide when claims for injury are to be brought. Where a plaintiff has failed to comply with this requirement, a court may not entertain the suit." The judgment of the district court is affirmed.

CHAPTER 8

CHAPTER OBJECTIVES

After studying this chapter, you should be able to:

1. Distinguish between felonies, misdemeanors, and violations.

2. Define and list the essential elements of a crime.

3. Describe criminal procedure, including arrest, indictment, arraignment, and the criminal trial.

4. List and describe crimes against persons and property.

5. Define major white-collar crimes, such as embezzlement, mail fraud, and bribery.

6. Explain the elements necessary to find criminal fraud.

7. Explain the constitutional safeguards against unreasonable searches and seizures.

8. Describe the Fifth Amendment's privilege against self-incrimination.

9. Explain the scope of the Foreign Corrupt Practices Act.

10. List and describe laws involving computer and Internet crimes.

Criminal Law and Process

It is better that ten guilty persons escape, than that one innocent suffer.

SIR WILLIAM BLACKSTONE,
COMMENTARIES ON THE LAWS OF ENGLAND (1809)

Introduction

For members of society to coexist peacefully and commerce to flourish, people and their property must be protected from injury by other members of society. Federal, state, and local governments' **criminal laws** are intended to accomplish this by providing an incentive for persons to act reasonably in society and imposing penalties on persons who violate them.

The United States has one of the most advanced and humane criminal law systems in the world. It differs from many other criminal law systems in several respects. First, a person charged with a crime in the United States is *presumed innocent until proven guilty*. The **burden of proof** is on the government to prove that the accused is guilty of the crime charged. Further, the accused must be found guilty "beyond a reasonable doubt." Conviction requires unanimous jury vote. Under many other legal systems, a person accused of a crime is presumed guilty unless the person can prove that he or she is not. A person charged with a crime in the United States also is provided with substantial constitutional safeguards during the criminal justice process—the protections against unreasonable search and seizure, against self-incrimination, against double jeopardy, and against cruel and unusual punishment, and the right to a public jury trial.

Some private lawyers specialize in criminal law by representing clients accused of criminal wrongdoing. Other lawyers work for the government, either for the prosecution team that represents the government in the criminal lawsuit against the defendant, or for a government-appointed defense counsel representing defendants who cannot afford a private attorney to represent them. Paralegals work for all of these criminal lawyers, and therefore require knowledge of the criminal legal process.

DEFINITION OF A CRIME

A **crime** is defined as any act done by an individual in violation of those duties that he or she owes to society and for the breach of which the law provides that the wrongdoer shall make amends to the public. Many activities have been considered crimes throughout the ages, whereas other crimes are of recent origin.

Penal Codes and Regulatory Statutes

Statutes are the primary source of criminal law. Most states have adopted comprehensive **penal codes** that define in detail the activities considered to be crimes within their jurisdiction and the penalties that will be imposed for committing these crimes. A comprehensive federal criminal code defines federal crimes (Title 18 of the U.S. Code). In addition, state and federal regulatory statutes often provide for criminal violations and penalties. The state and federal legislatures are continually adding to the list of crimes.

The penalty for committing a crime may be the imposition of a fine, imprisonment, both, or some other form of punishment (e.g., probation). Generally, imprisonment is imposed to

1. Incapacitate the criminal so he or she will not harm others in society.
2. Provide a means to rehabilitate the criminal.
3. Deter others from similar conduct.
4. Inhibit personal retribution by the victim.

Parties to a Criminal Action

In a criminal lawsuit, the government (not a private party) is the **plaintiff.** A lawyer called the **prosecutor, district attorney,** or in the federal system United States Attorney, represents the gov-

Meet

THE COURTHOUSE TEAM

Criminal Clerk of Court

In most jurisdictions the civil court records and the criminal court records are maintained in separate offices. The office of the criminal clerk of court maintains the official court files of criminal cases, including indictments, court proceedings, sentences and costs of prosecution records. Criminal defense requests and motions are also filed with the clerk of courts in most jurisdictions.

ernment. The accused is the **defendant.** The **defense attorney** represents the accused. If the accused cannot afford a defense lawyer, the government will provide one free of charge, called a **public defender.**

CLASSIFICATION OF CRIMES

All crimes can be classified into one of these categories: felonies, misdemeanors, or violations.

Felonies

Felonies are the most serious kinds of crimes. They include crimes that are *mala in se*—inherently evil. Most crimes against the person (murder, rape, and the like) and certain business-related crimes (such as embezzlement and bribery) are felonies in most jurisdictions. Felonies usually are punishable by imprisonment. In some jurisdictions, certain felonies (e.g., first-degree murder) are punishable by death. Federal law and some state laws require mandatory sentencing for specified crimes. Many statutes define different degrees of crimes (e.g., first-, second-, and third-degree murder) with each degree earning different penalties.

"This, ladies and gentleman, is Exhibit A, the sneakers that urged my client to Just Do It."

Misdemeanors

Misdemeanors are less serious than felonies. They are crimes *mala prohibita*—not inherently evil but prohibited by society. This category includes many crimes against property, such as robbery, burglary, and violations of regulatory statutes. Misdemeanors carry lesser penalties than felonies; they usually are punishable by fine and/or imprisonment for one year or less.

Violations

Crimes such as traffic violations and jaywalking are neither felonies nor misdemeanors. Called **violations,** these crimes usually are punishable by a fine. Occasionally, a few days of imprisonment are imposed.

ESSENTIAL ELEMENTS OF A CRIME

For a person to be found guilty of most crimes, a criminal act and criminal intent must be proven.

Criminal Act

The defendant must have actually performed the prohibited act. Under the common law, actual performance of the criminal act is called the *actus reus* (guilty act). Under the Model Penal Code, the prohibited act may be analyzed in terms of conduct, circumstances, and results. Killing someone without legal justification is an example of *actus reus*. Sometimes the omission of an act constitutes the requisite *actus reus*. For example, a crime has been committed if a taxpayer who is under a legal duty to file a tax return fails to do so. Merely thinking about committing a crime is not a crime because no action has been taken.

Criminal Intent

To be found guilty of a crime, the accused must be found to have possessed the requisite subjective state of mind (i.e., specific or general intent) when the act was performed. This is called the **mens rea** (evil intent) under the traditional common law analysis and *culpable mental state* under the Model Penal Code. The Model Penal Code has four levels of culpable mental state:

1. Purposeful (or intentional)
2. Knowingly
3. Recklessly
4. With criminal negligence.

Specific intent is found where the accused purposefully, intentionally, or with knowledge commits a prohibited act. *General intent* is found where there is a showing of recklessness or a lesser degree of mental culpability. The individual criminal statutes state whether the crime requires a showing of specific or general intent. Juries may infer an accused's intent from the facts and circumstances of the case. There is no crime if the requisite *mens rea* cannot be proven. Thus, no crime is committed if one person accidentally injures another person.

Some statutes impose criminal liability based on *strict* or *absolute liability*. A finding of *mens rea* is not required. Criminal liability is imposed if the prohibited act is committed. Absolute liability is often imposed by regulatory statutes, such as environmental laws.

CRIMINAL ACTS AS BASIS FOR TORT ACTIONS

An injured party may bring a *civil tort action* against a wrongdoer who has caused the party injury during the commission of a criminal act. Civil lawsuits are separate from the government's criminal action against the wrongdoer. In many cases, a person injured by a criminal act will not sue the criminal to recover civil damages. This is because the criminal is often *judgment proof*—that is, the criminal does not have the money to pay a civil judgment. Table 8.1 compares civil and criminal law.

CRIMINAL PROCEDURE

The court procedure for initiating and maintaining a criminal action is quite detailed. It encompasses both pretrial procedures and the actual trial. Pretrial criminal procedure consists of several distinct stages, including *arrest*, *indictment* or *information*, *arraignment*, and possible *plea bargaining*.

For centuries, some individuals—for various purposes, mostly financial in nature—have attempted to take the identity of other persons. Today, taking on the identity of another can be extremely lucrative, earning the spoils of another's credit cards, bank accounts, Social Security benefits, and such. The use of new technology—computers and the Internet—has made such identity fraud even easier. The victim of such fraud may be left with funds stolen, a dismantled credit history, and thousands of dollars in costs trying to straighten out the mess.

Identity fraud is the fastest growing financial fraud in the United States. Credit reporting firms say identity fraud cases have increased from 10,000 in 1990 to more than 500,000 cases per year today.

To combat such fraud, Congress passed the Identity Theft and Assumption Deterrence Act of 1998.

This law criminalizes identity fraud, making it a federal felony punishable with prison sentences ranging from 3 to 25 years. The Act also appoints a federal administrative agency, the Federal Trade Commission (FTC), to help victims restore their credit and erase the impact of the imposter. Law-enforcement officials suggest that you:

1. Never put your Social Security number on any document unless it is legally required.

2. Obtain and review copies of your credit report at least twice each year.

3. Use passwords other than maiden names and birthdays on bank accounts and other accounts that require personal identification numbers (PINs).

Arrest

Before the police can arrest a person for committing a crime, they usually must obtain an **arrest warrant** based upon a showing of **probable cause**—the substantial likelihood that the person either committed or is about to commit a crime. If the police do not have time to obtain a warrant (e.g., if the police arrive during the commission of a crime, when a person is fleeing from the scene of the crime, or when it is likely that evidence will be destroyed), the

ISSUE	CIVIL LAW	CRIMINAL LAW
\multicolumn{3}{l}{*Civil and criminal law compared.* **table 8.1**}
Party who brings the action	Plaintiff	Government
Trial by jury	Yes, except actions for equity	Yes
Burden of proof	Preponderance of evidence	Beyond a reasonable doubt
Jury vote	Judgment for plaintiff requires specific jury vote (e.g., 9 of 12 jurors)	Conviction requires unanimous jury vote
Sanctions and penalties	Monetary damages and equitable remedies (e.g., injunction, specific performance)	Imprisonment, capital punishment, fine, probation

police still may arrest the suspect. *Warrantless arrests*, too, are judged by the probable-cause standard. After a person is arrested, he or she is taken to the police station for *booking*—the administrative proceeding for recording the arrest, fingerprinting, and so on.

Indictment or Information

Accused persons must be formally charged with a crime before they can be brought to trial. This usually is done by the issuance of a *grand jury indictment* or a *magistrate's* (judge's) *information statement*. Evidence of serious crimes, such as murder, is usually presented to a *grand jury*. Most grand juries consist of between 6 and 24 citizens who are charged with evaluating the evidence presented by the government. Grand jurors sit for a fixed time, such as one year. If the grand jury determines that there is sufficient evidence to hold the accused for trial, it issues an **indictment.** Note that the grand jury does not determine guilt. If an indictment is issued, the accused will be held for later trial.

For lesser crimes (burglary, shoplifting, and such), the accused will be brought before a *magistrate* (judge). A magistrate who finds that there is enough evidence to hold the accused for trial will issue *information*. The case against the accused is dismissed if neither an indictment nor an information is issued.

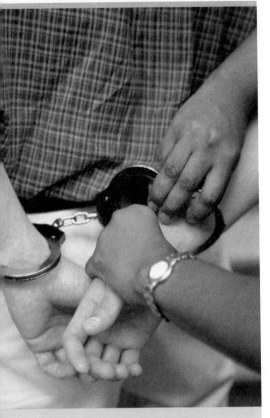

After arrest, the detainee is taken to the police station for booking.

Arraignment

If an indictment or information is issued, the accused is brought before a court for an **arraignment** proceeding during which the accused is (1) informed of the charges against him or her, and (2) asked to enter a *plea*. The accused may plead *guilty*, *not guilty*, or *nolo contendere*. A plea of *nolo contendere* means that the accused agrees to the imposition of a penalty but does not admit guilt. A *nolo contendere* plea cannot be used as evidence of liability against the accused at a subsequent civil trial. Corporate defendants often enter this plea. The government has the option of accepting a *nolo contendere* plea or requiring the defendant to plead guilty or not guilty. Depending on the nature of the crime, the accused may be released upon posting bail.

Plea Bargaining

Sometimes the accused and the government enter into a **plea bargain** agreement. The government engages in plea bargaining to save costs, avoid the risks of a trial, and prevent further overcrowding of the prisons. This type of arrangement allows the accused to admit to a lesser crime than charged. In return, the government agrees to impose a lesser penalty or sentence than might have been obtained had the case gone to trial. In the federal system, more than 90 percent plead guilty rather than go to trial.

THE CRIMINAL TRIAL

The criminal trial and the civil action trial have many similarities. The functions of the judge and jury are the same. The jury acts as the **trier of fact.** In cases in which the defendant exercises the right to proceed without a jury, also known as a **bench trial** (or *waiver trial*), the judge acts as the trier of fact. The judge also acts as the arbiter of procedural rules covering the conduct of the trial, and the judge is ultimately the one who applies the law to findings of fact, and guilt or innocence of the charges and who determines the sentence, fine, or other permitted forfeiture in cases of guilt. In some cases, such as murder trials, the jury also decides the sentence.

The order and presentation of evidence also are similar. The prosecution goes first and puts on its case, followed by the defense's presentation of its evidence. Motions for dismissal at the close of the prosecution's case are also similar to those in the civil action.

A significant difference is the concern in many cases to protect the record (the trial transcript). The defense counsel tends to be especially concerned with making appropriate objections on the record that can be used as the basis of an appeal. Prosecutors also are concerned that they not say anything on the record that the defendant can use as a basis for appeal in the event of a conviction.

Pretrial Discovery

A limited amount of pretrial discovery is permitted, with substantial restrictions to protect the identity of government informants and to prevent intimidation of witnesses. Defense attorneys often file motions to suppress evidence, which ask the court to exclude evidence from trial that the defendant believes the government obtained in violation of the defendant's constitutional rights, statute, or procedural rule. The government is under an obligation to provide **exculpatory** evidence to the defense attorney.

Under the Federal Rules of Criminal Procedure Rule 16, upon the defendant's request, the government must disclose and make available for inspection, copying, or photographing any relevant written or recorded statements made by defendant within the possession, custody, or control of the government, the existence of which is known, or where the exercise of due diligence may become known to the attorney for the government.

Determination of Guilt

At a criminal trial, unlike a civil-action trial, all jurors must *unanimously* agree before the accused is found *guilty* of the crime charged. If even one juror disagrees (i.e., has reasonable doubt) about the guilt of the

Meet THE COURTHOUSE TEAM

District Attorney–Prosecutor

In most jurisdictions, the individual who prosecutes criminal cases on behalf of the state is called the district attorney (DA) or prosecutor. In the federal system, the United States Attorney is the one who prosecutes federal criminal cases. The U.S. Attorney is appointed, whereas a district attorney is usually an elected official.

Subpoenas in Federal Criminal Cases

F.R.C.P. Rule 17 provides that the clerk of court or the magistrate judge hearing the matter shall issue subpoenas. These must be served by a person, not a party, who is no younger than 18 years of age. There is no provision for service by mail. All subpoenas must be accompanied by a check for the witness fee (typically $40 per day) and mileage (roundtrip to the courthouse), unless the subpoena is issued on behalf of the United States or the court has determined upon *ex parte* motion that the defendant is financially unable to pay.

SIDEBAR

accused, the accused is *not guilty* of the crime charged. If all of the jurors agree that the accused did not commit the crime, the accused is *innocent* of the crime charged.

After trial, the following rules apply:

- If the defendant is found guilty, he or she may appeal.
- If the defendant is found innocent, the government cannot appeal.
- If the jury cannot come to a unanimous decision about the defendant's guilt, the jury is considered a **hung jury.** The government may choose to retry the case before a new judge and jury.

CRIMES AFFECTING BUSINESS

Many crimes are committed against business property, often involving the theft, misappropriation, or fraudulent taking of property. The most important types of crimes against business property are discussed in the following paragraphs.

Robbery

At common law, **robbery** is defined as the taking of personal property from another person by the use of fear or force. For example, if a robber threatens to physically harm a storekeeper unless the victim surrenders the contents of the cash register, this is robbery. If a criminal pickpockets somebody's wallet, it is not robbery because there has been no use of force or fear. Robbery with a deadly weapon is generally considered *aggravated robbery* (or armed robbery) and carries a harsher penalty.

Burglary

At common law, **burglary** was defined as "breaking and entering a dwelling at night" with the intent to commit a felony. Modern penal codes have broadened this definition to include daytime thefts and thefts from offices and commercial and other buildings. In addition, most modern definitions of burglary have abandoned the "breaking-in" element. Thus, unauthorized entering of a building through an unlocked door is sufficient. Aggravated burglary (or armed burglary) carries stiffer penalties.

Larceny

At common law, **larceny** is defined as the wrongful and fraudulent taking of another person's personal property. Most personal property—including tangible property, trade secrets, computer programs, and other business property—is subject to larceny. The stealing of automobiles and car stereos, pickpocketing, and such are larceny. Neither the use of force nor the entry of a building is required. Some states distinguish between *grand larceny* and *petit larceny*, depending on the value of the property taken.

Theft

Some states have dropped the distinction among the crimes of robbery, burglary, and larceny. Instead, these states group these crimes under the general crime of *theft*. Most of these states distinguish between *grand theft* and *petit theft*, depending upon the value of the property taken.

Receiving Stolen Property

It is a crime for a person to (1) knowingly receive stolen property, and (2) intend to deprive the rightful owner of that property. Knowledge and intent can be inferred from the circumstances. The stolen property can be any tangible property (e.g., personal property, money, negotiable instruments, stock certificates, and so on).

Arson

At common law, **arson** was defined as the malicious or willful burning of the dwelling of another person. Modern penal codes expanded this definition to include the burning of all types of private, commercial, and public buildings. Thus, in most states, an owner who burns his or her own building to collect insurance proceeds can be found liable for arson. If arson is found, the insurance company does not have to pay the proceeds of any insurance policy on the burned property.

Forgery

The crime of **forgery** occurs if a written document is fraudulently made or altered and that change affects the legal liability of another person. Examples of forgery are counterfeiting, falsifying public records, and the material altering of legal documents. One of the most common forms of forgery is the signing of another person's signature to a check or changing the amount of a check. Note that signing another person's signature without intent to defraud is not forgery. For instance, forgery has not been committed if one spouse signs the other spouse's payroll check for deposit in a joint checking or savings account at the bank.

Extortion

The crime of **extortion** means the obtaining of property from another, with his or her consent, induced by wrongful use of actual or threatened force, violence, or fear. For example, extortion occurs when a person threatens to expose something about another person unless that other person gives money or property. The truth or falsity of the information is immaterial. Extortion of private persons is commonly called *blackmail*. Extortion of public officials is called *extortion "under color of official right."*

Sentencing Guidelines

The United States Sentencing Commission established the Sentencing Guidelines for the federal criminal justice system [18 U.S.C. § 3551 et. seq.]. If a defendant is found guilty, the court probation office prepares a report for the court and applies the Sentencing Guidelines to the individual defendant and the crimes for which he or she has been found guilty.

During sentencing, the court may consider the evidence produced at trial and also all relevant information that may be provided by the pretrial services officer, the U.S. attorney, and the defense attorney. In unusual circumstances, the court may depart from the sentence calculated according to the Sentencing Guidelines.

A sentence may include time in prison, a fine to be paid to the government, and monetary restitution to pay to crime victims. The court's probation officers assist the court in enforcing any conditions that are imposed as part of the criminal sentence.

Money Laundering

The term *money laundering* refers to the process by which criminals convert tainted proceeds into apparently legitimate funds or property. It applies equally to an international wire transfer of hundreds of millions of dollars in drug proceeds and the purchase of an automobile with funds robbed from a bank.

Money laundering is a federal crime. The following activities are among those that were criminalized by the Money Laundering Control Act:

- Knowingly engaging in a *financial transaction* involving the proceeds of some form of specified unlawful activity. Transactions covered include the sale of real property, personal property, intangible assets, and anything of value. [18 U.S.C. § 1956]

- Knowingly engaging in a *monetary transaction* by, through, or to a financial institution involving property of a value greater than $10,000, which is derived from specified unlawful activity. Monetary transaction is defined as a deposit, withdrawal, transfer between accounts, and use of a monetary instrument. [18 U.S.C. § 1957]

"Specified unlawful activity" includes narcotics activities and virtually any white-collar crime.

Money laundering statutes have been used to go after entities and persons involved in illegal check-cashing schemes, bribery, insurance fraud, Medicaid fraud, bankruptcy fraud, bank fraud, fraudulent transfer of property, criminal conspiracy, environmental crime, and other types of illegal activities.

Conviction for money laundering carries stiff penalties. Persons can be fined up to $500,000 or twice the value of the property involved, whichever is greater, and sentenced to up to 20 years in federal prison. In addition, violation subjects the defendant to provisions that mandate forfeiture to the government of any property involved in or traceable to the offense [18 U.S.C. §§ 981–982]. Any financial institution convicted of money laundering can have its charter revoked or its insurance of deposit accounts terminated.

To avoid running afoul of these increasingly complex statutes, banks and businesses must develop and implement policies and procedures to detect criminal activity and report money laundering by customers to the federal government.

Credit-Card Crimes

Substantial purchases in the United States are made with credit cards. This poses a problem if someone steals and uses another person's credit cards. Many states have enacted statutes that make the misappropriation and use of credit cards a separate crime. In other states, credit-card crimes are prosecuted under the forgery statute.

Bad Checks

Many states have enacted *bad check legislation*, which makes it a crime for a person to make, draw, or deliver a check at a time when that person knows that funds in the account are insufficient to cover the amount of the check. Some states require proof that the accused intended to defraud the payee of the check.

White-Collar Crimes

Certain types of crime that are prone to be committed by businesspersons are often referred to as **white-collar crimes.** These crimes usually involve cunning and deceit rather than physical force. Many of the white-collar crimes are discussed in the paragraphs that follow.

At Taubman Trial, Lovely Paralegal Holds the Balance

New York Observer, December 10, 2001   Ralph Gardner, Jr.

The surprise star of *U.S.A. v. Alfred Taubman* may turn out to be not Diana (Dede) Brooks, Sotheby's former chief executive, whom the defense spent the better part of the trial's final week attempting to portray as a sort of dominatrix in pearls and pumps, but Jade Burns. You need not feel inadequate if you've never heard of Ms. Burns. She's not a former member of Sotheby's titled board, or the ultimate expert on Rembrandt, or the recipient of a sweetheart loan from the auction house in exchange for the opportunity to sell her grandmother's Monet water lilies. Ms. Burns is a paralegal employed by the Department of Justice. And throughout the trial, she's sat at the prosecution table and ably and discreetly operated one of the computers that projects Sotheby's and Christie's notes, memos, board minutes, consignment contracts and other documents, incriminating or not, depending on your point of view, onto a giant screen and a collection of TV monitors strategically placed around the courtroom.

Mr. Taubman, Sotheby's former chairman and still its largest shareholder, is charged with conspiring with Sir Anthony Tennant, his opposite number at Christie's, to fix the auction business so that clients couldn't play the two houses against each other in search of more favorable terms. Sir Anthony is in Great Britain, where he can't be extradited; he's denied any wrongdoing. Ms. Brooks has pled guilty to collusion and awaits sentencing. She hopes that in exchange for her testimony against Mr. Taubman, she'll receive little (or, better yet, no) jail time. The jury spent the better part of Dec. 4 in deliberations, requesting documents and, before they quit for the night, a reading of the antitrust laws.

In light of all this, Ms. Burns, the government's last witness, showing up in the trial's final hours and on the spur of the moment, it seemed, appears an awfully small fish. However, since price-fixing never does much to stir the imagination, the case may turn on which side seems more sympathetic to the working-class jury. And in that regard, the paralegal, who is only 24, had very little competition: There seemed to be no heroes in this trial. The witness list included its share of overcompensated and overweight middle-aged men.

Ms. Burns' star turn came in response to a defense witness named Christine Nelson, an economic consultant who was being paid $425 an hour to testify that Mr. Taubman had done nothing wrong, based on her examination of data supplied to her by Sotheby's and Christie's. The prosecution has made much of a 1993 memo in Sir Anthony's handwriting that allegedly lays out the terms of his collusion deal with Mr. Taubman. However, in several areas where they'd agreed to stop competing, for example, in ceasing to give advances on single lots, or loans below Libor, the British equivalent of the prime rate, Ms. Nelson's analysis proved that the deal was disregarded. Of course, her study only examined the years 1993 to 1995. "Her chart simply started too early and ended too early," prosecutor John C. Greene charged in his summation rebuttal, rather than continuing on to 1999, when the alleged conspiracy started to unravel. She also ignored a possible logical explanation for her counter-intuitive findings, one offered by Christopher Davidge, Christie's former chief executive, when he testified earlier in the trial on loans below Libor: namely, that "the business was improving" and that, while the sheer number of such loans might be increasing, as a percentage of all transactions it might actually be diminishing. Finally, as the prosecution brought out on cross-examination, Ms. Nelson had no way of knowing whether the consignment contracts she studied may have been subject to preexisting, pre-1993 agreements between the auction houses and particular clients.

When Ms. Burns took the witness stand, one couldn't help but compare her to Ms. Nelson, whose Goody Two-Shoes manner didn't appear to endear her to the jury. (It's impossible to handicap a jury, but this one has offered few signs of affection for Mr. Taubman or his team. And shortly after Ms. Nelson stepped down after parts of two days spent on the witness stand, one of the jurors instructed Scott Muller, a Taubman lawyer, to turn off a light on a projection machine that was shining in the jury's eyes. When the lawyer promptly obeyed, the juror turned to a couple of buddies on the jury and gave them a wink and a "See, that'll show 'em" nod.)

Leave a person on a witness stand long enough, and they start to remind you of someone you hated in high school. And Ms. Nelson, particularly as she gamely sparred with Patricia Jannaco, the government lawyer cross-examining her, recalled the teacher's pet who scores 100 on the math final and throws off the entire grading curve. Ms. Burns also happens to be extremely pretty, perhaps even beautiful, though it's hard to tell since she keeps her hair pulled back and wears those nerdy, dark-framed glasses of the sort Tina Fey sports while giving the "Weekend Update" on Saturday Night Live. While the Berkeley philosophy major spent only a few fleeting moments on the witness stand, the government was able to get into evidence the fact that her charts covered the years up to and including 1998, unlike Ms. Nelson's (making one wonder what she might have been hiding), and also that Ms. Burns' data included information on sellers' commissions, the essence of the alleged collusion between Mr. Taubman and Mr. Tennant, showing the rates had gone up.

Besides Ms. Nelson, the defense called 13 other witnesses (the government offered five), whose contributions were of a more impressionistic nature. They testified to Mr. Taubman's excellence as a human being, even if he was a little vague on occasion, and to Ms. Brooks' unsympathetic tendencies.

Perhaps the most damaging testimony to Ms. Brooks came at the start of the defense's presentation, when Donaldson Pillsbury, Sotheby's in-house lawyer, testified that he never heard Mr. Taubman tell her, as she'd claimed, "You'll look good in stripes" during a meeting when he supposedly feared she'd squeal to the feds. Rather, Mr. Pillsbury said, Mr. Taubman actually asked rather amiably, "How do you think I'd look in stripes?" The ultimate question, of course, is whether the jury is wondering the same thing.

Mr. Taubman is little short of Sphinx-like as he sits at the defense table, the very model of aristocratic comportment, with the jury left to connect the dots as best it can to form a picture of his personality, one that's based mostly on the testimony of minions, some of whom had only fleeting contact with him. They painted a picture of an individual neither liked nor disliked, let alone loved or loathed, whose habits were more reminiscent of a brown bear than of a swashbuckling billionaire. (Mr. Taubman's net worth was estimated by his lawyers during their opening statements at between $700 million and $1 billion.)

Bernard Winograd, a former executive with Mr. Taubman's investment company in Michigan, whose holdings include Sotheby's, testified that "he does have a sleeping disorder and can occasionally fall asleep involuntarily." William Sheridan, Sotheby's current chief financial officer, volunteered that at board meetings his boss "was more concerned with what time lunch was going to be served and what was for lunch."

Ms. Brooks, on the other hand, was portrayed as the C.E.O. from heck, if not quite from hell, a Valkyrie in a business suit. George Bailey, Sotheby's managing director for Europe, recalled that she balked at agendas different from her own, including Mr. Taubman's. "She's a very emotional person," Mr. Bailey, whose British accent was as thick as Lyle's Golden Syrup, testified. "She used to get very upset." Michael Curle, a former Sotheby's finance director for Europe, once heard her snap at Mr. Bailey, "Alfred Taubman doesn't run this company, I do." And the billionaire apparently took it. "Mr. Taubman was pretty meek for a guy who owned all that stock," Mr. Sheridan said. "He'd just crawl back into his shell."

The central mystery of the case, of course, is who is Alfred Taubman, and why would he risk his reputation and immense wealth in something as potentially obvious as a price-fixing scheme? In answer to the latter question, lead prosecutor Greene quoted Adam Smith from 1776 (right around the time both auction houses were founded) in his closing argument, even though the defense fought mightily to prevent him from doing so. "People in the same trade seldom meet together for merriment and diversion," the economist observed, "but a conversation ends in a conspiracy against the public or in some contrivance to raise prices."

And then, of course, there's the possibility that Mr. Taubman is innocent. Sotheby's insiders have said that his defense team's portrayal of him as disinterested in the business isn't a cynical tactic to save him from the slammer, but the truth. He bought Sotheby's to mingle with lords and ladies, Kennedys and Duponts, they say, and left the nuts and bolts of crunching numbers to others. He really was out to lunch.

Mr. Taubman's true crime, the working-class jury may decide in these patriotic times, is that he seems to have aspired to being British. It was Mr. Bailey who stated that even though he wasn't aware that his chairman had met with Sir Anthony Tennant, it didn't surprise him. "No disrespect to Mr. Taubman," he stated delicately, "but he particularly enjoyed meeting people of title and position in the U.K." With that comment, it became clear whom Mr. Taubman models himself after as he sits there at the defense table, exquisitely well fed and beautifully tailored in his three-piece suits, not an American captain of business, but a British lord.

In his closing argument, Mr. Greene attacked what he described as the defense's "dumb and hungry" defense, pointing out that individuals who amass huge fortunes from scratch tend to have a certain faculty for numbers. Furthermore, Mr. Taubman sat on the boards of both Chase Manhattan Bank and Macy's. "Do you think they'd keep him on the boards if he is a know-nothing who only asked what is for lunch?" Mr. Greene inquired.

In Mr. Taubman's defense, at the time the conspiracy is alleged to have taken place, Sotheby's did have an excellent in-house chef. So if the chairman did often ask what was on the menu, the question may have been more a testimony to the sophistication of his palate than to a preoccupation with his animal needs. However, Mr. Taubman's attorney, Robert B. Fiske, Jr., chose not to highlight his client's good taste when his turn came to offer a summation. Rather, he called Mr. Greene's remark about the "dumb and hungry" defense "kind of an insult. It's an insult to Mr. Taubman and to the fine witnesses who came in here and testified."

What they testified to, according to Mr. Fiske, was that his client was a good and honorable man, and that Ms. Brooks was fully capable of hatching a conspiracy on her own and had the capacity and motive to do so. Mr. Fiske recalled his opening statement at the start of the 14-day trial, when he argued that Ms. Brooks found herself in dire straits back in 1994, shortly after becoming the C.E.O. of Sotheby's Holdings, when a contemporary sale cratered and the price of the company's stock plummeted, imperiling her nascent personal fortune in Sotheby's stock options.

The case was rather quite simple, Mr. Fiske told the haphazardly attentive jury (one of whom dozed on occasion; another, fortunately an alternate, appeared to be in R.E.M. sleep). It all boiled down to whom you believed. Ms. Brooks or Mr. Taubman. "You simply cannot believe Ms. Brooks, and you cannot believe her beyond a reasonable doubt," the lawyer, a former Whitewater prosecutor, charged. "She has no remorse about this at all."

Mr. Fiske dismissed Christopher Davidge, Christie's former chief executive and the government's other main witness, who, along with Christie's, received amnesty from prosecution for squealing first to the government about the alleged conspiracy, as someone who was being paid for his testimony and thus was not even worth considering. Mr. Fiske was referring to an $8 million severance package that Mr. Davidge received from Christie's in exchange for cooperating with the government's investigation into Sotheby's. "This is a one-witness case," Mr. Fiske told the jury. "She is an admitted liar with a powerful motive," that motive being to stay out of jail.

While Mr. Greene's summation was as focused as a satellite-guided missile hitting an Al Qaeda cave complex, "The agreement itself is the crime," he instructed the jury; "whether it is ever carried out, or succeeds or failed, doesn't matter," Mr. Fiske's closing argument was more complicated. For example, he reminded the jury that the only charge in the indictment concerned whether a conspiracy existed to fix sellers' prices, not such issues as guarantees, single-lot advances, or loans below Libor, describing those areas as a "side show." But he then went on to praise Ms. Nelson, whose charts dealt specifically with single-lot advances, loans below Libor, etc., but not at all with seller's commissions, describing her data as "unassailable." Ms. Burns' brief but charming testimony, alas, wasn't evoked by either the prosecution or the defense.

Perhaps the only masterpiece displayed at trial was a poster the prosecution created and had placed on an easel in front of the jury that showed the 12 meetings between Mr. Taubman and Sir Anthony. Though not quite rising to the level of Cubist collage, the government had cut-and-pasted the entries from Mr. Taubman's, his secretaries', and his handlers' daily planners into a sort of color-field painting, punctuated with Twomblyesque scribbled references to meetings with "a gentleman," "Tony," and, in one case, an individual denoted simply with four asterisks. Mr. Fiske characterized the meetings as wholly above board, however. "They were social friends," he noted, and besides, as chairman of their respective auction houses, the two had many legitimate subjects to discuss.

No matter how the case turns out, the jury seems to be getting along famously, at least those who manage to remain sentient, and they invariably enter the courtroom chuckling over some aside one of them has made to the others. And the members of the standing-room-only audience on the trial's last day, reporters, lawyers and a smattering of art-world types, seem to have no particular fear that the wounds this trial opened won't heal completely, even if Mr. Taubman's and Ms. Brooks' reputations lay in ruin. "I was thinking," said one Upper East Sider, "we should have an end-of-the-trial cocktail party with striped food."

Embezzlement

Unknown at common law, the crime of **embezzlement** is now a statutory crime. Embezzlement is the fraudulent conversion of property by a person to whom that property was entrusted. Typically, embezzlement is committed by an employer's employees, agents, or representatives (e.g., accountants, lawyers, trust officers, treasurers). Embezzlers often try to cover their tracks by preparing false books, records, or entries.

The key element here is that the stolen property was *entrusted* to the embezzler. This differs from robbery, burglary, and larceny, in which property is taken by someone not entrusted with the property. Consider this example: Embezzlement has been committed if a bank teller absconds with money that was deposited by depositors. The employer (the bank) entrusted the teller to take deposits from its customers.

"I plead guilty, Your Honor, but only in a nice, white-collar sort of way."

Criminal Fraud

Obtaining title to property through deception or trickery constitutes the crime of **criminal fraud,** also known as *false pretenses* or *deceit.* Consider this example: Robert Anderson, a stockbroker, promises Mary Greenberg, a prospective investor, that he will use any money she invests to purchase interests in oil wells. Based on this promise, Ms. Greenberg decides to make the investment. Mr. Anderson never intended to invest the money. Instead, he used the money for his personal needs. This is criminal fraud.

Mail and Wire Fraud

Federal law prohibits the use of mails or wires (e.g., telegraph or telephone) to defraud another person. These crimes are called **mail fraud** and **wire fraud,** respectively. The government often prosecutes a suspect under these statutes if there is insufficient evidence to prove the real crime that the criminal was attempting to commit or did commit. Wire fraud statutes are also sometimes used to prosecute Internet fraud.

Bribery

Bribery is one of the most prevalent forms of white-collar crime. A bribe can be in the form of money, property, favors, or anything else of value. The crime of commercial bribery prohibits the payment of bribes to private persons and businesses. This type of bribe is often called a *kickback* or a *payoff.* Intent is a necessary element of this crime. The offeror of a bribe commits the crime of bribery when the bribe is tendered. The offeree is guilty of the crime of bribery when he or she accepts the bribe. The offeror can be found liable for the crime of bribery even if the person to whom the bribe is offered rejects the bribe.

Consider this example: Harriet Landers is the purchasing agent for the ABCD Corporation and is in charge of purchasing equipment to be used by the corporation. Neal Brown, the sales representative of a company that makes equipment that can be used by the ABCD Corporation, offers to pay her a 10

Lawyer Charged with Bribing Skadden Paralegal in Insider Trading Scheme

New York Law Journal, November 21, 2000   Mark Hamblett

White Plains, N.Y., attorney Robert C. Schuster tried to bribe a paralegal at one of New York's largest law firms to obtain inside information on approaching mergers and acquisitions, federal prosecutors charged Monday. But authorities say the paralegal, who worked at Skadden, Arps, Slate, Meagher & Flom, turned the tables on Schuster by reporting the bribe attempt and then working as a confidential informant to help snare the attorney. Schuster, 32, allegedly offered the paralegal as much as $15,000 for advance notice of mergers and acquisitions being handled by Skadden.

In a complaint unsealed Monday following Schuster's arrest, prosecutors said the sole practitioner and former assistant district attorney was captured on tape talking to the paralegal and referring to the master stock market manipulator played by actor Michael Douglas in the movie "Wall Street."

"I'm not Gordon Gekko," Schuster reportedly said, "but . . . no risk, no reward."

Schuster, a prosecutor with the Cayuga County District Attorney's Office in Auburn from 1996 to 1997, pleaded not guilty to charges of securities fraud, wire fraud, and commercial bribery before Southern District Magistrate Judge Michael H. Dolinger. He was released on personal recognizance after he and his wife pledged their home to meet the bond of $200,000. The Millwood, N.Y., resident, a 1995 graduate of the Georgetown University Law Center, was also accused of violating securities laws in a civil complaint filed Monday by the Securities and Exchange Commission.

Assistant U.S. Attorney Timothy J. Coleman said in the complaint and an accompanying news release that Schuster was representing the paralegal on another matter when on Sept. 9 he offered $10,000—or $15,000, if necessary—for inside information on corporate mergers and acquisitions.

The paralegal, who remains unnamed, refused the offer and immediately reported the incident to Skadden management, which then alerted the authorities. However, the paralegal was persuaded to help with the investigation and draw Schuster into making incriminating statements on the phone and in person. The paralegal also agreed to wear a recording device when meeting Schuster in person to discuss the arrangement.

During meetings in October, Schuster was allegedly taped while promising the paralegal a "cut" of his profits should the scheme succeed, adding on one occasion that "the whole strategy has to be to know something before anyone else does." The Federal Bureau of Investigation had the paralegal give Schuster a fictitious tip about an upcoming takeover of a real company and, according to the complaint, Schuster ran with it, using his account at Fidelity Brokerage Services to buy 3,000 shares of the company for $153,750. He later gave the paralegal a $500 down payment for participating in the scheme.

On Oct. 4, the complaint continues, Schuster said he assumed that his "co-conspirator" was not wearing a recording device, stating "I am extremely security conscious . . . so I will be very, very cautious." Later, during the same conversation, Schuster muttered the old stockpicker's adage, "Pigs get fat; hogs get slaughtered."

Thomas Lee represented Schuster at arraignment.

percent kickback if she buys equipment from him. She accepts the bribe and orders the equipment. Both parties are guilty of bribery.

At common law, the crime of bribery was defined as the giving or receiving of anything of value in corrupt payment for an "official act" by a public official. Public officials include legislators, judges, jurors, witnesses at trial, administrative agency personnel, and other government officials. Modern penal codes also make it a crime to bribe public officials. For example, a developer who is constructing an apartment building cannot pay the building inspector to overlook a building code violation.

Ethical PERSPECTIVE   *Hughes Aircraft Downed as a Criminal Conspirator*

Hughes Aircraft Co., Inc. (Hughes), an aircraft manufacturer, contracted with the U.S. government to manufacture micro-electronic circuits, known as "hybrids," which are used as components in weapons defense systems. The contract required Hughes to perform tests on each hybrid. A Hughes employee, Donald LaRue, was the supervisor responsible for ensuring the accuracy of the hybrid testing process. LaRue falsely reported that all tests had been performed and that each hybrid had passed the test. When LaRue's subordinates called his actions to the attention of LaRue's supervisors, they did nothing about it. Instead, they responded that LaRue's decisions were his own and were not to be questioned. The United States sued Hughes and LaRue, charging criminal conspiracy to defraud the government. At trial, LaRue was acquitted, but Hughes was convicted of criminal conspiracy and fined $3.5 million. Hughes appealed its conviction, asserting that it should not be convicted of criminal conspiracy if its alleged co-conspirator, LaRue, was acquitted.

Should Hughes be acquitted as a matter of law because the same jury that convicted Hughes acquitted its alleged co-conspirator of the charge of criminal conspiracy? No. The court of appeals held that Hughes may be found guilty of criminal conspiracy even though its co-conspirator had been acquitted of the same crime, and affirmed.

The court of appeals, as a matter of law, held that the inconsistency of the jury verdicts of two defendants charged with criminal conspiracy does not mean that the convicted defendant should also be acquitted. The court noted that the jury may have been more lenient with defendant LaRue, an individual, than they were with Hughes, the corporate defendant. Moreover, the court stated that the jury could have found Hughes guilty of the required act of conspiracy based on evidence provided at trial by the other Hughes's employees that were called as witnesses. [*United States v. Hughes Aircraft Company, Inc.*, 20 F.3d 974 (9th Cir. 1994)]

Racketeer Influenced and Corrupt Organizations Act (RICO)

Organized crime has a pervasive influence on many parts of the U.S. economy. In 1980, Congress enacted the Organized Crime Control Act. The **Racketeer Influenced and Corrupt Organizations Act (RICO)** is part of this Act [18 U.S.C. §§ 1961–1968]. Originally, RICO was intended to apply only to organized crime, but the broad language of the RICO statute has been used against nonorganized crime defendants as well. RICO, which provides for both criminal and civil penalties, is one of the most important laws affecting business today.

RICO makes it a federal crime to acquire or maintain an interest in, use income from, or conduct or participate in the affairs of an "enterprise" through a "pattern" of "racketeering activity." An "enterprise" is defined as a corporation, a partnership, a sole proprietorship, another business or organization, and the government. *Racketeering activity* consists of a number of specifically enumerated federal and state crimes, including activities such as gambling, arson, robbery, counterfeiting, dealing in narcotics, and so on. Business-related crimes, such as bribery, embezzlement, mail fraud, wire fraud, and the like, also are considered racketeering.

During the 1970s, several scandals were uncovered in which American companies were found to have bribed foreign government officials to obtain lucrative contracts. Congressional investigations discovered that making such payments—or bribes—was pervasive in conducting international business. To prevent American companies from engaging in this type of conduct, the U.S. Congress enacted the Foreign Corrupt Practices Act of 1977 (FCPA) [15 U.S.C. § 78m]. Congress amended the FCPA as part of the Omnibus Trade and Competitiveness Act of 1988.

The FCPA attacks the problem in two ways. First, it requires firms to keep accurate books and records of all foreign transactions and install internal accounting controls to ensure that transactions and payments are authorized. Inadvertent or technical errors in maintaining books and records do not violate the FCPA.

Second, the FCPA makes it illegal for American companies, or their officers, directors, agents, or employees, to bribe a foreign official, a foreign political party official, or a candidate for foreign political office. A bribe is illegal only if it is meant to influence the awarding of new business or the retaining of a continuing business activity. Payments to secure ministerial, clerical, or routine government action (such as scheduling inspections, signing customs documents, unloading and loading of cargo, and the like) do not violate the FCPA.

The FCPA imposes criminal liability only in circumstances in which persons knowingly fail to maintain the proper system of accounting, pay the illegal bribe themselves, or supply a payment to a third party or agent knowing that it will be used as a bribe. A firm can be fined up to $2 million and an individual can be fined up to $100,000 and imprisoned for up to five years for violations of the FCPA.

The 1988 amendments created two defenses. One excuses a firm or a person charged with bribery under the FCPA if the firm or person can show that the payment was lawful under the written laws of that country. The other allows a defendant to show that a payment was a reasonable and bona fide expenditure related to the furtherance or execution of a contract.

Some people argue that the FCPA is too soft and permits U.S. firms to engage in the payment of bribes internationally that would otherwise be illegal in the United States. Others argue that the FCPA is difficult to interpret and apply, and that U.S. companies are placed at a disadvantage in international markets where commercial bribery is commonplace and firms from other countries are not hindered by laws similar to the FCPA.

To prove a *pattern of racketeering*, at least two predicate acts must be committed by the defendant within a 10-year period. For example, committing two different frauds would be considered a pattern. Individual defendants found criminally liable for RICO violations can be fined up to $25,000 per violation, imprisoned for up to 20 years, or both. In addition, RICO provides for the *forfeiture* of any property or business interests (even interests in a legitimate business) that were gained because of RICO violations. This provision allows the government to recover investments made with monies derived from racketeering activities. The government also may seek civil penalties for RICO violations. These include injunctions, orders of dissolution, reorganization of business, and divestiture of the defendant's interest in an enterprise.

Racketeering

In 1992, mob boss John Gotti was sentenced to life in prison after being convicted of criminal racketeering and murder charges. Gotti died in prison in 2002.

SIDEBAR

The Internet and Information Age ushered in a whole new world for education, business, and consumer transactions. But with it followed a new rash of digital crimes. Prosecutors and courts wrestled over how to apply existing laws written in a nondigital age to new Internet-related abuses. In many instances, criminal cases were dismissed because the statutory language of existing criminal laws could not be stretched to reach unauthorized computer breaches.

In 1996, Congress responded by enacting the Information Infrastructure Protection Act (IIP Act). In this new federal law, Congress addressed computer-related crimes as distinct offenses. Previously, the Computer Abuse Act outlawed knowingly damaging federal computers, but this Act did not cover nonfederal interest computers owned by businesses and individuals. Also, existing criminal acts required that unauthorized access to computer data had to be for the defendant's commercial benefit before it was illegal. The IIP Act cleared up both of these deficiencies in criminal law in the following ways:

- The IIP Act applies to all "protected computers," not only to federal computers. By statutory definition, a protected computer includes any computer that is used in interstate or foreign commerce.

Thus, the IIP Act provides protection for any computer attached to the Internet.

- The IIP Act does not require that the defendant accessed a protected computer for commercial benefit. The Act makes it clear that simply accessing and obtaining information from a protected computer in excess of one's authorization is unlawful.

The IIP Act makes it a criminal offense for anyone to intentionally access and obtain information from a protected computer without authorization. Thus, persons who transmit a computer virus over the Internet or hackers who trespass into Internet-connected computers may be criminally prosecuted under the IIP Act. Even merely observing data on a protected computer without authorization is sufficient to meet the requirement that the defendant has accessed a protected computer. Criminal penalties for violating the IIP Act include imprisonment for up to 10 years and fines.

The IIP Act gives the federal government a much-needed weapon for directly prosecuting cyber-crooks, hackers, and others who enter, steal, destroy, or look at others' computer data without authorization.

INCHOATE CRIMES

In addition to the substantive crimes discussed, a person can be held criminally liable for committing an **inchoate crime,** which includes incomplete crimes and crimes committed by nonparticipants. The most important inchoate crimes are discussed in the following paragraphs.

Criminal Conspiracy

When two or more persons enter into an *agreement* to commit a crime it is termed **criminal conspiracy.** To be liable for a criminal conspiracy, the conspirators must take an *overt act* to further the crime. The crime itself does not have to be committed, however.

Consider this example: Two securities brokers agreed over the telephone to commit a securities fraud. They also obtained a list of potential victims and prepared false financial statements necessary for the fraud. Because they entered into an agreement to commit a crime and took overt action, the brokers are guilty of the crime of criminal conspiracy even if they didn't carry out the securities fraud. The government usually brings criminal conspiracy charges if (1) the defendants have been thwarted in their efforts to commit the substantive crime, or (2) insufficient evidence is available to prove the substantive crime.

Attempt to Commit a Crime

The **attempt to commit a crime** is itself a crime. For example, suppose a person wants to kill his neighbor. He shoots at her but misses. The perpetrator is not liable for the crime of murder, but he is liable for the crime of attempted murder.

Aiding and Abetting the Commission of a Crime

Sometimes persons assist others in the commission of a crime. The act of **aiding and abetting** the commission of a crime is itself a crime. This concept, which is very broad, encompasses rendering support, assistance, or encouragement to the commission of a crime. Harboring a criminal after he or she has committed a crime is also considered aiding and abetting.

CONSTITUTIONAL SAFEGUARDS

When our forefathers drafted the U.S. Constitution, they included provisions that protect persons from unreasonable government intrusion and provide safeguards for those accused of crimes. Although these safeguards originally applied only to federal cases, the Fourteenth Amendment's Due Process Clause made them applicable to state criminal law cases as well. The most important constitutional safeguards and privileges are discussed in the following paragraphs.

Computer Crime

The use of computers to commit business crimes is increasing. Businesses must implement safeguards to prevent computer crimes.

SIDEBAR

Corporate Criminal Liability

A corporation is a fictitious legal person that is granted legal existence by the state only after meeting certain requirements. A corporation cannot act on its own behalf. Instead, it must act through *agents* such as managers, representatives, and employees.

The question of whether a corporation can be held criminally liable has intrigued legal scholars for some time. Originally, under the common law, it was generally held that corporations lacked the criminal mind (*mens rea*) to be held criminally liable. Modern courts, however, are more pragmatic. These courts have held that corporations are criminally liable for the acts of their managers, agents, and employees. In any event, because corporations cannot be put in prison, they usually are sanctioned with fines, loss of a license or franchise, and the like.

Corporate directors, officers, and employees are individually liable for crimes they personally commit, whether for personal benefit or on behalf of the corporation. In addition, under certain circumstances a corporate manager can be held criminally liable for the criminal activities of his or her subordinates. To be held criminally liable, the manager must have failed to supervise the subordinate appropriately. This is an evolving area of the law.

Fourth Amendment Protection Against Unreasonable Searches and Seizures

The *Fourth Amendment* to the U.S. Constitution protects persons and corporations from overzealous investigative activities by the government. It protects the rights of the people from **unreasonable search and seizure** by the government and permits people to be secure in their persons, houses, papers, and effects.

"Reasonable" search and seizure by the government is lawful. **Search warrants** based on probable cause are necessary in most cases. These warrants specifically state the place and scope of the authorized search. General searches beyond the specified area are forbidden. *Warrantless searches* generally are permitted only (1) incident to arrest, (2) where evidence is in "plain view," or (3) where evidence likely will be destroyed. Warrantless searches also are judged by the probable-cause standard.

Sevier County Courthouse completed 1896 in Sevierville, Tennessee.

Evidence obtained from an unreasonable search and seizure is considered tainted evidence ("fruit of a poisonous tree"). Under the **exclusionary rule,** such evidence can be prohibited from introduction at a trial or administrative proceeding against the person searched. This evidence, however, is freely admissible against other persons. The U.S. Supreme Court created a *good-faith exception* to the exclusionary rule. This exception allows evidence otherwise obtained illegally to be introduced as evidence against the accused if the police officers who conducted the unreasonable search reasonably believed they were acting pursuant to a lawful search warrant.

Generally, the government does not have the right to search business premises without a search warrant. But businesses in certain hazardous and regulated industries—such as sellers of firearms and liquor, coal mines, vehicle dismantling and automobile junkyards, and the like—are subject to warrantless searches if proper statutory procedures are met. A business also may give consent to search the premises, including employee desks and computers, because of the lack of privacy in those items.

Fifth Amendment Privilege Against Self-Incrimination

The *Fifth Amendment* to the U.S. Constitution provides that no person "shall be compelled in any criminal case to be a witness against himself." Thus, a person cannot be compelled to give testimony against himself or herself, although nontestimonial evidence (fingerprints, body fluids, and the like) may be required. A person who asserts this right is described as having "taken the Fifth." This protection applies to federal cases and is extended to state and local criminal cases through the Due Process Clause of the Fourteenth Amendment.

The protection against **self-incrimination** applies only to natural persons who are accused of crimes. Therefore, artificial persons (such as corporations and partnerships) cannot raise this protection against incriminating testimony. Thus, business records of corporations and partnerships are not protected

Kyllo v. United States

FACTS

In 1992, government agents suspected that marijuana was being grown in the home of Danny Kyllo, part of a triplex building in Florence, Oregon. Indoor marijuana growth typically requires high-intensity lamps. To determine whether an amount of heat was emanating from Kyllo's home consistent with the use of such lamps, federal agents used a thermal imager to scan the triplex. Thermal imagers detect infrared radiation and produce images of the radiation. The scan of Kyllo's home, which was performed from an automobile on the street, showed that the roof over the garage and a side wall of Kyllo's home were "hot." The federal agents concluded that Kyllo was using halide lights to grow marijuana in his house. The agents used this scanning evidence to obtain a search warrant authorizing a search of Kyllo's home. During the search, the agents found an indoor growing operation involving more than 100 marijuana plants.

Kyllo was indicted for manufacturing marijuana, a violation of federal criminal law. Kyllo moved to suppress the imaging evidence and the evidence it led to, arguing that it was an unreasonable search that violated the Fourth Amendment to the U.S. Constitution. The trial court disagreed with Kyllo and let the evidence be introduced and considered at trial. Kyllo then entered a conditional guilty plea and appealed the trial court's failure to suppress the challenged evidence. The court of appeals affirmed. The U.S. Supreme Court granted *certiorari* to hear the appeal.

ISSUE

Is the use of a thermal-imaging device aimed at a private home from a public street to detect relative amounts of heat within the home a "search" within the meaning of the Fourth Amendment?

IN THE LANGUAGE OF THE COURT

Scalia, Justice.

At the very core of the Fourth Amendment stands the right of a man to retreat into his own home and there be free from unreasonable governmental intrusion. With few exceptions, the question whether a warrantless search of a home is reasonable and hence constitutional must be answered no. On the other hand, the lawfulness of warrantless visual surveillance of a home has still been preserved. If fact we have held that visual observation is no "search" at all. We have applied the test on different occasions in holding that aerial surveillance of private homes and surrounding areas does not constitute a search. [*California v. Ciraolo*, 476 U.S. 207, 213, 106 S.Ct. 1809 (1986), and *Florida v. Riley*, 488 U.S. 445, 109 S.Ct. 693 (1989)]

The present case involves officers on a public street engaged in more than naked-eye surveillance of a home. The question we confront today is what limits there are upon this power of technology to shrink the realm of guaranteed privacy. We think that obtaining by sense-enhancing technology any information regarding the interior of the home that could not otherwise have been obtained without physical intrusion into a constitutionally protected area constitutes a search. This assures preservation of that degree of privacy against government that existed when the Fourth Amendment was adopted. On the basis of this criterion, the information obtained by the thermal imager in this case was the product of a search.

DECISION AND REMEDY

The U.S. Supreme Court held that the use of a thermal-imaging device aimed at a private home from a public street to detect relative amounts of heat within the home is a "search" within the meaning of the Fourth Amendment. The Supreme Court reversed and remanded the case for further proceedings.

Questions

1. Is the Fourth Amendment's prohibition against unreasonable search and seizure an easy standard to apply? Explain.

2. Did the police act ethically in obtaining the evidence in this case? Did Kyllo act ethically in trying to suppress the evidence?

3. How can the government catch entrepreneurs such as Kyllo? Explain.

from disclosure, even if they incriminate individuals who work for the business. But certain "private papers" of businesspersons (such as personal diaries) are protected from disclosure.

Immunity from Prosecution

On occasion, the government wants to obtain information from a suspect who has asserted his or her Fifth Amendment privilege against self-incrimination. The government can try to achieve this by offering the suspect **immunity from prosecution,** in which the government agrees not to use any evidence given by a person who has been granted immunity against that person. Once immunity is granted, the suspect loses the right to assert his or her Fifth Amendment privilege.

Grants of immunity often are given when the government wants the suspect to give information that will lead to the prosecution of other, more important criminal suspects. Partial grants of immunity also are available. For example, a suspect may be granted immunity from prosecution for a serious crime but not a lesser crime, in exchange for information.

Attorney–Client Privilege and Other Privileges

To obtain a proper defense, the accused person must be able to tell his or her attorney facts about the case without fear that the attorney will be called as a witness against the accused. The **attorney–client privilege** is protected by the Fifth Amendment. Either the client or the attorney can raise this privilege. For the privilege to apply, the information must be told to the attorney in his or her capacity as an attorney, and not as a friend or neighbor or other such relationship.

The following privileges also have been recognized under the Fifth Amendment:

1. Psychiatrist/psychologist–patient privilege,
2. Priest/minister/rabbi–penitent privilege,
3. Spouse–spouse privilege, and
4. Parent–child privilege.

There are some exceptions. For example, a spouse or a child who is beaten by a spouse or a parent may testify against the accused.

Fifth Amendment Protection Against Double Jeopardy

The **double jeopardy** clause of the Fifth Amendment protects persons from being tried twice for the same crime. For example, if the state tries a suspect for the crime of murder and the suspect is found innocent, the state cannot bring another trial against the accused for the same crime. But if the same criminal act involves several different crimes, the accused may be tried for each of the crimes without violating the double jeopardy clause. Suppose the accused kills two people during a robbery. The accused may be tried for two murders and the robbery.

If the same act violates the laws of two or more jurisdictions, each jurisdiction may try the accused. For instance, if an accused person kidnaps a person in one state and brings the victim across a state border into another state, the act violates the laws of two states and the federal government. Thus, three jurisdictions can prosecute the accused without violating the double jeopardy clause.

Sixth Amendment Right to a Public Jury Trial

The *Sixth Amendment* guarantees that criminal defendants have these rights:

1. The right to be tried by an impartial jury of the state or district in which the alleged crime was committed.
2. The right to confront (cross-examine) the witnesses against the accused.
3. The right to have the assistance of a lawyer.
4. The right to have a speedy trial.

The Speedy Trial Act requires that a criminal defendant be brought to trial within 70 days after indictment [18 U.S.C. § 3161(c)(1)]. The court may grant continuances to serve the "ends of justice."

Miranda 2000

Most people have not read and memorized the provisions of the U.S. Constitution. The U.S. Supreme Court recognized this fact when it decided the landmark case *Miranda v. Arizona* in 1966 [384 U.S. 436, 86 S.Ct. 1602]. In that case, the Supreme Court held that the Fifth Amendment privilege against self-incrimination is not useful unless a criminal suspect has knowledge of this right. Therefore, the Supreme Court required that the following warning—colloquially called the **Miranda rights**—be read to a criminal suspect before he or she is interrogated by the police or other government officials:

- You have the right to remain silent.
- Anything you say can and will be used against you.
- Your have the right to consult a lawyer, and to have a lawyer present with you during interrogation.
- If you cannot afford a lawyer, a lawyer will be appointed free of charge to represent you.

Any statements or confessions obtained from a suspect prior to being read his or her *Miranda* rights can be excluded from evidence at trial. *Miranda* has been criticized for letting guilty defendants go free. To combat this problem, the U.S. Congress enacted a statute, 18 U.S.C. Section 3501, which provided that a statement or confession by a suspect is admissible into evidence if it is "voluntarily" given even if the suspect has not been read his or her *Miranda* rights. Under this federal statute, many courts admitted into evidence confessions and other statements by defendants.

In 2000, the U.S. Supreme Court decided to revisit *Miranda* in *Dickerson v. United States* [120 S.Ct. 2326] to test the lawfulness of Section 3501 (voluntary admission of guilt). In that case, the criminal defendant Dickerson was indicted for bank robbery. Before trial, Dickerson moved to suppress an incriminating statement he had made to the Federal Bureau of Investigation (FBI) prior to being read his *Miranda* rights. The court of appeals applied Section 3501 and admitted the statement at trial. Dickerson appealed to the U.S. Supreme Court to keep the statement out of trial.

In a closely watched case, the Supreme Court upheld the *Miranda* ruling, finding that the *Miranda* decision was constitutionally based, and that Congress's attempt to lessen it by enacting Section 3501 was unconstitutional. In reaching its decision, the Supreme Court stated:

> We do not think there is justification for overruling *Miranda*. *Miranda* has become embedded in routine police practice to the point where the warnings have become part of our national culture. Whether or not we would agree with *Miranda's* reasoning and its resulting rule, were we addressing the issue in the first instance, the principles of stare decisis weigh heavily against overruling it now. We conclude that *Miranda* announced a constitutional rule that Congress may not supercede legislatively. Following the rule of stare decisis, we decline to overrule *Miranda* ourselves.

Thus, rather than being overturned or chipped away at, *Miranda* has been resurrected in its strict liability format: Police and government officials must read criminal suspects their *Miranda* rights. Otherwise the suspect's statements and confessions are inadmissible at trial.

Little did Christopher Columbus know in 1503 when he sailed past the Cayman Islands in the Caribbean that these tiny islands would become a bastion of international finance in the late twentieth and early twenty-first centuries. These tiny islands of 35,000 people host about 600 banks with more than $500 million in deposits. Why is so much money being hoarded there? The answer is: bank secrecy laws.

Every nation has banking laws, but all banking laws are not equal. What the Cayman Islands banking law provides is confidentiality. In most instances, no party other than the depositor has the right to know the identity of the depositor, account number, or amount in the account. In fact, most accounts are held in the name of trusts instead of the depositor's actual name. This bank secrecy law has attracted many persons to park their ill-gotten gains in a Cayman Islands bank. Often the bank is no more than a lawyer's office.

Switzerland was once the primary location for depositing money that did not want to be found. After some pressure from the United States and other countries, however, Switzerland entered into memoranda of understanding agreeing to cooperate with criminal investigations by these countries and to help uncover money deposited in Switzerland made through securities frauds and other crimes. Therefore, Switzerland has lost some of its luster as an international money hideout.

So Switzerland has been replaced by other places offering even more secret bank secrecy laws. The Cayman Islands is now the "Switzerland of the Caribbean," and there are several other bank secrecy hideouts around the world, including the Bahamas in the Caribbean, the country of Liechtenstein in Europe, the Isle of Jersey off Great Britain, and the micro-island of Niue in the South Pacific. These tiny countries and islands follow the adage: "Write a good law and they will come."

Eighth Amendment Protection Against Cruel and Unusual Punishment

The *Eighth Amendment* protects criminal defendants from **cruel and unusual punishment.** For example, it prohibits the torture of criminals. This clause, however, does not prohibit capital punishment.

Accountant–Client Privilege?

The common law has long recognized an attorney–client privilege that protects communications between a client and his or her lawyer from discovery in a lawsuit. This means that lawyers cannot testify against their own clients. The rationale for this rule is that if an attorney could be called to testify against a client, the client might choose to withhold information from the attorney. This might prevent the attorney from preparing the best defense.

Although a similar situation occurs when accountants are supplied with information and documents by their clients, the U.S. Supreme Court has found that there is no corresponding accountant–client privilege under federal law [*Couch v. U.S.*, 409 U.S. 322, 93 S.Ct. 611 (1973)]. Thus, an accountant could be called as a witness in cases involving federal securities laws, federal mail or wire fraud, or federal RICO.

Nevertheless, approximately 20 states have enacted special statutes that create an accountant–client privilege. An accountant cannot be called as a witness against a client in a court action in a state where these statutes are in effect. Federal courts do not recognize these laws, though.

Federal Antiterrorism Act of 2001

The devastating suicide attack on the World Trade Center in New York and the Pentagon in Washington, D.C., on September 11, 2001, shocked the nation. The attacks were organized and orchestrated by terrorists who crossed nations' borders easily, secretly planned and prepared for the attacks undetected, and financed the attacks with money located in banks in the United States, Great Britain, and other countries.

In response, Congress held hearings investigating how to counter such terrorist activities. Congress enacted a new federal Antiterrorism Act that assists the government in detecting and preventing terrorist activities, and investigating and prosecuting terrorists. The bill was signed into law by President George W. Bush on October 26, 2001. The Act contains the following main features.

- *Special intelligence court.* The Act authorizes a special intelligence court to issue expanded wiretap orders and subpoenas to obtain evidence of suspected terrorism.

- *Nationwide search warrant.* The Act created a nationwide search warrant to obtain evidence of terrorist activities. Previously, search warrants were limited to specific geographical locations.

- *Roving wiretaps.* The Act permits "roving wiretaps" on a person suspected of involvement in terrorism so that any telephone or electronic device used by the person may be monitored. Previously, officials had to obtain separate wiretap orders for each phone a suspect used, which increased the difficulty of monitoring terrorists who used multiple telephones, including cellular phones.

- *Sharing of information.* The Act permits sharing of evidence obtained during grand jury proceedings, and evidence obtained by government law enforcement and intelligence agencies such as the Federal Bureau of Investigation (FBI), Central Intelligence Agency (CIA), National Security Administration (NSA), Immigration and Naturalization Service (INS), U.S. Treasury Department, and other government agencies. Previously, sharing of such information was restricted.

- *Detention of noncitizens.* The Act gives the federal government authority to detain a nonresident in the United States for up to seven days without filing charges against that person if he or she is certified by the U.S. Attorney General as being under suspicion of involvement in terrorist activities. Nonresidents who are certified by a court as a threat to national security may be held for up to six months without a trial. Aliens who raise funds for terrorist organizations may be deported.

- *Bioterrorism provision.* The Act makes it illegal for people or groups to possess substances that can be used as biological or chemical weapons for any purpose besides a "peaceful" one.

- *Anti–money laundering provisions.* The Act includes several provisions to discover, trace, and impound bank accounts used to fund terrorist activities. The Act requires U.S. banks to determine sources of large overseas private bank accounts. Banks that refuse to disclose information on such accounts to U.S investigators are subject to sanctions, including loss of license to conduct banking operations. The U.S. Treasury Department may cut off all dealings in the United States of foreign banking institutions located in nations with bank secrecy laws that refuse to disclose information on bank accounts to U.S. investigators. U.S. banks are barred from doing business with offshore shell banks that have no connection to any regulated banking industry.

Proponents of the federal Antiterrorism Act argue that the new investigative and other powers granted by the Act are necessary to give law enforcement and intelligence agencies necessary tools to detect and prevent terrorist activities and to investigate and prosecute terrorists. Critics of the Act argue that civil liberties and many constitutional freedoms are trampled by provisions of the Act.

LEGAL TERMINOLOGY

Actus reus

Aiding and abetting

Arraignment

Arrest warrant

Arson

Attempt to commit a crime

Attorney–client privilege

Bench trial/waiver trial

Bribery

Burden of proof

Burglary

Crime

Criminal conspiracy

Criminal fraud

Criminal law

Cruel and unusual punishment

Defendant

Defense attorney

District attorney

Double jeopardy

Embezzlement

Exclusionary rule

Exculpatory

Extortion

Felony

Forgery

Hung jury

Immunity from prosecution

Inchoate crime

Indictment

Larceny

Mail fraud

Mens rea

Miranda rights

Misdemeanor

Penal code

Plaintiff

Plea bargain

Probable cause

Prosecutor

Public defender

Racketeer Influenced and Corrupt
    Organizations Act (RICO)

Robbery

Search warrant

Self-incrimination

Trier of fact

Unreasonable search and seizure

Violation

White-collar crime

Wire fraud

Summary

What Is a Crime?

Specifics of a Criminal Trial	1. The accused is *presumed innocent until proven guilty.* 2. The plaintiff (the government) bears the *burden of proof.* 3. The government must prove *beyond a reasonable doubt* that the accused is guilty of the crime charged. 4. The accused does not have to testify against himself or herself.
Definition	Any act done by a person in violation of those duties that he or she owes to society and for the breach of which the law provides a penalty.
Penal Codes	State and federal statutes that define many crimes. Criminal conduct is also defined in many *regulatory statutes.*
Parties to a Criminal Lawsuit	1. *Plaintiff:* The government, which is represented by the *prosecuting attorney* (or *prosecutor*). 2. *Defendant:* The person or business accused of the crime, who is represented by a *defense attorney.*
Classification of Crimes	1. *Felonies:* The most serious kinds of crimes. *Mala in se* (inherently evil). Usually punishable by imprisonment. 2. *Misdemeanors:* Less serious crimes. *Mala prohibita* (prohibited by society). Usually punishable by fine and/or imprisonment for less than one year. 3. *Violations:* Not a felony nor a misdemeanor. Generally punishable by a fine.
Elements of a Crime	1. *Actus reus:* guilty act. 2. *Mens rea:* evil intent.

Criminal Procedure and Process

Pretrial Criminal Procedure	1. *Arrest:* Made pursuant to an *arrest warrant* based upon a showing of "probable cause," or, where permitted, by a *warrantless* arrest. 2. *Indictment or information:* Grand juries issue *indictments;* magistrates (judges) issue *informations.* These formally charge the accused with specific crimes. 3. *Arraignment:* Accused is informed of the charges against him or her and enters a *plea* in court. The plea may be *not guilty, guilty,* or *nolo contendere.* 4. *Plea bargaining:* Government and accused may negotiate a settlement agreement wherein the accused agrees to admit to a lesser crime than charged. *(continued)*

Criminal Trial

Criminal Trial	1. *Conviction:* Requires unanimous vote of jury. 2. *Innocent:* Requires unanimous vote of jury. 3. *Hung jury:* Nonunanimous vote of the jury; the government may prosecute the case again.
Appeal	1. *Defendant:* May appeal his or her conviction. 2. *Plaintiff (government):* May not appeal a verdict of innocent.

Crimes Affecting Business

Robbery	The taking of personal property from another by fear or force.
Burglary	The unauthorized entering of a building to commit a felony.
Larceny	The wrongful taking of another's property other than from his person or building.
Theft	The wrongful taking of another's property, whether by robbery, burglary, or larceny.
Receiving Stolen Property	A person knowingly receives stolen property with the intent to deprive the rightful owner of that property.
Arson	The malicious and willful burning of another's building.
Forgery	Fraudulent making or altering of a written document that affects the legal liability of another person.
Extortion	Threat to expose something about another person unless that person gives up money or property.
Credit-card Crimes	The misappropriation or use of another person's credit card.
Bad check legislation	The making, drawing, or delivery of a check by a person when that person knows that there are insufficient funds in the account to cover the check.

White-Collar Crimes

Definition	Crimes that are prone to be committed by businesspersons that involve cunning and trickery rather than physical force.
Embezzlement	The fraudulent conversion of property by a person to whom the property was entrusted.
Criminal Fraud	Obtaining title to another's property through deception or trickery. Also called *false pretenses* or *deceit*.
Mail Fraud	The use of mail to defraud another person. *(continued)*

Wire Fraud	The use of wire (telephone or telegraph) to defraud another person.
Bribery	The offer of payment of money or property or something else of value in return for an unwarranted favor. The payor of a bribe is also guilty of the crime of bribery. 1. *Commercial bribery* is the offer of a payment of a bribe to a private person or a business. This is often referred to as a *kickback* or *payoff*. 2. Bribery of a public official for an "official act" is a crime.
Racketeer Influenced and Corrupt Organizations Act (RICO)	Makes it a federal crime to acquire or maintain an interest in, use income from, or conduct or participate in the affairs of an "enterprise" through a "pattern" of "racketeering activity." Criminal penalties include the *forfeiture* of any property or business interests gained by a RICO violation.

Inchoate Crimes

Definition	Crimes that are incomplete or that are committed by nonparticipants.
Criminal Conspiracy	When two or more persons enter into an *agreement* to commit a crime and take some *overt act* to further the crime.
Attempt to Commit a Crime	The attempt to commit a crime is a crime even if the commission of the intended crime is unsuccessful.
Aiding and Abetting the Commission of a Crime	Rendering support, assistance, or encouragement to the commission of a crime, or knowingly harboring a criminal after he or she has committed a crime.

Constitutional Safeguards

Fourth Amendment Protection Against Unreasonable Searches and Seizures	Protects persons and corporations from *unreasonable searches and seizures*.
	
	1. *Reasonable searches and seizures* based on *probable cause* are lawful:
	  a. *Search warrant:* Stipulates the place and scope of the search.
	  b. *Warrantless search:* Permitted only:
	    i. Incident to an arrest.
	    ii. Where evidence is in plain view.
	    iii. Where it is likely that evidence will be destroyed.
	
	2. *Exclusionary rule:* Evidence obtained from an unreasonable search and seizure is *tainted evidence* that may not be introduced at a government proceeding against the person searched.
	
	3. *Business premises:* Protected by the Fourth Amendment, except that certain *regulated industries* may be subject to warrantless searches authorized by statute.

Fifth Amendment Privilege Against Self-Incrimination	Provides that no person "shall be compelled in any criminal case to be a witness against himself." A person asserting this privilege is said to have taken the Fifth.

(continued)

Fifth Amendment Privilege Against Self-Incrimination, *continued*	1. *Nontestimonial evidence:* This evidence (e.g., fingerprints, body fluids, etc.) is not protected.
	 2. *Businesses:* The privilege applies only to natural persons; businesses cannot assert the privilege.
	 3. *Miranda rights:* A criminal suspect must be informed of his or her Fifth Amendment rights before the suspect can be interrogated by the police or government officials.
	 4. *Immunity from prosecution:* Granted by the government to obtain otherwise privileged evidence. The government agrees not to use the evidence given against the person who gave it.
	 5. *Attorney–client privilege:* An accused's lawyer cannot be called as a witness against the accused.
	 6. *Other privileges:* The following privileges have been recognized, with some limitations:
	   a. psychiatrist/psychologist–patient
	   b. priest/minister/rabbi–penitent
	   c. spouse–spouse; parent–child
	 7. *Accountant–client privilege:* None recognized at the federal level. Some states recognize this privilege in state law actions.

Fifth Amendment Protection Against Double Jeopardy	Protects persons from being tried twice by the same jurisdiction for the same crime. If the act violates the laws of two or more jurisdictions, each jurisdiction may try the accused.
Sixth Amendment Right to a Public Jury Trial	Guarantees criminal defendants the following rights: 1. To be tried by an impartial jury 2. To confront the witness 3. To have the assistance of a lawyer 4. To have a speedy trial
Eighth Amendment Protection Against Cruel and Unusual Punishment	Protects criminal defendants from cruel and unusual punishment. Capital punishment is permitted.

Working the Web

1. Check the U.S. Department of Justice website for information on the Freedom of Information Act and the principal FOIA contacts at various federal agencies at www.usdoj.gov/04foia/04_3.html.

2. Obtain a copy of *Your Right to Federal Records Questions and Answers on the Freedom of Information Act and Privacy Act* at www.pueblo.gsa.gov/cic_text/fed_prog/foia/foia.htm.

3. View the Privacy Act of 1974 at www.usdoj.gov/04foia/privstat.htm.

4. View a copy of the original document and information on the Bill of Rights at www.nara.gov/exhall/treasuresofcongress/page_3.html.

5. Obtain information on the United States Sentencing Commission at www.ussc.gov.

CRITICAL LEGAL THINKING AND WRITING

1. What obligation does the prosecution have to reveal to a defense attorney information helpful to the defense?

2. Why is counsel provided to criminal defendants without charge if they cannot afford to hire a lawyer?

3. Why is the burden of proof different in a criminal case than in a civil case?

4. What is the value in a plea bargain to the government? The defendant?

5. Why is the government not permitted to appeal a finding of not guilty in a criminal case?

6. Why would a person want to waive his or her Fifth Amendment right against self-incrimination?

7. When can a person be tried twice for the same act and not violate the double-jeopardy provision of the Fifth Amendment?

8. How can a corporation be punished for criminal acts?

9. How does the exclusionary rule protect the rights of the individual?

10. Should the standards of protection provided by the Constitution apply to nonresidents of the United States for crimes committed in the United States? Why or why not?

ETHICS: ANALYSIS AND DISCUSSION

1. Does the attorney–client privilege apply to those working as experts, such as accountants, for an attorney preparing a criminal case for trial? Would this be an extension of the attorney–client privilege?

2. Is the information given to a paralegal by a criminal client covered under the Fifth Amendment when he or she interviews a criminal?

3. What obligation does a paralegal have to make available exculpatory evidence discovered during investigation of a case?

Attorney–Client Privilege—Work Product Doctrine

There are few certainties in the area of ethics, for paralegals or in any profession. What qualifies as ethical conduct is in most cases based on state law and court interpretation applied to a set of facts. The citation listed below represents one legal opinion and is provided as a research starting point. Do not assume that the same rule applies in your jurisdiction. For the following:

- *Prepare a written statement based on your state law.*
- *Use your state bar association website as a starting point.*

You are working at a firm with a large client base that does not speak English. You are fluent in three languages and you are asked to translate for a firm attorney during an interview of a client in a criminal case. You take notes as you translate to be sure you are properly translating what is said. [*Von Bulow by Auersperg v. Von Bulow*, 811 F. 2nd 136 (2nd Cir. 1987).] Are the notes covered under the work product doctrine? Does the attorney–client privilege apply to what you heard?

CASES *for Discussion*

People v. Paulson

216 Cal.App.3d 1480, 265 Cal.Rptr. 579 (Cal.App. 1990)

9.1 FACTS

Lee Stuart Paulson owns the liquor license for "My House," a bar in San Francisco. The California Department of Alcoholic Beverage Control is the administrative agency that regulates bars in that state. The California Business and Professions Code, which the department administers, prohibits "any kind of illegal activity on licensed premises." On February 11, 1988, an anonymous informer tipped the department that narcotic sales were occurring on the premises of "My House" and that the narcotics were kept in a safe behind the bar on the premises.

A special department investigator entered the bar during its hours of operation, identified himself, and informed Paulson that he was conducting an inspection. The investigator, who did not have a search warrant, opened the safe without seeking Paulson's consent. Twenty-two bundles of cocaine, totaling 5.5 grams, were found in the safe. Paulson was arrested. At his criminal trial, Paulson challenged the lawfulness of the search.

ISSUE

Was the warrantless search of the safe a lawful search?

Center Art Galleries–Hawaii, Inc. v. United States

875 F.2d 747 (9th Cir. 1989)

9.2 FACTS

The Center Art Galleries–Hawaii sells artwork. Approximately 20 percent of its business involves art by Salvador Dali. The federal government, which suspected the center of fraudulently selling forged Dali artwork, obtained identical search warrants for six locations controlled by the center. The warrants commanded the executing officer to seize items which were "evidence of violations of federal criminal law." The warrants did not describe the specific crimes suspected and did not stipulate that only items pertaining to the sale of Dali's work could be seized. There was no evidence of any criminal activity unrelated to that artist.

ISSUE

Is the search warrant valid?

United States v. John Doe

465 U.S. 605, 104 S.Ct. 1237, 79 L.Ed.2d 552 (1984)

9.3 FACTS

John Doe is the owner of several sole-proprietorship businesses. In 1980, during the course of an investigation of corruption in awarding county and municipal contracts, a federal grand jury served several subpoenas on John Doe demanding the production of certain business records. The subpoenas demanded the production of the following records: (1) general ledgers and journals, (2) invoices, (3) bank statements and canceled checks, (4) financial statements, (5) telephone-company records, (6) safe-deposit box records, and (7) copies of tax returns. John Doe filed a motion in federal court seeking to quash the subpoenas, alleging that producing these business records would violate his Fifth Amendment privilege of not testifying against himself.

ISSUE

Do the records have to be disclosed?

People v. Shaw

10 Cal.App.4th 969, 12 Cal.Rptr.2d 665 (Cal. App. 1992)

9.4 FACTS

In 1979, Leo Shaw, an attorney, entered into a partnership agreement with three other persons to build and operate an office building. From the outset, it was agreed that Shaw's role was to manage the operation of the building. Management of the property was Shaw's contribution to the partnership; the other three partners contributed the necessary capital. In January 1989, the other partners discovered that the loan on the building was in default and that foreclosure proceedings were imminent. Upon investigation, they discovered that Shaw had taken approximately $80,000 from the partnership's checking account. After heated discussions, Shaw repaid $13,000. In May 1989, when no further payment was forthcoming, a partner filed a civil suit against Shaw and notified the police. The state filed a criminal complaint against Shaw on March 15, 1990. On April 3, 1990, Shaw repaid the remaining funds as part of a civil settlement. At his criminal trial in November 1990, Shaw argued that the repayment of the money was a defense to the crime of embezzlement.

ISSUE

Did Shaw act ethically in this case? Would your answer be different if he had really only "borrowed" the money and had intended to return it?

Department of Justice v. Landano

508 U.S. 165 (1993)   Supreme Court of the United States

Read the following case, excerpted from the U.S. Supreme Court's opinion. Review and brief the case. In your brief, answer the following questions:

1. Under what circumstances may a defendant obtain information under the Freedom of Information Act (FOIA)?

2. When may the government in a criminal case refuse to divulge information under the FOIA?

3. Is all information provided to the Federal Bureau of Investigation confidential and therefore not available under the FOIA?

4. Who has the burden of proof in FOIA cases?

O'Connor, J., delivered the opinion for a unanimous Court.

Exemption 7(D) of the Freedom of Information Act, 5 U.S.C. § 552 (FOIA), exempts from disclosure agency records "compiled for law enforcement purposes by criminal law enforcement authority in the course of a criminal investigation" if release of those records "could reasonably be expected to disclose" the identity of or information provided by a "confidential source" [§ 552(b)(7)(D)]. This case concerns the evidentiary showing that the Government must make to establish that a source is "confidential" within the meaning of Exemption 7(D). We are asked to decide whether the Government is entitled to a presumption that all sources supplying information to the Federal Bureau of Investigation (FBI or Bureau) in the course of a criminal investigation are confidential sources.

Respondent Vincent Landano was convicted in New Jersey state court for murdering Newark, New Jersey, police officer John Snow in the course of a robbery. The crime received considerable media attention. Evidence at trial showed that the robbery had been orchestrated by Victor Forni and a motorcycle gang known as "the Breed." There was testimony that Landano, though not a Breed member, had been recruited for the job. Landano always has maintained that he did not participate in the robbery, and that Forni, not he, killed Officer Snow. He contends that the prosecution withheld material exculpatory evidence in violation of *Brady v. Maryland*, 373 U.S. 83 (1963).

Landano apparently is currently pursuing a Brady claim in the state courts. Seeking evidence to support that claim, Landano filed FOIA requests with the FBI for information that the Bureau had compiled in the course of its involvement in the investigation of Officer Snow's murder. Landano sought release of the Bureau's files on both Officer Snow and Forni. The FBI released several hundred pages of documents. The Bureau redacted some of these, however, and withheld several hundred other pages altogether.

The information withheld under Exemption 7(D) included information provided by five types of sources: regular FBI informants; individual witnesses who were not regular informants; state and local law enforcement agencies; other local agencies; and private financial and commercial institutions. In the Government's view, all such sources should be presumed confidential. The deleted portions of the files were coded to indicate which type of source each involved.

Relying on legislative history, the court stated that a source is confidential within the meaning of Exemption 7(D) if the source received an explicit assurance of confidentiality or if there are circumstances "from which such an assurance could reasonably be inferred." An "assurance of confidentiality," the court said, is not a promise of absolute anonymity or secrecy, but "an assurance that the FBI would not directly or indirectly disclose the cooperation of the interviewee with the investigation unless such a disclosure is determined by the FBI to be important to the success of its law enforcement objective."

Exemption 7(D) permits the Government to withhold "records or information compiled for law enforcement purposes, but only to the extent that the production of such law enforcement records or information . . . could reasonably be expected to disclose the identity of a confidential source, including a state, local, or foreign agency or authority or any private institution which furnished information on a confidential basis, and, in the case of a record or information compiled by criminal law enforcement authority in the course of a criminal investigation, information furnished by a confidential source" [§ 552(b)(7)(D)]. The Government bears the burden of establishing that the exemption applies.

When FOIA was enacted in 1966, Exemption 7 broadly protected "'investigatory files compiled for law enforcement purposes except to the extent available by law to a private party.'" Congress adopted the current version of Exemption 7(D) in 1986. The 1986 amendment expanded "records" to "records or information," replaced the word "would" with the phrase "could reasonably be expected to," deleted the word "only" from before "confidential source," and clarified that a confidential source could be a state, local, or foreign agency or a private institution.

Under Exemption 7(D), the question is not whether the requested document is of the type that the agency usually treats as confidential, but whether the particular source spoke with an understanding that the communication would remain confidential. According to the Conference Report on the 1974 amendment, a source is confidential within the meaning of Exemption 7(D) if the source provided information under an express assurance of confidentiality or in circumstances from which such an assurance could be reasonably inferred. In this case, the Government has not attempted to demonstrate that the FBI made explicit promises of confidentiality to particular sources. That sort of proof apparently often is not possible: The FBI does not have a policy of discussing confidentiality with every source, and when such discussions do occur, agents do not always document them.

The precise question before us, then, is how the Government can meet its burden of showing that a source provided information on an implied assurance of confidentiality. The parties dispute two issues: the meaning of the word "confidential," and whether, absent specific evidence to the contrary, an implied assurance of confidentiality always can be inferred from the fact that a source cooperated with the FBI during a criminal investigation.

FOIA does not define the word "confidential." In common usage, confidentiality is not limited to complete anonymity or secrecy. A statement can be made "in confidence" even if the speaker knows the communication will be shared with limited others, as long as the speaker expects that the information will not be published indiscriminately. A promise of complete secrecy would mean that the FBI agent receiving the source's information could not share it even with other FBI personnel. Such information, of course, would be of little use to the Bureau.

We assume that Congress was aware of the Government's disclosure obligations under Brady and applicable procedural rules when it adopted Exemption 7(D). Congress also must have realized that some FBI witnesses would testify at trial. We therefore agree with the Court of Appeals that the word "confidential," as used in Exemption 7(D), refers to a degree of confidentiality less than total secrecy. A source should be deemed confidential if the source furnished information with the understanding that the FBI would not divulge the communication except to the extent the Bureau thought necessary for law enforcement purposes.

Considerations of "fairness" also counsel against the Government's rule. The Government acknowledges that its proposed presumption, though rebuttable in theory, is in practice all but irrebuttable. Once the FBI asserts that information was provided by a confidential source during a criminal investigation, the requester—who has no knowledge about the particular source or the information being withheld—very rarely will be in a position to offer persuasive evidence that the source in fact had no interest in confidentiality.

We agree with the Government that, when certain circumstances characteristically support an inference of confidentiality, the Government similarly should be able to claim exemption under Exemption 7(D) without detailing the circumstances surrounding a particular interview. Neither the language of Exemption 7(D) nor Reporters Committee, Page 178, however, supports the proposition that the category of all FBI criminal investigative sources is exempt.

But Congress did not expressly create a blanket exemption for the FBI; the language that it adopted requires every agency to establish that a confidential source furnished the information sought to be withheld under Exemption 7(D). In short, the Government offers no persuasive evidence that Congress intended for the Bureau to be able to satisfy its burden in every instance simply by asserting that a source communicated with the Bureau during the course of a criminal investigation. Had Congress meant to create such a rule, it could have done so much more clearly.

The Government has argued forcefully that its ability to maintain the confidentiality of all of its sources is vital to effective law enforcement. A prophylactic rule protecting the identities of all FBI criminal investigative sources undoubtedly would serve the Government's objectives, and would be simple for the Bureau and the courts to administer. But we are not free to engraft that policy choice onto the statute that Congress passed. For the reasons we have discussed, and consistent with our obligation to construe FOIA exemptions narrowly in favor of disclosure, we hold that the Government is not entitled to a presumption that a source is confidential within the meaning of Exemption 7(D) whenever the source provides information to the FBI in the course of a criminal investigation.

More narrowly defined circumstances, however, can provide a basis for inferring confidentiality. For example, when circumstances such as the nature of the crime investigated and the witness' relation to it support an inference of confidentiality, the Government is entitled to a presumption. In this case, the Court of Appeals incorrectly concluded that it lacked discretion to rely on such circumstances. Accordingly, we vacate the judgment of the Court of Appeals and remand the case for further proceedings consistent with this opinion. It is so ordered.

PART III

PARALEGAL SKILLS

Professional paralegals must develop a number of personal and professional skills. Verbal and written communication skills are crucial for paralegals, who will be interviewing clients and witnesses and developing professional relationships with the public. Paralegals should develop their ability to think and write critically while conducting legal research and preparing written reports. With the growth of electronic libraries and online resources, today's paralegals must be as comfortable with the computer and the Internet as with traditional research tools. All of these topics are covered in Part III of this book.

CHAPTER 9

CHAPTER OBJECTIVES

After studying this chapter, you should be able to:

1. Explain the paralegal's need for good communication skills.

2. State the purpose of investigating a claim.

3. Set forth the reasons for visiting the scene of the cause of action.

4. Use an example to illustrate the importance of a timeline in a case.

5. List some different types of questioning.

6. Differentiate between a moral and an ethical consideration.

7. Explain the concept of privileged communications.

8. Be able to conduct an effective interview and obtain information commonly kept by governmental agencies.

9. Explain the purpose of, and the limitation in, obtaining information under the federal Freedom of Information Act (FOIA).

10. Describe how to locate potential witnesses as part of the investigation of a case.

Interviewing and Investigation Skills

It is the spirit and not the form of law that keeps justice alive.

EARL WARREN

Introduction

Communication skills are at the heart of paralegals' ability to successfully conduct interviews and investigations. The paralegal must be prepared to be the first point of contact with the client. In some practices, clients are interviewed first by the supervising attorney and then referred to the paralegal for a detailed factual interview. In other practices, though, the paralegal is the first one to meet with the client and conduct the initial interview before referring the client to the supervising attorney.

The paralegal must be able to successfully interview clients, fact witnesses, expert witnesses, investigators, and others such as public records custodians who may have access to information necessary for the preparation of a case. The skill of the interviewer or investigator can determine the accuracy and completeness of the information obtained, and ultimately the outcome of the case. The impressions created and the relationship developed with a new client may be the deciding factor in whether the client stays with the firm or seeks other counsel. Professional relationships developed with public officials, public custodians of records, hospital records librarians, police investigators, and similar independent investigators can make the job of the paralegal much easier and ultimately benefit the client.

INVESTIGATING CLAIMS

The legal team must gather all of the relevant information about a cause of action before making a recommendation to a client to file a lawsuit or respond to a claim of wrongdoing. In most cases, before the first interview with the client is conducted, the paralegal has some indication of the area of law or the nature of the claim. It may be from a telephone interview when the client calls for an appointment, or from the referral from the supervising attorney to the paralegal to conduct the interview and investigation. If paralegals specialize in certain areas of law, they are likely to understand the underlying elements of the claims or rights the client wishes to assert. Those in general practice and those entering a new area have to understand the rules of law as they apply to that issue.

For example, in a products liability case, understanding the traditional, or common-law, law of negligence is not enough. One also must understand the law of **strict liability** for product defect cases as found in the **Restatement (Second) of Torts,** section 402A. Where negligence requires a breach of duty, strict liability is without fault in cases where the doctrine applies. An interview conducted strictly considering negligence as the basis for a legal action could improperly result in the client's being advised that he or she does not have a claim when, under the no-fault strict liability concept for defective products, an action might exist.

The first step is to determine the legal basis of a client's claim. With an understanding of the legal basis of the claim and the applicable law, an investigative plan can be prepared to obtain the necessary witness statements, locate physical evidence, and obtain photographs, reports, and other evidence for use in preparation for and at trial. Where a claim of negligence is to be made, photographic evidence may be essential in demonstrating the nature of the hazard.

For example, when a client has injured himself or herself as result of a fall in a store, photographs showing the hazardous condition should be obtained as quickly as possible. In the case of strict liability involving a product defect that caused injury or loss, preservation of the defective product or photographic documentation of the defect becomes essential as a matter of proof. Knowing what elements of the action must be proven dictates what evidence must be located in the form of witnesses, photographs, and physical evidence. Knowing the elements of the claim will ensure that the proper questions are asked in the interview, which then will dictate the necessary investigation steps.

A paralegal interviews a client.

A Defense Perspective

Most people quite naturally think of a lawsuit from the plaintiff's perspective. Most people think in terms of the violation of rights and resulting injury. In a perfect world, only legitimate actions would be filed and the law would provide a perfect remedy for all wrongs. But not every plaintiff is in the right, and some have been known to file frivolous or even fraudulent lawsuits.

The balance in the American legal system is achieved by a vigorous defense on behalf of the defendant. A plaintiff may claim, for example, that she slipped and was injured as a result of the negligence of a storeowner. The defendant storeowner might be innocent of any wrongdoing or breach of any duty. It is well to remember that for every plaintiff there is a defendant, and for each party there is a law firm, an attorney, and a paralegal.

Obtaining Official Reports

Most incidents giving rise to litigation have associated official reports. In the negligence action, it may be a police accident or incident report, emergency medical services report, fire department call report, or incident reports of safety violations by federal, state, or local authorities. These reports are filed in a central depository as public records. A useful starting point is to obtain any official reports associated with the case. These reports frequently indicate time, place, and the names of fact witnesses. In some cases, detailed diagrams or photographs may accompany the reports. Exhibit 9.1 is an example of a police accident report form.

Fact Analysis

Analyzing the facts starts with interviewing the clients and their recitation of the time, place, circumstances, and other people involved as participants or witnesses. Exhibit 9.2 is a sample client interview form. A complete analysis usually requires further field investigation of the location, the object involved, such as an automobile, and interviews of the parties and witnesses. One person's perception may not be reality. A client's recollection and description of the physical surroundings may not be proven by the investigator's visit to the location. What one person describes as a narrow, congested walkway may actually be a standard-width open sidewalk.

The ultimate trier of fact will be the jury, a panel of arbitrators, or a judge acting as the trier of fact. Therefore, analysis of the facts must be sufficient to justify the position taken and the presentation made in pursuing a client's claim or its defense in **arbitration** or in trial.

Locations

Careful analysis of a claim includes verification of the physical aspects of the actual location where the cause of action occurred. Ask any group of people to describe a location, and you're likely to get as many different descriptions as there are people in the group. How the person viewed the location, from the south, from the north, east, or west, may influence their description. Or the driver's view from behind the wheel of a large tractor–trailer might be different from the view from behind the wheel of a small sports car.

Investigation of a case should involve a trip to the location where the incident occurred. The trier of fact will be relying upon the plaintiff's and defendant's counsels to describe in their presentation the characteristics of the physical location. They also will be looking at the location from an impartial,

exhibit **9.1**   *Sample police accident report form.*

POLICE ACCIDENT REPORT

XX. REFER TO OVERLAY SHEETS   REPORTABLE ☐   NON - REPORTABLE ☐   PENNDOT USE ONLY

POLICE INFORMATION

1. INCIDENT NUMBER	
2. AGENCY NAME	
3. STATION/ PRECINCT	4. PATROL ZONE
5. INVESTIGATOR	BADGE NUMBER
6. APPROVED BY	BADGE NUMBER
7. INVESTIGATION DATE	8. ARRIVAL TIME

ACCIDENT INFORMATION

9. ACCIDENT DATE	10. DAY OF WEEK
11. TIME OF DAY	12. NUMBER OF UNITS
13. # KILLED	14. # INJURED	15. PRIV. PROP. ACCIDENT Y ☐ N ☐

16. DID VEHICLE HAVE TO BE REMOVED FROM THE SCENE?
UNIT 1   UNIT 2
Y ☐ N ☐   Y ☐ N ☐

17. VEHICLE DAMAGE
0 - NONE   UNIT 1 ☐
1 - LIGHT
2 - MODERATE
3 - SEVERE   UNIT 2 ☐

18. HAZARDOUS MATERIALS Y ☐ N ☐   19. PENNDOT PROPERTY Y ☐ N ☐

ACCIDENT LOCATION

20. COUNTY	CODE
21. MUNICIPALITY	CODE

PRINCIPAL ROADWAY INFORMATION

22. ROUTE NO. OR STREET NAME

23. SPEED LIMIT	24. TYPE HIGHWAY	25. ACCESS CONTROL

INTERSECTING ROAD:

26. ROUTE NO. OR STREET NAME

27. SPEED LIMIT	28. TYPE HIGHWAY	29. ACCESS CONTROL

IF NOT AT INTERSECTION:

30. CROSS STREET OR SEGMENT MARKER

31. DIRECTION FROM SITE N S E W	32. DISTANCE FROM SITE FT. MI.

33. DISTANCE WAS   MEASURED ☐   ESTIMATED ☐

34. CONSTRUCTION ZONE ☐   35. TRAFFIC CONTROL DEVICE   PRINCIPAL ☐   INTERSECTING ☐

UNIT # 1

36. LEGALLY PARKED? Y☐ N☐	37. REG. PLATE	38. STATE
39. PA TITLE OR OUT-OF-STATE VIN	
40. OWNER	
41. OWNER ADDRESS	
42. CITY, STATE & ZIPCODE	
43. YEAR	44. MAKE
45. MODEL - (NOT BODY TYPE)	46. INS. Y ☐ N ☐ UNK ☐
47. BODY TYPE	48. SPECIAL USAGE	49. VEHICLE OWNERSHIP
50. INITIAL IMPACT POINT	51. VEHICLE STATUS	52. TRAVEL SPEED
53. VEHICLE GRADIENT	54. DRIVER PRESENCE	55. DRIVER CONDITION
56. DRIVER NUMBER	57. STATE
58. DRIVER NAME	
59. DRIVER ADDRESS	
60. CITY, STATE & ZIPCODE	
61. SEX	62. DATE OF BIRTH	63. PHONE
64. COMM. VEH. Y☐ N☐	65. DRIVER CLASS	66. DRIVER SS#
67. CARRIER	
68. CARRIER ADDRESS	
69. CITY, STATE & ZIPCODE	
70. USDOT #	ICC #	PUC #
72. VEH. CONFIG.	73. CARGO BODY TYPE	74. GVWR
75. NO. OF AXLES	76. HAZARDOUS MATERIALS	77. RELEASE OF HAZ MAT Y ☐ N ☐ UNK ☐

UNIT # 2

36. LEGALLY PARKED? Y☐ N☐	37. REG. PLATE	38. STATE
39. PA TITLE OR OUT-OF-STATE VIN	
40. OWNER	
41. OWNER ADDRESS	
42. CITY, STATE & ZIPCODE	
43. YEAR	44. MAKE
45. MODEL - (NOT BODY TYPE)	46. INS. Y ☐ N ☐ UNK ☐
47. BODY TYPE	48. SPECIAL USAGE	49. VEHICLE OWNERSHIP
50. INITIAL IMPACT POINT	51. VEHICLE STATUS	52. TRAVEL SPEED
53. VEHICLE GRADIENT	54. DRIVER PRESENCE	55. DRIVER CONDITION
56. DRIVER NUMBER	57. STATE
58. DRIVER NAME	
59. DRIVER ADDRESS	
60. CITY, STATE & ZIPCODE	
61. SEX	62. DATE OF BIRTH	63. PHONE
64. COMM. VEH. Y☐ N☐	65. DRIVER CLASS	66. DRIVER SS#
67. CARRIER	
68. CARRIER ADDRESS	
69. CITY, STATE & ZIPCODE	
70. USDOT #	ICC #	PUC #
72. VEH. CONFIG.	73. CARGO BODY TYPE	74. GVWR
75. NO. OF AXLES	76. HAZARDOUS MATERIALS	77. RELEASE OF HAZ MAT Y ☐ N ☐ UNK ☐

AA-45 (1/92)   PAGE: _____   CENTER FOR HIGHWAY SAFETY

Sample police accident report form, continued.   *exhibit* **9.1**

78. RESPONDING EMS AGENCY	INCIDENT #:
79. MEDICAL FACILITY	ACCIDENT DATE:

80. PEOPLE INFORMATION

A	B	C	D	E	F	G	NAME	ADDRESS	H	I	J	K	L	M

81. ILLUMINATION   **82.** WEATHER
83. ROAD SURFACE

84. SCHOOL DISTRICT (IF APPLICABLE)

85. DESCRIPTION OF DAMAGED PROPERTY

OWNER

ADDRESS

PHONE

86. DIAGRAM

87. NARRATIVE - IDENTIFY PRECIPITATING EVENTS, CAUSATION FACTORS, SEQUENCE OF EVENTS, WITNESS STATEMENTS, AND PROVIDE ADDITIONAL DETAILS. LIKE INSURANCE INFORMATION AND LOCATION OF TOWED VEHILCES, IF KNOWN.

INSURANCE INFORMATION	COMPANY		INSURANCE INFORMATION	COMPANY
UNIT 1	POLICY NO		UNIT 2	POLICY NO

88. WINTESSES

NAME	ADDRESS	PHONE
NAME	ADDRESS	PHONE

89. VIOLATIONS INDICATED	90. SECTION NUMBERS (ONLY IF CHARGED)	TC NTC
UNIT 1		☐ ☐
UNIT 2		☐ ☐

	91. PROBABLE USE	92. TYPE TEST	93. RESULTS			91. PROBABLE USE	92. TYPE TEST	93. RESULTS		94. INVESTIGATION COMPLETE ?
UNIT 1			0.___ ___%	☐ NO TEST ☐ REFUSE ☐ UNK	UNIT 2			0.___ ___%	☐ NO TEST ☐ REFUSE ☐ UNK	YES ☐ NO ☐

AA-45 (1/92)   PAGE: _____   **CENTER FOR HIGHWAY SAFETY** *exhibit* 9.2   *Initial client interview form.*

CLIENT INTERVIEW CHECKLIST

CLIENT PERSONAL INFORMATION

Name

Address

City _____ State _____ Zip _____

Phone (hm) _____ (wk) _____ (cell) _____

How long at this address

Date of birth _____ Place of birth _____

Social Security No.

Prior address

City _____ State _____ Zip _____

Dates at this address

Employer:

Job description

Marital status _____ Maiden name _____

Spouse's name _____ Date of birth _____

Child's name _____ Date of birth _____

Child's name _____ Date of birth _____

Child's name _____ Date of birth _____

CASE INFORMATION

Case referred by

Case type: ☐ Appeal   ☐ Business   ☐ Corporate   ☐ Estate   ☐ Litigation
              ☐ Municipal   ☐ Real Estate   ☐ Tax   ☐ Trust   ☐ Other

Opposing party(ies)

Opposing party

Address

Opposing attorney

Address

Date of incident _____ Statute of limitation date _____

Summary of facts

neutral point of view, usually without prior familiarity with the location. The diagrams usually presented at trial are those of an aerial view with its sterile, one-dimensional presentation. Photographs from the points of view of all the participants can make the difference in understanding the duties and responsibilities of the litigants. Unlike diagrams of the location, these photographs more typically will be from the point of view of the plaintiff, defendant, or witness at ground level, or from behind the wheel of a vehicle, or looking out of a building window.

Tangible Evidence

Tangible evidence consists of the physical objects that may have caused the injury. These may include items as small as a giveaway toy from a fast-food restaurant swallowed by a 2-year-old, to a bottle that exploded, to a large automobile whose brakes failed or whose seat belts snapped. In some cases, the tangible evidence is essential to proving negligence or an element of strict liability in tort.

Much has been written of late about the effects of the plaintiffs' and defendants' failure to preserve critical evidence of this type. In some cases, failure to preserve the evidence has resulted in loss of the case by the plaintiff, and in other cases by the defendant.

It is important to understand the local rules with regard to **spoliation of evidence** and its effect on a cause of action. In determining the proper penalty for spoliation of evidence, courts are most likely to consider [*Schroeder v. Department of Transportation*, 551 Pa. 243, 710 A.2d 23, 26 (1998)]:

1. The degree of fault of the party who altered or destroyed the evidence.
2. The degree of prejudice suffered by the opposing party.
3. The availability of a lesser sanction that will protect the opposing party's rights and deter future similar conduct.

Following a Timeline

Causes of action should be viewed from the events leading up to the incident to the events and occurrences following the incident. (See Exhibit 9.3 for a sample timeline.) Few things in life that give rise to a potential claim occur in a vacuum. Usually some facts lead up to the incident and others follow the incident. The question may be, "Given the time in which the parties allege this happened, could this really have happened?" For example, could the parties have driven the 30 miles in 20 minutes through crowded rush-hour traffic on city streets? In a food-poisoning case, could ingestion of the food at noon have caused the reaction claimed by 1:00 P.M.? The claimant might have been negligent, or the first perceived wrongdoer perhaps was not the correct person, as most food-poisoning cases require 6 to 12 hours from ingestion of the tainted food until onset of symptoms of the illness.

The starting point is the time of the alleged injury. Also important, from a fault standpoint or defense standpoint, is what happened that led up to the incident. From the damages standpoint, what happened after the incident, including treatment and subsequent changes in the person's life or lifestyle, is important.

New Practices in Store for Future Law Office

PR Newswire New York, July 2, 2001

In the next decade the legal field could feature paperless work environments, redefined roles and responsibilities for partners and associates, and mergers between law firms and financial consulting businesses. These are just a few of the major findings from the Future Law Office research project conducted by The Affiliates, a leading staffing service specializing in attorneys, paralegals, and legal support professionals.

The Affiliates embarked on the national research project to gain a broader perspective on workplace trends impacting the legal field. The firm commissioned surveys of attorneys and legal administrators, consulted leading experts, and conducted extensive research to ascertain how the future law office would look and feel. The results of the project have been chronicled in a comprehensive white paper and are featured online at www.futurelawoffice.com.

"Changes are already taking place in the legal field that are defining how the future law office will take shape," said Kathleen Call, executive director of The Affiliates. "Our research identifies key areas that could significantly influence law firms and corporate legal departments as the decade unfolds."

Redefining the Legal Workforce

Legal professionals will have to adapt to offices that will look and operate differently than those they work in today, according to The Affiliates' research. Call said, "Everyone from lawyers to support specialists will need advanced computer and technical skills, expertise in specific practice areas, and an entrepreneurial business approach." Call noted that growth in responsibility will be the common theme for legal professionals. "Our research indicates that associates, including first- and second-year lawyers, will have increased interaction with clients and more accountability for their firm's profit growth," she said. "In addition, paralegals will assume heightened responsibilities, including some that currently are handled by new associates."

According to a recent poll by The Affiliates, more paralegals already are taking on expanded roles. Seventy-five percent of attorneys surveyed said they believe paralegals have more career-growth opportunities today than five years ago. For every legal professional, technology training will be essential to advancement. Eighty-three percent of attorneys polled said greater proficiency with the Internet will help their own careers in the coming years. In a companion survey, legal administrators chose Internet-related skills as the area of technical proficiency most likely to advance their careers in the future.

Among other workforce trends identified in the research:

- Many firms will offer staff members flextime, expanded retirement packages, more casual work environments, mentoring and career counseling, and child and elder care benefits. These options reflect a changing attitude by employers toward work–life balance for employees. Attorneys surveyed by The Affiliates cited showing appreciation for staff and maintaining high workplace morale among the most effective strategies for boosting employee satisfaction.

- The use of project professionals will grow throughout the legal field. Sixty-two percent of legal administrators surveyed expect their firm's use of project attorneys to increase over the next eight years; 59 percent of respondents predict their office's use of project teams will rise in this same period.

The Technology Revolution

The Affiliates' research shows that as the practice of law becomes a 24-hour, seven-day-a-week operation, law firms increasingly view technology as the key difference between themselves and their competitors. Technological advances will also reinforce relationships between client and attorney. Attorneys polled said that 75 percent of business communication will be conducted via email in the future. According to experts consulted by The Affiliates, security concerns will ease.

"Advanced encryption technology is already being developed that will enable the most sensitive information to be transmitted over the Internet," Call said. She added that attorneys will soon be able to file documents electronically with courts nationwide. E-filing, currently being tested in several jurisdictions, will automate the filing process and alleviate the need for sending physical copies of documents to courts or serving papers to parties involved in litigation.

Other technology trends identified in the research include:

- Application service providers (ASPs)—web portals offering case and document management systems—will allow firms to manage time and billing services, litigation support, and other key software through high-speed Internet connections.

- New technology will continue to increase the viability of telecommuting. Firms will issue laptop computers to most attorneys, enabling them to work from satellite locations. Ninety-eight percent of attorneys surveyed by The Affiliates believe that telecommuting will increase in the next decade.

The Right Look

The Affiliates' research suggests law office design will undergo dramatic changes in the coming years, including a move toward more egalitarian arrangements such as glass walls and similar-sized workspaces for all employees. In addition, noted Call, remote workers increasingly will influence office design decisions. To accommodate visiting attorneys and project professionals, offices will have hotelling areas with desks, telephones, and online access. In another of The Affiliates' surveys, legal administrators identified common offices used by telecommuters and common areas with moveable furniture as typical characteristics of future floor plans.

The traditional law library will also undergo changes. "While hard copies of books will always be part of a law practice, future libraries will be smaller, electronic and more user-friendly," Call said. Sixty-seven percent of attorneys polled by The Affiliates said that law libraries will decrease in size over the next 10 years.

Practice Area Specialization

"Increasingly the concept of the general practice attorney will become obsolete," said Call. The Affiliates'

research indicates there will be regional clusters of legal expertise nationwide—niche markets like Silicon Valley for intellectual property law or New York City for corporate law. Demographics, specialized education, and emerging economic trends will influence what is practiced in a particular region.

Other practice area trends identified in the Future Law Office research include:

- *Intellectual property, e-commerce, patent, and Internet issues.* Technology will continue to fuel growth in the number of firms specializing in these practice areas. Forty-eight percent of lawyers surveyed cited intellectual property as the hottest practice area for the coming decade.

- *Estate planning, medical technology (including privacy issues), elder law, and health care.* The aging baby boom generation will generate demand for these specializations.

- *Alternative dispute resolution (ADR).* With clients seeking ways to avoid lawsuits, issues that would normally find their way to court will be handled with greater frequency through ADR. Ninety-three percent of attorneys surveyed by The Affiliates said they would suggest ADR to their litigation clients as a viable option.

MDPs and Beyond

The Affiliates' findings suggest the legal field will see a shift toward multidisciplinary practices (MDPs). While current American Bar Association guidelines prohibit lawyers from sharing fees or forming partnerships with nonlawyers when activities involve law practice, by the close of the decade, more law firms will form alliances with accounting, management consulting, and real estate professionals to provide clients with a wide range of business services, research shows.

"We'll also see a renewed emphasis on marketing," Call said. "In response to increased competition from legal Web services and emerging MDPs, firms will focus on developing brand awareness." This finding is underscored by the results of The Affiliates' survey in which 94 percent of attorneys said law firm marketing would be important to their firms in the next 10 years.

Among other common business practices in the future law office:

- *Diverse billing procedures.* Increased emphasis on client service will lead to solutions such as value billing, in which fees are based on uniform standards—projecting the time required to complete a task, for example, and establishing a fee based on that time.

- *Online business opportunities.* Licensed lawyers, as well as nonattorneys, will capitalize on this trend. For example, websites managed by legal information brokers will enable individuals to download advice-oriented columns and materials as well as basic legal forms. Law firms will compete by offering legal services via their external websites.

The Affiliates provides law firms and corporate legal departments with project and full-time professionals including attorneys, paralegals, and legal support personnel. The Affiliates offers online job search services at www.affiliates.com. For more information on the Future Law Office project, including a listing of experts and research sources, please visit www.futurelawoffice.com.

Reproduced with permission of the copyright owner. Further reproduction or distribution is prohibited without permission.

exhibit 9.3 Timeline.

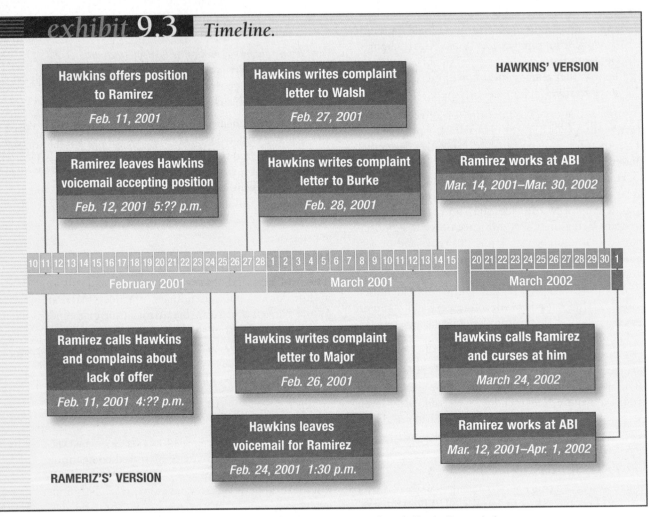

Timeline created using Time Map, from DecisionQuest, CaseSoft (www.casesoft.com). Used with permission.

Investigation Checklists

The investigation checklist (Exhibit 9.4) should not be viewed as a static document. The checklist should start with a listing all of the parties involved who should be interviewed, including initial fact witnesses. As additional parties and witnesses are interviewed, more people may have to be added to the list. Exhibit 9.5 is a witness information form. Investigation of locations and physical evidence may result in the need to examine other locations and evidence. Initial interviews also may result in the need to add one or more expert witnesses to the investigati1on checklist.

PREPARING FOR THE INTERVIEW

The first step in preparing for an interview or conducting an investigation is to understand the outcome desired. One of the desired outcomes in an initial interview with a new client is to instill confidence in the firm and its personnel. The fundamentally desired outcome of any interview is to obtain all of the needed relevant facts for the case that has been assigned. Understanding the goals of the interview or investigation, the background or cultural issues of the individual, or the nature of the situation will help in structuring a successful interview. Occasionally an interview has to be conducted without time for preparation, such as when the paralegal is asked to fill in for someone else at the last moment.

A checklist can be a valuable tool to be certain that all the information required for a certain type of case or other legal matter is obtained during the initial interview. The same checklist offers a good foundation for developing a more detailed interview plan when there is time for preparation.

> ### Interview Prep
>
> Physical surroundings, dress, and appearance for the interview are important in preparing for interviews and investigations.
>
> SIDEBAR

Physical Surroundings

The physical surroundings of the interview location can set the tone for the interview. Depending upon the purpose of the interview and the person being interviewed, the paralegal may wish to create a formal or informal environment. You probably can remember a situation in which someone interviewed you from across a desk. Didn't you feel a certain formality and possibly subservience to the interviewer? Contrast that situation with sitting in an informal setting with a low coffee table and living room-style chairs. This type of setting gives the meeting a more personal tone.

Setting a client at ease may be easier in the informal setting, whereas dealing with opposing counsel might be better handled in the formal "across the desk" type of meeting. In most cases the paralegal will want to create the impression of a competent professional, but in some situations, creating a more casual and less professional impression may be beneficial. Some witnesses are more cooperative and helpful when they feel as if they are in charge and are helping the paraprofessional because of their superiority.

Dress and Appearance

Remember the old saying, "first impressions count"? The impression a paralegal makes when walking into the room for the initial interview may set the stage for the entire relationship with the client or witness. Clothing, posture, and manner of greeting create the first impression.

exhibit 9.4   *Investigation checklist.*

INVESTIGATION CHECKLIST

Client name

Phone (hm) _____ (wk) _____ (cell) _____

Current address

Prior address(es)

Date of birth _____ Place of birth

Social Security No.

VEHICLE CLIENT OPERATING/PASSENGER

Owner and type of motor vehicle

Insurance Co. _____ Policy number

Insurance company contact _____ Phone

Date of incident _____ Time of day _____ Weather conditions

Location of incident

City, State _____ County _____ Municipality

Opposing party

Address

Phone (hm) _____ (wk) _____ (cell)

Owner and type of motor vehicle

Insurance Co. _____ Policy number

FACT WITNESSES

Name _____ Address

Name _____ Address

Name _____ Address

Name of ambulance

Name of hospital

Police report issued _____ Copy ordered

Photographs of scene taken

Name of treating physicians

EXPERT WITNESSES

Name _____ Address

Name _____ Address

Summary of cause of action

Attach detailed accident/incident description, accident reports and diagrams.

Witness information form.   exhibit 9.5

Witness Information

CLIENT PERSONAL DATA

Client Name	Case No.	File No.

Address	City, State, Zip	Phone

CASE DATA

File Label	Case Issue	Date

Responsible Attorney(s)

WITNESS DATA

Witness Name

Aliases, if any	US Citizen ☐ Yes ☐ No

Current Address	City, State, Zip	Phone

Past Address(es)

Date & Place of Birth	Sex	Race	Age	Current Marital Status ☐ Single ☐ Divorced
Name of Spouse	Number/Former Marriages		Number/Children	☐ Married ☐ Widowed ☐ Separated

Name of Children (natural & adopted)	Age	Name	Age

Current Employer

Address	City, State, Zip	Phone

Job Title	Supervisor	From	To

Previous Employer

Address	City, State, Zip	Phone

Job Title	Supervisor	From	To

Education/Name of School	City/State	From	To	Degree
High School				
College				
Technical/Other				

Witness for ☐ Plaintiff ☐ Defendant	Type of Witness ☐ Expert ☐ Character ☐ Eye Witness	Have you ever been a party or witness in a court suit? ☐ No ☐ Yes

If yes, where & when

OTHER PERTINENT DATA

Form 8567 • 9/86 **SYCOM** Madison, WI Printed in U.S.A.

Clothing sends a nonverbal message about the person and the firm or business. The impression a person makes upon walking into the room can enhance or destroy credibility. In the practice of law, or in a corporate law department, the unexpected can become the norm. Many attorneys, male and female alike, keep a "going-to-court suit" in the office just in case they need to have a more professional appearance at a moment's notice. When the new client comes in, they can change quickly while the receptionist or secretary buys them time to change to the "power" outfit.

A client may be offended by a paralegal's "casual Friday" appearance, believing the paralegal is not taking the matter seriously. However, the working paralegal usually doesn't have time to change when the unexpected arises, often being the one to "buy time" for the attorney. Therefore, paralegals must always be prepared to make a good impression and tailor their appearance appropriately as the situation warrants.

SIDEBAR

A Casual Look

Field interviews may require a casual appearance to put the potential witness at ease.

Cultural Sensitivity

Interviewers and investigators must be aware of cultural differences that can influence the results of interviews with clients, witnesses, personnel from the opposing law firm, and others. Of utmost importance is to pronounce correctly the names of the people with whom the paralegal has contact. For example, in some Asian cultures last names appear first and first names last. This may not be obvious when the business card is presented by a client of Asian origin and neither the first nor the last name is familiar.

Many non-Americans are uncomfortable with the informality of being called by their first name, even by their own attorney or paralegal. Titles are important in the form of address, including use of the term *doctor* to address those who have an academic doctorate and not just those with medical degrees.

Cultural issues in clothing also require sensitivity. Head coverings and floor-length dress are normal ways of dressing for a large segment of the world's population. Even in the United States, people whose cultural, ethnic, or religious backgrounds dictate more modest forms of dress may be offended by those they perceive as not respecting their traditions. For example, women paralegals may want to dress more conservatively when interviewing Moslem men and women so as not to appear contemptuous and create an impression of disrespect that can negatively affect the interview. And you can see that making an insensitive comment such as, "How can you wear all that clothing?" might be considered rude. Paralegals also should be aware of the religious calendar and religious or holy days when scheduling appointments. This adds to the overall positive impression.

People tend to think that others think, understand, and conduct themselves the same way we do. In a closed society, such as existed in Japan until the late 1940s and 1950s, this may have been true. But in the United States today, with its diverse cultures and assimilation into the American society of many religious and cultural groups, this is not true. We do not all read with the same level of understanding, nor do we all speak the same language or react the same

Religious Calendar:
www.interfaithcalendar.org/

way to verbal and written instructions. When interviewing clients and witnesses, we should try to determine how they perceive what we present and how the information will be perceived within their cultural understanding. For example, a well-meaning, caring, devoted parent who does not read English may understand verbal English but not appreciate the necessity of reading warning labels on over-the-counter medication.

Paralegals conducting interviews must be able to recognize these issues so they can present them well in their narrative reports. The supervising attorney will be using these reports in preparing the prosecution or the defense of the case, which makes accurate interpretation and representation of interviews essential.

CONDUCTING THE INTERVIEW

In the first meeting, the paralegal must make clear that he or she is a paralegal and not an attorney. During the first few minutes of the interview, paralegals must build a relationship with the interview subjects, let them understand the purpose of the interview, and eliminate any barriers that would prevent obtaining the necessary information. Sometimes the interviewees seem to be fully cooperative when in fact they are not cooperating. Or the subject matter may be embarrassing, or they may have a fear of authority figures, or they might be uncomfortable using certain terms necessary to describe the situation.

Effective interviewers learn the verbal and nonverbal cues that help them understand the reasons for interviewees' reluctance to answer questions. In some situations the solution is first to ask easy questions, such as the person's name and address. Once interviewees start speaking, they have less trouble answering well thought-out questions that build logically on the previous information. This is not always the case, though. In times of great stress, clients have been known to read the name from a nameplate in the office and state it as their own name! The interviewer must be careful to avoid embarrassing the interviewee and have prepared questions that can be answered easily and thereby help the person gain composure, such as, "My records show that you live at 123 South Main Street. Is that correct?" Or "How do you spell your name?"

Santa Barbara City Court house, California.

Leading Questions

Leading questions are those that suggest the desired answer. In conducting a cross-examination, lawyers in trial frequently use leading questions to force the witness to answer in a desired manner. An obvious example is, "Have you stopped kicking your dog?"

On direct examination, an attorney might ask a more direct and neutral question: "Have you ever kicked your dog?"

Leading questions do not lead to open-ended answers but are directed toward a desired answer: "You ran the red light, didn't you?"

Open-Ended Questions

Open-ended questions are designed to give interviewees an opportunity to tell their story without the limitation of yes-or-no answers. Open-ended questions create a **narrative opportunity** for the witness. For example: "Tell me about your life"; "Tell me about your life since the accident."

In fact interviews, the witness should receive the opportunity for open-ended narrative answers. Asking a question to solicit an answer that you desire may cut off information essential to your case. For example, you may want to know whether your client was at the scene of an accident and therefore ask the witness, "Did you see my client at the scene of the accident?" The answer to this question may be "yes" or "no." A better question would be, "Who was present at the scene of the accident?" This kind of question may lead to additional information on additional witnesses you may want to interview.

Similarly, the question, "How fast were the cars going prior to the impact?" is much better than, "Were the cars speeding before the impact?" In this context, the term "speeding" may be interpreted as exceeding the speed limit instead of going too fast for the conditions.

With the witness's statements from the interview in hand at the time of trial, the trial attorney might appropriately ask a leading question such as, "My client wasn't present at the scene of the accident, was she?" Or, "Isn't it true that the defendant was speeding before the impact?" With knowledge of the prior statement, there should be no surprise in the answer at trial. If there is, the prior statement can be used to impeach the credibility of the witness, if desired, as part of the trial strategy.

At times the interviewer may want to focus clients or witnesses by asking questions that give them a perspective of time or place, such as, "What did you observe at noon on Saturday?" or, "Tell me what happened on September 11, 2001." The tragedy of that day will haunt the memories of Americans and most of the rest of the world, so little stimulus will be needed to elicit where they were and what they observed. This is true of most traumatic events in people's lives—the loss of a loved one, the birth of a child, or a serious accident in which they were injured. Other days and times tend to blur and have to be brought to the consciousness of the witness by questions such as, "Let's think back to August 19, 2001" and, "What happened to you that day?"

ETHICAL VERSUS MORAL CONSIDERATIONS

At times in the investigation of a case, it is necessary to consider the difference between a moral consideration and an ethical consideration. A **moral obligation** is one based on one's own conscience or a person's perceived rules of correct conduct, generally in the person's own community. Some communities, for instance, may consider it to be morally improper to ask someone to give information about another person. An **ethical obligation,** for members of the legal team including those acting on behalf of a supervising attorney, are the responsibilities of the legal profession under the ABA Model Rules of Professional Conduct, including thoroughness in representing a client.

Is it ethically improper to ask someone to tell the truth surrounding the facts of a case that may lead to a neighbor, relative, or friend being subjected to liability for his or her actions? For the paralegal and the legal team, the primary ethical obligation is the duty to the client. It may offend some members of the legal team, for example, to ask a mother to testify against a child. This is a moral issue for the mother, in which the results may cause financial hardship or ruin upon awarding a verdict for causing injury as the result of negligent conduct, but ethics may require this course of conduct for the paralegal.

ABA Model Rules:

www.abanet.org/cpr/mrpc/mrpc_toc.html

PRIVILEGED COMMUNICATION

Certain forms of communication are considered privileged and not usable at trial unless the privilege is waived. Forms of **privileged communication** are:

1. Attorney–client communications
2. Doctor–patient communications
3. Priest–penitent communications
4. Spousal communications during marriage.

Each of these privileges can be waived. But the waiver must come from the client, the patient, the penitent, or the spouse making the statement with the belief that it is privileged. Changes in some of the rules of ethics, and by statute, may permit certain otherwise privileged communications to be revealed to prevent harm or injury to another. The spouse, the priest, or the doctor may have a moral issue in revealing what was communicated.

When the paralegal is acting on behalf of the attorney, communications between a client and the paralegal have the same privilege as those between the client and the attorney. Information gathered from the client as part of representation of the client and necessary for rendering competent legal advice is privileged. The paralegal, therefore, is in the same position as the attorney, the doctor, the priest, or the spouse to whom the confidential information has been communicated. Each must carefully guard the confidential information and not inadvertently or intentionally reveal the information. In some cases, such as when another person's life may be in danger, these people may be compelled by a court to testify even when they believe it is a violation of their moral duty to another person from whom they have received information

> ### Expert Witness
>
> (A) A party may depose any person who has been identified as an expert whose opinion may be presented at trial. If a report from the expert is required under (a)(2)(B) [Disclosure of Expert Testimony], the deposition shall not be conducted until after the report is provided. [F.R.C.P. 26(b)(4) Trial Preparation: Witness]
>
> SIDEBAR

EXPERT WITNESSES

Expert witnesses are individuals whose background, education, and experience are such that courts recognize them as qualified to give opinions based on a set of facts. The expert witness may be a doctor certified by a board of medical experts or a scientist or engineer specializing in an area of science such as flammability of fabrics. The report of these experts may be advice based on the facts of a potential case to determine whether there is sufficient evidence to believe that a wrong has occurred or malpractice committed. Without this report the lawyers may be obligated to advise clients that they have no actionable cause of action.

There is no clear rule on whether what is revealed to an expert in the preparation of a case is protected as part of the attorney–client privilege in the same manner as that revealed to a member of the trial team, including other attorneys, paralegals, and secretarial staff working on the case with the primary trial attorney. Almost certainly, anything revealed to an expert who is listed as an expert witness on the list of witnesses to be called at trial is discoverable.

Some law firms retain an expert to advise them but do not use that expert to testify. The advice and information provided by these experts to help in the preparation for trial may come under the privilege. Although the privilege is the client's, the paralegal and others on the legal team must be careful not to divulge privileged or confidential material without authorization.

The expert retained for background trial advice must have as much confidence in the legal team as the legal team has in the expert's advice and integrity. Some experts fear that the legal team will give them only selected information. With the limited information provided, they might give an expert opinion that is not what they would have given if they had received the complete set of facts.

Exhibit 9.6 indicates factors to be considered in arranging for an expert witness.

Checklist

DEPOSING EXPERT WITNESSES

Ask an expert witness these ten questions at deposition, even if you don't have time to ask anything else:

- ○ What opinions have you formed in this matter?
- ○ What did you do to reach those opinions?
- ○ How did you do that?
- ○ Why did you do that?
- ○ What results did you get?
- ○ How did the results affect your opinion?
- ○ Are there reliable authorities in this field?
- ○ What assumptions did you make in your work?
- ○ What tasks didn't you do?
- ○ Is this your current and accurate resume?

Source: Expert Rules: 100 (and More) Points You Need to Know About Expert Witnesses, 2d ed., by David M. Malone & Paul J. Zweir, National Institute for Trial Advocacy, 2000.

Expert witness form.   *exhibit* 9.6

EXPERT WITNESS CHECKLIST

BACKGROUND

Full name _____   Date of birth _____

Business address _____

Business telephone number _____   Business fax number _____

Business email address _____   Business web site _____

Locations of prior offices _____

Home address _____

Home telephone number _____

EDUCATION

Schools attended _____   Dates of attendance _____

Degrees or honors awarded _____

Continuing education courses _____

WORK HISTORY

Place of employment _____   Dates of employment _____

Job description _____

Reasons for leaving _____

Specific area of expertise _____

Published articles and books _____

Professional affiliations _____

Professional magazines subscribed to _____

Licenses and jurisdictions _____

Investigations or disciplinary action _____

PRIOR LEGAL EXPERIENCE

Ratio of plaintiff/defense cases _____

Prior clients including date (plaintiff or defendant) _____

Types of investigations with dates _____

Deposition testimony given with dates _____

Court testimony with dates _____

Legal references _____

AVAILABILITY

Vacation plans and dates _____   Potential meeting dates _____

FREEDOM OF INFORMATION ACT (FOIA)

The **Freedom of Information Act** is a federal statute designed to open to the public the information possessed by the federal government and its agencies. The federal government is a good source of information. Many of the documents required to be filed are available through the government, and frequently online, such as corporate filings with the Securities and Exchange Commission. Other information may be available by request, under the provisions of the Freedom of Information Act (FOIA), 5 U.S.C. § 552. Some limitations apply to the information available. The general exceptions, as found in the statute, are:

1. Classified documents concerning national defense and foreign policy.
2. Internal personnel rules and practices.
3. Exemptions under other laws that require information to be withheld, such as patent applications and income-tax returns.
4. Confidential business information and trade secrets.
5. Intra-agency and inter-agency internal communications not available by law to a party in litigation.
6. Protection of privacy of personnel and medical files and private lives of individuals.
7. Law-enforcement investigatory files.
8. Examination, operation, or condition reports of agencies responsible for the regulation and supervision of financial institutions.
9. Geological and geophysical information and data including maps concerning wells.

Exhibit 9.7 is the Freedom of Information/Privacy Act Request form.

SIDEBAR

Discovery

Always check the rules and consider the effect of taking discovery in an international dispute. Some countries, such as Japan, limit or prohibit the use in trial of material obtained during discovery.

LOCATING WITNESSES

Most witnesses can be located by use of directories. The Web has also become a valuable tool for locating witnesses.

Directories

Investigators usually keep a collection of telephone books of the areas in which they work. Rarely today does a person not have a telephone, even if it is an unlisted number. In addition to the standard-issue telephone directories, the cross-reference directory (also known as a "criss-cross directory") is a standard tool; these list phone numbers by address or by phone number instead of by name. Therefore, an address may be checked for a corresponding phone number—for example, determining the phone number located at 123 Main Street, or using the phone numbers listed at an address to determine the physical location or billing address of the phone.

Telephone directories are not limited to just the United States but typically are published in most parts of the world in one form or another. Companies and businesses also can be located by use of commercial or industrial telephone directories, both domestically and internationally.

In addition to telephone directories, directories are published by trade organizations, professional groups, and educational institutions. These direc-

FOIA/Privacy Act Request form. *exhibit* 9.7

U.S. Department of Justice
Immigration and Naturalization Service

Freedom of Information/Privacy Act Request

OMB NO. 1115-0087

The completion of this form is optional.

Any written format for Freedom of Information or Privacy Act requests is acceptable.

START HERE – Please type or print and read instructions on the reverse before completing this form.

1. Type of Request: *(Check appropriate box)*
   - ☐ Freedom of Information Act (FOIA) *(Complete all items except 7)*
   - ☐ Privacy Act (PA) *(Item 7 must be completed in addition to all other applicable items)*
   - ☐ Amendment *(PA only). Item 7 must be completed in addition to all other applicable items)*

2. Requester Information:

Name of Requester:		Daytime Telephone:
Address *(Street Number and Name)*:		Apt. No.
City:	State:	Zip Code:

   By my signature, I consent to the following:
   Pay all costs incurred for search, duplication, and review of materials up to $25.00, when applicable. *(See Instructions)*

   Signature of requester:
   - ☐ Deceased Subject – **Proof of death must be attached.** *(Obituary, Death Certificate or other proof of death required)*

3. Consent to Release Information. *(Complete if name is different from Requester)(Item 7 must be completed)*

Print Name of Person Giving Consent:	Signature of Person Giving Consent:

   By my signature, I consent to the following: (check applicable boxes)
   - ☐ Allow the Requester named in item 2 to see ☐ all of my records or ☐ a portion of my record. If a portion, specify what part *(i.e. copy of application)*

   (Consent is required for records for United States Citizens (USC) and Lawful Permanent Residents (LPR))

4. Action Requested *(Check One)*: ☐ Copy   ☐ In-Person Review

5. Information needed to search for records:
   Specific information, document(s), or record(s) desired: *Identify by name, date, subject matter, and location of information.)*

   Purpose: *(Optional; you are not required to state the purpose for your request; however, doing so may assist the INS in locating the records needed to respond to your request.)*

6. Data NEEDED on SUBJECT of Record: *(If data marked with asterisk (*) is not provided records may not be located)*

* Family Name	Given Name:	Middle Initial:
*Other names used, if any:	* Name at time of entry into the U.S.:	I-94 Admissions #:
* Alien Registration #:	* Petition or Claim Receipt #:	* Country of Birth:	*Date of Birth or Appx. Year
	Names of other family members that may appear on requested record(s): *(i.e., Spouse, Daughter, Son)*:	
Country of Origin *(Place of Departure)*:	Port-of-Entry into the U.S.	Date of Entry:
Manner of Entry: *(Air, Sea, Land)*	Mode of Travel: *(Name of Carrier)*	SSN:
Name of Naturalization Certifications:	Certificate #:	Naturalization Date:
Address at the time of Naturalization:	Court and Location:	

   Form G-639 (Rev. 7-25-00)N

---

7. Verification of Subject's Identity: *(See Instructions for Explanation)(Check One Box)*
   - ☐ In-Person with ID   ☐ Notarized Affidavit of Identity   ☐ Other *(Specify)* ____

   Signature of Subject of Record: Date: ____
   Telephone No.: ( ) - ____

   NOTARY *(Normally needed from individuals who are the subject of the records sought) (See below)* or a sworn declaration under penalty of perjury.
   Subscribed and sworn to before me this ____ day of ____ in the Year ____

   Signature of Notary ____   My Commission Expires ____

                                    OR

   If a declaration is provided in lieu of a notarized signature, it must state, at a minimum, the following: (Include Notary Seal or Stamp in this Space)

   If executed outside the United States: "I declare (certify, verify, or state) under penalty of perjury under the laws of the United States of America that the foregoing is true and correct.

   If executed within the United States, its territories, possessions, or commonwealths: "I declare (certify, verify, or state) under penalty of perjury that the foregoing is true and correct.

   Signature: ____   Signature: ____

   Form G-639 (Rev. 7-25-00)N Page 2

Checklist

INVESTIGATION INFORMATION SOURCES

Information Source	Web Address	Physical Location	Comments
Police Records–Local	www.		
Police Records–State	www.		
Birth Records	www.		
Death Records	www.		
Drivers License	www.		
Vehicle Registration	www.		
Corporate Records	www.		
Real Estate–Recorder	www.		
Real Estate–Tax	www.		
Real Estate–Land Mapping	www.		
Register of Wills	www.		
Trial Court	www.		
Federal District Court–Clerk's Office	www.	Room Federal Court House	
Federal Bankruptcy Court	www.		
Occupational License	www.		
Weather Reports	www.		

Personalize this list by adding the local or regional office Web addresses, mailing addresses, and room numbers for personal visits, and comments, with any applicable contact people, costs, or hours of operation.

tories may be limited to membership but can be useful in cases where the name and the association are known, but not the city, state, or country where the person can be found.

The Web

As paper is replaced by electronic media, directories are being placed online. Search engines can help locate individuals, businesses, and organizations on the Internet. Communications companies and other private firms offer a number of online white pages for individuals, and yellow pages for businesses. Many organizations and publishers of professional directories now offer their print directories online, such as the Web version of Martindale-Hubbell for attorneys (see Exhibit 9.8). These services may change or cancel their Web address and others may be added, so it is necessary to keep your list of websites up to date.

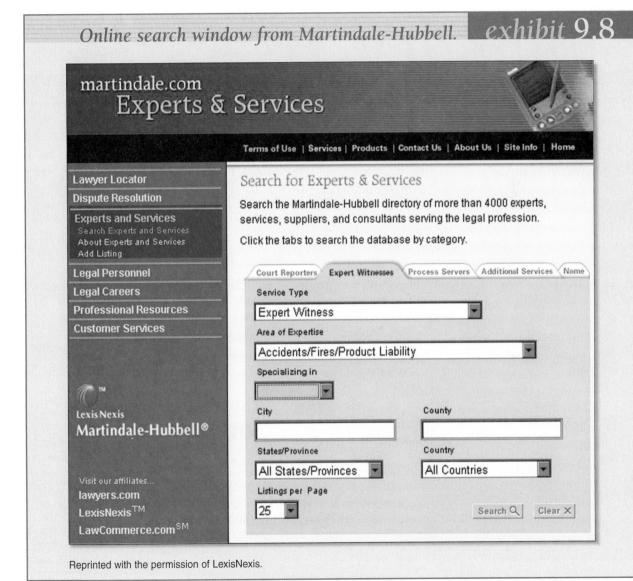

www

Martindale-Hubbell Legal Directory: http://lawyers. martindale.com/xp/Martindale/ home.xml

Online search window from Martindale-Hubbell.   *exhibit 9.8*

Reprinted with the permission of LexisNexis.

LEGAL TERMINOLOGY

Arbitration

Ethical obligation

Expert witness

Freedom of Information Act (FOIA)

Leading question

Moral obligation

Narrative opportunity

Open-ended questions

Privileged communication

Restatement (Second) of Torts

Spoliation of evidence

Strict liability

Summary

CHAPTER 9 INTERVIEWING AND INVESTIGATION SKILLS

Investigating Claims

Obtaining Official Reports	Most incidents giving rise to litigation have associated official reports. In the negligence action it may be a police accident or incident report, emergency medical services report, fire department call report, or incident reports of safety violations by federal, state, or local authorities. These reports are generally filed in a central depository as public records. It is a useful starting point to obtain any official reports associated with the case.
Fact Analysis	Starts with the interview of the client and recitation of the time, place, circumstances, and others involved as participants or as witnesses. A complete analysis usually requires further field investigation of location, object involved, and interviews of parties and witnesses.
Locations	Verification of physical aspects of actual location where the cause of action occurred.
Tangible Evidence	Includes physical objects that may have caused the injury. Requires understanding local rules with regard to "spoliation of evidence" and its effect on a cause of action. In determining proper penalty for spoliation of evidence, courts are most likely to consider (1) degree of fault of the party who altered or destroyed the evidence; (2) degree of prejudice suffered by opposing party, and (3) availability of a lesser sanction that will protect the opposing party's rights and deter future similar conduct.

(continued) |

Following a Timeline	Causes of action viewed from events leading up to the incident to events and occurrences following the incident.
Investigation Checklist	Starts with listing all parties involved who should be interviewed; as additional parties and witnesses are interviewed, additional people may be added to the list.

Preparing for the Interview

Outcome	1. First step is to understand the outcomes desired, one of which is to instill confidence in the firm and its personnel. 2. Desired outcome of any interview is to obtain all needed, relevant facts for the case.
Physical Surroundings	Depending upon purpose of interview and the person being interviewed, a formal or an informal environment may be desired.
Dress and Appearance	Clothing worn in an interview sends a nonverbal message about the paralegal and the firm or business, and the initial impression can enhance or destroy credibility.
Cultural Sensitivity	Interviewers and investigators must be aware of cultural differences and issues of clients and witnesses to avoid creating a negative impression.

Conducting the Interview

First Meeting	1. The paralegal must be careful to make clear that he or she is a paralegal and not an attorney. 2. Paralegal must build a relationship with the individual, let him or her understand the purpose of the interview, and eliminate any barriers that would prevent obtaining the necessary information.
Leading Questions	Questions that suggest the desired answer. Lawyers in conducting a cross-examination in trial frequently use leading questions to force the witness to answer in a desired manner.
Open-Ended Questions	Questions designed to create a narrative opportunity for the witness.

Ethical Versus Moral Considerations

Moral Obligations	Based on one's own conscience or perceived rules of correct conduct, generally in the person's own community.

(continued)

Ethical Obligations	Obligations of legal profession under ABA Model Rules of Professional Conduct, including thoroughness in representing a client.
Privileged Communications	
Forms	1. Attorney–client communications 2. Doctor–patient communications 3. Priest–penitent communications 4. Spousal communications during marriage
Waivers	These privileges can be waived, but the waiver must come from the client, the patient, the penitent, or the spouse making the statement with the belief that it is privileged.
Expert Witnesses	
Definition	Individuals whose background, education, and experience are such that courts will recognize them as qualified to give opinions based on a set of facts.
Freedom of Information Act (FOIA)	
Definition	A federal statute designed to open the information in the possession of the federal government and its agencies to the public.
Locating Witnesses	
Directories	1. Phone books 2. Cross-reference directories 3. Membership directories
The Web	Search engines can help locate individuals, businesses, and organizations on the Internet.

Working the Web

1. Using different Web search engines, locate information about yourself. For example, use a website that provides maps, such as MapQuest at www.mapquest.com, to locate the intersection nearest your home.

2. Use a search engine such as Findlaw to find an expert witness with a specialty of automobile tires, airplane accidents, and fire equipment, at http://marketcenter.findlaw.com/experts_consultants.html.

3. Check the listing for attornies in your city or town online in the Martindale Hubbell directory at http://lawyers.martindale.com/xp/ Martindale/Lawyer_Locator/Search_Lawyer_Locator/lawyer_search.xml.

4. Use the Martindale Hubbell site to locate an expert witness at http://lawyers.martindale.com/xp/Martindale/Experts_and_Services/ Search_Experts_and_Services/leg_search.xml.

Questions

CRITICAL LEGAL THINKING AND WRITING

1. Using the Facts in the *Palsgraf* case in Appendix A, prepare a list of witnesses who might be called in that case. Prepare an interview checklist for each of the witnesses.

2. Using the Facts in the *Palsgraf* case in Appendix A, prepare an investigative checklist including a list of the evidence that should be gathered in the case, including a list and description of any photographs needed.

3. In conducting an interview, when would it be appropriate to dress in "Friday casual" attire?

4. Why is it important to visit the site of the accident in a motor-vehicle case being prepared for trial?

5. Under what circumstances might it be advisable for someone else in the firm to handle an interview with a client or witness?

6. Why would someone feel a moral obligation not to answer questions in an interview?

7. Why would a law firm hire an expert witness and not call that person as a witness at trial?

8. How useful is the Freedom of Information Act in obtaining state or local government documents? Explain.

9. Complete the Investigation Information Source Checklist for your area.

10. Can a client restrict the use of information obtained as part of the investigation in preparation for trial even if doing so will have adverse consequences in the opinion of the attorney? Why or why not?

Questions

ETHICS: ANALYSIS AND DISCUSSION

1. Is it morally acceptable or ethically permissible to ask someone—such as a doctor, priest, spouse, or parent—who has information that has been communicated in confidence to breach that confidence as part of the interview or investigation in preparation for trial?

2. Under what circumstances should a paralegal decline to accept an assignment to conduct an interview or investigation? Why?

3. What steps should a paralegal take when she has determined that the case she is investigating is at the least frivolous or at worst fraudulent?

Practice Issue—Advising Status

There are few certainties in the area of ethics, for paralegals or in any profession. What qualifies as ethical conduct is in most cases based on state law and court interpretation applied to a set of facts. The citation listed below represents one legal opinion and is provided as a research starting point. Do not assume that the same rule applies in your jurisdiction. For the following:

- *Prepare a written statement based on your state law.*
- *Use your state bar association website as a starting point.*

You are assigned to interview a new client of the firm. You meet the client in the waiting room and say "Hello Mrs. Hannah, I'm Miss Ariel. I will be taking some information from you about your case. Please join me in the conference room." You then proceed to take all the information you need, thank the client, and say "We will be in touch with you. Can you find the way out?" The client leaves. [Canon 6 NFPA Ethics.] What obligation do you have to advise the client of your status as a paralegal?

Case

FOR DISCUSSION

Limitations on Obtaining Information in Criminal Cases Under the FOIA

The FOIA can be a good source of information in criminal cases as well as civil litigation. As with discovery-limitation exemptions in civil cases, additional exemptions exist under the Act in criminal cases. Landano was convicted in New Jersey state court for murdering a police officer during what may have been a gang-related robbery. In an effort to support his claim in subsequent state court proceedings that his rights were violated by withholding material exculpatory evidence, he filed Freedom of Information Act requests with the Federal Bureau of Investigation (FBI) for information it had compiled in connection with the murder investigation.

When the FBI redacted some documents and withheld others, Landano filed an action, seeking disclosure of the contents of the requested files. The court held that the government is not entitled to a presumption that all sources supplying information to the FBI in the course of a criminal investigation are confidential sources within the meaning of Exemption 7(D). Further, a source should be deemed "confidential" if the source furnished information with the understanding that the FBI would not divulge the communication except to the extent it thought necessary for law-enforcement purposes.

Questions

1. Does this unfairly subject an informant to potential harassment?
2. Does limiting information unfairly prevent the defendant from receiving a fair trial?
3. Does the limitation effectively limit any usefulness in making a request under the FOIA?

Read, and if assigned, brief this case. In your brief, answer the following questions.

1. What are the two conditions under which a document qualifies for exemption under the Freedom of Information Act, Exemption 5?
2. How is "agency" defined under the FOIA?
3. What is the "deliberative process" privilege? Does non-governmental litigation have an equivalent privilege?
4. What is the purpose of the deliberative process privilege?
5. What is the "general philosophy" behind the FOIA?

Justice Souter delivered the opinion of the Court. Documents in issue here, passing between Indian Tribes and the Department of the Interior, addressed tribal interests subject to state and federal proceedings to determine water allocations. The question is whether the documents are exempt from the disclosure requirements of the Freedom of Information Act, as "intra-agency memorandums or letters" that would normally be privileged in civil discovery [5 U.S.C. § 552(b)(5)]. We hold they are not.

I

... [T]he Department's Bureau of Indian Affairs (Bureau) filed claims on behalf of the Klamath Tribe alone in an Oregon state-court adjudication intended to allocate water rights. Since the Bureau is responsible for administering land and water held in trust for Indian tribes ... it consulted with the Klamath Tribe, and the two exchanged written memorandums on the appropriate scope of the claims ultimately submitted. ... The Bureau does not, however, act as counsel for the Tribe, which has its own lawyers and has independently submitted claims on its own behalf.[1]

... [T]he Klamath Water Users Protective Association is a nonprofit association of water users in the Klamath River Basin, most of whom receive water from the Klamath Project, and whose interests are adverse to the tribal interests owing to scarcity of water. The Association filed a series of requests with the Bureau under the Freedom of Information Act (FOIA) [5 U.S.C. § 552] seeking access to communications between the Bureau and the Basin Tribes during the rel-

evant time period. The Bureau turned over several documents but withheld others as exempt under the attorney work-product and deliberative process privileges. These privileges are said to be incorporated in FOIA Exemption 5, which exempts from disclosure "inter-agency or intra-agency memorandums or letters which would not be available by law to a party other than an agency in litigation with the agency" [§ 552(b)(5)]. The Association then sued the Bureau under FOIA to compel release of the documents. ...

Upon request, FOIA mandates disclosure of records held by a federal agency, see 5 U.S.C. § 552, unless the documents fall within enumerated exemptions. ...

A

Exemption 5 protects from disclosure "inter-agency or intra-agency memorandums or letters which would not be available by law to a party other than an agency in litigation with the agency" [5 U.S.C. § 552(b)(5)]. To qualify, a document must thus satisfy two conditions: Its source must be a Government agency, and it must fall within the ambit of a privilege against discovery under judicial standards that would govern litigation against the agency that holds it.

Our prior cases on Exemption 5 have addressed the second condition, incorporating civil discovery privileges. ... So far as they might matter here, those privileges include the privilege for attorney work-product and what is sometimes called the "deliberative process" privilege. Work-product protects "mental processes of the attorney" while deliberative process covers "docu-

---

[1] The Government is "not technically acting as [the Tribes'] attorney. That is, the Tribes have their own attorneys, but the United States acts as trustee" [Tr. of Oral Arg. 5]. "The United States has also filed claims on behalf of the Project and on behalf of other Federal interests" in the Oregon adjudication [Id. at 6]. The Hoopa Valley, Karuk, and Yurok Tribes are not parties to the adjudication. [Brief for Respondent 7]

ments reflecting advisory opinions, recommendations and deliberations comprising part of a process by which governmental decisions and policies are formulated." The deliberative process privilege rests on the obvious realization that officials will not communicate candidly among themselves if each remark is a potential item of discovery and front-page news, and its object is to enhance "the quality of agency decisions," . . . by protecting open and frank discussion among those who make them within the Government. . . .

The point is not to protect Government secrecy pure and simple, however, and the first condition of Exemption 5 is no less important than the second; the communication must be "inter-agency or intra-agency" [5 U.S.C. § 552(b)(5)] . . . . With exceptions not relevant here, "agency" means "each authority of the Government of the United States," . . . and "includes any executive department, military department, Government corporation, Government-controlled corporation, or other establishment in the executive branch of the Government . . . , or any independent regulatory agency." . . .

Although neither the terms of the exemption nor the statutory definitions say anything about communications with outsiders, some Courts of Appeals have held that in some circumstances a document prepared outside the Government may . . . qualify . . . under Exemption 5. . . .

> It is . . . possible . . . to regard as an intra-agency memorandum one that has been received by an agency, to assist it in the performance of its own functions, from a person acting in a governmentally conferred capacity other than on behalf of another agency—e.g., in a capacity as . . . consultant to the agency.

Typically, courts taking the latter view have held that the exemption extends to communications between Government agencies and outside consultants hired by them. . . . In such cases, the records submitted by outside consultants played essentially the same part in an agency's process of deliberation as documents prepared by agency personnel might have done. . . . [T]he fact about the consultant that is constant . . . is that the consultant does not represent an interest of its own, or the interest of any other client, when it advises the agency that hires it. Its only obligations are to truth and its sense of what good judgment calls for, and in those respects the consultant functions just as an employee would be expected to do.

B

. . . The Tribes, on the contrary, necessarily communicate with the Bureau with their own, albeit entirely legitimate, interests in mind. While this fact alone distinguishes tribal communications from the consultants' examples recognized by several Courts of Appeals, the distinction is even sharper, in that the Tribes are self-advocates at the expense of others seeking benefits inadequate to satisfy everyone.

. . . All of this boils down to requesting that we read an "Indian trust" exemption into the statute, a reading that is out of the question for reasons already explored. There is simply no support for the exemption in the statutory text, which we have elsewhere insisted be read strictly in order to serve FOIA's mandate of broad disclosure, which was obviously expected and intended to affect Government operations. In FOIA, after all, a new conception of Government conduct was enacted into law, "a general philosophy of full agency disclosure." Congress had to realize that not every secret under the old law would be secret under the new.

The judgment of the Court of Appeals is affirmed. *It is so ordered.*

CHAPTER 10

CHAPTER OBJECTIVES

After studying this chapter, you should be able to:

1. Explain the basic features of computer-assisted legal research programs.

2. Describe how to use the traditional law library resources to locate applicable statutes and court cases.

3. Explain the difference between primary and secondary sources.

4. Explain the need for parallel citation format.

5. Describe the function of connectors in computer research.

6. Outline the basic features of Lexis, Westlaw, Loislaw, and Versuslaw.

7. Explain the need to update prior legal research.

8. Name the online tools available for updating legal research.

9. Describe how *Shepard's* is compiled and used.

10. Demonstrate how to read traditional citations and use parallel citations.

Traditional and Computer Legal Research

This trial is a travesty; it's a travesty of a mockery of a sham of a mockery of a travesty of two mockeries of a sham. I move for a mistrial.

WOODY ALLEN, *BANANAS*

Introduction

One of the most important skills a paralegal can develop is the ability to find current relevant information in a timely manner. Knowing where to look is just as important as knowing what to look for. Clients expect their legal counsel to use the latest law in advising them. The paralegal is expected to be able to understand the relevant facts and find the current statutory law and case law. The frequent changes in court decisions and statutory enactments present a challenge to the legal profession. Traditional law libraries consisting of printed text may not provide the latest case, statute, or regulation for days or weeks because of the time required to assemble, print, and send out updates. Modern computer technology allows for more rapid distribution. Many courts now issue the electronic version of court opinions at the same time as the printed version. Instant availability is certainly a benefit if you are working on a similar case.

Although the ability to obtain current case law is important, in many cases an older common law case may still be precedent. The problem is that some electronic or online services, such as Versuslaw, may not have included the older cases in their database of available cases. When that happens, being able to find the case the old-fashioned way by checking through the books is a valuable skill. When using an electronic case service such as Versuslaw, the dates of the available cases should be checked to be certain that they cover the time period needed for the search.

RESEARCH STARTING POINT

Legal research is like a puzzle to be solved. Understanding the question is essential. A lot of time may be wasted if the paralegal takes the wrong research path, because the framer of the question has not been clear or the researcher is not clear on the information needed. At times the question is framed with some specificity:

Find the statute . . .
Get me the case of . . .

More often, however, the question is:

What is the law about . . . ?

Researchers first must understand the facts that apply to the case they are asked to research. Unlike the cases in textbooks and court opinions, the relevant facts and the specific area of substantive or procedural law in real life are usually not so clear. The initial interview information may have focused on what the client or the interviewer thought was the applicable law. Further research may indicate other areas of law that must be considered.

For example, what may seem to be a simple rear-end automobile accident caused by negligent driving may in actuality be a case of product liability caused by a manufacturing defect by the automobile manufacturer or the supplier of a defectively manufactured part, such as the tires. To analyze a case properly, the researcher must know the factual elements of a negligence case and of a product liability case. The researcher must understand the facts of the case at hand. Some facts are crucial to the case; others may or may not be important or have no legal significance.

Legal Briefs for the Court

Before starting your research, obtain a copy of the current *Local Rules of Court*. These may cover acceptable length, citation format, content requirement, number of copies, and binding format. It also may be helpful to contact the judge's law clerk or office assistant for any special requirements or preferences of the individual judge, such as size or style of type font preferred.

TRADITIONAL VERSUS COMPUTER-BASED LAW LIBRARIES

The traditional law library consisted of books in paper form, case reporters, legal encyclopedias, legal dictionaries, and a host of finding tools including paper card indexes and digests. (See Exhibits 10.1 and 10.2 for samples of traditional text reference materials.) Some modern law libraries are completely electronic, in the form of online computer services such as Westlaw,

Lexis, and Loislaw. Others combine traditional paper-based materials and electronic materials.

Paralegal students who grew up in the era of the ever-available online research sources provided by some high schools and colleges, frequently ask why they need to learn how to use a traditional "paper" law library. In the working world, not every office has access to all the latest computer resources, or the same ones. Ask anyone who has tried a case out of town or in a different courthouse and had to check an unexpected case or resource, about the availability of resources or lack of them.

At times paralegals accompany the lawyer to court. During the trial, they may be asked to slip out of the courtroom and conduct a quick bit of legal research. They may not be able to use a computer for legal research. In some courthouses, computers cannot be connected to outgoing phone lines for security reasons, and even cell phones are retained at the security desk. Other courthouses may not have a public computer terminal available in the law library. In these situations the paralegal must conduct the research quickly and accurately using traditional book methods. In short, the legal assistant must be able to find the information needed when the familiar resources are not available.

Computer research requires the use of appropriate search words to complete a successful search. As with any profession, the legal profession has its own vocabulary. These include words defined by the courts over the years to have specific meaning when used in a legal sense. For example, the legal definition of the term "holder" means a person to whom a negotiable instrument has been properly negotiated. To the layman, it may mean people holding something in their hands—not necessarily a negotiable instrument, or with any legal formality. Other words have a different meaning for a number of different groups. For example, to the medical community the word "head" means the top of a person's body; to the sailor it means a bathroom; and to a bartender it means the top of a beer.

People in all areas of life develop words and phrases that help them understand their fields of interest. In creating laws, legislatures use language in special ways that may not be clear to laypersons or even legal researchers who are not accustomed to the terminology of the lawmakers. The people who create indexes to legal references, such as the professional indexers from the Library of Congress and the indexers of the numerous private legal publications, each have their own vocabulary and method of indexing material.

Elmore County, Alabama, courthouse and jail complex.

For example, West Publishing Company editors index material using the 450 West Digest Topics. Unless the legal assistant understands what items are included under each index classification, it is difficult to find the items even with a fast computer search engine. The word "holder," for example, is listed in the *West Digest Index* as being under "Statutes," but as the word "holder" is defined above, it actually is found under the West Digest Topic "Bills and Notes." *Black's Law Dictionary* defines the same word in the language of the negotiable instrument law. Using the West Topic heading "Bills and Notes" and "holder" in a computer search will not return cases of negotiable

exhibit **10.1** *Sample of traditional Supreme Court reporter.*

98   OCTOBER TERM, 2000

Syllabus

BUSH ET AL. *v.* GORE ET AL.

CERTIORARI TO THE SUPREME COURT OF FLORIDA

No. 00–949.   Argued December 11, 2000—Decided December 12, 2000

On December 8, 2000, the Florida Supreme Court ordered, *inter alia*, that manual recounts of ballots for the recent Presidential election were required in all Florida counties where so-called "undervotes" had not been subject to manual tabulation, and that the manual recounts should begin at once. Noting the closeness of the election, the court explained that, on the record before it, there could be no question that there were uncounted "legal votes"—*i. e.,* those in which there was a clear indication of the voter's intent—sufficient to place the results of the election in doubt. Petitioners, the Republican candidates for President and Vice President who had been certified as the winners in Florida, filed an emergency application for a stay of this mandate. On December 9, this Court granted the stay application, treated it as a petition for a writ of certiorari, and granted certiorari.

Held: Because it is evident that any recount seeking to meet 3 U. S. C. § 5's December 12 "safe-harbor" date would be unconstitutional under the Equal Protection Clause, the Florida Supreme Court's judgment ordering manual recounts is reversed. The Clause's requirements apply to the manner in which the voting franchise is exercised. Having once granted the right to vote on equal terms, Florida may not, by later arbitrary and disparate treatment, value one person's vote over that of another. See, *e. g., Harper* v. *Virginia Bd. of Elections,* 383 U. S. 663, 665. The recount mechanisms implemented in response to the state court's decision do not satisfy the minimum requirement for nonarbitrary treatment of voters. The record shows that the standards for accepting or rejecting contested ballots might vary not only from county to county but indeed within a single county from one recount team to another. In addition, the recounts in three counties were not limited to so-called undervotes but extended to all of the ballots. Furthermore, the actual process by which the votes were to be counted raises further concerns because the court's order did not specify who would recount the ballots. Where, as here, a court orders a statewide remedy, there must be at least some assurance that the rudimentary requirements of equal treatment and fundamental fairness are satisfied. The State has not shown that its procedures include the necessary safeguards. Upon due consideration of the difficulties identified to this point, it is obvious that the recount cannot be conducted in compliance

Sample of traditional Supreme Court reporter, continued.   *exhibit* **10.1**

Cite as: 531 U. S. 98 (2000)   99

Syllabus

with the requirements of equal protection and due process without substantial additional work. The court below has said that the legislature intended the State's electors to participate fully in the federal electoral process, as provided in 3 U. S. C. §5, which requires that any controversy or contest that is designed to lead to a conclusive selection of electors be completed by December 12.   That date is here, but there is no recount procedure in place under the state court's order that comports with minimal constitutional standards.

772 So. 2d 1243, reversed and remanded.

Theodore B. Olson argued the cause for petitioners.   With him on the brief were *Douglas R. Cox, Thomas G. Hungar, Benjamin L. Ginsberg, Michael A. Carvin, Barry Richard, Miguel A. Estrada, George J. Terwilliger III, Timothy E. Flanigan, William K. Kelley, John F. Manning,* and *Bradford R. Clark.   Joseph P. Klock, Jr.,* argued the cause for Katherine Harris et al., respondents under this Court's Rule 12.6 in support of petitioners.   With him on the brief were *John W. Little III, Alvin F. Lindsay III, Ricardo M. Martinez-Cid,* and *Bill L. Bryant, Jr.*   Briefs in support of petitioners were filed by *William Kemper Jennings* for Glenda Carr et al.; by *Robert A. Destro* for Stephen Cruce et al.; and by *George S. LeMieux* and *Frederick J. Springer* for John E. Thrasher, all respondents under this Court's Rule 12.6.

David Boies argued the cause for respondents Gore et al. With him on the brief were *Laurence H. Tribe, Andrew J. Pincus, Thomas C. Goldstein, Jonathan S. Massey, Kendall Coffey,* and *Peter J. Rubin.**

---

*Briefs of *amici curiae* urging reversal were filed for the State of Alabama by *Bill Pryor,* Attorney General, and *Charles B. Campbell, Scott L. Rouse,* and *A. Vernon Barnett IV,* Assistant Attorneys General; for the Florida House of Representatives et al. by *Charles Fried, Einer Elhauge,* and *Roger J. Magnuson;* for William H. Haynes et al. by *Jay Alan Sekulow, Thomas P. Monaghan, Stuart J. Roth, Colby M. May, James M. Henderson, Sr., David A. Cortman, Griffin B. Bell, Paul D. Clement,* and *Jeffrey S. Bucholtz.*

Briefs of *amici curiae* urging affirmance were filed for the Brennan Center for Justice at New York University School of Law by *Burt Neuborne;* and for Robert A. Butterworth, Attorney General of Florida, by

exhibit **10.2**   *Page from Corpis Juris Secundum—a legal encyclopedia.*

§§ 58–59   SOCIAL SECURITY   81 C.J.S.

individual who died fully insured,[65] and have physical or mental impairments which, under regulations promulgated for the purpose, are deemed to be of such severity as to preclude engaging in any gainful activity.[66] The requirements for obtaining disability benefits by such persons are more restrictive than requirements for the insured individual himself.[67] The physical impairment necessary to a finding of disability is placed on a level of severity to be determined administratively,[68] and the regulations adopted to carry out the statutory provisions have been upheld.[69]

A claim for disability is judged solely by medical criteria,[70] without regard to non-medical factors[71] such as age, education, and work experience,[72] in contrast to the considerations given to an insured individual's age, education, and work experience, in determining his ability to engage in substantial gainful activity, as discussed supra § 56. An individual cannot qualify for disability insurance benefits unless suffering from an impairment listed in the appendix to the regulations applicable to disabilities, or from one or more unlisted impairments that singly or in combination are the medical equivalent of a listed impairment.[73] The benefits are to be paid only for a disabling medical impairment,[74] and not simply for the inability to obtain employment.[75]

§ 59.   Benefits of Disabled Child

A disabled child of an insured individual who is, or would have been, eligible for social security benefits, may be entitled to disability insurance benefits.

Research Note

Status as child eligible for benefits under statute generally is discussed supra § 41.

Library References

Social Security and Public Welfare ⬡123, 140.5.

Under the provisions of the Social Security Act,[76] disabled children of retired or disabled insured individuals, and of insured individuals who have died, may be paid benefits if they have been disabled since before they reached twenty-two years of age, and if they meet the other conditions of eligibility.[77] The purpose of the provision is to provide a measure of income and security to those who have lost a wage-earner on whom they depended,[78] or to provide support for the dependents of a disabled wage earner,[79] and not to replace only that support enjoyed by the child prior to the onset of disability.[80] The liberal perspective of the Act applies to the award of children's disability benefits.[81]

In order to be entitled to recover benefits under this provision, the child must have been disabled,[82] as defined elsewhere in the Act,[83] prior to attaining a specified age,[84] and must be un-

---

65. U.S.—Sullivan v. Weinberger, C.A. Ga., 493 F.2d 855, certiorari denied 95 S.Ct. 1958, 421 U.S. 967, 44 L.Ed.2d 455.

66. U.S.—Wokojance v. Weinberger, C. A.Ohio, 513 F.2d 210, certiorari denied 96 S.Ct. 106, 423 U.S. 856, 46 L.Ed.2d 82.

Hendrix v. Finch, D.C.S.C., 310 F. Supp. 513.

Baby sitting; domestic work
U.S.—Dixon v. Weinberger, C.A.Ga., 495 F.2d 202.

Time impairment manifest
U.S.—Sullivan v. Weinberger, C.A.Ga., 493 F.2d 855, certiorari denied 95 S.Ct. 1958, 421 U.S. 967, 44 L.Ed.2d 455.

67. U.S.—Wokojance v. Weinberger, C. A.Ohio, 513 F.2d 210, certiorari denied 96 S.Ct. 106, 423 U.S. 856, 46 L.Ed.2d 82.

Solis v. U. S. Secretary of Health, Ed. and Welfare, D.C.Puerto Rico, 372 F.Supp. 1223—Truss v. Richardson, D. C.Mich., 338 F.Supp. 741—Nickles v. Richardson, D.C.S.C., 326 F.Supp. 777.

68. U.S.—Gillock v. Richardson, D.C. Kan., 322 F.Supp. 354.

69. U.S.—Sullivan v. Weinberger, C.A. Ga., 493 F.2d 855, certiorari denied 95 S.Ct. 1958, 421 U.S. 967, 44 L.Ed.2d 455.

Gunter v. Richardson, D.C.Ark., 335 F.Supp. 907—Zanoviak v. Finch, D.C. Pa., 314 F.Supp. 1152—Frasier v. Finch, D.C.Ala., 313 F.Supp. 160, affirmed, C. A., 434 F.2d 597.

70. U.S.—Wokojance v. Weinberger, C. A.Ohio, 513 F.2d 210, certiorari denied 96 S.Ct. 106, 423 U.S. 856, 46 L.Ed.2d 82.

71. U.S.—Sullivan v. Weinberger, C.A. Ga., 493 F.2d 855, certiorari denied 95 S.Ct. 1958, 421 U.S. 967, 44 L.Ed.2d 455.

72. U.S.—Gillock v. Richardson, D.C. Kan., 322 F.Supp. 354.

73. U.S.—Wokojance v. Weinberger, C. A.Ohio, 513 F.2d 210, certiorari denied 96 S.Ct. 106, 423 U.S. 856, 46 L.Ed.2d 82.

Gillock v. Richardson, D.C.Kan., 322 F.Supp. 354—Hendrix v. Finch, D.C.S. C., 310 F.Supp. 513.

74. U.S.—Sullivan v. Weinberger, C.A. Ga., 493 F.2d 855, certiorari denied 95 S.Ct. 1958, 421 U.S. 967, 44 L.Ed.2d 455.

75. U.S.—Sullivan v. Weinberger, C.A. Ga., 493 F.2d 855, certiorari denied 95 S.Ct. 1958, 421 U.S. 967, 44 L.Ed.2d 455.

76. 42 U.S.C.A. § 402(d).

77. U.S.—Lowe v. Finch, D.C.Va., 297 F.Supp. 667—Blevins v. Fleming, D.C. Ark., 180 F.Supp. 287.

78. U.S.—Ziskin v. Weinberger, D.C. Ohio, 379 F.Supp. 124.

79. U.S.—Jimenez v. Weinberger, Ill., 94 S.Ct. 2496, 417 U.S. 628, 41 L.Ed.2d 363, appeal after remand, C.A., 523 F.2d 689, certiorari denied 96 S.Ct. 3200.

80. U.S.—Jimenez v. Weinberger, Ill., 94 S.Ct. 2496, 417 U.S. 628, 41 L.Ed.2d 363, appeal after remand, C.A., 523 F.2d 689, certiorari denied 96 S.Ct. 3200.

81. U.S.—Ziskin v. Weinberger, D.C. Ohio, 379 F.Supp. 124.

82. U.S.—Ziskin v. Weinberger, D.C. Ohio, 379 F.Supp. 124.

83. 42 U.S.C.A. § 423.

84. U.S.—Ziskin v. Weinberger, D.C. Ohio, 379 F.Supp. 124—Moon v. Richardson, D.C.Va., 345 F.Supp. 1182.

110

instrument holder. Using the terms "negotiable instrument" and "holder" as the search words in a computer search will yield the desired result. Because paralegals can never be sure whether the research will be done using a traditional paper library or a computer search, they must understand how each resource files the information.

Knowing how to use both traditional and computer methods, and recognizing the strengths and weaknesses of each system, is important in conducting searches. Traditional research may be better when general background research is needed and the paralegal isn't particularly familiar with an area of law. Indexing systems are grouped by concept, and once the legal assistants get into the right concept of law area, they can browse easily. The ability to flip pages back and forth when they are generally in the right area is particularly helpful in statutory research, as many of the computer-based systems perform that task slowly, if at all—and assuming the paralegal can figure out how the index has been developed to create the computer search term. In contrast, for a narrow, fact-based question, or if the research already has a citation or case name to work from, computer-based research is usually the best approach. Success in research depends on recognizing the best tools for a specific problem and using them efficiently.

TRADITIONAL LEGAL RESOURCES

The traditional law library usually consists of print copies of primary and secondary sources of the law. A **primary source** is the actual law itself; this includes the statutes and the case law. The cases you have been briefing in this text are primary sources. **Secondary sources** are not the laws themselves but instead are writings about the law, such as legal encyclopedias and digests. This textbook is a secondary source. A third set of resources is referred to as **finding tools**—publications, such as digests or the *Index to Legal Periodicals*, used to find primary and secondary sources. Frequently, sources contain both secondary sources and finding tools in one publication, such as the *American Law Reports*. Some services combine all three into one service or publication. Table 10.1 delineates primary and secondary sources and finding tools.

Research materials. **table 10.1**

PRIMARY SOURCES	SECONDARY SOURCES	FINDING TOOLS
Constitutions	Legal dictionaries	Digests
Statutes	Legal encyclopedias	Citators
Court decisions	Treatises	Indexes
Common-law cases	Law reviews	
Administrative regulations	Textbooks	
Ordinances	Legal periodicals	
Court rules		

Over time, each paralegal develops a personal search strategy based on the nature of the problem or issue to be researched and the resources available. When a legal issue is well-defined and a specific case or statute is in question, it may be possible to start with the original primary source. More likely, though, the research assignment will be less defined and may be just a set of facts describing a situation. A possible area of relevance of law may be suggested. This could be a specific area of law such as "driving too fast for conditions" or a general area of law such as "personal injury from an automobile accident."

The facts will determine the area of law. If the paralegal is unfamiliar with the area of law, the *relevant facts* may not be obvious. Secondary sources provide a good reference source to acquire a general understanding about an area of law. As you learn more about the specifics of the area of law and the essential elements of causes of actions, the relevant facts should become clearer. One of the advantages of using the traditional book form of research is the ability to flip pages back and forth and scan many items that can lead to a specific point of law. This is some times referred to as "the serendipity of research."

Often a combination of traditional and online research is needed for a case.

Computer search engines can lead to specific case law and statutes. The problem is in how to construct the search question. If you do not know the relevant facts to include, the resulting report may not be accurate. Computers, for the most part, are limited to finding only the things the search question specifically asks for. Learning the relevant facts to create the proper question may involve using the print resources first to determine the relevant facts or the proper terminology. For example, in a fair-use doctrine case of alleged copyright violation, is the status of the alleged violator as a nonprofit organization relevant?

Using Legal Reference Works

Most legal references have a set of common features. They generally have a section, usually in the introduction, that explains the coverage and how to use the specific book or service.

This usually includes the abbreviations used throughout the work (Exhibit 10.3), and the method of pagination—for example, standard page numbering or use of section numbers. A table of contents at the beginning of the work (Exhibit 10.4) provides a general list of major topics. The index at the end of the work provides the detailed coverage. Multivolume sets might have a separate set of volumes containing the index. Each volume also might contain an index for the specific volume.

Most legal works also contain a table of cases that are mentioned in the text. This is a useful feature when a case seems to be on point or relevant and the paralegal wants to research the area of law and other cases on the same issue. A table of statutes also may be included, to help the researcher find cases or discussions of a statute.

Sample list of abbreviations.   exhibit **10.3**

ABBREVIATIONS

A.	Atlantic Reporter	Binns' Just.	Binns' Justice
A.2d	Atlantic Reporter, Second Series	Biss.	Bissell's Reports, U.S.
Abb.	Abbott's Circuit Court Reports, U.S.	Black	Black's United States Supreme Court Reports
Abb.Adm.	Abbott's Admiralty Reports, U.S.	Blair	Blair County Law Reports
Adams L.J.	Adams County Legal Journal	Blatchf.C.C.	Blatchford's Reports, U.S.
Add.	Addison's Reports	Bond	Bond's Reports, U.S.
Am.Dec.	American Decisions	B.R.	Bankruptcy reports
Am.L.J.,N.S.	American Law Journal, New Series	Bright.E.C.	Brightly's Election Cases
Am.L.J.,O.S.	American Law Journal, Hall's	Bright.N.P.	Brightly's Nisi Prius Reports
Am.L.Reg.,N.S.	American Law Register, New Series	Browne	P. A. Browne's reports
Am.L.Reg.,O.S.	American Law Register, Old Series	Brock.	Brockenbrough's Reports, U.S.
Am.Rep.	American Reports	Bucks	Bucks County Law Reporter
Am.St.Rep.	American State Reports	C.A.	United States Court of Appeals
Ann.Cas.	American & English Annotated Cases	C.C.A.	United States Circuit Court of Appeals
Ashm.	Ashmead's Reports	Cambria	Cambria County Legal Journal
Baldw.	Baldwin's Reports, U.S.	Cambria C.R.	Cambria County Reports
Beaver	Beaver County Legal Journal	Camp.	Campbell's Legal Gazette Reports
Ben.	Benedict's Reports, U.S.	Cent.	Central Reporter
Berks	Berks County Legal Journal	C.C. (see Pa.C.C.)	County Court Reports
Binn.	Binney's Reports	Chest.	Chester County Reports

From Purdon's *Pennsylvania Statutes Annotated,* © 1994 by West Group, a Thomson Company. Reproduced with permission.

Updates

Print material is updated in a number of ways. One of the most frequent is the use of **pocket parts,** so called because they are slipped into a pocket in the back of the print volume. Usually these are annual updates, but they may be produced more or less frequently depending on the publisher and the need for updates. Also used are supplemental pamphlets, usually paperbacks, to supplement the annual updates. Some are issued monthly, and others quarterly or semiannually. It is essential that the pocket part or supplement be consulted. In statutory research, the main volumes may be many years old and sections of the law repealed. The pocket parts or other supplements, not the main volume, contain the latest information. For this reason, some researchers look at the pocket part first, before consulting the main volume. More and more frequently, additional updates are provided online. The paralegal must learn how each resource is updated and the frequency of the updates. Exhibit 10.5 is a sample pocket part supplement.

Research Strategy

SIDEBAR

Before starting your research, prepare a list of words and phrases from a general index or descriptive words index. Use them to create online searches and conduct hardcopy book research.

exhibit 10.4 *Sample table of contents.*

CHAPTER 9 Federal Estate Tax

Checklist

PRIMARY SOURCES

Case
- ○ Name
- ○ Citation

Federal statute
- ○ Federal citation
- ○ Popular name

State (name)
- ○ State citation
- ○ Popular name

Local jurisdiction name
- ○ Local citation
- ○ Popular name

Administrative regulations
- ○ Federal agency name
- ○ Citation

State agency name
- ○ Citation

Local agency name
- ○ Citation

Constitution
- ○ Federal citation
- ○ State citation

SECONDARY SOURCES

Encyclopedia—National
- ○ Name
- ○ Key or descriptive word

Encyclopedia—State
- ○ Name
- ○ Key or descriptive word

Treatises
- ○ Name
- ○ Citation

Restatement of law
- ○ Name
- ○ Citation

Periodicals
- ○ Citation

Practice Books
- ○ Name
- ○ Citation

Dictionary
- ○ Name

Digest
- ○ Name
- ○ Citation

exhibit **10.5**   *Sample pocket part supplement.*

13 Pa.C.S.A. § 1105   COMMERCIAL CODE

DIVISION 1
GENERAL PROVISIONS

CHAPTER 11

SHORT TITLE, CONSTRUCTION, APPLICATION
AND SUBJECT MATTER OF TITLE

§ 1105.   Territorial application of title; power of parties to choose applicable law

Notes of Decisions

Bankruptcy 6

1. In general

In re Eagle Enterprises, Inc., Bkrtcy.E.D.Pa. 1998, 223 B.R. 290, [main volume] affirmed 237 B.R. 269.

2. Law governing

When parties agree to apply foreign law, pursuant to which their contract to "lease" goods kept in Pennsylvania will be deemed a true "lease," despite fact that contract does not permit lessor to terminate agreement but affords him an option to purchase goods for nominal consideration, Pennsylvania law will not give effect to that choice. In re Eagle Enterprises, Inc., E.D.Pa.1999, 237 B.R. 269.

4. Third parties

In re Eagle Enterprises, Inc., Bkrtcy.E.D.Pa. 1998, 223 B.R. 290, [main volume] affirmed 237 B.R. 269.

6. Bankruptcy

While Chapter 7 debtor and equipment lessor were generally free, under Pennsylvania statute, to agree what law would govern their rights and duties, debtor and equipment lessor could not impose their choice of law on Chapter 7 trustee, as party who never agreed to choice-of-law provision, in order to prevent trustee from challenging parties' characterization, as equipment "lease," of agreement which required debtor to pay alleged rent throughout full term of lease, and which then allowed debtor to acquire equipment at end of lease for nominal consideration of one dollar, merely because lease would allegedly have been recognized as true lease under law of foreign country that parties chose to govern their agreement. In re Eagle Enterprises, Inc., E.D.Pa.1999, 237 B.R. 269.

CHAPTER 12

GENERAL DEFINITIONS AND PRINCIPLES OF INTERPRETATION

§ 1201.   General definitions

Notes of Decisions

11.   Lease or lease intended as security

Under Pennsylvania law, "lease" transaction in which "lessee" cannot terminate "lease" during its term, but may thereafter become owner of "leased" goods for no additional or nominal additional consideration, does not create lease, but rather a security interest. In re Eagle Enterprises, Inc., E.D.Pa.1999, 237 B.R. 269.

When parties agree to apply foreign law, pursuant to which their contract to "lease" goods kept in Pennsylvania will be deemed a true "lease," despite fact that contract does not permit lessor to terminate agreement but affords him an option to purchase goods for nominal consideration, Pennsylvania law will not give effect to that choice. In re Eagle Enterprises, Inc., E.D.Pa.1999, 237 B.R. 269.

13.   Security interest

Revised Pennsylvania statute defining term "security interest" seeks to correct shortcomings of its predecessor by focusing inquiry of lease/security interest analysis on economics of the transaction, rather than on intent of the parties. In re Kim, Bkrtcy.E.D.Pa.1999, 232 B.R. 324.

Whether, under Pennsylvania law, lease or security interest is created by a particular transaction is no longer within exclusive control of the parties and subject to possible manipulation through artful document drafting; rather, issue is to be determined by reference to uniform criteria set forth in revised statute defining term "security interest." In re Kim, Bkrtcy.E.D.Pa.1999, 232 B.R. 324.

In determining whether debtor's lease was a disguised security interest or a true lease under Pennsylvania law, bankruptcy court was required to consider entire "transaction" and was not constrained to look solely to documents signed by the parties which were designated "lease" or which made use of terms commonly found in leases, but could examine both parol and extrin-

4

Electronic Searching Strategy

"Searching is a process, not an event. . . . Searching a library is not about spending time and mental energy formulating the 'golden query' that retrieves your desired information in a single stroke. In practice, good online searching involves formulating a succession of queries until you are satisfied with the results. As you view results from one search, you'll come across additional leads that you did not identify in your original search. You can incorporate these new terms into your existing query or create a new one. After each query, evaluate its success by asking:

- Did I find what I was looking for?
- What better information could still be out there?
- How can I refine my query to find better information?

Issuing multiple queries can be frustrating or rewarding, depending on how long it takes you to identify the key material you need to answer your research problem."

Source: VersusLaw Research Manual, Part 1

CONSTRUCTING A SEARCH QUERY

Constructing a search query requires one to select a computer search index, then to create the query.

Creating a Computer Search

The three primary full-service online providers of computer research services—Lexis, Loislaw, and Westlaw—provide a broad range of legal materials including cases, statutes, and regulations. In addition, a limited-service search provider, VersusLaw, specializes in providing cases and limited access to additional items, such as the *Code of Federal Regulations.*

Search Method and Query

Each of the online providers uses words to find and retrieve documents. As part of the publication process, indexes are prepared of every word in the document, the words are tabulated for frequency, and a word index is prepared. The search you create searches this index. VersusLaw uses a full-text retrieval method that searches every word except "stop words"—words that are used too commonly in documents to be used in a search, such as "the," "not," "of," and "and." Exhibit 10.6 is the VersusLaw home page.

Creating the Query

When you conduct a search, you are asking the search engine to find the indexed words you have chosen. These may be legal specialty words or common English words. Single words may be in any of the Internet or legal search engines. Frequently you will be looking for more detailed information. Using combinations of words in the search can narrow the search results. In most cases, the most productive search contains a combination of words. This combination of words may consist of terms such as "strict liability," "legal malpractice," "automobile accident," or "reckless indifference," for example.

VersusLaw Research Manual:
www.versuslaw.com/Support/
R_Manual_Preface.asp

Lexis: www.lexisnexis.com/

Westlaw: www.westlaw.com/
about/

VersusLaw: www.versuslaw.com

Loislaw: www.loislaw.com

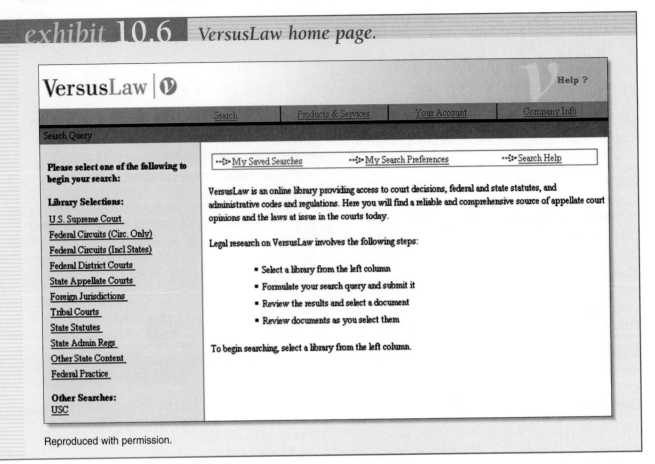

exhibit 10.6   VersusLaw home page.

Reproduced with permission.

Using Connectors

Connectors are instructions to the search engine to look for documents containing combinations of words. Connectors may be thought of as instructions to the search engine: Find me documents in which the words "strict" AND "liability" appear. The word AND is a connector that instructs the search not to return the documents in which only one of the words is found. Exhibit 10.7 shows a Loislaw search with the AND connector.

The connector OR instructs the search engine to find either term—the word "strict" OR the word "liability"—and retrieve the documents. Exhibit 10.8 depicts a Lexis search with the OR connector. The NOT connector instructs the search to eliminate certain words. For example, you may wish to review documents in which the word "malpractice" is found but *not* those with the word "medical."

In some cases it might be assumed that there will be other words between the desired terms, such as in the phrase "Paralegals are bound by the ethics of their profession." The NEAR connector helps you locate documents where the terms are near each other; for example: find "paralegal" NEAR "ethics." The NEAR connector allows you to search for words near each other by specifying the number of words apart that is acceptable. Exhibit 10.9 shows a Westlaw search using the NEAR connector.

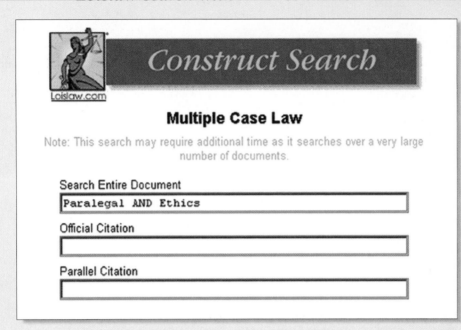

Loislaw search with AND connector. **exhibit 10.7**

Construct Search

Loislaw.com

Multiple Case Law

Note: This search may require additional time as it searches over a very large number of documents.

Search Entire Document

    Paralegal AND Ethics

Official Citation

Parallel Citation

Lexis search with OR connector. **exhibit 10.8**

- News
- Business
- Legal Research
  - Legal News
  - Law Reviews
  - Get a Case
    Shepard's® for U.S.
    Supreme Court
  - Federal Case Law
  - State Case Law
  - Area of Law by Topic
  - Federal Code
  - Federal Regulations
  - State Code
  - Tax Law
    Canadian Legislative
    Materials
    Canadian Statutes &
    Regulations
  - EU Law (CELEX)
    International Case

| Basic | Guided Search |

Federal Case Law   ○ *Tips*

Keyword and Additional Terms search the full text of cases. Only cases that match all the criteria you enter will be found.

Keyword: Paralegal OR Ethics
Entry Required   *e.g. speech OR expression*

Narrow search
with additional terms:
e.g. picketing OR demonstration

Court: Supreme Court Cases   ○ *Source List*

Date: ⊙ Previous two years

         ○ From: To: ○ *Examples*

         Search   Clear Form

Reprinted with the permission of Lexis-Nexis.

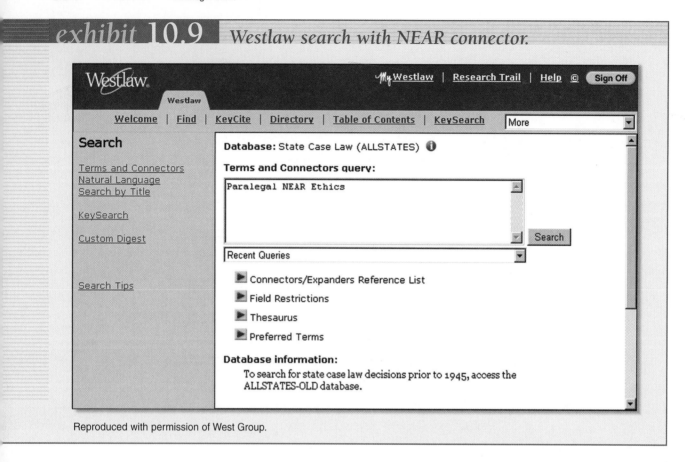

exhibit 10.9   *Westlaw search with NEAR connector.*

Reproduced with permission of West Group.

Exhibit 10.10 gives a comparison of these concepts, by VersusLaw, and Exhibit 10.11 gives a guide to connectors from Westlaw.

UPDATING LEGAL RESEARCH

The legal team always must use the most current statutory and case law in advising clients and arguing cases to the court. One of the features of the American legal system is its constant change. Courts attempt to meet the needs of a changing society by reviewing prior case law and, when appropriate, over-ruling or modifying it as the contemporary American view of justice dictates. The American legal system concept of **stare decisis** provides that we use prior case law as precedent but change the law as American society changes. Occasionally, existing case law may be held unconstitutional, such as happened with the landmark case of *Roe v. Wade*.

Knowing if the case law being used in a legal argument is the current case law is a vital part of the lawyer's obligation to the client and to the court. Up to the moment before the arguments are made to the court or the brief is submitted, a case that the attorney or the opponent is using as a basis for a legal argument may be overturned. The ethical obligation of candor to the court and of professional competency requires the use of current case law.

Comparison grid from VersusLaw.   *exhibit* 10.10

VersusLaw	LEXIS	Westlaw
Connectors		
and	and	and, &
or	or	or, *space*
not	and not	but not, %
Proximity operators		
w/n	w/n	w/n, /n
w/n	pre/n	pre/n, +n
Exact phrase match		
unlawful entry	unlawful entry	"unlawful entry"
Wild Cards - end of root words		
*	!	!
Wild Cards - single character		
?	*	*
Order of operators		
proximity operators, not, and, or	or, proximity operators, and, and not	or, proximity operators, and, but not

Reproduced with permission.

Westlaw guide to connectors.   *exhibit* 10.11

Using Connectors

Connector	You type	Westlaw retrieves documents
AND	&	containing both search terms: **work-place & safety**
OR	a space	containing either search term or both search terms: **landlord lessor**
Grammatical Connectors	/p	containing search terms in the same paragraph: **warrant! /p habitat!**
	/s	containing search terms in the same sentence: **danger! /s defect!**
	+s	in which the first term precedes the second within the same sentence: **capital +s gain**
Numerical Connectors	/n (where *n* is a number)	containing search terms within *n* terms of each other: **issues /5 fact**
	+n (where *n* is a number)	in which the first term precedes the second by *n* terms: **20 + 5 1080**
BUT NOT	%	not containing the term or terms following the percent symbol (%): **tax taxation % tax taxation /3 income**

Reproduced with permission from West Group.

Thus, an essential part of legal research for paralegals is to verify that they have the latest case or statute. The process is complicated by the method by which changes in statutes or case law are released to the public. Ultimately, new statutes and new case law are reported in a published form, both in paper and electronically, but not all publications are able to disseminate the information daily. Paper versions take time to print and distribute. Not all electronic versions are posted immediately. Therefore, it becomes important to know how quickly the reporting or electronic services of the law firm or practice distribute post-statutory changes and new cases. More and more courts have their own websites and release case opinions electronically along with the print versions to the public and publishing companies. For example, you can check decisions of the U. S. Supreme Court daily.

What is difficult is knowing if the new cases or new statutes affect the case being researched. When the court specially mentions a case being cited in a memo of law or court brief, the paralegal needs to know if the new case follows the older case law, reverses it, or in some way differs from the older case.

As soon as a case is entered into an electronic case law database, such as Westlaw, Lexis, Loislaw, or Versuslaw, a general search can be made for references to the case name or citation. Before it is entered, the same search will not show the newest reference. Even a reference to the case will not tell whether the case law has changed, only that another case has referred to it. Someone must actually read the case to see how the court has used it or referred to it in the opinion.

Shepard's

Long a standard tool of legal research in law libraries has been *Shepard's Citations*, a multivolume set of books listing cases and statutes by their respective citations and giving the citation of every other case in which the listed case was mentioned. The listings originally were compiled by editors who physically read through every case reported to find citations. These then were reported by case citation, with every other mention of the case reported by its citation in chronological fashion, with notations indicating if the opinion was reversed, affirmed, followed, overruled, and so on. The process of using *Shepard's* to check legal citations came to be called "Shepardizing," a term that many legal assistants still use, even when using other citation-checking services such as Westlaw's KeyCite. An advantage to the *Shepard's Citator* is the editorial symbol system used to indicate how the new case affects the case being checked, as shown in Exhibit 10.12.

The problem with the traditional paper form of Shepard's is the lag in time for the print version to be prepared and sent out to subscribers. *Shepard's* now provides the same service online through the Lexis service—subscribers can obtain the latest case information, to the day, by calling a toll-free number. One of the difficulties in using the print version of *Shepard's* is the number of hardbound volumes and paperback updates required to be consulted, and finding the latest update pamphlet if someone has misfiled it in the law library.

Shepard's *symbols showing effects of new cases.*   *exhibit* 10.12

Shepard's Signal

⬣ Warning — Strong negative treatment indicated. Includes:

- Overruled by
- Questioned by
- Superceded by
- Revoked
- Obsolete
- Rescinded

△ Caution — Possible negative treatment indicated. Includes:

- Limited
- Criticized by
- Clarified
- Modified
- Corrected

◆ Positive — Positive treatment indicated. Includes:

- Followed
- Affirmed
- Approved

Ⓐ Citing References with Analysis — Other cases cited the case and assigned some analysis that is not considered positive or negative. Includes:

- Appeal denied by
- Writ of certiorari denied

Ⓘ Citation Information — References have not applied any analysis to the citation. For example the case was cited by law reviews, ALR® Annotations, or in other case law not warranting an analysis. Example: Cited By

Reprinted with the permission of LexisNexis.

Many educational institutions and public libraries subscribe to the web-based LexisNexis Academic Universe. *Shepard's* citation service (Exhibit 10.13) usually is available for the U. S. Supreme Court as part of the service, but other federal and state *Shepard* citation services may not be included because of the cost of the additional license fees involved.

Westlaw provides the same function, calling its service KeyCite. Loislaw offers a case reference search called GlobalCite.

GlobalCite™

Loislaw **GlobalCite** provides a reverse chronological list of the case law, statutes in the order of the highest number of citation occurrences, the regulations listed in relevancy order, and reference to other databases in the Loislaw library. Exhibit 10.14 shows a GlobalCite screen.

KeyCite™

KeyCite is the Westlaw online citation update service. The Westlaw KeyCite is a combination citator and case finder (see Exhibit 10.15). Unlike other similar services, KeyCite uses the West Key number system and West Headnotes.

exhibit **10.13** *Shepard's citation service.*

Edit Search | FOCUS | Print/Save Options | E-Mail

KWIC™ | Full

Shepard's® - 240 Citing References

All Neg | All Pos | Any | Custom Restrictions | Unrestricted

▲ 365 U.S. 127

Signal: ▲ Caution - Possible negative treatment
Citation: 365 U.S. 127
Restrictions: Analysis: Followed, Criticized, Dissenting Op.

Eastern R. Presidents Conference v. Noerr Motor Freight, Inc., 365 U.S. 127, 5 L. Ed. 2d 464, 81 S. Ct. 523, 1961 U.S. LEXIS 2128, 1961 Trade Cas. (CCH) P69927

PRIOR HISTORY (4 citing references) ♦ Hide Prior History

Noerr Motor Freight, Inc. v. Eastern R. Presidents Conference, 155 F. Supp. 768, 1957 U.S. Dist. LEXIS 3019, 1957 Trade Cas. (CCH) P68827 (D. Pa. 1957)

Affirmed by:

Noerr Motor Freight, Inc. v. Eastern R. Presidents Conference, 273 F.2d 218, 1959 U.S. App. LEXIS 5485, 1959 Trade Cas. (CCH) P69546 (3d Cir. Pa. 1959)

▶ **Reversed by (CITATION YOU ENTERED):**

Eastern R. Presidents Conference v. Noerr Motor Freight, Inc., 365 U.S. 127, 5 L. Ed. 2d 464, 81 S. Ct. 523, 1961 U.S. LEXIS 2128, 1961 Trade Cas. (CCH) P69927 (1961)

Reprinted with the permission of LexisNexis.

exhibit **10.14** *Loislaw GlobalCite screen.*

GlobalCite Results

Loislaw.com

U.S. 7th Circuit Court of Appeals Reports
LAWLINE v. AMERICAN BAR ASS'N. , 956 F.2d 1378 (7th Cir. 1992)
20 Found. (1 - 20 shown)

Click the case name to view the document.

Arkansas Cases
CAMBIANO v. NEAL, 342 Ark. 691 (2000)
00-283.
Opinion delivered November 16, 2000. [Substituted Opinion on Denial of
Petition for Rehearing delivered December 15, 2000]

interests of consumer protection and the integrity of the legal system.
Further we hold that it is no more restrictive than necessary and is thus
constitutional. In Lawline v. American Bar Association, 956 F.2d 1378 (7th
Cir. 1992), the United States Court of Appeals for the Eleventh Circuit held
that Illinois had the right to regulate the practice of law

LOIS Federal District Court Opinions: Non-Referenced
TSAU v. NATIONAL SCIENCE FOUNDATION, (N.D. III. 2000)

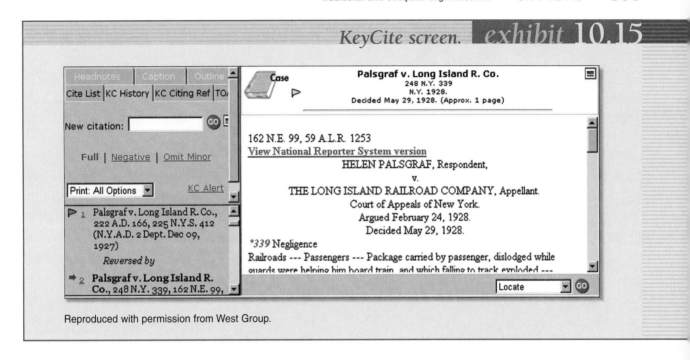

KeyCite screen.   *exhibit* **10.15**

Reproduced with permission from West Group.

PARALLEL CITATIONS

Most cases are reported in more than one service or set of books. A **parallel citation** is a cite to the same material, usually a case, in another source. Frequently a state has an official publication, such as the court's own publication, and a private publication, such as the *West Reporter*. In some cases, West was and is the official reporter, and there may not be a parallel print source. One of the many uses of *Shepard's* is to find the parallel citation to other locations for the same case.

Shepard's also provides update information on statutory citations. Amendments and repeals of statutory information are listed in *Shepard's*. Citations to any cases in which the statute has been cited also are listed, with information on how the case law considered the statute.

Checklist

RESEARCH SEARCH ITEMS

○ Client:	○ Date:
○ Issue:	
○ Search terms and phrases:	
○ Search combinations used:	

Checklist

RESEARCH SOURCES CHECKED				
CHECKED	SOURCE	CITATION	POCKET PART CHECKED ▼	WEB LOCATION
PRIMARY SOURCES				
	State statute			www.
	USC			www.
	USCA			www.
	CFR			www.
	Local ordinance			www. www.
SECONDARY SOURCES				
	State digest			www.
	Federal digest			www.
	ALR			www. www.
	Encyclopedia			www.
	State			www.
	C.J.S.			www.
	Periodicals			www.
	Treatises			www.

LEGAL TERMINOLOGY

Connector
Finding tool
GlobalCite
KeyCite
Parallel citation
Pocket part
Primary source
Relevant fact
Secondary source
Stare decisis

Summary

CHAPTER 10 TRADITIONAL AND COMPUTER LEGAL RESEARCH

Traditional and Computer Research

Online Law Libraries	1. Westlaw 3. Loislaw 2. Lexis 4. VersusLaw
Research Services	1. *Shepard's* 2. KeyCite 3. GlobalCite
Research Starting Point	1. The question typically is framed with some specificity. 2. Researchers must understand the facts that apply to the case they are asked to research.
Traditional Versus Computer-Based Law Libraries	1. *Traditional law library:* Books in paper form, case reporters, legal encyclopedias, legal dictionaries, and finding tools including paper card indexes and digests. 2. *Modern law library:* Electronic, with online computer services such as Westlaw, Lexis, and Loislaw. 3. Not every office will have access to all the latest computer resources, or the same ones.
Traditional Legal Resources	1. *Primary source:* The actual law itself, including statutes and case law. 2. *Secondary sources:* Not the laws themselves, but writings about the law, such as legal encyclopedias and digests. 3. *Finding tools.* *(continued)*

Computer Research	
Constructing a Search Query	Each online provider uses words to find and retrieve documents. As part of the publication process, indexes are prepared of every word in the document, the words are tabulated for frequency, and a word index is prepared. The search you create searches this index.
Creating a Computer Search	Search engine is used to find the indexed words you have chosen; may be legal specialty words or common English words. Using combinations of words in the search can narrow the search results.

Search Method and Query	
Connectors in Legal Research	1. AND—instructs the search not to return documents in which only one of the words is found. 2. OR—instructs search engine to find either term. 3. NEAR—may be used to find occurrence of desired words within a set number of words of each other.
Updating Legal Research	1. *Shepard's:* A multivolume set of books listing cases and statutes by their respective citations and giving the citation of every other case in which the listed case was mentioned; checking citations is often called "Shepardizing." 2. *GlobalCite* (Loislaw): Provides a reverse chronological list of the case law, a list of statutes in the order of the highest number of citation occurrences, regulations in relevancy order, and reference to other databases in Loislaw library. 3. *KeyCite* (Westlaw): Online citation update service.
Parallel Citation	A citation to the same material, usually a case, in another source.
Statutory Law Updates	*Shepard's* provides update information on amendments and repeals of statutory information. Citations to any cases in which the statute has been cited are also listed, with information on how the case law considered the statute.

Working the Web

1. Search the term "paralegal ethics" using at least two different general search engines such as:
   a. www.google.com
   b. www.yahoo.com
   c. www.altavista.com
2. Search the term "paralegal ethics" using two or more legal research sites (if available to you), such as Westlaw, Lexis, Loislaw, or VersusLaw. Are the results the same?
3. Find the features that Westlaw offers for research and writing at its website at www.westlaw.com.
4. Find the features, including those without charge, that Lexis offers for research and writing at its websites at www.lexisnexis.com and www.lexisone.com.
5. Find the features that Loislaw offers for research and writing at its website at www.loislaw.com.
6. Find the features that VersusLaw offers for research and writing at its website at www.versuslaw.com.

Questions

CRITICAL LEGAL THINKING AND WRITING

1. Using the facts in the *Palsgraf* case in Appendix A, prepare a search query using connectors to locate the law or a similar case in your jurisdiction. Run the search using an online legal research service, if available.
2. Why does a paralegal have to be familiar with both traditional and electronic research tools and methods?
3. Why does the paralegal have to know how quickly changes in statutory and case law are updated by online and traditional primary and secondary sources?
4. Why is knowledge of the underlying law in an area important in constructing a question for online research?
5. How can a researcher be certain that a case that seems to be on point is still the current case law?
6. Why should secondary sources not be relied upon in citing binding authority?
7. Why would a researcher use a traditional paper resource before using an online research tool?
8. How does the use of connectors help in conducting online research? Give an example.

9. Why might an identical search query return different results?

10. Why must researchers clearly understand the question they are being asked to research? How can they be certain they do?

ETHICS: ANALYSIS AND DISCUSSION

1. Is there an ethical obligation under the Model Rules to perform legal research competently? Explain.

2. What is the ethical obligation under the Model Rules to provide the court with legal authority that is not favorable to your client's legal position?

3. What is the ethical obligation to "Shepardize" cases and statutes before submitting a brief or memo of law to the court?

For answers, look at American Bar Association Rule 3.3, Candor Toward the Tribunal, and Rule 1.1, Competence (ABA *Model Rules of Professional Conduct*, 2002).

Confidentiality

There are few certainties in the area of ethics, for paralegals or in any profession. What qualifies as ethical conduct is in most cases based on state law and court interpretation applied to a set of facts. The citation listed below represents one legal opinion and is provided as a research starting point. Do not assume that the same rule applies in your jurisdiction. For the following:

- *Prepare a written statement based on your state law.*
- *Use your state bar association website as a starting point.*

You are waiting for a fax needed for a case on which you are working. While you are standing by the fax machine, a fax comes in from an attorney at an opposing firm containing a letter about settlement that was clearly intended for the attorney's client and not for opposing counsel. Your best friend in the office is the paralegal who is working on that case at the other law office. She is stressed out by the case and made the mistake of dialing your fax number. From your reading of the letter it appears the information will be of major help in your law office winning the case. [*ABA Formal Ethics Opinion, State Compensation Insurance Fund v. The WPS, Inc.*, 70 CA 4644; 82 C.R.2 799 (1999)] Do you quietly return the fax to your friend and say nothing to anyone? Do you read it carefully to be sure of the contents? Do you return it to opposing counsel? Do you tell your supervising attorney about the letter? The contents?

Case

FOR DISCUSSION

American Geophysical Union v. Texaco Inc.   37 F.3d 881 (2d Cir. 1994)

Copying of Material for Future Research and Law Library Archives from Copyrighted Magazines and Journals

Most researchers understand that misuse of copyright material may subject them to liability under the copyright laws. The case of *American Geophysical Union v. Texaco* illustrates the potential liability in regularly copying copyrighted articles for personal archives. Researchers of Texaco regularly made copies of articles for future reference from the works of the plaintiff and 82 other publishers of scientific and technical journals. Texaco raised the defense of "fair use" as permitted under the copyright law.

Fair use as a defense depends on four tests: (1) the purpose and character of the use—including whether for nonprofit educational purposes or commercial use; (2) the nature of copyright work—the law generally recognizes a greater need to disseminate factual works than works of fiction or fantasy; (3) amount and substantiality of portion used—was the quantity used reasonable in relation to the purpose of the copying? (4) effect on potential market or value—will the copying have an impact on the sale of the works, and is there an efficient mechanism for the licensing of the works?

Questions

1. How does copyright law apply to a student copying copyrighted materials while doing research for a class project?
2. Would the answer be the same if the student were doing the research as part of an assignment while working in a law office?
3. Does it matter if the work copied is a court case or an article by an expert in automobile airbags liability? Why?

Hart v. Massanari

266 F.3d 1155 (2001)　　　　　　　　United States Court of Appeals, Ninth Circuit

Read, and if assigned, brief this case. In your brief, answer the following questions.

1. Why are unpublished dispositions (opinion) of courts not valid as precedent in future cases?

2. What is the difference between controlling authority and persuasive authority?

3. How does a court decide if it is bound by an earlier decision?

4. Why does this court believe it is important, in writing an opinion of the court, to recite all the relevant facts?

5. What is the effect of binding precedent on other courts?

Kozinski, Circuit Judge.

Appellant's . . . brief cites . . . an unpublished disposition, not reported in the *Federal Reporter*. . . . The full text . . . is marked with the following notice: "This disposition is not appropriate for publication and may not be cited to or by the courts of this circuit. . . ." Unpublished dispositions and orders of this Court are not binding precedent . . . [and generally] may not be cited to or by the courts of this circuit." . . . [9th Cir.R.36-3.]

We ordered counsel to show cause as to why he should not be disciplined for violating Ninth Circuit Rule 36-3. Counsel responds by arguing that Rule 36-3 may be unconstitutional . . . [relying] . . . on the Eighth Circuit's opinion in *Anastasoff v. United States*, [which] while vacated, continues to have persuasive force. . . .

A. Anastasoff held that Eighth Circuit Rule 28A(i), . . . that unpublished dispositions are not precedential* . . . violates Article III of the Constitution. . . . We believe that Anastasoff overstates the case. . . .

Anastasoff focused on one aspect of the way federal courts do business—the way they issue opinions—and held that they are subject to a constitutional limitation derived from the [constitutional] framers' conception of what it means to exercise the judicial power. . . . We question whether the "judicial power" clause contains any limitation at all, separate from the specific limitations of Article III and other parts of the Constitution. . . . The term "judicial power" in Article III is more likely descriptive than prescriptive. . . .

B. Modern federal courts are the successors of the English courts that developed the common law. . . . Common law judges did not make law as we understand

that concept; rather, they "found" the law with the help of earlier cases that had considered similar matters. An opinion was evidence of what the law is, but it was not an independent source of law. . . . The idea that judges declared rather than made the law remained firmly entrenched in English jurisprudence until the early nineteenth century. . . . For centuries, the most important sources of law were not judicial opinions themselves, but treatises that restated the law. . . .

The modern concept of binding precedent . . . came about only gradually over the nineteenth and early twentieth centuries. Lawyers began to believe that judges made, not found, the law. This coincided with monumental improvements in the collection and reporting of case authorities . . . and [as] a more comprehensive reporting system began to take hold, it became possible for judicial decisions to serve as binding authority. . . .

II

Federal courts today do follow some common law traditions. When ruling on a novel issue of law, they will generally consider how other courts have ruled on the same issue. . . . Law on point is the law. If a court must decide an issue governed by a prior opinion that constitutes binding authority, the later court is bound to reach the same result, even if it considers the rule unwise or incorrect. Binding authority must be followed unless and until overruled by a body competent to do so.

In determining whether it is bound by an earlier decision, a court considers not merely the "reason and spirit of cases" but also "the letter of particular precedents." . . . This includes not only the rule announced, but also the facts giving rise to the dispute, other rules considered and rejected, and the views expressed in response to any dissent or concurrence. Thus, when crafting binding authority, the precise language employed is often crucial to the contours and scope of the rule announced.

. . . A decision of the Supreme Court will control that corner of the law unless and until the Supreme Court itself overrules or modifies it. . . . Thus, the first panel to consider an issue sets the law not only for all the inferior courts in the circuit, but also future panels of the court of appeals. Once a panel resolves an issue in a precedential opinion, the matter is deemed resolved, unless overruled by the court itself sitting en banc, or by the Supreme Court. . . .

Controlling authority has much in common with persuasive authority. Using the techniques developed at common law, a court confronted with apparently controlling authority must parse the precedent in light of the facts presented and the rule announced. Insofar as there may be factual differences between the current case and the earlier one, the court must determine whether those differences are material to the application of the rule or allow the precedent to be distinguished on a principled basis. . . . But there are also very important differences between controlling and persuasive authority. . . . [I]f a controlling precedent is determined to be on point, it must be followed. . . . Thus, an opinion of our court is binding within our circuit, not elsewhere. . . .

III

While we agree with Anastasoff that the principle of precedent was well established in the common law courts by the time Article III of the Constitution was written, we do not agree that it was known and applied in the strict sense in which we apply binding authority today. . . .

In writing an opinion, the court must be careful to recite all facts that are relevant to its ruling, while omitting facts that it considers irrelevant. Omitting relevant facts will make the ruling unintelligible to those not already familiar with the case; including inconsequential facts can provide a spurious basis for distinguishing the case in the future. . . .

While federal courts of appeals generally lack discretionary review authority, they use their authority to decide cases by unpublished—and nonprecedential—dispositions to achieve the same end. . . . That a case is decided without a precedential opinion does not mean it is not fully considered. . . . The disposition is not written in a way that makes it suitable for governing future cases. . . . An unpublished disposition is, more or less, a letter from the court to parties familiar with the facts, announcing the result and the essential rationale of the court's decision. . . .

IV

We conclude that Rule 36-3 is constitutional. We also find that counsel violated the rule. Nevertheless, we are aware that Anastasoff may have cast doubt on our rule's constitutional validity. Our rules are obviously not meant to punish attorneys who, in good faith, seek to test a rule's constitutionality. We therefore conclude that the violation was not willful and exercise our discretion not to impose sanctions.

The order to show cause is DISCHARGED.

---

* Our rule operates . . . differently from . . . the Eighth Circuit . . . Rule 28A(i) [that] says that "[u]npublished decisions are not precedent." [W]e say that unpublished dispositions are "not binding precedent." . . . Our rule . . . prohibits citation of an unpublished disposition to any of the courts of our circuit. The Eighth Circuit's rule allows citation . . . , but provides that the authority is persuasive rather than binding.

CHAPTER 11

CHAPTER OBJECTIVES

After studying this chapter, you should be able to:

1. Explain the need for proper citation format.

2. Describe how to use appropriate traditional citation format.

3. Explain the Universal Citation Format.

4. Describe the *Bluebook* citation format.

5. Describe the AWLD Citation Format.

6. Define the ethical duty of candor to the court.

7. Differentiate the writing style in preparing an internal memo of law and the style for writing a court memo of law.

8. Explain the need for a clear definition of the facts and assignment before preparing a memorandum.

9. Explain the need to write for the intended audience.

10. Describe the impact of Federal Rule of Civil Procedure 11 on submitting briefs to the court.

Critical Legal Thinking and Writing

Justice is the end of government. It is the end of civil society. It ever has been, and ever will be pursued, until it be obtained, or until liberty be lost in the pursuit.

JAMES MADISON

Introduction

Critical legal thinking is the process of identifying legal issues, determining the relevant facts, and applying the applicable law to come to a conclusion that answers the legal question the issues present. A written opinion by a court is an example of critical legal thinking combined with writing. In the law office this is frequently seen in the office memorandum of law and the legal case brief submitted to a court.

COURT BRIEF AND OFFICE MEMORANDUM WRITING STYLES

Both the brief and the memorandum may be on the exact same set of facts, legal issue, and applicable law, but the writing style is totally different. The **memorandum** is a working document for the legal team to be used in the preparation and presentation of a case. As a result, it has to be an objective analysis of the case, including factual subtleties and analysis of the applicable law with any alternate interpretations. The brief written for the court is designed to provide written advocacy of the client's position and must be written to convince the court to adopt a position favorable to the client.

Candor to the Court

Comment to *Model Rules of Professional Conduct* Rule 3.3. The comment states in relevant part:

> The advocate's task is to present the client's case with persuasive force. Performance of that duty while maintaining confidences of the client is qualified by the advocate's duty of candor to the tribunal. . . . Legal argument based on a knowingly false representation of law constitutes dishonesty toward the tribunal.

A lawyer is not required to make a disinterested exposition of the law, but must recognize the existence of pertinent legal authorities. . . . (a)(3), an advocate has a duty to disclose directly adverse authority in the controlling jurisdiction which has not been disclosed by the opposing party. The underlying concept is that legal argument is a discussion seeking to determine the legal premises properly applicable to the case.

Checklist

MEMORANDUM OF LAW TEMPLATE

- ○ To:
- ○ From:
- ○ Date:
- ○ Subject:
- ○ Facts
- ○ Issue(s)
- ○ Discussion
- ○ Conclusion

HONESTY

Above all is an obligation to be honest with the court, called the **duty of candor.** The legal team has an ethical obligation not to mislead the court. Just one brief that intentionally distorts or hides the truth or intentionally misleads the court can destroy a legal career. Even if it doesn't result in sanctions, suspension, or disbarment, judges talk with their colleagues, and a bad reputation for integrity to the court is hard to correct. At the least, the court always will remember that the attorney did shoddy work and may give more credibility to the opposing side in the future, even if later cases by the offending attorney are better prepared and more accurately on point.

OFFICE MEMORANDUM

In doing research and preparing the memorandum of law, the legal assistant must be careful to include all the relevant applicable statutes and case law. Some paralegals are intimidated by the gruff and sometime downright nasty attitude of lawyers, particularly trial counsel in the middle of a stressful case. They are afraid that the lawyer will "shoot the messenger." The reality is that the attorney *must* know the weaknesses in the case along with the strengths. Nothing is more upsetting to the attorney, whether in court or in a meeting with a client or opposing counsel, than to be surprised by a case, facts, or law that has not been covered in the office memorandum of law.

Office memoranda are frequently indexed by subject and filed in the office for future reference. If the same or a similar fact pattern requires research, these provide a good starting point and can be a major time-saver. So that a memorandum may be indexed properly, the facts upon which the conclusion is based must be clearly stated. All statutes, regulations, and cases must be cited properly so anyone reading the memorandum in the future can look them up. Listing relevant websites used in the preparation is also helpful.

PERSPECTIVE

Email

When sending confidential information through electronic mail (whether direct link, commercial service, or Internet), there is a reasonable expectation of privacy. Use of electronic mail will not affect the confidentiality of client communications under South Carolina Rule of Professional Conduct 1.6.

Starting Point

The starting point for the legal researcher is to understand the specific assignment. What is it that you have been asked to research? For the memorandum of law, it usually is to answer a question:

> *What is the current law on . . . ?*
> *What happens if . . . ?*
> *What is the procedure for . . . ?*

Before starting an assignment, the paralegal must be certain what is really being asked. Any questions should be resolved by asking the person for whom the memorandum is being prepared: "What does the attorney expect?" Where the paralegal's knowledge of the subject area is sufficient, he or she may know that certain facts may change the outcome—such as the requirement in some states that a subscribing witness to a decedent's will cannot be a beneficiary. Before starting, paralegals must be sure to have all the relevant facts, then restate what they believe they are being asked to research in the form of a statement of the question. For example: "You have asked for the law on the rights of individuals to . . . ."

Facts

Paralegals, of course, must have a clear statement of the facts from which to work. The facts relied upon in writing the memo must be part of the ultimate final memorandum. Other people may read the memorandum. They need to understand the specific facts upon which the analysis is based, particularly if

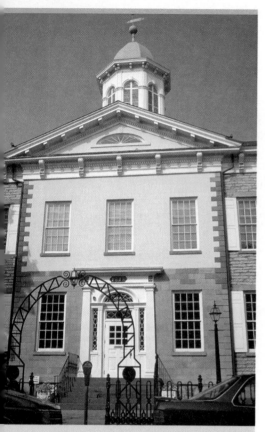

County courthouse, Kingston, New York.

they read it at a time when the paralegal is not available to answer questions, such as the middle of a case, out ill, on vacation, or after the paralegal has left the firm. It also is frequently necessary to recite other facts not relied upon and the reason for not considering them—that the result would be different. An example is a notation that this fact pattern is based upon the participants all being over the age of majority for contracting, or over the age to purchase and consume alcoholic beverages.

Analysis

A memorandum must present both sides of the issue and, in that respect, be a neutral, unbiased, objective presentation of applicable laws as they apply to the facts of the case. Issues that the opposing attorney or the judge may raise should be considered and presented. A good analysis will include a discussion of how the fact pattern may differ in cases that are not on point but may be used by opposing counsel.

The memorandum the paralegal prepares may be the basis for the court brief that the attorney or someone else will prepare. To be able to meet the ethical obligation to the court, the person who presents a persuasive argument favoring the client must know all the relevant statutory and case law.

Editing and Rewriting

The written word is a reflection of the writer. Everyone who reads the memorandum will measure the researcher's reputation and skill level. Each person who reads the memorandum will measure the writer's communication skills. The paralegal, however, may be writing for a certain audience, and someone other than that might read the memorandum, unaware of the intended reader.

Certain elements of writing style transcend the audience. For example:

Is it clear?

Are the words used properly?

Is the spelling correct?

Is it written using proper English grammar?

If it is being written for an audience for whom English is a second language, is that made clear?

Where there are variations in translation of foreign language terms, have these been clarified? For example, were the facts translated from words spoken by someone from Spain or someone from Puerto Rico, from someone who speaks Northern High German or Bavarian Southern German or Swiss German?

CITATIONS

A legal **citation** is a reference to the source of the information that allows someone else to find the case or other material mentioned in a document. The form of the citation must allow others to find the material. The format must be one that others in the legal community generally accept and use. If a person in California submits a brief to a court, a person in New York or in Florida must be able to use the citation to locate the items referred to in the document in a traditional legal library or electronic law source such as Loislaw, VersusLaw, Lexis, or Westlaw.

All legal authorities can be divided into two groups—primary authority and secondary authority. **Primary authority** includes constitutions, statutes, cases, and administrative regulations. Everything else is a **secondary authority** explaining the primary authority or a finding tool providing a method of locating primary authority. With a consistent citation format, the reader can determine the source of the authority mentioned and find the applicable primary source (constitution, statute, regulation, or case) or secondary source or finding tool (treatise, encyclopedia, digest, or dictionary).

Traditional Sources (Print)

The traditional method for publishing primary and secondary authority is the paper form, including books, collections of books, and series of books. Where a case, statute, or regulation is available in more than one series of books, such as the official reporter of the state and a private publication such as those published by West Publishing, the citation to both locations—known as parallel citations—is required. The citation form is basically the same:

Volume	Book or Series	Page
232	Atlantic 2d	44

In this example, written as 232 A.2d 44, 232 refers to the volume in the Atlantic 2d series reporter service of West Publishing Company, and 44 refers to the page on which the authority may be found.

Bluebook

The most commonly used guide to citation form is the publication *The Bluebook: A Uniform System of Citation*. This is the generally accepted authority for proper citation form unless the rules of a particular court dictate a different citation format. For example, the executive administrator of the Superior Court of Pennsylvania issued this notice:

> Pennsylvania Superior Court will be issuing opinions containing a Universal Citation. This citation will be as follows:
>
> Jones v. Smith, 1999 PA Super, 1.
>
> The second number is a Court-issued number on the opinion. Each opinion will also have numbered paragraphs, to be used for pinpoint citation, e.g., Jones v. Smith, 1999 PA Super, 1,15. Citation to opinions that have not yet been issued an Atlantic 2d citation are to be in the Universal Citation number. After the official citation has been issued, citation is to be only the official citation, and not the Universal Citation.

Effectively the old citation format, citing to the book, is still to be used.

Legal Citations— Tradition or Innovation?

Judges and lawyers in some states are abandoning the longstanding tradition of putting citations in the body of a document and now are putting the citations at the bottom of the document in the footnotes. They claim it makes reading legal opinions easier by eliminating the interference of the citations with the flow of words.

SIDEBAR

Legal Citations Are on Trial in Innovation v. Tradition

The New York Times July 8, 2001

For a couple of centuries, judges and lawyers have been including arcane numbers smack in the middle of their writing. They call them sentence citations—see, e.g., *Bush v. Gore*, 531 U.S. 98, 121 S. Ct. 525, 148 L. Ed. 2d 388 (2000).

Lots of people call them annoying. Now, at the prompting of one of the country's leading authorities on legal writing, lawyers and judges are joining the ranks of the complainers. In court opinions and legal briefs, they are flouting convention by tucking those numbers into footnotes. In the process, they are irritating some of their colleagues and changing the look of legal documents from coast to coast. They say they are also taking an important step toward making the law slightly more comprehensible to people who have not spent three years in law school.

But the defenders of legal tradition say the rebels are ruining a superior system of legal citation with unorthodox ideas. "It's a nuisance" and "aggravating" and "an obstacle to proper opinion writing," said Ned E. Doucet Jr., chief judge of a Louisiana appeals court that divided over the issue this spring. He exchanged tartly conflicting decisions with another judge over whether the new approach was a violation of all they held dear.

Still, some lawyers and judges in Texas, Michigan, Delaware, California, Alaska, and many other states are trying the new, cleaner look in legal documents by putting their citations at the bottom of the page. Legal citations can include references to the date, volume, and page number of legal publications where precedents can be found. Some converts say they are making the switch to democratize the law because the public is put off by strings of numbers that can make legal prose seem even more impenetrable than it is.

"We hear that all the time: 'Your opinions are oatmeal; they're not readable,'" said a Michigan Court of Appeals judge, William C. Whitbeck. "Judges see this as one way to respond."

Most of the judges did not think of the idea themselves. They have an authority to cite on the question: Bryan A. Garner, a silver-penned legal writing specialist who is, among other things, the editor of *Black's Law Dictionary*, a volume that has ruled the world of legal language since 1891. Mr. Garner, 42, has 12 books in print on language and legal writing. He revels in his role as the persnickety stylist for a linguistically challenged profession. Based in Dallas, he travels the country lecturing to lawyers and judges about how to avoid being "a workaday hack," as he put it to 150 New York lawyers the other day.

Mr. Garner's standing is such that a new book of his on American language was the subject of an occasionally playful critique by the novelist David Foster Wallace in *Harper's* magazine in April. Mr. Wallace suggested that sticklers like Mr. Garner may very likely have been "savagely and repeatedly Wedgied" in their grammatical adolescences. It is a charge Mr. Garner smilingly denies to audiences of chortling lawyers. Mr. Garner was recently named "the E. B. White of legal prose" by a San Francisco legal newspaper, *The Recorder*; and he has wide influence in the legal profession. The power of Mr. Garner's name has lent credibility to the movement for "citational footnotes." But the battle against entrenched tradition would not be possible, he said, were it not for the sheer logic of the idea of denuding legal prose of numbers.

In the legal profession, Mr. Garner said, "we have certain conventions—mind-numbing conventions—that keep us from writing coherently, and one of those is that we have these constant hiccups." Nobody really likes hearing that his writing is full of hiccups like this.* So Mr. Garner has made points.

Christopher W. Madel, a Minneapolis lawyer, changed the citation method he learned in law school after attending a Garner seminar. "You're reading, you're understanding," Mr. Madel said. "Then all of a sudden, there's an obscure 'Deposition, paragraph 48 at 7.' It makes no sense."

Rodney Davis, a California appeals judge in Sacramento, was also persuaded. After hearing Mr. Garner in October, Associate Justice Davis tried taking all the numbers out of the text of his decisions. He was stunned to see his words all by themselves. "Once

William Glaberson

I dropped the citations down to the bottom of the page and looked at what was left, it became apparent that what was left read like legal code," he said. "It would be very difficult to understand what I was saying."

But plenty of judges and lawyers say Mr. Garner is a false prophet. Some say the footnote approach undermines respect for precedent. In a 1999 article in a state bar journal, Mark E. Steiner, an assistant professor at the South Texas College of Law in Houston, warned fellow lawyers that Mr. Garner's ideas about putting citations in footnotes were catching on. Mr. Garner, he wrote, had a "Rasputin-like influence" over Texas judges. Since then, Mr. Steiner said in an interview, his views about Mr. Garner's proposal have grown extreme.

Scott Turow, the best-selling writer and practicing lawyer, said the idea of putting citations in footnotes would only make legal briefs confusing. "By the time your eyes get to the bottom of the page," Mr. Turow said, "you forget whether you're looking for footnote 22 or 23."

In San Francisco, Judge Joanne C. Parrilli, a state appeals judge, agreed. She said she tried the Garner approach, but all the looking up and down at footnotes "produced a certain amount of optical indigestion."

On the Delaware Supreme Court, Justice Joseph T. Walsh is the lone holdout on a bench where the four other justices have been putting their citations in footnotes. Justice Walsh explained his allegiance to the traditional method. Whatever his colleagues in Delaware may be doing, he said, Mr. Garner has yet to win a single convert on the highest court of the land. "If it's good enough for the Supreme Court," Justice Walsh said, "it's good enough for me."

Informed over lunch of Justice Walsh's assertion, Mr. Garner displayed the understated feistiness that makes him a hit on the continuing legal education circuit. "Although I have the highest respect for the justices of the U. S. Supreme Court," he said, "most of their opinions cannot be held up as literary models by any means." The Supreme Court's public information officer, Kathy Arberg, declined to comment.

Mr. Garner's willingness to experiment no matter whose literary feelings are hurt is a characteristic of many of his followers. "I love change," said Judge Billie Colombaro Woodard, the Louisiana judge who irked colleagues by writing opinions in the new style in April.

Chief Judge Doucet, who presides over the 12-judge court that hears appeals from a large area of southern Louisiana, agreed with the ruling Judge Woodard made in a workers' compensation case. But he refused to sign her opinion. He wrote his own, calling the use of footnotes "contrary to this court's officially adopted citation rules." Judge Woodard then filed a response calling Judge Doucet's opinion a "disconcerting" attack on judicial independence.

In an interview, Judge Doucet said a "bunch of judges" had been offended by the citational footnotes because that is not the way writing is done in rulings. Judge Woodard acknowledged that her colleagues' reactions were less than effusive. "I may be tarred and feathered and run out of town," she said. But she added that it was important for judges to experiment with ways of making legal opinions more accessible to ordinary people.

Many lawyers and judges agree that stripping the numbers out of their paragraphs might make them more readable. But it might be wrong to suggest that anything will make people wade through court decisions, said J. Michael Luttig, a judge on the United States Court of Appeals for the Fourth Circuit in Richmond. "It would make it more accessible, but the lay public still won't read legal opinions," Judge Luttig said, sounding a little forlorn. "They're too complex, laborious, and uninteresting to the lay public."

---

* For opinions using the new citational footnotes, see *TXU Elec. Co. v. Public Util. Comm'n of Texas*, 44 Tex. Sup. Ct. J. 854, 2001 WL 618186 Tex. LEXIS 53 (Tex. 2001) (Owen, J., concurring); *Shaw v. State Farm Mut. Auto Ins. Co.*, 19 P.3d 588, 2001 Alas. LEXIS 24 (2001).

ALWD Citation Format

A new citation format, written by the **Association of Legal Writing Directors (ALWD),** is provided in the *ALWD Citation Manual, A Professional System of Citation.* The ALWD is a society for professors who coordinate legal writing instruction in legal education.

One of the attributes of the manual, as set out in the preface, is that it is "a set of rules that reflects a consensus in the legal profession about how citations should function." The ALWD manual includes, in addition to the general citation rules, an appendix containing court citation rules for the individual states.

Universal Citation Format

The *Universal Citation Guide* represents an attempt by the American Association of Law Libraries (AALL), Committee on Citation Formats, to create a set of universal citation rules for American law that are vendor (publisher) neutral and medium (print and electronic) neutral (see Exhibit 11.1).

The various formats of electronic distribution require a system of citation that can be applied consistently to allow researchers to find the referenced authority regardless of the research tool used. Whereas the traditional, paper or book-based, citation uses information based on internal page numbers, the **Universal Citation Format** relies upon the courts to use numbered paragraphs in their opinions. Any publisher of the case law then can preserve the information provided by the court including the citation references to the case and paragraph.

Anyone who has read and compared a case in a book with a case online is aware that the page size and the display are different. Unless the online computer display is in a photo-image format, such as Adobe PDF, locating a specific page or reference can be difficult. Librarians and courts are recognizing the need for pinpoint citations for the on-screen user.

Paralegal preparing memoranda of law in a law library.

The Universal Citation Format represents an attempt to solve this problem. The difficulty with some courts is the requirement that the Universal Citation Format be used only until the hard copy is published, at which time the traditional citation must be used. As a result, you may see the following citation format within documents:

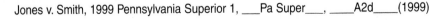

Jones v. Smith, 1999 Pennsylvania Superior 1, ___Pa Super___, ____A2d____(1999)

in which the blank spaces are provided to insert the ultimate volume and page number in the print version when it is available. Exhibit 11.2 lists court name abbreviations.

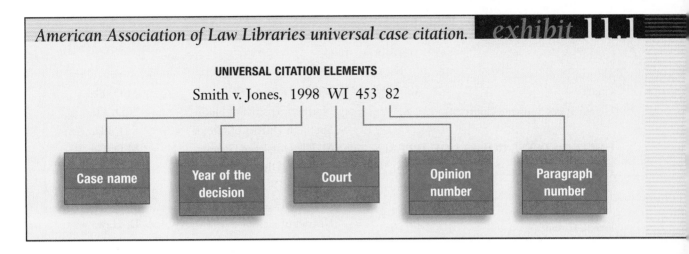

American Association of Law Libraries universal case citation. *exhibit* **11.1**

UNIVERSAL CITATION ELEMENTS

Smith v. Jones, 1998 WI 453 82

| Case name | Year of the decision | Court | Opinion number | Paragraph number |

Other Citation Formats

Many states, including Pennsylvania, have adopted as their official citation format one that originally was created by publishers such as West Publishing Company. These sometimes are referred to as **vendor-specific citation formats.** The West Publishing Company format is based on the West Regional Reporter system and its publications of federal material.

New methods of electronic information technology, in the form of databases, CD-ROMs, and the Internet, have created a number of problems with the traditional citation format. Some of the vendors have claimed copyright protection for their pagination systems.

In 1985, West Publishing Company in a case against Mead Data Central successfully argued that the wholesale use of its *pagination* by a competing online publisher infringed West's copyright interest in the arrangement of cases in its court reports. And in a 1998 case involving Matthew Bender & Company and West Publishing Company, the Second Circuit held that West's pagination was not protected by copyright. Obviously, all claims to a pagination system or citation system that is vendor-specific will result in some action to protect the corporate claim for copyright, trademark, or potential patent for some electronic methodology.

Cite Checking

Cite checking is the process of verifying that the proper citation format has been used in a document. The term also means checking the referenced case or statute to determine that it is valid and that it has not been repealed or overturned. The strictness with which the citation rules must be applied, as well as the method—*Bluebook*, *ALWD Citation Manual*, or Universal Citation Format—depends on the wishes and demands of the attorney for whom the document is prepared or the court or judge to whom it is submitted. Some courts view the presentation of improper citation format with a jaundiced eye, just as they view improper punctuation, improper spelling, and bad grammar. Others are upset if the citation to the paper references or online legal research service available to them is not used.

exhibit **11.2**   *Federal court name abbreviations.*

Court	Abbrev.
United States Supreme Court	U.S.

UNITED STATES COURTS OF APPEALS

First Circuit	1st Cir.
Second Circuit	2d Cir.
Third Circuit	3d Cir.
Fourth Circuit	4th Cir.
Fifth Circuit	5th Cir.
Sixth Circuit	6th Cir.
Seventh Circuit	7th Cir.
Eighth Circuit	8th Cir.
Ninth Circuit	9th Cir.
Tenth Circuit	10th Cir.
Eleventh Circuit	11th Cir.
D.C. Circuit	D.C. Cir.
Federal Circuit	Fed. Cir.

UNITED STATES DISTRICT COURTS

Middle District of Alabama	M.D. Ala.
Northern District of Alabama	N.D. Ala.
Southern District of Alabama	S.D. Ala.
District of Alaska	D. Alaska
District of Arizona	D. Ariz.
Eastern District of Arkansas	E.D. Ark.
Western District of Arkansas	W.D. Ark.
Central District of California	C.D. Cal.
Eastern District of California	E.D. Cal.
Northern District of California	N.D. Cal.
Southern District of California	S.D. Cal.
District of the Canal Zone	D.C.Z.

(Note: The D.C.Z. ceased to exist on March 31, 1982.)

District of Colorado	D. Colo.
District of Connecticut	D. Conn.
District of Delaware	D. Del.
District of D.C.	D.D.C.

Middle District of Florida	M.D. Fla.
Northern District of Florida	N.D. Fla.
Southern District of Florida	S.D. Fla.
Middle District of Georgia	M.D. Ga.
Northern District of Georgia	N.D. Ga.
Southern District of Georgia	S.D. Ga.
District of Guam	D. Guam
District of Hawaii	D. Haw.
District of Idaho	D. Idaho
Central District of Illinois	C.D. Ill.
Northern District of Illinois	N.D. Ill.
Southern District of Illinois	S.D. Ill.
Northern District of Indiana	N.D. Ind.
Southern District of Indiana	S.D. Ind.
Northern District of Iowa	N.D. Iowa
Southern District of Iowa	S.D. Iowa
District of Kansas	D. Kan.
Eastern District of Kentucky	E.D. Ky.
Western District of Kentucky	W.D. Ky.
Eastern District of Louisiana	E.D. La.
Middle District of Louisiana	M.D. La.
Western District of Louisiana	W.D. La.
District of Maine	D. Me.
District of Maryland	D. Md.
District of Massachusetts	D. Mass.
Eastern District of Michigan	E.D. Mich.
Western District of Michigan	W.D. Mich.
District of Minnesota	D. Minn.
Northern District of Mississippi	N.D. Miss.
Southern District of Mississippi	S.D. Miss.
Eastern District of Missouri	E.D. Mo.
Western District of Missouri	W.D. Mo.
District of Montana	D. Mont.
District of Nebraska	D. Neb.
District of Nevada	D. Nev.
District of New Hampshire	D.N.H.
District of New Jersey	D.N.J.

Federal court name abbreviations, continued.   *exhibit* **11.2**

District of New Mexico	**D.N.M.**	Western District of Washington	**W.D. Wash.**
Eastern District of New York	**E.D.N.Y.**	Northern District of West Virginia	**N.D.W. Va.**
Northern District of New York	**N.D.N.Y.**	Southern District of West Virginia	**S.D.W. Va.**
Southern District of New York	**S.D.N.Y.**	Eastern District of Wisconsin	**E.D. Wis.**
Western District of New York	**W.D.N.Y.**	Western District of Wisconsin	**W.D. Wis.**
Eastern District of North Carolina	**E.D.N.C.**	District of Wyoming	**D. Wyo.**
Middle District of North Carolina	**M.D.N.C.**		
Western District of North Carolina	**W.D.N.C.**	**MILITARY COURTS**	
District of North Dakota	**D.N.D.**	United States Court of Appeals for the Armed Forces	**Armed Forces App.**
District of the Northern Mariana Islands	**D.N. Mar. I.**	United States Court of Veterans Appeals	**Vet. App.**
Northern District of Ohio	**N.D. Ohio**	United States Air Force Court of Criminal Appeals	**A.F. Crim. App.**
Southern District of Ohio	**S.D. Ohio**		
Eastern District of Oklahoma	**E.D. Okla.**	United States Army Court of Criminal Appeals	**Army Crim. App.**
Northern District of Oklahoma	**N.D. Okla.**		
Western District of Oklahoma	**W.D. Okla.**	United States Coast Guard Court of Criminal Appeals	**Coast Guard Crim. App.**
District of Oregon	**D. Or.**		
Eastern District of Pennsylvania	**E.D. Pa.**	United States Navy-Marine Corps Court of Criminal Appeals	**Navy-Marine Crim. App.**
Middle District of Pennsylvania	**M.D. Pa.**		
Western District of Pennsylvania	**W.D. Pa.**		
District of Puerto Rico	**D.P.R.**	**BANKRUPTCY COURTS**	
District of Rhode Island	**D.R.I.**	Each United States District Court has a corresponding bankruptcy court. To cite a bankruptcy court, add Bankr. to the district court abbreviation.	
District of South Carolina	**D.S.C.**		
District of South Dakota	**D.S.D.**		
Eastern District of Tennessee	**E.D. Tenn.**	*Examples:*	
Middle District of Tennessee	**M.D. Tenn.**	Bankr. N.D. Ala.	
Western District of Tennessee	**W.D. Tenn.**	Bankr. D. Mass.	
Eastern District of Texas	**E.D. Tex.**		
Northern District of Texas	**N.D. Tex.**	**OTHER FEDERAL COURTS**	
Southern District of Texas	**S.D. Tex.**	Court of Federal Claims	**Fed. Cl.**
Western District of Texas	**W.D. Tex.**	Court of Customs and Patent Appeals	**Cust. & Pat. App.**
District of Utah	**D. Utah**		
District of Vermont	**D. Vt.**	Court of Claims	**Ct. Cl.**
Eastern District of Virginia	**E.D. Va.**	Claims Court	**Cl. Ct.**
Western District of Virginia	**W.D. Va.**	Court of International Trade	**Ct. Intl. Trade**
District of the Virgin Islands	**D.V.I.**	Tax Court	**Tax**
Eastern District of Washington	**E.D. Wash.**		

Reprinted from *ALWD Citation Manual: A Professional System of Citation*, with the permission of Aspen Law and Business.

exhibit **11.3** *Comparison of* Bluebook *and ALWD Manual parts.*

BLUEBOOK	ALWD MANUAL
Part 1 General standards of citation and style	Part 1 Introductory material
Part 2 Specific rules for citation to cases, statutes, books, periodicals, foreign materials, international materials, and so forth	Part 2 Citation basics
	Part 3 Citation format for print versions
	Part 4 Citation format for electronic materials
Part 3 Tables to be used in conjunction with the rules, including state and foreign jurisdiction citation formats	Part 5 Incorporating citations into documents
	Part 6 How to quote material
	Part 7 Appendices, including local jurisdictional requirements

Bluebook and ALWD Compared

Which citation format is used depends on the local custom and courts in which the firm or supervising attorney practices (and the wishes of your instructors!). The two forms most commonly used—the *Bluebook* and the *ALWD Manual*—have a number of similarities. Both of these documents are divided into parts and rules, the *Bluebook* into three parts and the *ALWD Manual* into seven parts, as indicated in Exhibit 11.3.

The parts are further divided into rules (see Table 11.1). The *Bluebook* has 20 basic rules, and the *ALWD* 50 rules. Most of the rules have a common pattern, and some are the same, such as *Bluebook* Rule 12–Statutes, and *ALWD* Rule 14 on the method of citing the United State Code: 18 U.S.C. § 1965 (1994). Others are minor variations in presentation, such as *Bluebook* Rule 10.2.2, which provides "Do not abbreviate 'United States'" and *ALWD* Rule 12.2 (g) "United States as party: Cite as U. S. Omit 'America.'"

Sample *Bluebook* citation formats:

Rule 11 Constitutions:	U.S.Const.art.I, § 9, cl.2.
Rule 10 Cases:	United States v Shaffer Equip. Co., 11 F.3d 450 (4th Cir. 1993)
Rule 12 Statutes:	42 U.S. C. § 1983 (1994)

Sample *ALWD* citation formats:

Rule 13 Constitutions:	U.S. Const.art. IV, § 5(b)
Rule 12 Cases:	Brown v. Bd. Of Educ., 349 U.S. 294
	U.S. v. Chairse, 18 F.Supp. 2d 1021 (D. Minn. 1998)
Rule 14 Statutory Codes, Session Laws, SlipLaws:	18 U.S.C. § 1965 (1994)

Comparison of selected ALWD and Bluebook rules.   *table* 11.1

RULE	*ALWD* CITATION	*BLUEBOOK* CITATION	DIFFERENCES
Typeface (Rule 1)	Ordinary type and *italics* (or <u>underlining</u>). No distinctions based on type of document (law review v. court document) or placement of citation within the paper.	Ordinary type, *italics* (or <u>underlining</u>), and small caps. Different fonts required depending on type of document and where source is cited within the paper.	*ALWD* has one set of conventions, not two. *ALWD* eliminates small caps as a typeface.
Spacing (Rule 2)	F. Supp. F.3d	F. Supp. F.3d	No substantial differences.
Capitalization (Rule 3)	*Federal Civil Procedure before Trial*	*Federal Civil Procedure Before Trial*	*ALWD* eliminates the "and prepositions of four or fewer letters" part of the *Bluebook,* which brings legal citation closer to non-legal style.
Ordinal Numbers (Rule 4)	1st, 2d, 3d, 4th	1st, 2d, 3d, 4th	No substantial differences.
Page spans (Rule 5)	125-126 **or** 125-26	125-26	*ALWD* gives a choice on how to present a page span; you may retain all digits or drop repetitive digits and retain two digits on the right hand side of the span, as in *Bluebook* 3.3(d).
Footnotes and endnotes (Rule 7)	n. 7 nn. 12-13	n.7 nn.12-13	*ALWD* requires a space after n. or nn. abbreviation.
Supra and *infra* (Rule 10)	*Supra* n. 45.	*Supra* note 45.	Under *ALWD*, abbreviate note as "n." and place a space after the period.
Id. (Rule 11.3)	*Id.* at 500.	*Id.* at 500.	Basically similar rules. *ALWD* eliminates the "5 *id.* in a row" rule found in *Bluebook* 10.9.
Cases (Rule 12)	*Brown v. Bd. of Educ.,* 349 U.S. 294, 297 (1955). *MBNA Am. Bank, N.A. v. Cardoso,* 707 N.E.2d 189 (Ill. App. 1st Dist. 1998). [required inclusion of district court information]	*Brown v. Board of Educ.,* 349 U.S. 294, 297 (1955). *MBNA Am. Bank, N.A. v. Cardoso,* 707 N.E.2d 189 (Ill. App. Ct. 1st Dist. 1998). [permissive inclusion of district information]	Case names are always italicized. Under *ALWD*, first word of a party's name may be abbreviated. *Bluebook*'s 17th edition will be consistent with this rule. Do not have to abbreviate words in case names. For those who want to abbreviate, Appendix 3 provides a longer list of words. *ALWD* eliminates the "multiple date" rule found in *Bluebook* 10.5. *ALWD* uses S. instead of So. for the regional reporter. *ALWD* requires division and district information for state appellate courts. "Ct." is eliminated from most court abbreviations. *(continued)*

table 11.1 *Comparison of ALWD and Bluebook rules, continued.*

RULE	*ALWD* CITATION	*BLUEBOOK* CITATION	DIFFERENCES
Constitutions (Rule 13)	U.S. Const. amend. V	U.S. Const. amend. V.	No substantial differences.
Statutes (Rule 14)	18 U.S.C. § 1965 (1994).	18 U.S.C. § 1965 (1994).	No substantial differences.
Legislative Materials (Rules 15 and 16)	Sen. Res. 35, 106th Cong. (1999).	S. Res. 35, 106th Cong. (1999).	*ALWD* abbreviates Senate as "Sen." instead of "S." to avoid confusion with other abbreviations. Most forms are relatively consistent.
Court Rules (Rule 17)	Fed. R. Civ. P. 11 (1999).	Fed. R. Civ. P. 11.	*ALWD* requires a date, even for current rules, to help avoid confusion.
Administrative Materials (Rules 19 and 20)	42 C.F.R. § 422.206(a) (1999). 64 Fed. Reg. 12473 (Mar. 12, 1999).	42 C.F.R. § 422.206(a) (1999). 64 Fed. Reg. 12473 (1999).	C.F.R. citation is the same. *ALWD* requires an exact date for Fed. Reg. citations.
Books and Treatises (Rule 22)	Charles Alan Wright, Arthur R. Miller & Mary Kay Kane, *Federal Practice and Procedure* vol. 6A, § 1497, 70-79 (2d ed., West 1990). OR Charles Alan Wright et al., *Federal Practice and Procedure* vol. 6A, § 1497, 70-79 (2d ed., West 1990).	6A Charles Alan Wright et al., *Federal Practice and Procedure* § 1497, at 70-79 (2d ed. 1990).	Under *ALWD* you may, but are not required to, use et al. for more than two authors. The *Bluebook*'s 17th edition will be consistent with this rule. *ALWD* places volume information after the title, just like any other subdivision. *ALWD* separates subdivisions with a comma, but no "at." *ALWD* requires that the publisher be included.
Legal Periodicals (Rule 23)	L. Ray Patterson, *Legal Ethics and the Lawyer's Duty of Loyalty*, 29 Emory L.J. 909, 915 (1980). Hope Viner Samborn, *Navigating Murky Waters*, 85 ABA J. 28 (July 1998). Tara Burns Koch, Student Author, *Betting on Brownfields—Does Florida's Brownfields Redevelopment Act Transform Liability into Opportunity?*, 28 Stetson L. Rev. 171 (1998).	L. Ray Patterson, *Legal Ethics and the Lawyer's Duty of Loyalty*, 29 Emory L.J. 909, 915 (1980). Hope Viner Samborn, *Navigating Murky Waters*, A.B.A. J., July 1998, at 28 Tara Burns Koch, Comment, *Betting on Brownfields—Does Florida's Brownfields Redevelopment Act Transform Liability into Opportunity?*, 28 Stetson L. Rev. 171 (1998).	*ALWD* eliminates most distinctions between consecutively and nonconsecutively paginated articles; includes longer date for nonconsecutively paginated journals, but does so within the parenthetical. *ALWD* uses the term "Student Author" to replace Note, Comment, etc.
A.L.R. Annotations (Rule 24)	Marjorie A. Caner, *Validity, Construction, and Application of Stalking Statutes*, 29 A.L.R.5th 487, 489 (1995).	Marjorie A. Caner, Annotation, *Validity, Construction, and Application of Stalking Statutes*, 29 A.L.R.5th 487, 489 (1995).	*ALWD* eliminates the "Annotation" reference.
Legal dictionaries (Rule 25)	*Black's Law Dictionary* 101 (Bryan A. Garner ed., 7th ed., West 1999).	*Black's Law Dictionary* 101 (7th ed. 1999).	*ALWD* treats dictionaries like treatises.
Legal Encyclopedias (Rule 26)	11 C.J.S. *Bonds* § 21 (1995). 76 Am. Jur. 2d *Trusts* §§ 1-4 (1992 & Supp. 1999).	11 C.J.S. *Bonds* § 21 (1995). 76 Am. Jur. 2d *Trusts* §§ 1-4 (1992 & Supp. 1999).	No substantial differences; however, *ALWD* provides expanded coverage and includes a list of many abbreviations for state encyclopedias.

Comparison of ALWD and Bluebook rules, continued.   *table* 11.1

RULE	*ALWD* CITATION	*BLUEBOOK* CITATION	DIFFERENCES
Websites (Rule 40)	Federal Judicial Center, *Federal Judicial Center Publications* <http://www.fjc.gov/pubs.html> (accessed July 10, 1999).	Federal Judicial Center, *Federal Judicial Center Publications* (visited July 10, 1999) <http://www.fjc.gov/pubs.html>.	*ALWD* moved the date to end to be more consistent with other sources. *ALWD* uses "accessed" instead of "visited" to give a more professional tone and be consistent with non-legal citation guides.
Neutral Citation (Rule 43)	*ALWD* indicates that neutral citation may be used (not limited to cases). *ALWD* also indicates that a parallel citation to a print source should also be used. *ALWD* permits use of the citation format used by the state whose case is being cited, the citation used on the source, or the form suggested by the AALL.	The *Bluebook* indicates that a public domain citation for cases should be used when available and allows a parallel citation.	
Signals (Rule 45)	"No signal" is not treated like a signal. No signal is used for direct support and quotations. Signals are *e.g., see, cf., contra, compare . . . with, but see, but cf.,* and *see generally.*	[no signal]: Cited authority (i) identifies the source of a quotation, or (ii) identifies an authority referred to in text. *See:* Cited authority *directly states or clearly supports the proposition.*	*ALWD* returns to long-used definitions. The *Bluebook*'s 17th edition will return to 15th-edition signals. *ALWD* eliminates the *accord* and *see also* signals because they are too close to other signals. Under *ALWD*, all signals may be separated with semicolons. *ALWD* does not have a comma after *e.g.*
Order of Citations (Rule 46)	*ALWD* lists federal and state court cases first by jurisdiction, then in reverse chronological order.	The *Bluebook* lists federal and state court cases in reverse chronological order.	
Quotations (Rule 48)	*ALWD* says to block-indent passages if they contain at least 50 words OR if they exceed four lines of typed text.	The *Bluebook* says to block-indent passages if they contain at least 50 words.	*ALWD* does not require counting the exact number of words in long quotations.

Reprinted from *ALWD Citation Manual: A Professional System of Citation,* with the permission of Aspen Law and Business.

Association of Legal Writing
    Directors (ALWD)
Citation
Cite checking
Critical legal thinking
Duty of candor

Memorandum
Primary authority
Secondary authority
Universal Citation Format
Vendor-specific citation format

Summary

CHAPTER 11 CRITICAL LEGAL THINKING AND WRITING

Critical Legal Thinking

Definition	The process of identifying legal issues, determining the relevant facts, and applying the applicable law to come to a conclusion that answers the legal question the issues present. The paralegal must understand the audience for whom the document is being prepared: the client, the supervising attorney and other members of the legal team, or the court.

Critical Legal Writing

Standards	1. The language used must be clear to the intended reader. 2. The writer must make an honest presentation of the facts and argument. 3. Arguments advocating a new interpretation to the existing law, as well as the current law, must be clearly stated. 4. The ethical obligation to the court must be obeyed, including the presentation of adverse authority in the jurisdiction. 5. Factual variation must be presented, and the sources used clearly identified by proper citation in a format acceptable to the reader.

Court Brief and Office Memorandum Writing Styles

Differences	Both the brief and the memorandum may be on the exact same set of facts, legal issue, and applicable law, but the writing style is totally different. 1. The memorandum is a working document for the legal team to be used in preparation and presentation of a case. 2. The brief written for the court provides written advocacy of the client's position and must be written to convince the court to adopt a position favorable to the client.

(continued)

Duty of Candor	There is an obligation to be honest with the court and not to mislead the court.
Office Memorandum	1. Office memoranda are frequently indexed by subject and filed in the office for future reference; if the same or a similar fact pattern requires research, it is a good starting point and can be a major time-saver.
	2. The paralegal must understand the specific assignment. What have you been asked to research? For the memorandum of law, it usually is the answer to a question.
	3. The facts relied upon in writing the memo must be a part of the final memorandum; other people who read the memorandum need to understand the specific facts.
	4. A memorandum must present both sides of the issue, and in that respect be a neutral, unbiased, objective presentation of applicable laws as they apply to the facts of the case. Issues that the opposing attorney or the judge may raise should be considered and presented. A good analysis includes a discussion of how the fact pattern may differ in cases that are not on point.
	5. The written word is a reflection of the writer. Everyone who reads the memorandum will measure the writer's reputation and level of researching skill.

Citations

Purpose	A citation should allow someone else to find the case or other material mentioned in a document, and the form of citation must do this. The format must be generally accepted and used by others in the legal community.
Traditional Sources (Print) Citation Format	Basic paper or traditional citation form: Volume • Book or Series • Page e. g., 232 Atlantic 2d 44 232 refers to the volume in the Atlantic 2d series reporter service of West Publishing Company, and 44 refers to the page on which the authority may be found.
Bluebook Citation Format	*Bluebook* has been the generally accepted authority for proper citation form unless the rules of a particular court dictated a different citation format.
ALWD Manual Citation Format	A citation format authority written by Association of Legal Writing Directors.
Universal Citation Format	Traditional, paper or book-based citation used information based on internal page numbers; Universal Citation Format relies upon the courts to provide numbered paragraphs in their opinions.

(continued)

Cite Checking	Document must be checked to verify that the proper citation format has been used, and that the referenced cases and statutes are valid and the cases have not been repealed or overturned. The strictness with which the citation rules must be applied, as well as the method—*Bluebook*, *ALWD*, or Universal Citation Format—depends on the wishes and demands of the attorney for whom the document is being prepared, or the court or judge to whom it is submitted.

Working the Web

1. Bookmark for future reference the citation primer based on the 17th edition of the *Bluebook* at the Cornell University LII website, at www.law.cornell.edu/citation.

2. Find and download the comparison between the *Bluebook* rules and the *ALWD* rule at www.alwd.org.

3. Locate and download any updates to the *ALWD* manual from www.alwd.org.

4. Check your local and state courts online for any citation requirements or rules.

5. Take the tour of *Shepard's* at the Lexis website at www.lexis.com.

Questions
CRITICAL LEGAL THINKING AND WRITING

1. Prepare a memo of law based on the following facts, using your state law and ethics rules.

   A client who is traveling in Asia requests a paralegal to immediately forward to him by email a copy of an opinion letter, which was mailed to his home. The opinion letter contains a summary of the facts, including details about opposing parties, strategy, and potential violations of law. Are there any ethical issues? May the paralegal send it as requested?

2. Prepare a memo of law on the question: Is there a continuing duty to advise the court of any changes in the law or facts after the case has been presented? (*Triverton Board of License Commissioners v. Patore*, 469 U.S. 238)

3. How does the general duty to inform the court preserve the integrity of the judicial process? (*Hazel-Atlas Glass Co. v. Hartford-Empire Co.*, 322 U.S. 238)

4. Are sanctions against attorneys for failing to observe a duty of candor to the court an appropriate remedy? [*Beam v. IPCO Corp.*, 838 F.2d 242 (7th Cir. 1998)]

5. What are the relevant facts in the *Palsgraf v. LIRR* case found in Appendix A? What facts are interesting but not relevant facts? Create a search query using the facts in the *Palsgraf* case, and search the case law of your jurisdiction using these relevant facts. Prepare a short brief of the latest case you find, including proper *Bluebook* and *ALWD* citation format.

6. What questions should a paralegal ask before preparing a memo of law or a brief?

7. Why should both sides of a case be presented in an office memo of law?

8. Why would an attorney request that all parallel citations be listed for each case listed in a memo of law?

9. How would knowing the intended audience influence the writing of a memo of law or a legal brief?

10. What level of confidentiality should be attached to the preparation and handling of a memo of law? Why?

ETHICS: ANALYSIS AND DISCUSSION

1. What are the ethical issues in failing to properly cite authorities used in a document?

2. What are the ethical obligations in arguing to the court for a change in the law and not the current law?

3. What are the ethical obligations to the client when analysis of the law indicates there is no valid claim?

Unauthorized Practice of Law—Supervision

There are few certainties in the area of ethics, for paralegals or in any profession. What qualifies as ethical conduct is in most cases based on state law and court interpretation applied to a set of facts. The citation listed below represents one legal opinion and is provided as a research starting point. Do not assume that the same rule applies in your jurisdiction. For the following:

- *Prepare a written statement based on your state law.*
- *Use your state bar association website as a starting point.*

You have been working for a legal specialist in estate law for a number of years and have taken a number of advanced courses in the field. You are highly regarded in the paralegal community as the person to call for help in the field. Your supervising attorney decides to take a three-week bicycle trip through the Swiss Alps and leaves you in charge of the office.

During his absence you give a talk to a local senior citizens group on the advantages of preparing a will. You meet with most of the people in the audience after the talk and tell them a simple will can be prepared for $25 (your office's standard fee) and proceed to take the information from them for a will. You prepare the individual wills and send copies marked DRAFT to each person along with an invoice for the $25 fee with a note to return the fee if they wish to have the will completed. Everyone accepts and sends in the fee.

Upon his return the attorney looks over the wills and tells you they are "letter perfect," and says "It's just what I would have done." [*Cincinnati Bar v. Kathman*, 92 Ohio St. 92 (2001) quoting *People v. Cassidy*, 884 P.2d 309 (Colo. 1994).] What are the legal and ethical issues?

FOR DISCUSSION

United States v. Shaffer Equipt. Co.   11 F.3d 450 (4th Cir. 1993)

Issue: Continuing Duty to Inform Court of Changes in the Law

Government counsel learned that its expert witness had lied about his credentials and that the witness had lied in other litigation. The attorney did not immediately notify the court or opposing counsel. In finding against the government, the court extended the duty of candor to include a continuing duty to inform the court of any development that may conceivably affect the outcome of litigation.

Questions

1. Is preserving the integrity of the judicial process more important than the duty to vigorously pursue a client's case?

2. Is there a duty to inform the court when an attorney suspects that a client may have committed perjury?

3. What additional burden is placed on the paralegal in preparing material for a case in light of this decision?

CASE FOR BRIEFING

Golden Eagle Distributing Corp. v. Burroughs

801 F.2d. 1531 (9th Cir. 1986)   United States Court of Appeals, Ninth Circuit

Read, and if assigned, brief this case. In your brief, answer the following questions.

1. What is the intent of Federal Rules of Civil Procedure Rule 11?

2. What test does the court use to determine if sanctions should be imposed under FRCP Rule 11?

3. What is meant by the "ethical duty of candor"?

4. Is there a conflict between the attorney's ethical obligations under the ABA Model Rules and the requirements of FRCP 11?

5. Do attorneys have any duty to cite cases adverse to their case? Explain.

Schroeder, Circuit Judge.

This is an appeal from the imposition of sanctions under Rule 11 of the Federal Rules of Civil Procedure as amended in 1983. The appellant, a major national law firm, raises significant questions of first impression.

The relevant portions of the amended Rule provide: Every pleading, motion, and other paper of a party represented by an attorney shall be signed by at least one attorney. . . . The signature of an attorney . . . constitutes a certificate by him that he has read the pleading, motion, or other paper; that to the best of his knowledge, information, and belief formed after reasonable inquiry, it is well grounded in fact and is warranted by existing law or a good faith argument for the extension, modification, or reversal of existing law. . . . If a pleading, motion, or other paper is signed in violation of this rule, the court, upon motion or upon its own initiative, shall impose upon the person who signed it, a represented party, or both, an appropriate sanction. . . .

In this appeal, we must decide whether the district court correctly interpreted Rule 11.

. . . Golden Eagle Distributing Corporation filed the underlying action in Minnesota state court for fraud, negligence, and breach of contract against Burroughs, because of an allegedly defective computer system. Burroughs removed the action to the federal district court in Minnesota. Burroughs then moved pursuant to 28 U.S.C. § 1404(a) to transfer the action to the Northern District of California. . . . Burroughs next filed the motion for summary judgment, which gave rise to the sanctions at issue here. It argued that the California, rather than the Minnesota, statute of limitations applied and that all of Golden Eagle's claims were time-barred under California law. It also contended that Golden Eagle's claim for economic loss arising from negligent manufacture lacked merit under California law. Golden Eagle filed a response, arguing that Minnesota law gov-

erned the statute of limitations question and that Burroughs had misinterpreted California law regarding economic loss. . . .

After a hearing, the district judge denied Burroughs' motion and directed the Kirkland & Ellis attorney who had been responsible for the summary judgment motion to submit a memorandum explaining why sanctions should not be imposed under Rule 11. . . . Proper understanding of this appeal requires some comprehension of the nature of Burroughs' arguments and the faults which the district court found with them. . . .

Kirkland & Ellis's opening memorandum argued that Golden Eagle's claims were barred by California's three-year statute of limitations. The question was whether the change of venue from Minnesota to California affected which law applied. . . . In imposing sanctions, the district court held that Kirkland & Ellis's argument was "misleading" because it suggested that there already exists a *forum non conveniens* exception to the general rule that the transferor's law applies. . . . [The case cited] raised the issue but did not decide it. . . . Kirkland & Ellis's corollary argument, that a Minnesota court would have dismissed the case on *forum non conveniens* grounds, was found to be "misleading" because it failed to note that one prerequisite to such a dismissal is that an alternative forum be available. . . .

Kirkland & Ellis also argued that Golden Eagle's claim for negligent manufacture lacked merit because Golden Eagle sought damages for economic loss, and such damages are not recoverable under California law [as demonstrated in the *Seely* case]. . . . The district court sanctioned Kirkland & Ellis for not citing three cases whose holdings it concluded were adverse to *Seely:* . . . The district court held that these omissions violated counsel's duty to disclose adverse authority, embodied in Model Rule 3.3, Model Rules of Professional Conduct Rule 3.3 (1983), which the court viewed as a "necessary corollary to Rule 11."

. . . The district court's application of Rule 11 in this case strikes a chord not otherwise heard in discussion of this Rule. The district court did not focus on whether a sound basis in law and in fact existed for the defendant's motion for summary judgment. Indeed it indicated that the motion itself was nonfrivolous. . . . Rather, the district court looked to the manner in which the motion was presented. The district court in this case held that Rule 11 imposes upon counsel an ethical "duty of candor." . . . It said:

The duty of candor is a necessary corollary of the certification required by Rule 11. A court has a right to expect that counsel will state the controlling law fairly and fully; indeed, unless that is done the court cannot perform its task properly. A lawyer must not misstate the law, fail to disclose adverse authority (not disclosed by his opponent), or omit facts critical to the application of the rule of law relied on. . . .

With the district court's salutary admonitions against misstatements of the law, failure to disclose directly adverse authority, or omission of critical facts, we have no quarrel. It is, however, with Rule 11 that we must deal. The district court's interpretation of Rule 11 requires district courts to judge the ethical propriety of lawyers' conduct with respect to every piece of paper filed in federal court. This gives us considerable pause. . . .

The district court's invocation of Rule 11 has two aspects. The first, which we term "argument identification," is the holding that counsel should differentiate between an argument "warranted by existing law" and an argument for the "extension, modification, or reversal of existing law." The second is the conclusion that Rule 11 is violated when counsel fails to cite what the district court views to be directly contrary authority.

. . . The text of the Rule . . . does not require that counsel differentiate between a position which is supported by existing law and one that would extend it. The Rule on its face requires that the motion be either one or the other. . . . The district court's ruling appears to go even beyond the principle of Rule 3.3 of the ABA Model Rules, which proscribes "knowing" false statements of material fact or law. The district court made no finding of a knowing misstatement, and, given the well-established objective nature of the Rule 11 standard, such a requirement would be inappropriate. Both the earnest advocate exaggerating the state of the current law without knowingly misrepresenting it, and the unscrupulous lawyer knowingly deceiving the court, are within the scope of the district court's interpretation.

This gives rise to serious concerns about the effect of such a rule on advocacy. It is not always easy to decide whether an argument is based on established law or is an argument for the extension of existing law. Whether the case being litigated is . . . materially the same as earlier precedent is frequently the very issue which prompted the litigation in the first place. Such questions can be close.

Sanctions under Rule 11 are mandatory. . . . In even a close case, we think it extremely unlikely that a judge, who has already decided that the law is not as a lawyer argued it, will also decide that the loser's position was warranted by existing law. Attorneys who adopt an aggressive posture risk more than the loss of the motion if the district court decides that their argument is for an extension of the law which it declines to make. What is at stake is often not merely the monetary sanction but the lawyer's reputation.

The "argument identification" requirement adopted by the district court therefore tends to create a conflict between the lawyer's duty zealously to represent his client, Model Code of Professional Responsibility Canon 7, and the lawyer's own interest in avoiding rebuke. The concern on the part of the bar that this type of requirement will chill advocacy is understandable. . . .

. . . Were the scope of the rule to be expanded as the district court suggests, mandatory sanctions would ride on close decisions concerning whether or not one case is or is not the same as another. We think Rule 11 should not impose the risk of sanctions in the event that the court later decides that the lawyer was wrong. The burdens of research and briefing by a diligent lawyer anxious to avoid any possible rebuke would be great. And the burdens would not be merely on the lawyer. If the mandatory provisions of the Rule are to be interpreted literally, the court would have a duty to research authority beyond that provided by the parties to make sure that they have not omitted something.

The burden is illustrated in this case, where the district court based its imposition of sanctions in part upon Kirkland & Ellis's failure to cite authorities which the court concluded were directly adverse to a case it did cite. The district court charged the appellant with constructive notice of these authorities because they were identified in Shepard's as "distinguishing" the case Kirkland & Ellis relied on.

. . . Amended Rule 11 of the Federal Rules of Civil Procedure does not impose upon the district courts the burden of evaluating under ethical standards the accuracy of all lawyers' arguments. Rather, Rule 11 is intended to reduce the burden on district courts by sanctioning, and hence deterring, attorneys who submit motions or pleadings which cannot reasonably be supported in law or in fact. We therefore reverse the district court's imposition of sanctions for conduct which it felt fell short of the ethical responsibilities of the attorney. Reversed.

How to Brief a Case

Critical Legal Thinking

Judges apply *legal reasoning* in reaching a decision in a case. That is, the judge must specify the issue presented by the case, identify the key facts in the case and the applicable law, and then apply the law to the facts to come to a conclusion that answers the issue presented. This process is called **critical legal thinking.** Skills of analysis and interpretation are important in deciding legal cases.

Key Terms

Before you embark upon the study of law, you should know the following key legal terms.

Plaintiff   The party who originally brought the lawsuit.

Defendant   The party against whom the lawsuit has been brought.

Petitioner or Appellant   The party who has appealed the decision of the trial court or lower court. The petitioner may be either the plaintiff or defendant, depending on who lost the case at the trial court or lower court level.

Respondent or Appellee   The party who must answer the petitioner's appeal. The respondent may be either the plaintiff or defendant, depending upon which party is the petitioner. In some cases, both the plaintiff *and* the defendant may disagree with the trial court's or lower court's decision, and both parties may appeal the decision.

Briefing a Case

It is often helpful for a student to "brief" a case in order to clarify the legal issues involved and to gain a better understanding of the case.

The procedure for briefing a case is as follows. The student must summarize, or brief, the court's decision in no more than 400 words (some professors may shorten or lengthen this limit). The assignment's format is highly structured, consisting of five parts, each of which is numbered and labeled:

Part	Maximum Words
1. Case name and citation	25
2. A summary of the key facts in the case	125
3. The issue presented by the case, stated as a one-sentence question answerable only by *yes* or *no*	25
4. The court's resolution of the issue (the "holding")	25
5. A summary of the court's reasoning justifying the holding	<u>200</u>
Total words	*400*

Briefing a case consists of making a summary of each of the following items of the case.

1. Case Name and Citation

The name of the case should be placed at the beginning of each briefed case. The case name usually contains the names of the parties to the lawsuit. Where there are multiple plaintiffs or defendants, however, some of the names of the parties may be omitted from the case name. Abbreviations are also often used in case names.

The case citation, which consists of a number plus the year in which the case was decided, such as "126 L.Ed.2d 295 (1993)," is set forth below the case name. The case citation identifies the book in the law library in which the case may be found. For example, the case in the above citation may be found in volume 126 of the *Supreme Court Reporter Lawyer's Edition (Second)*, page 295. The name of the court that decided the case should be set forth below the case name.

2. Summary of the Key Facts in the Case

The important facts of a case should be stated briefly. Extraneous facts and facts of minor importance should be omitted from the brief. The facts of the case can usually be found at the beginning of the case, but not necessarily. Important facts may be found throughout the case.

3. Issue Presented by the Case

It is crucial in the briefing of a case to identify the issue presented to the court to decide. The issue on appeal is most often a legal question, although questions of fact are sometimes the subject of an appeal. The issue presented in each case is usually quite specific and should be asked in a one-sentence question that is answerable only by a *yes* or *no*. For example, the issue statement, "Is Mary liable?" is too broad. A more proper statement of the issue would be, "Is Mary liable to Joe for breach of the contract made between them based on her refusal to make the payment due on September 30?"

4. Holding

The "holding" is the decision reached by the present court. It should be *yes* or *no*. The holding should also state which party won.

5. Summary of the Court's Reasoning

When an appellate court or supreme court issues a decision, which is often called an *opinion*, the court will normally state the reasoning it used in reaching its decision. The rationale for the decision may be based on the specific facts of the case, public policy, prior law, or other matters. In stating the reasoning of the court, the student should reword the court's language into the student's own language. This summary of the court's reasoning should pick out the meat of the opinions and weed out the nonessentials.

Following are two U.S. Supreme Court opinions for briefing. The case is presented in the language of the U.S. Supreme Court. A "Brief of the Case" follows each of the two cases. A third case, from the New York State Court of Appeals, is also included for briefing.

FOR BRIEFING

Harris v. Forklift Systems, Inc.
510 U.S. 17, 114 S.Ct. 367, 126 L.Ed.2d 295

CASE NAME	
CITATION	1993 U.S. LEXIS 7155 (1993)
COURT	Supreme Court of the United States

OPINION OF THE COURT. O'CONNOR, JUSTICE

FACTS. Teresa Harris worked as a manager at Forklift Systems, Inc., an equipment rental company, from April 1985 until October 1987. Charles Hardy was Forklift's president. Throughout Harris's time at Forklift, Hardy often insulted her because of her gender and often made her the target of unwanted sexual innuendos. Hardy told Harris on several occasions, in the presence of other employees, "You're a woman, what do you know" and "We need a man as the rental manager"; at least once, he told her she was "a dumb-ass woman." Again in front of others, he suggested that the two of them "go to the Holiday Inn to negotiate Harris' raise." Hardy occasionally asked Harris and other female employees to get coins from his front pants pocket. He threw objects on the ground in front of Harris and other women, and asked them to pick the objects up. He made sexual innuendos about Harris' and other women's clothing.

In mid-August 1987, Harris complained to Hardy about his conduct. Hardy said he was surprised that Harris was offended, claimed he was only joking, and apologized. He also promised he would stop and based on his assurance Harris stayed on the job. But in early September, Hardy began anew: While Harris was arranging a deal with one of Forklift's customers, he asked her, again in front of other employees, "What did you do, promise the guy some sex Saturday night?" On October 1, Harris collected her paycheck and quit.

LOWER COURTS' OPINIONS. Harris then sued Forklift, claiming that Hardy's conduct had created an abusive work environment for her because of her gender. The United States District Court for the Middle District of Tennessee found this to be "a close case," but held that Hardy's conduct did not create an abusive environment. The court found that some of Hardy's comments offended Harris, and would offend the reasonable woman," but that they were not "so severe as to be expected to seriously affect Harris' psychological well-being." A reasonable woman manager under like circumstances would have been offended by Hardy, but his conduct would not have risen to the level of interfering with that person's work performance. The United States Court of Appeals for the Sixth Circuit affirmed in a brief unpublished decision.

ISSUE. We granted certiorari to resolve a conflict among the Circuits on whether conduct, to be actionable as "abusive work environment" harassment, must "seriously affect an employee's psychological well-being" or lead the plaintiff to "suffer injury."

STATUTE BEING INTERPRETED. Title VII of the Civil Rights Act of 1964 makes it "an unlawful employment practice for an employer . . . to discriminate against any individual with respect to his compensation, terms, conditions, or privileges of employment, because of such individual's race, color, religion, sex, or national origin." 42 U.S.C. §2000e-2(a)(1).

U.S. SUPREME COURT'S REASONING. When the workplace is permeated with discriminatory intimidation, ridicule, and insult that is sufficiently severe or pervasive to alter the conditions of the victim's employment and create an abusive working environment, Title VII is violated. This standard takes a middle path between making actionable any conduct that is merely offensive and requiring the conduct to cause a tangible psychological injury. Mere utterance of an epithet which engenders offensive feelings in an employee does not sufficiently affect the conditions of employment to implicate Title VII. Conduct that is not severe or pervasive enough to create an objectively hostile or abusive work environment—an environment that a reasonable person would find hostile or abusive—is beyond Title VII's purview. Likewise, if the victim does not subjectively perceive the environment to be abusive, the conduct has not actually altered the conditions of the victim's employment, and there is no Title VII violation.

But Title VII comes into play before the harassing conduct leads to a nervous breakdown. A discriminatorily abusive work environment, even one that does not seriously affect employees' psychological well-being, can and often will detract from employees' job performance, discourage employees from remaining on the job, or keep them from advancing in their careers. Moreover, even without regard to these tangible effects, the very fact that the discriminatory conduct was so severe or pervasive that it created a work environment abusive to employees because of their race, gender, religion, or national origin offends Title VII's broad rule of workplace equality.

HOLDING. We therefore believe the district court erred in relying on whether the conduct "seriously affected plaintiff's psychological well-being" or led her to "suffer injury." Such an inquiry may needlessly focus the factfinder's attention on concrete psychological harm, an element Title VII does not require. So long as the environment would reasonably be perceived, and is perceived, as hostile or abusive, there is no need for it also to be psychologically injurious. This is not, and by its nature cannot be, a mathematically precise test. But we can say that whether an environment is "hostile" or "abusive" can be determined only by looking at all the circumstances.

We therefore reverse the judgment of the Court of Appeals, and remand the case for further proceedings consistent with this opinion.

CONCURRING OPINION. GINSBURG, JUSTICE

The critical issue, Title VII's text indicates, is whether members of one sex are exposed to disadvantageous terms or conditions of employment to which members of the other sex are not exposed. The adjudicator's inquiry should center, dominantly, on whether the discriminatory conduct has reasonably interfered with the plaintiff's work performance. To show such interference, the plaintiff need not prove that his or her tangible productivity has declined as a result of the harassment.

Brief of the Case: *Harris v. Forklift Systems, Inc.*

1. Case Name, Citation, and Court

Harris v. Forklift Systems, Inc.
126 L.Ed.2d. 295 (1993)
United States Supreme Court

2. Summary of the Key Facts

A. While Harris worked at Forklift, Hardy continually insulted her because of her gender and made her the target of unwanted sexual innuendos.

B. This conduct created an abusive and hostile work environment, causing Harris to terminate her employment.

C. Harris sued Forklift, alleging sexual harassment in violation of Title VII of the Civil Rights Act of 1964, which makes it an unlawful employment practice for an employer to discriminate in employment because of an individual's sex.

3. The Issue

Must an employee prove that she suffered psychological injury before she can prove a Title VII claim for sexual harassment against her employer?

4. The Holding

No. The Supreme Court remanded the case for further proceedings consistent with its opinion.

5. Summary of the Court's Reasoning

The Supreme Court held that a workplace that is permeated with discriminatory intimidation, ridicule, and insult so severe that it alters the conditions of the victim's employment creates an abusive and hostile work environment that violates Title VII. The Court held that the victim is not required to prove that she suffered tangible psychological injury to prove her Title VII claim. The Court noted that Title VII comes into play before the harassing conduct leads the victim to have a nervous breakdown.

FOR BRIEFING

PGA TOUR, Inc. v. Martin
121 S.Ct. 1879, 149 L.Ed.2d 904 (2001)

CASE NAME
CITATION   2001 U.S. LEXIS 4115
COURT   Supreme Court of the United States

OPINION OF THE COURT. STEVEN, JUSTICE

ISSUE. This case raises two questions concerning the application of the Americans with Disabilities Act of 1990 [42 U.S.C. § 12101 *et seq.*] to a gifted athlete: first, whether the Act protects access to professional golf tournaments by a qualified entrant with a disability; and second, whether a disabled contestant may be denied the use of a golf cart because it would "fundamentally alter the nature" of the tournaments to allow him to ride when all other contestants must walk.

FACTS. Petitioner PGA TOUR, Inc., a nonprofit entity formed in 1968, sponsors and cosponsors professional golf tournaments conducted on three annual tours. About 200 golfers participate in the PGA TOUR; about 170 in the NIKE TOUR; and about 100 in the SENIOR PGA TOUR. PGA TOUR and NIKE TOUR tournaments typically are 4-day events, played on courses leased and operated by petitioner. The revenues generated by television, admissions, concessions, and contributions from cosponsors amount to about $300 million a year, much of which is distributed in prize money. The "Conditions of Competition and Local Rules," often described as the "hard card," apply specifically to petitioner's professional tours. The hard cards for the PGA TOUR and NIKE TOUR require players to walk the golf course during tournaments, but not during open qualifying rounds. On the SENIOR PGA TOUR, which is limited to golfers age 50 and older, the contestants may use golf carts. Most seniors, however, prefer to walk.

RESPONDENT. Casey Martin is a talented golfer. As an amateur, he won 17 Oregon Golf Association junior events before he was 15, and won the state championship as a high school senior. He played on the Stanford University golf team that won the 1994 National Collegiate Athletic Association (NCAA) championship. As a professional, Martin qualified for the NIKE TOUR in 1998 and 1999, and based on his 1999 performance, qualified for the PGA TOUR in 2000. In the 1999 season, he entered 24 events, made the cut 13 times, and had 6 top-10 finishes, coming in second twice and third once.

Martin is also an individual with a disability as defined in the Americans with Disabilities Act of 1990 (ADA or Act). Since birth he has been afflicted with Klippel-Trenaunay-Weber Syndrome, a degenerative circulatory disorder that obstructs the flow of blood from his right leg back to his heart. The disease is progressive; it causes severe pain and has atrophied his right leg. During the latter part of his college career, because of the progress of the disease, Martin could no longer walk an 18-hole golf course. Walking not only caused him pain, fatigue, and anxiety, but also created a significant risk of hemorrhaging, developing blood clots, and fracturing his tibia so badly that an amputation might be required.

When Martin turned pro and entered the petitioner's Qualifying-School, the hard card permitted him to use a cart during his successful progress through the first two stages. He made a request, supported by detailed medical records, for permission to use a golf cart during the third stage. Petitioner refused to review those records, or to waive its walking rule for the third stage. Martin therefore filed this action.

DISTRICT COURT'S DECISION
994 F.SUPP. 1242 [DISTRICT: OREGON (1998)] At trial, petitioner PGA TOUR did not contest the conclusion that Martin has a disability covered by the ADA, or the fact that his disability prevents him from walking the course during a round of golf. Rather, petitioner asserted that the condition of walking is a substantive rule of competition, and that waiving it as to any individual for any reason would fundamentally alter the nature of the competition. Petitioner's evidence included the testimony of a number of experts, among them some of the greatest golfers in history. Arnold Palmer, Jack Nicklaus, and Ken Venturi explained that fatigue can be a critical factor in a tournament, particularly on the last day when psychological pressure is at a maximum. Their testimony makes it clear that, in their view, permission to use a cart might well give some players a competitive advantage over other players who must walk.

The judge found that the purpose of the rule was to inject fatigue into the skill of shot-making, but that the fatigue injected "by walking the course cannot be deemed significant under normal circumstances." Furthermore, Martin presented evidence, and the judge found, that even with the use of a cart, Martin must walk over a mile during an 18-hole round, and that the fatigue he suffers from coping with his disability is "undeniably greater" than the fatigue his able-bodied competitors endure from walking the course. As a result, the judge concluded that it would "not fundamentally alter the nature of the PGA Tour's game to accommodate him with a cart." The judge accordingly entered a permanent injunction requiring petitioner to permit Martin to use a cart in tour and qualifying events.

COURT OF APPEALS DECISION
204 F.3D 994 [9TH CIRCUIT (2000)] The Court of Appeals concluded that golf courses remain places of public accommodation during PGA tournaments. On the merits, because there was no serious dispute about the fact that permitting Martin to use a golf cart was both a reasonable and a necessary solution to the problem of providing him access to the tournaments, the Court of Appeals regarded the central dispute as whether such permission would "fundamentally alter" the nature of the PGA TOUR or NIKE TOUR. Like the District Court, the Court of Appeals viewed the issue not as "whether use of carts generally would fundamentally alter the competition, but whether the use of a cart by Martin would do so." That issue turned on "an intensively fact-based inquiry," and, the court concluded, had been correctly resolved by the trial judge. In its words, "all that the cart does is permit Martin access to a type of competition in which he otherwise could not engage because of his disability."

FEDERAL STATUTE BEING INTERPRETED. Congress enacted the ADA in 1990 to remedy widespread discrimination against disabled individuals. To effectuate its sweeping purpose, the ADA forbids discrimination against disabled individuals in major areas of public life, among them employment (Title I of the Act), public services (Title II), and public accommodations (Title III). At issue now is the applicability of Title III to petitioner's golf tours and qualifying rounds, in particular to petitioner's treatment of a qualified disabled golfer wishing to compete in those events.

U.S. SUPREME COURT'S REASONING. It seems apparent, from both the general rule and the comprehensive definition of "public accommodation," that petitioner's golf tours and their qualifying rounds fit comfortably within the coverage of Title III, and Martin within its protection. The events occur on "golf courses," a type of place specifically identified by the Act as a public accommodation. Section 12181(7)(L). In this case, the narrow dispute is whether allowing Martin to use a golf cart, despite the walking requirement that applies to the PGA TOUR, the NIKE TOUR, and the third stage of the Qualifying-School, is a modification that would "fundamentally alter the nature" of those events.

As an initial matter, we observe that the use of carts is not itself inconsistent with the fundamental character of the game of golf. From early on, the essence of the game has been shot-making—using clubs to cause a ball to progress from the teeing ground to a hole some distance away with as few strokes as possible. Golf carts started appearing with increasing regularity on American golf courses in the 1950's. Today they are everywhere. And they are encouraged. For one thing, they often speed up play, and for another, they are great revenue producers. There is nothing in the Rules of Golf that either forbids the use of carts, or penalizes a player for using a cart.

Petitioner, however, distinguishes the game of golf as it is generally played from the game that it sponsors in the PGA TOUR, NIKE TOUR, and the last stage of the Qualifying-School—golf at the "highest level." According to petitioner, "the goal of the highest-level competitive athletics is to assess and compare the performance of different competitors, a task that is meaningful only if the competitors are subject to identical substantive rules." The waiver of any possibly "outcome-affecting" rule for a contestant would violate this principle and therefore, in petitioner's view, fundamentally alter the nature of the highest level athletic event. The walking rule is one such rule, petitioner submits, because its purpose is "to inject the element of fatigue into the skill of shot-making," and thus its effect may be the critical loss of a stroke. As a consequence, the reasonable modification Martin seeks would fundamentally alter the nature of petitioner's highest level tournaments.

The force of petitioner's argument is, first of all, mitigated by the fact that golf is a game in which it is impossible to guarantee that all competitors will play under exactly the same conditions or that an individual's ability will be the sole determinant of the outcome. For example, changes in the weather may produce harder greens and more head winds for the tournament leader than for his closest pursuers. A lucky bounce may save a shot or two. Whether such happenstance events are more or less probable than the likelihood that a golfer afflicted with Klippel-Trenaunay-Weber Syndrome would one day qualify for the NIKE TOUR and PGA TOUR, they at least demonstrate that pure chance may have a greater impact on the outcome of elite golf tournaments than the fatigue resulting from the enforcement of the walking rule.

Further, the factual basis of petitioner's argument is undermined by the District Court's finding that the fatigue from walking during one of petitioner's 4-day tournaments cannot be deemed significant. The District Court credited the testimony of a professor in physiology and expert on fatigue, who calculated the calories expended in walking a golf course (about five miles) to be approximately 500 calories—"nutritionally less than a Big Mac." What is more, that energy is expended over a 5-hour period, during which golfers have numerous intervals for rest and refreshment. In fact, the expert concluded, because golf is a low intensity activity, fatigue from the game is primarily a psychological phenomenon in which stress and motivation are the key ingredients. And even under conditions of severe heat and humidity, the critical factor in fatigue is fluid loss rather than exercise from walking. Moreover, when given the option of using a cart, the majority of golfers in petitioner's tournaments have chosen to walk, often to relieve stress or for other strategic reasons. As NIKE TOUR member Eric Johnson testified, walking allows him to keep in rhythm, stay warmer when it is chilly, and develop a better sense of the elements and the course than riding in a cart. As we have demonstrated, the walking rule is at best peripheral to the nature of petitioner's athletic events, and thus it might be waived in individual cases without working a fundamental alteration.

HOLDING AND REMEDY. Under the ADA's basic requirement that the need of a disabled person be evaluated on an individual basis, we have no doubt that allowing Martin to use a golf cart would not fundamentally alter the nature of petitioner's tournaments. As we have discussed, the purpose of the walking rule is to subject players to fatigue, which in turn may influence the outcome of tournaments. Even if the rule does serve that purpose, it is an uncontested finding of the District Court that Martin "easily endures greater fatigue even with a cart than his able-bodied competitors do by walking." The purpose of the walking rule is therefore not compromised in the slightest by allowing Martin to use a cart. A modification that provides an exception to a peripheral tournament rule without impairing its purpose cannot be said to "fundamentally alter" the tournament. What it can be said to do, on the other hand, is to allow Martin the chance to qualify for and compete in the athletic events petitioner

offers to those members of the public who have the skill and desire to enter. That is exactly what the ADA requires. As a result, Martin's request for a waiver of the walking rule should have been granted.

The judgment of the Court of Appeals is affirmed. It is so ordered.

DISSENTING OPINION. SCALIA, JUSTICE

In my view today's opinion exercises a benevolent compassion that the law does not place it within our power to impose. The judgment distorts the text of Title III, the structure of the ADA, and common sense. I respectfully dissent.

The Court, for its part, assumes that conclusion for the sake of argument, but pronounces respondent to be a "customer" of the PGA TOUR or of the golf courses on which it is played. That seems to me quite incredible. The PGA TOUR is a professional sporting event, staged for the entertainment of a live and TV audience. The professional golfers on the tour are no more "enjoying" (the statutory term) the entertainment that the tour provides, or the facilities of the golf courses on which it is held, than professional baseball players "enjoy" the baseball games in which they play or the facilities of Yankee Stadium. To be sure, professional baseball players *participate* in the games, and *use* the ballfields, but no one in his right mind would think that they are *customers* of the American League or of Yankee Stadium. They are themselves the entertainment that the customers pay to watch. And professional golfers are no different. A professional golfer's practicing his profession is not comparable to John Q. Public's frequenting "a 232-acre amusement area with swimming, boating, sun bathing, picnicking, miniature golf, dancing facilities, and a snack bar."

Having erroneously held that Title III applies to the "customers" of professional golf who consist of its practitioners, the Court then erroneously answers—or to be accurate simply ignores—a second question. The ADA requires covered businesses to make such reasonable modifications of "policies, practices, or procedures" as are necessary to "afford" goods, services, and privileges to individuals with disabilities; but it explicitly does not require "modifications that would fundamentally alter the nature" of the goods, services, and privileges. Section 12182(b)(2)(A)(ii). In other words, disabled individuals must be given *access* to the same goods, services, and privileges that others enjoy.

A camera store may not refuse to sell cameras to a disabled person, but it is not required to stock cameras specially designed for such persons. It is hardly a feasible judicial function to decide whether shoe stores should sell single shoes to one-legged persons and if so at what price, or how many Braille books the Borders or Barnes and Noble bookstore chains should stock in each of their stores. Eighteen-hole golf courses, 10-foot-high basketball hoops, 90-foot baselines, 100-yard football fields—all are arbitrary and none is essential. The only support for any of them is tradition and (in more modern times) insistence by what has come to be regarded as the ruling body of the sport—both of which factors support the PGA TOUR's position in the present case. One can envision the parents of a Little League player with attention deficit disorder trying to convince a judge that their son's disability makes it at least 25% more difficult to hit a pitched ball. (If they are successful, the only thing that could prevent a court order giving a kid four strikes would be a judicial determination that, in baseball, three strikes are metaphysically necessary, which is quite absurd.)

Agility, strength, speed, balance, quickness of mind, steadiness of nerves, intensity of concentration—these talents are not evenly distributed. No wild-eyed dreamer has ever suggested that the managing bodies of the competitive sports that test precisely these qualities should try to take account of the uneven distribution of God-given gifts when writing and enforcing the rules of competition. And I have no doubt Congress did not authorize misty-eyed judicial supervision of such revolution. The year was 2001, and "everybody was finally equal." K. Vonnegut, Harrison Bergeron, in *Animal Farm and Related Readings* 129 (1997).

Brief of Case: *PGA TOUR, Inc. v. Martin*

1. Case Name, Citation, and Court

PGA TOUR, Inc. v. Martin
121 S.Ct. 1879, 2001 LEXIS 415 (2001)
Supreme Court of the United States

2. Summary of the Key Facts

A. PGA TOUR, Inc. is a nonprofit organization that sponsors professional golf tournaments.

B. The PGA establishes rules for its golf tournaments. A PGA rule requires golfers to walk the golf course, and not use golf carts.

C. Casey Martin is a professional golfer who suffers from Klippel-Trenaunay-Weber Syndrome, a degenerative circulatory disorder that atrophied Martin's right leg and causes him pain, fatigue, and anxiety when walking.

D. When Martin petitioned the PGA to use a golf cart during golf tournaments, the PGA refused.

E. Martin sued the PGA, alleging discrimination against a disabled individual in violation of the American with Disabilities Act of 1990, a federal statute.

3. Issue

Does the Americans with Disabilities Act require the PGA to accommodate Martin by permitting him to use a golf cart while playing in PGA golf tournaments?

4. Holding

Yes. The Supreme Court held that the PGA must allow Martin to use a golf cart when competing in PGA golf tournaments. Affirmed.

5. Court's Reasoning

The Supreme Court held that:

A. Martin was disabled and covered by the Act.

B. Golf courses are "public accommodations" covered by the Act.

C. The use of golf carts is not a fundamental characteristic of the game of golf.

D. Other than the PGA rule, there is no Rule of Golf that forbids the use of golf carts.

E. It is impossible to guarantee all players in golf will play under the exact same conditions, so allowing Martin to use a golf cart gives him no advantage over other golfers.

F. Martin, because of his disease, will probably suffer more fatigue playing golf using a golf cart than other golfers will suffer without using a cart.

G. The PGA's "walking rule" is only peripheral to the game of golf and not a fundamental part of golf.

H. Allowing Martin to use a golf cart will not fundamentally alter the PGA's highest-level professional golf tournaments.

FOR BRIEFING

Palsgraf v. Long Island R.R. Co.	CASE NAME	
248 N.Y. 339 (1928)	CITATION	162 N.E. 99
	COURT	Court of Appeals of the State of New York

OPINION OF THE COURT. CARDOZO, Ch. J.

FACTS. Plaintiff was standing on a platform of defendant's railroad after buying a ticket to go to Rockaway Beach. A train stopped at the station, bound for another place. Two men ran forward to catch it. One of the men reached the platform of the car without mishap, though the train was already moving. The other man, carrying a package, jumped aboard the car, but seemed unsteady as if about to fall. A guard on the car, who had held the door open, reached forward to help him in, and another guard on the platform pushed him from behind. In this act, the package was dislodged, and fell upon the rails. It was a package of small size, about fifteen inches long, and was covered by a newspaper. In fact it contained fireworks, but there was nothing in its appearance to give notice of its contents. The fireworks when they fell exploded. The shock of the explosion threw down some scales at the other end of the platform, many feet away. The scales struck the plaintiff, causing injuries for which she sues.

The conduct of the defendant's guard, if a wrong in its relation to the holder of the package, was not a wrong in its relation to the plaintiff, standing far away. Relatively to her it was not negligence at all. Nothing in the situation gave notice that the falling package had in it the potency of peril to persons thus removed. Negligence is not actionable unless it involves the invasion of a legally protected interest, the violation of a right. "Proof of negligence in the air, so to speak, will not do" (Pollock, *Torts* [11th ed.], p. 455; *Martin v. Herzog*, 228 N.Y. 164, 170; cf. Salmond, Torts [6th ed.], p.24). "Negligence is the absence of care, according to the circumstances" (WILLES, J., in *Vaughan v. Taff Vale Ry. Co.*, 5 H. & N. 679, 688; 1 Beven, Negligence [4th ed.], 7; *Paul v. Consol. Fireworks Co.*, 212 N.Y. 117; *Adams v. Bullock*, 227 N.Y. 208, 211; *Parrott v. Wells-Fargo Co.*, 15 Wall. [U.S.] 524). The plaintiff as she stood upon the platform of the station might claim to be protected against intentional invasion of her bodily security. Such invasion is not charged. She might claim to be protected against unintentional invasion by conduct involving in the thought of reasonable men an unreasonable hazard that such invasion would ensue. These, from the point of view of the law, were the bounds of her immunity, with perhaps some rare exceptions, survivals for the most part of ancient forms of liability, where conduct is held to be at the peril of the actor (*Sullivan v. Dunham*, 161 N.Y. 290 Page 342). If no hazard was apparent to the eye of ordinary vigilance, an act innocent and harmless, at least to outward seeming, with reference to her, did not take to itself the quality of a tort because it happened to be a wrong, though apparently not one involving the risk of bodily insecurity, with reference to some one else. "In every instance, before negligence can be predicated of a given act, back of the act must be sought and found a duty to the individual complaining, the observance of which would have averted or avoided the injury" (McSHERRY, C.J., in *W. Va. Central R. Co. v. State*, 96 Md. 652, 666; cf. *Norfolk & Western Ry. Co. v. Wood*, 99 Va. 156, 158, 159; *Hughes v. Boston & Maine R.R. Co.*, 71 N.H. 279, 284; *U.S. Express Co. v. Everest*, 72 Kan. 517; *Emry v. Roanoke Nav. Co.*, 111 N.C. 94, 95; *Vaughan v. Transit Dev. Co.*, 222 N.Y. 79; *Losee v. Clute*, 51 N.Y. 494; *DiCaprio v. N.Y.C.R.R. Co.*, 231 N.Y. 94; 1 Shearman & Redfield on Negligence, § 8, and cases cited; Cooley on Torts [3d ed.], p. 1411; Jaggard on Torts, vol. 2, p.826; Wharton, *Negligence*, § 24; Bohlen, *Studies in the Law of Torts*, p. 601). "The ideas of negligence and duty are strictly correlative" (BOWEN, L.J., in *Thomas v. Quartermaine*, 18 Q.B.D. 685, 694). The plaintiff sues in her own right for a wrong personal to her, and not as the vicarious beneficiary of a breach of duty to another.

A different conclusion will involve us, and swiftly too, in a maze of contradictions. A guard stumbles over a package which has been left upon a platform. It seems to be a bundle of newspapers. It turns out to be a can of dynamite. To the eye of ordinary vigilance, the bundle is abandoned waste, which may be kicked or trod on with impunity. Is a passenger at the other end of the platform protected by the law against the unsuspected hazard concealed beneath the waste? If not, is the result to be any different, so far as the distant passenger is concerned, when the guard stumbles over a valise which a truckman or a porter has left upon the walk? The passenger far away, if the victim of a wrong at all, has a cause of action, not derivative, but original and primary. His claim to be protected against invasion of his bodily security is neither greater nor less because the act resulting in the invasion is a wrong to another far removed. In this case, the rights that are said to have been violated, the interests said to have been invaded, are not even of the same order. The man was not injured in his person nor even put in danger. The purpose of the act, as well as its effect, was to make his person safe. If there was a wrong to him at all, which may very well be doubted, it was a wrong to a property interest only, the safety of his package. Out of this wrong to property, which threatened injury to nothing else, there has passed, we are told, to the plaintiff by derivation or succession a right of action for the invasion of an interest of another order, the right to bodily security. The diversity of interests emphasizes the futility of the effort to build the plaintiff's right upon the basis of a wrong to some one else. The gain is one of emphasis, for a like result would follow if the interests were the same. Even then, the orbit of the danger as disclosed to the eye of reasonable vigilance would be the orbit of the duty. One who jostles one's neighbor in a crowd does not invade

the rights of others standing at the outer fringe when the unintended contact casts a bomb upon the ground. The wrongdoer as to them is the man who carries the bomb, not the one who explodes it without suspicion of the danger. Life will have to be made over, and human nature transformed, before prevision so extravagant can be accepted as the norm of conduct, the customary standard to which behavior must conform. The argument for the plaintiff is built upon the shifting meanings of such words as "wrong" and "wrongful," and shares their instability. What the plaintiff must show is "a wrong" to herself, i.e., a violation of her own right, and not merely a wrong to some one else, nor conduct "wrongful" because unsocial, but not "a wrong" to any one. We are told that one who drives at reckless speed through a crowded city street is guilty of a negligent act and, therefore, of a wrongful one irrespective of the consequences. Negligent the act is, and wrongful in the sense that it is unsocial, but wrongful and unsocial in relation to other travelers, only because the eye of vigilance perceives the risk of damage. If the same act were to be committed on a speedway or a race course, it would lose its wrongful quality. The risk reasonably to be perceived defines the duty to be obeyed, and risk imports relation; it is risk to another or to others within the range of apprehension (Seavey, Negligence, Subjective or Objective, 41 H.L. Rv. 6; *Boronkay v. Robinson & Carpenter*, 247 N.Y. 365). This does not mean, of course, that one who launches a destructive force is always relieved of liability if the force, though known to be destructive, pursues an unexpected path. "It was not necessary that the defendant should have had notice of the particular method in which an accident would occur, if the possibility of an accident was clear to the ordinarily prudent eye" (*Munsey v. Webb*, 231 U.S. 150, 156; *Condran v. Park & Tilford*, 213 N.Y. 341, 345; *Robert v. U.S.E.F. Corp.*, 240 N.Y. 474, 477). Some acts, such as shooting, are so imminently dangerous to any one who may come within reach of the missile, however unexpectedly, as to impose a duty of prevision not far from that of an insurer. Even today, and much oftener in earlier stages of the law, one acts sometimes at one's peril (Jeremiah Smith, Tort and Absolute Liability, 30 H.L. Rv. 328; Street, *Foundations of Legal Liability*, vol. 1, pp. 77, 78). Under this head, it may be, fall certain cases of what is known as transferred intent, an act willfully dangerous to A resulting by misadventure in injury to B (*Talmage v. Smith*, 101 Mich. 370, 374) These cases aside, wrong is defined in terms of the natural or probable, at least when unintentional (*Parrot v. Wells-Fargo Co.* [The Nitro-Glycerine Case], 15 Wall. [U.S.] 524). The range of reasonable apprehension is at times a question for the court, and at times, if varying inferences are possible, a question for the jury. Here, by concession, there was nothing in the situation to suggest to the most cautious mind that the parcel wrapped in newspaper would spread wreckage through the station. If the guard had thrown it down knowingly and willfully, he would not have threatened the plaintiff's safety, so far as appearances could warn him. His conduct would not have involved, even then, an unreasonable probability of invasion of her bodily security. Liability can be no greater where the act is inadvertent.

Negligence, like risk, is thus a term of relation. Negligence in the abstract, apart from things related, is surely not a tort, if indeed it is understandable at all (BOWEN, L.J., in *Thomas v. Quartermaine*, 18 Q.B.D. 685, 694). Negligence is not a tort unless it results in the commission of a wrong, and the commission of a wrong imports the violation of a right, in this case, we are told, the right to be protected against interference with one's bodily security. But bodily security is protected, not against all forms of interference or aggression, but only against some. One who seeks redress at law does not make out a cause of action by showing without more that there has been damage to his person. If the harm was not willful, he must show that the act as to him had possibilities of danger so many and apparent as to entitle him to be protected against the doing of it though the harm was unintended. Affront to personality is still the keynote of the wrong. Confirmation of this view will be found in the history and development of the action on the case. Negligence as a basis of civil liability was unknown to mediaeval law (8 Holdsworth, *History of English Law*, p. 449; Street, *Foundations of Legal Liability*, vol. 1, pp. 189, 190). For damage to the person, the sole remedy was trespass, and trespass did not lie in the absence of aggression, and that direct and personal (Holdsworth, op. cit. p. 453; Street, op. cit. vol. 3, pp. 258, 260, vol. 1, pp. 71, 74.) Liability for other damage, as where a servant without orders from the master does or omits something to the damage of another, is a plant of later growth (Holdsworth, op. cit. 450, 457;Wigmore, *Responsibility or Tortious Acts*, vol. 3, *Essays in Anglo-American Legal History*, 520, 523, 526, 533). When it emerged out of the legal soil, it was thought of as a variant of trespass, an offshoot of the parent stock. This appears in the form of action, which was known as trespass on the case (Holdsworth, op. cit. p. 449; cf. *Scott v. Shepard*, 2 Wm. Black. 892; Green, *Rationale of Proximate Cause*, p. 19). The victim does not sue derivatively, or by right of subrogation, to vindicate an interest invaded in the person of another. Thus to view his cause of action is to ignore the fundamental difference between tort and crime (Holland, *Jurisprudence* [12th ed.], p.328). He sues for breach of a duty owing to himself.

The law of causation, remote or proximate, is thus foreign to the case before us. The question of liability is always anterior to the question of the measure of the consequences that go with liability. If there is no tort to be redressed, there is no occasion to consider what damage might be recovered if there were a finding of a tort. We may assume, without deciding, that negligence, not at large or in the abstract, but in relation to the plaintiff, would entail liability for any and all consequences, however novel or extraordinary (*Bird v. St. Paul F. & M. Ins. Co.*, 224 N.Y. 47, 54; *Ehrgott v. Mayor, etc., of N Y*, 96 N.Y. 264; *Smith v. London & S.W. Ry. Co.*, L.R. 6 C.P. 14; 1 Beven, Negligence, 106; Street, op. cit. vol. 1, p.

90; Green, *Rationale of Proximate Cause*, pp. 88, 118; cf. *Matter of Polemis*, L.R. 1921, 3 K.B. 560; 44 *Law Quarterly Review*, 142). There is room for argument that a distinction is to be drawn according to the diversity of interests invaded by the act, as where conduct negligent in that it threatens an insignificant invasion of an interest in property results in an unforeseeable invasion of an interest of another order, as, e.g., one of bodily security. Perhaps other distinctions may be necessary. We do not go into the question now. The consequences to be followed must first be rooted in a wrong.

HOLDING. The judgment of the Appellate Division and that of the Trial Term should be reversed, and the complaint dismissed, with costs in all courts.

DISSENTING OPINION. ANDREWS, J.

Assisting a passenger to board a train, the defendant's servant negligently knocked a package from his arms. It fell between the platform and the cars. Of its contents the servant knew and could know nothing. A violent explosion followed. The concussion broke some scales standing a considerable distance away. In falling they injured the plaintiff, an intending passenger.

Upon these facts may she recover the damages she has suffered in an action brought against the master? The result we shall reach depends upon our theory as to the nature of negligence. Is it a relative concept—the breach of some duty owing to a particular person or to particular persons? Or where there is an act which unreasonably threatens the safety of others, is the doer liable for all its proximate consequences, even where they result in injury to one who would generally be thought to be outside the radius of danger? This is not a mere dispute as to words. We might not believe that to the average mind the dropping of the bundle would seem to involve the probability of harm to the plaintiff standing many feet away whatever might be the case as to the owner or to one so near as to be likely to be struck by its fall. If, however, we adopt the second hypothesis we have to inquire only as to the relation between cause and effect. We deal in terms of proximate cause, not of negligence.

Negligence may be defined roughly as an act or omission which unreasonably does or may affect the rights of others, or which unreasonably fails to protect oneself from the dangers resulting from such acts. Here I confine myself to the first branch of the definition. Nor do I comment on the word "unreasonable." For present purposes it sufficiently describes that average of conduct that society requires of its members.

There must be both the act or the omission, and the right. It is the act itself, not the intent of the actor, that is important. (*Hover v. Barkhoof*, 44 N.Y. 113; *Mertz v. Connecticut Co.*, 217 N.Y. 475.) In criminal law both the intent and the result are to be considered. Intent again is material in tort actions, where punitive damages are sought, dependent on actual malice—not on merely reckless conduct. But here neither insanity nor infancy lessens responsibility. (*Williams v. Hays*, 143 N.Y. 442.)

As has been said, except in cases of contributory negligence, there must be rights which are or may be affected. Often though injury has occurred, no rights of him who suffers have been touched. A licensee or trespasser upon my land has no claim to affirmative care on my part that the land be made safe. (*Meiers v. Koch Brewery*, 229 N.Y. 10.) Where a railroad is required to fence its tracks against cattle, no man's rights are injured should he wander upon the road because such fence is absent. (*DiCaprio v. N.Y.C.R.R.*, 231 N.Y. 94.) An unborn child may not demand immunity from personal harm. (Drobner v. Peters, 232 N.Y. 220.)

But we are told that "there is no negligence unless there is in the particular case a legal duty to take care, and this duty must be one which is owed to the plaintiff himself and not merely to others." (Salmond Torts [6th ed.], 24.) This, I think too narrow a conception. Where there is the unreasonable act, and some right that may be affected there is negligence whether damage does or does not result. That is immaterial. Should we drive down Broadway at a reckless speed, we are negligent whether we strike an approaching car or miss it by an inch. The act itself is wrongful. It is a wrong not only to those who happen to be within the radius of danger but to all who might have been there—a wrong to the public at large. Such is the language of the street. Such the language of the courts when speaking of contributory negligence. Such again and again their language in speaking of the duty of some defendant and discussing proximate cause in cases where such a discussion is wholly irrelevant on any other theory. (*Perry v. Rochester Line Co.*, 219 N.Y. 60.) As was said by Mr. Justice HOLMES many years ago, "the measure of the defendant's duty in determining whether a wrong has been committed is one thing, the measure of liability when a wrong has been committed is another." (*Spade v. Lynn & Boston R.R. Co.*, 172 Mass. 488.) Due care is a duty imposed on each one of us to protect society from unnecessary danger, not to protect A, B or C alone.

It may well be that there is no such thing as negligence in the abstract. "Proof of negligence in the air, so to speak, will not do." In an empty world negligence would not exist. It does involve a relationship between man and his fellows. But not merely a relationship between man and those whom he might reasonably expect his act would injure. Rather, a relationship between him and those whom he does in fact injure. If his act has a tendency to harm some one, it harms him a mile away as surely as it does those on the scene. We now permit children to recover for the negligent killing of the father. It was never prevented on the theory that no duty was owing to them. A husband may be compensated for the loss of his wife's services. To say that the wrongdoer was negligent as to the husband as well as to the wife is merely an attempt to fit facts to theory. An insurance company paying a fire loss recovers its payment of the negligent incendiary. We speak of subrogation—of suing in the right of the insured.

Behind the cloud of words is the fact they hide, that the act, wrongful as to the insured, has also injured the company. Even if it be true that the fault of father, wife or insured will prevent recovery, it is because we consider the original negligence not the proximate cause of the injury. (Pollock, *Torts* [12th ed.], 463.)

In the well-known *Polemis* case (1921, 3 K.B. 560), SCRUTTON, L.J., said that the dropping of a plank was negligent for it might injure "workman or cargo or ship." Because of either possibility the owner of the vessel was to be made good for his loss. The act being wrongful the doer was liable for its proximate results. Criticized and explained as this statement may have been, I think it states the law as it should be and as it is. (*Smith v. London & Southwestern Ry. Co.*, [1870-71] 6 C.P. 14; *Anthony v. Slaid*, 52 Mass. 290; *Wood v. Penn. R.R.Co.*, 177 Penn. St. 306; *Trashansky v. Hershkovitz*, 239 N.Y. 452.)

The proposition is this. Every one owes to the world at large the duty of refraining from those acts that may unreasonably threaten the safety of others. Such an act occurs. Not only is he wronged to whom harm might reasonably be expected to result, but he also who is in fact injured, even if he be outside what would generally be thought the danger zone. There needs be duty due the one complaining but this is not a duty to a particular individual because as to him harm might be expected. Harm to some one being the natural result of the act, not only that one alone, but all those in fact injured may complain. We have never, I think, held otherwise. Indeed in the Di Caprio case we said that a breach of a general ordinance defining the degree of care to be exercised in one's calling is evidence of negligence as to every one. We did not limit this statement to those who might be expected to be exposed to danger. Unreasonable risk being taken, its consequences are not confined to those who might probably be hurt.

If this be so, we do not have a plaintiff suing by "derivation or succession." Her action is original and primary. Her claim is for a breach of duty to herself—not that she is subrogated to any right of action of the owner of the parcel or of a passenger standing at the scene of the explosion.

The right to recover damages rests on additional considerations. The plaintiff's rights must be injured, and this injury must be caused by the negligence. We build a dam, but are negligent as to its foundations. Breaking, it injures property down stream. We are not liable if all this happened because of some reason other than the insecure foundation. But when injuries do result from our unlawful act we are liable for the consequences. It does not matter that they are unusual, unexpected, unforeseen and unforeseeable. But there is one limitation. The damages must be so connected with the negligence that the latter may be said to be the proximate cause of the former.

These two words have never been given an inclusive definition. What is a cause in a legal sense, still more what is a proximate cause, depend in each case upon many considerations, as does the existence of negligence itself. Any philosophical doctrine of causation does not help us. A boy throws a stone into a pond. The ripples spread. The water level rises. The history of that pond is altered to all eternity. It will be altered by other causes also. Yet it will be forever the resultant of all causes combined. Each one will have an influence. How great only omniscience can say. You may speak of a chain, or if you please, a net. An analogy is of little aid. Each cause brings about future events. Without each the future would not be the same. Each is proximate in the sense it is essential. But that is not what we mean by the word. Nor on the other hand do we mean sole cause. There is no such thing.

Should analogy be thought helpful, however, I prefer that of a stream. The spring, starting on its journey, is joined by tributary after tributary. The river, reaching the ocean, comes from a hundred sources. No man may say whence any drop of water is derived. Yet for a time distinction may be possible. Into the clear creek, brown swamp water flows from the left. Later, from the right comes water stained by its clay bed. The three may remain for a space, sharply divided. But at last, inevitably no trace of separation remains. They are so commingled that all distinction is lost.

As we have said, we cannot trace the effect of an act to the end, if end there is. Again, however, we may trace it part of the way. A murder at Sarajevo may be the necessary antecedent to an assassination in London twenty years hence. An overturned lantern may burn all Chicago. We may follow the fire from the shed to the last building. We rightly say the fire started by the lantern caused its destruction.

A cause, but not the proximate cause. What we do mean by the word proximate" is, that because of convenience, of public policy, of a rough sense of justice, the law arbitrarily declines to trace a series of events beyond a certain point. This is not logic. It is practical politics. Take our rule as to fires. Sparks from my burning haystack set on fire my house and my neighbor's. I may recover from a negligent railroad. He may not. Yet the wrongful act as directly harmed the one as the other. We may regret that the line was drawn just where it was, but drawn somewhere it had to be. We said the act of the railroad was not the proximate cause of our neighbor's fire. Cause it surely was. The words we used were simply indicative of our notions of public policy. Other courts think differently. But somewhere they reach the point where they cannot say the stream comes from any one source.

Take the illustration given in an unpublished manuscript by a distinguished and helpful writer on the law of torts. A chauffeur negligently collides with another car which is filled with dynamite, although he could not know it. An explosion follows. A, walking on the sidewalk nearby, is killed. B, sitting in a window of a building opposite, is cut by flying glass. C, likewise sitting in a window a block away, is similarly injured. And a further illustration. A nursemaid, ten blocks away, startled by the noise, involuntarily drops a baby from her arms to the walk. We are told that C may not

recover while A may. As to B it is a question for court or jury. We will all agree that the baby might not. Because, we are again told, the chauffeur had no reason to believe his conduct involved any risk of injuring either C or the baby. As to them he was not negligent.

But the chauffeur, being negligent in risking the collision, his belief that the scope of the harm he might do would be limited is immaterial. His act unreasonably jeopardized the safety of any one who might be affected by it. C's injury and that of the baby were directly traceable to the collision. Without that, the injury would not have happened. C had the right to sit in his office, secure from such dangers. The baby was entitled to use the sidewalk with reasonable safety.

The true theory is, it seems to me, that the injury to C, if in truth he is to be denied recovery, and the injury to the baby is that their several injuries were not the proximate result of the negligence. And here not what the chauffeur had reason to believe would be the result of his conduct, but what the prudent would foresee, may have a bearing. May have some bearing, for the problem of proximate cause is not to be solved by any one consideration.

It is all a question of expediency. There are no fixed rules to govern our judgment. There are simply matters of which we may take account. We have in a somewhat different connection spoken of "the stream of events." We have asked whether that stream was deflected—whether it was forced into new and unexpected channels. (*Donnelly v. Piercy Contracting Co.*, 222 N.Y. 210). This is rather rhetoric than law. There is in truth little to guide us other than common sense.

There are some hints that may help us. The proximate cause, involved as it may be with many other causes, must be, at the least, something without which the event would not happen. The court must ask itself whether there was a natural and continuous sequence between cause and effect. Was the one a substantial factor in producing the other? Was there a direct connection between them, without too many intervening causes? Is the effect of cause on result not too attenuated? Is the cause likely, in the usual judgment of mankind, to produce the result? Or by the exercise of prudent foresight could the result be foreseen? Is the result too remote from the cause, and here we consider remoteness in time and space. (*Bird v. St. Paul F. & M. Ins. Co.*, 224 N.Y. 47, where we passed upon the construction of a contract—but something was also said on this subject.) Clearly we must so consider, for the greater the distance either in time or space, the more surely do other causes intervene to affect the result. When a lantern is overturned the firing of a shed is a fairly direct consequence. Many things contribute to the spread of the conflagration—the force of the wind, the direction and width of streets, the character of intervening structures, other factors. We draw an uncertain and wavering line, but draw it we must as best we can.

Once again, it is all a question of fair judgment, always keeping in mind the fact that we endeavor to make a rule in each case that will be practical and in keeping with the general understanding of mankind.

Here another question must be answered. In the case supposed it is said, and said correctly, that the chauffeur is liable for the direct effect of the explosion although he had no reason to suppose it would follow a collision. "The fact that the injury occurred in a different manner than that which might have been expected does not prevent the chauffeur's negligence from being in law the cause of the injury." But the natural results of a negligent act—the results which a prudent man would or should foresee—do have a bearing upon the decision as to proximate cause. We have said so repeatedly. What should be foreseen? No human foresight would suggest that a collision itself might injure one a block away. On the contrary, given an explosion, such a possibility might be reasonably expected. I think the direct connection, the foresight of which the courts peak, assumes prevision of the explosion, for the immediate results of which, at least, the chauffeur is responsible.

It may be said this is unjust. Why? In fairness he should make good every injury flowing from his negligence. Not because of tenderness toward him we say he need not answer for all that follows his wrong. We look back to the catastrophe, the fire kindled by the spark, or the explosion. We trace the consequences—not indefinitely, but to a certain point. And to aid us in fixing that point we ask what might ordinarily be expected to follow the fire or the explosion.

This last suggestion is the factor which must determine the case before us. The act upon which defendant's liability rests is knocking an apparently harmless package onto the platform. The act was negligent. For its proximate consequences the defendant is liable. If its contents were broken, to the owner; if it fell upon and crushed a passenger's foot, then to him. If it exploded and injured one in the immediate vicinity, to him also as to A in the illustration. Mrs. Palsgraf was standing some distance away. How far cannot be told from the record—apparently twenty-five or thirty feet. Perhaps less. Except for the explosion, she would not have been injured. We are told by the appellant in his brief "it cannot be denied that the explosion was the direct cause of the plaintiff's injuries." So it was a substantial factor in producing the result—there was here a natural and continuous sequence—direct connection. The only intervening cause was that instead of blowing her to the ground the concussion smashed the weighing machine which in turn fell upon her. There was no remoteness in time, little in space. And surely, given such an explosion as here it needed no great foresight to predict that the natural result would be to injure one on the platform at no greater distance from its scene than was the plaintiff. Just how no one might be able to predict. Whether by flying fragments, by broken glass, by wreckage of machines or structures no one could say. But injury in some form was most probable.

Under these circumstances I cannot say as a matter of law that the plaintiff's injuries were not the proximate result of the negligence. That is all we have before us. The court refused to so charge. No request was made to submit the matter to the jury as a question of fact, even would that have been proper upon the record before us.

The judgment appealed from should be affirmed, with costs.

NATIONAL FEDERATION OF PARALEGAL ASSOCIATIONS, INC.

Model Code of Ethics and Professional Rsponsibility and Guidelines for Enforcement*

PREAMBLE

The National Federation of Paralegal Associations, Inc. ("NFPA") is a professional organization comprised of paralegal associations and individual paralegals throughout the United States and Canada. Members of NFPA have varying backgrounds, experiences, education and job responsibilities that reflect the diversity of the paralegal profession. NFPA promotes the growth, development and recognition of the paralegal profession as an integral partner in the delivery of legal services.

In May 1993 NFPA adopted its Model Code of Ethics and Professional Responsibility ("Model Code") to delineate the principles for ethics and conduct to which every paralegal should aspire.

Many paralegal associations throughout the United States have endorsed the concept and content of NFPA's Model Code through the adoption of their own ethical codes. In doing so, paralegals have confirmed the profession's commitment to increase the quality and efficiency of legal services, as well as recognized its responsibilities to the public, the legal community, and colleagues.

Paralegals have recognized, and will continue to recognize, that the profession must continue to evolve to enhance their roles in the delivery of legal services. With increased levels of responsibility comes the need to define and enforce mandatory rules of professional conduct. Enforcement of codes of paralegal conduct is a logical and necessary step to enhance and ensure the confidence of the legal community and the public in the integrity and professional responsibility of paralegals.

In April 1997 NFPA adopted the Model Disciplinary Rules ("Model Rules") to make possible the enforcement of the Canons and Ethical Considerations contained in the NFPA Model Code. A con-current determination was made that the Model Code of Ethics and Professional Responsibility, formerly aspirational in nature, should be recognized as setting forth the enforceable obligations of all paralegals.

The Model Code and Model Rules offer a framework for professional discipline, either voluntarily or through formal regulatory programs.

§1.
NFPA MODEL DISCIPLINARY RULES AND ETHICAL CONSIDERATION

1.1 A Paralegal Shall Achieve and Maintain a High Level of Competence.

ETHICAL CONSIDERATIONS

EC-1.1(a) A paralegal shall achieve competency through education, training, and work experience.

EC-1.1(b) A paralegal shall aspire to participate in a minimum of twelve (12) hours of continuing legal education, to include at least one (1) hour of ethics education, every two (2) years in order to remain current on developments in the law.

EC-1.1(c) A paralegal shall perform all assignments promptly and efficiently.

1.2 A Paralegal Shall Maintain a High Level of Personal and Professional Integrity.

ETHICAL CONSIDERATIONS

EC-1.2(a) A paralegal shall not engage in any ex parte communications involving the courts or any other adjudicatory body in an attempt to exert undue influence or to obtain advantage or the benefit of only one party.

EC-1.2(b) A paralegal shall not communicate, or cause another to communicate, with a party the paralegal knows to be represented by a lawyer in a pending matter without the prior consent of the lawyer representing such other party.

EC-1.2(c) A paralegal shall ensure that all timekeeping and billing records prepared by the paralegal are thorough, accurate, honest, and complete.

EC-1.2(d) A paralegal shall not knowingly engage in fraudulent billing practices. Such practices may include, but are not limited to: inflation of hours billed to a client or employer; misrepresentation of the nature of tasks performed; and/or submission of fraudulent expense and disbursement documentation.

EC-1.2(e) A paralegal shall be scrupulous, thorough and honest in the identification and maintenance of all funds, securities, and other assets of a client and shall provide accurate accounting as appropriate.

EC-1.2(f) A paralegal shall advise the proper authority of non-confidential knowledge of any dishonest or fraudulent acts by any person pertaining to the handling of the funds, securities or other assets of a client. The authority to whom the report is made shall depend on the nature and circumstances of the possible misconduct, (e.g., ethics committees of law firms, corporations and/or paralegal associations, local or state bar associations, local prosecutors, administrative agencies, etc.). Failure to report such knowledge is in itself misconduct and shall be treated as such under these rules.

1.3 A Paralegal Shall Maintain a High Standard of Professional Conduct.

ETHICAL CONSIDERATIONS

EC-1.3(a) A paralegal shall refrain from engaging in any conduct that offends the dignity and decorum of proceedings before a court or other adjudicatory body and shall be respectful of all rules and procedures.

EC-1.3(b) A paralegal shall avoid impropriety and the appearance of impropriety and shall not engage in any conduct that would adversely affect his/her fitness to practice. Such conduct may include, but is not limited to: violence, dishonesty, interference with the administration of justice, and/or abuse of a professional position or public office.

EC-1.3(c) Should a paralegal's fitness to practice be compromised by physical or mental illness, causing that paralegal to commit an act that is in direct violation of the Model Code/Model Rules and/or the rules and/or laws governing the jurisdiction in which the paralegal practices, that paralegal may be protected from sanction upon review of the nature and circumstances of that illness.

EC-1.3(d) A paralegal shall advise the proper authority of non-confidential knowledge of any action of another legal professional that clearly demonstrates fraud, deceit, dishonesty, or misrepresentation. The authority to whom the report is made shall depend on the nature and circumstances of the possible misconduct, (e.g., ethics committees of law firms, corporations and/or paralegal associations, local or state bar associations, local prosecutors, administrative agencies, etc.). Failure to report such knowledge is in itself misconduct and shall be treated as such under these rules.

EC-1.3(e) A paralegal shall not knowingly assist any individual with the commission of an act that is in direct violation of the Model Code/Model Rules and/or the rules and/or laws governing the jurisdiction in which the paralegal practices.

EC-1.3(f) If a paralegal possesses knowledge of future criminal activity, that knowledge must be reported to the appropriate authority immediately.

1.4 A Paralegal Shall Serve the Public Interest by Contributing to the Improvement of the Legal System and Delivery of Quality Legal Services, Including Pro Bono Publico Services.

ETHICAL CONSIDERATIONS

EC-1.4(a) A paralegal shall be sensitive to the legal needs of the public and shall promote the development and implementation of programs that address those needs.

EC-1.4(b) A paralegal shall support efforts to improve the legal system and access thereto and shall assist in making changes.

EC-1.4(c) A paralegal shall support and participate in the delivery of Pro Bono Publico services directed toward implementing and improving access to justice, the law, the legal system or the paralegal and legal professions.

EC-1.4(d) A paralegal should aspire annually to contribute twenty-four (24) hours of Pro Bono Publico services under the supervision of an attorney or as authorized by administrative, statutory or court authority to:

1. persons of limited means; or
2. charitable, religious, civic, community, governmental and educational organizations in matters that are designed primarily to address the legal needs of persons with limited means; or
3. individuals, groups or organizations seeking to secure or protect civil rights, civil liberties or public rights.

1.5 A Paralegal Shall Preserve All Confidential Information Provided by the Client or Acquired from Other Sources Before, During, and After the Course of the Professional Relationship.

ETHICAL CONSIDERATIONS

EC-1.5(a) A paralegal shall be aware of and abide by all legal authority governing confidential information in the jurisdiction in which the paralegal practices.

EC-1.5(b) A paralegal shall not use confidential information to the disadvantage of the client.

EC-1.5(c) A paralegal shall not use confidential information to the advantage of the paralegal or of a third person.

EC-1.5(d) A paralegal may reveal confidential information only after full disclosure and with the client's written consent; or, when required by law or court order; or, when necessary to prevent the client from committing an act that could result in death or serious bodily harm.

EC-1.5(e) A paralegal shall keep those individuals responsible for the legal representation of a client fully informed of any confidential information the paralegal may have pertaining to that client.

EC-1.5(f) A paralegal shall not engage in any indiscreet communications concerning clients.

1.6 A Paralegal Shall Avoid Conflicts of Interest and Shall Disclose Any Possible Conflict to the Employer or Client, as Well as to the Prospective Employers or Clients.

ETHICAL CONSIDERATIONS

EC-1.6(a) A paralegal shall act within the bounds of the law, solely for the benefit of the client, and shall be free of compromising influences and loyalties. Neither the paralegal's personal or business interest, nor those of other clients or third persons, should compromise the paralegal's professional judgment and loyalty to the client.

EC-1.6(b) A paralegal shall avoid conflicts of interest that may arise from previous assignments, whether for a present or past employer or client.

EC-1.6(c) A paralegal shall avoid conflicts of interest that may arise from family relationships and from personal and business interests.

EC-1.6(d) In order to be able to determine whether an actual or potential conflict of interest exists a paralegal shall create and maintain an effective recordkeeping system that identifies clients, matters, and parties with which the paralegal has worked.

EC-1.6(e) A paralegal shall reveal sufficient non-confidential information about a client or former client to reasonably ascertain if an actual or potential conflict of interest exists.

EC-1.6(f) A paralegal shall not participate in or conduct work on any matter where a conflict of interest has been identified.

EC-1.6(g) In matters where a conflict of interest has been identified and the client consents to continued representation, a paralegal shall comply fully with the implementation and maintenance of an Ethical Wall.

1.7 A Paralegal's Title Shall be Fully Disclosed.

ETHICAL CONSIDERATIONS

EC-1.7(a) A paralegal's title shall clearly indicate the individual's status and shall be disclosed in all business and professional communications to avoid misunderstandings and misconceptions about the paralegal's role and responsibilities.

EC-1.7(b) A paralegal's title shall be included if the paralegal's name appears on business cards, letterhead, brochures, directories, and advertisements.

EC-1.7(c) A paralegal shall not use letterhead, business cards or other promotional materials to create a fraudulent impression of his/her status or ability to practice in the jurisdiction in which the paralegal practices.

EC-1.7(d) A paralegal shall not practice under color of any record, diploma, or certificate that has been illegally or fraudulently obtained or issued or which is misrepresentative in any way.

EC-1.7(e) A paralegal shall not participate in the creation, issuance, or dissemination of fraudulent records, diplomas, or certificates.

1.8 A Paralegal Shall Not Engage in the Unauthorized Practice of Law.

ETHICAL CONSIDERATIONS

EC-1.8(a) A paralegal shall comply with the applicable legal authority governing the unauthorized practice of law in the jurisdiction in which the paralegal practices.

§2.
NFPA GUIDELINES FOR THE ENFORCEMENT OF THE MODEL CODE OF ETHICS AND PROFESSIONAL RESPONSIBILITY

2.1 Basis for Discipline

2.1(a) Disciplinary investigations and proceedings brought under authority of the Rules shall be conducted in accord with obligations imposed on the paralegal professional by the Model Code of Ethics and Professional Responsibility.

2.2 Structure of Disciplinary Committee

2.2(a) The Disciplinary Committee ("Committee") shall be made up of nine (9) members including the Chair.

2.2(b) Each member of the Committee, including any temporary replacement members, shall have demonstrated working knowledge of ethics/professional responsibility-related issues and activities.

2.2(c) The Committee shall represent a cross-section of practice areas and work experience. The following recommendations are made regarding the members of the Committee.

1) At least one paralegal with one to three years of law-related work experience.

2) At least one paralegal with five to seven years of law related work experience.

3) At least one paralegal with over ten years of law-related work experience.

4) One paralegal educator with five to seven years of work experience; preferably in the area of ethics/ professional responsibility.

5) One paralegal manager.

6) One lawyer with five to seven years of law-related work experience.

7) One lay member.

2.2(d) The Chair of the Committee shall be appointed within thirty (30) days of its members' induction. The Chair shall have no fewer than ten (10) years of law-related work experience.

2.2(e) The terms of all members of the Committee shall be staggered. Of those members initially appointed, a simple majority plus one shall be appointed to a term of one year, and the remaining members shall be appointed to a term of two years. Thereafter, all members of the Committee shall be appointed to terms of two years.

2.2(f) If for any reason the terms of a majority of the Committee will expire at the same time, members may be appointed to terms of one year to maintain continuity of the Committee.

2.2(g) The Committee shall organize from its members a three-tiered structure to investigate, prosecute and/or adjudicate charges of misconduct. The members shall be rotated among the tiers.

2.3 Operation of Committee

2.3(a) The Committee shall meet on an as-needed basis to discuss, investigate, and/or adjudicate alleged violations of the Model Code/Model Rules.

2.3(b) A majority of the members of the Committee present at a meeting shall constitute a quorum.

2.3(c) A Recording Secretary shall be designated to maintain complete and accurate minutes of all Committee meetings. All such minutes shall be kept confidential until a decision has been made that the matter will be set for hearing as set forth in Section 6.1 below.

2.3(d) If any member of the Committee has a conflict of interest with the Charging Party, the Responding Party, or the allegations of misconduct, that member shall not take part in any hearing or deliberations concerning those allegations. If the absence of that member creates a lack of a quorum for the Committee, then a temporary replacement for the member shall be appointed.

2.3(e) Either the Charging Party or the Responding Party may request that, for good cause shown, any member of the Committee not participate in a hearing or deliberation. All such requests shall be honored. If the absence of a Committee member under those circumstances creates a lack of a quorum for the Committee, then a temporary replacement for that member shall be appointed.

2.3(f) All discussions and correspondence of the Committee shall be kept confidential until a decision has been made that the matter will be set for hearing as set forth in Section 6.1 below.

2.3(g) All correspondence from the Committee to the Responding Party regarding any charge of misconduct and any decisions made regarding the charge shall be mailed certified mail, return receipt requested, to the Responding Party's last known address and shall be clearly marked with a "Confidential" designation.

2.4 Procedure for the Reporting of Alleged Violations of the Model Code/Disciplinary Rules

2.4(a) An individual or entity in possession of non-confidential knowledge or information concerning possible instances of misconduct shall make a confidential written report to the Committee within thirty (30) days of obtaining same. This report shall include all details of the alleged misconduct.

2.4(b) The Committee so notified shall inform the Responding Party of the allegation(s) of misconduct no later than ten (10) business days after receiving the confidential written report from the Charging Party.

2.4(c) Notification to the Responding Party shall include the identity of the Charging Party, unless, for good cause shown, the Charging Party requests anonymity.

2.4(d) The Responding Party shall reply to the allegations within ten (10) business days of notification.

2.5 Procedure for the Investigation of a Charge of Misconduct

2.5(a) Upon receipt of a Charge of Misconduct ("Charge"), or on its own initiative, the Committee shall initiate an investigation.

2.5(b) If, upon initial or preliminary review, the Committee makes a determination that the charges are either without basis in fact or, if proven, would not constitute professional misconduct, the Committee shall dismiss the allegations of misconduct. If such determination of dismissal cannot be made, a formal investigation shall be initiated.

2.5(c) Upon the decision to conduct a formal investigation, the Committee shall:

1) mail to the Charging and Responding Parties within three (3) business days of that decision notice of the commencement of a formal investigation. That notification shall be in writing and shall contain a complete explanation of all Charge(s), as well as the reasons for a formal investigation and shall cite the applicable codes and rules;

2) allow the Responding Party thirty (30) days to prepare and submit a confidential response to the Committee, which response shall address each charge specifically and shall be in writing; and

3) upon receipt of the response to the notification, have thirty (30) days to investigate the Charge(s). If an extension of time is deemed necessary, that extension shall not exceed ninety (90) days.

2.5(d) Upon conclusion of the investigation, the Committee may:

1) dismiss the Charge upon the finding that it has no basis in fact;

2) dismiss the Charge upon the finding that, if proven, the Charge would not constitute Misconduct;

3) refer the matter for hearing by the Tribunal; or

4) in the case of criminal activity, refer the Charge(s) and all investigation results to the appropriate authority.

2.6 Procedure for a Misconduct Hearing Before a Tribunal

2.6(a) Upon the decision by the Committee that a matter should be heard, all parties shall be notified and a hearing date shall be set. The hearing shall take place no more than thirty (30) days from the conclusion of the formal investigation.

2.6(b) The Responding Party shall have the right to counsel. The parties and the Tribunal shall have the right to call any witnesses and introduce any documentation that they believe will lead to the fair and reasonable resolution of the matter.

2.6(c) Upon completion of the hearing, the Tribunal shall deliberate and present a written decision to the parties in accordance with procedures as set forth by the Tribunal.

2.6(d) Notice of the decision of the Tribunal shall be appropriately published.

2.7 Sanctions

2.7(a) Upon a finding of the Tribunal that misconduct has occurred, any of the following sanctions, or others as may be deemed appropriate, may be imposed upon the Responding Party, either singularly or in combination:

1) letter of reprimand to the Responding Party; counseling;

2) attendance at an ethics course approved by the Tribunal; probation;

3) suspension of license/authority to practice; revocation of license/authority to practice;

4) imposition of a fine; assessment of costs; or

5) in the instance of criminal activity, referral to the appropriate authority.

2.7(b) Upon the expiration of any period of probation, suspension, or revocation, the Responding Party may make application for reinstatement. With the application for reinstatement, the Responding Party must show proof of having complied with all aspects of the sanctions imposed by the Tribunal.

2.8 Appellate Procedures 2.8(a) The parties shall have the right to appeal the decision of the Tribunal in accordance with the procedure as set forth by the Tribunal.

DEFINITIONS

"Appellate Body" means a body established to adjudicate an appeal to any decision made by a Tribunal or other decision-making body with respect to formally-heard Charges of Misconduct.

"Charge of Misconduct" means a written submission by any individual or entity to an ethics committee, paralegal association, bar association, law enforcement agency, judicial body, government agency, or other appropriate body or entity, that sets forth non-confidential information regarding any instance of alleged misconduct by an individual paralegal or paralegal entity.

"Charging Party" means any individual or entity who submits a Charge of Misconduct against an individual paralegal or paralegal entity.

"Competency" means the demonstration of: diligence, education, skill, and mental, emotional, and physical fitness reasonably necessary for the performance of paralegal services.

"Confidential Information" means information relating to a client, whatever its source, that is not public knowledge nor available to the public. ("Non-Confidential Information" would generally include the name of the client and the identity of the matter for which the paralegal provided services.)

"Disciplinary Hearing" means the confidential proceeding conducted by a committee or other designated body or entity concerning any instance of alleged misconduct by an individual paralegal or paralegal entity.

"Disciplinary Committee" means any committee that has been established by an entity such as a paralegal association, bar association, judicial body, or government agency to: (a) identify, define and investigate general Ethical Considerations and concerns with respect to paralegal practice; (b) administer and enforce the Model Code and Model Rules and; (c) discipline any individual paralegal or paralegal entity found to be in violation of same.

"Disclose" means communication of information reasonably sufficient to permit identification of the significance of the matter in question.

"Ethical Wall" means the screening method implemented in order to protect a client from a conflict of interest. An Ethical Wall generally includes, but is not limited to, the following elements: (1) prohibit the paralegal from having any connection with the matter; (2) ban discussions with or the transfer of documents to or from the paralegal; (3) restrict access to files; and (4) educate all members of the firm, corporation, or entity as to the separation of the paralegal (both organizationally and physically) from the pending matter. For more information regarding the Ethical Wall, see the NFPA publication entitled "The Ethical Wall—Its Application to Paralegals."

"Ex parte" means actions or communications conducted at the instance and for the benefit of one party only, and without notice to, or contestation by, any person adversely interested.

"Investigation" means the investigation of any charge(s) of misconduct filed against an individual paralegal or paralegal entity by a Committee.

"Letter of Reprimand" means a written notice of formal censure or severe reproof administered to an individual paralegal or paralegal entity for unethical or improper conduct.

"Misconduct" means the knowing or unknowing commission of an act that is in direct violation of those Canons and Ethical Considerations of any and all applicable codes and/or rules of conduct.

"Paralegal" is synonymous with "Legal Assistant" and is defined as a person qualified through education, training, or work experience to perform substantive legal work that requires knowledge of legal concepts and is customarily, but not exclusively performed by a lawyer. This person may be retained or employed by a lawyer, law office, governmental agency, or other entity or may be authorized by administrative, statutory, or court authority to perform this work.

"Pro Bono Publico" means providing or assisting to provide quality legal services in order to enhance access to justice for persons of limited means; charitable, religious, civic, community, governmental and educational organizations in matters that are designed primarily to address the legal needs of persons with limited means; or individuals, groups or organizations seeking to secure or protect civil rights, civil liberties or public rights.

"Proper Authority" means the local paralegal association, the local or state bar association, Committee(s) of the local paralegal or bar association(s), local prosecutor, administrative agency, or other tribunal empowered to investigate or act upon an instance of alleged misconduct.

"Responding Party" means an individual paralegal or paralegal entity against whom a Charge of Misconduct has been submitted.

"Revocation" means the recision of the license, certificate or other authority to practice of an individual paralegal or paralegal entity found in violation of those Canons and Ethical Considerations of any and all applicable codes and/or rules of conduct.

"Suspension" means the suspension of the license, certificate or other authority to practice of an individual paralegal or paralegal entity found in violation of those Canons and Ethical Considerations of any and all applicable codes and/or rules of conduct.

"Tribunal" means the body designated to adjudicate allegations of misconduct.

OUTLINE OF AND EXCERPTS FROM THE
ABA MODEL RULES OF PROFESSIONAL CONDUCT, 2002 *

American Bar Association: www.abanet.org
The full text of the rules may be viewed on the ABA website.

Rule 1.0 Terminology

CLIENT–LAWYER RELATIONSHIP

Rule 1.1 Competence

Rule 1.2 Scope of Representation and Allocation of Authority Between Client and Lawyer

Rule 1.3 Diligence

Rule 1.4 Communications

Rule 1.5 Fees

Rule 1.6 Confidentiality of Information

(a) A lawyer shall not reveal information relating to the representation of a client unless the client gives informed consent, the disclosure is impliedly authorized in order to carry out the representation or the disclosure is permitted by paragraph

(b) A lawyer may reveal information relating to the representation of a client to the extent the lawyer reasonably believes necessary:

(1) to prevent reasonably certain death or substantial bodily harm;

(2) to secure legal advice about the lawyer's compliance with these Rules;

(3) to establish a claim or defense on behalf of the lawyer in a controversy between the lawyer and the client, to establish a defense to a criminal charge or civil claim against the lawyer based upon conduct in which the client was involved, or to respond to allegations in any proceeding concerning the lawyer's representation of the client; or

(4) to comply with other law or a court order.

Comment:

[1] This Rule governs the disclosure by a lawyer of information relating to the representation of a client during the lawyer's representation of the client. See Rule 1.18 for the lawyer's duties with respect to information provided to the lawyer by a prospective client, Rule 1.9(c)(2) for the lawyer's duty not to reveal information relating to the lawyer's prior representation of a former client and Rules 1.8(b) and 1.9(c)(1) for the lawyer's duties with respect to the use of such information to the disadvantage of clients and former clients.

[2] A fundamental principle in the client-lawyer relationship is that, in the absence of the client's informed consent, the lawyer must not reveal information relating to the representation. See Rule 1.0(e) for the definition of informed consent. This contributes to the trust that is the hallmark of the client-lawyer relationship. The client is thereby encouraged to seek legal assistance and to communicate fully and frankly with the lawyer even as to embarrassing or legally damaging subject matter. The lawyer needs this information to represent the client effectively and, if necessary, to advise the client to refrain from wrongful conduct. Almost without exception, clients come to lawyers in order to determine their rights and what is, in the complex of laws and regulations, deemed to be legal and correct. Based upon experience, lawyers know that almost all clients follow the advice given, and the law is upheld.

[3] The principle of client-lawyer confidentiality is given effect by related bodies of law: the attorney-client privilege, the work product doctrine and the rule of confidentiality established in professional ethics. The attorney-client privilege and work-product doctrine apply in judicial and other proceedings in which a lawyer may be called as a witness or otherwise required to produce evidence concerning a client. The rule of client-lawyer confidentiality applies in situations other than those where evidence is sought from the lawyer through compulsion of law. The confidentiality rule, for example, applies not only to matters communicated in confidence by the client but also to all information relating to the representation, whatever its source. A lawyer may not disclose such information except as authorized or required by the Rules of Professional Conduct or other law. See also Scope.

[4] Paragraph (a) prohibits a lawyer from revealing information relating to the representation of a client. This prohibition also applies to disclosures by a lawyer that do not in themselves reveal protected information but could reasonably lead to the discovery of such information by a third person. A lawyer's use of a hypothetical to discuss

issues relating to the representation is permissible so long as there is no reasonable likelihood that the listener will be able to ascertain the identity of the client or the situation involved.

Authorized Disclosure

[5] Except to the extent that the client's instructions or special circumstances limit that authority, a lawyer is impliedly authorized to make disclosures about a client when appropriate in carrying out the representation. In some situations, for example, a lawyer may be impliedly authorized to admit a fact that cannot properly be disputed or to make a disclosure that facilitates a satisfactory conclusion to a matter. Lawyers in a firm may, in the course of the firm's practice, disclose to each other information relating to a client of the firm, unless the client has instructed that particular information be confined to specified lawyers.

Disclosure Adverse to Client

[6] Although the public interest is usually best served by a strict rule requiring lawyers to preserve the confidentiality of information relating to the representation of their clients, the confidentiality rule is subject to limited exceptions. Paragraph (b)(1) recognizes the overriding value of life and physical integrity and permits disclosure reasonably necessary to prevent reasonably certain death or substantial bodily harm. Such harm is reasonably certain to occur if it will be suffered imminently or if there is a present and substantial threat that a person will suffer such harm at a later date if the lawyer fails to take action necessary to eliminate the threat. Thus, a lawyer who knows that a client has accidentally discharged toxic waste into a town's water supply may reveal this information to the authorities if there is a present and substantial risk that a person who drinks the water will contract a life-threatening or debilitating disease and the lawyer's disclosure is necessary to eliminate the threat or reduce the number of victims.

[7] A lawyer's confidentiality obligations do not preclude a lawyer from securing confidential legal advice about the lawyer's personal responsibility to comply with these Rules. In most situations, disclosing information to secure such advice will be impliedly authorized for the lawyer to carry out the representation. Even when the disclosure is not impliedly authorized, paragraph (b)(2) permits such disclosure because of the importance of a lawyer's compliance with the Rules of Professional Conduct.

[8] Where a legal claim or disciplinary charge alleges complicity of the lawyer in a client's conduct or other misconduct of the lawyer involving representation of the client, the lawyer may respond to the extent the lawyer reasonably believes necessary to establish a defense. The same is true with respect to a claim involving the conduct or representation of a former client. Such a charge can arise in a civil, criminal, disciplinary or other proceeding and can be based on a wrong allegedly committed by the lawyer against the client or on a wrong alleged by a third person, for example, a person claiming to have been defrauded by the lawyer and client acting together. The lawyer's right to respond arises when an assertion of such complicity has been made. Paragraph (b)(3) does not require the lawyer to await the commencement of an action or proceeding that charges such complicity, so that the defense may be established by responding directly to a third party who has made such an assertion. The right to defend also applies, of course, where a proceeding has been commenced.

[9] A lawyer entitled to a fee is permitted by paragraph (b)(3) to prove the services rendered in an action to collect it. This aspect of the rule expresses the principle that the beneficiary of a fiduciary relationship may not exploit it to the detriment of the fiduciary.

[10] Other law may require that a lawyer disclose information about a client. Whether such a law supersedes Rule 1.6 is a question of law beyond the scope of these Rules. When disclosure of information relating to the representation appears to be required by other law, the lawyer must discuss the matter with the client to the extent required by Rule 1.4. If, however, the other law supersedes this Rule and requires disclosure, paragraph (b)(4) permits the lawyer to make such disclosures as are necessary to comply with the law.

[11] A lawyer may be ordered to reveal information relating to the representation of a client by a court or by another tribunal or governmental entity claiming authority pursuant to other law to compel the disclosure. Absent informed consent of the client to do otherwise, the lawyer should assert on behalf of the client all nonfrivolous claims that the order is not authorized by other law or that the information sought is protected against disclosure by the attorney-client privilege or other applicable law. In the event of an adverse ruling, the lawyer must consult with the client about the possibility of appeal to the extent required by Rule 1.4. Unless review is sought, however, paragraph (b)(4) permits the lawyer to comply with the court's order.

[12] Paragraph (b) permits disclosure only to the extent the lawyer reasonably believes the disclosure is necessary to accomplish one of the purposes specified. Where practicable, the lawyer should first seek to persuade the client to take suitable action to obviate the need for disclosure. In any case, a disclosure adverse to the client's interest should be no greater than the lawyer reasonably believes necessary to accomplish the purpose. If the disclosure will be made in connection with a judicial proceeding, the disclosure should be made in a manner that limits access to

the information to the tribunal or other persons having a need to know it and appropriate protective orders or other arrangements should be sought by the lawyer to the fullest extent practicable.

[13] Paragraph (b) permits but does not require the disclosure of information relating to a client's representation to accomplish the purposes specified in paragraphs (b)(1) through (b)(4). In exercising the discretion conferred by this Rule, the lawyer may consider such factors as the nature of the lawyer's relationship with the client and with those who might be injured by the client, the lawyer's own involvement in the transaction and factors that may extenuate the conduct in question. A lawyer's decision not to disclose as permitted by paragraph (b) does not violate this Rule. Disclosure may be required, however, by other Rules. Some Rules require disclosure only if such disclosure would be permitted by paragraph (b). See Rules 1.2(d), 4.1(b), 8.1 and 8.3. Rule 3.3, on the other hand, requires disclosure in some circumstances regardless of whether such disclosure is permitted by this Rule. See Rule 3.3(c).

Withdrawal

[14] If the lawyer's services will be used by the client in materially furthering a course of criminal or fraudulent conduct, the lawyer must withdraw, as stated in Rule 1.16(a)(1). After withdrawal the lawyer is required to refrain from making disclosure of the client's confidences, except as otherwise permitted by Rule 1.6. Neither this Rule nor Rule 1.8(b) nor Rule 1.16(d) prevents the lawyer from giving notice of the fact of withdrawal, and the lawyer may also withdraw or disaffirm any opinion, document, affirmation, or the like. Where the client is an organization, the lawyer may be in doubt whether contemplated conduct will actually be carried out by the organization. Where necessary to guide conduct in connection with this Rule, the lawyer may make inquiry within the organization as indicated in Rule 1.13(b).

Acting Competently to Preserve Confidentiality

[15] A lawyer must act competently to safeguard information relating to the representation of a client against inadvertent or unauthorized disclosure by the lawyer or other persons who are participating in the representation of the client or who are subject to the lawyer's supervision. See Rules 1.1, 5.1 and 5.3.

[16] When transmitting a communication that includes information relating to the representation of a client, the lawyer must take reasonable precautions to prevent the information from coming into the hands of unintended recipients. This duty, however, does not require that the lawyer use special security measures if the method of communication affords a reasonable expectation of privacy.

Special circumstances, however, may warrant special precautions. Factors to be considered in determining the reasonableness of the lawyer's expectation of confidentiality include the sensitivity of the information and the extent to which the privacy of the communication is protected by law or by a confidentiality agreement. A client may require the lawyer to implement special security measures not required by this Rule or may give informed consent to the use of a means of communication that would otherwise be prohibited by this Rule.

Former Client

[17] The duty of confidentiality continues after the client-lawyer relationship has terminated. See Rule 1.9(c)(2). See Rule 1.9(c)(1) for the prohibition against using such information to the disadvantage of the former client.

Rule 1.7 Conflict of Interest: Current Clients

(a) Except as provided in paragraph (b), a lawyer shall not represent a client if the representation involves a concurrent conflict of interest. A concurrent conflict of interest exists if:

(1) the representation of one client will be directly adverse to another client; or

(2) there is a significant risk that the representation of one or more clients will be materially limited by the lawyer's responsibilities to another client, a former client or a third person or by a personal interest of the lawyer.

(b) Notwithstanding the existence of a concurrent conflict of i\nterest under paragraph (a), a lawyer may represent a client if:

(1) the lawyer reasonably believes that the lawyer will be able to provide competent and diligent representation to each affected client;

(2) the representation is not prohibited by law;

(3) the representation does not involve the assertion of a claim by one client against another client represented by the lawyer in the same litigation or other proceeding before a tribunal; and

(4) each affected client gives informed consent, confirmed in writing.

Comment:

General Principles

[1] Loyalty and independent judgment are essential elements in the lawyer's relationship to a client. Concurrent conflicts of interest can arise from the lawyer's responsibilities to another client, a former client or a third person or from the lawyer's own interests. For specific Rules regarding certain concurrent conflicts of interest, see Rule 1.8. For former client conflicts of interest, see Rule 1.9.

For conflicts of interest involving prospective clients, see Rule 1.18. For definitions of "informed consent" and "confirmed in writing," see Rule 1.0(e) and (b).

[2] Resolution of a conflict of interest problem under this Rule requires the lawyer to: 1) clearly identify the client or clients; 2) determine whether a conflict of interest exists; 3) decide whether the representation may be undertaken despite the existence of a conflict, i.e., whether the conflict is consentable; and 4) if so, consult with the clients affected under paragraph (a) and obtain their informed consent, confirmed in writing. The clients affected under paragraph (a) include both of the clients referred to in paragraph (a)(1) and the one or more clients whose representation might be materially limited under paragraph (a)(2).

[3] A conflict of interest may exist before representation is undertaken, in which event the representation must be declined, unless the lawyer obtains the informed consent of each client under the conditions of paragraph (b). To determine whether a conflict of interest exists, a lawyer should adopt reasonable procedures, appropriate for the size and type of firm and practice, to determine in both litigation and non-litigation matters the persons and issues involved. See also Comment to Rule 5.1. Ignorance caused by a failure to institute such procedures will not excuse a lawyer's violation of this Rule. As to whether a client-lawyer relationship exists or, having once been established, is continuing, see Comment to Rule 1.3 and Scope.

[4] If a conflict arises after representation has been undertaken, the lawyer ordinarily must withdraw from the representation, unless the lawyer has obtained the informed consent of the client under the conditions of paragraph (b). See Rule 1.16. Where more than one client is involved, whether the lawyer may continue to represent any of the clients is determined both by the lawyer's ability to comply with duties owed to the former client and by the lawyer's ability to represent adequately the remaining client or clients, given the lawyer's duties to the former client. See Rule 1.9. See also Comments [5] and [29].

[5] Unforeseeable developments, such as changes in corporate and other organizational affiliations or the addition or realignment of parties in litigation, might create conflicts in the midst of a representation, as when a company sued by the lawyer on behalf of one client is bought by another client represented by the lawyer in an unrelated matter. Depending on the circumstances, the lawyer may have the option to withdraw from one of the representations in order to avoid the conflict. The lawyer must seek court approval where necessary and take steps to minimize harm to the clients. See Rule 1.16. The lawyer must continue to protect the confidences of the client from whose representation the lawyer has withdrawn. See Rule 1.9(c).

Identifying Conflicts of Interest: Directly Adverse

[6] Loyalty to a current client prohibits undertaking representation directly adverse to that client without that client's informed consent. Thus, absent consent, a lawyer may not act as an advocate in one matter against a person the lawyer represents in some other matter, even when the matters are wholly unrelated. The client as to whom the representation is directly adverse is likely to feel betrayed, and the resulting damage to the client-lawyer relationship is likely to impair the lawyer's ability to represent the client effectively. In addition, the client on whose behalf the adverse representation is undertaken reasonably may fear that the lawyer will pursue that client's case less effectively out of deference to the other client, i.e., that the representation may be materially limited by the lawyer's interest in retaining the current client. Similarly, a directly adverse conflict may arise when a lawyer is required to cross-examine a client who appears as a witness in a lawsuit involving another client, as when the testimony will be damaging to the client who is represented in the lawsuit. On the other hand, simultaneous representation in unrelated matters of clients whose interests are only economically adverse, such as representation of competing economic enterprises in unrelated litigation, does not ordinarily constitute a conflict of interest and thus may not require consent of the respective clients.

[7] Directly adverse conflicts can also arise in transactional matters. For example, if a lawyer is asked to represent the seller of a business in negotiations with a buyer represented by the lawyer, not in the same transaction but in another, unrelated matter, the lawyer could not undertake the representation without the informed consent of each client.

Identifying Conflicts of Interest: Material Limitation

[8] Even where there is no direct adverseness, a conflict of interest exists if there is a significant risk that a lawyer's ability to consider, recommend or carry out an appropriate course of action for the client will be materially limited as a result of the lawyer's other responsi- bilities or interests. For example, a lawyer asked to represent several individuals seeking to form a joint venture is likely to be materially limited in the lawyer's ability to recommend or advocate all possible positions that each might take because of the lawyer's duty of loyalty to the others. The conflict in effect forecloses alternatives that would otherwise be available to the client. The mere possibility of subsequent harm does not itself require disclosure and consent. The critical questions are the likelihood that a difference in interests will eventuate and, if it does, whether it will materially interfere with the lawyer's independent professional judgment in considering alternatives

or foreclose courses of action that reasonably should be pursued on behalf of the client.

Lawyer's Responsibilities to Former Clients and Other Third Persons

[9] In addition to conflicts with other current clients, a lawyer's duties of loyalty and independence may be materially limited by responsibilities to former clients under Rule 1.9 or by the lawyer's responsibilities to other persons, such as fiduciary duties arising from a lawyer's service as a trustee, executor or corporate director.

Personal Interest Conflicts

[10] The lawyer's own interests should not be permitted to have an adverse effect on representation of a client. For example, if the probity of a lawyer's own conduct in a transaction is in serious question, it may be difficult or impossible for the lawyer to give a client detached advice. Similarly, when a lawyer has discussions concerning possible employment with an opponent of the lawyer's client, or with a law firm representing the opponent, such discussions could materially limit the lawyer's representation of the client. In addition, a lawyer may not allow related business interests to affect representation, for example, by referring clients to an enterprise in which the lawyer has an undisclosed financial interest. See Rule 1.8 for specific Rules pertaining to a number of personal interest conflicts, including business transactions with clients. See also Rule 1.10 (personal interest conflicts under Rule 1.7 ordinarily are not imputed to other lawyers in a law firm).

[11] When lawyers representing different clients in the same matter or in substantially related matters are closely related by blood or marriage, there may be a significant risk that client confidences will be revealed and that the lawyer's family relationship will interfere with both loyalty and independent professional judgment. As a result, each client is entitled to know of the existence and implications of the relationship between the lawyers before the lawyer agrees to undertake the representation. Thus, a lawyer related to another lawyer, e.g., as parent, child, sibling or spouse, ordinarily may not represent a client in a matter where that lawyer is representing another party, unless each client gives informed consent. The disqualification arising from a close family relationship is personal and ordinarily is not imputed to members of firms with whom the lawyers are associated. See Rule 1.10.

[12] A lawyer is prohibited from engaging in sexual relationships with a client unless the sexual relationship predates the formation of the client-lawyer relationship. See Rule 1.8(j).

Interest of Person Paying for a Lawyer's Service

[13] A lawyer may be paid from a source other than the client, including a co-client, if the client is informed of that fact and consents and the arrangement does not compromise the lawyer's duty of loyalty or independent judgment to the client. See Rule 1.8(f). If acceptance of the payment from any other source presents a significant risk that the lawyer's representation of the client will be materially limited by the lawyer's own interest in accommodating the person paying the lawyer's fee or by the lawyer's responsibilities to a payer who is also a co-client, then the lawyer must comply with the requirements of paragraph (b) before accepting the representation, including determining whether the conflict is consentable and, if so, that the client has adequate information about the material risks of the representation.

Prohibited Representations

[14] Ordinarily, clients may consent to representation notwithstanding a conflict. However, as indicated in paragraph (b), some conflicts are nonconsentable, meaning that the lawyer involved cannot properly ask for such agreement or provide representation on the basis of the client's consent. When the lawyer is representing more than one client, the question of consentability must be resolved as to each client.

[15] Consentability is typically determined by considering whether the interests of the clients will be adequately protected if the clients are permitted to give their informed consent to representation burdened by a conflict of interest. Thus, under paragraph (b)(1), representation is prohibited if in the circumstances the lawyer cannot reasonably conclude that the lawyer will be able to provide competent and diligent representation. See Rule 1.1 (competence) and Rule 1.3 (diligence).

[16] Paragraph (b)(2) describes conflicts that are nonconsentable because the representation is prohibited by applicable law. For example, in some states substantive law provides that the same lawyer may not represent more than one defendant in a capital case, even with the consent of the clients, and under federal criminal statutes certain representations by a former government lawyer are prohibited, despite the informed consent of the former client. In addition, decisional law in some states limits the ability of a governmental client, such as a municipality, to consent to a conflict of interest.

[17] Paragraph (b)(3) describes conflicts that are nonconsentable because of the institutional interest in vigorous development of each client's position when the clients are aligned directly against each other in the same litigation or other proceeding before a tribunal. Whether clients are

aligned directly against each other within the meaning of this paragraph requires examination of the context of the proceeding. Although this paragraph does not preclude a lawyer's multiple representation of adverse parties to a mediation (because mediation is not a proceeding before a "tribunal" under Rule 1.0(m)), such representation may be precluded by paragraph (b)(1).

Informed Consent

[18] Informed consent requires that each affected client be aware of the relevant circumstances and of the material and reasonably foreseeable ways that the conflict could have adverse effects on the interests of that client. See Rule 1.0(e) (informed consent). The information required depends on the nature of the conflict and the nature of the risks involved. When representation of multiple clients in a single matter is undertaken, the information must include the implications of the common representation, including possible effects on loyalty, confidentiality and the attorney-client privilege and the advantages and risks involved. See Comments [30] and [31] (effect of common representation on confidentiality).

[19] Under some circumstances it may be impossible to make the disclosure necessary to obtain consent. For example, when the lawyer represents different clients in related matters and one of the clients refuses to consent to the disclosure necessary to permit the other client to make an informed decision, the lawyer cannot properly ask the latter to consent. In some cases the alternative to common representation can be that each party may have to obtain separate representation with the possibility of incurring additional costs. These costs, along with the benefits of securing separate representation, are factors that may be considered by the affected client in determining whether common representation is in the client's interests.

Consent Confirmed in Writing

[20] Paragraph (b) requires the lawyer to obtain the informed consent of the client, confirmed in writing. Such a writing may consist of a document executed by the client or one that the lawyer promptly records and transmits to the client following an oral consent. See Rule 1.0(b). See also Rule 1.0(n) (writing includes electronic transmission). If it is not feasible to obtain or transmit the writing at the time the client gives informed consent, then the lawyer must obtain or transmit it within a reasonable time thereafter. See Rule 1.0(b). The requirement of a writing does not supplant the need in most cases for the lawyer to talk with the client, to explain the risks and advantages, if any, of representation burdened with a conflict of interest, as well as reasonably available alternatives, and to afford the client a reasonable opportunity to consider the risks and alterna-

tives and to raise questions and concerns. Rather, the writing is required in order to impress upon clients the seriousness of the decision the client is being asked to make and to avoid disputes or ambiguities that might later occur in the absence of a writing.

Revoking Consent

[21] A client who has given consent to a conflict may revoke the consent and, like any other client, may terminate the lawyer's representation at any time. Whether revoking consent to the client's own representation precludes the lawyer from continuing to represent other clients depends on the circumstances, including the nature of the conflict, whether the client revoked consent because of a material change in circumstances, the reasonable expectations of the other client and whether material detriment to the other clients or the lawyer would result.

Consent to Future Conflict

[22] Whether a lawyer may properly request a client to waive conflicts that might arise in the future is subject to the test of paragraph (b). The effectiveness of such waivers is generally determined by the extent to which the client reasonably understands the material risks that the waiver entails. The more comprehensive the explanation of the types of future representations that might arise and the actual and reasonably foreseeable adverse consequences of those representations, the greater the likelihood that the client will have the requisite understanding. Thus, if the client agrees to consent to a particular type of conflict with which the client is already familiar, then the consent ordinarily will be effective with regard to that type of conflict. If the consent is general and open-ended, then the consent ordinarily will be ineffective, because it is not reasonably likely that the client will have understood the material risks involved. On the other hand, if the client is an experienced user of the legal services involved and is reasonably informed regarding the risk that a conflict may arise, such consent is more likely to be effective, particularly if, e.g., the client is independently represented by other counsel in giving consent and the consent is limited to future conflicts unrelated to the subject of the representation. In any case, advance consent cannot be effective if the circumstances that materialize in the future are such as would make the conflict nonconsentable under paragraph (b).

Conflicts in Litigation

[23] Paragraph (b)(3) prohibits representation of opposing parties in the same litigation, regardless of the clients' consent. On the other hand, simultaneous representation of parties whose interests in litigation may conflict, such as coplaintiffs or codefendants, is governed by paragraph (a)(2). A conflict may exist by reason of substantial dis-

crepancy in the parties' testimony, incompatibility in positions in relation to an opposing party or the fact that there are substantially different possibilities of settlement of the claims or liabilities in question. Such conflicts can arise in criminal cases as well as civil. The potential for conflict of interest in representing multiple defendants in a criminal case is so grave that ordinarily a lawyer should decline to represent more than one codefendant. On the other hand, common representation of persons having similar interests in civil litigation is proper if the requirements of paragraph (b) are met.

[24] Ordinarily a lawyer may take inconsistent legal positions in different tribunals at different times on behalf of different clients. The mere fact that advocating a legal position on behalf of one client might create precedent adverse to the interests of a client represented by the lawyer in an unrelated matter does not create a conflict of interest. A conflict of interest exists, however, if there is a significant risk that a lawyer's action on behalf of one client will materially limit the lawyer's effectiveness in representing another client in a different case; for example, when a decision favoring one client will create a precedent likely to seriously weaken the position taken on behalf of the other client. Factors relevant in determining whether the clients need to be advised of the risk include: where the cases are pending, whether the issue is substantive or procedural, the temporal relationship between the matters, the significance of the issue to the immediate and long-term interests of the clients involved and the clients' reasonable expectations in retaining the lawyer. If there is significant risk of material limitation, then absent informed consent of the affected clients, the lawyer must refuse one of the representations or withdraw from one or both matters.

[25] When a lawyer represents or seeks to represent a class of plaintiffs or defendants in a class-action lawsuit, unnamed members of the class are ordinarily not considered to be clients of the lawyer for purposes of applying paragraph (a)(1) of this Rule. Thus, the lawyer does not typically need to get the consent of such a person before representing a client suing the person in an unrelated matter. Similarly, a lawyer seeking to represent an opponent in a class action does not typically need the consent of an unnamed member of the class whom the lawyer represents in an unrelated matter.

Nonlitigation Conflicts

[26] Conflicts of interest under paragraphs (a)(1) and (a)(2) arise in contexts other than litigation. For a discussion of directly adverse conflicts in transactional matters, see Comment [7]. Relevant factors in determining whether there is significant potential for material limita-

tion include the duration and intimacy of the lawyer's relationship with the client or clients involved, the functions being performed by the lawyer, the likelihood that disagreements will arise and the likely prejudice to the client from the conflict. The question is often one of proximity and degree. See Comment [8].

[27] For example, conflict questions may arise in estate planning and estate administration. A lawyer may be called upon to prepare wills for several family members, such as husband and wife, and, depending upon the circumstances, a conflict of interest may be present. In estate administration the identity of the client may be unclear under the law of a particular jurisdiction. Under one view, the client is the fiduciary; under another view the client is the estate or trust, including its beneficiaries. In order to comply with conflict of interest rules, the lawyer should make clear the lawyer's relationship to the parties involved.

[28] Whether a conflict is consentable depends on the circumstances. For example, a lawyer may not represent multiple parties to a negotiation whose interests are fundamentally antagonistic to each other, but common representation is permissible where the clients are generally aligned in interest even though there is some difference in interest among them. Thus, a lawyer may seek to establish or adjust a relationship between clients on an amicable and mutually advantageous basis; for example, in helping to organize a business in which two or more clients are entrepreneurs, working out the financial reorganization of an enterprise in which two or more clients have an interest or arranging a property distribution in settlement of an estate. The lawyer seeks to resolve potentially adverse interests by developing the parties' mutual interests. Otherwise, each party might have to obtain separate representation, with the possibility of incurring additional cost, complication or even litigation. Given these and other relevant factors, the clients may prefer that the lawyer act for all of them.

Special Considerations in Common Representation

[29] In considering whether to represent multiple clients in the same matter, a lawyer should be mindful that if the common representation fails because the potentially adverse interests cannot be reconciled, the result can be additional cost, embarrassment and recrimination. Ordinarily, the lawyer will be forced to withdraw from representing all of the clients if the common representation fails. In some situations, the risk of failure is so great that multiple representation is plainly impossible. For example, a lawyer cannot undertake common representation of clients where contentious litigation or negotiations between them are imminent or contemplated. Moreover,

because the lawyer is required to be impartial between commonly represented clients, representation of multiple clients is improper when it is unlikely that impartiality can be maintained. Generally, if the relationship between the parties has already assumed antagonism, the possibility that the clients' interests can be adequately served by common representation is not very good. Other relevant factors are whether the lawyer subsequently will represent both parties on a continuing basis and whether the situation involves creating or terminating a relationship between the parties.

[30] A particularly important factor in determining the appropriateness of common representation is the effect on client-lawyer confidentiality and the attorney-client privilege. With regard to the attorney-client privilege, the prevailing rule is that, as between commonly represented clients, the privilege does not attach. Hence, it must be assumed that if litigation eventuates between the clients, the privilege will not protect any such communications, and the clients should be so advised.

[31] As to the duty of confidentiality, continued common representation will almost certainly be inadequate if one client asks the lawyer not to disclose to the other client information relevant to the common representation. This is so because the lawyer has an equal duty of loyalty to each client, and each client has the right to be informed of anything bearing on the representation that might affect that client's interests and the right to expect that the lawyer will use that information to that client's benefit. See Rule 1.4. The lawyer should, at the outset of the common representation and as part of the process of obtaining each client's informed consent, advise each client that information will be shared and that the lawyer will have to withdraw if one client decides that some matter material to the representation should be kept from the other. In limited circumstances, it may be appropriate for the lawyer to proceed with the representation when the clients have agreed, after being properly informed, that the lawyer will keep certain information confidential. For example, the lawyer may reasonably conclude that failure to disclose one client's trade secrets to another will not adversely affect representation involving a joint venture between the clients and agree to keep that information confidential with the informed consent of both clients.

[32] When seeking to establish or adjust a relationship between clients, the lawyer should make clear that the lawyer's role is not that of partisanship normally expected in other circumstances and, thus, that the clients may be required to assume greater responsibility for decisions than when each client is separately represented. Any limitations on the scope of the representation made necessary as a result of the common representation should be fully explained to the clients at the outset of the representation. See Rule 1.2(c).

[33] Subject to the above limitations, each client in the common representation has the right to loyal and diligent representation and the protection of Rule 1.9 concerning the obligations to a former client. The client also has the right to discharge the lawyer as stated in Rule 1.16.

Organizational Clients

[34] A lawyer who represents a corporation or other organization does not, by virtue of that representation, necessarily represent any constituent or affiliated organization, such as a parent or subsidiary. See Rule 1.13(a). Thus, the lawyer for an organization is not barred from accepting representation adverse to an affiliate in an unrelated matter, unless the circumstances are such that the affiliate should also be considered a client of the lawyer, there is an understanding between the lawyer and the organizational client that the lawyer will avoid representation adverse to the client's affiliates, or the lawyer's obligations to either the organizational client or the new client are likely to limit materially the lawyer's representation of the other client.

[35] A lawyer for a corporation or other organization who is also a member of its board of directors should determine whether the responsibilities of the two roles may conflict. The lawyer may be called on to advise the corporation in matters involving actions of the directors. Consideration should be given to the frequency with which such situations may arise, the potential intensity of the conflict, the effect of the lawyer's resignation from the board and the possibility of the corporation's obtaining legal advice from another lawyer in such situations. If there is material risk that the dual role will compromise the lawyer's independence of professional judgment, the lawyer should not serve as a director or should cease to act as the corporation's lawyer when conflicts of interest arise. The lawyer should advise the other members of the board that in some circumstances matters discussed at board meetings while the lawyer is present in the capacity of director might not be protected by the attorney-client privilege and that conflict of interest considerations might require the lawyer's recusal as a director or might require the lawyer and the lawyer's firm to decline representation of the corporation in a matter.

Rule 1.8 Conflict of Interest: Current Clients: Specific Rules

Rule 1.9 Duties to Former Clients

Rule 1.10 Imputation of Conflicts of Interest: General Rule

Rule 3.3 Candor Toward the Tribunal

(a) A lawyer shall not knowingly:

(1) make a false statement of fact or law to a tribunal or fail to correct a false statement of material fact or law previously made to the tribunal by the lawyer;

(2) fail to disclose to the tribunal legal authority in the controlling jurisdiction known to the lawyer to be directly adverse to the position of the client and not disclosed by opposing counsel; or

(3) offer evidence that the lawyer knows to be false. If a lawyer, the lawyer's client, or a witness called by the lawyer, has offered material evidence and the lawyer comes to know of its falsity, the lawyer shall take reasonable remedial measures, including, if necessary, disclosure to the tribunal. A lawyer may refuse to offer evidence, other than the testimony of a defendant in a criminal matter, that the lawyer reasonably believes is false.

(b) A lawyer who represents a client in an adjudicative proceeding and who knows that a person intends to engage, is engaging or has engaged in criminal or fraudulent conduct related to the proceeding shall take reasonable remedial measures, including, if necessary, disclosure to the tribunal.

(c) The duties stated in paragraphs (a) and (b) continue to the conclusion of the proceeding, and apply even if compliance requires disclosure of information otherwise protected by Rule 1.6.

(d) In an ex parte proceeding, a lawyer shall inform the tribunal of all material facts known to the lawyer that will enable the tribunal to make an informed decision, whether or not the facts are adverse.

Comment:

[1] This Rule governs the conduct of a lawyer who is representing a client in the proceedings of a tribunal. See Rule 1.0(m) for the definition of "tribunal." It also applies when the lawyer is representing a client in an ancillary proceeding conducted pursuant to the tribunal's adjudicative authority, such as a deposition. Thus, for example, paragraph (a)(3) requires a lawyer to take reasonable remedial measures if the lawyer comes to know that a client who is testifying in a deposition has offered evidence that is false.

[2] This Rule sets forth the special duties of lawyers as officers of the court to avoid conduct that undermines the integrity of the adjudicative process. A lawyer acting as an advocate in an adjudicative proceeding has an obligation to present the client's case with persuasive force. Performance of that duty while maintaining confidences of the client, however, is qualified by the advocate's duty of candor to the tribunal. Consequently, although a lawyer in an adversary proceeding is not required to present an impartial exposition of the law or to vouch for the evidence submitted in a cause, the lawyer must not allow the tribunal to be misled by false statements of law or fact or evidence that the lawyer knows to be false.

Representations by a Lawyer

[3] An advocate is responsible for pleadings and other documents prepared for litigation, but is usually not required to have personal knowledge of matters asserted therein, for litigation documents ordinarily present assertions by the client, or by someone on the client's behalf, and not assertions by the lawyer. Compare Rule 3.1. However, an assertion purporting to be on the lawyer's own knowledge, as in an affidavit by the lawyer or in a statement in open court, may properly be made only when the lawyer knows the assertion is true or believes it to be true on the basis of a reasonably diligent inquiry. There are circumstances where failure to make a disclosure is the equivalent of an affirmative misrepresentation. The obligation prescribed in Rule 1.2(d) not to counsel a client to commit or assist the client in committing a fraud applies in litigation. Regarding compliance with Rule 1.2(d), see the Comment to that Rule. See also the Comment to Rule 8.4(b).

Legal Argument

[4] Legal argument based on a knowingly false representation of law constitutes dishonesty toward the tribunal. A lawyer is not required to make a disinterested exposition of the law, but must recognize the existence of pertinent legal authorities. Furthermore, as stated in paragraph (a)(2), an advocate has a duty to disclose directly adverse authority in the controlling jurisdiction that has not been disclosed by the opposing party. The underlying concept is that legal argument is a discussion seeking to determine the legal premises properly applicable to the case.

Offering Evidence

[5] Paragraph (a)(3) requires that the lawyer refuse to offer evidence that the lawyer knows to be false, regardless of the client's wishes. This duty is premised on the lawyer's obligation as an officer of the court to prevent the trier of fact from being misled by false evidence. A lawyer does not violate this Rule if the lawyer offers the evidence for the purpose of establishing its falsity.

[6] If a lawyer knows that the client intends to testify falsely or wants the lawyer to introduce false evidence, the lawyer should seek to persuade the client that the evidence should not be offered. If the persuasion is ineffective and the lawyer continues to represent the client, the lawyer must refuse to offer the false evidence. If only a portion of a witness's testimony will be false, the lawyer may call the witness to testify but may not elicit or otherwise permit the witness to present the testimony that the lawyer knows is false.

[7] The duties stated in paragraphs (a) and (b) apply to all lawyers, including defense counsel in criminal cases. In some jurisdictions, however, courts have required counsel to present the accused as a witness or to give a narrative statement if the accused so desires, even if counsel knows that the testimony or statement will be false. The obligation of the advocate under the Rules of Professional Conduct is subordinate to such requirements. See also Comment [9].

[8] The prohibition against offering false evidence only applies if the lawyer knows that the evidence is false. A lawyer's reasonable belief that evidence is false does not preclude its presentation to the trier of fact. A lawyer's knowledge that evidence is false, however, can be inferred from the circumstances. See Rule 1.0(f). Thus, although a lawyer should resolve doubts about the veracity of testimony or other evidence in favor of the client, the lawyer cannot ignore an obvious falsehood.

[9] Although paragraph (a)(3) only prohibits a lawyer from offering evidence the lawyer knows to be false, it permits the lawyer to refuse to offer testimony or other proof that the lawyer reasonably believes is false. Offering such proof may reflect adversely on the lawyer's ability to discriminate in the quality of evidence and thus impair the lawyer's effectiveness as an advocate. Because of the special protections historically provided criminal defendants, however, this Rule does not permit a lawyer to refuse to offer the testimony of such a client where the lawyer reasonably believes but does not know that the testimony will be false. Unless the lawyer knows the testimony will be false, the lawyer must honor the client's decision to testify. See also Comment [7].

Remedial Measures

[10] Having offered material evidence in the belief that it was true, a lawyer may subsequently come to know that the evidence is false. Or, a lawyer may be surprised when the lawyer's client, or another witness called by the lawyer, offers testimony the lawyer knows to be false, either during the lawyer's direct examination or in response to cross-examination by the opposing lawyer. In such situations or if the lawyer knows of the falsity of testimony elicited from the client during a deposition, the lawyer must take reasonable remedial measures. In such situations, the advocate's proper course is to remonstrate with the client confidentially, advise the client of the lawyer's duty of candor to the tribunal and seek the client's cooperation with respect to the withdrawal or correction of the false statements or evidence. If that fails, the advocate must take further remedial action. If withdrawal from the representation is not permitted or will not undo the effect of the false evidence, the advocate must make such disclosure to the tribunal as is reasonably necessary to remedy the situation, even if doing so requires the lawyer to reveal information that otherwise would be protected by Rule 1.6. It is for the tribunal then to determine what should be done - making a statement about the matter to the trier of fact, ordering a mistrial or perhaps nothing.

[11] The disclosure of a client's false testimony can result in grave consequences to the client, including not only a sense of betrayal but also loss of the case and perhaps a prosecution for perjury. But the alternative is that the lawyer cooperate in deceiving the court, thereby subverting the truth-finding process which the adversary system is designed to implement. See Rule 1.2(d). Furthermore, unless it is clearly understood that the lawyer will act upon the duty to disclose the existence of false evidence, the client can simply reject the lawyer's advice to reveal the false evidence and insist that the lawyer keep silent. Thus the client could in effect coerce the lawyer into being a party to fraud on the court.

Preserving Integrity of Adjudicative Process

[12] Lawyers have a special obligation to protect a tribunal against criminal or fraudulent conduct that

undermines the integrity of the adjudicative process, such as bribing, intimidating or otherwise unlawfully communicating with a witness, juror, court official or other participant in the proceeding, unlawfully destroying or concealing documents or other evidence or failing to disclose information to the tribunal when required by law to do so. Thus, paragraph (b) requires a lawyer to take reasonable remedial measures, including disclosure if necessary, whenever the lawyer knows that a person, including the lawyer's client, intends to engage, is engaging or has engaged in criminal or fraudulent conduct related to the proceeding.

Duration of Obligation

[13] A practical time limit on the obligation to rectify false evidence or false statements of law and fact has to be established. The conclusion of the proceeding is a reasonably definite point for the termination of the obligation. A proceeding has concluded within the meaning of this Rule when a final judgment in the proceeding has been affirmed on appeal or the time for review has passed.

Ex Parte Proceedings

[14] Ordinarily, an advocate has the limited responsibility of presenting one side of the matters that a tribunal should consider in reaching a decision; the conflicting position is expected to be presented by the opposing party. However, in any ex parte proceeding, such as an application for a temporary restraining order, there is no balance of presentation by opposing advocates. The object of an ex parte proceeding is nevertheless to yield a substantially just result. The judge has an affirmative responsibility to accord the absent party just consideration. The lawyer for the represented party has the correlative duty to make disclosures of material facts known to the lawyer and that the lawyer reasonably believes are necessary to an informed decision.

Withdrawal

[15] Normally, a lawyer's compliance with the duty of candor imposed by this Rule does not require that the lawyer withdraw from the representation of a client whose interests will be or have been adversely affected by the lawyer's disclosure. The lawyer may, however, be required by Rule 1.16(a) to seek permission of the tribunal to withdraw if the lawyer's compliance with this Rule's duty of candor results in such an extreme deterioration of the client-lawyer relationship that the lawyer can no longer competently represent the client. Also see Rule 1.16(b) for the circumstances in which a lawyer will be permitted to seek a tribunal's permission to withdraw. In connection with a request for permission to withdraw that is premised on a client's misconduct, a lawyer may reveal information relating to the representation only to the extent reasonably necessary to comply with this Rule or as otherwise permitted by Rule 1.6.

Rule 3.4 Fairness to Opposing Party and Counsel

Rule 3.5 Impartiality and Decorum of the Tribunal

Rule 3.6 Trial Publicity

Rule 3.7 Lawyer as Witness

Rule 3.8 Special Responsibilities of a Prosecutor

Rule 3.9 Advocate in Nonadjudicative Proceedings

TRANSACTIONS WITH PERSONS OTHER THAN CLIENTS

Rule 4.1 Truthfulness in Statements to Others

Rule 4.2 Communication with Person Represented by Counsel

Rule 4.3 Dealing with Unrepresented Person

Rule 4.4 Respect for Rights of Third Persons

LAW FIRMS AND ASSOCIATIONS

Rule 5.1 Responsibilities of a Partner or Supervisory Lawyer

Rule 5.2 Responsibilities of a Subordinate Lawyer

Rule 5.3 Responsibilities Regarding Nonlawyer Assistants

With respect to a nonlawyer employed or retained by or associated with a lawyer:

(a) a partner, and a lawyer who individually or together with other lawyers possesses comparable managerial authority in a law firm shall make reasonable efforts to ensure that the firm has in effect measures giving reasonable assurance that the person's conduct is compatible with the professional obligations of the lawyer;

(b) a lawyer having direct supervisory authority over the nonlawyer shall make reasonable efforts to ensure that the person's conduct is compatible with the professional obligations of the lawyer; and

(c) a lawyer shall be responsible for conduct of such a person that would be a violation of the Rules of Professional Conduct if engaged in by a lawyer if:

(1) the lawyer orders or, with the knowledge of the specific conduct, ratifies the conduct involved; or

(2) the lawyer is a partner or has comparable managerial authority in the law firm in which the person is

employed, or has direct supervisory authority over the person, and knows of the conduct at a time when its consequences can be avoided or mitigated but fails to take reasonable remedial action.

Comment:

[1] Lawyers generally employ assistants in their practice, including secretaries, investigators, law student interns, and paraprofessionals. Such assistants, whether employees or independent contractors, act for the lawyer in rendition of the lawyer's professional services. A lawyer must give such assistants appropriate instruction and supervision concerning the ethical aspects of their employment, particularly regarding the obligation not to disclose information relating to representation of the client, and should be responsible for their work product. The measures employed in supervising nonlawyers should take account of the fact that they do not have legal training and are not subject to professional discipline.

[2] Paragraph (a) requires lawyers with managerial authority within a law firm to make reasonable efforts to establish internal policies and procedures designed to provide reasonable assurance that nonlawyers in the firm will act in a way compatible with the Rules of Professional Conduct. See Comment [1] to Rule 5.1. Paragraph (b) applies to lawyers who have supervisory authority over the work of a nonlawyer. Paragraph (c) specifies the circumstances in which a lawyer is responsible for conduct of a nonlawyer that would be a violation of the Rules of Professional Conduct if engaged in by a lawyer.

Rule 5.4 Professional Independence of a Lawyer

Rule 5.5 Unauthorized Practice of Law

A lawyer shall not:

(a) practice law in a jurisdiction where doing so violates the regulation of the legal profession in that jurisdiction; or

(b) assist a person who is not a member of the bar in the performance of activity that constitutes the unauthorized practice of law.

Comment:

[1] A lawyer may practice law only in a jurisdiction in which the lawyer is authorized to practice. A lawyer may be admitted to practice law in a jurisdiction on a regular basis or may be authorized by court rule or order or by law to practice for a limited purpose or on a restricted basis. Paragraph (a) applies to unauthorized practice of law by a lawyer, whether through the lawyer's direct action or by the lawyer assisting another person.

[2] The definition of the practice of law is established by law and varies from one jurisdiction to another. Whatever

the definition, limiting the practice of law to members of the bar protects the public against rendition of legal services by unqualified persons. This Rule does not prohibit a lawyer from employing the services of paraprofessionals and delegating functions to them, so long as the lawyer supervises the delegated work and retains responsibility for their work. See Rule 5.3.

[3] A lawyer may provide professional advice and instruction to nonlawyers whose employment requires knowledge of the law; for example, claims adjusters, employees of financial or commercial institutions, social workers, accountants and persons employed in government agencies. Lawyers also may assist independent nonlawyers, such as paraprofessionals, who are authorized by the law of a jurisdiction to provide particular law-related services. In addition, a lawyer may counsel nonlawyers who wish to proceed pro se.

[4] Other than as authorized by law or this Rule, a lawyer who is not admitted to practice generally in this jurisdiction violates paragraph (b) if the lawyer establishes an office or other systematic and continuous presence in this jurisdiction for the practice of law. Presence may be systematic and continuous even if the lawyer is not physically present here. Such a lawyer must not hold out to the public or otherwise represent that the lawyer is admitted to practice law in this jurisdiction. See also Rules 7.1(a) and 7.5(b).

[5] There are occasions in which a lawyer admitted to practice in another United States jurisdiction, and not disbarred or suspended from practice in any jurisdiction, may provide legal services on a temporary basis in this jurisdiction under circumstances that do not create an unreasonable risk to the interests of their clients, the public or the courts. Paragraph (c) identifies four such circumstances. The fact that conduct is not so identified does not imply that the conduct is or is not authorized. With the exception of paragraphs (d)(1) and (d)(2), this Rule does not authorize a lawyer to establish an office or other systematic and continuous presence in this jurisdiction without being admitted to practice generally here.

[6] There is no single test to determine whether a lawyer's services are provided on a "temporary basis" in this jurisdiction, and may therefore be permissible under paragraph (c). Services may be "temporary" even though the lawyer provides services in this jurisdiction on a recurring basis, or for an extended period of time, as when the lawyer is representing a client in a single lengthy negotiation or litigation.

[7] Paragraphs (c) and (d) apply to lawyers who are admitted to practice law in any United States jurisdiction, which includes the District of Columbia and any state, territory or commonwealth of the United States. The word

"admitted" in paragraph (c) contemplates that the lawyer is authorized to practice in the jurisdiction in which the lawyer is admitted and excludes a lawyer who while technically admitted is not authorized to practice, because, for example, the lawyer is on inactive status.

[8] Paragraph (c)(1) recognizes that the interests of clients and the public are protected if a lawyer admitted only in another jurisdiction associates with a lawyer licensed to practice in this jurisdiction. For this paragraph to apply, however, the lawyer admitted to practice in this jurisdiction must actively participate in and share responsibility for the representation of the client.

[9] Lawyers not admitted to practice generally in a jurisdiction may be authorized by law or order of a tribunal or an administrative agency to appear before the tribunal or agency. This authority may be granted pursuant to formal rules governing admission pro hac vice or pursuant to informal practice of the tribunal or agency. Under paragraph (c)(2), a lawyer does not violate this Rule when the lawyer appears before a tribunal or agency pursuant to such authority. To the extent that a court rule or other law of this jurisdiction requires a lawyer who is not admitted to practice in this jurisdiction to obtain admission pro hac vice before appearing before a tribunal or administrative agency, this Rule requires the lawyer to obtain that authority.

[10] Paragraph (c)(2) also provides that a lawyer rendering services in this jurisdiction on a temporary basis does not violate this Rule when the lawyer engages in conduct in anticipation of a proceeding or hearing in a jurisdiction in which the lawyer is authorized to practice law or in which the lawyer reasonably expects to be admitted pro hac vice. Examples of such conduct include meetings with the client, interviews of potential witnesses, and the review of documents. Similarly, a lawyer admitted only in another jurisdiction may engage in conduct temporarily in this jurisdiction in connection with pending litigation in another jurisdiction in which the lawyer is or reasonably expects to be authorized to appear, including taking depositions in this jurisdiction.

[11] When a lawyer has been or reasonably expects to be admitted to appear before a court or administrative agency, paragraph (c)(2) also permits conduct by lawyers who are associated with that lawyer in the matter, but who do not expect to appear before the court or administrative agency. For example, subordinate lawyers may conduct research, review documents, and attend meetings with witnesses in support of the lawyer responsible for the litigation.

[12] Paragraph (c)(3) permits a lawyer admitted to practice law in another jurisdiction to perform services on a temporary basis in this jurisdiction if those services are in or reasonably related to a pending or potential arbitration, mediation, or other alternative dispute resolution proceeding in this or another jurisdiction, if the services arise out of or are reasonably related to the lawyer's practice in a jurisdiction in which the lawyer is admitted to practice. The lawyer, however, must obtain admission pro hac vice in the case of a court-annexed arbitration or mediation or otherwise if court rules or law so require.

[13] Paragraph (c)(4) permits a lawyer admitted in another jurisdiction to provide certain legal services on a temporary basis in this jurisdiction that arise out of or are reasonably related to the lawyer's practice in a jurisdiction in which the lawyer is admitted but are not within paragraphs (c)(2) or (c)(3). These services include both legal services and services that nonlawyers may perform but that are considered the practice of law when performed by lawyers.

[14] Paragraphs (c)(3) and (c)(4) require that the services arise out of or be reasonably related to the lawyer's practice in a jurisdiction in which the lawyer is admitted. A variety of factors evidence such a relationship. The lawyer's client may have been previously represented by the lawyer, or may be resident in or have substantial contacts with the jurisdiction in which the lawyer is admitted. The matter, although involving other jurisdictions, may have a significant connection with that jurisdiction. In other cases, significant aspects of the lawyer's work might be conducted in that jurisdiction or a significant aspect of the matter may involve the law of that jurisdiction. The necessary relationship might arise when the client's activities or the legal issues involve multiple jurisdictions, such as when the officers of a multinational corporation survey potential business sites and seek the services of their lawyer in assessing the relative merits of each. In addition, the services may draw on the lawyer's recognized expertise developed through the regular practice of law on behalf of clients in matters involving a particular body of federal, nationally-uniform, foreign, or international law.

[15] Paragraph (d) identifies two circumstances in which a lawyer who is admitted to practice in another United States jurisdiction, and is not disbarred or suspended from practice in any jurisdiction, may establish an office or other systematic and continuous presence in this jurisdiction for the practice of law as well as provide legal services on a temporary basis. Except as provided in paragraphs (d)(1) and (d)(2), a lawyer who is admitted to practice law in another jurisdiction and who establishes an office or other systematic or continuous presence in this jurisdiction must become admitted to practice law generally in this jurisdiction.

[16] Paragraph (d)(1) applies to a lawyer who is employed by a client to provide legal services to the client

or its organizational affiliates, i.e., entities that control, are controlled by, or are under common control with the employer. This paragraph does not authorize the provision of personal legal services to the employer's officers or employees. The paragraph applies to in-house corporate lawyers, government lawyers and others who are employed to render legal services to the employer. The lawyer's ability to represent the employer outside the jurisdiction in which the lawyer is licensed generally serves the interests of the employer and does not create an unreasonable risk to the client and others because the employer is well situated to assess the lawyer's qualifications and the quality of the lawyer's work.

[17] If an employed lawyer establishes an office or other systematic presence in this jurisdiction for the purpose of rendering legal services to the employer, the lawyer may be subject to registration or other requirements, including assessments for client protection funds and mandatory continuing legal education.

[18] Paragraph (d)(2) recognizes that a lawyer may provide legal services in a jurisdiction in which the lawyer is not licensed when authorized to do so by federal or other law, which includes statute, court rule, executive regulation or judicial precedent.

[19] A lawyer who practices law in this jurisdiction pursuant to paragraphs (c) or (d) or otherwise is subject to the disciplinary authority of this jurisdiction. See Rule 8.5(a).

[20] In some circumstances, a lawyer who practices law in this jurisdiction pursuant to paragraphs (c) or (d) may have to inform the client that the lawyer is not licensed to practice law in this jurisdiction. For example, that may be required when the representation occurs primarily in this jurisdiction and requires knowledge of the law of this jurisdiction. See Rule 1.4(b).

[21] Paragraphs (c) and (d) do not authorize communications advertising legal services to prospective clients in this jurisdiction by lawyers who are admitted to practice in other jurisdictions. Whether and how lawyers may communicate the availability of their services to prospective clients in this jurisdiction is governed by Rules 7.1 to 7.5.

Effective Learning: How to Study

Everyone learns differently. Some people seem to absorb information like a sponge while others must work hard to soak up any information. Although it is true that some people have photographic memories, they are few and far between. Most likely the people who seem to absorb information "like a sponge" have learned how to maximize their learning experiences. Most of us do not take the time to figure out how we learn best and as a result probably spend more time than necessary to achieve the same level of results as more proficient learners. Have you ever wondered how some people, who are just average students, seem to always get A's? If you were to ask them, they would probably tell you that they spend more time than most people studying and preparing, or that they have learned how to study more effectively and efficiently in the time they have available. A good starting point is to determine how you learn best and work out methods to maximize the time and effort you have available.

LEARNING STYLES

A learning style is the way you learn most effectively. Everyone has his or her own learning style; there are no "better" or "correct" ways to learn. Somewhere in your school career you may have been given tests to determine your personal learning styles, such as the Hogan/Champagne Personal Style Indicator or the Kolb Learning Style Inventory. These and similar assessments are available through most school advisors and guidance counselors. If you want help in determining your learning styles, take the initiative for your own success and immediately make an appointment with someone who can administer an assessment.

Learning styles fall into these categories:

- independent (competitive) versus collaborative
- structured versus unstructured
- auditory versus visual
- spatial versus verbal
- practical versus creative
- applied versus conceptual
- factual versus analytical
- emotional versus logical

It sounds like a lot to consider, but taking a few minutes to determine which learning style best suits you can save you countless hours of frustration—hours that could be better devoted to studying or other activities.

Independent vs. Collaborative

Do you prefer working with a group or independently? Some people find it easier to avoid all distractions by working alone; others prefer working in a study group and sharing information as part of the learning process.

If you prefer working independently, you may want to obtain additional course information from study guides and computer assisted instruction. You may prefer lecture-format classes to small discussion courses. If you prefer working collaboratively, you may wish to form study groups early in the semester or find a tutor to work with, and you should choose courses that include small discussion groups or group projects.

Structured vs. Unstructured

Structured learners feel more comfortable when they formalize their study habits, for example, by selecting a definite time and place in which to study every day. If you are a structured learner, you may find it useful to create to-do lists and keep a written schedule of classes, study times, and activities.

Unstructured learners tend to resist formalizing their study plan and try to avoid feeling "locked-in." The unstructured learner tends to procrastinate. Procrastinators need to find ways to give more structure to their learning activities. One method is to join a study group of students who are more organized.

Auditory vs. Visual

Auditory learners learn best by listening. Visual learners learn best from what they see. For visual learners, it is not always possible to learn everything by listening to lectures or by reading and watching video presentations. Auditory learners may find it more efficient to listen to lectures and then read related material. Visual learners may do better reading the book first and then attending lectures. Auditory learners may also find group discussion and study group activities beneficial.

Spatial vs. Verbal

Spatial learners are better at reading and interpreting maps, charts, and other graphics. Verbal learners prefer to read words rather than interpret graphics. Spatial learners need to create and incorporate their own diagrams, maps, timelines, and other such graphics into their notes. Verbal learners need to translate or obtain translations of graphics into words. A useful technique for verbal learners is to take notes that describe the material, including the graphics, in such a way that a visually impaired student could understand the graphic representation from the verbal description. Teaming up with a visually impaired student may be mutually beneficial.

Practical vs. Creative

Practical learners tend to be methodical and systematic. They prefer specific instruction that is directed and focused. Creative learners prefer experimentation and creative activities. Practical learners may benefit from creating an organized study plan for each course, including detailed to-do lists and a calendar. For the creative learner, courses that allow writing and other creative approaches may be more satisfying.

Applied vs. Conceptual

Applied learners want to know how information can be applied to given situations. The conceptual learner is not so much concerned with the application as with the underlying concepts. Applied learners need to focus on ways in which the ideas presented in courses and lectures can be applied. Taking of notes that include examples for applying the concepts helps them recall the concepts later. Conceptual learners may find it useful to consider the concepts in a broader context than that of the narrow lecture presentation.

Factual vs. Analytical

Factual learners are good with details and enjoy learning interesting and unusual facts. They prefer objective tests. Analytical learners like to break a topic down into its component parts in order to understand how the parts relate to each other. Analytical learners prefer essay exams that allow them to demonstrate how their knowledge relates to the question. Factual learners may want to make lists of facts, which they can associate with prior knowledge. Analytical learners may want to analyze the organization as they read a textbook, looking for trends and patterns.

Emotional vs. Logical

Emotional learners tend to prefer human-interest stories to material that presents just facts and logic. Logical learners prefer to understand the factual basis, including statistics, of an argument. Emotional learners may find that reading biographical sketches helps them understand factual subjects.

PUTTING IT ALL TOGETHER

1. Understand yourself. From the previous list of types of learners, select the descriptions in each category that best fit your style of learning. Look back at courses and classes you have taken in which you have done well or that you enjoyed the most. You may see a pattern that will help you understand your learning style.

2. Set goals. Determine your personal and occupational goals. Do you want a career working with people or with things? Do you want a professional career working directly with people or behind the scenes supporting others? What courses will help you acquire the skills and knowledge you need to achieve these goals?

3. Make a plan. At the end of your educational path should be a goal. It may be a personal goal to be an outstanding parent or partner, or it may be a goal to be a generalist or a specialist in an occupation or profession. To achieve these goals you will need to focus on courses that give you the necessary skills and knowledge. Within the courses may be options that accommodate your learning style, such as large lecture classes versus small group discussion classes, face-to-face courses versus distance learning courses, and so on. Create a personal plan that allows for flexibility as your goals or interests change—a good foundation will allow you more flexibility in courses and curriculum. Don't be afraid to admit that you did not enjoy some courses you expected to enjoy or that you enjoyed some classes you never thought would give you pleasure. Such insights may help you fine-tune your personal and professional goals.

4. Check your progress. Periodically assess how well you are doing in individual classes as well as in your overall program of study. Use the opportunity to assess why you are doing better than you expected in some classes and not as well in others. You may need to adjust your overall plan or merely your learning methods. Or, outside influences such as work, family, or personal issues may be interfering with your learning. Periodic self-assessment is the first step to modifying your goals.

5. Make adjustments. As your goals change, so will your plan. Don't be afraid to make the adjustments necessary to achieve your goals or to change your goals as your interests change. Life rarely follows a straight path. Be adaptable and make adjustments when necessary.

SCHEDULING TIME

Most people use a calendar to keep track of information such as birthdays, appointments, or upcoming events. They may include vacations, concerts, or other special events or activities. Depending on your personal style, you might include to-do lists or an hour-by-hour schedule of classes and other activities. Scheduling school and study time is helpful to most students.

Whichever method works best for you, use it to track the amount of time you spend in all of your activities so that you can budget your time more accurately. When scheduling, keep in mind that there is a limit to everyone's power of concentration. Don't schedule so many activities that they exceed your mental or physical abilities.

SUPPLEMENTAL LEARNING AIDS

1. Study guides. Most textbooks have a study guide that will give you additional information; they frequently include sample tests and quizzes. Your instructor may or may not require the use of a study guide. If you need additional reinforcement, you may want to purchase a study guide even if it is not a required part of the course.

2. Flash cards. Flash cards are available for many courses in college bookstores. However, you will learn more by preparing your own and customizing them to the course you are taking. On the front side of an index card write a word, phrase, or concept, and write the definition or explanation on the reverse side. With a properly prepared set of flash cards, you may not need to refer to the text or your notes when studying for a test.

3. Companion websites. Many publishers offer companion websites for their textbooks. Many of these websites are available on the publisher's website without cost or for a nominal fee. Often these websites are the equivalent of an online study guide. Others offer self-tests. The publisher may post information that has become available since the publication of the textbook.

4. Outlining. Few people have a photographic memory or the ability to absorb material on one reading. The following approach can help you use your textbook effectively.

a. *How long is the chapter?* Check the length of the chapter and your reading assignment before you start. Most textbooks are filled with graphics and illustrations that reduce the amount of actual reading time to a manageable level.

b. *Scan the chapter.* Scan the material to get a feel for what will be covered.

c. *Chapter objectives.* At the beginnings of chapters, most textbooks list what you should learn from reading the chapter. These chapter objectives help you focus on important topics, information, and themes.

d. *Read the chapter.* Quickly read through the chapter to get an overall sense of the material and how the sections relate to each other.

e. *Underline the important items.* After you have read quickly through the chapter, go back over the material and underline the items you believe are important in pencil.

f. *Go to class.* From the instructor's lecture and class discussion you may find that what you think is important changes.

g. *Highlight the important material.* After class, use a highlighter to highlight what you now believe to be the important information in the text. You will probably find that it is substantially less than what you underlined in pencil.

h. *Make your flash cards.* From the highlighted information, create a set of flash cards for each chapter.

5. Tutors. Not everyone can afford the luxury of a personal tutor. However, most colleges and universities have a tutoring center or some form of tutoring assistance. If you are having difficulty, don't be afraid to ask for help before it is too late. At the beginning of the semester determine what personalized help is available for each course. You may not need to use this information, but having it will reduce your anxiety and panic if you realize that you need some help. Don't be afraid to ask your instructor for help. Your instructor wants you to succeed. If you are doing everything you can to be successful in a class, the instructor should be more than happy to help you or direct you for help.

6. Study groups. If you are the type of learner who benefits from working with others, form a study group at the beginning of each semester in each course. After the first class ask if there are others who wish to form a study group, or post a notice on the course bulletin board website. One advantage of study groups is the opportunity to share class notes as well as ideas. Verbal learners can benefit from having visual learners in the study group who can interpret and explain charts, graphs, and maps. Study groups can motivate procrastinators to complete tasks on time.

7. Tests. Most students suffer from some form of test anxiety. At the beginning of each course, ask the instructor the exam schedule and the type of tests he or she will be giving. Some schools maintain copies of all tests that students can use for practice. If your school does not maintain these, ask your instructors if they will make available sample tests and quizzes. Practice tests may be available in the study guide for the text or on a companion website. If you are in a study group, members can prepare practice tests as part of test preparation.

For more detailed information about study skills, see Judy M. Roberts, *Effective Study Skills: Maximizing Your Academic Potential* (Prentice Hall, 1998).

The Constitution of the United States of America

PREAMBLE

We the People of the United States, in Order to form a more perfect Union, establish Justice, insure domestic Tranquility, provide for the common defense, promote the general Welfare, and secure the Blessings of Liberty to ourselves and our Posterity, do ordain and establish this Constitution for the United States of America.

ARTICLE I

Section 1. All legislative Powers herein granted shall be vested in a Congress of the United States, which shall consist of a Senate and House of Representatives.

Section 2. The House of Representatives shall be composed of Members chosen every second Year by the People of the several States, and the Electors in each State shall have the Qualifications requisite for Electors of the most numerous Branch of the State Legislature.

No Person shall be a Representative who shall not have attained to the Age of twenty five Years, and been seven Years a Citizen of the United States, and who shall not, when elected, be an Inhabitant of that State in which he shall be chosen.

Representatives and direct Taxes shall be apportioned among the several States which may be included within this Union, according to their respective Numbers, which shall be determined by adding to the whole Number of free Persons, including those bound to Service for a Term of Years, and excluding Indians not taxed, three fifths of all other Persons. The actual Enumeration shall be made within three Years after the first Meeting of the Congress of the United States, and within every subsequent Term of ten Years, in such Manner as they shall by Law direct. The Number of Representatives shall not exceed one for every thirty Thousand, but each State shall have at Least one Representative; and until such enumeration shall be made, the State of New Hampshire shall be entitled to chuse three, Massachusetts eight, Rhode-Island and Providence Plantations one, Connecticut five, New-York six, New Jersey four, Pennsylvania eight, Delaware one, Maryland six, Virginia ten, North Carolina five, South Carolina five, and Georgia three.

When vacancies happen in the Representation from any State, the Executive Authority thereof shall issue Writs of Election to fill such Vacancies.

The House of Representatives shall chuse their Speaker and other Officers; and shall have the sole Power of Impeachment.

Section 3. The Senate of the United States shall be composed of two Senators from each State, chosen by the Legislature thereof for six Years; and each Senator shall have one Vote.

Immediately after they shall be assembled in Consequence of the first Election, they shall be divided as equally as may be into three Classes. The Seats of the Senators of the first Class shall be vacated at the Expiration of the second Year, of the second Class at the Expiration of the fourth Year, and of the third Class at the Expiration of the sixth Year, so that one third may be chosen every second Year; and if Vacancies happen by Resignation, or otherwise, during the Recess of the Legislature of any State, the Executive thereof may make temporary Appointments until the next Meeting of the Legislature, which shall then fill such Vacancies.

No Person shall be a Senator who shall not have attained to the Age of thirty Years, and been nine Years a Citizen of the United States, and who shall not, when elected, be an Inhabitant of that State for which he shall be chosen.

The Vice President of the United States shall be President of the Senate, but shall have no Vote, unless they be equally divided.

The Senate shall chuse their other Officers, and also a President pro tempore, in the Absence of the Vice President, or when he shall exercise the Office of President of the United States.

The Senate shall have the sole Power to try all Impeachments. When sitting for that Purpose, they shall be on Oath or Affirmation. When the President of the United States is tried, the Chief Justice shall preside: And no Person shall be convicted without the Concurrence of two thirds of the Members present.

Judgment in Cases of Impeachment shall not extend further than to removal from Office, and disqualification to hold and enjoy any Office of honor, Trust or Profit under the United States: but the Party convicted shall nevertheless be liable and subject to Indictment, Trial, Judgment and Punishment, according to Law.

Section 4. The Times, Places and Manner of holding Elections for Senators and Representatives, shall be prescribed in each State by the Legislature thereof; but the Congress may at any time by Law make or alter such Regulations, except as to the Places of chusing Senators.

The Congress shall assemble at least once in every Year, and such Meeting shall be on the first Monday in December, unless they shall by Law appoint a different Day.

Section 5. Each House shall be the Judge of the Elections, Returns and Qualifications of its own Members, and a Majority of each shall constitute a Quorum to do Business; but a smaller Number may adjourn from day to day, and may be authorized to compel the Attendance of absent Members, in such Manner, and under such Penalties as each House may provide.

Each House may determine the Rules of its Proceedings, punish its Members for disorderly Behaviour, and, with the Concurrence of two thirds, expel a Member.

Each House shall keep a Journal of its Proceedings, and from time to time publish the same, excepting such Parts as may in their Judgment require Secrecy; and the Yeas and Nays of the Members of either House on any question shall, at the Desire of one fifth of those Present, be entered on the Journal.

Neither House, during the Session of Congress, shall, without the Consent of the other, adjourn for more than three days, nor to any other Place than that in which the two Houses shall be sitting.

Section 6. The Senators and Representatives shall receive a Compensation for their Services, to be ascertained by Law, and paid out of the Treasury of the United States. They shall in all Cases, except Treason, Felony and Breach of the Peace, be privileged from Arrest during their Attendance at the Session of their respective Houses, and in going to and returning from the same; and for any Speech or Debate in either House, they shall not be questioned in any other Place.

No Senator or Representative shall, during the Time for which he was elected, be appointed to any civil Office under the Authority of the United States, which shall have been created, or the Emoluments whereof shall have been encreased during such time; and no Person holding any Office under the United States, shall be a Member of either House during his Continuance in Office.

Section 7. All Bills for raising Revenue shall originate in the House of Representatives; but the Senate may propose or concur with Amendments as on other Bills.

Every Bill which shall have passed the House of Representatives and the Senate, shall, before it become a Law, be presented to the President of the United States: If he approve he shall sign it, but if not he shall return it, with his Objections to that House in which it shall have originated, who shall enter the Objections at large on their Journal, and proceed to reconsider it.If after such Reconsideration two thirds of that House shall agree to pass the Bill, it shall be sent, together with the Objections, to the other House, by which it shall likewise be reconsidered, and if approved by two thirds of that House, it shall become a Law. But in all such Cases the Votes of both Houses shall be determined by yeas and Nays, and the Names of the Persons voting for and against the Bill shall be entered on the Journal of each House respectively. If any Bill shall not be returned by the President within ten Days (Sundays excepted) after it shall have been presented to him, the Same shall be a Law, in like Manner as if he had signed it, unless the Congress by their Adjournment prevent its Return, in which Case it shall not be a Law.

Every Order, Resolution, or Vote to which the Concurrence of the Senate and House of Representatives may be necessary (except on a question of Adjournment) shall be presented to the President of the United States; and before the Same shall take Effect, shall be approved by him, or being disapproved by him, shall be repassed by two thirds of the Senate and House of Representatives, according to the Rules and Limitations prescribed in the Case of a Bill.

Section 8. The Congress shall have Power To lay and collect Taxes, Duties, Imposts and Excises, to pay the Debts and provide for the common Defence and general Welfare of the United States; but all Duties, Imposts and Excises shall be uniform throughout the United States;

To borrow Money on the credit of the United States;

To regulate Commerce with foreign Nations, and among the several States, and with the Indian Tribes;

To establish an uniform Rule of Naturalization, and uniform Laws on the subject of Bankruptcies throughout the United States;

To coin Money, regulate the Value thereof, and of foreign Coin, and fix the Standard of Weights and Measures;

To provide for the Punishment of counterfeiting the Securities and current Coin of the United States;

To establish Post Offices and post Roads;

To promote the Progress of Science and useful Arts, by securing for limited Times to Authors and Inventors the exclusive Right to their respective Writings and Discoveries;

To constitute Tribunals inferior to the supreme Court;

To define and punish Piracies and Felonies committed on the high Seas, and Offences against the Law of Nations;

To declare War, grant Letters of Marque and Reprisal, and make Rules concerning Captures on Land and Water;

To raise and support Armies, but no Appropriation of Money to that Use shall be for a longer Term than two Years;

To provide and maintain a Navy;

To make Rules for the Government and Regulation of the land and naval Forces;

To provide for calling forth the Militia to execute the Laws of the Union, suppress Insurrections and repel Invasions;

To provide for organizing, arming, and disciplining, the Militia, and for governing such Part of them as may be employed in the Service of the United States, reserving to the States respectively, the Appointment of the Officers, and the Authority of training the Militia according to the discipline prescribed by Congress;

To exercise exclusive Legislation in all Cases whatsoever, over such District (not exceeding ten Miles square) as may, by Cession of particular States, and the Acceptance of Congress, become the Seat of the Government of the United States, and to exercise like Authority over all Places purchased by the Consent of the Legislature of the State in which the Same shall be, for the Erection of Forts, Magazines, Arsenals, dock-Yards, and other needful Buildings;—And

To make all Laws which shall be necessary and proper for carrying into Execution the foregoing Powers, and all other Powers vested by this Constitution in the Government of the United States, or in any Department or Officer thereof.

Section 9. The Migration or Importation of such Persons as any of the States now existing shall think proper to admit, shall not be prohibited by the Congress prior to the Year one thousand eight hundred and eight, but a Tax or duty may be imposed on such Importation, not exceeding ten dollars for each Person.

The Privilege of the Writ of Habeas Corpus shall not be suspended, unless when in Cases of Rebellion or Invasion the public Safety may require it.

No Bill of Attainder or ex post facto Law shall be passed.

No Capitation, or other direct, Tax shall be laid, unless in Proportion to the Census or enumeration herein before directed to be taken.

No Tax or Duty shall be laid on Articles exported from any State.

No Preference shall be given by any Regulation of Commerce or Revenue to the Ports of one State over those of another; nor shall Vessels bound to, or from, one State, be obliged to enter, clear, or pay Duties in another.

No Money shall be drawn from the Treasury, but in Consequence of Appropriations made by Law; and a regular Statement and Account of the Receipts and Expenditures of all public Money shall be published from time to time.

No Title of Nobility shall be granted by the United States: And no Person holding any Office of Profit or Trust under them, shall, without the Consent of the Congress, accept of any present, Emolument, Office, or Title, of any kind whatever, from any King, Prince, or foreign State.

Section 10. No State shall enter into any Treaty, Alliance, or Confederation; grant Letters of Marque and Reprisal; coin Money; emit Bills of Credit; make any Thing but gold and silver Coin a Tender in Payment of Debts; pass any Bill of Attainder, ex post facto Law, or Law impairing the Obligation of Contracts, or grant any Title of Nobility.

No State shall, without the Consent of the Congress, lay any Imposts or Duties on Imports or Exports, except what may be absolutely necessary for executing it's inspection Laws: and the net Produce of all Duties and Imposts, laid by any State on Imports or Exports, shall be for the Use of the Treasury of the United States; and all such Laws shall be subject to the Revision and Controul of the Congress.

No State shall, without the Consent of Congress, lay any Duty of Tonnage, keep Troops, or Ships of War in time of Peace, enter into any Agreement or Compact with another State, or with a foreign Power, or engage in War, unless actually invaded, or in such imminent Danger as will not admit of delay.

ARTICLE II

Section 1. The executive Power shall be vested in a President of the United States of America. He shall hold his Office during the Term of four Years, and, together with the Vice President, chosen for the same Term, be elected, as follows:

Each State shall appoint, in such Manner as the Legislature thereof may direct, a Number of Electors, equal to the whole Number of Senators and Representatives to which the State may be entitled in the Congress: but no Senator or Representative, or Person holding an Office of Trust or Profit under the United States, shall be appointed an Elector.

The Electors shall meet in their respective States, and vote by Ballot for two Persons, of whom one at least shall not be an Inhabitant of the same State with themselves. And they shall make a List of all the Persons voted for, and of the Number of Votes for each; which List they shall sign and certify, and transmit sealed to the Seat of the Government of the United States, directed to the President of the Senate. The President of the Senate shall, in the Presence of the Senate and House of Representatives, open all the Certificates, and the Votes shall then be counted. The Person having the greatest Number of Votes shall be the President, if such Number be a Majority of the whole Number of Electors appointed; and if there be more than one who have such Majority, and have an equal Number of Votes, then the House of Representatives shall immediately chuse by Ballot one of them for President; and if no Person have a Majority, then from the five highest on the List the said House shall in like Manner chuse the President. But in chusing the President, the Votes shall be taken by States, the Representation from each State having one Vote; A quorum for this purpose shall consist of a Member or Members from two thirds of the States, and a Majority of all the States shall be necessary to a Choice. In every Case, after the Choice of the President, the Person having the greatest Number of Votes of the Electors shall be the Vice President. But if there should remain two or more who have equal Votes, the Senate shall chuse from them by Ballot the Vice President.

The Congress may determine the Time of chusing the Electors, and the Day on which they shall give their Votes; which Day shall be the same throughout the United States.

No Person except a natural born Citizen, or a Citizen of the United States, at the time of the Adoption of this Constitution, shall be eligible to the Office of President; neither shall any Person be eligible to that Office who shall not have attained to the Age of thirty five Years, and been fourteen Years a Resident within the United States.

In Case of the Removal of the President from Office, or of his Death, Resignation, or Inability to discharge the Powers and Duties of the said Office, the Same shall devolve on the Vice President, and the Congress may by Law provide for the Case of Removal, Death, Resignation or Inability, both of the President and Vice President, declaring what Officer shall then act as President, and such Officer shall act accordingly, until the Disability be removed, or a President shall be elected.

The President shall, at stated Times, receive for his Services, a Compensation, which shall neither be increased nor diminished during the Period for which he shall have been elected, and he shall not receive within that Period any other Emolument from the United States, or any of them.

Before he enter on the Execution of his Office, he shall take the following Oath or Affirmation:—"I do solemnly swear (or affirm) that I will faithfully execute the Office of President of the United States, and will to the best of my Ability, preserve, protect and defend the Constitution of the United States."

Section 2. The President shall be Commander in Chief of the Army and Navy of the United States, and of the Militia of the several States, when called into the actual Service of the United States; he may require the Opinion, in writing, of the principal Officer in each of the executive Departments, upon any Subject relating to the Duties of their respective Offices, and he shall have Power to grant Reprieves and Pardons for Offences against the United States, except in Cases of Impeachment.

He shall have Power, by and with the Advice and Consent of the Senate, to make Treaties, provided two thirds of the Senators present concur; and he shall nominate, and by and with the Advice and Consent of the Senate, shall appoint Ambassadors, other public Ministers and Consuls, Judges of the supreme Court, and all other Officers of the United States, whose Appointments are not herein otherwise provided for, and which shall be established by Law: but the Congress may by Law vest the Appointment of such inferior Officers, as they think proper, in the President alone, in the Courts of Law, or in the Heads of Departments.

The President shall have Power to fill up all Vacancies that may happen during the Recess of the Senate, by granting Commissions which shall expire at the End of their next Session.

Section 3. He shall from time to time give to the Congress Information of the State of the Union, and recommend to their Consideration such Measures as he shall judge necessary and expedient; he may, on extraordinary Occasions, convene both Houses, or either of them, and in Case of Disagreement between them, with Respect to the Time of Adjournment, he may adjourn them to such Time as he shall think proper; he shall receive Ambassadors and other public Ministers; he shall take Care that the Laws be faithfully executed, and shall Commission all the Officers of the United States.

Section 4. The President, Vice President and all civil Officers of the United States, shall be removed from Office on Impeachment for, and Conviction of, Treason, Bribery, or other high Crimes and Misdemeanors.

ARTICLE III

Section 1. The judicial Power of the United States shall be vested in one supreme Court, and in such inferior Courts as the Congress may from time to time ordain and establish. The Judges, both of the supreme and inferior Courts, shall hold their Offices during good Behaviour, and shall, at stated Times, receive for their Services a Compensation, which shall not be diminished during their Continuance in Office.

Section 2. The judicial Power shall extend to all Cases, in Law and Equity, arising under this Constitution, the Laws of the United States, and Treaties made, or which shall be made, under their Authority;—to all Cases affecting Ambassadors, other public Ministers and Consuls;—to all Cases of admiralty and maritime Jurisdiction;—to Controversies to which the United States shall be a Party;—to Controversies between two or more States;— between a State and Citizens of another State;—between Citizens of different States;—between Citizens of the same State claiming Lands under Grants of different States, and between a State, or the Citizens thereof, and foreign States, Citizens or Subjects.

In all Cases affecting Ambassadors, other public Ministers and Consuls, and those in which a State shall be Party, the supreme Court shall have original Jurisdiction. In all the other Cases before mentioned, the supreme Court shall have appellate Jurisdiction, both as to Law and Fact, with such Exceptions, and under such Regulations as the Congress shall make.

The Trial of all Crimes, except in Cases of Impeachment, shall be by Jury; and such Trial shall be held in the State where the said Crimes shall have been committed; but when not committed within any State, the Trial shall be at such Place or Places as the Congress may by Law have directed.

Section 3. Treason against the United States, shall consist only in levying War against them, or in adhering to their Enemies, giving them Aid and Comfort. No Person shall be convicted of Treason unless on the Testimony of two Witnesses to the same overt Act, or on Confession in open Court.

The Congress shall have Power to declare the Punishment of Treason, but no Attainder of Treason shall work Corruption of Blood, or Forfeiture except during the Life of the Person attainted.

ARTICLE IV

Section 1. Full Faith and Credit shall be given in each State to the public Acts, Records, and judicial Proceedings of every other State. And the Congress may by general Laws prescribe the Manner in which such Acts, Records and Proceedings shall be proved, and the Effect thereof.

Section 2. The Citizens of each State shall be entitled to all Privileges and Immunities of Citizens in the several States.

A Person charged in any State with Treason, Felony, or other Crime, who shall flee from Justice, and be found in another State, shall on Demand of the executive Authority of the State from which he fled, be delivered up, to be removed to the State having Jurisdiction of the Crime.

No Person held to Service or Labour in one State, under the Laws thereof, escaping into another, shall, in Consequence of any Law or Regulation therein, be discharged from such Service or Labour, but shall be delivered up on Claim of the Party to whom such Service or Labour may be due.

Section 3. New States may be admitted by the Congress into this Union; but no new State shall be formed or erected within the Jurisdiction of any other State; nor any State be formed by the Junction of two or more States, or Parts of States, without the Consent of the Legislatures of the States concerned as well as of the Congress.

The Congress shall have Power to dispose of and make all needful Rules and Regulations respecting the Territory or other Property belonging to the United States; and nothing in this Constitution shall be so construed as to Prejudice any Claims of the United States, or of any particular State.

Section 4. The United States shall guarantee to every State in this Union a Republican Form of Government, and shall protect each of them against Invasion; and on Application of the Legislature, or of the Executive (when the Legislature cannot be convened), against domestic Violence.

ARTICLE V

The Congress, whenever two thirds of both Houses shall deem it necessary, shall propose Amendments to this Constitution, or, on the Application of the Legislatures of two thirds of the several States, shall call a Convention for proposing Amendments, which, in either Case, shall be valid to all Intents and Purposes, as Part of this Constitution, when ratified by the Legislatures of three fourths of the several States, or by Conventions in three fourths thereof, as the one or the other Mode of Ratification may be proposed by the Congress; Provided that no Amendment which may be made prior to the Year One thousand eight hundred and eight shall in any Manner affect the first and fourth Clauses in the Ninth Section of the first Article; and that no State, without its Consent, shall be deprived of its equal Suffrage in the Senate.

ARTICLE VI

All Debts contracted and Engagements entered into, before the Adoption of this Constitution, shall be as valid against the United States under this Constitution, as under the Confederation.

This Constitution, and the Laws of the United States which shall be made in Pursuance thereof; and all Treaties made, or which shall be made, under the Authority of the United States, shall be the supreme Law of the Land; and the Judges in every State shall be bound thereby, any Thing in the Constitution or Laws of any State to the Contrary notwithstanding.

The Senators and Representatives before mentioned, and the Members of the several State Legislatures, and all executive and judicial Officers, both of the United States and of the several States, shall be bound by Oath or Affirmation, to support this Constitution; but no religious Test shall ever be required as a Qualification to any Office or public Trust under the United States.

ARTICLE VII

The Ratification of the Conventions of nine States, shall be sufficient for the Establishment of this Constitution between the States so ratifying the Same.

AMENDMENTS TO THE CONSTITUTION OF THE UNITED STATES

[Amendments I-X make up the Bill of Rights]

AMENDMENT I

Congress shall make no law respecting an establishment of religion, or prohibiting the free exercise thereof; or abridging the freedom of speech, or of the press; or the right of the people peaceably to assemble, and to petition the Government for a redress of grievances.

AMENDMENT II

A well regulated Militia, being necessary to the security of a free State, the right of the people to keep and bear Arms, shall not be infringed.

AMENDMENT III

No Soldier shall, in time of peace be quartered in any house, without the consent of the Owner, nor in time of war, but in a manner to be prescribed by law.

AMENDMENT IV

The right of the people to be secure in their persons, houses, papers, and effects, against unreasonable searches and seizures, shall not be violated, and no Warrants shall issue, but upon probable cause, supported by Oath or affirmation, and particularly describing the place to be searched, and the persons or things to be seized.

AMENDMENT V

No person shall be held to answer for a capital, or otherwise infamous crime, unless on a presentment or indictment of a Grand Jury, except in cases arising in the land or naval forces, or in the Militia, when in actual service in time of War or public danger; nor shall any person be subject for the same offence to be twice put in jeopardy of life or limb; nor shall be compelled in any criminal case to be a witness against himself, nor be deprived of life, liberty, or property, without due process of law; nor shall private property be taken for public use, without just compensation.

AMENDMENT VI

In all criminal prosecutions, the accused shall enjoy the right to a speedy and public trial, by an impartial jury of the State and district wherein the crime shall have been committed, which district shall have been previously ascertained by law, and to be informed of the nature and cause of the accusation; to be confronted with the witnesses against him; to have compulsory process for obtaining witnesses in his favor, and to have the Assistance of Counsel for his defence.

AMENDMENT VII

In suits at common law, where the value in controversy shall exceed twenty dollars, the right of trial by jury shall be preserved, and no fact tried by a jury, shall be otherwise reexamined in any Court of the United States, than according to the rules of the common law.

AMENDMENT VIII

Excessive bail shall not be required, nor excessive fines imposed, nor cruel and unusual punishments inflicted.

AMENDMENT IX

The enumeration in the Constitution, of certain rights, shall not be construed to deny or disparage others retained by the people.

AMENDMENT X

The powers not delegated to the United States by the Constitution, nor prohibited by it to the States, are reserved to the States respectively, or to the people.

AMENDMENT XI

The Judicial power of the United States shall not be construed to extend to any suit in law or equity, commenced or prosecuted against one of the United States by Citizens of another State, or by Citizens or Subjects of any Foreign State.

AMENDMENT XII

The Electors shall meet in their respective states and vote by ballot for President and Vice-President, one of whom, at least, shall not be an inhabitant of the same state with themselves; they shall name in their ballots the person voted for as President, and in distinct ballots the person voted for as Vice-President, and they shall make distinct lists of all persons voted for as President, and of all persons voted for as Vice-President, and of the number of votes for each, which lists they shall sign and certify, and transmit sealed to the seat of the government of the United States, directed to the President of the Senate; — the President of the Senate shall, in the presence of the Senate and House of Representatives, open all the certificates and the votes shall then be counted; — The person having the greatest number of votes for President, shall be the President, if such number be a majority of the whole number of Electors appointed; and if no person have such majority, then from the persons having the highest numbers not exceeding three on the list of those voted for as President, the House of Representatives shall choose immediately, by ballot, the President. But in choosing the President, the votes shall be taken by states, the representation from each state having one vote; a quorum for this purpose shall consist of a member or members from two-thirds of the states, and a majority of all the states shall be necessary to a choice. [And if the House of Representatives shall not choose a President whenever the right of choice shall devolve upon them, before the fourth day of March next following, then the Vice-President shall act as President, as in case of the death or other constitutional disability of the President. —]* The person having the greatest number of votes as Vice-President, shall be the Vice-President, if such number be a majority of the whole number of Electors appointed, and if no person have a majority, then from the two highest numbers on the list, the Senate shall choose the Vice-President; a quorum for the purpose shall consist of two-thirds of the whole number of

Senators, and a majority of the whole number shall be necessary to a choice. But no person constitutionally ineligible to the office of President shall be eligible to that of Vice-President of the United States.

AMENDMENT XIII

Section 1. Neither slavery nor involuntary servitude, except as a punishment for crime whereof the party shall have been duly convicted, shall exist within the United States, or any place subject to their jurisdiction.

Section 2. Congress shall have power to enforce this article by appropriate legislation.

AMENDMENT XIV

Section 1. All persons born or naturalized in the United States, and subject to the jurisdiction thereof, are citizens of the United States and of the State wherein they reside. No State shall make or enforce any law which shall abridge the privileges or immunities of citizens of the United States; nor shall any State deprive any person of life, liberty, or property, without due process of law; nor deny to any person within its jurisdiction the equal protection of the laws.

Section 2. Representatives shall be apportioned among the several States according to their respective numbers, counting the whole number of persons in each State, excluding Indians not taxed. But when the right to vote at any election for the choice of electors for President and Vice-President of the United States, Representatives in Congress, the Executive and Judicial officers of a State, or the members of the Legislature thereof, is denied to any of the male inhabitants of such State, being twenty-one years of age,* and citizens of the United States, or in any way abridged, except for participation in rebellion, or other crime, the basis of representation therein shall be reduced in the proportion which the number of such male citizens shall bear to the whole number of male citizens twenty-one years of age in such State.

Section 3. No person shall be a Senator or Representative in Congress, or elector of President and Vice-President, or hold any office, civil or military, under the United States, or under any State, who, having previously taken an oath, as a member of Congress, or as an officer of the United States, or as a member of any State legislature, or as an executive or judicial officer of any State, to support the Constitution of the United States, shall have engaged in insurrection or rebellion against the same, or given aid or comfort to the enemies thereof. But Congress may by a vote of two-thirds of each House, remove such disability.

Section 4. The validity of the public debt of the United States, authorized by law, including debts incurred for payment of pensions and bounties for services in suppressing insurrection or rebellion, shall not be questioned. But neither the United States nor any State shall assume or pay any debt or obligation incurred in aid of insurrection or rebellion against the United States, or any claim for the loss or emancipation of any slave; but all such debts, obligations and claims shall be held illegal and void.

Section 5. The Congress shall have the power to enforce, by appropriate legislation, the provisions of this article.

AMENDMENT XV

Section 1. The right of citizens of the United States to vote shall not be denied or abridged by the United States or by any State on account of race, color, or previous condition of servitude—

Section 2. The Congress shall have the power to enforce this article by appropriate legislation.

AMENDMENT XVI

The Congress shall have power to lay and collect taxes on incomes, from whatever source derived, without apportionment among the several States, and without regard to any census or enumeration.

AMENDMENT XVII

The Senate of the United States shall be composed of two Senators from each State, elected by the people thereof, for six years; and each Senator shall have one vote. The electors in each State shall have the qualifications requisite for electors of the most numerous branch of the State legislatures.

When vacancies happen in the representation of any State in the Senate, the executive authority of such State shall issue writs of election to fill such vacancies: Provided, That the legislature of any State may empower the executive thereof to make temporary appointments until the people fill the vacancies by election as the legislature may direct.

This amendment shall not be so construed as to affect the election or term of any Senator chosen before it becomes valid as part of the Constitution.

AMENDMENT XVIII

Section 1. After one year from the ratification of this article the manufacture, sale, or transportation of intoxicating liquors within, the importation thereof into, or the exportation thereof from the United States and all territory subject to the jurisdiction thereof for beverage purposes is hereby prohibited.

Section 2. The Congress and the several States shall have concurrent power to enforce this article by appropriate legislation.

Section 3. This article shall be inoperative unless it shall have been ratified as an amendment to the Constitution by the legislatures of the several States, as provided in the Constitution, within seven years from the date of the submission hereof to the States by the Congress.

AMENDMENT XIX

The right of citizens of the United States to vote shall not be denied or abridged by the United States or by any State on account of sex.

Congress shall have power to enforce this article by appropriate legislation.

AMENDMENT XX

Section 1. The terms of the President and the Vice President shall end at noon on the 20th day of January, and the terms of Senators and Representatives at noon on the 3d day of January, of the years in which such terms would have ended if this article had not been ratified; and the terms of their successors shall then begin.

Section 2. The Congress shall assemble at least once in every year, and such meeting shall begin at noon on the 3d day of January, unless they shall by law appoint a different day.

Section 3. If, at the time fixed for the beginning of the term of the President, the President elect shall have died, the Vice President elect shall become President. If a President shall not have been chosen before the time fixed for the beginning of his term, or if the President elect shall have failed to qualify, then the Vice President elect shall act as President until a President shall have qualified; and the Congress may by law provide for the case wherein neither a President elect nor a Vice President shall have qualified, declaring who shall then act as President, or the manner in which one who is to act shall be selected, and such person shall act accordingly until a President or Vice President shall have qualified.

Section 4. The Congress may by law provide for the case of the death of any of the persons from whom the House of Representatives may choose a President whenever the right of choice shall have devolved upon them, and for the case of the death of any of the persons from whom the Senate may choose a Vice President whenever the right of choice shall have devolved upon them.

Section 5. Sections 1 and 2 shall take effect on the 15th day of October following the ratification of this article.

Section 6. This article shall be inoperative unless it shall have been ratified as an amendment to the Constitution by the legislatures of three-fourths of the several States within seven years from the date of its submission.

AMENDMENT XXI

Section 1. The eighteenth article of amendment to the Constitution of the United States is hereby repealed.

Section 2. The transportation or importation into any State, Territory, or Possession of the United States for delivery or use therein of intoxicating liquors, in violation of the laws thereof, is hereby prohibited.

Section 3. This article shall be inoperative unless it shall have been ratified as an amendment to the Constitution by conventions in the several States, as provided in the Constitution, within seven years from the date of the submission hereof to the States by the Congress.

AMENDMENT XXII

Section 1. No person shall be elected to the office of the President more than twice, and no person who has held the office of President, or acted as President, for more than two years of a term to which some other person was elected President shall be elected to the office of President more than once. But this Article shall not apply to any person holding the office of President when this Article was proposed by Congress, and shall not prevent any person who may be holding the office of President, or acting as President, during the term within which this Article becomes operative from holding the office of President or acting as President during the remainder of such term.

Section 2. This article shall be inoperative unless it shall have been ratified as an amendment to the Constitution by the legislatures of three-fourths of the several States within seven years from the date of its submission to the States by the Congress.

AMENDMENT XXIII

Section 1. The District constituting the seat of Government of the United States shall appoint in such manner as Congress may direct:

A number of electors of President and Vice President equal to the whole number of Senators and Representatives in Congress to which the District would be entitled if it were a State, but in no event more than the least populous State; they shall be in addition to those appointed by the States, but they shall be considered, for the purposes of the election of President and Vice President, to be electors appointed by a State; and they shall meet in the District and perform such duties as provided by the twelfth article of amendment.

Section 2. The Congress shall have power to enforce this article by appropriate legislation.

AMENDMENT XXIV

Section 1. The right of citizens of the United States to vote in any primary or other election for President or Vice President, for electors for President or Vice President, or for Senator or Representative in Congress, shall not be denied or abridged by the United States or any State by reason of failure to pay poll tax or other tax.

Section 2. The Congress shall have power to enforce this article by appropriate legislation.

AMENDMENT XXV

Section 1. In case of the removal of the President from office or of his death or resignation, the Vice President shall become President.

Section 2. Whenever there is a vacancy in the office of the Vice President, the President shall nominate a Vice President who shall take office upon confirmation by a majority vote of both Houses of Congress.

Section 3. Whenever the President transmits to the President pro tempore of the Senate and the Speaker of the House of Representatives his written declaration that he is unable to discharge the powers and duties of his office, and until he transmits to them a written declaration to the contrary, such powers and duties shall be discharged by the Vice President as Acting President.

Section 4. Whenever the Vice President and a majority of either the principal officers of the executive departments or of such other body as Congress may by law provide, transmit to the President pro tempore of the Senate and the Speaker of the House of Representatives their written declaration that the President is unable to discharge the powers and duties of his office, the Vice President shall immediately assume the powers and duties of the office as Acting President.

Thereafter, when the President transmits to the President pro tempore of the Senate and the Speaker of the House of Representatives his written declaration that no inability exists, he shall resume the powers and duties of his office unless the Vice President and a majority of either the principal officers of the executive department or of such other body as Congress may by law provide, transmit within four days to the President pro tempore of the Senate and the Speaker of the House of Representatives their written declaration that the President is unable to discharge the powers and duties of his office. Thereupon Congress shall decide the issue, assembling within forty-eight hours for that purpose if not in session. If the Congress, within twenty-one days after receipt of the latter written declaration, or, if Congress is not in session, within twenty-one days after Congress is required to assemble, determines by two-thirds vote of both Houses that the President is unable to discharge the powers and duties of his office, the Vice President shall continue to discharge the same as Acting President; otherwise, the President shall resume the powers and duties of his office.

AMENDMENT XXVI

Section 1. The right of citizens of the United States, who are eighteen years of age or older, to vote shall not be denied or abridged by the United States or by any State on account of age.

Section 2. The Congress shall have power to enforce this article by appropriate legislation.

AMENDMENT XXVII

No law, varying the compensation for the services of the Senators and Representatives, shall take effect, until an election of representatives shall have intervened.

Courts—Alternative Dispute Resolution—Government

U.S. Courts	www.uscourts.gov
U.S. Tax Court	www.ustaxcourt.gov/ustcweb.htm
U.S. Court of Federal Claims	www.uscfc.uscourts.gov/
U.S. Court of International Trade	www.uscit.gov/
U.S Court for the Federal Circuit	www.fedcir.gov/
U.S. Supreme Court	www.supremecourtus.gov
National Mediation Board	www.nmb.gov
American Arbitration Association	www.adr.org
Pacer System	http://pacer.psc.uscourts.gov/
U.S. Court of Appeals	www.uscourts.gov/courtsofappeals.html
Internal Revenue Service	www.irs.gov
Government Printing Office	www.gpo.gov/
Code of Federal Regulations	www.access.gpo.gov/nara/cfr/index.html

Legal Research

VersusLaw	www.versuslaw.com/
Lexis	www.lexisnexis.com/
Westlaw	www.westlaw.com/
Library of Congress	www.loc.gov
Loislaw	www.loislaw.com
Cornell University LII	www.law.cornell.edu/citation
ALWD Manual	www.alwd.org

Legal Organizations

American Bar Association	www.abanet.org
National Federation of Paralegal Associations, Inc	www.paralegals.org
National Association of Legal Assistants	www.nala.org
American Association of Legal Administrators	www.alanet.org/home.html
American Association for Paralegal Education	www.aafpe.org
ABA Standing Committee on Legal Assistants	www.abanet.org/legalassts
Legal Nurse Consultants	www.aalnc.org

State Bar Associations

Alabama	www.alabar.org	Montana	www.montanabar.org
Alaska	www.alaskabar.org	Nebraska	www.nebar.org
Arizona	www.azbar.org.org	Nevada	www.nvbar.org
Arkansas	www.arkbar.org	New Hampshire	www.nhbar.org
California	www.calbar.org	New Jersey	www.njsba.com
Colorado	www.cobar.org	New Mexico	www.nmbar.org
Connecticut	www.ctbar.org	New York	www.nysba.org
Delaware	www.dsba.org	North Carolina	www.ncbar.com
District of Columbia	www.dcbar.org	North Dakota	www.sband.org
Florida	www.flabar.org	Ohio	www.ohiobar.org
Georgia	www.gabar.org	Oklahoma	www.okbar.org
Hawaii	www.hsba.org	Oregon	www.osbar.org
Idaho	www2.state.id.us/isb/	Pennsylvania	www.pa-bar.org
Illinois	www.isba.org	Rhode Island	www.ribar.com
Indiana	www.inbar.org	South Carolina	www.scbar.org
Iowa	www.iowabar.org	South Dakota	www.sdbar.org
Kansas	www.ksbar.org	Tennessee	www.tba.org
Kentucky	www.kybar.org	Texas	www.texasbar.com
Louisiana	www.lsba.org	Utah	www.utahbar.org
Maine	www.maine.org	Vermont	www.vtbar.org
Maryland	www.msba.org	Virginia	www.vsb.org
Massachusetts	www.massbar.org	Washington	www.wsba.org
Michigan	www.michbar.org	West Virginia	www.wvbar.org
Minnesota	www.mnbar.org	Wisconsin	www.wisbar.org
Mississippi	www.msbar.org	Wyoming	www.wyomingbar.org
Missouri	www.mobar.org		

Other

Religious calendar	www.interfaithcalendar.org/
AOL	www.aol.com
Compuserve	WWW.compuserve.com
The Affiliate	www.futurelawoffice.com/practice.html
Adobe Systems	www.adobe.com
Mapquest	www.mapquest.com

Internet Search Engines

AltaVista	www.altavista.com
Ask Jeeves	www.askjeeves.com
Dogpile	www.dogpile.com
Excite	www.excite.com
Google	www.google.com
Metacrawler	www.metacrawler.com
Netscape	www.netscape.com
Yahoo!	www.yahoo.com
Findlaw	www.findlaw.com

a priori   Desde antes, del pasado.

AAA Siglas para **American Arbitration Association** Asociación de Arbitraje.

ABA Siglas para **American Bar Association** Colegio de Abogados Estadounidenses.

accept   Aceptar, admitir, aprobar, recibir reconocer.

accession   Accesión, admisión, aumento, incremento.

accord   Acuerdo, convenio, arreglo, acordar, conceder.

acquittal   Absolución, descargo, veredicto de no culpable.

act   Acto, estatuto, decreto, actuar, funcionar.

actionable   Justiciable, punible, procesable.

adjourn   Levantar, posponer, suspender la sesión.

adjudicate   Adjudicar, decidir, dar fallo a favor de, sentenciar, declarar.

administrative   Administrativo, ejecutivo.

administrative agency   Agencia administrativa.

administrative hearing   Juicio administrativo.

administrative law   Derecho administrativo.

administrative law judge   Juez de derecho, Administrativo.

administrator   Administrador.

admit   Admitir, conceder, reconocer, permitir entrada, confesar, asentir.

adverse   Adverso, contrario, opuesto.

adverse possession   Posesión adversa.

advice   Consejo, asesoramiento, notificación.

affected class   Clase afectada, grupo iscriminado.

affidavit   Declaración voluntaria, escrita y bajo uramento, afidávit, atestiguación, testificata.

affirmative action   Acción positiva.

affirmative defense   Defensa justificativa.

after acquired property   Propiedad adquirida con garantía adicional.

against   En contra.

agency   Agencia, oficina, intervención.

agent   Agente, representante autorizado.

aggrieved party   Parte dañada, agraviada, perjudicada.

agreement   Acuerdo, arreglo, contrato, convenio, pacto.

alibi   Coartada.

alien   Extranjero, extraño, foráneo.

annul   Anular, cancelar, invalidar, revocar, dejar sin efecto.

answer   Contestación, réplica, respuesta, alegato.

antecedent   Antecedente, previo, preexistente.

appeal   Apelar, apelación.

appear   Aparecer, comparecer.

appellate court   Tribunal de apelaciones.

appellate jurisdiction   Competencia de apelación.

applicable   Aplicable, apropiado, pertinente a, lo que puede ser aplicado.

arraign   Denunciar, acusar, procesar, instruir de cargos hechos.

arrears   Retrasos, pagos atrasados, decursas.

arrest   Arresto, arrestar, aprehensión, aprehender, detener.

arson   Incendio intencional.

articles of incorporation   Carta de organización corporativa.

assault   Agresión, asalto, ataque, violencia carnal, agredir, atacar, acometer.

assault and battery Amenazas y agresión, asalto.

assign Asignar, ceder, designar, hacer cesión, traspasar, persona asignada un derecho.

attachment Secuestro judicial.

attorney Abogado, consejero, apoderado.

award Fallo, juicio, laudo, premio.

bail Caución, fianza.

bail bondsman Fiador, fiador judicial.

bailee Depositario de bienes.

bailment Depósito, encargo, depósito mercantil, depósito comercial.

bailment For hire, depósito oneroso.

bailor Fiador.

bankruptcy Bancarrota, quiebra, insolvencia.

battery Agravio, agresión.

bearer bond Título mobiliario.

bearer instrument Título al portador.

bench Tribunal, los jueces, la magistratura.

beneficiary Beneficiario, legatario.

bequeath Legar.

bilateral contract Contrato bilateral.

bill of lading Póliza de embarque, boleto de carga, documento de tránsito.

bill of rights Las primeras diez enmiendas a la Constitución de los Estados Unidos de América.

binder Resguardo provisional, recibo para garantizar el precio de un bien inmueble.

birth certificate Acta de nacimiento, partida de nacimiento, certificado de nacimiento.

blue sky laws Estatutos para prevenir el fraude en la compraventa de valores.

bond Bono, título, obligación, deuda inversionista, fianza.

booking Término dado en el cuartel de policía al registro de arresto y los cargos hechos al arrestado.

breach of contract Violación, rotura, incumplimiento de contrato.

brief Alegato, escrito memorial.

burglary Escalamiento, allanamiento de morada.

buyer Comprador.

bylaws Estatutos sociales, reglamentos internos.

capacity to contract capacidad contractual.

case Causa, caso, acción legal, proceso, proceso civil, asunto, expediente.

case law Jurisprudencia.

cashier's check Cheque bancario.

cease and desist order Orden judicial de cese.

censure Censura.

certificate of deposit Certificado de depósito.

certified check Cheque certificado.

certify Certificar, atestiguar.

charge Cobrar, acusar, imputar.

charitable trust Fideicomiso caritativo.

chattel Bienes muebles, bártulos.

cheat Fraude, engaño, defraudador, trampa, tramposo, estafar.

check Cheque, talón, comprobación.

cite Citación, citar, referir, emplazar.

citizenship Ciudadanía.

civil action Acción, enjuiciamiento civil, demanda.

civil law Derecho civil.

Claims Court Tribunal federal de reclamaciones.

client Cliente.

closing arguments Alegatos de clausura.

closing costs Gastos ocasionados en la venta de bienes raíces.

clue Pista, indicio.

codicil Codicilo.

coercion Coerción, coacción.

collateral Colateral, auxiliar, subsidiario, seguridad colateral, garantía prendaria.

collect Cobrar, recobrar, recaudar.

collision Choque, colisión.

common law Derecho consuetudinario.

comparative negligence Negligencia comparativa.

compensatory damages Indemnización compensatoria por daños y perjuicios, daños compensatorios.

competency Competencia, capacidad legal.

concurrent conditions Condiciones concurrentes.

concurrent jurisdiction Jurisdicción simultanea, conocimiento acumulativo.

concurrent sentences Sentencias que se cumplen simultáneamente.

concurring opinion Opinión coincidente.

condemn Condenar, confiscar, expropiar.

condition precedent Condición precedente.

condition subsequent Condición subsecuente.

confession   Confesión, admisión.

confidential   Confidencial, íntimo, secreto.

confiscation   Confiscación, comiso, decomiso.

consent decree   Decreto por acuerdo mutuo.

consequential damages   Daños especiales.

consideration   Contraprestación.

consolidation   Consolidación, unión, concentración.

courts   Cortes o tribunales establecidas por la constitución.

constructive delivery   Presunta entrega.

contempt of court   Desacato, contumacia o menosprecio a la corte.

contract   Contrato, convenio, acuerdo, pacto.

contributory negligence   Negligencia contribuyente.

conversion   Conversión, canje.

conviction   Convicción, fallo de culpabilidad, convencimiento, sentencia condenatoria, condena.

copyright   Derecho de autor, propiedad literaria, propiedad intelectual, derecho de impresión.

corroborate   Corroborar, confirmar.

counterclaim   Contrademanda, excepción de compensación.

counteroffer   Contra oferta.

covenant for quiet enjoyment   Convenio de disfrute y posesión pacífica.

creditor   Acreedor.

crime   Crimen, delito.

criminal act   Acto criminal.

criminal law   Derecho penal.

cross examination   contrainterrogatorio, repregunta.

cure   Curar, corregir.

damages   Daños y perjuicios, indemnización pecuniaria.

DBA   Sigla para **doing business as** En negociación comercial.

deadly force   Fuerza mortífera.

debt   Deuda, débito.

debtor   Deudor.

decision   Decisión judicial, fallo, determinación auto, sentencia.

deed   Escritura, título de propiedad, escritura de traspaso.

defamation   Difamación, infamación.

default   Incumplir, faltar, no comparecer, incumplimiento.

defendant   Demandado, reo, procesado, acusado.

delinquent   Delincuente, atrasado en pagos, delictuoso.

denial   Denegación, negación, denegatoria.

deponent   Deponente, declarante.

deportation   Deportación, destierro.

deposition   Deposición, declaración bajo juramento.

detain   Detener, retardar, retrasar.

devise   Legado de bienes raíces.

direct examination   Interrogatorio directo, interrogatorio a testigo propio.

directed verdict   Veredicto expedido por el juez, veredicto por falta de pruebas.

disaffirm   Negar, rechazar, repudiar, anular.

discharge   Descargo, cumplimiento, liberación,

disclose   Revelar.

discovery   Revelación de prueba, exposición reveladora.

discriminate   Discriminar.

dismiss   Despedir, desechar, desestimar

dissenting opinion   Opinión en desacuerdo.

dissolution   Disolución, liquidación.

diversity of citizenship   Diversidad de ciudadanías, ciudadanías diferentes.

dividend   Acción librada, dividendo.

divorce   Divorcio, divorciar.

docket   Orden del día, lista de casos en la corte.

double jeopardy   Non bis in idem.

driving under the influence   Manejar bajo los efectos de bebidas alcohólicas o drogas.

duress   Coacción.

earnest money   Arras, señal.

easement   Servidumbre.

edict   Edicto, decreto, auto.

embezzlement   Malversación de fondos.

eminent domain   Dominio eminente.

encroachment   Intrusión, usurpación, invasión, uso indebido.

encumbrance   Gravamen, afectación, cargo.

enforce   Hacer cumplir, dar valor, poner en efecto.

entitlement   Derecho, título.

equal protection clause Cláusula de protección de igualdad ante la ley.

equal protection of the law Igualdad ante la ley.

equity Equidad. Derecho equitativo.

escheat Reversión al estado al no haber herederos.

estate Bienes, propiedad, caudal hereditario, cuerpo de la herencia, caudal, derecho, título, interés sobre propiedad.

estop Impedir, detener, prevenir.

ethics Sistema ético.

eviction Evicción, desalojo, desalojamiento, desahucio, lanzamiento.

evidence Testimonio, prueba, pruebas documentales, pieza de prueba.

examination Examen, reconocimiento, interrogatorio.

executed contract Contrato firmado, contrato ejecutado.

execution Ejecución, desempeño, cumplimiento.

executory contract Contrato por cumplirse.

executory interests Intereses futuros.

exempt Franquear, exentar, exencionar, eximir, libre, franco, exento, inmune.

exoneration Exoneración, descargo, liberación.

expert witness Testigo perito.

express contract Contrato explícito.

expropriation Expropiación, confiscación.

eyewitness Testigo ocular o presencial.

fact Hecho falsificado.

failure to appear Incomparecencia.

fault Falta, defecto, culpa, negligencia.

fee Honorarios, retribución, cuota, cargo, derecho, dominio, asesoría, propiedad, bienes raíces.

fee simple estate Propiedad en dominio pleno.

felon Felón, autor de un delito.

felony Delito mayor o grave.

fiduciary Fiduciario.

find against Fallar o decidir en contra.

find for Fallar o decidir a favor.

finding Determinación de los hechos.

fine Multa, castigo.

fixture Accesorio fijo.

foreclose Entablar juicio hipotecario, embargar bienes hipotecados.

forgery Falsificación.

franchise Franquicia, privilegio, patente, concesión social, derecho de votar.

fraud Fraude, engaño, estafa, trampa, embuste, defraudación.

full disclosure Revelación completa.

garnishment Embargo de bienes.

gift Regalo, dádiva, donación.

gift causa mortis Donación de propiedad en expectativa de muerte.

gift inter vivos Donación entre vivos.

gift tax Impuesto sobre donaciones.

good and valid consideration Causa contractual válida.

good faith Buena fe.

goods Mercaderías, bienes, productos.

grace period Período de espera.

grantee Concesionario, cesionario.

grantor Otorgante, cesionista.

grievance Agravio, injuria, ofensa, queja formal.

gross negligence Negligencia temeraria, negligencia grave.

habitation Habitación, lugar donde se vive.

harassment Hostigamiento.

hearing Audiencia, vista, juicio.

hearsay Testimonio de oídas.

holder Tenedor, poseedor.

holding Decisión, opinión, tenencia posesión, asociación, grupo industrial.

holographic will Testamento hológrafo.

homeowner Propietario, dueño de casa.

homestead Casa, solariega, hogar, heredad, excepción de embargo, bien de familia.

hung jury Jurado sin veredicto.

identify Identificar, verificar, autenticar.

illegal Ilegal, ilícito, ilegítimo.

illegal entry Entrada ilegal.

illegal search Registro domiciliario, allanamiento ilegal, cacheo ilegal.

immunity Inmunidad, exención.

implied warranty Garantía implícita.

impossibility of performance Imposibilidad de cumplimiento.

impound Embargar, incautar, confiscar, secuestrar.

inadmissible Inadmisible, inaceptable.

income   Ingreso, ganancia, entrada, renta, rédito.

incriminate   Incriminar, acriminar.

indictment   Procesamiento, acusación por jurado acusatorio, inculpatoria.

indorsement   Endose, endoso, respaldo, garantía.

informant   Informador, denunciante, delator.

information   Información, informe, acusación por el fiscal, denuncia.

informed consent   Conformidad por información.

inherit   Heredar, recibir por herencia.

injunction   Mandato judicial, amparo, prohibición judicial, interdicto.

innocent   Inocente, no culpable.

inquiry   Indagatoria judicial, pesquisa.

insufficient evidence   Prueba insuficiente.

interrogation   Interrogación.

interstate commerce   Comercio interestatal.

intestate   Intestado, intestar, sin testamento.

intestate succession   Sucesión hereditaria.

investigation   Investigación, indagación, encuesta.

issue   Emisión, cuestión, punto, edición, número, tirada, sucesión, descendencia, resultado, decisión.

jail   Cárcel, calabozo, encarcelar.

joint tenancy   Condominio.

judge   Magistrado, juez, juzgar, adjudicar, enjuiciar, fallar.

judgment   Sentencia, fallo, juicio, decisión, dictamen, criterio.

judicial proceeding   Proceso o diligencia judicial.

judicial review   Revisión judicial.

jump bail   Fugarse bajo fianza.

jurisdiction   Jurisdicción, fuero competencia.

jury   Jurado

landlord   Arrendatario, propietario.

larceny   Hurto, latrocinio, ladronicio.

law   Ley, derecho.

lease   Contrato de arrendamiento, arrendamiento, arriendo, contrato de locación, arrendar, alquilar.

leasehold estate   Bienes forales.

legatee   Legatario, asignatario.

lender   Prestamista.

lessee   Arrendatario, locatario, inquilino.

lessor   Arrendatario, arrendador, arrendante, locador.

letter of credit   Letra de crédito.

liability   Responsiva, responsabilidad.

libel   Libelo por difamación por escrito.

license   Licencia, permiso, privilegio, matrícula, patente, título, licenciar, permitir.

lien   Gravamen, derecho prendario o de retención, embargo preventivo.

life estate   Hipoteca legal, dominio vitalicio.

limited liability company   Sociedad de responsabilidad limitada.

limited partnership   Sociedad en comandita, sociedad comanditaria.

litigated   Pleiteado, litigado, sujeto a litigación.

majority opinion   Opinión que refleja la mayoría de los miembros de la corte de apelaciones.

maker   Otorgante, girador.

malice   Malicia, malignidad, maldad.

malpractice   Incompetencia profesional.

manslaughter   Homicidio sin premeditación.

material witness   Testigo esencial.

mechanics lien   Gravamen de construcción.

mediation   Mediación, tercería, intervención, interposición.

medical examiner   Médico examinador.

merger   Fusión, incorporación, unión, consolidación.

minor   Menor, insignificante, pequeño, trivial.

misdemeanor   Delito menor, fechoría.

mitigation of damages   Mitigación de daños, minoración, atenuación.

monetary damages   Daños pecuniarios.

mortgage   Hipoteca, gravamen, hipotecar, gravar.

motion to dismiss   Petición para declaración sin lugar.

motion to suppress   Moción para suprimir, reprimir o suspender.

motive   Motivo.

murder   Asesinato, asesinar, homicidio culposo.

naturalization   Naturalización.

negligence   Negligencia, descuido, imprudencia.

negotiable   Negociable.

negotiate   Negociar, agenciar, hacer efectivo, traspasar, tratar.

net assets   Haberes netos.

notice   Aviso, notificación, advertencia, conocimiento.

novation Novación, delegación de crédito.

nuisance Daño, molestia, perjuicio.

nuncupative will Testamento abierto.

oath Juramento.

objection Objeción, oposición, disconformidad, recusación, impugnación, excepción, réplica, reclamación.

obstruction of justice Encubrimiento activo.

offer Oferta, ofrecimiento, propuesta, ofrecer, proponer.

omission Omisión, falla, falta.

opinion Opinión, dictamen, decisión de la corte.

oral argument Alegato oral.

order instrument Instrumento de pago a la orden.

owe Deber, estar en deuda, adeudo.

owner Dueño, propietario, poseedor.

pain and suffering Angustia mental y dolor físico.

pardon Perdón, indulto, absolución, indultar, perdonar.

parol evidence rule Principio que prohíbe la modificación de un contrato por prueba verbal.

parole Libertad vigilada.

partnership Sociedad, compañía colectiva, aparcería, consorcio, sociedad personal.

patent Patente, obvio, evidente, aparente, privilegio de invención, patentar.

penalty Pena, multa, castigo, penalidad, condena.

pending Pendiente, en trámite, pendiente de, hasta que.

per capita Por cabeza.

performance Cumplimiento, desempeño, ejecución, rendimiento.

perjury Perjurio, testimonio falso, juramento falso.

personal property Bienes personales, bienes mobiliarios.

plea bargain Declaración de culpabilidad concertada.

plea of guilty Alegación de culpabilidad.

pleadings Alegatos, alegaciones, escritos.

pledge Prenda, caución, empeño, empeñar, dar en prenda, pignorar.

police power Poder policial.

policy Póliza, escritura, práctica política.

possession Posesión, tenencia, goce, disfrute.

possibility of reverter Posibilidad de reversión.

power of attorney Poder de representación, poder notarial, procura.

precedent Precedente, decisión previa por el mismo tribunal.

preemptive right Derecho de prioridad.

prejudicial Dañoso, perjudicial.

preliminary hearing Audiencia preliminar.

premeditation Premeditación.

presume Presumir, asumir como hecho basado en la experiencia, suponer.

prevail Prevalecer, persuadir, predominar, ganar, triunfar.

price discrimination Discriminación en el precio.

principal Principal, jefe, de mayor importancia, valor actual.

privileged communication Comunicación privilegiada.

privity Coparticipación, intereses comunes.

procedural Procesal.

proceeds Ganancias.

profit Ganancia, utilidad, lucro, beneficio.

prohibited Prohibido.

promise Promesa.

promissory estoppel Impedimento promisorio.

promissory note Pagaré, vale, nota de pago.

proof Prueba, comprobación, demostración.

prosecutor Fiscal, abogado público acusador.

proximate cause Causa relacionada.

proxy Poder, delegación, apoderado, mandatario.

punishment Pena, castigo.

punitive damages Indemnización punitiva por daños y perjuicios, daños ejemplares.

qualification Capacidad, calidad, preparación.

qualified indorsement Endoso limitado endoso con reservas.

quasi contract Cuasicontrato.

query Pregunta, interrogación.

question of fact Cuestión de hecho.

question of law Cuestión de derecho.

quiet enjoyment Uso y disfrute.

quitclaim deed Escritura de traspaso de finiquito.

race discrimination Discriminación racial.

rape Estupro, violación, ultraje, rapto, violar.

ratification Ratificación, aprobación, confirmación.

ratify Aprobar, confirmar, ratificar, convalidar, adoptar.

real property   Bienes raíces, bienes inmuebles, arraigo.

reasonable doubt   Duda razonable.

rebut   Rebatir, refutar, negar, contradecir.

recognizance   Obligación impuesta judicialmente.

recordation   Inscripción oficial, grabación.

recover   Recobrar, recuperar, obtener como resultado de decreto.

redress   Reparación, compensación, desagravio, compensar, reparar, satisfacer, remediar.

regulatory agency   Agencia reguladora.

reimburse   Reembolsar, repagar, compensar, reintegrar.

rejoinder   Respuesta, réplica, contrarréplica.

release   Descargo, liberación, librar, relevar, descargar, libertar.

relevance   Relevancia.

remainder   Resto, restante, residuo, derecho expectativo a un bien raíz.

remedy   Remedio, recurso.

remuneration   Remuneración, compensación.

reply   Réplica, contestación, contestar, responder.

reprieve   Suspensión de la sentencia, suspensión, indulto, indultar, suspender.

reprimand   Reprender, regañar, reprimenda, reprensión.

repudiate   Repudiar, renunciar, rechazar.

rescission   Rescisión, abrogación, cancelación de un contrato.

respondeat superior   Responsabilidad civil al supervisor.

respondent   Apelado, demandado.

restitution   Restitución, devolución.

restraining order   Inhibitoria, interdicto, orden de amparo.

retain   Retener, emplear, guardar.

reversion   Reversión, derecho de sucesión.

revocation   Revocación, derogación, anulación.

reward   Premio.

right of first refusal   Retracto arrendaticio.

right of subrogation   Derecho de sustituir.

right of survivorship   Derecho de supervivencia entre dueños de propiedad mancomunada.

right to work laws   Leyes que prohíben la filiación sindical como requisito para poder desempeñar un puesto, derecho de trabajo.

rights   Derechos.

robbery   Robo, atraco.

ruling   Determinación oficial, auto judicial.

sale   Venta.

sale on approval   Venta por aprobación.

satisfaction   Satisfacción, liquidación, cumplimiento, pago, finiquito.

scope of authority   Autoridad explícitamente otorgada o implícitamente concedida.

search and seizure   Allanamiento, registro e incautación.

search warrant   Orden de registro o de allanamiento.

secured party   Persona con interés asegurado.

secured transaction   Transacción con un interés asegurado.

securities   Valores, títulos, obligaciones.

security agreement   Acuerdo que crea la garantía de un interés.

security deposit   Deposito de seguridad.

seize   Arrestar, confiscar, secuestrar, incautar.

settlement   Arreglo, composición, ajuste, liquidación, componenda, acomodo.

sex discrimination   Discriminación sexual.

sexual harassment   Acoso sexual.

shoplifting   Ratería en tiendas.

signature   Firma.

slander   Calumnia, difamación oral, calumniar.

source of income   Fuente de ingresos.

specific performance   Prestación específica contractual.

split decision   Decisión con opiniones mixtas.

spousal abuse   Abuso conyugal.

stare decisis   Vinculación con decisiones judiciales anteriores.

state of mind   Estado de ánimo, estado mental.

statement   Alegación, declaración, relato, estado de cuentas.

statutory foreclosure   Ejecución hipotecaria estatutaria.

statutory law   Derecho estatutario.

statutory rape   Estupro, violación de un menor de edad.

steal   Robar, hurtar, robo, hurto.

stock   Acciones, capital, existencias, semental.

stock option   Opción de comprar o vender acciones.

stop payment order   Suspensión de pago.

strict liability   Responsabilidad rigurosa.

sublease   Subarriendo, sublocación, subarrendar.

subpoena   Citación, citatorio, comparendo, cédula de citación, citación judicial, subpoena.

sue   Demandar, procesar.

summary judgment   Sentencia sumaria.

summon   Convocar, llamar, citar.

suppress   Suprimir, excluir pruebas ilegalmente obtenidas, reprimir, suspender.

surrender   Rendir, entregar, entrega, rendirse, entregarse.

surviving spouse   Cónyuge sobreviviente.

suspect   Sospecha, sospechar, sospechoso

tangible evidence   Prueba real.

tangible property   Propiedad tangible, bienes tangibles.

tenancy at sufferance   Tenencia o posesión por tolerancia.

tenancy at will   Tenencia o inquilinato sin plazo fijo.

tenancy by the entirety   Tenencia conyugal.

tenancy for life   Tenencia vitalicia.

tenancy for years   Inquilinato por tiempo fijo.

tender   Propuesta, oferta, presentar.

testator   Testador.

testify   Atestar, atestiguar, dar testimonio.

theft   Hurto.

title   Título, derecho de posesión, rango, denominación.

tort   Agravio, torticero, entuerto, daño legal, perjuicio, acto ilícito civil.

Totten trust   Fideicomiso bancario Totten.

trade name   Nombre comercial, marca de fábrica, marca comercial.

trademark   Marca registrada, marca industrial.

transgression   Ofensa, delito, transgresión.

trespass   Transgresión, violación de propiedad ajena, translimitación, traspasar, violar, infringir, transgredir.

trial court   Tribunal de primera instancia.

trust   Fideicomiso, confianza, confidencia, confianza, crédito, combinación, consorcio, grupo industrial.

truth   Verdad, verdadero, veracidad.

try   Probar, juzgar.

ultra vires   Mas allá de la facultad de actuar.

unanimous verdict   Veredicto unánime.

unbiased   Imparcial, neutral.

unconditional pardon   Perdón, amnistía, indulto incondicional.

unconscionable   Reprochable, repugnante, desmedido.

under arrest   Arrestado, bajo arresto.

underwrite   Subscribir, asegurar, firmar.

undisclosed   Escondido, no revelado.

undue influence   Influencia indebida, coacción, abuso de poder.

unenforceable   Inejecutable.

unilateral contract   Contrato unilateral.

unlawful   Ilegal, ilícito, ilegítimo.

unsound mind   Privado de razón, de mente inestable.

usury   Usura, agiotaje, logrería.

vagrancy   Vagancia, vagabundeo.

validity   Validez, vigencia.

valuable consideration   Causa contractual con cierto valor, causa contractual onerosa.

venue   Partido judicial.

verbal contract   Contrato verbal.

verbatim   Al pié de la letra.

verdict   Veredicto, fallo, sentencia, decisión.

victim   Víctima.

voidable   Anulable, cancelable.

wage   Salario, jornal, sueldo.

waive   Renunciar, ceder, suspender, abdicar.

waiver   Renunciar, desistir, ceder, suspender, abdicar, renuncia.

warrant   Autorización, resguardo, comprobante, certificado, justificación, decisión judicial.

warranty   Garantía, seguridad.

warranty of habitability   Garantía de habitabilidad.

welfare   Asistencia pública.

will   Testamento, voluntad.

willful misconduct   Mala conducta intencional.

withhold   Retener, detener.

witness   Testigo, declarante, atestar, testificar, atestiguar.

writ of attachment   Mandamiento de embargo.

writ of certiorari   Pedimento de avocación.

writ of execution   Auto de ejecución, ejecutoria.

GLOSSARY

Abatement   A principle stating that if the property the testator leaves is not sufficient to satisfy all the beneficiaries named in a will and there are both general and residuary bequests, the residuary bequest is paid last—(abated first).

Acceptance   A manifestation of assent by the offeree to the terms of the offer in a manner invited or required by the offer as measured by the objective theory of contracts.

Actus reus   "Guilty act"—actual performance of criminal act.

Ademption   A principle stating that if a testator leaves a specific devise of property to a beneficiary but the property is no longer in the estate when the testator dies, the beneficiary receives nothing.

Administrative agencies   Agencies that the legislative and executive branches of federal and state governments establish to set rules and regulations.

Administrative law judge (ALJ)   A judge presiding over administrative proceedings who decides questions of law and fact concerning the case.

Administrative Procedure Act (APA)   A law establishing certain administrative procedures that federal administrative agencies must follow in conducting their affairs.

Administrative subpoena   An order that directs the subject of the subpoena to disclose the requested information.

Administrator or administratrix   A court-appointed personal representative who administers the estate during its settlement phase when no one is named in the will or if the decedent dies intestate.

Adverse possession   the wrongful possession of someone else's property; the adverse possessor may obtain title to that property if certain statutory requirements are met.

Affirm   To agree with; to let stand.

Agency   The principal–agent relationship; the fiduciary relationship "which results from the manifestation of consent by one person to another that the other shall act in his behalf and subject to his control, and consent by the other so to act" (Restatement [Second] of Agency).

Agency by ratification   An agency that occurs when (1) a person misrepresents himself or herself as another's agent when in fact he or she is not, and (2) the purported principal ratifies the unauthorized act.

Agent   The party who agrees to act on behalf of another, such as a person who has been authorized to sign a negotiable instrument on behalf of another person.

Agreement   The manifestation by two or more persons of the substance of a contract.

Aiding and abetting   Rendering support, assistance, or encouragement to the commission of a crime; harboring a criminal after he or she has committed a crime.

Air-space parcel   A property right that is a three-dimensional cube of air above the surface of the earth.

Alien corporation   A corporation that is incorporated in another country.

Alternative dispute resolution (ADR)   Methods of resolving disputes other than litigation.

American Association for Paralegal Education (AAfPE)   National organization of paralegal educators and institutions offering paralegal education programs.

American Bar Association (ABA)   Largest professional legal organization in the United States.

American Inventors Protection Act   A law that reorganized the U.S. Patent and Trademark Office (PTO), granting it new regulatory powers for inventions and patents and upgrading the PTO Commissioner to Assistant Secretary of Commerce with advisory powers.

Americans with Disabilities Act (ADA)   A law that imposes obligations on employers and providers of public transportation, telecommunications, and public facilities to accommodate individuals with disabilities.

Analytical skill   The ability to follow a step-by-step process to solve a problem.

Answer   Defendant's written response to plaintiff's complaint, filed with the court and served on plaintiff.

Anticybersquatting Consumer Protection Act
Legislation aimed at preventing "cybersquatters" who register domain names based on names of famous companies and people and hold them "hostage."

Apparent agency (agency by estoppel)   (1) Agency that arises when a principal creates the appearance of an agency that in actuality does not exist; (2) agency that arises when a franchisor creates the appearance that a franchisee is its agent when in fact an actual agency does not exist.

Appeal   The act of asking an appellate court to overturn a decision after the trial court's final judgment has been entered.

Appellant   The appealing party in an appeal; also known as *petitioner.*

Appellee   Responding party in an appeal; also known as *respondent.*

Arbitration   A form of alternative dispute resolution in which the parties choose an impartial third party to hear and decide the dispute.

Arraignment   A hearing during which the accused is brought before a court and is (1) informed of the charges against him or her, and (2) asked to enter a plea.

Arrest warrant   A document for a person's detainment based upon a showing of probable cause that the person committed the crime.

Arson   Willfully or maliciously burning another's building.

Article 2 (Sales) of Uniform Commercial Code   Article of the Uniform Commercial Code that governs sale of goods.

Article 2A (Leases) of Uniform Commercial Code   Article of the Uniform Commercial Code that governs lease of goods.

Articles of incorporation (corporate charter)   The basic governing document of the corporation; must be filed with the secretary of state of the state of incorporation.

Articles of limited liability partnership   A public document that must be filed with the secretary of state to form a limited liability partnership.

Assault   Either (1) the threat of immediate harm or offensive contact, or (2) any action that arouses reasonable apprehension of imminent harm; actual physical contact is unnecessary.

Associate's degree   A college degree in science (AS) or arts (AA) or applied arts (AAS), generally requiring two years of full-time study.

Association of Legal Writing Directors (ALWD)   A society for professors who coordinate legal writing instruction in legal education.

Assumption of the risk   A defense a defendant can use against a plaintiff who knowingly and voluntarily enters into or participates in a risky activity that results in injury; defendant must prove that (1) plaintiff knew and appreciated the risk, and (2) plaintiff voluntarily assumed the risk.

Attachment   Seizure by creditors of property in debtor's possession to collect on a debt while their lawsuit is pending.

Attempt to commit a crime   Trying to commit a crime but not completing it.

Attestation   Action of a will being witnessed by two or three objective and competent people.

Attorney–client privilege   A rule that says a client can tell his or her lawyer anything about the case without fear that the attorney will be called as a witness against the client.

Attorney-in-fact   Agent who has power of attorney; does not actually have to be an attorney.

Bachelor's degree   A college degree generally requiring four years of full-time study.

Bailee   Holder of goods who is not a seller or a buyer (e.g., a warehouse).

Bailment   A transaction whereby an owner transfers his or her personal property to another to be held, stored, delivered, or for some other purpose; title to the property does not transfer.

Bailor   Owner of property in a bailment.

Barrister   A lawyer in the English legal system who is brought cases by a solicitor and litigates the cases.

Battery   Unauthorized and harmful or offensive physical contact with another person; direct physical contact is not necessary.

Bench trial   Trial without a jury; also called a *waiver trial.*

Beneficiary   (1) A person or organization designated in the will to receive all or a portion of the testator's property at the time of the testator's death. (2) The person for whose benefit a trust is created. (3) The person who is to receive life insurance proceeds when the insured dies. (4) The creditor in a deed of trust and note transaction.

Bequest   A gift of personal property by will; also known as a *legacy.*

Berne Convention   An international copyright treaty to which the United States and many other nations are signatories.

Bill of Rights   Constitutional Amendments I through X.

Biosafety protocol   An agreement sponsored by United Nations in which countries agreed that all genetically engineered foods will be clearly labeled with the phrase "May contain living modified organisms."

Board of directors   A panel of decision makers, the members of which are elected by the shareholders of a corporation.

Bluebook, The   A uniform system of citation published by the *Harvard Law Review.*

Bona fide occupational qualification (BFOQ)   Employment discrimination based on a protected class (other than race or color) that is lawful if it is job-related and a business necessity.

Breach of the duty of care   Failure to exercise care or to act as a reasonable person would act.

Bribery   A person's giving another person money, property, favors, or anything else of value in exchange for a favor; often called a payoff or "kickback."

Briefs   Documents submitted by the parties' attorneys to the judge; contain legal support for their side of the case.

Burden of proof   The weight a plaintiff carries in proving the allegations made in his or her complaint.

Burglary   Taking personal property from another's home, office, or commercial or other type of building.

Business judgment rule   A rule that protects the decisions of board of directors, which acts on an informed basis, in good faith, and in the honest belief that the action taken is in the best interests of the corporation and its shareholders.

Causation   Concept that a person who commits a negligent act is not liable unless his or her act was the cause of the plaintiff's injuries. Two types: (1) causation in fact (actual cause), and (2) proximate cause (legal cause).

Causation in fact   Actual cause of negligence.

Certification mark   A mark certifying that goods and services are of a certain quality or originate from particular geographical areas.

Certified legal assistant (CLA)   Designation by National Association of Legal Assistants for those who take and pass NALA certification program two-day comprehensive examination.

Chain of distribution   All manufacturers, distributors, wholesalers, retailers, lessors, and subcomponent manufacturers involved in a transaction.

Chain-style franchise   License by franchisor to franchisee to make and sell its products or distribute services to the public from a retail outlet serving an exclusive territory.

Charitable trust   A trust created for the benefit of a segment of society or society in general.

Chief justice   The U.S. Supreme Court justice responsible for administration of the Court.

Child custody   A divorce issue concerning who is to be the child's primary caregiver (or joint custodian) and the amount of time the noncustodial parent is to spend with the child (parenting time).

Child support   Entitlement of children to be financially supported by their parents upon divorce, based on the parents' earning ability.

Circuits   The geographical area served by a U.S. court of appeals.

Citation   A reference to the source of the information.

Cite checking   (1) Verifying that the proper citation format has been used in a document and (2) checking the referenced case to determine its validity and that it has not been repealed or overturned.

Civil law system   A major legal system derived from the Roman Empire, in which a civil code and statutes interpreting it are the sole sources of law; thus, case law and court decisions do not have the force of law.

Civil litigation   Involves legal action to resolve disputes between parties (as contrasted with criminal litigation).

Closing arguments   Statements made by plaintiff's and defendant's attorneys to the jury at the end of a trial to try to convince the jury to render a verdict for their client.

Codicil   A separate document that must be executed to amend a will; must be executed with the same formalities as a will.

Codified law   Statutes organized into code books, organized by topic.

Collective mark   A mark used by cooperatives, associations, and fraternal organizations.

Color discrimination   Employment discrimination based upon skin color prohibited under Title VII of Civil Rights Act of 1964.

"Coming and going"   A rule that says a principal is generally not liable for injuries caused by its agents and employees while they are on their way to or from work.

Commerce Clause   A clause of the U.S. Constitution that grants Congress the power "to regulate commerce with foreign nations, and among the several states, and with Indian tribes."

Commitment   The dedication to finish that which one starts out to do or complete.

Common-law marriage   A marriage recognized by some states without a marriage license between the parties.

Common stock certificate   A document that represents a common shareholder's investment in a corporation.

Common stockholder   A person who owns common stock.

Communication   The act of expressing oneself in written or spoken words.

Community property   A form of co-ownership in which husband and wife share equally in the fruits of the marital partnership.

Comparative negligence   A doctrine that applies to strict liability actions that says a plaintiff who is contributorily negligent for his or her injuries is responsible for a proportional share of the damages.

Compensatory damages   (1) An award of money intended to compensate a nonbreaching party for the loss of the bargain; they place the nonbreaching party in the same position as if the contract had been fully performed by restoring the "benefit of the bargain." (2) Damages that are generally equal to the difference between the value of the goods as warranted and the actual value of the goods accepted at the time and place of acceptance.

Complaint   Document the plaintiff files with the court and serves on the defendant to initiate a lawsuit.

Complete performance   Action that occurs when a party to a contract renders performance exactly as required by the contract; discharges that party's obligations under the contract.

Computer Software Copyright Act   Amended the Copyright Act of 1976 to include computer programs in the list of tangible items protected by copyright law.

Conciliation   A form of mediation in which the parties choose an interested third party to act as the mediator.

Concurring opinion   Issued by a justice who agrees with the outcome of a case but not the reason proffered by other justices, to set forth his or her reasons for deciding the case.

Condition precedent   A condition that requires the occurrence (or nonoccurrence) of an event before a party is obligated to perform a duty under a contract.

Condominium   A common form of ownership in a multiple-dwelling building in which the purchaser has title to the individual unit and owns the common areas as a tenant in common with the other condominium owners.

Conflict checking   Comparing current and prior representations of parties and matters handled to verify that the acceptance of a new client or legal matter will not present a conflict of interest for the firm.

Conflict of interest   The representation of one client being directly adverse to the interest of another client.

Connector   Instructions to a search engine to look for combinations of words; include "and," "near," and "or."

Consequential damages   Foreseeable damages that arise from circumstances outside a contract; to be liable for these damages, the breaching party must know or have reason to know that the breach will cause special damages to the other party.

Consideration   Something of legal value given in exchange for a promise.

Consolidation   (1) Act of a court to combine two or more separate lawsuits into one lawsuit. (2) The combining of two or more corporations to form an entirely new corporation.

Constructive trust   An equitable trust imposed by law to avoid fraud, unjust enrichment, and injustice.

Contempt of court   A party to a lawsuit may be held in contempt of court for refusing to comply with the court's orders; punishment may include a fine or jail time.

Contract   An agreement that is enforceable by a court of law or equity.

Contracts contrary to public policy   Contracts that have a negative impact on society or interfere with the public's safety and welfare.

Contractual capacity   One of the requirements of a valid contract is that both parties must have the capacity to contract; those not having capacity include minors, mentally incompetent persons, and intoxicated persons.

Contributory negligence (1) A doctrine that says a plaintiff who is partially at fault for his or her own injury cannot recover against the negligent defendant. (2) A defense that says a person who is injured by a defective product but has been negligent and has contributed to his or her own injuries cannot recover from the defendant.

Conversion of personal property A tort that deprives a true owner of the use and enjoyment of his or her personal property by taking over such property and exercising ownership rights over it.

Cooperative (1) A voluntary joining together of businesses that provides services to its members. (2) A form of co-ownership of a multiple-dwelling building in which a corporation owns the building and the residents own shares in the corporation.

Co-ownership Two or more persons own a piece of real property; forms of co-ownership include joint tenancy, tenancy in common, tenancy by the entirety, community property, condominium, and cooperative.

Copyright The exclusive legal right to reproduce, publish, and sell a literary, musical, or artistic work.

Copyright infringement The copying of a substantial and material part of the plaintiff's copyrighted work without permission; copyright holder may recover damages and other remedies against the infringer.

Corporation A fictitious legal entity that (1) is created according to statutory requirements, and (2) is a separate taxpaying entity for federal income tax purposes.

Counteroffer A response by an offeree that contains terms and conditions different from or in addition to those of the offer; a counteroffer terminates an offer.

Court of Appeals for the Federal Circuit A court of appeals in Washington, D.C. that has special appellate jurisdiction to review the decisions of the claims court, the Patent and Trademark Office, and the Court of International Trade.

Court of record A state's general-jurisdiction trial court, in which testimony and evidence are recorded and stored for future reference.

Covenant An unconditional promise to perform.

Crime Violation of a statute for which the government imposes a punishment.

Criminal conspiracy Two or more persons entering into an agreement to commit a crime and taking an overt act to further the crime.

Criminal fraud Obtaining title to property through deception or trickery; also known as *false pretenses* or *deceit*.

Criminal law Federal, state, and local government laws for the purpose of defining crimes and setting forth punishments for those found guilty of violating criminal laws.

Critical legal thinking The process of specifying the issue presented by a case, identifying the key facts in the case and applicable law, and then applying the law to the facts to come to a conclusion that answers the issue presented.

Cross-complaint Document filed by defendant against plaintiff to seek damages or some other remedy.

Cross-examination Questioning of a witness following direct examination; precedes redirect examination and recross examination.

Cruel and unusual punishment A clause in the Eighth Amendment that protects criminal defendants from torture or other abusive punishment.

Cultural sensitivity Awareness of the differences in the way people behave, based on religious and ethnic backgrounds and belief systems, and reacting appropriately.

"Danger invites rescue" Doctrine that provides that a rescuer who is injured while going to someone's rescue can sue the person who caused the dangerous situation.

Deed Document that describes a person's ownership interest in a piece of real property.

Defamation of character False statement(s) made by one person about another; in court, the plaintiff must prove that (1) the defendant made an untrue statement of fact about the plaintiff, and (2) the statement was intentionally or accidentally published to a third party.

Default judgment If a defendant does not file an answer to a plaintiff's complaint, a default judgment is entered against him or her, establishing the defendant's liability.

Defendant The party against whom a lawsuit is brought.

Defendant's case Process by which the defendant (1) rebuts the plaintiff's evidence, (2) proves affirmative defenses, and (3) proves allegations made in a cross-complaint.

Defense attorney Attorney working on behalf of the defendant.

Deferred posting rule A rule that allows banks to fix an afternoon hour of 2:00 P.M. or later as a cutoff hour for the purpose of processing items.

Delegation doctrine A doctrine that says when an administrative agency is created, it receives certain powers and the agency can use only those legislative, judicial, and executive powers bestowed on it.

De novo appeal   To appeal to a higher court as if there has been no prior decision.

Deponent   Party who gives a deposition.

Deposition   Oral testimony given under oath by a party or witness and transcribed prior to trial.

Digital Millennium Copyright Act   Enacted in 1998 to protect "wrappers" and encryption technology of copyrighted works from infringement; imposes civil and criminal penalties.

Direct examination   The initial questioning of witnesses in a case by an attorney; often followed by cross-examination, redirect examination, and recross examination.

Disaffirm   The act of a minor to rescind a contract under the infancy doctrine; may be done orally, in writing, or by the minor's conduct.

Discovery   A legal process during which both parties engage in various activities to find facts of the case from the other party and witnesses prior to trial.

Dissenting opinion   Issued by a justice who does not agree with the court's decision, setting forth the reasons for his or her dissent.

Distinctiveness of a mark   The quality of a brand name that has acquired a secondary meaning; necessary to be trademarked.

District attorney–prosecutor   The lawyer representing the government in a criminal lawsuit.

Diversity of citizenship   A case between (1) citizens of different states, (2) a citizen of a state and a citizen or subject of a foreign country, and (3) a citizen of a state and a foreign country where a foreign country is the plaintiff.

Divorce   Legal proceeding whereby a married couple legally undo their marriage.

Doctrine of strict liability   A tort doctrine that makes manufacturers, distributors, wholesalers, retailers, and others in the chain of distribution of a defective product liable for damages caused by the defect, irrespective of fault.

"Doing business as" (d.b.a.)   Operating under a trade name.

Domain name   A unique name that identifies an individual's or company's website.

Domestic corporation   A corporation in the state in which it was formed.

Double jeopardy   A clause in the Fifth Amendment that protects persons from being tried twice for the same crime.

Dram shop act   State statutes that make taverns and bartenders liable for injuries caused to or by patrons who are served too much alcohol.

Dual-purpose mission   An errand or other act that a principal requests of an agent while the agent is on his or her own personal business.

Due Process Clause   A clause in the Fourteenth Amendment to the U.S. Constitution that provides that no person shall be deprived of "life, liberty, or property" without due process of the law.

Duty not to willfully or wantonly injure   The obligation an owner owes a trespasser to prevent intentional injury or harm to the trespasser when the trespasser is on the owner's premises.

Duty of candor   The obligation to be honest with the court.

Duty of care   (1) The obligation we all owe each other not to cause any unreasonable harm or risk of harm; a breach is negligence. (2) An obligation owed by a member of a member-managed LLC and a manager of a manager-managed LLC not to engage in (a) a known violation of law, (b) intentional conduct, (c) reckless conduct, or (d) grossly negligent conduct that injures the LLC. (3) An obligation that corporate directors and officers have to use care and diligence when acting on behalf of the corporation.

Duty of loyalty   (1) An obligation of directors and officers not to act adversely to the interests of the corporation and to subordinate their personal interests to those of the corporation and its shareholders. (2) An obligation of a partner not to act adversely to the interests of the partnership.

Duty of ordinary care   The obligation of an owner to an invitee or a licensee to prevent injury or harm when the invitee or licensee steps on the owner's premises.

Duty of reasonable care   The obligation of a reasonable bailee in like circumstances to protect the bailed property.

Duty of utmost care   An obligation of care, going beyond ordinary care, that says common carriers and innkeepers have a responsibility to provide security to their passengers or guests.

Easement   A right to use someone else's land without owning or leasing it.

Economic Espionage Act   A law enacted in 1996 that makes it a federal crime to steal another's trade secret.

Elective course   An educational offering not required as part of a program of study.

Electronic mail (email)   Written communication between individuals and businesses using computers connected to the Internet or an internal network.

Embezzlement   Fraudulent conversion of property by a person to whom that property was entrusted.

Employer–employee relationship   A relationship that results when an employer hires an employee to perform some form of physical service.

Employment-at-will   Employment without an employment contract.

Employment-related injury   Injury arising out of and in the course of employment, under the Workers' Compensation Act.

Entity theory   An approach holding that partnerships are separate legal entities that can have title to personal and real property, transact business in the partnership name, sue in the partnership name, and the like.

Enumerated powers   Certain powers delegated to the federal government by the states.

Environmental Protection Agency (EPA)   An administrative agency created by the U.S. Congress in 1970 to coordinate implementation and enforcement of federal environmental protection laws.

Equal Access to Justice Act   A law enacted to protect persons from harassment by federal administrative agencies.

Equitable distribution   In property division in divorce, the doctrine that takes into account issues of rearing a family rather than being in the workplace, age and medical condition of the parties, and the contribution to the education or professional or business success by one spouse to the other.

Escheat   Goes to; used to describe property that goes to the state when an individual dies intestate (without a will).

Estate   Ownership rights in real property; the bundle of legal rights of the owner to possess, use, and enjoy property.

Estate *pur autre vie*   A life estate measured in the life of a third party.

Estray statutes   Statutes that permit a finder of mislaid or lost property to clear title to the property if (1) the finder reports the found property to the appropriate government agency and turns over possession of the property to this agency, (2) either the finder or the government agency posts notices and publishes advertisements describing the lost property, and (3) a specified amount of time has passed without the rightful owner's reclaiming the property.

Ethical obligation   The obligation to conform to a set of ethics, in general or that of a profession, such as the ABA Model Rules for lawyers.

Ethical wall   An environment in which an attorney or a paralegal is isolated from a particular case or client to avoid a conflict of interest or to protect a client's confidences and secrets.

Exclusionary rule   A rule that says evidence obtained from an unreasonable search and seizure generally can be prohibited from introduction at a trial or administrative proceeding against the person searched.

Exclusive agency contract   A contract between a principal and an agent that says the principal cannot employ any agent other than the exclusive agent.

Exculpatory clause   A contractual provision that relieves one or both parties to the contract from tort liability for ordinary negligence.

Executive branch of government   The part of the federal government that consists of the President and Vice President.

Executive order   An order issued by a member of the executive branch of the government, such as the President.

Executive powers   Authority granted to administrative agencies, such as the investigation and prosecution of possible violations of statutes, administrative rules, and administrative orders.

Executor or executrix   A personal representative named in a will to administer an estate during its settlement phase.

Expert witnesses   Those individuals whose background, education, and experience are such that courts will recognize them as qualified to give opinions based on a set of facts.

Express agency   An agency that occurs when a principal and an agent expressly agree to enter into an agency agreement with each other.

Express contract   An agreement in written or oral words.

Express trust   A trust created voluntarily by the settlor.

Extortion   Threat to expose something about another person unless that other person gives money or property; often called "blackmail."

Fair-use doctrine   A doctrine that permits certain limited use of a copyright by someone other than the copyright holder without the permission of the copyright holder.

False imprisonment The intentional confinement or restraint of another person without authority or justification and without that person's consent.

Family law The practice of law concerning marriage, divorce, and child custody and support.

Federal administrative agencies Administrative agencies that are part of the executive or legislative branch of government.

Federal question A case arising under the U.S. Constitution, treaties, or federal statutes and regulations.

Federal Rules of Appellate Procedure (F.R.A.P.) Rules governing appeals in both civil and criminal cases to the federal appellate court.

Federal Rules of Civil Procedure Rules governing civil trials in the federal system.

Federalism The U.S. form of government, in which the federal government and the 50 state governments share powers.

Fee simple absolute (fee simple) A type of ownership of real property that grants the owner the fullest bundle of legal rights that a person can hold in real property.

Fee simple defeasible (qualified fee) A type of ownership of real property that grants the owner all the incidents of a fee simple absolute except that it may be taken away if a specified condition occurs or does not occur.

Felony The most serious type of crime; most crimes against the person and some business-related crimes are felonies.

File server The central computer in a network computer system that controls the flow of information over the network.

Final order rule A rule that says the decision of an administrative agency must be final before judicial review can be sought.

Finding tools Publications, such as digests or the *Index to Legal Periodicals*, used to find primary and secondary sources.

Fireman's rule A rule stating that a firefighter who is injured while putting out a fire may not sue the party whose negligence caused the fire.

Fixture Personal property that is permanently affixed to the real property, such as built-in cabinets in a house.

Force majeure **clause** Clause in a contract that excuses nonperformance of the contract if certain events occur.

Foreign corporation A corporation in any state or jurisdiction other than the one in which it was formed.

Forgery Unauthorized signature of a maker, drawer, or indorser.

Forum-selection clause Contract provision that designates a certain court to hear any dispute concerning nonperformance of the contract.

Franchise An arrangement whereby the franchisor (owner) licenses another party to use the franchisor's trade name, trademarks, commercial symbols, patents, copyrights, and other property in the distribution and selling of goods and services.

Franchisee The party who is licensed by the franchisor in a franchise situation.

Fraud Intentional misrepresentation.

Freedom of Information Act (FOIA) A law enacted to give the public access to documents in the possession of federal administrative agencies.

Freehold estate An estate in which the owner has a present possessory interest in the real property.

Frolic and detour A situation in which an agent does something during the course of his or her employment to further his or her own interests rather than the principal's.

Fully disclosed agency An agency that results if the third party entering into a contract knows (1) that the agent is acting as an agent for a principal, and (2) the actual identity of the principal.

Future interest The interest that a grantor retains for himself or herself or a third party.

General gift Testamentary gift that does not identify the specific property from which the gift is to be made.

General-jurisdiction trial court A court that hears cases of a general nature that are not within the jurisdiction of limited-jurisdiction trial courts; testimony and evidence at trial are recorded and stored for future reference.

General partner Partner in a limited partnership who invests capital, manages the business, and is personally liable for partnership debts.

General partnership An association of two or more persons to carry on as co-owners of a business for profit [UPA § 6(1)].

General power of attorney A type of power of attorney that confers broad powers on the agent to act in any matters on the principal's behalf.

General practice A law firm that handles all types of cases.

Generic name   A term for a mark that has become a common term for a product line or type of service and therefore has lost its trademark protection.

Gift promise   An unenforceable promise because it lacks consideration.

GlobalCite   The Loislaw reverse chronological list of case law; statutes in the order of the highest number of citation occurrences; regulations in relevancy order; and references to other databases in the Loislaw library.

Good Samaritan law   Statute that relieves medical professionals from liability for ordinary negligence when they stop and render aid to victims in emergency situations.

Government in the Sunshine Act   A law that opens certain federal administrative agency meetings to the public.

Grantee   The party to whom an interest in real property is transferred.

Grantor   The party who transfers an ownership interest in real property.

Guest statute   Statute providing that if a driver of a vehicle voluntarily and without compensation gives a ride to another person, the driver is not liable to the passenger for injuries caused by driver's ordinary negligence.

Heirs   Relatives who receive property under intestacy statutes when a person dies without a will.

Holographic will   Will that is entirely handwritten and signed by the testator.

Hung jury   A jury that cannot come to a unanimous decision about the defendant's guilt; the government may choose to retry the case.

Illegal contract   A contract to perform an unlawful act; cannot be enforced by either party to the contract.

Immunity from prosecution   The government's agreeing not to use any evidence given by a person granted immunity against that person.

Implied agency   An agency that occurs when a principal and an agent do not expressly create an agency but it is inferred from the conduct of the parties.

Implied-in-fact contract   Contracts that are implied from the action and conduct of the parties rather than stated in oral or written words.

Implied trust   A trust that is imposed by law or from the conduct of the parties.

Implied warranty of habitability   A warranty that provides that the leased premises must be fit, safe, and suitable for ordinary residential use.

Inchoate crimes   Incomplete crimes or crimes committed by nonparticipants, including criminal conspiracy, attempt to commit a crime, and aiding and abetting the commission of a crime.

Incidental beneficiary   A party who unintentionally benefits from another's contract.

Indemnification   Right of a partner to be reimbursed for expenditures incurred on behalf of a partnership.

Independent contractor   "A person who contracts with another to do something for him who is not controlled by the other nor subject to the other's right to control with respect to his physical conduct in the performance of the undertaking" (Restatement [Second] of Agency).

Indictment/information   The charge of having committed a crime, based on the judgment of a grand jury.

Infancy doctrine   A doctrine that allows minors to disaffirm (cancel) most contracts they have entered into with adults.

Injunction   A court order prohibiting a person from doing a certain act.

In personam jurisdiction   A court's authority over the parties to a lawsuit; also called *personal jurisdiction*.

In rem jurisdiction   Authority to hear a case because of jurisdiction over the property of the lawsuit; literally, "jurisdiction over the thing."

Inside director   A member of a board of directors who is also an officer of the corporation.

Intangible property   Rights that cannot be reduced to physical form, including stock certificates, certificates of deposit, bonds, and copyrights.

Intentional infliction of emotional distress   A tort that says a person whose extreme and outrageous conduct intentionally or recklessly causes severe emotional distress to another person is liable for that emotional distress; also known as *tort of outrage*.

Intentional misrepresentation   Fraud or deceit; occurs when an agent makes an untrue statement that he or she knows is not true.

Intentional tort   A category of torts requiring that the defendant intended to do the act that caused the plaintiff's injuries; occurs when a person has intentionally committed a wrong against (1) another person or his or her character, or (2) another person's property.

Intermediate appellate court (court of appeal)   A court that hears appeals from trial courts.

Internet A collection of millions of computers that provide a network of electronic connections between computers.

Internet search engine A program designed to search for a word or set of words on the Internet.

Internet service provider (ISP) Organization providing local or toll-free access to connect to the Internet.

Interpersonal skills The ability to work with others.

Interpretive rules Rules issued by administrative agencies that explain existing statutory language as they understand it.

Interrogatories Written questions submitted by one party to another party; the questions must be answered in writing within a stipulated time.

Interstate commerce Movement of goods between states, or business that affects commerce between states.

Intervention The act of others to join as parties to an existing lawsuit.

Inter vivos A trust created by a grantor (settlor) during his or her lifetime.

Intestacy statute A state statute dictating how property is to be distributed to heirs of an individual who dies without a will.

Intestate succession The application of a state's intestacy statutes to determine how property is to be distributed to heirs when an individual dies without an heir.

Intrastate commerce Movement of goods within states, or business that affects commerce within states.

Invasion of the right to privacy A tort that constitutes the violation of a person's right to live his or her life without being subjected to unwarranted and undesired publicity.

Invitee A person who has been expressly or impliedly invited onto owner's premises for mutual benefit of both parties.

Joint and several liability Condition of a partnership in which the partners are jointly and severally liable for tort liability of the partnership; this means that the plaintiff can sue one or more of the partners separately. If successful, the plaintiff can recover the entire amount of the judgment from any or all of the defendant-partners.

Joint liability An aspect of a partnership in which the partners are both or all liable for contracts and debts of the partnership; this means that a plaintiff must name the partnership and all of the partners as defendants in a lawsuit.

Joint tenancy Form of co-ownership that includes the right of survivorship.

Joint will A will executed by two or more testators.

Judgment Official decision of the court.

Judgment notwithstanding the verdict (j.n.o.v.) In a civil case, the judge's overturning the jury's verdict if he or she finds bias or jury misconduct.

Judicial branch of government The part of the federal government that consists of the Supreme Court and other federal courts.

Judicial decision Written opinion explaining the reasoning in an individual lawsuit; issued by federal and state courts.

Jurisdiction Authority of a court to hear a case.

Jurisprudence Philosophy or science of law.

Jury deliberation Process by which a jury discusses the facts and evidence they have witnessed in a trial.

Jury instructions Directions given by judge to jury informing them of the law to be applied in the case.

Just Compensation Clause Clause in the U.S. Constitution mandating that the government compensate owners and lessees for property taken under the power of eminent domain.

KeyCite The Westlaw on-line citation update service.

LAN Local area network.

Land Real property consisting of land and buildings and other structures permanently attached to the land.

Landlord/lessor Owner who transfers a leasehold.

Land-use control Collective term for the laws that regulate the possession, ownership, and use of real property.

Larceny Taking another's personal property other than from his or her person or building.

Law A body of rules of action or conduct prescribed by controlling authority, and having binding legal force; must be obeyed and followed by citizens subject to sanctions or legal consequences.

Law court A court that developed and administered a uniform set of laws decreed by the kings and queens subsequent to William the Conqueror; emphasized legal procedure over merits.

Leading questions Questions that suggest the desired answer.

Lease A transfer of the right to possession and use of real property for a set term in return for certain consideration; rental agreement between landlord and tenant.

Leasehold estate (leasehold)   A tenant's interest in the property.

Legal assistant   A person qualified by education, training, or work experience who is employed or retained by a lawyer, law office, corporation, governmental agency, or other entity who performs specifically delegated substantive legal work for which a lawyer is responsible; *paralegal* is an equivalent term.

Legislative branch of government   The part of the federal government that consists of Congress (the Senate and the House of Representatives).

Libel   A false statement that appears in a letter, newspaper, magazine, book, photograph, movie, video, and so on.

License   (1) A contract that transfers limited rights in intellectual property and informational rights. (2) A contract that grants a person the right to enter upon another's property for a specified and usually short period of time. (3) A government document conferred on people in certain types of industries or professions.

Licensee   The party who is given limited rights in or access to intellectual property and informational rights owned by the licensor.

Licensing power   Statute that requires a person or business to obtain a license from the government prior to engaging in a specified occupation or activity.

Life estate   An interest in the land for a person's lifetime; upon that person's death, the interest is transferred to another party.

Limited-jurisdiction trial court   A court that hears matters of a specialized or limited nature.

Limited liability   Liability of shareholders or limited partners only to the extent of their capital contribution; they generally are not personally liable for debts and obligations of the corporation or partnership.

Limited liability company (LLC)   An unincorporated business entity that combines the most favorable attributes of general partnerships, limited partnerships, and corporations.

Limited liability partnership (LLP)   A type of partnership in which all (limited) partners have limited liability.

Limited partner   Partner in a limited partnership who invests capital but does not participate in management and is not personally liable for partnership debts beyond capital contributions.

Limited partnership   A type of partnership that has two types of partners: (1) general partners, and (2) limited partners.

Limited partnership agreement (articles of limited partnership)   Terms and conditions regarding operation, termination, and dissolution of a partnership; a document that sets forth the rights and duties of the general and limited partners.

Liquidated damages   Damages specified in a contract rather than determined by the court; paid upon a breach of contract established in advance.

Litigation   The process of bringing, maintaining, and defending a lawsuit.

Living will   A will that a person makes before catastrophe strikes and he or she becomes unable to express it because of illness or accident, stipulating that his or her life is not to be prolonged indefinitely by artificial means.

Long-arm statute   A statute that extends a state's jurisdiction to nonresidents who were not served a summons within the state.

Mail fraud   The use of mail to defraud another person.

Mala in se   Term describing crimes that are inherently evil, such as murder, rape, and other crimes against persons.

Mala prohibita   Term describing crimes that are not inherently evil but are prohibited by society; these include non-felony crimes against property, such as robbery.

Malicious prosecution   A lawsuit in which the original defendant sues the original plaintiff; a civil action for damages.

Mark   Any trademark, service mark, certification mark, or collective mark that can be trademarked.

Marriage   A voluntary agreement between a man and a woman to become husband and wife.

Material breach–inferior performance   A breach of contract that occurs when a party renders inferior performance of his or her contractual duties.

Mediation   A form of alternative dispute resolution in which the parties choose a neutral third party to act as mediator of the dispute.

Memorandum   Working document for the legal team, used in preparing for and presenting the case.

Mens rea   From Latin, "evil intent"—possessing the requisite state of mind to commit a prohibited act.

Merchant court   Separate set of courts established in England to administer "law of merchants."

Merchant protection statutes   Statutes that allow merchants to stop, detain, and investigate suspected shoplifters without being held liable for false imprisonment if (1) there are reasonable grounds for the suspicion, (2) suspects are detained for only a reasonable time, and (3) investigations are conducted in a reasonable manner.

Minor breach–substantial performance   A breach of contract that occurs when a party renders substantial performance of his or her contractual duties.

Miranda rights   The colloquial name for the warning required to be read to a criminal suspect before he or she is interrogated by the police or other government officials; established by the U.S. Supreme Court in the landmark case *Miranda v. Arizona.*

Misappropriation of the right to publicity   An attempt by another person to appropriate a living person's name or identity for commercial purposes.

Misdemeanor   A crime that is less serious than a felony and is not inherently evil.

Model Guidelines for the Utilization of Legal Assistant Services   A set of guidelines by ABA policy-making body, the House of Delegates, intended to govern conduct of lawyers when utilizing paralegals or legal assistants.

Model Rules of Professional Conduct   A recommended set of ethics and professional conduct guidelines for lawyers, prepared by American Bar Association, originally released in 1983; prior release was Model Code of Professional Conduct.

Modem   A device for converting computer information into an electronic format that will allow it to be transmitted over telephone lines, cable lines, and radio waves.

Moral obligation   An obligation based on one's own conscience or a person's perceived rules of correct conduct.

Motion for judgment on the pleadings   Motion alleging that if all the facts presented in the pleadings are taken as true, the party making the motion would win the lawsuit when the proper law is applied to these asserted facts.

Motion for summary judgment   Motion asserting that there are no factual disputes to be decided by the jury; if so, the judge can apply the proper law to the undisputed facts and decide the case without a jury.

Motivation test   A test to determine the liability of a principal; if the agent's motivation in committing an intentional tort is to promote the principal's business, the principal is liable for any injury caused by the tort.

Multinational corporation   A single economic unit composed of companies of different nationalities connected by shareholding, managerial control, or contractual agreement.

Mutual benefit bailment   A bailment that benefits both the bailor and the bailee; the bailee owes a duty of reasonable care to protect the bailed property.

Mutual (reciprocal) wills   Wills in which two or more testators execute separate wills leaving their property to each other on the condition that the survivor leave the remaining property on his or her death as agreed by the testators; also called reciprocal wills.

Narrative opportunity   An opportunity to tell a story or answer a question without a limitation.

National Association of Legal Assistants (NALA)   Professional organization for legal assistants that provides continuing education and professional certification for paralegals, incorporated in 1975.

National Federation of Paralegal Associations (NFPA)   Professional organization of state and local paralegal associations founded in 1974.

National origin discrimination   Employment discrimination based on national heritage, prohibited under Title VII of Civil Rights Act of 1964.

Necessaries of life   Food, clothing, shelter, medical care, and other items considered necessary to the maintenance of life.

Negligence   (1) Tort related to defective products in which the defendant has breached a duty of due care and caused harm to the plaintiff. (2) Failure of a corporate director or officer to exercise the duty of care while conducting the corporation's business.

Negligence per se   Tort in which the violation of a statute or ordinance constitutes breach of the duty of care.

Negligent infliction of emotional distress   Tort that permits a person to recover for emotional distress caused by defendant's negligent conduct.

Networking   Establishing and maintaining contact with others, asking questions and exchanging information.

No Electronic Theft (NET) Act   A 1997 law that criminalizes certain copyright infringement.

No-fault divorce   Divorce without an allegation of fault.

Nonconforming uses   Uses and buildings that already exist in a zoned area that are permitted to continue even though they do not fit within new zoning ordinances.

Noncupative will   Oral will that is made before a witness during the testator's last illness.

Nondisclosure agreement (NDA)   An enforceable contract swearing the signatory to secrecy regarding confidential information.

Nurse paralegals   Nurses who have medical work experience and combine it with paralegal skills.

Offer   Manifestation of willingness to enter into a bargain, to justify another person's understanding that the assent to that bargain is invited and will conclude it.

Offeree   The party to whom an offer to enter into a contract is made.

Offeror   The party who makes an offer to enter into a contract.

Officers (of corporation)   Employees of a corporation appointed by the board of directors to manage day-to-day operations of the corporation.

Older Workers Benefit Protection Act (OWBPA)   A law prohibiting age discrimination in employee benefits.

One-year rule   An executory contract stating that if it cannot be performed by its own terms within one year of its formation, it must be in writing.

Open-ended questions   Questions designed to create a narrative opportunity for the witness.

Opening statements   Comments made at the beginning of a trial by the attorneys to the jury summarizing the factual and legal issues of the case.

Operating agreement   An agreement entered into among members that governs the affairs and business of a limited liability company and the relations among members, managers, and the LLC.

Order   Decision issued by an administrative law judge.

Ordinances   Laws enacted by local government bodies such as cities and municipalities, counties, school districts, and water districts.

Organizational meeting   A meeting that must be held by the initial directors of a corporation after the articles of incorporation are filed.

Outside director   A member of a board of directors who is not an officer of the corporation.

PACER (Public Access to Court Electronic Records)   An electronic public-access service allowing users to obtain case and docket information from federal appellate, district, and bankruptcy courts and from the U.S. Party/ Case Index.

Paralegal   A person qualified by education, training, or work experience who is employed or retained by a lawyer, law office, corporation, governmental agency, or other entity who performs specifically delegated substantive legal work for which a lawyer is responsible; equivalent term is *legal assistant*.

Paralegal Advanced Competency Exam (PACE)   National Association of Paralegal Association's certification program that requires the paralegal to have two years of experience and a bachelor's degree and have completed a paralegal course at an accredited school.

Parallel citation   A citation to the same material, usually a case, in another source.

Partially disclosed agency   An agency that occurs if the agent discloses his or her agency status but does not reveal the principal's identity and the third party does not know the principal's identity from another source.

Partnership   Two or more natural or artificial (corporation) persons who have joined together to share ownership and profit or loss.

Partnership agreement   A written agreement that the partners sign; also called *articles of partnership*.

Partnership at will   A partnership with no fixed duration.

Partnership for a term   A partnership with a fixed duration.

Patent   Registration of an invention that is novel, useful, and nonobvious, as conferred by the United States Patent and Trademark Office.

Patent infringement   Unauthorized use of another's patent.

Penal codes   A collection of criminal statutes.

***Per capita* distribution**   A distribution of the estate that makes each grandchild and great-grandchild of the deceased inherit equally with the children of the deceased.

Periodic tenancy   A tenancy created when a lease specifies intervals at which payments are due but does not specify duration of the lease.

Personal property   Property that consists of tangible property such as automobiles, furniture, and jewelry, as well as intangible property such as securities, patents, and copyrights.

***Per stirpes* distribution**   A distribution of an estate that makes grandchildren and great-grandchildren of the deceased inherit by representation of their parent.

Petition for certiorari   A petition asking U.S. Supreme Court to hear one's case.

Petitioner   The party appealing the decision of an administrative agency.

Piercing the corporate veil A doctrine that says if a shareholder dominates a corporation and uses it for improper purposes, a court of equity can disregard the corporate entity and hold the shareholder personally liable for the corporation's debts and obligations.

Plaintiff The party who files a complaint; in the case of criminal law, the government.

Plaintiff's case Process in which the plaintiff introduces evidence to prove the allegations contained in his or her complaint.

Plant life and vegetation Real property that is growing in or on the surface of the land.

Plea bargain An agreement by an accused to admit to a lesser crime than charged; in return, the government agrees to impose a lesser sentence than might have been obtained had the case gone to trial.

Pleadings The paperwork filed with a court to initiate and respond to a lawsuit.

Pocket Part A method of updating a printed volume by inserting a pamphlet in the back of the bound volume in a pocket cut into the inside back cover for that purpose.

Police powers The power of states to regulate private and business activity within their borders.

Power of attorney An express agency agreement used to give an agent the power to sign legal documents on behalf of the principal.

Precedent A rule of law established in a court decision; lower courts must follow precedent established by higher courts.

Preemption doctrine The concept that federal law takes precedent over state or local law.

Pretrial hearing A hearing before a trial to facilitate settlement of a case; also called a *pretrial settlement conference*.

Primary authority The actual law itself; this includes statutes and case law.

Primary source The actual law itself; this includes statutes and case law.

Principal A person who authorizes an agent to sign a negotiable instrument on his or her behalf.

Principal–agent relationship A relationship in which an employer hires an employee and gives that employee authority to act and enter into contracts on his or her behalf.

Principal–independent contractor relationship A relationship that results when a person or business that is not an employee is employed by a principal to perform a certain task on his or her behalf.

Privacy Act A law stipulating that federal administrative agencies can maintain only information about an individual that is relevant and necessary to accomplish a legitimate agency purpose.

Privileged communication Certain forms of communication not usable at trial unless the privilege is waived; includes attorney–client communications, doctor–patient communications, priest–penitent communications, and spousal communications during marriage.

Pro bono Work without compensation for individuals and organizations that otherwise could not afford legal assistance.

Probable cause The substantial likelihood that the person either committed or is about to commit a crime.

Probate (settlement of the estate) The process of a deceased's property being collected, debts and taxes paid, and the remainder of the estate distributed.

Procedural due process Type of due process that requires the respondent to be given (1) proper and timely notice of the allegations or charges against him or her, and (2) an opportunity to present evidence on the matter.

Procedural law Rules defining the ways in which the rights and obligations of individuals will be enforced.

Production of documents A form of discovery in which one party requests that another party produce all documents relevant to the case prior to trial.

Professional malpractice Liability of a professional who breaches his or her duty of ordinary care.

Proprietary school Private, as opposed to public, institution, generally for profit, offering training and education.

Prosecutor The lawyer representing the government in a criminal lawsuit.

Protocol The format dictating the arrangement of information.

Proximate cause A point along a chain of events caused by a negligent party after which this party is no longer legally responsible for the consequences of his or her actions. Also termed *legal cause*.

Public defender Attorney provided by the government to represent a defendant who cannot afford legal representation.

Public-use doctrine A doctrine that says a patent may not be granted if the public used the invention for more than one year prior to filing of the patent application.

Punitive damages   Damages awarded to punish the defendant, to deter the defendant from similar conduct in the future, and to set an example for others.

***Quasi in rem* jurisdiction**   Authority allowed a plaintiff who obtains a judgment in one state to try to collect the judgment by attaching property of the defendant located in another state.

Quasi- or implied-in-law contract   An equitable doctrine whereby a court may award monetary damages to a plaintiff for providing work or services to a defendant even though no actual contract existed; this doctrine intends to prevent unjust enrichment and unjust detriment.

Quiet title   An action brought by a party seeking an order of the court declaring who has title to disputed property; the court "quiets title" by its decision.

Quitclaim deed   A type of deed that provides the least amount of protection because the grantor conveys only whatever interest he or she has in the property.

Racketeer Influenced and Corrupt Organizations Act (RICO)   Federal statute that authorizes civil lawsuits against defendants for engaging in a pattern of racketeering activities; provides for both criminal and civil penalties for securities fraud.

Real property   The land itself, as well as buildings, trees, soil, minerals, timber, plants, and other things permanently affixed to the land.

Rebuttal   Presentation of a case (calling witnesses and putting forth evidence) by the plaintiff's attorney to rebut the defendant's case.

Record   The recorded summary of a trial court proceeding, including memorandum, trial transcript, and evidence produced at trial.

Recross examination   An attorney asks questions of the witness, following direct examination, cross-examination, and redirect examination.

Redirect examination   An attorney asks questions of the witness, following direct examination and cross-examination.

Reformation   An equitable doctrine that permits the court to rewrite a contract to express the parties' true intentions.

Regular meeting of board of directors   A meeting held by a board of directors at the time and place established in the bylaws.

Relevant facts   Those facts that tend to prove or disprove a matter.

Remainder   The right of possession returning to a third party upon expiration of a limited or contingent estate.

Remainderman   The person to receive the trust corpus upon termination of a trust.

Remand   An appellate court finds that the lower court has made an error that can be corrected and sends the case back to the lower court to take further action or conduct further proceedings.

Repealed   Abolishment of an existing law by formal action.

Reply   Court document filed by original plaintiff to answer defendant's cross-complaint.

Residuary gift   Gift of the estate left after the debts, taxes, and specific and general gifts have been paid.

Res ipsa loquitur   Tort in which the presumption of negligence arises because (1) the defendant was in exclusive control of the situation, and (2) the plaintiff would not have suffered injury but for someone's negligence.

Resourcefulness   The ability to meet and handle situations and find solutions to problems.

Restatement (Second) of Torts   A compilation of model tort law principles drafted by legal scholars. The Restatement is not law.

Resulting trust   A trust created by the conduct of the parties.

Resume   A short description of a person's educational, work experience, and other related and supporting information that is used in evaluating a person's potential qualifications for a position in a firm or an organization.

Reverse   An appellate court decision indicating that the lower court has made a substantial error in deciding a case.

Reverse discrimination   Discrimination against a group that usually is thought of as a majority.

Reversion   A right of possession that returns to the grantor after expiration of a limited or contingent estate.

Revised Model Business Corporation Act (RMBCA)   A revision of the MBCA in 1984 that arranged the provisions of the Act more logically, revised the language to be more consistent, and made substantial changes in the provisions.

Revised Uniform Limited Partnership Act (RULPA)   A 1976 revision of the ULPA that updates the comprehensive law for the formation, operation, and dissolution of limited partnerships.

Right of survivorship   Rule stating that a deceased partner's right in specific partnership property vests with the remaining partners upon his or her death.

Robbery   Taking personal property from another person by use of fear or force.

Rules and regulations   A legislative function adopted by administrative agencies to interpret the statutes they are authorized to enforce.

S corporations   Corporations that elect to be taxed under the Subchapter S Revision Act (as opposed to C corporations, all other corporations).

Search warrant   Document authorizing the police to search a designated place for specified contraband, articles, items, or documents; must be based on probable cause.

Secondary authority   Writings about the law, such as legal encyclopedias and digests.

Secondary meaning   The distinctiveness that results when an ordinary term has become a brand name; necessary for a trademark.

Secondary source   Writings about the law, such as legal encyclopedias and digests.

Self-incrimination   The Fifth Amendment protection stating that no person shall be compelled in any criminal case to be a witness against himself or herself.

Service mark   A mark that distinguishes the services of the holder from those of its competitors.

Service of process   Serving a summons on a defendant to obtain personal jurisdiction over him or her.

Settlement conference   Parties meet before the trial for the purpose of facilitating settlement of the case.

Settlor   Person who creates a trust. Also termed *trustor* or *transferor*.

Sex discrimination   Discrimination against a person solely because of his or her gender.

Sexual harassment   Lewd remarks, touching, intimidation, posting pinups, and other verbal or physical conduct of a sexual nature that occurs on the job.

Shareholders   Owners of corporations.

Simultaneous deaths   Under the Uniform Simultaneous Death Act, a provision that each deceased person's property is distributed as if he or she survived.

Slander   Oral defamation of character.

Small-claims court   A court that hears civil cases involving small dollar amounts.

Social host liability   Rule providing that social hosts are liable for injuries caused by guests who become intoxicated at a social function; this rule is not in effect in all states.

Sole proprietorship   A form of business in which the owner is actually the business; the business is not a separate legal entity.

Solicitor   In the English legal system, a lawyer who deals directly with clients but does not try cases.

Special federal courts   Federal courts that hear matters of limited jurisdiction: U.S. tax court, U.S. court of federal claims, U.S. court of international trade; U.S. bankruptcy court.

Special power of attorney   A type of power of attorney that limits the agent to acts specifically enumerated in an agreement.

Specialty practice   A firm that engages in a specialized area of law.

Specific gift   Testamentary gift of a specifically named piece of property.

Specific performance   A decree of the court that orders a seller or lessor to perform his or her obligations under the contract; usually occurs when the goods in question are unique, such as art or antiques.

Spendthrift trust   A trust that removes all control over the trust from the beneficiary.

Spoliation of evidence   Destruction or loss of evidence.

Standing to sue   Plaintiff's having some stake in the outcome of the lawsuit.

Stare decisis   From Latin, "to stand by the decision"; adherence to precedent.

State administrative agencies   Administrative agencies that states create to enforce and interpret state law.

State supreme court   Highest court in a state court system; hears appeals from intermediate state courts and certain trial courts.

Statement of policy   A written document issued by an administrative agency announcing a proposed course of action that the agency intends to follow in the future.

Statute of Frauds   State statute that requires certain types of contracts to be in writing.

Statute of limitations   Statute that establishes the time period during which a lawsuit must be brought; if the lawsuit is not brought within this period, the injured party loses the right to sue.

Strict liability   Liability without fault.

Subject-matter jurisdiction   A court's authority to hear only certain types of cases or certain topics.

Subpoena   A court order.

Substantive due process   Type of due process that requires that government statutes, ordinances, regulations, or other laws be clear on their face and not overly broad in scope.

Substantive law   The law of the case, as opposed to procedural law.

Substantive rules   Government regulations that have the force of law and must be adhered to by the persons and businesses covered.

Subsurface rights   Rights to the earth located beneath the surface of the land; also called *mineral rights*.

Summons   A court order directing a defendant to appear in court and answer the complaint.

Supremacy Clause   A clause in the U.S. Constitution that establishes that the federal Constitution, treaties, federal laws, and federal regulations are the supreme law of the land.

Tangible property   All real property and physically defined personal property such as goods, animals, and minerals.

Tangible writing   Writing that can be physically seen.

Tenancy at sufferance   A tenancy created when a tenant retains possession of property after the expiration of another tenancy or a life estate without the owner's consent.

Tenancy at will   A lease that may be terminated at any time by either party.

Tenancy for years   A tenancy created when the landlord and the tenant agree on a specific duration for the lease.

Tenancy in common/tenancy by the entirety   A form of co-ownership in which the interest of a surviving tenant in common passes to the deceased tenant's estate and not to the co-tenants.

Tenant/lessee   The party to whom a leasehold is transferred.

Tender of performance   An unconditional and absolute offer by a contracting party to perform his or her obligations under the contract.

Testamentary capacity   The Statute of Wills requirement that the testator must have been of legal age and "sound mind."

Timekeeping   Keeping track of billable time to ensure that the law firm will be properly compensated for its advice and efforts on behalf of clients.

Title insurance   Insurance that owners of real property purchase to ensure that they have clear title to the property.

Title VII of Civil Rights Act of 1964 (Fair Employment Practices Act)   Law intended to eliminate job discrimination based on five protected classes: race, color, religion, sex, and national origin.

Tort   French for a "wrong."

Totten trust   A trust created when a person deposits money in a bank account in his or her own name and holds it as a trustee for the benefit of another person.

Trademark   A distinctive mark, symbol, name, word, motto, or device that identifies the goods of a particular business.

Trademark infringement   Unauthorized use of another's mark; the holder may recover damages and other remedies from the infringer.

Trade secret   An idea that makes a franchise successful but does not qualify for trademark, patent, or copyright protection; a product formula, pattern, design, compilation of data, customer list, or other business secret.

Transferred intent doctrine   A doctrine under which the law transfers the perpetrator's intent from the target to the actual victim of an act.

Treaty   A compact made between two or more nations.

Trespass to land   A tort that interferes with an owner's right to exclusive possession of land.

Trespass to personal property   A tort that occurs whenever one person injures another person's personal property or interferes with that person's enjoyment of his or her personal property.

Trespasser   A person who has no invitation, permission, or right to be on another's property.

Trier of fact   Jury in a jury trial; or the judge if not a jury trial.

Trust   A legal arrangement established when a person (trustor) transfers title to property to another person (trustee) to be managed for the benefit of specifically named persons (beneficiaries).

Trust corpus The property held in trust. Also termed *trust res.*

Trustee (1) Holder of legal title of the real property in a deed of trust and note transaction. (2) Person who holds legal title to trust corpus and manages the trust for the benefit of the beneficiary(ies).

UCC Section 201 (Statute of Frauds) A rule that requires all contracts for the sale of goods costing $500 or more and lease contracts involving payments of $1,000 or more to be in writing.

Unauthorized practice of law (UPL) Giving legal advice, if legal rights may be affected, by anyone not licensed to practice law.

Unconscionable contract Also called a *contract of adhesion,* such a contract is found to be unjust if one party possessed severely unequal bargaining power, if the dominant party unreasonably used its bargaining power to obtain oppressive or manifestly unfair contract terms, and if the adhering party had no reasonable alternative.

Undisclosed agency An agency that occurs when the third party is unaware of either (1) the existence of an agency, or (2) the principal's identity.

Undue influence One person's taking advantage of another person's mental, emotional, or physical weakness and unduly persuading that person to enter into a contract: the persuasion by the wrongdoer must overcome the free will of the innocent party.

Uniform Commercial Code (UCC) Comprehensive statutory scheme including laws that cover aspects of commercial transactions.

Uniform Computer Information Transactions Act (UCITA) A model Act that provides uniform and comprehensive rules for contracts involving computer information transactions and software and information licenses.

Uniform Limited Liability Company Act (ULLCA) A model law that provides comprehensive and uniform rules for the formation, operation, and dissolution of limited liability companies.

Uniform Partnership Act (UPA) Model act that codifies partnership law; most states have adopted the UPA in whole or in part.

Uniform Probate Code (UPC) A model law promulgated to establish consistent rules for the creation of wills, administration of estates, and resolution of conflicts in settling estates.

Uniform resource locator (URL) Specific address for an Internet site.

Unintentional tort or negligence A doctrine that says a person is liable for harm that is the foreseeable consequence of his or her actions.

Universal citation format A system that relies upon the courts to number all paragraphs in every opinion to allow researchers to find the referenced authority regardless of the electronic or other research tool used.

Unreasonable search and seizure Any search and seizure by the government that violates the Fourth Amendment to the U.S. Constitution.

Unsecured credit Credit that does not require any security (collateral) to protect payment of the debt.

U.S. Constitution Fundamental law of the United States of America; ratified by the states in 1788.

U.S. courts of appeals The federal court system's intermediate appellate courts.

U.S. district courts The federal court system's trial courts of general jurisdiction.

U.S. Supreme Court Court created by Article III of the U.S. Constitution; the highest court in the land, located in Washington, D.C.

Variance An exception that permits a type of building or use in an area that otherwise would not be allowed by a zoning ordinance.

Vendor-specific citation format A citation format originally created by publishers for their works.

Venue Location or jurisdiction in which an incident occurred or where the parties to a lawsuit reside; lawsuits must be heard by the court with nearest jurisdiction.

Verdict Decision reached by a jury.

Violation A crime that is neither a felony nor a misdemeanor; usually is punishable by a fine.

Warranty deed A type of deed that contains the greatest number of warranties and provides the most protection to grantees.

Web browser A software program that allows a person to use a computer to access and search the Internet.

White-collar crimes Crimes usually involving cunning and deceit rather than physical force; often committed by businesspersons.

Will A declaration of how a person wants his or her property distributed upon death.

Wire fraud Use of the telephone or telegraph to defraud another person.

Withholding delivery   The act of seller or lessor purposefully refusing to deliver goods to buyer or lessee upon breach of sales or lease contract by buyer or lessee or insolvency of buyer or lessee.

Witness   An individual asked to testify in court, under oath.

Work product doctrine   A qualified immunity from discovery for "work product of the lawyer" except on a substantial showing of "necessity or justification" of certain written statements and memoranda prepared by counsel in representation of a client, generally in preparation for trial.

Workers' compensation   Protection for workers providing compensation for injuries that occur on the job.

World Wide Web   An electronic connection of millions of computers that support a standard set of rules for the exchange of information.

Writ of certiorari   An official notice that the U.S. Supreme Court will review one's case.

Wrongful dissolution   A member's withdrawing from (1) a term limited liability company prior to expiration of the term, or (2) an at-will limited liability company when the operating agreement eliminates a member's power to withdraw.

Wrongful termination of an agency   (1) Ending a franchise without just cause. (2) Termination of an agency contract in violation of terms of the agency contract; nonbreaching party may recover damages from breaching party.

Zoning ordinances   Local laws adopted by municipalities and local governments to regulate land use within their boundaries; they are adopted and enforced to protect the health, safety, morals, and general welfare of the community.

INDEX

Case Index

INDEX

Subject Index

GLOSSARY OF LATIN TERMS AND PHRASES

Pronunciation Key

Stress. The symbol (´), as in **mother** (muth´er), and **red´ wine´**, marks primary stress; any syllable immediately followed by (´) is pronounced with greater emphasis than syllables not marked (´). The symbol (ʻ), as used following the second syllables of **grandmother** (grand´muth·er), and **ice´ wa·ter**, marks secondary stress; a syllable marked for secondary stress is pronounced with less emphasis than one marked (´) but with more than those bearing no stress mark.

a	act, bat, marry	g	give, trigger, beg	l	low, mellow, all, bottle (bot l)	ōō	ooze, fool, too	û(r)	urge, burn, cur
ā	age, paid, say					ou	out, loud, cow	v	voice, river, live
â(r)	air, dare, Mary	h	hit, behave, hear	m	my, summer, him	p	pot, supper, stop	w	witch, away
ä	ah, part, balm					r	read, hurry, near	y	yes, onion
b	back, cabin, cab	hw	which, nowhere	n	now, sinner, on, button (but n)	s	see, passing, miss	z	zoo, lazy, those
ch	child, teacher, beach	i	if, big, mirror, furniture	ng	sing, Washington	sh	shoe, fashion, push	zh	treasure, mirage
d	do, madder, bed	ī	ice, bite, pirate, deny	o	ox, bomb, wasp	t	ten, matter, bit	ə	occurs in unaccented syllables to indicate the sound of the reduced vowel in alone, system, easily, gallop, circus
e	edge, set, merry			ō	over, boat, no	th	thin, ether, path		
ē	equal, seat, bee, mighty	j	just, tragic, fudge	ô	order, ball, raw	th	that, either, smooth		
ēr	ear, mere	k	keep, token, make	oi	oil, joint, joy	u	up, sun		
f	fit, differ, puff			ōō	book, tour				

ᵊ occurs between **i** and **r** and between **ou** and **r** to show triphthongal quality, as in **fire** (fiᵊr), **hour** (ouᵊr)

Source: *Random House Dictionary of the English Language* (2nd Edition). New York: Random House, 1987.

---

a fortiori with stronger reason; much more — ā fôr shē ôr´ī

a posteriori from the effect to the cause; from what comes after — ā po ster ē or´ī

a prendre to take; to seize — ä pron dûr

a priori from the cause to the effect; from what comes before — ā prī ôr´ī

ab initio from the beginning — äb i nit´ē ō

actio criminalis a criminal action — ak shē ō kri mä nā lis

actio damni injuria an action for damages — ak shē ō dam nī in ju rē ä

actio ex delicto an action arising out of fault — ak shē ō eks da lik tō

ad damnum to the damage; money loss claimed by the plaintiff — ad dam´nəm

ad hoc for one special purpose — ad hok´

ad infinitum indefinitely; forever — ad in fə ni´tem

ad litem for the suit — ad´lı´tem

ad respondendum to make answer — ad re spon den dəm

additur addition by a judge to the amount of damages awarded by a jury — a də tər

amicus curiae friend of the court — əmı´kəs kyŏŏr ē

animus furandi intent to steal — an´əməs fu ran dī

animus testandi intent to make a will — an əməs tes tən dī

anno Domini (A.D.) in the year of our Lord — an´ō dom´ə nī

ante before — an´tē

arguendo in arguing — ar gŏō en dō

assumpsit he promised — ə sump´sit

bona fide in good faith — bō´nə fīd´

caveat beware — kav´ēät

caveat emptor let the buyer beware — kav ēät emp´tôr

caveat venditor let the seller beware — kav ēat ven də tər

certiorari to be informed of; to be assured — sûr´shē ə râr ī

cestui que trust beneficiary of a trust — setē kə trəst

compos mentis sound of mind — kom pəs men təs

consortium fellowship of husband and wife — kən sôr´shē əm

contra against — kon´trə

coram before; in the presence of — kôr´am

corpus delicti body of the crime — kôr´pəs di lik´tī

corpus juris body of law — kôr´pəs jŏŏr´is

cum testamento annexo with the will annexed — kum tes tə men tō an nek sō

damnum absque injuria loss without injury in the legal sense — dam nəm abs kwē in ju ri ya

de facto in fact; actually — dē fak´tō

de jure according to law; rightfully — dē jû rē

de minimis of little importance — dē mi nə məs

de novo anew, afresh, a second time — dē nō´vō

dictum unessential statement or remark in a court decision — dik´təm

doli capax capable of criminal intent; able to distinguish between right and wrong — dō lī kā paks

duces tecum bring with you — dŏŏ´sēz te´kəm

ergo therefore; hence — ûr´gō

et al abbreviation for et alii; and others — et al´

et seq abbreviation for et sequentia; and the following

et ux abbreviation for et uxor; and wife

et vir and husband — et vēr´

ex contractu out of a contract — eks kən trak tōō

ex delicto out of a tort or wrong — eks´də lik tō

ex officio by virtue of an office — eks´ə fish´ēō´

ex parte apart from; one side only — eks pär´te

ex post facto after the fact — eks´pōst´fak·tō

forum non conveniens inconvenient court — for´əm non kən vēn(i) yenz

gratis without reward or consideration — grat´is

habeas corpus you have the body — hā bē əs kôr´pəs

habendum to have thus; clause in a deed that defines extent of ownership — hə ben dəm

ibid abbreviation for ibidem; in the same place — ib´id

id abbreviation for idem; the same — id